RESEARCH METHODS FOR
CRIMINAL JUSTICE
AND CRIMINOLOGY

SECOND EDITION

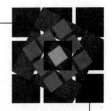

MICHAEL G. MAXFIELD

Indiana University

EARL BABBIE

Chapman University

West/Wadsworth

I(T)P® An International Thomson Publishing Company

Belmont, CA • Albany, NY • Bonn • Boston • Cincinnati • Detroit • Johannesburg • London • Madrid
Melbourne • Mexico City • New York • Paris • Singapore • Tokyo • Toronto • Washington

Criminal Justice Editor: Sabra Horne
Development Editor: Sheryl Symington
Assistant Editor: Claire Masson
Senior Editorial Assistant: Kate Barrett
Marketing Manager: Mike Dew
Production: Greg Hubit Bookworks
Print Buyer: Karen Hunt

Permissions Editor: Robert Kauser
Text and Cover Designer: Norman Baugher
Copy Editor: Carol Reitz
Compositor: G & S Typesetters, Inc.
Printer: R. R. Donnelley & Sons Company,
  Crawfordsville

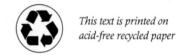

*This text is printed on
acid-free recycled paper*

Printed in the United States of America
 2 3 4 5 6 7 8 9 10

For more information, contact Wadsworth Publishing Company, 10 Davis Drive, Belmont, CA 94002, or electronically at http://www.thomson.com/wadsworth.html

International Thomson Publishing Europe
Berkshire House 168–173
High Holborn
London WC1V 7AA, England

Thomas Nelson Australia
102 Dodds Street
South Melbourne 3205
Victoria, Australia

Nelson Canada
1120 Birchmount Road
Scarborough, Ontario
Canada M1K 5G4

International Thomson Editores
Seneca 53
Col. Polanco
11560 México D.F., México

International Thomson Publishing GmbH
Königswinterer Strasse 418
53227 Bonn, Germany

International Thomson Publishing Asia
221 Henderson Road
#05–10 Henderson Building
Singapore 0315

International Thomson Publishing Japan
Hirakawacho Kyowa Building, 3F
2-2-1 Hirakawacho
Chiyoda-ku, Tokyo 102, Japan

Library of Congress Cataloging-in-Publication Data
Maxfield, Michael G.
  Research methods for criminal justice and criminology /
Michael G. Maxfield, Earl Babbie—2nd ed.
    p. cm.
  Includes bibliographical references and index.
    ISBN 0-534-52164-9 (alk. paper)
   1. Criminal justice, Administration of—Research—Methodology.
 2. Criminology—Research—Methodology. I. Babbie, Earl R. II. Title.
HV7419.5.M38 1998
364'.072—dc20   97-28501

Contents in Brief

PART 1
AN INTRODUCTION TO CRIMINAL JUSTICE INQUIRY 1

1 Crime, Criminal Justice, and Scientific Inquiry 2
2 Theory and Criminal Justice Research 25
3 Causation and Validity 46

PART 2
STRUCTURING CRIMINAL JUSTICE INQUIRY 67

4 General Issues in Research Design 68
5 Concepts, Operationalization, and Measurement 93
6 Measuring Crime 118
7 Experimental and Quasi-experimental Designs 146
8 Ethics and Criminal Justice Research 175

PART 3
MODES OF OBSERVATION 195

9 Overview of Data Collection and Sampling 196
10 Survey Research and Other Ways of Asking Questions 231
11 Field Research 261
12 Agency Records, Content Analysis, and Secondary Data 291

PART 4
PULLING IT ALL TOGETHER 319

13 Program Evaluation and Policy Analysis 320
14 Interpreting Data 353
15 Pulling It All Together: Annotated Examples 389

APPENDIXES A1

A: Using the Library: Traditional and Computer-Based Information Sources A2
B: National Criminal Justice Reference Service A9
C: The Research Report A13
D: Sources of Secondary Data A20
E: Distribution of Chi Square A28

Bibliography B1
Glossary G1
Indexes I1

Contents in Detail

Preface

PART 1
**AN INTRODUCTION TO CRIMINAL JUSTICE
INQUIRY   1**

CHAPTER 1
**Crime, Criminal Justice, and Scientific
Inquiry   2**

Introduction: Why Study Research
   Methods?   3

What Is This Book About?   3
   Two Realities   3
   The Role of Science   5

Personal Human Inquiry   5
   Tradition   6
   Authority   7

Errors in Personal Human Inquiry   8
   Inaccurate Observation   8
   Overgeneralization   9
   Selective Observation   10
   Illogical Reasoning   10
   Ideology and Politics   10
   To Err Is Human   10

The Foundations of Social Science   11
   Theory, Not Philosophy or Belief   11
   Regularities   13
   What About Exceptions?   13
   Aggregates, Not Individuals   13
   A Variable Language   14
   Variables and Relationships   16

Differing Avenues for Inquiry   18
   Idiographic and Nomothetic Explanations   18
   Inductive and Deductive Reasoning   19
   Qualitative and Quantitative Data   20

Ethics and Criminal Justice Research   22

Knowing Through Experience: Summing Up
   and Looking Ahead   22

Main Points   23

Review Questions and Exercises   24

Additional Readings   24

CHAPTER 2
Theory and Criminal Justice Research   25

Introduction   26

The Creation of Social Science Theory   26
   The Traditional Model of Science   26
   Two Logical Systems   29
   Terms Used in Theory Construction   34

Theory in Criminal Justice   38
   Law Breaking   39
   Policy Responses   41
   Theory, Research, and Public Policy   41
   Ecological Theories of Crime and Crime
      Prevention Policy   42

Main Points   43

Review Questions and Exercises   44

Additional Readings   44

CHAPTER 3
Causation and Validity   46

Introduction   47

Determinism and Social Science   47
   Causation in the Natural Sciences   47
   Finding Causes in Social Science   47
   Reasons Have Reasons   48
   Determinism in Perspective   48

Idiographic and Nomothetic
   Models of Explanation   49

Criteria for Causality   50
   Necessary and Sufficient Causes   51
   Molar, Not Micromediational,
      Causal Statements   54
   Errors of Reasoning   54

Validity and Causal Inference   55
  Statistical Conclusion Validity   56
  Internal Validity   57
  Construct Validity   57
  External Validity   58
  Validity and Causal Inference Summarized   59
  Does Drug Use Cause Crime?   59

Linking Measurement and Association   61
  The Traditional Deductive Model   61
  The Interchangeability of Indexes   62

Main Points   64

Review Questions and Exercises   64

Additional Readings   65

PART 2
STRUCTURING CRIMINAL JUSTICE INQUIRY   67

CHAPTER 4
General Issues in Research Design   68

Introduction   69

Purposes of Research   69
  Exploration   69
  Description   70
  Explanation   71
  Application   71

Units of Analysis   72
  Individuals   73
  Groups   73
  Organizations   74
  Social Artifacts   74
  Units of Analysis in Review   75
  The Ecological Fallacy   76
  Reductionism   77

The Time Dimension   78
  Cross-sectional Studies   78
  Longitudinal Studies   78
  Approximating Longitudinal Studies   80
  Retrospective Studies   80
  The Time Dimension Summarized   83

How to Design a Research Project   83
  The Research Process   83
  Getting Started   85
  Conceptualization   86
  Choice of Research Method   86
  Operationalization   87

  Population and Sampling   87
  Observations   87
  Data Processing   87
  Analysis   88
  Application   88
  Review   88

The Research Proposal   89
  Elements of a Research Proposal   90

Answers to Units of Analysis Exercise   91

Main Points   91

Review Questions and Exercises   91

Additional Readings   92

CHAPTER 5
**Concepts, Operationalization,
and Measurement   93**

Introduction   94

Conceptions and Concepts   94
  Conceptualization   95
  Indicators and Dimensions   96
  Confusion over Definitions and Reality   97
  Creating Conceptual Order   97

Operationalization Choices   99
  Measurement   101
  Exhaustive and Exclusive Measurement   103
  Levels of Measurement   104
  Implications of Levels of Measurement   105

Criteria for Measurement Quality   106
  Reliability   107
  Validity   109

Composite Measures   112
  Typologies   112
  An Index of Disorder   113

Measurement Summary   115

Main Points   115

Review Questions and Exercises   116

Additional Readings   117

CHAPTER 6
Measuring Crime   118

Introduction   119

General Issues in Measuring Crime   119
  What Offenses?   119

What Units of Analysis? 120
What Purpose? 121

Crimes Known to Police 122
Uniform Crime Reports 123
UCR and Criteria for Measurement Quality 124
Incident-Based Police Records 125
National Incident-Based Reporting System 125
NIBRS and Criteria for
  Measurement Quality 127

Measuring Crime Through Surveys 128
National Crime Victimization Survey 128
NCVS Redesign 130
Comparing Victim Surveys and Crimes Known
  to Police 132

Surveys of Offending 133
National Household Survey on Drug Abuse 134
Monitoring the Future 135
Validity and Reliability of
  Self-report Measures 136
Self-report Surveys Summarized 137

Drug Surveillance Systems 137
Drug Use Forecasting 137
Drug Abuse Warning Network 138
Pulse Check 139

Measuring Crime for Specific Purposes 140

Measuring Crime: Summary 142

Main Points 143

Review Questions and Exercises 144

Additional Readings 144

CHAPTER 7
Experimental and Quasi-experimental
Designs 146

Introduction 147

Topics Appropriate to Experiments 147

The Classical Experiment 148
Independent and Dependent Variables 148
Pretesting and Posttesting 148
Experimental and Control Groups 149
Double-Blind Experiment 151
Selecting Subjects 151
Randomization 152

Experiments and Causal Inference 152
Experiments and Threats to Validity 153

Threats to Internal Validity 153
Ruling Out Threats to Internal Validity 156
Generalizability 158
Threats to Construct Validity 158
Threats to External Validity 159
Threats to Statistical Conclusion Validity 160

Variations in the Classical Experimental
  Design 160

Quasi-experimental designs 162
Nonequivalent-Groups Designs 162
Cohort Designs 165
Time-Series Designs 166
Variations in Time-Series Designs 168
Gun Control, Homicide, and Suicide 170

Experimental and Quasi-experimental
  Designs Summarized 172

Main Points 173

Review Questions and Exercises 174

Additional Readings 174

CHAPTER 8
Ethics and Criminal Justice Research 175

Introduction 176

Ethical Issues in Criminal Justice Research 176
No Harm to Participants 177
Voluntary Participation 178
Anonymity and Confidentiality 179
Deceiving Subjects 180
Analysis and Reporting 181
Legal Liability 181
Special Problems 182

Promoting Compliance with Ethical
  Principles 184
Institutional Review Boards 184
Institutional Review Board Requirements
  and Researcher Rights 187

Two Ethical Controversies 188
Trouble in the Tearoom 188
Simulating a Prison 189

Discussion Examples 191

Main Points 192

Review Questions and Exercises 193

Additional Readings 193

PART 3
MODES OF OBSERVATION   195

CHAPTER 9
Overview of Data Collection and Sampling   196

Introduction   197

Three Sources of Data   197
Asking Questions   198
Making Observations   198
Examining Written Records   199
Sources of Data Compared   200

General Issues in Data Collection   200
Measurement Validity and Reliability   201
Obtrusive and Unobtrusive Measures   201
Be Careful, But Be Creative   204

Sampling   204

The Logic of Probability Sampling   205
Conscious and Unconscious Sampling Bias   206
*Representativeness and Probability
    of Selection   207*

Sampling Concepts and Terminology   207

Probability Sampling Theory and
    Sampling Distribution   209
Probability Sampling Theory   210
The Sampling Distribution of Ten Cases   210
Binomial Sampling Distribution   211

Populations and Sampling Frames   217

Types of Sampling Designs   217
Simple Random Sampling   218
Systematic Sampling   218
Stratified Sampling   219
Disproportionate Stratified Sampling   219
Multistage Cluster Sampling   220
*Multistage Cluster Sampling
    with Stratification   221*

Illustration: Two National Crime Surveys   223
National Crime Victimization Survey   223
British Crime Survey   224

Probability Sampling in Review   225

Nonprobability Sampling   225
Purposive or Judgmental Sampling   225
Quota Sampling   226
Reliance on Available Subjects   227
Snowball Sampling   228

Main Points   228

Review Questions and Exercises   230

Additional Readings   230

CHAPTER 10
**Survey Research and Other Ways
of Asking Questions   231**

Introduction   232

Topics Appropriate to Survey Research   232
Counting Crime   233
Self-reports   233
Perceptions and Attitudes   233
Policy Proposals   234
Targeted Victim Surveys   234
Other Evaluation Uses   234
General-Purpose Crime Surveys   235

Guidelines for Asking Questions   235
Open-Ended and Closed-Ended Questions   235
Questions and Statements   236
Make Items Clear   236
Short Items Are Best   236
Avoid Negative Items   236
Avoid Biased Items and Terms   237
Tips on Self-report Items   237

Questionnaire Construction   239
General Questionnaire Format   240
Contingency Questions   240
Matrix Questions   241
Ordering Questions in a Questionnaire   243

Self-administered Questionnaires   243
Mail Distribution and Return   244
Warning Mailings, Cover Letters   245
Monitoring Returns   245
Follow-up Mailings   246
Acceptable Response Rates   246

In-person Interview Surveys   247
The Role of the Interviewer   247
General Rules for Interviewing   247
Coordination and Control   248

Telephone Surveys   249
Computer-Assisted Interviewing   250

Comparison of the Three Methods   251

Strengths and Weaknesses
    of Survey Research   253

Other Ways of Asking Questions   255
  Specialized Interviewing   255
  Focus Groups   256

Should You Do It Yourself?   257

Main Points   258

Review Questions and Exercises   259

Additional Readings   260

CHAPTER 11
Field Research   **261**

Introduction   262

Topics Appropriate to Field Research   263

The Various Roles of the Observer   264

Asking Questions   266

Preparing for the Field   267
  Access to Formal Organizations   267
  Access to Subcultures   270
  Selecting Cases for Observation   271
  Sampling in Field Research   273
  Recording Observations   274
  Field Notes   275
  Structured Observations   276

Linking Field Observations and Other Data   278

Illustrations of Field Research   279
  Shoplifting   279
  How Many People Wear Seat Belts?   282
  Bars and Violence   283

Strengths and Weaknesses of Field
     Research   285
  Validity   286
  Reliability   287
  Generalizability   287

Main Points   288

Review Questions and Exercises   289

Additional Readings   289

CHAPTER 12
**Agency Records, Content Analysis,
and Secondary Data**   **291**

Introduction   292

Topics Appropriate for Agency Records   292

Types of Agency Records   294
  Published Statistics   294
  Nonpublic Agency Records   296
  New Data Collected by Agency Staff   300

Units of Analysis and Sampling   302
  Units of Analysis   302
  Sampling   303

Reliability and Validity   303
  *Sources of Reliability and
     Validity Problems*   304

Content Analysis   308
  *Units of Analysis and Sampling in
     Content Analysis*   309
  Coding in Content Analysis   311
  Illustrations of Content Analysis   312

Secondary Analysis   314
  Sources of Secondary Data   315
  *Advantages and Disadvantages of
     Secondary Data*   316

Main Points   316

Review Questions and Exercises   317

Additional Readings   317

PART 4
PULLING IT ALL TOGETHER   **319**

CHAPTER 13
Program Evaluation and Policy Analysis   **320**

Introduction   321

Topics Appropriate for Evaluation Research
     and Policy Analysis   321
  The Policy Process   322
  Linking the Process to Evaluation   323

Getting Started   325
  Evaluability Assessment   326
  Problem Formulation   327
  Measurement   328

Designs for Program Evaluation   332
  Randomized Evaluation Designs   332
  *Home Detention:
     Two Randomized Studies*   335
  Quasi-experimental Designs   337

Nonexperimental Evaluation Studies 340
Other Types of Evaluation Studies 341

Policy Analysis 341
Modeling Prison Populations 342

Political Context of Applied Research 346
Evaluation and Stakeholders 346
Politics and Objectivity 348

Main Points 350

Review Questions and Exercises 351

Additional Readings 351

CHAPTER 14
Interpreting Data 353

Introduction 354

Descriptive Statistics 354
Univariate Analysis 354
Subgroup Comparisons 362
Bivariate Analysis 362
Multivariate Analysis 365
Measures of Association 370

Inferential Statistics 376
Univariate Inferences 376
Tests of Statistical Significance 377
The Logic of Statistical Significance 377
Chi Square 382
*Cautions in Interpreting
Statistical Significance* 384

Main Points 386

Review Questions and Exercises 387

Additional Readings 388

CHAPTER 15
Pulling It All Together: Annotated Examples 389

Introduction 390

National Institute of Justice Research
Plan 1995–96 391
Writing Your Grant Proposal 392

Juvenile Victimization and Offending 394
Research Program Statement 394
*Proposal: Longitudinal Design Using
Available Data* 395
The Research Report 398

Crime Commission Rates 400
Research Program Statement 401
Proposal: Inmate Self-report Survey 401
The Research Report 408

Conclusion 410

APPENDIXES A1

A: Using the Library: Traditional and
Computer-based Information Sources A2

B: National Criminal Justice
Reference Service A9

C: The Research Report A13

D: Sources of Secondary Data A20

E: Distribution of Chi Square A28

Bibliography B1

Glossary G1

Indexes I1

Preface

One of my[1] most oddly rewarding teaching experiences took place not in the classroom but on the streets of downtown Indianapolis. On my way to a meeting with staff from the Indiana Department of Correction, I recognized a student from the previous semester's research methods class. Ryan was seated on a shaded bench, clipboard in hand, watching pedestrians make their way down the sidewalk. After we had exchanged greetings, I learned that Ryan had landed a summer internship with the city's planning department and was currently at work conducting a study of pedestrian traffic.

"Ha!" I exclaimed, recalling student complaints about how research methods are not relevant (what I have since referred to as "Ryan's lament"), "and you whined about how you were never going to use the stuff we talked about in class."

Ryan responded that the systematic study of pedestrians was interesting and admitted that some course topics did in fact relate to his work as an intern. He also said something about not really knowing what actual research involved until he began his current project. Ryan remained attentive to people passing by while we chatted for a few minutes. I was pleased to see that he was a careful observer, applying some of the skills he learned in my course only a few weeks after the semester's end.

Later, thinking more about the encounter, I recognized the need to change my approach to teaching the course. Ryan clearly enjoyed his experience in doing research but he had not recognized how much fun research could be until after he had left the classroom. As a result, I restruc-

tured the course to involve students more actively in the research process. I resolved to be more diligent in linking fundamental concepts of research methods to a broad spectrum of examples, and I became determined to show students how they, like Ryan, could apply systematic inquiry and observation techniques to a wide variety of situations in criminal justice and other policy areas.

Collaborating with Earl Babbie to produce this textbook, I joined a colleague whose writing embodied my efforts to engage students in the learning process. Earl's classic text, *The Practice of Social Research,* has always been an enviable model of clarity—generating student interest while still presenting a rigorous treatment of social science research methods.

As has always been the case with *Practice,* our text illustrates principles of doing research with examples specifically selected to appeal to students. We have sought to convey something of the excitement in doing research that Ryan discovered as he observed pedestrians in downtown Indianapolis.

A Familiar, Comfortable Approach

This text has several distinctive features. Anyone who has taught with or learned from *The Practice of Social Research* will recognize much in our collaborative effort. This enables instructors of criminal justice research methods to organize their course around a familiar approach, capitalizing on the strengths and popularity of Earl Babbie's superb text. At the same time, we have designed our book to address the particular needs of research methods for criminal justice and criminology.

---

1. In this preface, first person singular is Maxfield while first person plural is Maxfield and Babbie.

Features of the New Edition

The first edition of our text, *Research Methods for Criminal Justice and Criminology,* retained much of the raw material from *Practice,* albeit revised and otherwise adapted for students in criminology and criminal justice. In preparing the second edition, we stayed with what has proved to be a popular formula. But we have also responded to suggestions from several people—reviewers, colleagues, and instructors—who used the first edition.

One new chapter has been added; certain features of some individual chapters have been supplemented; and other smaller changes are found throughout the book. Here's an overview of what's new in this edition.

Measuring Crime

More than one reviewer suggested adding more detail and depth to our discussion of measuring crime, a topic we included in the general measurement chapter in the first edition. We enthusiastically concur, and are very pleased to add a new chapter devoted exclusively to that important measurement problem.

The new Chapter 6 expands our discussion from the first edition, but goes beyond that in two ways. First, we describe recent and developing changes in victim surveys and crimes known to police. We describe revisions to the National Crime Victimization Survey (NCVS) screening questions and probes, showing how the new procedures have increased counts of certain types of offenses. Similarly, participation in the National Incident-Based Reporting System (NIBRS) has become more widespread. We describe NIBRS in much greater detail than we did in the first edition, and present some state-level data that illustrate how incident-based reporting produces different measures of crime.

The second major addition to material on measuring crime expands our discussion of self-report surveys and other "nontraditional" measures. This includes more detail on two national self-report series—Monitoring the Future and the National Household Survey of Drug Abuse. With expanded discussion of these two series we can better illustrate how self-report measures differ from victim surveys and crimes known to police. In addition, we describe three special efforts to measure different dimensions of drug use in specific populations. Chapter 6 concludes with a discussion of why it's often necessary to develop still other measures of crime for special purposes.

What results is a coverage of crime measurement that is unprecedented in research methods textbooks. At the same time, we have been careful to present this new material at a level that is readily understood by undergraduates.

Composite Measures

Moving our coverage of crime measurement to its own chapter made it possible to describe composite measures in more detail, as suggested by reviewers and users of the first edition. The general chapter on measurement (Chapter 5) explains how and why composite measures are used, and presents examples of typologies and indexes.

Field Methods

We expanded our treatment of field methods (Chapter 11) to include additional material on ethnographic research. This includes examples from recent studies of offenders and drug use. We also describe snowball sampling in greater detail (in Chapters 9 and 11), again drawing on recent studies as examples. Reviewers and others have also pointed out that field research raises particular ethical questions, so we have added examples of field-based ethical issues (Chapter 8). Together, these changes strengthen our discussion of field methods, and we are grateful to our reviewers for steering us in that direction.

Applied Examples

Several boxes and other special features have been added to this edition; most present additional examples of applied criminal justice research. In doing this, we have sought to illustrate the uses of research for practicing criminal justice professionals. Justice agencies are increasingly using crime analysis, problem-solving, and evaluation techniques. Additional applied examples illustrate these uses and should be especially helpful to students who aspire to careers in criminal justice operations or management.

Longitudinal Research

Chapter 4 includes an expanded treatment of the time dimension, an increasingly important concern in both basic and applied research. In part this change responds to suggestions from users of the first edition. It also reflects my recent collaboration with Cathy Spatz Widom in a study of the long-term consequences of child abuse.

Internet and Technology

The first edition urged students to try the state-of-the-art research tool, "Gopher," to find resources and data. While it's impossible to publish a traditional textbook that has any hope of keeping up on computer and telecommunications developments, we have woven updated material on the Internet into various parts of the text. Students will find references to web sites for publications and data.

For example, the latest professional codes addressing ethical questions (Chapter 8) are from web pages maintained by the American Psychological Association and the American Sociological Association. Tables illustrating NIBRS and NCVS revisions cite web-based sources that students can verify themselves. Chapter 14 on interpreting data presents some tables constructed from a General Social Survey data file that can be accessed and analyzed on-line. We invite students to replicate our calculations and learn about data analysis by doing their own. Finally, appendixes on the National Criminal Justice Reference Service, sources of secondary data, and web-based references have been updated to reflect the state of affairs as of Spring 1997.

In addition, a data disk, which you will find packaged in the back of this book, provides both SPSS and ASCII formats of real data. Suggested exercises appear for relevant chapters, allowing and encouraging further practice using criminal justice data collected from actual surveys and sources.

Notable First Edition Features Retained and Updated

Measurement

Many people believe that measurement presents the greatest challenge in doing social science research. We feel this is especially true for criminal justice. Students frequently alternate between being shrewd skeptics about measurement and being uncritical consumers of media reports about crime, violence, drug use, or whatever havoc happens to be in fashion. Two chapters (Chapters 5 and 6) are devoted to this topic in the second edition; throughout the text we remind students to be careful but creative when it comes to measurement.

Design Building Blocks

Research methods seems to be one of those courses where students feel driven to memorize the book, lectures, practice questions, last semester's notes purchased from a friend, or whatever. The strange vocabulary of the subject probably encourages this tendency, which seems to be especially troublesome when teaching research design. All those Xs and Os must be faithfully recorded, memorized, and associated with the right label.

Although the XO diagrams in Chapter 7 will be familiar to many instructors, we encourage students to become engaged in learning research methods by describing how common research designs represent creative uses of design building blocks. In Chapter 7 and elsewhere we describe how the fundamentals of subject selection, making observations, and administering or withholding a treatment represent basic building blocks of design. Rather than trying to shoehorn a research problem into some pattern of Xs and Os that appears in their books, we urge students to learn what these building blocks represent and what different building blocks can be expected to accomplish.

Agency Records As Data Sources

Criminal justice, perhaps more than any other social science, commonly draws on a bewildering variety of information produced by public agencies. Reported crimes represent only the most well-known example. Students (and many researchers) too often readily accept data produced by some government organization as reliable if not valid. Following our general maxim "be careful but be creative," Chapter 12 guides students through the promises and pitfalls of agency records. We describe some everyday problems researchers encounter in using such data, common sources of those problems, how to detect them, and how to deal with them. Several examples illustrate the important lessons in Chapter 12.

Reviewers and colleagues reacted favorably to the first edition's discussion of agency records. This chapter remains a unique feature of our text, and we have added material to reflect the growing sophistication of data management systems in justice agencies.

Survey Research and Sampling

One of the strengths of *The Practice of Social Research* has always been a comprehensive but eminently readable treatment of sampling and survey methods. Our criminal justice text (in Chapters 9 and 10) retains Earl's general approach, but it also points to some of the more specialized criminal justice applications. These range from victim and self-report surveys to specialized interviews with nonprobability samples. Again, our approach focuses on arming students with the principles of survey methods so that they can adapt these general tools to a variety of uses.

Applied Research and Policy Experiments

We have devoted a chapter to applied criminal justice research; Chapter 13 examines program evaluation and policy analysis. Additionally, we link policy and management applications to virtually every stage of the research process, from theory in Chapter 2 through data interpretation in Chapter 14. We feel this approach is crucial for two complementary reasons. First, students whose interests center on criminal justice policy must understand that applied research is as dependent on theory and reasoned expectations as is basic research. Second, basic research in criminology or criminal justice is usually conducted in some applied context, so the researcher interested in some causal proposition about, say, drug use and violence must recognize that these are not simply abstract constructs. Most measures of drug use and violence will be operationalized with legal or policy definitions of those constructs in mind.

Randomized field experiments have become the designs of choice for many applied studies. In our chapters on experimental and quasi-experimental designs (Chapter 7) and applied research (Chapter 13), we have much to say about the advantages of randomized designs. However, we take care to caution students that all designs have weaknesses and no design is well suited for all research purposes. Unfortunately, the weaknesses of randomized experiments are sometimes overlooked by their champions and by many textbooks. Our treatment of this topic, encouraging students to think carefully and creatively, is more balanced and will enable students to better recognize appropriate and inappropriate uses of experiments.

Ethics

Among the social sciences, criminology and criminal justice probably present the widest array of questions about research ethics. Our treatment of this important topic (Chapter 8) again combines discussion of general principles with emphasis on the particular problems encountered by criminal justice researchers.

Statistics

Chapter 14 guides students through fundamental principles of descriptive and inferential statistics. Our coverage of this topic is conceptual and brief, reflecting our view that criminal justice research design, measurement, and data collection require the concerted attention of students for a full semester. We also believe that understanding these issues is a necessary foundation for doing meaningful statistical analysis. Future producers and consumers of criminal justice research must understand how concepts become observations and how observations become data before they learn the details of data analysis.

At the same time, our approach to statistics is both thorough and conceptually sound. As a result, instructors who wish to cover data analysis in more detail (perhaps in a second semester course) will find Chapter 14 an excellent point of departure.

Suggestions for Instructors

All instructors have their own preferences in teaching research methods—topics to emphasize, pedagogical styles, course requirements, and so forth. Here are a few tips on how to incorporate certain distinctive features of this text into different approaches to teaching the course.

An Example of the Case Method

Chapter 15 reflects my experience teaching in a public affairs program where I learned something of the case method, which is standard pedagogy in law schools and business schools. While the chapter is not a true case study, it represents a mirror image of much of the book. Other chapters center on concepts and principles, introducing examples to illustrate various points. Chapter 15 presents two examples in detail, referring readers to earlier chapters for conceptual treatment of points that are illustrated.

You may wish to use Chapter 15 as something of a model to develop your own extended examples (cases) that students can then consult throughout the course. In this way, cases can feed into course projects. They can also form the basis for exercises or exam questions at various points in the course. Or you can work up cases that more closely reflect your own substantive interests, perhaps even your own research.

In either event, we suggest that instructors

read Chapter 15 carefully when planning the course. The examples may suggest other ways you can use case studies.

Appendixes

Many instructors in research methods courses have their students prepare a research design or a complete proposal as a term project. Chapters 4 and 15 provide general guidelines for preparing research proposals. Four of the appendixes will be especially valuable for such projects; you may wish to point them out early in the semester.

Appendix A includes examples and general information about evolving library and information technology. Depending on the availability of tools and resources on your campus, we suggest you supplement Appendix A with guides or manuals that document campus facilities and routines.

Appendix B describes the National Criminal Justice Reference Service (NCJRS), a specialized library and information tool for criminal justice research and policy development. NCJRS was rather late in developing a useful web site, but now provides ready access to publications issued by Justice Department agencies. We also steer students to the excellent web site maintained by the Bureau of Justice Statistics (BJS).

Appendix C presents guidelines on writing research reports. If your course will require a proposal or research report, we recommend that students review this appendix early in the term. See also Chapters 4 and 15 for further information on proposals. You may wish to either supplement or modify our suggestions to reflect your own preferences.

Appendix D describes major sources of secondary data, most notably the National Archive of Criminal Justice Data (NACJD) and the Interuniversity Consortium for Political and Social Research (ICPSR). Following one of the examples presented in Chapter 15, students might prepare a proposal that uses data obtained from one of those sources. If suitable resources are accessible, students can retrieve information about NACJD and ICPSR holdings through the Internet and web. Appendix D presents an example of how to do this, retrieving information about data used in research examples discussed elsewhere in the text.

Supplements

We have also provided numerous teaching resources to facilitate ease of instruction as well as student comprehension. The supplement package includes:

- An Instructor's Manual with very detailed chapter outlines, key terms, homework exercises, and numerous test questions in a variety of formats.
- A Computerized Test Bank, available in Macintosh, Windows, and DOS versions, featuring true/false, multiple-choice, short-answer, and essay questions.

For the student, we have:

- A Study Guide featuring fill-in outlines, which aid students in taking notes but do not substitute for reading the chapter; key terms; and self-tests for each chapter.
- Blankenship and Vito's *Your Research: Data Analysis for Criminal Justice and Criminology*—an easy-to-use data analysis and graphics program with an accompanying workbook. This software is available for PC's.
- *The Internet Investigator*—this colorful trifold pamphlet lists the most popular Internet addresses for criminal-justice-related websites.

Acknowledgments

Several reviewers made perceptive and useful comments on various drafts of the book. We are especially grateful to them for their insights and suggestions: Allan R. Barnes, University of Alaska at Anchorage; Brian Byers, Ball State University; Tom Durkin, University of Florida; Mark M. Lanier, University of Central Florida; and Joan McDermott, Southern Illinois University at Carbondale.

Other colleagues offered suggestions, comments, and advice: Dick Andzenge, St. Cloud State University; Patricia Brantingham, Simon Fraser University; Jan Chaiken, Bureau of Justice Statistics (BJS); Scott Decker, University of Missouri at St. Louis; Bob Hardt, State University of New York at Albany; John Kennedy, Indiana University; and Cathy Spatz Widom, State University of New York at Albany.

I am also grateful to Jeremy Travis, National Institute of Justice (NIJ), for hosting me as a Visiting Fellow at the institute. My fellowship enabled me to meet and work with colleagues outside the normal university environment; this has been extremely valuable. Many people helped in many ways: Barbara Boland, NIJ Visiting Fellow; Tony Fabelo, Texas Criminal Justice Policy Council; Sally Hillsman, NIJ; Bob Kirchner, Bureau of Justice Assistance; Pam Lattimore, NIJ; Michael Maltz, BJS and Northeastern University; Phyllis McDonald, NIJ; Roger Przybylski, Illinois Criminal Justice Information Authority; Winnie Reed, NIJ; and Ed Zedlewski, NIJ.

I was privileged to enjoy the hospitality of the Rutgers University School of Criminal Justice as a visiting faculty member during 1997. I thank Ronald Clarke for inviting me to Rutgers. Thanks also to students who offered comments on draft materials for the second edition: Nigel Cohen, Yakenya Goldsberg, Kimberly Jones, Douglas Koski, Jarret Lovell, Timothy O'Boyle, William Sousa, and Michael Wagers. In addition, Gisela Bichler-Robertson kindly prepared a box on safety audits (in Chapter 11), and Tracey Rutnik helped me out in countless ways.

Finally, Earl and I are very grateful for the patient, professional assistance from people at Wadsworth: Kate Barrett, Michael Dew, Heather Dutton, Sabra Horne, and Greg Hubit.

North River, New York

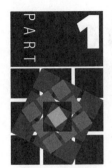

An Introduction to Criminal Justice Inquiry

WHAT comes to mind when you encounter the word *science?* What do you think of when we describe criminal justice as a social science? For some, science is mathematics; for others, it is white coats and laboratories. It is often confused with technology or equated with difficult high school or college courses.

Science is, of course, none of these things per se, but it is difficult to specify exactly what science is. Scientists, in fact, disagree on the proper definition. Some would object to the idea of social science; others might question whether criminal justice can be a social science.

For the purposes of this book, we will look at science as a method of inquiry—a way of learning and knowing things about the world around us. Contrasted with other ways of learning and knowing about the world, science has some special characteristics. We'll examine these traits in this opening set of chapters. We'll also see how the scientific method of inquiry—a way of learning and knowing things—can be applied to the study of crime and criminal justice.

Part 1 of the book is intended to lay the groundwork for the discussions that follow in the rest of the book—to examine the fundamental characteristics and issues that make science different from other ways of knowing things. In

Chapter 1, we'll begin with a look at native human inquiry, the sort of thing you've been doing all your life. In the course of that examination, we'll see some of the ways people go astray in trying to understand the world around them, and we'll consider the primary characteristics of scientific inquiry that guard against those errors.

Chapter 2 deals specifically with the social scientific approach to criminal justice inquiry, and the links between theory and research. The lessons of Chapter 1 are applied in the study of crime and criminal justice. You will discover that, although special considerations arise in studying people and organizations, the basic logic of all science is the same.

In their attempt to develop generalized understanding, scientists seek to discover patterns of interrelationships among variables. Often, these interrelationships take a cause-and-effect form. Chapter 3 addresses the nature and logic of causation as appropriate to criminal justice research. This theoretical chapter lays the basis for later chapters on analytic techniques.

The overall purpose of Part 1 is to construct a backdrop against which to view more specific aspects of research design and execution. By the time you complete the chapters in Part 1, you'll be ready to look at some of the more concrete aspects of criminal justice research.

CHAPTER 1

Crime, Criminal Justice, and Scientific Inquiry

What You'll Learn in This Chapter

We'll examine the way people learn about their world and the mistakes they make along the way. We'll also begin to see what makes science different from other ways of knowing things.

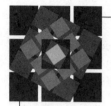

INTRODUCTION: WHY STUDY RESEARCH METHODS?

WHAT IS THIS BOOK ABOUT?
Two Realities
The Role of Science

PERSONAL HUMAN INQUIRY
Tradition
Authority

ERRORS IN PERSONAL HUMAN INQUIRY
Inaccurate Observation
Overgeneralization
Selective Observation
Illogical Reasoning
Ideology and Politics
To Err Is Human

THE FOUNDATIONS OF SOCIAL SCIENCE
Theory, Not Philosophy or Belief
Regularities
What About Exceptions?

Aggregates, Not Individuals
A Variable Language
Variables and Relationships

DIFFERING AVENUES FOR INQUIRY
Idiographic and Nomothetic Explanations
Inductive and Deductive Reasoning
Qualitative and Quantitative Data

ETHICS AND CRIMINAL JUSTICE RESEARCH

KNOWING THROUGH EXPERIENCE: SUMMING UP AND LOOKING AHEAD

MAIN POINTS

REVIEW QUESTIONS AND EXERCISES

ADDITIONAL READINGS

■ INTRODUCTION: WHY STUDY RESEARCH METHODS?

Spending a semester studying criminal justice methodology may not be high on your list of "Fun Things to Do." Perhaps you are or plan to be a criminal justice professional and you are thinking, "Why do I have to study research methods? When I graduate, I will be working in probation (or law enforcement, or corrections, or court services), not conducting research! I would benefit more from learning about probation counseling (or police management, or corrections policy, or court administration)."

Fair enough. As a criminal justice professional, you should expect to become a consumer of research. For example, in the section "Two Realities," we will discuss how the Kansas City Preventive Patrol Experiment appeared to contradict traditional views about law enforcement—that a visible patrol force prevents crime. A police officer, supervisor, or executive should be able to understand how the research was conducted and how the study's findings might apply in his or her department. [As it happens, the methods used in the Kansas City study have been criticized (see, for example, Larson, 1975), although the study's fundamental conclusions are generally accepted.] Since police practices vary somewhat from city to city, a police executive would benefit from being able to understand research methods and how to interpret findings.

Most criminal justice professionals, especially those in supervisory roles, routinely review various types of performance reports and statistical tabulations. An understanding of research methods can help decision makers critically evaluate such reports and recognize when methods are properly and improperly applied. The box entitled "Home Detention" describes an example of how knowledge of research methods can help policymakers avoid mistakes.

One objective of this book, therefore, is to help future professionals become informed consumers of research. In the past 25 years or so, thousands of criminal justice research and evaluation studies have been conducted. The National Criminal Justice Reference Service responds to more than 5,000 requests for information about recent research per month, distributing documents to criminal justice professionals and researchers around the world (National Criminal Justice Reference Service, 1996). Many such reports are prepared specifically to keep the criminal justice community informed and up to date with new research developments. In addition, the Internet is a rapidly growing source of information about criminal justice research and policy.

In other courses you take or in your job, you may also become a producer of research. Probation officers frequently try out new approaches to supervising or counseling clients. Police officers try new methods of working with the community and with witnesses and suspects. It has become essential in many cities and states to estimate how changes in sentencing policy might affect jail and prison populations. Determining whether such changes are effective is an example of applied research. A "problem-solving" approach is used in more and more police departments, and in many other justice agencies as well.

■ WHAT IS THIS BOOK ABOUT?

This book is about knowing things. Although you will come away from the book knowing some things you don't know right now, our primary purpose is to help you look at *how* you know things, not *what* you know.

Two Realities

Ultimately, we live in a world of two realities. Part of what we know could be called our *experiential reality:* the things we know from direct experience. If you dive into a glacial stream flowing down through the Canadian Rockies, you don't need anyone to tell you it's cold. You notice that all by yourself. The first time you step on a thorn, you know it hurts even before anyone tells you. The other part of what we know could be called our *agreement reality:* things we consider real because we've been told they're real, and everyone else seems to agree they are real. A big part of

Home Detention

HOME detention with electronic monitoring (ELMO) was widely adopted as an alternative punishment throughout the United States in the 1980s. The technology for this new sanction was developed from advances in telecommunications and computer systems. Prompted by growing prison and jail populations, not to mention sales pitches by equipment manufacturers, criminal justice officials embraced ELMO. Questions about the effectiveness of these programs quickly emerged, however, and led to research to determine whether the technology worked. Comprehensive evaluations were conducted in Marion County (Indianapolis), Indiana. Selected findings from these studies illustrate the importance of understanding research methods in general, and the meaning of various ways to measure program success in particular.

ELMO programs directed at three groups of people were studied: (1) convicted adult offenders, (2) adults charged with a criminal offense and awaiting trial, and (3) juveniles convicted of burglary or theft. People in each of the three groups were assigned to home detention for a specified period of time. They could complete the program in one of three ways: (1) successful release after serving their term; (2) removal due to rule violations, such as being arrested again or violating program rules; or (3) running away, or "absconding."

The agencies that administered each program were required to submit regular reports to county officials on how many persons completed their home detention terms in each category. The accompanying table summarizes the program completion types during the evaluation study:

	Convicted Adults	Pretrial Adults	Juveniles
Success	81%	73%	99%
Rule violation	14	13	1
Abscond	5	14	0

growing up in any society, in fact, is learning to accept what everybody around you "knows" is so. If you don't know those same things, you can't really be a part of the group. If you were to seriously question a geography professor whether the sun really sets in the west, you'd quickly find yourself set apart from other people. The first reality is a product of our own experience; the second is a product of what people have told us.

To illustrate the difference between agreement and experiential realities, let's consider the example of preventive police patrol. Using the term *preventive* implies that when police patrol their assigned beats, they prevent crime. Police do not prevent all crime, of course, but it is a commonsense belief that a visible, mobile police force will prevent some crimes. In fact, the value of patrol in preventing crime was a fundamental tenet of police operations for many years. O. W. Wilson, a legendary police chief in Chicago and the author of an influential book on police administration, wrote that patrol was an indispensable service that prevented crime by eliminating incentives and opportunities for misconduct (Wilson and McLaren, 1963:320). A 1967 report on policing by President Lyndon Johnson's Commission on Law Enforcement and Administration of Justice (1967:1) stated that "the heart of the police effort against crime is patrol. . . . The object of patrol is to disperse policemen in a way that will eliminate or reduce the opportunity for misconduct and to increase the probability that a criminal will be apprehended while he is committing a crime or immediately thereafter."

Seven years later the Police Foundation, a private research organization, published results from an experimental study that presented a dramatic challenge to conventional wisdom. Known as the "Kansas City Preventive Patrol Experiment," this study compared police beats with three levels of preventive patrol: (1) control beats, with one car per beat; (2) proactive beats, with two or three

These figures, reported by agencies to county officials, indicate that the juvenile program was a big success; virtually all juveniles were successfully released.

Now consider some additional information on each program collected by the evaluation team. Data were gathered on new arrests of program participants and on the number of successful computerized telephone calls to participants' homes:

	Convicted Adults	Pretrial Adults	Juveniles
New arrest	5%	1%	11%
Successful calls	53	52	17

The table shows that many more juveniles were arrested, and juveniles successfully answered a much lower percentage of telephone calls to their homes. What happened?

The simple answer is that the staff responsible for administering the juvenile program were not keeping track of offenders. The ELMO equipment was not maintained properly, and police were not visiting the homes of juveniles as planned. Since staff were not keeping track of program participants, they were not aware that many juveniles were violating the conditions of home detention. And because they were unable to detect violations, they naturally reported that the vast majority of young burglars and thieves completed their home detention successfully.

A county official who relied on only agency reports of program success would have made a big mistake in judging the juvenile program to be 99 percent successful. On the other hand, an informed consumer of such reports would have been skeptical of a 99 percent success rate and searched for more information.

Source: Adapted from Maxfield and Baumer (1991) and Baumer, Maxfield, and Mendelsohn (1993).

---

cars per beat; and (3) reactive beats, with no routine preventive patrol. After almost one year, researchers examined data from the three types of beats and found no differences in crime rates, citizen satisfaction with police, fear of crime, or other measures of police performance (Kelling, Pate, Dieckman, and Brown, 1974).

Researchers and law enforcement professionals alike were surprised by these findings. For the record, Kelling and associates never claimed they had proven that preventive patrol had no impact on crime. Instead, they argued that police should work more closely with neighborhood residents, and that routine patrol might be more effective if it were combined with other strategies that used police resources in a more thoughtful way.

Other studies conducted in the 1970s cast doubt on other fundamental assumptions about police practices. Responding quickly to crime reports made no difference in arrests, according to additional research in Kansas City (Van Kirk, 1977). Criminal investigation by police detectives was rarely effective in producing an arrest (Greenwood, 1975).

We mention these examples not to attack routine law enforcement practices. Our point is to show that systematic research on policing has illustrated how traditional beliefs, agreement reality, can be misleading. Simply increasing the number of police officers on patrol will not reduce crime because police patrol often lacks direction. Faster response time to calls for police assistance does not increase arrests because there is often a long delay between the time a crime occurs and when it is reported to police. Clever detective work seldom solves crimes because investigators get most of their information from reports prepared by patrol officers, who in turn get their information from victims and witnesses.

Traditional beliefs about patrol effectiveness, response time, and detective work are examples of agreement reality, while the research projects that produced alternative views about each law enforcement practice represent experiential reality. These studies are examples of **empirical research**,[1] the production of knowledge based on experience or observation. In each case, researchers conducted studies of police and based their conclusions on experience. Empirical research is a way of knowing things about crime and criminal justice, and explaining how to conduct empirical research is the purpose of this book.

By focusing on empirical research, we do not intend to downplay the importance of other ways of knowing things. Law students, for example, are trained in how to interpret statutes and judicial opinions. Historians take courses on methods of historical interpretation, mathematics majors learn numerical analysis, and students of philosophy study logic. If you are a criminal justice major, many of the other courses you take—say, a course on theories of crime and deviance—will add to your agreement reality.

The Role of Science

Science offers an approach to both agreement reality and experiential reality. Scientists have certain criteria that must be met before they will agree on the reality of something they haven't personally experienced. In general, an assertion must have both *logical* and *empirical* support: It must make sense, and it must agree with observations in the world. Why do earthbound scientists accept the assertion that it's cold on the dark side of the moon? First, it makes sense because the surface heat of the moon comes from the sun's rays. Second, scientific measurements made on the moon's dark side confirm the assertion. So scientists accept the reality of things they don't personally experience—they accept an agreement reality—but they have special standards for doing so.

More to the point of this book, however, science offers a special approach to the discovery of reality through personal experience. It offers a

special approach to the business of inquiry. *Epistemology* is the science of knowing; *methodology* (a subfield of epistemology) might be called "the science of finding out." This book offers an examination and presentation of criminal justice methodology; we're going to concern ourselves with how social science methods can be used to better understand crime and criminal justice policy. To understand scientific inquiry, let's first look at the kinds of inquiry we all do each day.

■ PERSONAL HUMAN INQUIRY

Practically all people would like to predict their future circumstances. We seem quite willing, moreover, to undertake this task using *causal* and *probabilistic* reasoning. First, we generally recognize that future circumstances are somehow caused or conditioned by present ones. We learn that getting an education will affect how much money we earn later in life, and that running stoplights may bring an unhappy encounter with an alert traffic officer. As students, we learn that studying hard will result in better examination grades.

Second, people learn that such patterns of cause and effect are probabilistic in nature: The effects occur more often when the causes occur than when the causes are absent—but not always. Thus, students learn that studying hard produces good grades in most instances, but not every time. We recognize the danger of ignoring stoplights without believing that every such violation will produce a traffic ticket.

We will return to these concepts of causality and probability throughout the book. As we'll see, science makes them more explicit and provides techniques for dealing with them more rigorously than does casual human inquiry.

As we look at our own personal inquiry, it is important to distinguish between prediction and understanding. Often, we are able to predict without understanding; you may be able to predict rain when your trick knee aches. And often, even if we don't understand why, we are willing to act on the basis of a demonstrated predictive ability. The racetrack buff who finds that the third-

---

[1] Words in **boldface** are defined in the glossary at the end of the book.

ranked horse in the third race of the day always wins will probably keep betting without knowing, or caring, why it works out that way.

The attempt to predict is often placed in a context of knowledge and understanding. If you can understand why things are related to one another, why certain regular patterns occur, you can predict better than if you simply observe and remember those patterns. For example, college dormitories are often targets of burglary during semester breaks. If you understand something about the opportunity structure of burglary (it's more likely when a suitably motivated offender knows that a dwelling will be unoccupied), you would be able to predict that hanging a sign on your room, "Off to Daytona Beach! See you in two weeks!" invites trouble. Thus, human inquiry attempts to answer both *what* and *why* questions, and we pursue these goals by observing and figuring out.

Our attempts to learn about the world are only partly linked to direct personal inquiry or experience. Another, much larger, part comes from the agreed-on knowledge that others give us. This agreement reality both assists and hinders our attempts to find out for ourselves. Two important sources of secondhand knowledge—tradition and authority—deserve brief consideration here.

Tradition

Each of us inherits a culture made up, in part, of firmly accepted knowledge about the workings of the world. We may learn from others that planting corn in the spring will gain the greatest assistance from the gods, that the circumference of a circle is approximately twenty-two sevenths of its diameter, or that driving to the left of center (in the United States) is dangerous. We may test a few of these "truths" on our own, but we simply accept the great majority of them. These are the things that "everybody knows."

Tradition, in this sense, has some clear advantages for human inquiry. By accepting what everybody knows, you are spared the overwhelming task of starting from scratch in your search for regularities and understanding. Knowledge is cumulative, and an inherited body of information

and understanding is the jumping-off point for the development of more knowledge.

At the same time, tradition may be detrimental to human inquiry. If you seek a fresh and different understanding of something that everybody already understands and has always understood, you might be treated as a fool for your efforts. More to the point, however, it will probably never occur to you to seek a different understanding of something that is already understood and obvious.

Authority

Despite the power of tradition, new knowledge appears every day. Aside from your own personal inquiries, throughout your life you will learn about the new discoveries and understandings of others. Your acceptance of this new knowledge often depends on the status of the discoverer. You are more likely to believe a judge who declares that your next traffic violation will bring a suspension of your driver's license, for example, than to believe your parents when they say the same thing.

Like tradition, authority can both help and hinder human inquiry. We do well to trust the judgment of the person who has special training, expertise, and credentials in a matter, especially in the face of contradictory arguments on a given question. At the same time, inquiry can be greatly hindered by the legitimate authority who errs within his or her own special province. Biologists, after all, do make mistakes in the field of biology, and biological knowledge changes over time. Most of us assume that over-the-counter medications are safe when taken as directed, trusting the authority of drug manufacturers and some distant government agency. However, in the late 19th century, our trust might have led us to buy a box of Bayer Heroin (Inciardi, 1986). The box entitled "Arrest and Domestic Violence" illustrates the difficult problems that can result when criminal justice policy accepts too quickly the results from criminal justice research.

Inquiry is also hindered when we depend on the authority of experts speaking outside their realm of expertise. For example, consider the

Arrest and Domestic Violence

IN 1983, preliminary results were released from a study on the deterrent effects of ar-rest in cases of domestic violence. The study reported that male abusers who were arrested were less likely to commit future assaults, compared to offenders who were not arrested. Conducted by researchers from the Police Foundation, the study used rigorous experimental methods adapted from the natural sciences. Criminal justice scholars generally believed the research was well designed and executed. Public officials were quick to embrace the study's findings that arresting domestic violence offenders deterred them from future violence.

Here, at last, was empirical evidence to support an effective policy in combating domestic assaults. Results of the Minneapolis Domestic Violence Experiment were widely disseminated, in part due to aggressive efforts by the researchers to publicize their findings (Sherman and Cohn, 1989). The Attorney General of the United States recommended that police departments make arrests in all cases of misdemeanor domestic violence. Within five years, more than 80 percent of law enforcement agencies in U.S. cities adopted arrest as the preferred way for responding to domestic assaults (Sherman, 1992a:2).

Several things contributed to the rapid adoption of arrest policies to deter domestic violence. First, the experimental study was conducted carefully by highly respected researchers. Results were also widely publicized in newspapers, in professional journals, and on television programs. Officials could understand the study, and most believed that its findings made sense. Finally, mandating arrest in less serious cases of domestic violence was a straightforward and politically attractive approach to a growing problem.

political or religious leader, lacking any biochemical expertise, who declares marijuana to be a dangerous drug. The advertising industry plays heavily on this misuse of authority by having popular athletes discuss the nutritional value of breakfast cereals and having movie actors evaluate the performance of automobiles.

Both tradition and authority, then, are double-edged swords in the search for knowledge about the world. Simply put, they provide us with a starting point for our own inquiry, but they may lead us to start at the wrong point or push us off in the wrong direction.

■ ERRORS IN PERSONAL HUMAN INQUIRY

Aside from the potential dangers of relying on tradition and authority, we often stumble and fall down when we set out to learn for ourselves. Now we'll mention some of the common errors we make in our own casual inquiries and look at the ways science provides safeguards against those errors.

Inaccurate Observation

The keystone of inquiry is observation. We can never understand the way things are without first having something to understand. We have to know *what* before we can explain *why*. On the whole, however, people are pretty sloppy, even unconscious, observers of the flow of events in life. We fail to observe things right in front of us and mistakenly observe things that aren't so. You probably don't recall, for example, what your instructor was wearing on the first day of this class. If you had to guess now, you'd probably be wrong.

In contrast to casual human inquiry, scientific observation is a conscious activity. Simply making observation more deliberate helps to reduce error. If you had gone to the first class meeting with a conscious plan to observe and record what your instructor was wearing, you'd be more accurate.

Sherman and Berk (1984) urged caution in uncritically embracing the results of their study. Others stated that similar research should be conducted in other cities to check on the Minneapolis findings (Lempert, 1984). Recognizing this, the U.S. National Institute of Justice sponsored more experiments—known as replications—in six other cities. Not everyone was happy about the new studies. A feminist group in Milwaukee opposed the replication in that city because it believed the effectiveness of arrest had already been proven (Sherman and Cohn, 1989:138).

Results from the replication studies now question the effectiveness of arrest policies. In three cities, no deterrent effect was found in police records of domestic violence. In other cities, there was no evidence of deterrence for longer periods (6–12 months), and in three cities, researchers found that violence escalated when offenders were arrested (Sherman, 1992a:30). For example, Sherman and others (1992:167) report that in Milwaukee, "The initial deterrent effects observed for up to thirty days quickly disappear. By one year later [arrests] produce an escalation effect." Arrest works in some cases but not in others. As so often happens, the criminal justice response to domestic assaults must carefully consider the characteristics of offenders and the nature of the relationship between offender and victim.

After police departments throughout the country embraced arrest policies following the Minneapolis study, researchers were faced with the difficult task of explaining why initial results must be qualified. Arrest seems to make sense; officials and the general public believed what they read in the papers and saw on television. Changing their minds by reporting complex findings is more difficult.

In many cases, using both simple and complex measurement devices helps to guard against inaccurate observations. Moreover, they add a degree of precision well beyond the capacity of the unassisted human senses. Suppose, for example, that you had taken color photographs of your instructor on the first day.

Overgeneralization

When we look for patterns among the specific things we observe around us, we often assume that a few similar events are evidence of a general pattern. Probably the tendency to overgeneralize is greatest when there is pressure to reach a general understanding, yet it also occurs casually in the absence of pressure. Whenever overgeneralization does occur, it can misdirect or impede inquiry.

Imagine you are a rookie police officer newly assigned to foot patrol in an urban neighborhood. Your sergeant wants to meet with you at the end of your shift to discuss what you think are the major law enforcement problems on the beat. Eager to earn favor with your supervisor, you interview the managers of a few stores in a small shopping area. If each mentions vandalism as the biggest concern, you might report that vandalism is the major problem on your beat, even though many residents believe drug dealing contributes to the neighborhood problems of burglary, street robbery, and vandalism. Overgeneralization leads to misrepresentation and simplification of problems on your beat.

Criminal justice researchers guard against overgeneralization by committing themselves in advance to a sufficiently large sample of observations and by being attentive to how representative those observations are. The replication of inquiry provides another safeguard. Replication means repeating a study, checking to see whether similar results are produced each time. The study may also be repeated under slightly varied conditions or in different locations. The box entitled "Arrest and Domestic Violence" describes an example of why replication can be especially important in applied research.

Selective Observation

One danger of overgeneralization is that it may lead to selective observation. Once you have concluded that a particular pattern exists and have developed a general understanding of why, you will be tempted to pay attention to future events and situations that correspond with the pattern and to ignore those that don't. Racial, ethnic, and other prejudices depend heavily on selective observation for their persistence.

A research design will often specify in advance the number and kind of observations to be made as a basis for reaching a conclusion. If we wanted to learn whether men were more likely than women to support long prison sentences for rapists, we would decide to make a specified number of observations on that question in a research project. We might select a thousand people to be interviewed. Even if the first ten women supported long sentences and the first ten men opposed them, we would continue to interview everyone selected for the study and record each observation. Then we would base our conclusion on an analysis of all the observations, not just those first ten.

Illogical Reasoning

People have various ways of handling observations that contradict their judgments about the way things are. Surely one of the most remarkable creations of the human mind is "the exception that proves the rule." That idea doesn't make any sense at all. An exception can draw attention to a rule or to a supposed rule, but in no system of logic can it *prove* the rule it contradicts. Yet we often use this pithy saying to brush away contradictions with a simple stroke of illogic.

What statisticians have called the *gambler's fallacy* is another illustration of illogic in day-to-day reasoning. A consistent run of either good or bad luck is presumed to foreshadow its opposite. An evening of bad luck at poker may kindle the belief that a winning hand is just around the corner; many a poker player has stayed in a game too

long because of that mistaken belief. Conversely, an extended period of good weather may lead you to worry that it is certain to rain on the weekend picnic.

Although all of us sometimes fall into embarrassingly illogical reasoning, scientists avoid this pitfall by using systems of logic consciously and explicitly. Chapter 2 will examine the logic(s) of science in more depth. For now, it is sufficient to note that logical reasoning is a conscious activity for social scientists.

Ideology and Politics

Crime is, of course, an important social problem, and a great deal of controversy surrounds policies for dealing with crime. Many people feel strongly one way or another about the death penalty, gun control, or long prison terms for drug users as approaches to reducing crime. There is ongoing disagreement about the scope of racial bias in police practices and sentencing policies. These kinds of ideological or political views can undermine objectivity in the research process. Criminal justice professionals may have special difficulty separating ideology and politics from a more detached, scientific approach to the study of crime.

Criminologist Samuel Walker (1994:16) compares ideological bias in criminal justice research to theology: "The basic problem . . . is that faith triumphs over facts. For both liberals and conservatives, certain ideas are unchallenged articles of faith, almost like religious beliefs that remain unshaken by empirical facts."

Most researchers have their own beliefs about public policy, including policies for dealing with crime. The danger lies in allowing such beliefs to distort how research problems are defined and how research results are interpreted. The scientific approach to the study of crime and criminal justice policy guards against, but does not prevent, ideology and theology from coloring the research process. With empirical research, articles of faith are compared with experience.

To Err Is Human

We have described some of the ways we go astray in our attempts to know and understand the world and some of the ways that science protects its inquiries from these pitfalls. For the most part, social science differs from our casual, day-to-day inquiry in two important respects. First, scientific inquiry is a conscious activity. Although we engage in continuous observation in daily life, much of it is unconscious or semiconscious. In social scientific inquiry, we make a conscious decision to observe, and we stay awake while we do it. Second, social scientific inquiry is more careful than our casual efforts; we are more wary of making mistakes and take special precautions to avoid error.

Nothing we've said should lead you to conclude that social science methods offer total protection against the errors that people commit in personal inquiry. Not only do individuals make every kind of error we've looked at, but social scientists as a group also fall into the pitfalls and stay trapped for long periods of time.

■ THE FOUNDATIONS OF SOCIAL SCIENCE

Science is sometimes characterized as *logico-empirical*. This ugly term carries an important message: The two pillars of science are (1) logic or rationality and (2) observation. A scientific understanding of the world must make sense and agree with what we observe. Both of these elements are essential to social science and relate to three major aspects of the overall scientific enterprise: theory, data collection, and data analysis.

As a gross generalization, scientific theory deals with the logical aspect of science; data collection deals with the observational aspect, and data analysis looks for patterns in what is observed. Most of this book deals with issues related to data collection—demonstrating how to conduct empirical research—but you should recognize that social science involves all three elements. With this in mind, Chapters 2 and 3 deal with the theoretical context of designing and executing research, and Chapter 14 presents a conceptual introduction to the statistical analysis of data. Figure 1-1 offers a schematic view of how the book addresses these three aspects of social science.

Let's turn now to some of the fundamental issues that distinguish social science from other ways of looking at social phenomena.

Theory, Not Philosophy or Belief

Social scientific theory has to do with what *is*, not what should be. This means that scientific theory—and, more broadly, science itself—cannot settle debates on value. Social science cannot determine whether, for example, police who carry firearms (as in the United States) are "better" than police who do not carry firearms (as in England) except in terms of some agreed-on criteria. We could determine scientifically whether armed or unarmed police are more respected by the citizens they serve only if we could agree on some measures of citizen respect, and our conclusion in that case would depend totally on the measures we had agreed on.

By the same token, if we could agree that conviction rate, say, or average sentence length was a good measure of a prosecutor's quality, then we would be in a position to determine scientifically whether a prosecutor in one city was better or worse than a prosecutor in another city. Again, however, our conclusion would be inextricably tied to the criteria agreed on. As a practical matter, people are seldom able to agree on criteria for determining issues of value, so science is seldom of any use in settling such debates.

This issue will be considered in more detail in Chapter 13 when we look at *evaluation research*. As you'll see, criminal justice research has become increasingly involved in studying whether or not programs achieve their intended goals. One of the biggest problems faced by evaluation researchers is getting people to agree on the criteria for success and failure. Yet such criteria are essential if social scientific research is to tell us anything useful about matters of value.

As an example, consider the dilemma of identifying a good parole officer. On the one hand, a parole officer whose clients are rarely cited for violations and returned to prison might be considered a good officer. However, parole officers might attain low violation rates by ignoring transgressions by people they are supposed to supervise—in

FIGURE 1-1

Social Science = Theory + Data Collection + Data Analysis

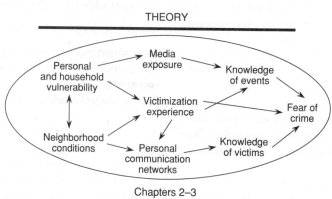

THEORY

Chapters 2–3

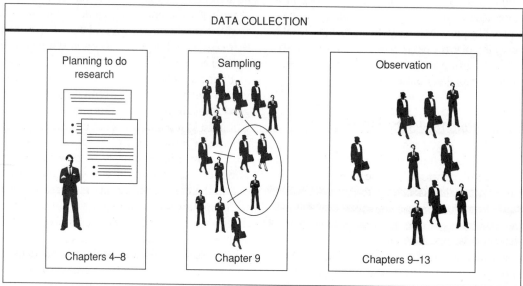

DATA COLLECTION

Planning to do research

Chapters 4–8

Sampling

Chapter 9

Observation

Chapters 9–13

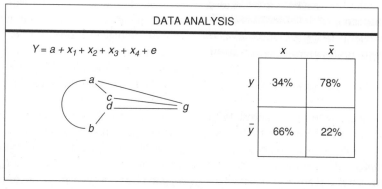

DATA ANALYSIS

$$Y = a + x_1 + x_2 + x_3 + x_4 + e$$

	x	$\bar{x}$
y	34%	78%
$\bar{y}$	66%	22%

Chapter 14

effect, by not supervising them at all. So we might view a parole officer who frequently cites parolees for violations as being especially attentive to his or her job. We might also consider other factors in judging parole officers. Someone who routinely cites parolees for trivial rule infractions would not necessarily be considered a good officer, especially if such actions swell already crowded prisons.

Thus, social science can assist us in knowing only what is and why. It can be used to address the question of what ought to be only when people agree on the criteria for deciding what's better than something else. But this agreement seldom occurs. With that understanding, let's turn now to some of the fundamentals that social scientists use to develop theories about what is and why.

Regularities

Ultimately, social scientific theory aims to find patterns of regularity in social life. This assumes, of course, that life is regular, not totally chaotic or random. That assumption applies to all science, but it is sometimes a barrier for people when they first approach social science.

Certainly at first glance, the subject matter of the physical sciences appears to be more regular than that of the social sciences. A heavy object, after all, falls to earth every time we drop it, but a judge may sentence one person to prison while another is given probation even though each is convicted of the same offense. Similarly, ice always melts when heated enough, but seemingly honest people sometimes steal. Examples like these, though true, can lead us to lose sight of the high degree of regularity in social affairs.

A vast number of formal norms in society create regularity. For example, only persons who have reached a certain age may receive a driver's license. In the National Football League, only men are allowed to participate in combat on the field. Such formal prescriptions, then, regulate, or regularize, social behavior.

Aside from formal prescriptions, other social norms can be observed that create more regularities. Teenagers tend to commit more crimes than middle-age people. When males commit murder, they usually kill another male, but female murderers more often kill men. On the average, white urban residents view police more favorably than nonwhites do. Judges receive higher salaries than police. Probation officers have more empathy for people they supervise than prison guards do.

We have noted that regularities exist in social life, and that science assumes that regularity exists in whatever is to be studied. Therefore, logically, social behavior should be susceptible to scientific analysis. But is that necessarily the case? After all, police officers in large cities often earn more than small-town judges. Or are these kinds of irregularities worthy of scientific study? So males murder other males, while females rarely murder other females. What's the point?

What About Exceptions?

The objection that there are always exceptions to any social regularity is inappropriate. It is not important that a particular police officer earns more money than a particular judge if judges earn more than police officers overall. The pattern still exists. Social regularities represent probabilistic patterns, and a general pattern does not have to be reflected in 100 percent of the observable cases to still be a pattern.

This rule applies in the physical sciences as well as the social sciences. In genetics, for example, the mating of a blue-eyed person with a brown-eyed person will probably result in a brown-eyed offspring. The birth of a blue-eyed child does not challenge the observed regularity, however, because the geneticist states only that the brown-eyed offspring is *more likely* and, furthermore, that brown-eyed offspring will be born only in a certain percentage of the cases. The social scientist makes a similar, probabilistic prediction: that women overall are less likely to murder anybody, but when they do, their victims are most often males.

Aggregates, Not Individuals

Social regularities do exist, then, and they are both susceptible to and worthy of theoretical and empirical study. Implicit in the preceding statement, however, is a point that needs to be made explicit. Social scientists study primarily social patterns rather than individual ones. All the regular patterns we've mentioned have reflected the aggregate or combined actions and situations of many individuals. Although social scientists study motivations that affect individuals, aggregates are more often the subject of social science research.

Focusing on aggregate patterns rather than on individuals distinguishes the activities of the criminal justice researcher from the daily routines of many criminal justice practitioners. Consider, for example, the problem of processing and classifying persons newly admitted to a correctional facility. Prison staff administer psychological tests and review the prior record of each new inmate to determine security risk and program need for that individual, and to decide what kind of job might best suit the person. A researcher who is studying whether white inmates tended to be assigned to more desirable jobs than nonwhite inmates would be more interested in patterns of job assignment. The focus would be on aggregates of white and nonwhite persons rather than the assignment for any particular individual.

Social scientific theories deal then, typically, with aggregated, not individual, behavior. Their purpose is to explain why aggregated patterns of behavior are so regular even when the individuals who participate in them change over time. In another important sense, social science doesn't even seek to explain people. Its aim is to understand the systems within which people operate, the systems that explain why people do what they do. The elements in such a system are not people but variables.

A Variable Language

Our natural attempts at understanding usually take place at the concrete, idiosyncratic level. That's just the way we think. Imagine that someone says to you, "Women are too soft-hearted to be criminal court judges." You are likely to "hear" that comment in terms of what you know about the speaker. If it's your old Uncle Albert who, you recall, is also strongly opposed to daylight savings time, zip codes, and electricity, you are likely to

think his latest pronouncement simply fits into his rather odd point of view about things in general.

If, on the other hand, the statement comes from a city council candidate who is trailing a female challenger and who has begun making other statements about women being emotionally unfit for public office, not understanding politics, and the like, you may "hear" his latest comment in the context of this political challenge.

In both of these examples, you understand the thoughts of a particular, concrete individual. In social science, however, we go beyond that level of understanding to seek insights into classes or types of individuals. In the two examples above, we might use terms like *old-fashioned* or *bigot* to describe the person who made the comment. In other words, we try to identify the concrete individual with some set of similar individuals, and that identification operates on the basis of abstract concepts.

One implication of this approach is that we can make sense out of more than one person. In understanding what makes the bigoted politician think the way he does, then, we'll also learn about other people who are "like him." This is possible because, in an important sense, we have not been studying bigots as much as we have been studying bigotry.

Bigotry is considered a **variable** in this case because it varies. Some people in an observed group are more bigoted than others. Social scientists may be interested in understanding the system of variables that causes bigotry to be high in one instance and low in another. Bigotry is not the only variable here. Gender, age, and economic status also vary among the observed group.

The idea of a system composed of variables may be foreign to you, so here's another example. Consider the problem of whether police should make arrests in cases of domestic violence. The subject of a police officer's attention in handling a domestic assault is the individual case. Of course each case includes a victim and an offender, and police are concerned with preventing further harm to the victim. The officer must decide whether to arrest an assailant or take some other action. By contrast, a criminal justice researcher's subject matter is different: Does arrest as a general policy prevent future assaults? The researcher may study the police officer's case (victim and offender), but for the researcher that case is relevant only as a situation where arrest policy might be invoked, which is what the researcher is really studying.

This is not to say that criminal justice researchers don't care about real people. They certainly do. Their ultimate purpose in studying domestic violence cases is to protect potential victims from future assaults. But in their actual research, victims and offenders are relevant only for what they reveal about the effectiveness of arrest policy.

Social science involves the study of two kinds of concepts: variables and the **attributes** that compose them. Social scientific theories are written in a variable language, and people get involved only as the carriers of those variables. Here's what social scientists mean by variables and attributes.

Attributes are characteristics or qualities that describe some object—in this case, a person. Examples are bigot, old-fashioned, female, married, repeat offender, white, unemployed, and intoxicated. Any quality you might use to describe yourself or someone else is an attribute.

Variables, on the other hand, are logical groupings of attributes. Thus, for example, "male" and "female" are attributes, and "gender" is the variable composed of those two attributes. The variable "occupation" is composed of attributes like "dentist," "professor," and "truck driver." "Prior record" is a variable composed of a set of attributes such as "prior convictions," "prior arrests without convictions," and "no prior arrests."

Sometimes it helps to think of attributes as the categories that make up a variable. See Figure 1-2 for a schematic view of what social scientists mean by variables and attributes.

The relationship between attributes and variables lies at the heart of both description and explanation in science. For example, we might describe a prosecutor's office in terms of the variable "gender" by reporting the observed frequencies of the attributes "male" and "female": "The office staff is 70 percent men and 30 percent women." An incarceration rate can be thought of as a de-

scription of the variable "incarceration status" of a state's population in terms of the attributes "incarcerated" and "not incarcerated." Even the report of family income for a city is a summary of attributes composing the income variable: $17,124; $24,980; $76,000; and so forth.

The relationship between attributes and variables is more complicated as we try to explain things. Here's a simple example involving two variables: type of defense attorney and sentence. For the sake of simplicity, let's assume that the variable "defense attorney" has only two attributes: "private attorney" and "public defender." (Chapter 5 will discuss how such things are defined and measured.) Similarly, let's give the variable "sentence" two attributes: "probation" and "prison."

Now let's suppose that 90 percent of people represented by public defenders are sentenced to prison and the other 10 percent are sentenced to probation. And let's suppose that 30 percent of people with private attorneys go to prison and the other 70 percent receive probation. This is shown visually in Figure 1-3A.

Figure 1-3A illustrates a relationship between the variables "defense attorney" and "sentence." This relationship can be seen by the pairings of attributes on the two variables. There are two predominant pairings: (1) persons represented by private attorneys who are sentenced to probation and (2) persons represented by public defenders who are sentenced to prison. Here are two other useful ways of viewing that relationship.

First, let's imagine that we play a game in which we bet on your ability to guess whether a person is sentenced to prison or probation. We'll pick the people one at a time (not telling you which ones we've picked), and you have to guess which sentence each person receives. We'll do it for all 20 people in Figure 1-3A. Your best strategy in this case is to always guess prison because 12 out of the 20 people are categorized that way. Thus, you'll get 12 right and 8 wrong, for a net success of 4.

Now let's suppose that we pick a person from the figure and then we have to tell you whether the person has a private attorney or a public defender. Your best strategy now is to guess prison

FIGURE 1-2
Variables and Attributes

A.

Some Common Criminal Justice Concepts
Female
Probation
Thief
Gender
Sentence
Property crime
Middle-aged
Age
Auto theft
Occupation

B.

Two Different Kinds of Concepts	
Variables	Attributes
Gender	Female
Sentence	Probation
Property crime	Auto theft
Age	Middle-aged
Occupation	Thief

C.

The Relationship Between Variables and Attributes	
Variables	Attributes
Gender	Female, male
Age	Young, middle-aged, old
Sentence	Fine, prison, probation
Property crime	Auto theft, burglary, larceny
Occupation	Judge, lawyer, thief

for each person with a public defender and probation for each person represented by a private attorney. If you follow that strategy, you will get 16 right and 4 wrong. Your improvement in guessing sentence by knowing type of defense attorney is an illustration of what we mean by the variables being related. You would have made a probabilistic statement that was based on some empirical observations about the relationship between type of lawyer and type of sentence.

Second, by contrast, let's consider how the 20 people would be distributed if type of defense attorney and sentence were unrelated. This is illustrated in Figure 1-3B. Notice that half the people

have private attorneys and half have public defenders. Also notice that 12 of the 20 (60 percent) are sentenced to prison. If 6 of the 10 people in each group were sentenced to prison, we would conclude that the two variables were unrelated. Then knowing what type of attorney a person had would not be of any value to you in guessing whether that person was sentenced to prison or probation.

Variables and Relationships

We will look more closely at the nature of the relationships between variables later in this book. In particular, we'll see some of the ways rela-

FIGURE 1-3
Illustration of Relationships Between Two Variables

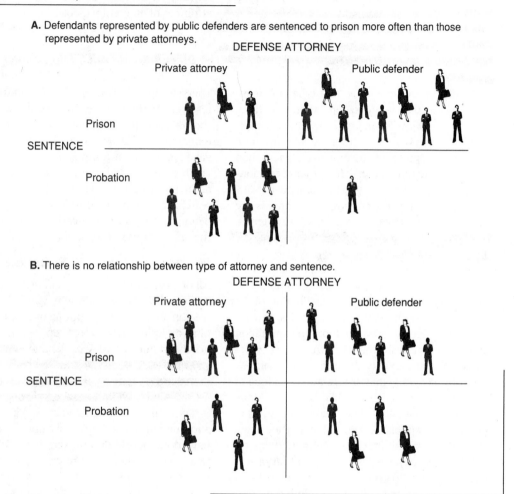

A. Defendants represented by public defenders are sentenced to prison more often than those represented by private attorneys.

B. There is no relationship between type of attorney and sentence.

tionships can be discovered and interpreted in research analysis. Still, it is important that you have a general understanding of relationships now to appreciate the logic of social scientific theories and their use in criminal justice research.

Theories describe the relationships that might logically be expected among variables. The expectation often involves the notion of causation. A person's attributes on one variable are expected to cause, predispose, or encourage a particular attribute on another variable. In the example just given, it appeared that having a private attorney or a public defender caused a person to be sentenced to probation or prison, respectively. It seems there is something about having a public defender that leads people to be sentenced to prison more often than if they were represented by a private attorney.

As we'll discuss in more detail later in the book, type of defense attorney and sentence in this example are regarded as independent and dependent variables, respectively. These two concepts are implicit in causal models, and we'll devote all of Chapter 3 to the notion of causation. In this example, we assume that criminal sentences are determined or caused by something; the type of sentence depends on something—hence, it is called the **dependent variable.** The dependent variable depends on an **independent variable;** in this case, sentence depends on type of defense attorney.

Notice, at the same time, that type of defense attorney might be found to depend on something else—our subjects' employment status, for example. People who have full-time jobs are more likely to be represented by private attorneys than those who are unemployed. In this latter relationship, the type of attorney is the dependent variable and the subject's employment status is the independent variable. In cause-and-effect terms, **the independent variable is the cause, and the dependent variable is the effect.**

So, how does this relate to theory? Our discussion of Figure 1-3 has involved the interpretation of data. We looked at the distribution of the 20 people in terms of the two variables. In constructing a theory, we would form an expectation about the relationship between the two variables based on what we know about each. For example, we know generally that private attorneys tend to be more experienced than public defenders. Many people fresh out of law school gain a few years of experience as public defenders before they begin to work in private practice. Logically, then, we would expect more experienced private attorneys to be better able to get more lenient sentences for their clients. We might further explore this question by examining the relationship between attorney experience and sentence, perhaps comparing inexperienced public defenders with public defenders who had been working for a few years. Pursuing this line of reasoning, we could also compare experienced private attorneys with private attorneys who had just completed law school.

Notice that the theory has to do with the variables "defense attorney" and "sentence" (and maybe years of experience), not with individual people per se. People are the carriers of those two variables, so the relationship between the variables can be seen by observing people. Ultimately, however, the theory is constructed of a variable

language. It describes the associations that might logically be expected to exist between particular attributes of different variables.

■ DIFFERING AVENUES FOR INQUIRY

There is no one way of doing criminal justice research. If there were, this would be a much shorter book. In fact, much of the power and potential of social science research lies in the many valid approaches it comprises.

Three broad and interrelated distinctions underlie many of the variations of social science research. Although it is possible to see them as competing choices, a good researcher masters each of the orientations we are about to describe.

Idiographic and Nomothetic Explanations

All of us go through life explaining things; we do it every day. You explain why you did poorly or well on an exam, why your favorite team is winning or losing, why you keep getting speeding tickets. In our everyday explanations, we engage in two distinct forms of causal reasoning, idiographic and nomothetic explanation, although we do not ordinarily distinguish them.

Sometimes we attempt to explain a single situation exhaustively. Thus, for example, you may have done poorly on an exam because: (1) you had forgotten there was an exam that day, (2) it was in your worst subject, (3) a traffic jam made you late to class, (4) your roommate kept you up the night before the exam with loud music, and (5) the police kept you until dawn demanding to know what you had done with your roommate's stereo, and what you had done with your roommate for that matter. Given all these circumstances, it is no wonder that you did poorly on the exam.

This type of causal reasoning is *idiographic* explanation. "Idio-" in this context means unique, separate, peculiar, or distinct, as in the word "idiosyncrasy." When we have completed an idiographic explanation, we feel that we fully understand the many causes of what happened in a particular instance. At the same time, the scope of our explanation is limited to the case at hand. While parts of the idiographic explanation might apply to other situations, our intention is to explain one case fully.

Now consider a different kind of explanation. For example, every time you study with a group, you do better on the exam than if you study alone; or your favorite team does better at home than on the road; or you get more speeding tickets on weekends than during the week. This type of explanation—called *nomothethic*—seeks to explain a class of situations or events rather than a single one. Moreover, it seeks to explain "efficiently," using only one or just a few explanatory factors. Finally, it settles for partial rather than full explanation of a type of situation.

In each of the preceding nomothetic examples, you might qualify your causal statements with phrases like "on the whole," "usually," or "all else being equal." Thus, you usually do better on exams when you've studied in a group, but there have been exceptions in both directions. Similarly, your team has won some games on the road and lost some at home. And last week you got a speeding ticket on the way to Tuesday's chemistry class, but you did not get one over the weekend. Such exceptions are an acceptable price to pay for a broader range of overall explanation.

Both the idiographic and the nomothetic approaches to understanding can be useful to you in your daily life. By the same token, both idiographic and nomothetic reasoning are powerful tools for criminal justice research. The researcher who seeks an exhaustive understanding of the inner workings of a particular juvenile gang or the rulings of an individual judge is engaging in idiographic research. The aim is to understand that particular group as fully as possible.

In an in-depth study of a group of New York cocaine dealers, Terry Williams (1989) recognized that the dealers he interviewed and observed were not necessarily typical of dealers in other cities, or even in other parts of New York. While Williams gained key insights into how drug rings operate generally, his immediate goal was to understand and describe the activities of a small group of dealers. Spending more than 1,200 hours in the field,

Williams describes the activities of "Max" and his crew in rich detail.

Sometimes, however, the aim is a more generalized understanding, across a class of events, even though the level of understanding is inevitably more superficial. For example, researchers who seek to uncover the chief factors that lead to juvenile delinquency are pursuing a nomothetic inquiry. They might discover, for example, that children who frequently skip school are more likely to have records of delinquency than those who attend school regularly. This explanation would extend well beyond any single juvenile, but it would do so at the expense of incomplete explanation.

In contrast to the Williams (idiographic) study of a cocaine crew, Avshalom Caspi and associates (1994) sought to understand relationships between certain personality traits and delinquency. Although they could not conclusively answer the question, Is there a criminal personality?, Caspi and associates found regularities in personality profiles among research subjects in Dunedin, New Zealand, and Pittsburgh, Pennsylvania. This is an illustration of the nomothetic approach to understanding.

As you can see then, social scientists have access to two distinct logics of explanation. Just as physicists treat light sometimes as a particle and other times as a wave, so social scientists can alternate between searching for broad, albeit less detailed, universals today and probing more deeply into the narrowly particular tomorrow. Both are good science, both are rewarding, and both can be fun.

Inductive and Deductive Reasoning

The distinction between inductive and deductive reasoning exists in your daily life, as well as in criminal justice research. You might take two different routes to reach the conclusion that you do better on exams if you study with others. First, you might find yourself puzzling, halfway through your college career, why you do so well on exams sometimes and more poorly at other times. You might list all the exams you've taken, noting how well you did on each. Then you try to recall any circumstances shared by all the good exams or by all the poor ones. Did you do better on multiple-choice exams or essay exams? Morning exams or afternoon exams? Exams in the natural sciences, the humanities, or the social sciences? Times when you studied alone or in a group? It suddenly occurs to you that you have almost always done better on exams when you studied with others, better than when you studied alone. This is known as the *inductive* mode of inquiry.

Inductive reasoning moves from the specific to the general. It moves from a set of particular observations to the discovery of a pattern that represents some degree of order among all the varied events under examination. Notice, incidentally, that your discovery doesn't necessarily tell you why the pattern exists—just that it does.

Here's the second and very different way you might reach the same conclusion about studying for exams. As you approach your first set of exams in college, you might wonder about the best ways to study. You might consider how much you should review the readings, how much you should focus on your class notes. Should you study at a measured pace over time or pull an all-nighter just before the exam? Among these musings, you might ask whether you should get together with other students in the class or just study on your own. You decide to evaluate the pros and cons of both options. Studying with others might not be as efficient because a lot of time might be spent on things you understand already. Or the group might get distracted from studying. On the other hand, you can understand something even better when you've explained it to someone else. And other students might understand parts of the course that you've been having trouble with. Several minds can reveal perspectives that might have escaped you.

So, you add up the pros and the cons and conclude, logically, that you'd benefit from studying with others. This seems reasonable to you, just as it seems true "in theory." To see whether the process is true in practice, you test your idea by studying alone for half your exams and studying with others for the other exams. This second approach is known as the deductive mode of inquiry.

Deductive reasoning moves from the general to the specific. It moves from (1) a pattern that might be logically or theoretically expected to (2) observations that test whether the expected pattern actually occurs in the real world. Notice that deduction begins with *why* and moves to *whether,* while induction moves in the opposite direction.

As we'll see later in this book, both of these approaches are valid avenues for criminal justice and other social science research. Moreover, we'll see how they work together to provide ever more powerful and complete understandings.

Quantitative and Qualitative Data

Most simply put, the distinction between quantitative and qualitative data is the distinction between numerical and nonnumerical data. When you say someone is witty, that's a qualitative assertion. When you say that person has appeared three times in a local comedy club, you are attempting to quantify your assessment.

All observations are qualitative at the outset, whether it is your experience of someone's sense of humor, the location of a pointer on a measuring scale, or a checkmark entered in a questionnaire. None of these things is inherently numerical or quantitative, but sometimes it is useful to convert them to a numerical form. Quantification often makes our observations more explicit, can make it easier to aggregate and summarize data, and opens up the possibility of statistical analyses, ranging from simple averages to complex formulas and mathematical models.

Quantification involves focusing your attention and specifying meaning. For example, someone asks whether your friends tend to be older or younger than you. A quantitative answer seems easy. You recall how old each of your friends is, calculate an average, and see whether it is older or younger than you. Case closed.

Or is it? Although we focused our attention on "older or younger" as the number of years people have been alive, sometimes people mean something different with that idea. We might really mean "maturity" or "worldliness." Thus, your friends may tend to be a little younger than you in age but act more mature. Or we might have been thinking of how young or old your friends look or maybe the variation in their life experiences, their worldliness. All these other meanings are lost in the quantitative calculation of average age.

In addition to greater detail, qualitative data seem to carry a greater richness of meaning than do quantified data. Think of the cliché, "He is older than his years." The meaning of that expression is destroyed by attempts to specify how much older.

This richness of meaning is partly a function of ambiguity. If the expression meant something to you when you read it, that meaning comes from your own experiences, from people you have known who might fit the description of being "older than their years," or perhaps times you have heard someone use that expression. Two things are certain: (1) your understanding of the expression is different from ours, and (2) you don't know exactly what either of us means by the expression.

Earl Babbie has a young friend, Ray Zhang, who was responsible for communications at the 1989 freedom demonstrations at Tiananmen Square in Beijing. Following the Army clampdown on the demonstrations, Ray fled south, was arrested, and then was released with orders to return to Beijing. Instead, he escaped from China and made his way to Paris. Eventually, he came to the United States, where he resumed the graduate studies he had to abandon in fleeing his homeland. Ray has had to deal with the difficulties of getting enrolled in school without any transcripts from China, studying in a foreign language, meeting his financial needs, and doing all this on his own, thousands of miles from his family. Through all this, Ray still speaks of one day returning to China to build a system of democracy.

You'll probably agree that Ray sounds like someone who is both worldly and "older than his years." This qualitative description, while it fleshes out the meaning of the phrase, still does not equip us to say how much older or even to compare Ray with someone else without the risk of disagreeing as to which one is more "worldly."

This concept can be quantified to a certain extent, however. For example, we could make a list of life experiences that contribute to what we mean by "worldliness":

Getting married
Getting divorced
Having a parent die
Seeing a murder committed
Being arrested
Being fired from a job
Running away with a rock band

We could quantify people's worldliness by how many of these experiences they have had: The more such experiences, the more worldly we say they are. If we think that some experiences are more powerful than others, we can give those experiences more points than others. Once we have decided on the specific experiences to be considered and the number of points each warrants, scoring people and comparing their worldliness would be pretty straightforward.

To quantify a concept like worldliness, we must be explicit about what we mean. By focusing specifically on what we will include in our measurement of the concept, however, we also exclude the other possible meanings. Inevitably, then, any quantitative measure will be more superficial than the corresponding qualitative description. This is the trade-off.

What a dilemma! Which approach should you choose? Which is better? Which is more appropriate to criminal justice research?

The good news is that you don't need to choose. Both qualitative and quantitative methods are useful and legitimate. You will discover that some research situations and topics are more suited to qualitative examination, others more suited to quantification, and still others may require elements of both approaches. Michael Quinn Patton (1990:13) puts it this way: "Research, like diplomacy, is the art of the possible."

■ *ETHICS AND CRIMINAL JUSTICE RESEARCH*

Most of this book is designed to teach you specific techniques of social scientific research in criminal justice. Our goal is to help you understand the different techniques available to criminal justice researchers, and which particular methods are best suited for different situations. Some vital nonscientific concerns also shape the activities of criminal justice researchers.

Chapter 8 of this book deals extensively with the issue of research ethics, but we would like to introduce that topic now. Ethics is especially important in studying crime and criminal justice, because our interest often focuses on human behavior that is illegal. You would do well to keep these ethical considerations in mind as you learn about the logic and techniques of criminal justice research.

The foremost ethical rule of social science research is: *Bring no harm to research subjects.* Although no researcher plans to hurt people intentionally, this ethical rule applies to inadvertent or accidental harm as well. Research subjects might be indirectly harmed in several ways. A gang member observed talking with a researcher might be physically harmed by other gang members. Victims of crime can suffer psychological harm when asked to describe their experiences. Research subjects engaged in criminal activities may experience legal or economic harm if their activities become known to officials or employers. Finally, research subjects may be harmed through embarrassment or violation of privacy. Eliminating the potential for harm to subjects is not always possible, but researchers use several general strategies to minimize possible harm. Maintaining the confidentiality of data that might be gathered during a criminal justice research project is one of the most widely used strategies.

Another basic ethical rule of research is: *Participation should be voluntary.* Again, in principle, this appears a pretty simple rule to follow. An experimenter who forced people to participate in the experiment would be roundly criticized. When someone calls and asks you to participate in a telephone survey, you are free to refuse. Yet when we go into the field to observe transactions in a street drug market, we don't ask permission of all buyers and sellers who come to our attention. Or if we trace arrest records for convicted burglars after they are released from prison, we can't really say they are volunteering for our study. Researchers sometimes debate whether a particular study did or did not violate this established ethical principle.

Not harming subjects and voluntary participation are the most fundamental ethical issues in criminal justice and other forms of social science research. We will discuss these and others in Chapter 8. We'll see that different approaches to criminal justice research often raise different kinds of ethical questions. For now, you should be aware of the importance of ethical issues and the need to consider them throughout the research process.

■ *KNOWING THROUGH EXPERIENCE: SUMMING UP AND LOOKING AHEAD*

This chapter introduced you to the foundation of criminal justice research: empirical research, learning through experience. Each avenue for inquiry—nomothetic or idiographic description, inductive or deductive reasoning, qualitative or quantitative data—is fundamentally empirical.

You may find it helpful to think of criminal justice research as organized around two activities: measurement and interpretation. Researchers measure aspects of reality and then draw conclusions about the meaning of what they have measured. All of us are observing all the time, but measurement refers to something more deliberate and rigorous. Part 2 of this book describes ways of structuring observations to produce more deliberate, rigorous measures. As we will see, your ability to interpret observations in criminal justice depends crucially on how those observations are structured. After structuring observations, you have to actually measure them. Whereas physical scientists sometimes use tensiometers, spectrographs, and other such equipment for measurement, criminal justice researchers use a variety of techniques examined in Part 3 of this book.

The other key to criminal justice research is interpretation. Much of interpretation is based on data analysis, which we will introduce in Chapter 14. More generally, however, interpretation is very much dependent on how observations are structured, a point that is repeated throughout the book.

When you put the pieces together—measurement and interpretation—you are in a position to describe, explain, or predict something. Chapter 13 will focus on the applications of criminal justice research in selecting and evaluating policy actions.

■ *MAIN POINTS*

- Inquiry is a natural human activity that people use to seek a general understanding of the world around them.
- Much of what we know, we know by agreement rather than by direct experience.
- Tradition and authority are important sources of knowledge.
- When we understand through experience, we make observations and seek patterns of regularities in what we observe. Empirical research produces knowledge through systematic observation.
- In day-to-day inquiry, we often make mistakes. Science offers protection against such mistakes.
- Whereas people often observe inaccurately, such errors are avoided in science by making observation a careful and deliberate activity.
- Sometimes we jump to general conclusions on the basis of only a few observations. Scientists avoid overgeneralizaton through replication—the repeating of studies.
- Once a conclusion has been reached, we sometimes ignore evidence that contradicts

that conclusion, paying attention only to evidence that confirms it. Scientists commit themselves in advance to making a complete set of observations, regardless of whether or not a pattern emerges early in the process.

- Sometimes people simply reason illogically. Scientists avoid this by being as careful and deliberate in their reasoning as in their observations.
- The scientific study of crime guards against, but does not prevent, ideological and political beliefs from influencing the research process.
- Social science involves three fundamental aspects: theory, data collection, and data analysis.
- Social scientific theory addresses what is, not what should be. Theory should not be confused with philosophy or belief.
- Social science looks for regularities in social life.
- Social scientists are interested in explaining human aggregates, not individuals.
- An attribute is a characteristic, such as male or young.
- A variable is a logical set of attributes. "Gender," for example, is a variable made up of the attributes "male" and "female."
- Although social scientists observe people, they are primarily interested in discovering relationships that connect variables.
- Idiographic explanations seek to understand specific cases.
- Nomothetic explanations seek a generalized understanding of many cases.
- Inductive theories find general patterns within specific observations.
- Deductive theories predict specific events based on general theories.
- Quantitative data are numerical; qualitative data are not.
- Social science research ethics prohibit bringing harm to subjects.
- Participation in social research should be voluntary.

■ *REVIEW QUESTIONS AND EXERCISES*

1. Review the common errors of personal inquiry discussed in this chapter. Find a newspaper article or a letter to the editor about crime that illustrates one of those errors. Discuss how a scientist would avoid making that error.
2. List five criminal justice variables and the attributes making up those variables.

■ *ADDITIONAL READINGS*

Babbie, Earl, *The Sociological Spirit* (Belmont, CA: Wadsworth, 1994). A primer in some sociological points of view. It introduces some of the concepts commonly used in the social sciences.

Babbie, Earl, *Observing Ourselves: Essays in Social Research* (Belmont, CA: Wadsworth, 1986). A collection of essays that expand some of the philosophical issues in social scientific research, including objectivity, paradigms, determinism, concepts, reality, causation, and values.

Gallup, George, Jr., Roper, Burns, Yankelovich, Daniel, and others, "Polls That Made a Difference," *Public Perspective,* May–June 1990, pp. 17–21. Several public opinion researchers talk about social research polls that have had a great impact on everyday life.

Hoover, Kenneth R., *The Elements of Social Scientific Thinking* (New York: St. Martin's Press, 1992). An excellent overview of the key elements in social scientific analysis.

McDermott, M. Joan, "The Personal Is Empirical: Feminism, Research Methods, and Criminal Justice Education," *Journal of Criminal Justice Education,* Vol. 3, no. 2 (Fall 1992), 237–249. A discussion of recent challenges to "malestream" approaches to empirical criminal justice research. McDermott suggests various themes that have emerged in feminist writings on research methods, including a suggestion that feminist researchers strive to bridge qualitative and quantitative approaches.

Watson, James, *The Double-Helix* (New York: New American Library, 1968). An informal and candid research biography describing the discovery of the DNA molecule, written by a principal in the drama. This account should serve as a healthy antidote to the traditional view of science as totally cool, rational, value-free, and objectively impersonal.

2 Theory and Criminal Justice Research

What You'll Learn in This Chapter

You'll see what distinguishes scientific theory from everyday reasoning and how the social scientific approach to criminal justice research is linked to theory. This chapter will lay a foundation for your understanding of research techniques discussed throughout the rest of the book.

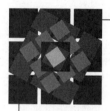

INTRODUCTION

THE CREATION OF SOCIAL SCIENCE THEORY
The Traditional Model of Science
Two Logical Systems
Terms Used in Theory Construction

THEORY IN CRIMINAL JUSTICE
Law Breaking
Policy Responses
Theory, Research, and Public Policy
Ecological Theories of Crime and Crime
  Prevention Policy

MAIN POINTS

REVIEW QUESTIONS AND EXERCISES

ADDITIONAL READINGS

■ INTRODUCTION

One of the livelier academic debates of recent years has focused on the scientific status of subjects gathered under the heading of social sciences. Basically at issue is whether human behavior can be studied scientifically.

The movement toward social science has represented a redirection and, in some cases, a renaming of established academic disciplines. Increasingly, departments of government have been replaced by departments of political science. There are today few university departments of social studies, whereas sociology departments abound. Departments of police science or forensic studies were formed in a few universities in the 1930s and 1940s. In the later part of the 20th century, departments of criminal justice have become more common. Departments of criminology are also found, although criminology is sometimes studied in departments of sociology.

In many cases, the movement toward social science has brought a greater emphasis on systematic explanation where the previous emphasis was on description. In political science, emphasis is now on explaining political behavior rather than describing political institutions. The growth of such subfields as econometrics has had this effect in economics, as has historiography in history. Criminal justice and criminology have followed this same trend. Research on the causes of crime and the effects of criminal justice policy has supplemented a previous emphasis on describing strategies for police investigation or corrections management. Understandably, professionals trained and experienced in the more traditional orientations of these fields have objected to the new directions.

This book is grounded in the position that human social behavior can be subjected to scientific study as legitimately as can the physicist's atoms or the biologist's cells. The study of crime and criminal justice concentrates on particular types of human behavior and is, therefore, no less subject to scientific study. This chapter describes the overall logic of social scientific inquiry as it applies to criminology and criminal justice.

■ THE CREATION OF SOCIAL SCIENCE THEORY

In Chapter 1, we looked at some of the foundations of social scientific research as a mode of inquiry involving both logic and observation. Now we'll examine the relationship between theory and research in more depth. First comes a look at "the scientific method" as it is traditionally taught. Following that, we'll see there are actually two models describing the relationship between theory and research in the practice of social science. The chapter concludes with a look at the important links between theory, research, and policy.

The Traditional Model of Science

Instruction in the scientific method, especially in the physical sciences, tends to create a particular picture in students' minds of how science operates. Although this traditional model of science tells only a part of the story, it is important that you understand the basic logic of that model.

The three main elements in the traditional model of science, which are typically presented in a chronological order of execution, are theory, operationalization, and observation. Let's look at each in turn.

Theory According to the traditional model of science, the scientist begins with an interest in some aspect of the real world. Suppose, for example, you were interested in discovering some of the broad social factors that contribute to the concentration of crime in urban areas. What kinds of major social problems and characteristics of urban areas are associated with higher levels of crime?

As you think about this question, you will probably suggest things like population density, crowded housing conditions, poverty, unemployment, limited economic opportunity, weakened family ties, and the absence of appropriate role models. As described by Marvin Krohn (1991), these are some of the ideas that influenced the development of social disorganization theories of crime. In the early part of the 20th century, sociologists began to examine the social disruption produced by rapid population growth in the city of Chicago. What came to be known as the "Chicago School" of criminology began with more general studies on the roots of a broad spectrum of social problems.

Sociologists Ernest Burgess and Robert Park described Chicago's growth as a pattern of concentric zones (Burgess, 1925; Park and Burgess, 1921). At the core was the city's central business district, or downtown area. As Chicago grew outward, the city developed in a pattern of circles centered around the core. Each area, from the downtown core to outlying suburbs, displayed particular patterns of land use. Commerce and industry were concentrated in downtown areas, while wealthy families occupied residential areas in outer circles. Lower-income migrants to Chicago settled in transition zones between the core and more distant areas.

Transition zones were so labeled because of the continuous flow of people moving in and out of the areas. Higher-income residents tended to move outward to avoid the influx of industrial activity expanding from the city's core area. Outward-moving families were replaced by lower-income immigrants from Europe (and later white and black migrants from depressed southern states) who were moving to the city to pursue economic opportunity or escape political oppression. Persons moving into transition zones found housing that was deteriorating and crowded but close to the factory jobs that had attracted them to Chicago. Because poverty afforded them little choice, they settled there in large numbers. As their economic situation improved, people moved outward and were replaced by new in-migrants, thus continuing the cycle of transition.

Burgess argued that these patterns of population movement and neighborhood conditions weakened family, neighborhood social institutions, and other collective ties, thus producing a general phenomenon he termed *social disorganization*. Several problems were believed to result from social disorganization, including higher rates of disease, mental illness, and crime. These ideas form the basis of the social disorganization theory of crime.

The kinds of social conditions Burgess described in transition zones suggest other possible explanations for the concentration of crime in these areas. For example, if 20th-century immigrants from Europe (and, later, low-income migrants from the American South) were concentrated in transition zones, such groups might bring cultural differences to urban areas that produced crime and other social ills. In other words, crime in transition zones might be the result of a concentration of individuals from particular cultural backgrounds in those areas, rather than the consequence of social disorganization.

How would you settle the question of whether social disorganization or cultural differences accounted for the concentration of crime in transition zones? The second step in the traditional model of science helps us move toward an answer.

Operationalization   Operationalization is simply the specification of the steps, procedures, or operations that you go through to actually identify and measure the variables you want to observe. Chapter 5 of this book describes that topic in more depth. In the present example, operationalization involves deciding how to measure things like crime, social disorganization, and cultural background.

While Park and Burgess were developing their general theories of urban growth and its social consequences, Shaw and McKay began a series of studies that tested the social disorganization explanation for crime in transition zones. Their landmark study, originally published in 1942, described how important concepts were operationalized (Shaw and McKay, 1969).

First, they chose three indicators of delinquency to measure crime, each obtained from official city records: (1) alleged delinquents brought before juvenile court, (2) juveniles committed to institutions, and (3) alleged delinquents dealt with by police but not brought before a juvenile court. In later chapters, we will discuss common problems with using such measures, but for now it is interesting to note that Shaw and McKay recognized these limitations and discussed them in an insightful manner.

Second, social disorganization was measured even less directly, as is often the case in social research. Indicators were constructed from census data and information provided by local agencies. Some indicators were: families on relief (an earlier version of welfare and unemployment payments), average monthly rent, home ownership, occupational status, and ethnicity. Their measure of ethnicity was whether or not a head of household was born in another country, referred to as "foreign-born." The percentage of black families also expressed ethnicity.

These indicators made it possible to compare delinquency to social disorganization and ethnic background, but how could Shaw and McKay determine which of these two factors was more important in explaining delinquency? Recall for a moment the concept of transition zones: People were continuously moving into and out of the neighborhoods between core commercial zones and more wealthy residential areas. The notion of transition implies population movement, and the mobility of urban residents in Chicago offered an answer.

Shaw and McKay compared changes in delinquency rates over time, examining three time periods: 1900–1906, 1917–1923, and 1927–1933. They also examined delinquency for different ethnic groups within each zone. If cultural differences accounted for crime, then delinquency rates in outer zones should increase as people from different cultural backgrounds moved out of transition zones and into more stable residential areas. On the other hand, if social disorganization produced delinquency, then the pattern of lower rates in outer zones and higher rates in transition zones should remain stable, despite the outward movement of ethnic groups.

One additional step was necessary: to operationalize urban zones. As noted, earlier work by Park and Burgess described concentric zones. They identified five in Chicago: Zones I and II were the inner core and transition areas; farther out, zone III included the homes of working-class families, zone IV was a higher-income residential area, and zone V was a suburban or outer area. Within

each zone were several distinct neighborhoods. Shaw and McKay divided the city of Chicago into 140 areas of approximately one square mile each, so that several areas were included in each of the five zones. These 140 areas represented units of analysis. Chapter 4 will discuss units of analysis and the problems that sometimes accompany defining them. For now, it is only important that you recognize these 140 areas as units that include aggregations of individuals.

Observation   The final step in the traditional model of science involves actual observation—looking at the world and making measurements of what is seen. Having developed theoretical expectations and having created a strategy for looking, we need only to look at the way things are. Sometimes this step involves conducting experiments, sometimes interviewing people, sometimes visiting what you're interested in and watching it. Sometimes the observations are structured around the testing of specific hypotheses; sometimes the inquiry is less structured. For Shaw and McKay, it meant poring through published statistics in search of data relevant to their operationalization, and then grouping data on delinquency and other indicators into 140 areas.

Comparing delinquency between ethnic groups, they found that rates were higher for all groups in core areas and transition zones. Although there was wide variation within groups— foreign-born, black, and native white—similar rates for each group were found in the same types of zones. Comparing rates over time, Shaw and McKay (1969:162, 315) found that as foreign-born families moved to outer zones, delinquency rates remained lower in those areas than in inner zones. Summarizing these findings, they concluded:

■ In the face of these facts it is difficult to sustain the contention that, by themselves, the factors of race, nativity, and nationality are vitally related to the problem of juvenile delinquency. It seems necessary to conclude, rather, that the significantly higher rates of delinquents found among the children of Negroes, the foreign born, and more recent immigrants are closely related to existing differences in their respective patterns of geographical distribution within the city. . . . Moreover, the fact that in Chicago the rates of delinquents for many years have remained relatively constant in the areas adjacent to centers of commerce and heavy industry, despite successive changes in the nativity and nationality composition of the population, supports emphatically the conclusion that the delinquency-producing factors are inherent in the community.

Although later research has challenged some of the conclusions Shaw and McKay reached, social disorganization theory continues to influence theory and research in criminal justice and other fields. For example, sociologist William Julius Wilson (1987) argues that limited opportunities for upward economic mobility and outward residential mobility have contributed to a host of chronic social problems, including crime, among inner-city residents in the late 20th century. Contemporary environmental theories of crime, which emphasize such concepts as urban form and its influence on human behavior, are rooted in the earlier work of Park and Burgess, and Shaw and McKay (for example, see Brantingham and Jeffery, 1991).

Notice how the research by Shaw and McKay was based on a more general theory of the links between the conditions of urban neighborhoods and a broad class of social ills. They had certain expectations about the pattern they would find in the numbers if a particular theoretical explanation was accurate. Operationalizing delinquency as an example of a social problem, they found higher rates of delinquency in transition zones, regardless of ethnic or cultural composition. In themselves, of course, these particular data did not prove the case; they did not provide definitive evidence that social disorganization produced delinquency. These data, however, were part of a weight of evidence that Shaw and McKay amassed. In addition to Chicago, they used similar measures to examine delinquency in other cities and found similar patterns.

We chose this example for three reasons. First, it illustrates the traditional model of scientific research, moving from theory to operationalization to observation. Second, it is more realistic than the hypothetical example of a simple physics experiment you might recall from discussions of the scientific method in a science class. Finally, contemporary research in criminal justice continues to build on this theoretical view of the relationships between crime and the urban environment.

Figure 2-1 provides a schematic diagram of the traditional model of scientific inquiry. In it, we see the researcher beginning with an interest in something or an idea about it. Next comes the development of a theoretical understanding. The theoretical considerations result in a hypothesis, or an expectation about the way things ought to be in the world if the theoretical expectations are correct. The notation $Y = f(X)$ is a conventional way of saying that Y (for example, delinquency) is a function of (is in some way caused by) X (for example, substandard housing). At that level, however, X and Y have general rather than specific meanings.

In the operationalization process, general concepts are translated into specific indicators. The lowercase x, for instance, is a concrete indicator of capital X. As an example, census data on the number of housing units that lack indoor plumbing (x) is a concrete indicator of substandard housing (X). This operationalization process results in the formation of a testable hypothesis: For example, did the rate of delinquency among Italian immigrants actually decline as they moved from transition zones to outer residential areas? Observations aimed at finding out are part of what is typically called **hypothesis testing.**

Although this traditional model of science provides a clear and understandable guide to how you could study something carefully and logically, it presents only a part of the picture. Let's look at the other parts now.

Two Logical Systems

The traditional model of science uses what is called *deductive logic* (see **deduction** in the glossary at the back of this book). In this section, we will examine deductive logic as it fits into social

FIGURE 2-1
The Traditional Image of Science

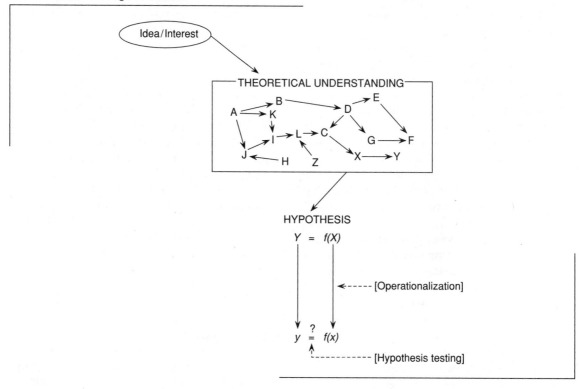

scientific research, and particularly, we will contrast it with *inductive logic* (see **induction** in the glossary). W. I. B. Beveridge (1950:113), a philosopher of science, describes these two systems of logic as follows:

◼ Logicians distinguish between inductive reasoning (from particular instances to general principles, from facts to theories) and deductive reasoning (from the general to the particular, applying a theory to a particular case). In induction one starts from observed data and develops a generalization which explains the relationships between the objects observed. On the other hand, in deductive reasoning one starts from some general law and applies it to a particular instance.

The classic illustration of deductive logic is the familiar syllogism "All people are mortal; Socrates is a person; therefore, Socrates is mortal." This syllogism, or logical argument, presents a theory and its operationalization. To prove it, you might

perform an empirical test of Socrates's mortality. That is essentially the approach discussed as the traditional model.

Using inductive logic, you might begin by noting that Socrates is mortal and observing a number of other people as well. You might then note that all the observed people are mortals, thereby arriving at the tentative conclusion that all people are mortal.

A Deductive Illustration   Why is there so much plea bargaining in criminal courts? What accounts for differences in conviction rates and sentence length among people convicted of similar offenses? These were among the questions addressed by James Eisenstein and Herbert Jacob (1977) in a study of court processing in three U.S. cities. Their research provides a good example of the deductive approach.

They began by identifying the shortcomings of popular views of criminal court outcomes. Differences in defendant characteristics, judicial characteristics, and the formal requirements of court procedure were not satisfactory explanations. Furthermore, they argued, previous studies of criminal courts had failed to disentangle the combined influence of differences in judges, lawyers, defendants, and court procedures.

Their novel approach was to view trial courts as organizations and to appeal to various theories of organization behavior to explain trial court outcomes. Courts in the United States (in contrast to courts in some other countries) are formally adversarial organizations, meaning that attorneys representing each side are supposed to do battle before a neutral judge. Maybe, said Eisenstein and Jacob, but even though prosecutors and defense lawyers are formal adversaries, they do work together to achieve the common goal of processing defendants, and therefore they have incentives to cooperate with each other. Similarly, judges are supposed to play a neutral role, but they also have to manage their courtrooms and move along large numbers of cases in a timely fashion.

Viewing the judge, prosecutor, and defense attorney as a workgroup helps explain their mutual incentives. In organization theory, workgroups are small collections of people who share responsibility for certain tasks. If the workgroup is stable, where its members work together over some period of time, individuals in the group come to know one another and develop shared incentives for maintaining group cohesion and harmony. Among the shared goals of courtroom workgroups are disposing of caseloads and reducing uncertainty, which means that group members share information about cases and try to avoid surprises. Of course, they also want to do justice, but justice is an elusive concept; other goals are easier to identify and have more immediate relevance to the workgroup. Finally, like most people who must work together, judges, prosecutors, and defense attorneys find their jobs more pleasant and easier if they get along with one another.

Eisenstein and Jacob drew several hypotheses from this theory, most notably that plea bargaining would be more common in courts with stable workgroups. Let's break this hypothesis down into parts to see how it deduces a specific prediction about trial courts from general organization theory. First, the longer people work together in a small group (stability), the better they will come to know one another and pursue common goals in a cooperative way. Second, members of the courtroom workgroup have a common goal of processing cases. Third, plea bargains are the products of negotiation. Therefore, stable courtroom workgroups will more often process cases through negotiated pleas of guilty than through formal trials.

Having framed this hypothesis (and others), Eisenstein and Jacob gathered data from felony courts (those that handle more serious crimes) in three cities: Baltimore, Chicago, and Detroit. Their findings generally supported the workgroup hypothesis by comparing the characteristics of court organization with indicators of case outcomes. However, they found that certain other features of court organization also helped explain case processing.

Plea bargaining was common in Chicago and Detroit for slightly different reasons, each consistent with organizational features. Judges, prosecutors, and public defenders in Chicago were regularly assigned to specific courtrooms for extended periods. This, and the traditional politics of accommodation in Chicago, promoted plea bargaining, which was how 70 percent of convicted defendants were processed.

Detroit courts had less stable workgroups but used a system of court administration that played a much stronger role in managing caseloads compared to Chicago. Judges and prosecutors took active steps to promote the rapid settlement of cases. As a result, 82 percent of convicted defendants pleaded guilty in plea bargains. The more aggressive management also resulted in faster processing of cases than in Chicago.

The situation was different in Baltimore. Court management was haphazard, judges were regularly rotated to different courtrooms, and there was a great deal of turnover among prosecutors. As a result, courtroom workgroups were less stable and the informal goals of negotiation gave way to more formal processing of felony cases—only 45 percent were settled by plea bargains. Eisenstein and Jacob also point out that in Baltimore, where neither informal workgroup norms nor formal court management was very strong, there tended to be greater differences in sentences between judges. That is, where formal and informal organization controls were weaker, individual differences in sentencing became more common.

This research example clearly illustrates the deductive model. Beginning with general, theoretical expectations about the impact of organization characteristics on court operations, Eisenstein and Jacob derived concrete hypotheses that linked specific measurable variables. The actual empirical data could then be analyzed to determine whether the deductive expectations were supported by empirical reality.

An Inductive Illustration Often, social scientists begin constructing a theory by observing aspects of social life, seeking to discover patterns that may point to more or less universal principles. Barney Glaser and Anselm Strauss (1967) coined the term *grounded theory* to describe this inductive method of theory construction. Field research—the direct observation of events in progress (discussed in depth in Chapter 11)—is frequently used to develop theories through observation. Or survey research (see Chapter 10) may reveal patterns of attitudes that suggest particular theoretical explanations. Here's an example.

During the 1960s and 1970s, marijuana use on America's college campuses was a subject of considerable discussion in the popular press. Some people were troubled by marijuana's popularity; others welcomed it. What interests us here is why some students smoked marijuana and others didn't. A survey of students at the University of Hawaii (Takeuchi, 1974) provided the data needed to answer that question.

At the time of the study, countless explanations were being offered for drug use. People who opposed drug use often suggested that marijuana smokers were academic failures who turned to drugs rather than face the rigors of college life. Those in favor of marijuana, on the other hand,

often spoke of the search for new values: Marijuana smokers, they said, were people who had seen through the hypocrisy of middle-class values.

David Takeuchi's (1974) analysis of the data gathered from University of Hawaii students, however, did not support any of the explanations being offered. Those who reported smoking marijuana had essentially the same academic records as those who didn't smoke it, and both groups were equally involved in traditional "school spirit" activities. Both groups seemed to feel equally well integrated into campus life.

There were differences, however:

1. Women were less likely than men to smoke marijuana.
2. Asian students (a large proportion of the University of Hawaii student body) were less likely to smoke marijuana than non-Asians.
3. Students living at home were less likely to smoke marijuana than those living in apartments.

The three variables independently affected the likelihood of a student's smoking marijuana. About 10 percent of the Asian women living at home had smoked marijuana, as contrasted with about 80 percent of the non-Asian men living in apartments. And the researchers discovered a powerful pattern of drug use before they had an explanation for that pattern.

In this instance, the explanation took a peculiar turn. Instead of explaining why some students smoked marijuana, the researchers explained why some didn't. Assuming that all students had some motivation for trying drugs, the researchers suggested that students differed in the degree of "social constraints" that prevented them from following through on that motivation.

American society is, on the whole, more tolerant of men than of women when it comes to deviant behavior. Consider, for example, a group of men getting drunk and boisterous. We tend to dismiss such behavior with references to "camaraderie" and "having a good time," whereas a group of women behaving similarly would be regarded with disapproval. The researchers reasoned, therefore, that women would have more to lose by smoking marijuana than men would. Being female, then, provided a constraint against smoking marijuana.

Students who lived at home had obvious constraints against smoking marijuana in comparison with students who lived on their own. Aside from differences in opportunity, those living at home were seen as being more dependent on their parents, and hence more vulnerable to additional punishment for breaking the law.

Finally, the Asian subculture in Hawaii has traditionally placed a higher premium on obedience to the law than other subcultures, so Asian students would have more to lose if they were caught violating the law by smoking marijuana.

Overall, then, a "social constraints" theory was offered as the explanation for observed differences in the likelihood of smoking marijuana. The more constraints a student had, the less likely he or she would be to smoke marijuana. It bears repeating that the researchers had no thoughts about such a theory when their research began. The theory was developed out of an examination of the data—the inductive approach.

Inductive Theory and Justice Policy   Consider a different way of looking at inductive theory building, suggested by Barbara Hart, Legal Director of the Pennsylvania Coalition Against Domestic Violence.[1] Speaking on the topic of how to increase the utilization of criminal justice research by justice professionals, Hart argued that the development of grounded theory was commonplace among many practitioners. By this she meant that probation officers, judges, case managers, victim service counselors, and others tend to formulate general explanations to fit the patterns they observe in individual cases. As Hart put it: "Practitioners engage in theory building as they interpret experience."

Such theory may then guide the future actions of justice professionals, until they discover cases

or patterns of cases that don't fit their theory. See the box entitled "Grounded Theory and Community Prosecution" for an example.

A Graphic Contrast   Figure 2-2 shows a graphic comparison of the deductive and inductive methods. In both cases, we are interested in the relationship between the number of hours spent studying for an exam and the grade earned on that exam. Using the deductive method, we begin by examining the matter logically. Doing well on an exam reflects a student's ability to recall and manipulate information. Both of these abilities should be increased by exposure to the information before the exam. In this fashion, we arrive at a hypothesis suggesting a positive relationship between the number of hours spent studying and the grade earned on the exam. We say *positive* because we expect grades to increase as the hours of studying increase. If increased hours produced lower grades, that would be called a negative relationship. The hypothesis is represented by the graph in part 1(a) of Figure 2-2.

Our next step, using the deductive method, is to make observations relevant to testing our hypothesis. The shaded area in part 1(b) of the figure represents perhaps hundreds of observations of different students, noting how many hours they studied and what grades they got. Finally, in part 1(c) of the figure, we compare the hypothesis and the observations. Because observations in the real world seldom (if ever) match our expectations perfectly, we must decide whether the match is close enough to consider the hypothesis confirmed. Put differently, can we conclude that the hypothesis describes the general pattern that exists, granting some variations in real life?

Now let's address the same research question using the inductive method. In this case, we begin—as in part 2(a) of the figure—with a set of observations. Curious about the relationship between hours spent studying and grades earned, we might simply arrange to collect some relevant data. Then we'd look for a pattern that best represents or summarizes our observations. In part 2(b) of the figure, the pattern is shown as a curved

---

[1] From remarks at the Family Violence Cluster Conference, National Institute of Justice, Washington, DC, July 12, 1995.

Grounded Theory and Community Prosecution

by Barbara Boland

LIKE community policing, community prosecution differs from traditional ways of handling crime in two respects. First, community policing and prosecution involve working with community organizations and ordinary residents. Second, police and prosecutors try to identify patterns of crime and related problems rather than just respond to individual incidents as they occur. "Look for patterns, and look for help" is one way to summarize this approach: Focus on problems rather than incidents; cooperate with community residents and others rather than responding to a crime report or prosecuting a case in isolation of other organizations.

A community prosecutor who worked in a Portland, Oregon, neighborhood initially assumed that the concerns of area residents centered on serious crime problems produced by repeat offenders. However, conventional notions about crime and appropriate responses were

quickly changed once the prosecutor began talking with neighborhood residents. They wanted something done about prostitution, public drinking, drug use, vandalism, littering, assaults, garbage, and thefts from cars—problems that did not match the traditional notions of serious crime.

One particular area in the neighborhood, Sullivan's Gulch, illustrates what troubled residents. A natural depression where two railroad lines intersect, Sullivan's Gulch had long attracted transients who set up illegal camps in the area, sometimes remaining for extended stays. By the late 1980s, the number of illegal campers had exploded. Gulch dwellers wandered into nearby commercial and residential areas to buy and consume liquor, to litter, loiter, urinate, and fight. None of these problems were serious crimes, and such nuisance reports were seldom recorded in crime counts. But they nonetheless troubled neighborhood residents and undermined efforts to revitalize commerce in the area.

After talking with area residents and business owners and thinking about the problem, the

line running through the center of the curving mass of points.

The pattern found among the points in this case—and shown in part 2(c) of the figure—suggests that with 1 to 15 hours of studying, each additional hour generally produces a higher grade on the exam. With 15 to about 25 hours, however, more study seems to slightly lower the grade. Studying more than 25 hours, on the other hand, results in a return to the initial pattern: More hours produce higher grades. Using the inductive method, then, we end up with a tentative conclusion about the pattern of the relationship between the two variables. The conclusion is *tentative* because the observations we have made cannot be taken as a test of the pattern; those observations are the source of the pattern we've created.

In actual practice, then, theory and research interact through a continuous alternation of de-

duction, induction, deduction, and so forth. Walter Wallace (1971) has represented this process nicely as a circle, which is presented in a modified form in Figure 2-3.

In summary, the scientific norm of logical reasoning provides a bridge between theory and research—a two-way bridge. Scientific inquiry in practice typically involves an alternation between deduction and induction. During the deductive phase, we reason *toward* observations; during the inductive phase, we reason *from* observations. Both logic and observation are essential. In practice, both deduction and induction are routes to the construction of social theories.

Terms Used in Theory Construction

In this section, we will discuss some of the terms used in connection with the creation of scientific theories. We've already been using some of

community prosecutor reasoned that traditional approaches like stepped-up patrol, police visibility, and arrests might work for a time. The increased police presence could not be maintained over a long period, however, and problems would no doubt reappear after police moved on to other areas.

Instead, the prosecutor arranged an initial police sweep to disperse campers from the Gulch. This was accompanied by a city-sponsored clean-up that removed tents, derelict structures, and countless truckloads of debris. The next step was a cooperative effort among police and area residents. Signs reading "No Camping" on one side and listing nearby homeless shelters on the reverse were posted in the area. Citizens were enlisted to patrol the Gulch on a regular basis and to notify police about the appearance of any campsites. Encouraged by the support they had received from police and the prosecutor's office, area residents were diligent in watching for campers and dissuading new arrivals from setting up camp.

Resident concerns about Sullivan's Gulch offer a classic example of the links between disorder and crime, as described in the article "Broken Windows" by James Wilson and George Kelling (1982) and a later book by Wesley Skogan (1990a). The "broken windows" theory of crime holds that: ". . . serious crime flourishes in areas where disorderly behavior goes unchecked" (Wilson and Kelling, 1982:34).

Listening to the concerns of residents and business owners near Sullivan's Gulch and observing the area first-hand, the neighborhood prosecutor "built" a theory. His theory was based on street-level experience, experience that differed from the prevailing suite-level perspective of traditional prosecution. The theory was inductive, grounded in observations that were then used to formulate more general statements about the links between disorder and serious crime in an area of Portland. And these links suggested a theory of action that guided justice policy.

Adapted from Boland (1996:36–37).

---

these terms because we know you have a general idea of what they mean in everyday language. Now, however, it is important to examine their meanings.

Objectivity and Subjectivity   We recognize that some things fall into the realm of attitudes, opinions, and subjective points of view: We say that the question of whether Bach or Beethoven was the better composer is a subjective matter, dependent on the experiences and tastes of the person who is making such a judgment. But we also feel that the existence of the book in your hands is an objective matter, independent of your experience of it. *Objective* is typically defined as "independent of mind," but our awareness of what might objectively exist comes to us through our minds. As a working principle, we substitute **intersubjective agreement** for **objectivity:** If several of us agree that something exists, then we treat that thing

as though it had objective existence. This book can be seen as a discussion of the logic and procedures by which social scientists come to intersubjective agreement, or how they come to agree on what's real.

Observation   The "experience" of whatever may or may not really exist typically refers to the operation of the human senses. In the case of social research, this is typically limited to seeing, hearing, and—less commonly—touching. The term *observation* is generally used in reference to such information gathering. (Part 3 of this book is devoted to the modes of observation used by social scientists.)

Fact   Although the notion of a *fact* is as complex for philosophers as is the notion of reality, it is generally used in the context of social scientific research to mean some phenomenon that has been observed. It is a fact, for example, that Bill Clinton

FIGURE 2-2
Deductive and Inductive Methods

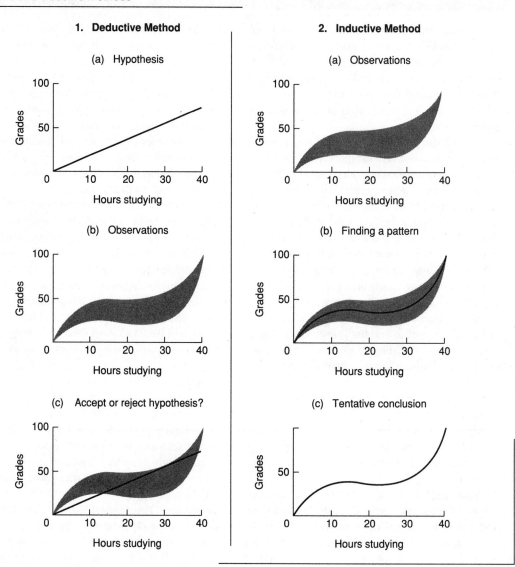

defeated Robert Dole in the 1996 presidential election.

Law Abraham Kaplan (1964:91) defines laws as universal generalizations about classes of facts. The law of gravity is a classic example: Bodies are attracted to each other in proportion to their masses and inversely proportional to the distance separating them.

Laws in science must be truly universal, however, and not merely accidental patterns found among a specific set of facts. It is a fact, Kaplan (1964:92) points out, that in each of the U.S. presidential elections from 1920 to 1960, the major candidate with the longest name won. That is not a law, however, as shown in three of the next four elections. It was a coincidence.

FIGURE 2-3
The Wheel of Science

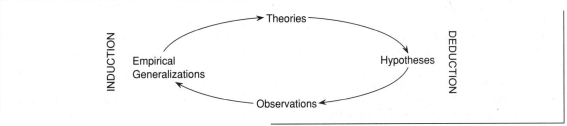

Source: Adapted from Walter Wallace, *The Logic of Science in Sociology* (New York: Aldine deGruyter, 1971). Copyright © 1971 by Walter L. Wallace. Used by permission.

Laws are sometimes also called *principles* and are important statements about what is so. We speak of them as being "discovered" because laws are not created by scientists. Also, laws in and of themselves do not explain anything. They just summarize the way things are. Explanation is a function of theory, and theories are created, as we'll see next.

Theory   A theory is a systematic explanation for the observed facts and laws that relate to a particular aspect of life—juvenile delinquency, for example, or perhaps social stratification, political revolution, or the like. Kenneth Hoover (1992: 34) defines *theory* as "a set of related propositions that suggest why events occur in the manner that they do."

Jonathan Turner (1974:3) has examined several elements of theory. We are going to consider three of them briefly: concepts, variables, and statements.

Concepts   Turner (1974:5) calls concepts the "basic building blocks of theory." They are abstract elements that represent classes of phenomena within the field of study. The concepts relevant to a theory of juvenile delinquency, for example, would include *juvenile* and *delinquency* for starters. *Peer group*—the people you hang around with and identify with—would be another relevant concept. *Social disorganization* was a central concept in the theory of delinquency tested by Shaw and McKay. *School performance* might also be relevant to a theory of juvenile delinquency.

Variables   A *variable* is a concept's empirical counterpart. Whereas concepts are in the domain of theory, variables can be observed and can take different values; they vary. Thus, variables require more specificity than concepts. For instance, as a variable, income might be specified as annual family income reported in response to a survey question. Chapter 5 will pursue the matter of how variables are measured in considerable detail.

Statements   A theory comprises several types of *statements*. Principles or laws, as discussed previously, are one type. Another type of statement is the *axiom*, a fundamental assertion—taken to be true—on which the theory is grounded. *Propositions* are a third type of statement: conclusions drawn about the relationships among concepts, based on the logical interrelationships among the axioms. To clarify, an axiom is an assumption about reality, while a proposition expresses relationships among axioms.

For example, in a theory of juvenile delinquency, we might begin with axioms such as "Everyone desires material comforts" and "The ability to obtain material comforts legally is greater for the upper class than for the working class." These axioms might reasonably lead us to the proposition: "Working-class youths would be more likely to break the law to gain material comforts than would upper-class youths."

Hypotheses   A **hypothesis** is a specified expectation about empirical reality, derived from propositions. If we continue the present example, a theory might contain the hypothesis "Working-class youths have higher delinquency rates than upper-class youths." Such a hypothesis could then be tested through research, as we saw in the earlier example of social disorganization and delinquency.

Paradigm   No one ever starts out with a completely clean slate to create a theory. The concepts that are the building blocks of theory are not created out of nothing. When we mentioned juvenile delinquency as an example of a topic for theory construction, you already had some implicit ideas about it. If we had asked you to list some concepts that would be relevant to a theory of juvenile delinquency, you would have been able to make suggestions. We might say that you already have a general point of view—a frame of reference or paradigm. A *paradigm* is a fundamental model or scheme that organizes our view of something.

This may strike you as uncomfortably similar to the definition of theory, and this is a natural point of confusion. The primary distinction is based on organization and structure. In Hoover's (1992:66) view, "A theory is a collection of hypotheses linked by some kind of logical framework." A paradigm is a much less structured way of viewing things that nonetheless affects how we approach research problems. It may be helpful to think of a paradigm as a pair of tinted glasses; everything you look at reflects the tint, no matter how you structure your observations. A theory serves to structure more carefully what we see through the paradigm's lenses, but what we see is still tinted.

Although a paradigm doesn't necessarily answer important questions, it tells us where, and often how, to look for the answers. And, as we'll see repeatedly, where you look largely determines the answers you'll find. Thomas Kuhn (1970:37) describes the importance of paradigms this way:

■ One of the things a scientific community acquires with a paradigm is a criterion for choosing problems that, while the paradigm is taken for granted, can be assumed to have solutions. To a great extent these are the only problems that the community will admit as scientific or encourage its members to undertake. Other problems, including many that had previously been standard, are rejected as metaphysical, as the concern of another discipline, or sometimes as just too problematic to be worth the time. A paradigm can, for

that matter, even insulate the community from those socially important problems that are not reducible to the puzzle form, because they cannot be stated in terms of the conceptual and instrumental tools the paradigm supplies.

Kuhn's chief interest was in how science advances. Although some progress is the slow, steady, and incremental improvement of established paradigms (Kuhn calls this *normal science*), he suggests that major scientific progress takes the form of *paradigm shifts,* as established, agreed-on paradigms are thrown out in favor of new ones. Thus, for example, Newtonian physics was replaced by Einstein's relativity in what Kuhn calls a *scientific revolution.*

We suggest that you compare the concept of paradigm to the world of fashion. Just as styles of clothing go in and out of fashion, paradigms that influence criminal justice come and go. We hope some styles and paradigms are gone forever: Contemporary men are free from the powdered wigs of the 18th century, women no longer suffer whalebone corsets (good for whales, too), and Western public officials have stopped amputating the hands of thieves. Some good ideas have stood the test of time. Summer shorts are blessings for women and men alike. Similarly, the early research by Park and Burgess and by Shaw and McKay pointed to the role of social disorganization as a cause of crime in the most disadvantaged urban areas, and their insights continue to influence contemporary research.

■ THEORY IN CRIMINAL JUSTICE

Because criminal justice draws on several disciplines—such as sociology, economics, geography, political science, psychology, anthropology, and biology—different paradigms, or frames of reference, have influenced criminal justice theory, research, and policy. Let's consider some examples, beginning with a general way of grouping theories in criminal justice. We emphasize that the following section presents *examples* of theories and is not intended to include a complete or even representative inventory.

At the risk of oversimplification, it is useful to consider two broad approaches to criminal justice research: law breaking and policy responses. Studies that focus on law breaking are interested in questions about why people commit crimes. Other studies are interested in how criminal justice institutions respond to crime as a policy problem, and how those institutions are managed. If you think about this distinction for a moment, you will realize that there may be considerable overlap between the two approaches. Of course, criminal justice policy is interested in why people commit crimes. By the same token, studies that focus on law breaking may suggest ways that public policy encourages or discourages crime.

This distinction, imperfect as it is, offers a useful way to discuss criminal justice theories and their links to individual disciplines.

Law Breaking

Theories rooted in biology dominated early research on crime, beginning most prominently with the work of an Italian physician, Cesare Lombroso, who tried to identify types of criminals based on their behavior and physical anatomy. Although Lombroso's research and conclusions have long since been discredited and often ridiculed, biological and genetic approaches to the study of criminality continue. For example, Sarnoff Mednick and colleagues have conducted studies to compare criminal behavior in persons who are adopted with criminal behavior by their biological parents and adoptive parents. Finding that adopted males who are criminals were more likely to have a biological father with a criminal record than an adopted father with a criminal record, they conclude that genetic factors influence criminality (Mednick, Gabrielli, and Hutchings, 1984).

In a fascinating study of homicide, Daly and Wilson (1988) draw on Charles Darwin's theory of sexual selection. Beginning with Darwin's principle that a species must reproduce to survive, Daly and Wilson point out that physiological differences between males and females promote conflict among males, but not among females. During their lifetime, females can produce a limited

number of offspring. The nine-month gestation period for human females means that through the childbearing years—say, ages 16 to 46—a woman can produce a maximum of about 30 children. But human males, by mating with more than one female, can produce a hypothetically unlimited number of children. From Darwin's principle of sexual selection, Daly and Wilson argue that an individual human male has incentives to mate with many females and produce a large number of offspring. Since this applies to all human males, they compete for female mates and their competition may take the form of fatal violence. Daly and Wilson (1988:147–148) present historical homicide statistics from several countries—ranging from 13th-century England to contemporary Miami—to show that males kill males about 100 times more often than females kill females.

Theory from the discipline of psychology also influences studies of law breaking, by linking such concepts as intelligence and personality traits to aggressive behavior, drug abuse, and crime. Early studies applying psychological theories showed that delinquent boys, for example, were more likely than nondelinquent boys to have such personality traits as impulsiveness and feelings of resentment (Glueck and Glueck, 1950). More recent research examines how childhood and developmental patterns are related to crime, delinquency, and more general antisocial behavior.

Research on criminal careers is one of the most prominent, but controversial, applications of developmental theories. Criminal career studies examine such concepts as when criminal or delinquent behavior begins, how long it continues, the extent to which the number of crimes committed increases, and when a criminal career ends. Blumstein, Cohen, Roth, and Visher (1986) call these concepts *onset, persistence, escalation,* and *desistance,* respectively.

Theories from the discipline of sociology have had the greatest influence on research on law breaking in the United States in the last half century. Psychologists are more interested in individual behavior, while sociologists are concerned with social relationships. In the view of Gottfredson and Hirschi (1990:75), psychologists see crime as behavior learned by individuals, while sociologists see it as group behavior.

We have already mentioned the early development of theories of social disorganization. Social strain theory begins with the assumption that people in modern society are socialized to pursue success, monetary or otherwise. When they encounter obstacles to achieving success, they experience frustration or strain. Rebellion is one possible reaction to such strain, involving, almost by definition, the rejection of social values. General social values may be replaced with other values that may lead to crime.

Conflict theory is closely associated with sociology but also has roots in political science. Conflict theory rejects absolute definitions of crime and criminality. Instead, crime is a *label* produced by social values and political power, both of which are embodied in criminal law. In connection with crime, politics involves conflict over social and other values. The winners of such conflict define certain behavior and acts as crimes, and the losers—people whose behavior is rejected—are labeled as criminals.

Political scientist Ted Robert Gurr (1976) advocates a version of conflict theory by focusing not only on crime, but also on the more general concept of public order. In Gurr's view, political leaders (and would-be leaders) apply the labels *crime* and *civil strife* to distinguish acts that threaten individuals (crime) from acts that threaten political stability. Both types of threats to public order include violence, but incidents of criminal violence are individual acts, while civil strife represents collective violence. In elaborating this approach, Gurr examines crime and civil strife in Western and Eastern societies from the early 1800s through 1970. For a contemporary example that illustrates Gurr's concept of public order, consider events following the breakup of Yugoslavia. Newspaper reports described how rape, most often viewed as an individual act of violence, was used as an instrument of collective violence intended to undermine the stability of a political regime. Mass law breaking was a product of political conflict.

Economists are interested in how people make choices, most often under a fundamental assump-

tion of rationality. People engage in behavior to maximize satisfaction, and such behavior is rational. Rationality, therefore, is the framework through which an economic theory of law breaking would view individual behavior.

In seeking to maximize satisfaction, individuals weigh the costs and benefits of various actions: If benefits outweigh costs, the behavior is rational. Since the calculation of costs and benefits is subjective, and people may have incomplete information about potential costs and benefits, different individuals may have different ideas about what is rational. A burglar, for example, may overestimate how much profit might be made from selling a stolen television or might underestimate the chances of getting caught. Reuter, MacCoun, and Murphy (1990) apply economic theories of labor force participation to explain the actions of drug dealers in Washington, D.C. Dealers make calculated choices about the relative benefits and costs of selling drugs, and implicitly compare them with the benefits and costs of engaging in some other occupation.

Our final theory of law breaking integrates principles from different social science disciplines. Environmental explanations link criminal behavior to physical and social space. As described by Paul and Patricia Brantingham (1991:12–13), the application of social ecology to criminology has two components. First, the physical features of a city—urban form—are partly the results of conflict over a scare resource, space. Cities are densely populated because land costs are high and many people want to locate near jobs, shopping, and entertainment. Second, human behavior is affected by physical form. People behave differently in the downtown areas of large cities, for example, than they do in suburban shopping malls.

Different urban forms present greater or lesser opportunities for crime by bringing potential offenders and victims close to each other. For example, the Brantinghams (1991:49) describe how dispersed shopping areas and strip developments are especially vulnerable to high rates of property crime. This is because such shopping areas are designed to provide convenient access to large numbers of people in automobiles. As much as shoppers, property offenders value ease of access and anonymity and are therefore attracted to dispersed shopping centers and strip developments in large metropolitan areas.

Policy Responses

Each of the disciplines mentioned above has also influenced studies of how government officials and people in general respond to crime as a policy problem. We mentioned the influence of organization theory (drawing on psychology and sociology) on the study of criminal courts by Eisenstein and Jacob (1977).

The disciplines of economics and psychology are evident in most studies of deterrence. Criminal justice policy from law making to corrections seeks to deter individuals from committing crimes by threatening to punish them. Whether or not the threat of punishment can deter criminal acts depends on three elements: certainty, severity, and celerity. Deterrence works best when individuals are certain that they will be caught and punished and when their punishment is severe enough to represent a real threat. *Celerity* is another word for swiftness—how quickly does punishment follow the crime—and is used primarily because "certainty, severity, and swiftness" does not sound as good. Much deterrence research seeks to find out which of these three factors is most important.

Throughout U.S. history, different paradigms associated with punishment come and go. Rehabilitation, retribution, and incapacitation are paradigms in that they represent fundamental frames of reference about the purposes of punishment. Rehabilitation is a paradigm that sees punishment or other sanctions as instruments to change behavior. Research has been unable to show much consistent success in rehabilitating wrongdoers. As a result, other paradigms have influenced policy approaches to punishment. Retribution, with biblical origins, is the belief that society has a legitimate interest in punishing criminals, simply for the sake of expressing disapproval. Incapacitation has enjoyed recent popularity among officials and researchers alike. This paradigm assumes that society is protected from further harm when criminals are incarcerated; in prison, criminals lack the capacity to commit further crimes against the general public.

When coupled with research on criminal careers, the principle of incapacitation is potentially interesting to public officials by suggesting that sentencing policy could be more selective. Criminal career research has found that most delinquents and young adult criminals "grow out" of crime; their offending desists as they become older. However, criminal careers for some people persist and escalate. These findings suggest that prison sentences should be used more selectively, to incapacitate people who do not grow out of crime or to incapacitate people until they grow out of crime.

It is not difficult to see that the implications of incapacitation are controversial. In addition to the ethical problem of locking people up until they reach a certain age, there is the prediction problem: Social science methods are not sufficiently accurate to enable judges to predict who should be incapacitated (Gottfredson and Gottfredson, 1994).

Theory, Research, and Public Policy

Because crime is an important social problem, rather than simply a social artifact of interest to researchers, much research in criminal justice is closely linked to public policy. It is interesting and important to determine why some people commit crimes while others do not, but such research takes on added meaning when we consider how new knowledge can be used to formulate policy. Research on criminal justice policy is an example of *applied research;* research results are applied to specific questions about how government officials and the general public should respond to crime.

Criminal justice theory is just as important in structuring applied research questions as it is in directing basic research. Theory, research, and criminal justice policy are linked in two ways. First, as we have seen, theory is used to guide basic research. Results from basic research may suggest specific policy actions. For example, a presiding judge in Phoenix who wishes to process cases faster would be wise to learn about empirical research on trial courts. Eisenstein and Jacob found that court administrators in Detroit scheduled meetings between prosecutor and defense attorneys where plea bargains were discussed, and they required that reports of such meetings be forwarded to judges. The Phoenix presiding judge might then direct all judges to require pretrial meetings between prosecutors and defense attorneys to negotiate the terms of plea bargains.

To understand the second way criminal justice theory and policy are related, consider the similarities between hypotheses and specific programs. Earlier in this chapter, we said that hypotheses are specified expectations about empirical reality. This statement is also true of policy programs: They are specified expectations about what empirical reality will result from some specific policy action. Theories of social disorganization include "if–then" statements such as: "If an urban neighborhood exhibits signs of social disorder, then crime and delinquency in that neighborhood will be higher compared to neighborhoods with fewer signs of social disorder." This implies a public policy if–then statement: "If we implement a new program to reduce social disorder in an urban neighborhood, then crime and delinquency will decline."

Complementary if–then statements such as these underlie the rationale for community policing and actions taken by Portland's community prosecutor (see the box earlier in this chapter). Under community-based crime control strategies, police and prosecutors take action against neighborhood problems of social disorder that may contribute to crime and juvenile delinquency.

So theory, research, and policy are related in two similar ways: (1) theory structures research, which in turn is consulted to develop policy, and (2) policies take the form of if–then statements, which implies that they are subject to empirical tests. The second way theory is linked to policy forms the basis for evaluation research—studies that assess whether or not some program is achieving its intended goals. A program is simply a hypothesis that some specific action will produce some specific result. A program may therefore be empirically evaluated in the same way a research hypothesis can be empirically evaluated.

To illustrate the relationships between theory, research, and policy, we now turn to some intellectual descendants of Shaw and McKay.

Ecological Theories of Crime and Crime Prevention Policy

In his introduction to a collection of case studies on situational crime prevention, Ronald Clarke (1992b) describes how this approach to criminal justice policy evolved from more general ecological theories of crime.

The word *ecological* is significant: Just as humans and other organisms are affected by environmental forces in nature (weather, ozone depletion, water quality), human behavior is partially a function of the physical and social environment in which that behavior takes place. If you think for a moment, you will recognize that this fundamental principle is consistent with social disorganization theory: Crime is more common in urban transition zones where the physical environment (crowded housing) is unpleasant and the social environment (poverty, unemployment, and disease) is undesirable.

Ecological theories rooted in research by Shaw and McKay eventually influenced the thinking of architects and city planners, whose work focuses on the design of buildings, streets, parks, and other physical features of the urban landscape. One of the most influential works that blended concepts of urban design and criminal justice was Oscar Newman's (1972) book *Defensible Space*. Newman argued that urban housing should be constructed to enhance the ability of residents to monitor and control their environment. Too often, the design of large public housing projects in U.S. cities made it difficult for residents to distinguish threatening strangers from neighbors going about their business.

At about the same time Newman's book appeared, similar ideas about the link between urban design, human behavior, and crime were influencing the development of crime prevention policy in England. Drawing also on the economics paradigm of rational choice, researchers in the

British Home Office Research Unit extended Newman's ideas about how the physical environment affected potential victims (be they people or places), proposing that decisions made by criminals were also influenced by urban design (Clarke and Mayhew, 1980; Cornish and Clarke, 1986). Offenders may not formally weigh the costs and benefits of committing a crime, but Cornish and Clarke assert that offenders do evaluate potential targets and make choices based at least in part on opportunities.

Such reasoning led Clarke and others to propose crime prevention policies that try to reduce the opportunities for crime. This approach is called *situational crime prevention*, defined by Clarke (1992b:4) as "opportunity-reducing measures that are (1) directed at highly specific forms of crime (2) that involve the management, design or manipulation of the immediate environment in as systematic and permanent a way as possible (3) so as to increase the effort and risks of crime and reduce the rewards as perceived by a wide range of offenders." Clarke describes several examples of situational crime prevention techniques. The effort required to steal a car can be increased by steering wheel locks; rewards of theft from automobiles can be reduced if car owners install removable stereo systems; the risks (to thieves) of auto theft can be increased by more thoughtful design of parking lots.

This example illustrates the deductive approach to moving from theory to policy development. Situational crime prevention policies were deduced, over a period of years, from earlier theories that described the relationships between crime and the physical and social environment of urban areas.

Now consider how Clarke's description of the steps involved in designing specific situational crime prevention programs illustrates the inductive approach to policy development (1992b:5):

1. Collect data about the nature and dimensions of the specific crime problem;
2. analysis of the situational conditions that . . . facilitate the commission of the crimes in question;
3. systematic study of possible means of blocking opportunities for these particular crimes, including analysis of costs;
4. implementation of the most promising, feasible and economic measures; and
5. monitoring of results and dissemination of experience.

Points 1 and 2 involve collecting data and searching for patterns; points 3 and 4 are equivalent to formulating a tentative conclusion and operating hypothesis based on the observed patterns. The final step is the applied research counterpart to hypothesis testing: Monitor and evaluate results and then report whether or not the program achieved its intended objectives.

Throughout this chapter, we have seen various aspects of the links between theory and research in criminal justice inquiry. In the deductive model, research is used to test theories. In the inductive model, theories are developed from the analysis of research data. Whereas we have discussed two logical models for linking theory and research, actual criminal justice inquiries have developed a great many variations on these themes. Sometimes theoretical issues are introduced merely as a background for empirical analyses. Other studies cite selected empirical data to bolster theoretical arguments.

The ground we've covered in this chapter should make you even more aware that there is no simple cookbook recipe for conducting criminal justice research. It is far more open-ended than the traditional view of science would suggest. Ultimately, science rests on two pillars: logic and observation. As we'll see throughout this book, they can be fit together in many patterns.

■ *MAIN POINTS*

- Whether human social behavior can be studied "scientifically" has been debated for some time. It can.
- The traditional image of science includes theory, operationalization, and observation.

- Social scientific theory and research are linked through two logical methods: (1) Deduction involves the derivation of expectations or hypotheses from theories, and (2) induction involves the development of generalizations from specific observations.
- Grounded theory is a term used in reference to the creation of theory based on observation more than on deduction.
- Science is a process involving an alternation of deduction and induction.
- Although people speak of science as being "objective," that quality is difficult to define and demonstrate. More accurately, intersubjective agreement means that different scientists—even those with different points of view—can agree in their observations and conclusions.
- A fact usually refers to something that has been observed.
- A law in science is a universal generalization about a class of facts.
- A theory is a systematic explanation for a set of facts and laws.
- A paradigm is a fundamental model or scheme that organizes our view of something.
- Theory in criminology and criminal justice is frequently adapted from other disciplines in the social and, less often, natural sciences.
- Theories in criminology and criminal justice can be grouped into two general, and often overlapping, categories: law breaking and policy responses.
- Criminal justice theory, research, and policy are linked in two ways: (1) Theory influences basic research, which may suggest new policy developments, and (2) policies are formulated like hypotheses and may therefore be subject to empirical test.

■ REVIEW QUESTIONS AND EXERCISES

1. Consider the possible relationship between education and deterrence theory. Describe how that relationship might be examined through (a) deductive and (b) inductive reasoning.
2. Select an article describing applied research from some academic journal. Describe the relationships among theory, research, and policy in that article.
3. After reviewing the wheel of science in Figure 2-3, redraw the figure to include "justice policy" in the circle. Explain why you chose to place justice policy in that particular place.

■ ADDITIONAL READINGS

Clarke, Ronald V., "Situational Crime Prevention," in Michael Tonry and David Farrington (eds.), *Crime and Justice: An Annual Review of Research* (Chicago: University of Chicago Press, 1995), pp. 91–150. In this essay, Clarke lays out the genesis of situational crime prevention, linking it to past and evolving theories of crime and delinquency. This is an excellent example of synthesizing theory, research, crime prevention policy, and research methods.

Gottfredson, Michael R., and Hirschi, Travis, *A General Theory of Crime* (Stanford, CA: Stanford University Press, 1990). This book presents a good example of a comprehensive theory, in which the authors argue that crime should be viewed as one type of human behavior that has much in common with other types of behavior. Along the way, the authors comment on how theories from different social and natural science disciplines contribute to theory in criminology and criminal justice.

Kaplan, Abraham, *The Conduct of Inquiry* (San Francisco: Chandler, 1964). A standard reference volume on the logic and philosophy of science and social science. Though rigorous and scholarly, it is eminently readable and continually related to the real world of inquiry.

Kuhn, Thomas, *The Structure of Scientific Revolutions,* 2d ed. (Chicago: University of Chicago Press, 1970). An exciting and innovative recasting of the nature of scientific development. Kuhn disputes the notion of gradual change and modification in science, arguing instead that established "paradigms" tend to persist until the weight of contradictory evidence brings about their rejection and replacement by new paradigms. This short book is at once stimulating and informative.

Simpson, Sally, "Strategy, Structure, and Corporate Crime: The Historical Context of Anticompetitive Behavior," in Freda Adler and William S. Laufer (eds.), *New Directions in Criminological Theory, Advances in Criminological Theory*, Vol. 4 (New Brunswick, NJ: Transaction Publishers, 1993). Simpson's article is an excellent example of synthesizing theory from other social sciences to generate theory in criminal justice. Organization and economic theory, together with historical analysis of industrial technology, are integrated to explain varying patterns of illegal corporate practices.

Weiss, Carol H., "Nothing As Practical As Good Theory: Exploring Theory-based Evaluation for Comprehensive Community Initiatives for Children and Families," in James P. Connell, Anne C. Kubisch, Lisbeth B. Schorr, and Carol H. Weiss (eds.), *New Approaches to Evaluating Community Initiatives: Concepts, Methods, and Contexts* (Washington, DC: Aspen Institute, 1995), pp. 65–92. A well-known evaluation researcher, Weiss describes how public officials implicitly use theories of impact to guide their actions. She offers sound advice on how theories can improve research and evaluation in complex policy areas.

CHAPTER 3 *Causation and Validity*

What You'll Learn in This Chapter

Here you'll see how the notions of cause and effect relate to social science. You'll learn about both the technical and logical aspects of causation.

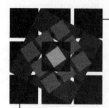

INTRODUCTION

DETERMINISM AND SOCIAL SCIENCE
Causation in the Natural Sciences
Finding Causes in Social Science
Reasons Have Reasons
Determinism in Perspective

IDIOGRAPHIC AND NOMOTHETIC MODELS OF EXPLANATION

CRITERIA FOR CAUSALITY
Necessary and Sufficient Causes
Molar, Not Micromediational,
    Causal Statements
Errors of Reasoning

VALIDITY AND CAUSAL INFERENCE
Statistical Conclusion Validity
Internal Validity
Construct Validity
External Validity
Validity and Causal Inference Summarized
Does Drug Use Cause Crime?

LINKING MEASUREMENT AND ASSOCIATION
The Traditional Deductive Model
The Interchangeability of Indexes

MAIN POINTS

REVIEW QUESTIONS AND EXERCISES

ADDITIONAL READINGS

■ *INTRODUCTION*

Implicit in much of what has been said so far in this book are the notions of cause and effect. One of the chief goals of scientists is to explain why things are the way they are. Typically, we do that by specifying the causes for the way things are: Some things are caused by other things.

The general notion of causation is both simple and complex. On the one hand, we could have ignored the issue altogether in this book. We could simply use the terms *cause* and *effect,* and you would have little difficulty understanding them. On the other hand, an adequate discourse on causation would require a whole book or a series of books. We decided to adopt a middle ground, providing more than a commonsense perspective on causation but not attempting to be definitive.

You will notice that much of our discussion in this chapter describes issues of causation and validity for social science in general. Recall from Chapters 1 and 2 that criminal justice research and theory are most strongly rooted in the social sciences, and that social science research methods are adapted from those used in the physical sciences. There are many important and difficult questions about causality and validity in criminal justice, but our basic approach requires stepping back a bit to consider the larger picture of how we can or cannot assert that some cause actually produces some effect.

We'll begin with the subject of determinism in social science. Having done that, we'll return briefly to the topic of deductive and inductive logic, with deterministic assumptions added. Next, we'll consider some appropriate and inappropriate criteria for causality, introducing the concept of validity. The chapter will conclude with a discussion of the links between measurement and association.

■ *DETERMINISM AND SOCIAL SCIENCE*

The deterministic perspective to be discussed now contrasts with a freewill image of human behavior that we all take for granted in our daily lives. The fundamental issue is this: Is your behavior

the product of your personal willpower or the product of forces and factors in the world that you cannot control and may not even recognize? We are going to look at that issue in more depth here. Once we have completed our examination, we'll be in a position to look at the place of causation in social scientific research.

Causation in the Natural Sciences

The deterministic model of explanation is evident throughout the natural sciences. Physical growth, for example, is caused by a number of factors. We can affect the growth of plants by varying the amount of light, water, and nutrients they receive. We also know that the growth rate of human beings is affected by the nutrients they receive. But the desire to grow or not to grow is irrelevant—for humans just as for plants. We acknowledge that nutrition greatly overshadows our free will in the matter of growth.

The point of this example is to show that the natural sciences operate on the basis of a deterministic cause-and-effect model, and that model is often applied to human beings as well as to plants and inanimate objects. For the most part, we accept the deterministic model as appropriate in such cases. We recognize that our free will is limited by certain deterministic constraints.

Finding Causes in Social Science

Essentially the same deterministic cause-and-effect model is used in the social sciences. It is usually so implicit that we may forget the nature of the model we are using, so let us illustrate how social science might proceed with that model. Imagine that you have received a multi-million-dollar grant from the National Science Foundation to find the causes of delinquency. That's certainly a laudable aim, and many government and private foundations have spent considerable sums supporting such research. Let's suppose you receive the money and spend it on your research. Now you are ready to send your project report off to the foundation. Here's what the report says:

■ After an exhaustive examination of the subject, we have discovered that some children become delinquents, and the reason for that is that they want to commit delinquent acts. Other children do not become delinquents, and the reason is that they do not want to commit delinquent or criminal acts.

Obviously, this paragraph would not be a satisfactory conclusion for a research project aimed at finding out what causes delinquency. When we look for the causes of delinquency, we look for the reasons: the things that make some people commit delinquent acts while others do not. More satisfactory reasons might include lack of parental supervision, peer-group association, early childhood experiences, and amount and kind of education. We know, for example, that parental supervision tends to reduce delinquency. That's the kind of causal explanation we accept as the end product of social research.

Now let's look at the logic of such an explanation a little more closely. What does it say about the people involved in the research conclusion— the subjects of study? Fundamentally, it says that people turned out to be delinquents or not delinquents as a result of something they did not themselves control or choose. It's as though they came to a fork in the road, with one turn representing delinquency and the other representing no delinquency. They were propelled down one or the other road by forces such as parental supervision, childhood experiences, and similar factors they neither controlled nor were even aware of. They turned out delinquent or not delinquent for reasons beyond their control.

The same model applies when criminal justice researchers address policy questions. What are the factors that cause a neighborhood to become a center for drug trafficking? A neighborhood does not "want" to be a thriving drug market, and if we knew what caused drug activity to become concentrated in some particular area, we might be able to take steps to reduce the problem—so the implicit reasoning goes.

Reasons Have Reasons

Sometimes people protest this reasoning by arguing that individuals make personal choices about things like whether or not to commit a delinquent act. For example, let's assume you have never committed a delinquent act, defined here as a nontraffic criminal offense committed by someone under age 18. We conclude from some research that the reasons you were not a delinquent are that you never had friends who were delinquents, and that your parents attentively supervised your after-school and weekend social life. Didn't you choose to follow your parents' advice and not associate with troublemakers in high school? Aren't you and the choices you made the reason you were not involved in delinquency?

The problem with this view is that reasons have reasons. *Why* did you choose to avoid being friends with delinquents? Let's say you thought that by avoiding the wrong crowd, you would stay out of trouble yourself. That makes sense, and we might say that your desire to stay out of trouble was influenced by your parents.

Clearly, it is not possible—in this book—to deal with all the particular reasons you might have had for not becoming a juvenile delinquent, but you can see that your life has unfolded in a particular way for various reasons. Moreover, no matter what reason you had at any specific step in the process, your reason would have a reason. The ultimate implication of this discussion is that your being delinquent or not can be traced back through a long and complex chain of reasons that explain why you turned out the way you did. You made choices, but your choices were influenced by many other things.

Whenever we undertake explanatory social science research—when we set out to discover the causes of delinquency, for example—we adopt a model of human behavior that assumes people have little individual freedom of choice. We don't say that, of course, but if you look at the implications of asking, Why are people delinquent?, you'll see that it's so.

Determinism in Perspective

As you probably realize, the issue of determinism versus freedom is a complex one, which philosophers have debated for thousands of years and will probably debate for thousands more. It is perhaps ultimately one of those "open questions" that is more valuable in the asking than it would be in the answering. We are not going to resolve it here.

Our purpose in raising the issue of determinism is to engage you in the question and to alert you to its place in criminal justice research. When people set out to learn the skills of explanatory research, the implicit assumption that human behavior is determined by social and other forces sometimes disturbs them. New researchers may harbor a concern about whether they are learning to demonstrate that they themselves have no free will, no personal freedom in determining the course of their own lives. To the extent that this concern grows and festers, it interferes with learning analytic skills and techniques. Our purpose in this discussion has been to confront the issue head on rather than leaving it for you to discover later.

Having said all that, let us clarify what is *not* part of the deterministic model. First, social scientists do not believe that all human actions, thoughts, and feelings are determined, nor do they lead their lives as though they believed that. Second, the deterministic model does not assume that causal patterns are simple. Nor does the model assume we are all controlled by the same factors and forces: Your reasons for not becoming a delinquent were surely somewhat different from someone else's reasons. Moreover, the deterministic model at the base of explanatory social science does not suggest that we now know all the answers about what causes what or that we ever will.

Finally, as we'll see later, social science typically operates on the basis of a *probabilistic* causal model. We say that certain factors make delinquency more or less likely within groups of people. Thus, teenagers with weak family bonds are more likely to commit delinquent acts than teenagers with strong family bonds (Elliott, Huizinga, and Ageton, 1985). This does not mean that all of the former and none of the latter will become delinquent.

To summarize, the kind of understanding we seek as we analyze criminal justice research data inevitably involves a deterministic model of human behavior. In looking for the reasons people are the way they are and do the things they do, we implicitly assume that their characteristics and actions are determined by the forces and factors that influence them. You do not need to believe that human actions and decisions are totally determined, nor do you have to lead your life as though you were, but you must be willing to use deterministic logic in looking for explanations when you engage in criminal justice research.

■ IDIOGRAPHIC AND NOMOTHETIC MODELS OF EXPLANATION

You have probably recognized that the preceding discussion, which probed the multiplicity of reasons that account for a specific behavior, illustrated the *idiographic model of explanation*. This model aims at explanation by enumerating the many, perhaps unique, considerations that lie behind a given action. Of course, we can never list all those reasons in practice. Nevertheless, it is important to realize that the idiographic model is used frequently in many different contexts.

Clinical psychologists tend to use the idiographic model as they seek to explain the aberrant behavior of a patient. A judge, in response to a plea of extenuating circumstances, may seek to examine all the various considerations that have resulted in the particular crime. A correctional intake worker considers the criminal history, education, and psychological profile of a newly committed offender in recommending a work assignment. And most of us use the idiographic model in attempting to understand the actions of the people around us.

Although the idiographic model of explanation is often used in daily life and in social research, other situations and purposes call for a different approach: the *nomothetic model of explanation*. This model does not involve an exhaustive enumeration of all the considerations that lie behind a particular action or event. Rather, the nomothetic model is designed to discover those considerations that are most important in explaining general classes of actions or events.

Suppose we want to find out why judges sentence some convicted drug offenders to prison terms, while others are given probation. The judges we talk to might give us several reasons for their sentencing decisions. Suppose one judge gave us 47 different reasons that one drug offender was sentenced to prison. We'd probably feel we had a pretty complete explanation for that particular sentence. In fact, if we found another case that had those same 47 reasons, we would feel pretty confident in predicting that that case would result in a prison sentence.

The nomothetic model of explanation, on the other hand, involves isolating a few considerations that provide a partial explanation for the sentences imposed by many judges or all judges. For example, the offender's prior record would be a consideration of general importance in determining the sentencing decisions of all judges. Most defendants with many previous convictions would probably be sentenced to prison, and most of those with no previous arrests or convictions for drug use would probably receive probation and suspended sentences. Of course, this single consideration would not provide a complete explanation for judges' sentencing decisions. Some first-time offenders receive prison sentences; some offenders with prior convictions get probation. We might also expect variation among judges in different cities and different states in the relationship between prior record and sentence. The goal of the nomothetic model of explanation is to provide the greatest amount of explanation with the fewest number of causal variables to uncover general patterns of cause and effect.

The nomothetic model of explanation is inevitably *probabilistic* in its approach to causation. In the best of all practical worlds, the nomothetic model indicates there is a very high (or very low) probability or likelihood that a given action will occur whenever a limited number of specified considerations are present. Adding more specified considerations typically increases the degree of explanation, but the basic simplicity of the model calls for balancing a high degree of explanation with a small number of specified considerations. We make probabilistic statements to gain this balance.

Social scientists sometimes are criticized for dehumanizing the people they study. This charge is lodged specifically against the nomothetic model of explanation. The charge is even more severe when social scientists analyze matters of great human concern. Judges, for example, may feel offended if a criminal justice researcher claims that available prison capacity has more influence on sentencing decisions than does any consideration of justice by the court. Any judge can quickly point out that there is much more to sentencing offenders than checking out the availability of prison space. And indeed there is, as the use of the idiographic model in the case of any particular sentencing decision would reveal. But is the idiographic model any less dehumanizing than the nomothetic model?

If all actions—including sentencing decisions—are a product of prior considerations, is it any more dehumanizing to seek partial but general explanations using only a few of those considerations than to seek total explanation using them all? Predicting a drug offender's sentence by counting the 47 specific reasons used by a particular judge is no less deterministic than predicting a sentence using fewer reasons. Yet it may seem more dehumanizing to seek a smaller number of reasons to explain behavior in general than to consider the many reasons that explain any particular action by an individual person.

It is important for you to realize that a careful listing of all the individual reasons for sentencing an individual offender, or for any other action, involves the acknowledgment of a deterministic perspective. You're still trying to determine all the causes that explain why someone was sentenced. This process is logically no different from the deterministic perspective that permits us to state the importance of prison capacity in a judge's sentencing. You should realize that nomothetic explanations are inherently deterministic because they try to completely explain why something happens.

■ CRITERIA FOR CAUSALITY

None of the preceding discussion provides much practical guidance about how to discover causal relationships in scientific research. Regarding idiographic explanation, Joseph Maxwell (1996: 87–88) speaks of the validity of an explanation and says the main criteria are (1) its credibility or believability and (2) whether alternative explanations ("rival hypotheses") were seriously considered and found wanting. The first criterion relates to earlier comments about logic as one of the foundations of science. We demand that our explanations make sense, even if the logic is sometimes complex. The second criterion reminds us of Sherlock Holmes's dictum that when all other possibilities have been eliminated, the remaining explanation must be the truth.

Regarding nomothetic explanation, we will discuss three specific criteria for causality, as described by Thomas Cook and Donald Campbell (1979). The actual use of these criteria will be illustrated in Chapter 7 on experimental design and in Chapter 13 on evaluation methods.

The first requirement in a causal relationship between two variables is that the cause precede the effect in time. It makes no sense to imagine something being caused by something else that happened later on. A bullet leaving the muzzle of a gun does not cause the gunpowder to explode; it works the other way around.

As simple and obvious as this criterion may seem, we will discover endless problems in this regard in criminal justice research. Often the time order connecting two variables is simply unclear. Which comes first: drug use or crime? And even when the time order seems essentially clear, exceptions can often be found. For example, we normally assume that obtaining a master's degree in management is a cause of more rapid advancement in a state department of corrections. Yet corrections executives might pursue graduate education after they have been promoted and they recognize that advanced training in management skills will help them do their job better.

The second requirement in a causal relationship is that the two variables be empirically correlated with each other. It would make no sense to say that exploding gunpowder causes a bullet to leave the muzzle of a gun if, in observed reality, a bullet did not come out after the gunpowder exploded.

Again, criminal justice research has difficulties with this seemingly obvious requirement. In the probabilistic world of nomothetic models of explanation at least, there are few perfect correlations. Most judges sentence repeat drug dealers to prison, but some don't. We are forced to ask, therefore, how strong the empirical relationship must be for that relationship to be considered causal.

The third requirement for a causal relationship is that the observed empirical correlation between two variables cannot be explained away as being due to the influence of some third variable that causes both of them. For example, you may observe that your left knee generally aches just before it rains, but this does not mean that your joints influence the weather. A third variable, relative humidity, is the cause of both your aching knee and the rain.

The box entitled "Correlation and Causality" shows that correlation does not necessarily point to a particular causal relationship.

To review, most social researchers consider two variables to be causally related—that is, one causes the other—if (1) the cause precedes the effect in time, (2) there is an empirical correlation between them, and (3) the relationship is not found to result from the effects of some third variable on each of the two initially observed. Any relationship that satisfies all these criteria is causal, and these are the only criteria.

Necessary and Sufficient Causes

Recognizing that virtually all causal relationships in criminal justice are probabilistic is central to understanding other points about cause. Within the probabilistic model, it is useful to distinguish two types of causes: necessary and sufficient causes. A *necessary cause* is a condition that, by and large, *must* be present for the effect to follow. For example, it is necessary for someone to be charged with a criminal offense in order to be convicted, but being charged is not enough; you must plead guilty or be found guilty by the court. Figure 3-1A illustrates that relationship.

A *sufficient cause*, on the other hand, is a condition that pretty much guarantees the effect in question. Thus, for example, pleading guilty to some criminal charge is a sufficient cause for being convicted, although you could be convicted through a trial as well. Figure 3-1B illustrates this state of affairs.

Correlation and Causality

by Charles Bonney
Department of Sociology, Eastern Michigan University

HAVING demonstrated a statistical relationship between a hypothesized "cause" and its presumed "effect," many people (sometimes including researchers who should know better) are only too eager to proclaim "proof" of causation. Let's take an example to see why "it ain't necessarily so."

Imagine you have conducted a study on college students and have found an inverse correlation between marijuana smoking (variable M) and grade point average (variable G)—that is, those who smoke tend to have lower GPAs than those who do not, and the more smoked, the lower the GPA. You might therefore claim that smoking marijuana lowers one's grades (in symbolic form, $M \rightarrow G$), giving as an explanation, perhaps, that marijuana adversely affects memory, which would naturally have detrimental consequences on grades.

However, if an inverse correlation is all the evidence you have, a second possibility exists. Getting poor grades is frustrating; frustration often leads to escapist behavior; getting stoned is a popular means of escape; ergo, low grades cause marijuana smoking ($G \rightarrow M$)! Unless you can establish which came first, smoking or low grades, this explanation is supported by the correlation just as plausibly as the first.

Let's introduce another variable into the picture: the existence and/or extent of emotional problems (variable E). It could certainly be plausibly argued that having emotional problems may lead to escapist behavior, including marijuana smoking. Likewise it seems reasonable to suggest that emotional problems are likely to adversely affect grades. That correlation of marijuana smoking and low grades may exist for the same reason that runny noses and sore throats tend to go together—*neither* is the cause of the other, but rather, both are the consequences of some third variable ($E \rightarrow M$, and $E \rightarrow G$). Unless you can rule out such third variables, this explanation too is just as well supported by the data as is the first (or the second).

Then again, perhaps students smoke marijuana primarily because they have friends who smoke, and get low grades because they are simply not as bright or well prepared or industrious

FIGURE 3-1A
Necessary Cause

Not Charged   Charged

Convicted

Not Convicted

as their classmates, and the fact that it's the same students in each case in your sample is purely coincidental. Unless your correlation is so strong and so consistent that mere coincidence becomes highly unlikely, this last possibility, while not supported by your data, is not precluded either.

Incidentally, this particular example was selected for two reasons. First of all, *every one* of the above explanations for such an inverse correlation has appeared in a national magazine at one time or another. And second, *every one* of them is probably doomed to failure because it turns out that, among college students, most studies indicate a *direct* correlation—that is, it is those with higher GPAs who are more likely to be marijuana smokers! Thus, with tongue firmly in cheek, we may reanalyze this finding:

1. Marijuana relaxes a person, clearing away other stresses, thus allowing more effective study; hence, $M \to G$.

   or

2. Marijuana is used as a reward for really hitting the books or doing well ("Wow,

man! An 'A'! Let's go get high!"); hence, $G \to M$.

or

3. A high level of curiosity (E) is definitely an asset to learning and achieving high grades and may also lead one to investigate "taboo" substances; hence, $E \to M$, and $E \to G$.

or

4. Again coincidence, but this time the samples just happened to contain a lot of brighter, more industrious students whose friends smoke marijuana!

The obvious conclusion is this: If *all* of these are possible explanations for a relationship between two variables, then no one of them should be too readily singled out. Establishing that two variables tend to occur together is a *necessary* condition for demonstrating a causal relationship, but it is not by itself a *sufficient* condition. It is a fact, for example, that human birthrates are higher in areas of Europe where there are lots of storks, but as to the meaning of that relationship . . . !

FIGURE 3-1B
Sufficient Cause

The discovery of a necessary and sufficient cause is the most satisfying outcome in research. If you were studying juvenile delinquency, it would be nice to discover a single condition that (1) had to be present for delinquency to develop and (2) always resulted in delinquency. Then you would surely feel that you knew precisely what caused juvenile delinquency. Unfortunately, we seldom discover causes that are both necessary and sufficient, nor, in practice, are causes 100 percent necessary or 100 percent sufficient.

Molar, Not Micromediational, Causal Statements

Natural scientists and engineers are often interested in making very specific, detailed statements about cause. For example, most of us vaguely understand that lamps come on when switches are turned because electricity is doing some magical thing through plugs and wires. A physicist understands the process differently: Flipping a switch closes a circuit that allows electrons to move through a conductor to the element of an incandescent lamp, which glows because electrical resistance slows the flow of electrons and produces heat; this all happens very fast.

Cook and Campbell (1979) refer to such detailed specifications of cause as *micromediational* causal statements. A physicist's explanation of why a light comes on is a micromediational statement about cause. However, most of us get along just fine in life without understanding the micromediational details of excitable electrons, resistance, and heat. We have what Cook and Campbell call a *molar* understanding of the process: Flipping a switch causes a light to come on.

In criminal justice and other social science research, molar statements about cause can be meaningful even when micromediational details are not known. For example, police officers know that consuming large quantities of alcohol inhibits the ability of people to operate motor vehicles safely. They do not have to know the micromediational details of physiology and neurochemical reactions. Corrections officials understand that crowded conditions in prisons cause inmate dissatisfaction and possibly violence, but they cannot specify a micromediational process explaining why this is so.

Molar statements about cause and effect can be at least as useful as micromediational statements. For example, if your car will not start some cold, damp morning, a mechanic's molar explanation—"bad distributor cap"—would be more useful to you than a physicist's micromediational explanation: "An internal combustion engine is based on several principles of thermodynamics and electromechanical resistance . . . ."

Social science research can therefore productively investigate molar questions about cause. You should recognize that this is consistent with our probabilistic approach. Our statements about cause-and-effect relationships normally describe tendencies rather than infallible laws, and we can propose useful molar statements without being able to specify micromediation.

Errors of Reasoning

Cause and effect are essential to scientific explanation, and yet we've seen that they are more complex than meets the eye. They are also fundamental to our day-to-day lives, and people commonly make errors in their assessment of causation. It will be useful, therefore, to look at some examples from daily life. See if you can detect the error before reading our explanation.

Early in the history of the AIDS epidemic, the *San Francisco Chronicle* (September 6, 1984) carried an article about research that claimed a link between fluoridation of the water and AIDS. In part, the claim hinged on the assertion that "while half the country's communities have fluoridated water supplies and half do not, 90 percent of AIDS cases are coming from fluoridated areas and only 10 percent are coming from nonfluoridated areas." Can you see any flaws in this reasoning?

First, you should always be wary when data about communities are used to draw conclusions about individuals; we'll examine this further in Chapter 4. In this instance, "half the communities" may not contain half the population. Indeed, large cities are probably more likely to fluoridate their water than small towns are. Logically, it would be possible for the fluoridated communities to have 90 percent of the nation's population, in which case they should have 90 percent of the AIDS cases even if there were no relationship between AIDS and fluoridation.

Second, it's possible that "cosmopolitan/progressive" social values might affect both lifestyles associated with AIDS and the decision to fluoridate the water supply. In that case, AIDS and fluoridation could be statistically correlated without being causally linked.

The headline "Attend class regularly—it'll help your grades" summarized the conclusions of a study reported in *USA Today* on September 4, 1985. The results of a ten-year study of undergraduates at the University of Michigan indicated that class attendance was related to grades achieved.

■ Students with the lowest attendance earned the poorest grades. Those who attended 79 percent of classes or less ended up in the low C range; 90 percent and above scored above a B average.

Students who sat up front got "significantly higher grades," but Walsh [the researcher] thinks they could be more interested in the subjects.

Can you see anything in the concluding remark that might challenge the causal assertion about attendance and grades? The explanation that being interested in a subject would account for both sitting up front and getting good grades suggests the same possibility regarding attendance and grades. Maybe "interest in the subject" is the primary cause of good grades, and it also results in better attendance and in sitting up front in class.

Sometimes it's possible to detect failures of causal reasoning on logical grounds alone, when there is no possibility of examining empirical data. Again, concern for AIDS offers an example. It has been argued by some that the AIDS epidemic represents God's displeasure with certain human behaviors—specifically, homosexuality and drug use. Evangelist Don Boys spoke to the sexual issue in a guest editorial in *USA Today* on October 7, 1985: "The AIDS epidemic indicates that morality has broken its mooring and drifted into a miasmic swamp, producing disease, degeneracy, and

death. . . . God's plan is for each man to have one woman—his wife—for a lifetime, and be faithful to her."

The flaw in this case is not just that AIDS has become increasingly common among heterosexual, married couples or that some hemophiliac young people have contracted AIDS through tainted blood transfusions. It is legitimate to use a probabilistic model of causation in this context, and homosexual men are, in fact, more likely to contract AIDS than heterosexual men. If AIDS is an indication of "God's plan," however, then lesbians must be the most favored of all because AIDS is rarest among lesbian women.

None of these illustrations of faulty causal reasoning is intended as an indictment of the perpetrators. All of us fall into such errors. It has been said that the problem with "common sense" is that it's not all that common. Our purpose in these examples has been twofold. First, we want to sensitize you to faulty causal reasoning by pointing out some of the ways it shows up in daily life. Perhaps that alone will help you avoid some errors, recognize them in the reasoning of others, or both. Second, we want to use such examples as a backdrop for you to understand the power of careful, scientific reasoning. Although scientists are not immune to logical error, the procedures of science offer some degree of protection from it. We want to make that protection available to you.

■ VALIDITY AND CAUSAL INFERENCE

Paying careful attention to cause-and-effect relationships is crucial in criminal justice research. Cause and effect are also important in applied studies, where a researcher may be interested in whether or not, for example, a new determinant sentencing law actually causes an increase in the prison population.

When we are concerned with whether or not we are correct in inferring that a cause produced some effect, we are concerned with the **validity** of causal inference. Cook and Campbell (1979:37) define validity as "the best available approximation to the truth or falsity of propositions, including propositions about cause." They go on to note that *approximation* is an important word because one can never be absolutely certain about cause. This is especially true in our probabilistic, molar approach to uncovering cause-and-effect relationships.

When we consider whether or not our cause-and-effect statements are true, we consider whether or not they are valid. Cook and Campbell (1979) describe a number of different **validity threats** in causal inference—reasons we might be incorrect in stating that some cause produced some effect. Here we will summarize the threats to four general categories of validity: statistical conclusion validity, internal validity, construct validity, and external validity. Chapter 7 will examine each type in more detail, linking the issue of validity to different ways of designing research. Although their book is sometimes difficult to read, Cook and Campbell provide a thorough and interesting discussion of various threats to validity.

Statistical Conclusion Validity

Statistical conclusion validity refers to our ability to determine whether a change in the suspected cause is statistically associated with a change in the suspected effect. This corresponds with one of the first questions asked by researchers: Are two variables related to each other? For example, if we suspect that using illegal drugs causes people to commit crimes, one of the first things we would be interested in is the covariation between drug use and crime. If drug users and nonusers committed equal rates of crime, and if about the same proportions of criminals and noncriminals used drugs, there would be no statistical relationship between measures of drug use and criminal offending.

There may be some technical reasons that we cannot find covariation between drug use and crime, however. Perhaps we do not have good measures of either the cause or the effect. Having deficient measures of either drug use or crime may be one reason we cannot demonstrate a statistical relationship between the two. Chapter 5 will consider measurement problems in more de-

tail, but one of that chapter's central points is that illegal behaviors, such as using drugs and committing other crimes, can be very difficult to measure with accuracy. If measures are not accurate, we may not be able to detect statistical patterns.

Another common threat to statistical conclusion validity is basing conclusions on a small number of cases. For example, let's say you studied ten drug users and ten nonusers and compared the numbers of times these subjects were arrested for other crimes over a six-month period. You might find that the ten users were arrested an average of three times, while nonusers averaged two arrests in six months. There is a difference in arrest rates, but is it a significant difference? Statistically, the answer would be no because so few drug users were included in your study. The discussion of sampling in Chapter 9 and interpreting data in Chapter 14 will introduce the principles of statistical significance, but the basic point is a simple one: Researchers cannot have much confidence in making statements about cause if their findings are based on a small number of cases.

Threats to statistical conclusion validity can have the opposite effect of suggesting that covariation is present when in fact there is no cause-and-effect relationship. The reasons for this are again somewhat technical and require a basic understanding of statistical inference, a topic we will discuss in Chapter 14. However, some of the superstitious behavior exhibited by gamblers provides a rough-and-ready example. Let's say you like to play state lotteries; nothing serious, you just buy a couple tickets a week. Many people play a system where they pick numbers that correspond to their date of birth or the license number of their car. Expecting these lucky numbers to influence your chances of winning the lottery is an example of failing to recognize that winning numbers are picked by a random process. If you always picked your birthday—say, July 7, 1977 (7777)—and bought two tickets per week for five years, your lucky number might come up simply by chance in the random system used to pick winning numbers. There would be no statistical conclusion validity to the inference that consistently picking your birthday caused you to win the lottery. Your winning would be due to the random effects of how numbers are selected.

Internal Validity

Internal validity threats also challenge causal statements that are based on some observed relationship. An observed association between two variables has internal validity if the relationship is in fact causal and not due to the effects of some other variable. Whereas statistical conclusion threats are most often due to random error, however, internal validity problems have their source in nonrandom or systematic error. Simply put, threats to the internal validity of a proposed causal relationship between two indicators usually arise from the effects of some third variable. You should recognize the similarity between this validity threat and the third requirement for establishing a causal relationship, described earlier.

If, for example, you observed that convicted drug users sentenced to probation were rearrested less often than drug users sentenced to prison, you might be tempted to infer that prison sentences cause recidivism. Although being in prison might have some impact on whether one committed more crimes in the future, in this case it would be important to look for other causes of recidivism. One likely candidate is prior criminal record. Convicted drug users without prior criminal records are more likely to be sentenced to probation, while persons with previous convictions more often receive prison terms. Research on criminal careers has found that the probability of reoffending increases with the number of prior arrests and convictions (Chaiken and Chaiken, 1982). In this case, a third variable—prior convictions—may explain some or all of the observed tendency of prison sentences to be associated with recidivism. Prior convictions are associated with both sentence—prison or probation—and subsequent convictions.

Construct Validity

This type of validity is concerned with how well an observed relationship between variables represents the underlying causal process of interest. In a sense, **construct validity** refers to generalizing from what we observe and measure to the real-world things in which we are interested. The concept of construct validity is closely related to issues in measurement, the subject of Chapter 5.

To illustrate construct validity, we adapt an example from Cook and Campbell (1979) on the concept of supervision. They describe how a researcher might study the effects of supervision on factory workers, where supervision is defined as standing within speaking distance and watching the work of a machinist. Let's consider the supervision of police officers. We might be interested in whether close supervision causes police officers to write more traffic tickets. We could define "close supervision" in this way: A police sergeant drives his own marked police car in such a way as to always keep a patrol car in view.

This would certainly qualify as close supervision, but you may recognize a couple of problems. First, two marked patrol cars present a very visible presence to motorists, who might drive more prudently and thus reduce the opportunities for patrol officers to write traffic tickets. Second, and more central to the issue of construct validity, this represents a narrow definition of the construct "close supervision." Patrol officers may be closely supervised in other ways that cause them to write more traffic tickets. Sergeants could closely supervise their officers by reviewing their ticket production at the end of each shift. Supervising subordinates by keeping them in view is only one way of exercising control over their behavior. It may be appropriate for factory workers, but it is not practical for police, representing a very limited version of the construct "supervision."

The well-known Kansas City Preventive Patrol Experiment, mentioned in Chapter 1, provides another example of construct validity problems. Recall that the experiment sought to determine whether routine preventive patrol caused reductions in crime and fear of crime and increases in arrests. This causal proposition was tested by comparing measures of crime, fear, and arrests in proactive beats (with twice the normal level of preventive patrol), reactive beats (with no preventive patrol), and control beats (with normal levels of preventive patrol). Results from this experiment found no significant differences in crime, fear, and arrests.

Richard Larson (1975) discusses several difficulties with the experiment's design. One important problem relates to the visibility of police presence, a central concept in preventive patrol. It is safe to assume that the ability of routine patrol to prevent crime and enhance feelings of safety depends crucially on the visibility of police. It makes sense to assume further that withdrawing preventive patrol, as was done in the reactive beats, reduces the visibility of police. But by how much? Larson explores this question in detail and suggests that two other features of police operations during the Kansas City experiment partially compensated for the absence of preventive patrol and produced a visible police presence.

First, the different types of experimental beats were adjacent to one another; one reactive beat shared borders with three control and three proactive beats. This enhanced the visibility of police in reactive beats in two ways: (1) police in adjoining proactive and control beats sometimes drove around the perimeter of reactive beats, and (2) police often drove through reactive beats on their way to some other part of the city.

Second, many Kansas City police officers were skeptical about the experiment and feared that withdrawing preventive patrol in reactive beats would create problems. Partly as a result, police who responded to calls for service in the reactive areas more frequently used lights and sirens when driving to the location of complaints. A related action was that police units not assigned to the calls for service nevertheless drove into the reactive beats to provide backup service.

Each of these actions produced a visible police presence in the reactive beats. People who lived in these areas were unaware of the experiment and, as you might expect, did not know whether a police car happened to be present because it was on routine patrol, was on its way to some other part of the city, or was responding to a call for assistance. And, of course, the use of lights and sirens makes police cars much more visible.

Larson's point is that the construct of police visibility is only partly represented by routine preventive patrol. A visible police presence was produced in Kansas City through other means. Therefore, the researchers' conclusion that routine preventive patrol does not cause a reduction in crime or an increase in arrests suffers from threats to construct validity. Construct validity is a frequent problem in applied studies, where researchers may oversimplify complex policies and policy goals.

External Validity

Do findings about preventive patrol in Kansas City apply to preventive patrol in San Francisco? Are community crime prevention organizations successful in combating drug use throughout a city, or do they work best in areas with only minor drug problems? Electronic monitoring may be suitable as an alternative sentence for convicted offenders, but can it work as an alternative to jail for defendants awaiting trial? Such questions are examples of issues in **external validity:** Do research findings about cause and effect apply equally to different cities, neighborhoods, and populations?

In a general sense, external validity is concerned with whether research findings from one study can be reproduced in another study, often under different conditions. The tool of replication, as mentioned in Chapter 1, is used to check on the external validity of research results.

External validity may also refer to the correspondence between basic research under controlled conditions and the real-world application of research findings. Will a drug tested on laboratory animals have the same effects in experimental trials with humans? If experimental trials of a new drug produce the desired effects, will the same results be obtained when the drug is available to the general public?

Because crime problems and criminal justice responses can vary so much from city to city, or state to state, researchers and public officials are often especially interested in external validity. For example, in their evaluation of programs to reduce the fear of crime, Pate, Wycoff, Skogan, and Sherman (1986) conducted experiments in two very different cities—Houston, Texas, and Newark, New Jersey. Houston is physically large and sprawling, reflecting sustained economic and population growth through 1980. In contrast, Newark is an older, more densely populated city that had fallen on hard economic times. Pate and associates took account of the physical, social, and economic differences between the two cities in developing specific experimental actions to reduce the fear of crime, thus enhancing the external validity of their study.

The fear-of-crime evaluation found that certain fear-reduction policies had varying effects. For example, neighborhood police storefront offices and foot patrol in Houston had beneficial effects among white residents and home owners, but these programs had no impact on fear among renters and African American residents (Wycoff, Skogan, Pate, and Sherman, 1985a, 1985b). The extent to which a program intervention caused a desired effect varied across program targets, thus limiting the external validity of certain fear-reduction policies.

Validity and Causal Inference Summarized

The four types of validity threats can be grouped into two categories: bias and generalizability. Internal and statistical conclusion validity threats are related to systematic and nonsystematic bias, respectively. Nonsystematic problems with statistical procedures, or the systematic bias introduced by some alternative explanation for an observed relationship, can call into question the inference that some cause produced some effect. Failing to consider the more general cause-and-effect constructs that operate in an observed cause-and-effect relationship results in research findings that cannot be generalized to real-world behaviors and conditions. And a cause-and-effect relationship observed in one setting or at one time may not operate in the same way in a different setting or different time.

Cook and Campbell (1979:39) summarize their discussion of these four validity threats by linking them to the types of questions that researchers ask in trying to establish cause and effect. Test your understanding by writing the name of each validity threat after the appropriate question from Cook and Campbell.

1. Is there a relationship between two variables? _Statistical_
2. Given that there is a relationship, is it plausibly causal from one operational variable [cause] to the other [effect], or would the same relationship have been obtained in the absence of any treatment of any kind? _internal_
3. Given that the relationship is plausibly causal and is reasonably known to be from one variable to another, what particular cause-and-effect constructs are involved in the relationship? _Construct_
4. Given that there is probably a causal relationship from construct A to construct B, how generalizable is this relationship across persons, settings, and times? _external_

Does Drug Use Cause Crime?

By way of illustrating issues of validity and causal inference, we will consider the relationship between drug use and crime. Few assumptions about cause and effect in criminal justice are as prevalent as the presumed link between drugs and crime. Drug addiction is thought to cause people who are desperate for a fix and unable to secure legitimate income to commit crimes in order to support their habit. Decades of popular culture, basic research, and criminal justice policy have explored this issue.

Discussing the validity of claims that drug use causes crime requires thinking more carefully about two central concepts—drug use and crime—and considering the various ways these concepts might be related. Jan and Marcia Chaiken (1990) provide unusually careful and well-reasoned insights into this issue. Our discussion borrows heavily from their work. We will first touch on issues in basic research on the drugs–crime connection and then discuss the implications of this research for criminal justice policy.

First is the question of temporal order: Which comes first, drug use or crime? Research summarized by Chaiken and Chaiken provides no conclusive answer. In an earlier study of prison inmates, Chaiken and Chaiken (1982) found that 12 percent of their adult subjects committed crimes after using drugs for at least two years; 15 percent began drug use two or more years after they began committing predatory crimes. Studies of juveniles revealed similar findings: "About 50 percent of delinquent youngsters are delinquent before they start using drugs; about 50 percent start concurrently or after" (Chaiken and Chaiken, 1990:235; based on data from Elliott and Huizinga, 1984).

Many studies have found that some drug users commit crimes and some criminals use drugs, but Chaiken and Chaiken (1990:234) conclude that "drug use and crime participation are weakly related as contemporaneous products of factors generally antithetical to traditional United States lifestyles." Stated somewhat differently, drug use and crime (as well as delinquency) are each deviant activities produced by other underlying causes. There is a statistical association between drug use and crime, but other factors mean the relationship is not directly causal, thus questioning the internal validity of causal statements about drug use and crime.

To assess the construct validity of research on drugs and crime, it is important to consider different patterns of each behavior. Many adolescents in the United States experiment with drugs, just as many—especially males—may commit delinquent acts or petty crimes. A large number of adults may be occasional users of illegal drugs.

Chaiken and Chaiken suggest that applying a criminal careers paradigm, mentioned in Chapter 2, to both drug use and crime can help sort out the different patterns of each. Recall that onset, frequency, desistance, persistence, and escalation are central concepts for understanding criminal careers. For many people, experimentation with drugs begins in adolescence but desists soon thereafter. Among people whose use persists beyond experimentation, frequency of use varies widely. Similar differences characterize criminal careers; some begin early, escalate, and persist, while others desist following sporadic delinquency.

The point is that many different patterns of drug use, delinquency, and adult criminality can be found. Because there is no simple way to describe either construct, searching for a single cause-and-effect relationship is certain to misrepresent a complex causal process.

Both construct and external validity are concerned with generalizations. Problems with the external validity of research on drugs and crime are similar to those revolving around construct validity. The relationship between occasional marijuana use and delinquency among teenagers is different from that between occasional cocaine use and adult crime; each relationship varies from that between heroin addiction and persistent criminal behavior among adults.

The issue of external validity comes into sharper focus when we shift from basic research that seeks to uncover fundamental causal relationships to criminal justice policy. Chaiken and Chaiken argue that any unitary policy that seeks to reduce the use of all drugs among all population groups will have little effect on serious crime. By now, you should recognize that this is because there is no simple cause-and-effect relationship between the use of all types of drugs, by all types of people, and crime. Most occasional juvenile and adult users of all drugs do not commit serious acquisitive crimes. This is also true among persistent users of drugs other than heroin, cocaine, and crack. About half of incarcerated persons who have been persistent offenders never used drugs. Only among that group of persistent offenders who regularly use a variety of drugs, including heroin and cocaine, can drug control policy cause much of a reduction in crime (Chaiken and Chaiken, 1990:235).

Basic and applied research on the important question of cause-and-effect relationships among drug use and crime readily illustrates threats to the validity of causal inference. It is often difficult to find a relationship because there is so much variation in drug use and crime participation (statistical conclusion validity threat). A large number of studies have demonstrated that when statistical relationships are found, both drug use and crime can be attributed to other, often multiple, causes (internal validity threat). Different patterns among different population groups mean that there are no readily identifiable cause-and-effect constructs. Because of these differences, policies developed to counter drug use among the population as a whole cannot be expected to have much of an impact on serious crime.

None of the above is to say that there is no cause-and-effect relationship between drug use and crime. Chaiken and Chaiken show that there is no simple relationship.

■ LINKING MEASUREMENT AND ASSOCIATION

As we have seen, one of the key elements that determines causation in science is an empirical correlation between the cause and the effect. All too often, however, the process of measuring variables is seen as separate from that of determining the associations between variables. This view is incorrect, or at the very least misleading.

This section addresses the intimate links between measurement and association within the context of causal inference. To do that, we'll review the traditional deductive model of science. Then we'll examine some alternative images of science. In this latter regard, we'll consider the notion of the interchangeability of indexes.

The Traditional Deductive Model

The traditional perspective on the scientific method, as you'll recall, involves a series of steps:

1. Theory construction
2. Derivation of theoretical hypotheses
3. Operationalization of concepts
4. Collection of empirical data
5. Empirical testing of hypotheses

Let's illustrate this view of the scientific research process with an example.

Theory Construction Faced with an interesting aspect of the natural or social world, the scientist creates an abstract deductive theory to describe it. This is largely a logical exercise. Let's assume for the moment that a social scientist is interested in deviant behavior. A theory of deviant behavior is constructed on the basis of some existing theory, such as social control theory, which focuses on the coercive and persuasive forces that establish and maintain social order. Among other things, this theory includes a variety of concepts relevant to the causes of deviant behavior.

Derivation of Theoretical Hypotheses On the basis of this total theory of deviant behavior, the scientist derives hypotheses about the various concepts that make up the theory. Continuing our example, we suppose that the scientist logically derives the hypothesis that juvenile delinquency is a function of supervision: As supervision increases, juvenile delinquency decreases.

Operationalization of Concepts The next step is to specify empirical indicators that represent the theoretical concepts. Although theoretical concepts must be somewhat abstract and perhaps vague, the empirical indicators must be precise and specific (as we'll examine in detail in Chapter 5). Thus, in our example, the scientist might operationalize the concept "juvenile" as anyone under 18 years of age, "delinquency" as being arrested for a criminal act, and "supervision" as the presence of a nonworking adult in the home.

The effect of operationalization is to convert the theoretical hypothesis into an empirical one. In this case, the empirical hypothesis is that among persons under 18 years of age, those who live in homes with a nonworking adult will be less likely to be arrested for a criminal act than will those without a nonworking adult in the home.

Collection of Empirical Data Based on the operationalization of theoretical concepts, researchers collect data relating to the empirical indicators. In the present example, they might conduct a survey of persons under 18 years of age. Among other things, the survey questionnaire would ask juveniles whether they live in a home with a nonworking adult and whether they have ever been arrested for a criminal act.

Empirical Testing of Hypotheses After the data have been collected, the final step is the statistical testing of the hypothesis. The scientist determines, empirically, whether those juveniles who have a nonworking adult in the home are less likely to have been arrested for criminal acts than those with no nonworking adult at home. The confirmation or disconfirmation of the empirical hypothesis is then used to accept or reject the theoretical hypothesis.

Although this traditional image of scientific research can be a useful model for you to have in mind, it tends to conceal some of the practical problems that crop up in most actual research. In particular, two basic problems prevent the easy application of this model in practice.

First, theoretical concepts seldom permit unambiguous operationalization. Because concepts are abstract and general, every specification of empirical indicators must be an approximation. In our example, it is unlikely that the general concept of supervision is adequately represented by the presence of a nonworking adult in the home. The presence of such an adult does not assure supervision of the juvenile, and in some homes that lack such an adult, other arrangements may be made for the juvenile's supervision.

Being arrested for a criminal act cannot be equated with the abstract concept of delinquency. Some juveniles may engage in delinquent behavior without being arrested; others may be arrested falsely. Moreover, the specification of juvenile as a person under age 18 is arbitrary. Other specifications might have been made, and probably none would be unambiguously correct. Every empirical indicator has some defects; all could be improved on, and the search for better indicators is an endless one.

Second, the empirical associations between variables are almost never perfect. If all juveniles who have nonworking adults in the home had never been arrested and all those without such adults had been arrested, we might conclude that the hypothesis had been confirmed. Or if both groups had exactly the same records, we might conclude that the hypothesis had been rejected. Neither eventuality is likely in practice, however. Many variables are related empirically to one another to some extent. Specifying the extent that represents acceptance of the hypothesis and the extent that represents rejection is also arbitrary.

Ultimately, then, scientists use imperfect indicators of theoretical concepts to discover imperfect associations. And these imperfections conspire with one another against our ability to demonstrate cause and effect.

Measurement and association are interrelated concepts. The social scientist must handle both simultaneously and logically. Rather than moving through a fixed set of steps, the researcher moves back and forth through them endlessly. Often theoretical constructions are built around the previously observed associations between empirical indicators. Partial theoretical constructions may suggest new empirical data to be examined, and so forth. After each activity, you hope to understand your subject matter a little better. The "critical experiment" that ultimately determines the fate of an entire theory is rare indeed.

Scientific research, then, is a never-ending enterprise aimed at understanding some phenomenon. To that end, you continually measure and examine associations, and you must constantly be aware of the relationships between them.

The Interchangeability of Indexes

Paul Lazarsfeld (1959), in his discussions of the **interchangeability of indexes,** has provided an important conceptual tool for our understanding of the relationship between measurement and association and has partially resolved the two problems discussed in the preceding section. His comments grew out of the recognition that any concept has several possible indicators.

Let's suppose you are interested in how decisions are made to set bail for persons who are arrested and charged with some crime. Traditionally, bail decisions were based on judgments about whether a defendant, if released from jail, would appear for trial or flee. In more recent years, decisions have also considered whether defendants might commit additional crimes while out on bail. Your interest is more in the traditional criteria, and you believe that defendants' ties to the community affect whether or not they will appear for trial. That's certainly a reasonable expectation, but what do you mean by ties to the community?

There are several possible indicators: having a full-time job, length of employment, holding elected office, owning a home, living with a spouse, having a rental lease, having a telephone and being listed in the phone book, length of residence in the community, and so forth.

Let us return for the moment to the notion of a theoretical hypothesis, $Y = f(X)$, introduced in Chapter 2. It suggests that some dependent variable (Y), appearance at trial in this case, can be explained as an effect of the independent variable (X), community ties. Lazarsfeld recognized that a concept like community ties can have several possible indicators; we might write these as x_1, x_2, x_3, and so forth. Although there may be reasons for believing that some of the indicators are better than others, Lazarsfeld argued, if they all are indicators of the same concept, they should be essentially interchangeable in testing relationships. Thus, whereas the traditional model of science suggests that we test one relationship, represented by the equation $y = f(x)$, we can use all the possible indicators of ties to the community. So, we test all these empirical hypotheses: $y = f(x_1)$, $y = f(x_2)$, $y = f(x_3)$, and so forth. Rather than having one test of the hypothesis, we have several, as indicated schematically in Figure 3-2.

In terms of our present example, we might be asking whether those who have a full-time job are more likely to appear at trial than those who are unemployed, whether those who are living with their spouse will appear more often than those living alone, whether persons listed in the phone book are more likely to appear at trial than those who do not have telephone service, and so forth. You may already have anticipated a new dilemma. If the traditional view of the scientific method led us to a single imperfect empirical association, now we may be faced with several empirical associations, none of which is perfect and some of which may conflict with one another. Thus, even if we have specified a particular extent of association that will be sufficient to confirm the causal hypothesis, we may discover that the tests involving x_1, x_3, and x_5 meet that specified criterion, but the tests involving x_2 and x_4 do not.

FIGURE 3-2
The Interchangeability of Indexes

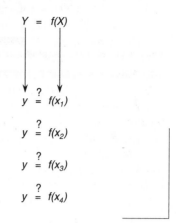

Our dilemma is seemingly compounded. In fact, however, the situation really may be clarified.

Using the notion of the interchangeability of indexes, we accept a theoretical hypothesis as a general proposition if it is confirmed by all the specified empirical tests. If, for example, appearing at trial is a function of community ties in a broadly generalized sense, then appearance at trial should be related to every empirical indicator of community ties. If, however, we discover that only certain indicators of community ties have this property, then we have specified the kinds of community ties for which the proposition holds. In practice, this may help us to understand and reconceptualize ties to the community in more precise terms.

It is important to realize what we have accomplished through this process. Rather than routinely testing a fixed cause-and-effect hypothesis relating to community ties and appearance at trial, we have a better defined understanding of the nature of that association. That will make sense, however, only if we view the goal of science as understanding rather than simply as theory construction and hypothesis testing.

The implication of the preceding comments is that measurement and association are importantly intertwined. The measurement of a variable makes little sense outside the empirical and theoretical contexts of the associations to be tested. Asked "How should I measure community ties?," the experienced scientist will reply, "What is your purpose for measuring it?" The "proper" way of measuring a given variable depends heavily on the variables to be associated with it.

You should now have a sense of the explanatory purpose of criminal justice research. Though it is not our only purpose in research, we often wish to explain why people think and act as they do. Typically, we ask what causes what. We have introduced the notion of causation early in the book so that you can hold it up as a backdrop for the related discussions that follow.

■ MAIN POINTS

- Explanatory scientific research depends implicitly on the notion of cause and effect.
- Explanatory social scientific research depends implicitly on a deterministic image of human behavior, at least in part.
- The idiographic model of explanation aims at a complete understanding of a particular phenomenon, using all relevant causal factors.
- The nomothetic model of explanation aims at a general understanding—not necessarily complete—of a class of phenomena, using the smallest number of the most relevant causal factors.
- Most explanatory social research uses a probabilistic model of causation. X may be said to cause Y if it is seen to have some influence on Y.
- The two important types of causes are necessary and sufficient causes. X is a necessary cause of Y if Y cannot happen without X having happened. X is a sufficient cause of Y if Y always happens when X happens. The most satisfying scientific discovery is a necessary and sufficient cause.
- Three basic requirements determine a causal relationship in scientific research: (1) The independent variable must occur earlier in time than the dependent variable, (2) the independent (cause) and dependent (effect) variables must be empirically related to each other, and (3) the observed relationship cannot be explained away as the artificial product of the effect of another earlier variable.
- Although natural scientists often make detailed, micromediational statements about cause, that is seldom possible in social science. Researchers in criminal justice and other social sciences are most commonly interested in molar statements combined with the probabilistic model of cause.
- When scientists consider whether causal statements are true or false, they are concerned with the validity of causal inference.
- Four classes of threats to validity correspond to the types of questions researchers ask in trying to establish cause and effect. Threats to statistical conclusion validity and internal validity arise from bias. Construct and external validity threats may limit our ability to generalize from an observed relationship to a real-world causal process or to similar relationships among different subjects, in different settings, or at different times.
- A perfect statistical relationship between two variables is not an appropriate requirement for causation in social research. We may say that a causal relationship exists between X and Y even though X is not the total cause of Y.
- The interchangeability of indexes suggests that if several specific, though imperfect, indicators of one variable are similarly related to another variable, then we may assume that the first variable—in general—is related to the second. Thus, we may conclude that X is related to Y even though we cannot satisfactorily define X.

■ REVIEW QUESTIONS AND EXERCISES

1. Discuss one of the following statements in terms of what you have learned about the criteria of causation and threats to the validity of causal inference. What cause-and-effect rela-

tionships are implied? What are some alternative explanations?

    a. Guns don't kill people; people kill people.

    b. Capital punishment prevents murder.

    c. Marijuana is a gateway drug that leads to the use of other drugs.

2. Several times we have discussed the relationship between drug use and crime. Describe the conditions that would lead us to conclude that drug use is:

    a. A necessary cause

    b. A sufficient cause

    c. A necessary and sufficient cause

3. Why did you choose to attend the college you are now attending? Create an idiographic explanation by listing all the factors that led to your choice. Now think of reasons your friends decided to attend college. Develop a nomothetic explanation that partially tells why you and all your friends made their particular college choices.

■ ADDITIONAL READINGS

Beck, E. M., and Tolnay, Stewart E., "The Killing Fields of the Deep South: The Market for Cotton and the Lynching of Blacks, 1882–1930," *American Sociological Review,* Vol. 55 (August 1990), pp. 526–539. This analysis of the structural causes of lynchings in the South illustrates the type of causal analysis that social scientists often undertake. Some of the variables examined are inflation, the price of cotton, and the proportion of blacks in the population.

Cook, Thomas D., and Campbell, Donald T., *Quasi-experimentation: Design and Analysis Issues for Field Settings* (Boston: Houghton Mifflin, 1979). This book is considered by many social science researchers to be a definitive discussion of cause and threats to the validity of causal inference. See especially Chapters 1 and 2 for details.

Hirschi, Travis, and Selvin, Hanan, *Principles of Survey Analysis* (New York: Free Press, 1973), especially Part II. Excellent statements on causation within a practical framework. The book is readable, stimulating, and generally just plain excellent.

Kaplan, Abraham, *The Conduct of Inquiry* (San Francisco: Chandler, 1964). A philosopher's perspective on social research. Especially in his discussions of explanation (Part 9), Kaplan lays the logical foundation for an understanding of the nature and analysis of causal relationships in social science.

Rosenberg, Morris, *The Logic of Survey Analysis* (New York: Basic Books, 1968). A clear and practical statement of how the social researcher addresses causation. In his opening chapter, Rosenberg discusses the general meaning of causal relationships. In the concluding two chapters, he describes the process through which a researcher may arrive at causal conclusions.

2 Structuring Criminal Justice Inquiry

POSING questions properly is often more difficult than answering them. Indeed, a properly phrased question often seems to answer itself. You may have discovered the answer to a question just in the process of making the question clear to someone else.

At base, scientific research is a process for achieving generalized understanding through observation. Part 3 of this book describes some of the specific methods of observation for criminal justice research. Part 2 deals with the posing of proper questions, the structuring of inquiry.

Chapter 4 addresses the beginnings of research. It examines some of the purposes of inquiry, the units of analysis and points of focus in criminal justice research, and the reasons scientists get involved in research projects.

Chapter 5 deals with the specification of what it is you want to study—a process called *conceptualization*—and the measurement of the concepts you specify. We're going to look at some of the terms that we use casually in everyday life, and we'll see how essential it is to get clear about what we really mean by such terms when we do research. Once we are clear on what we mean when we use certain terms, we are in a position to create measurements of what those terms refer to. The process of devising steps or operations for measuring what we want to study is called *operationalization.*

Chapter 6 focuses on a specific, and perennially difficult, measurement problem: measuring crime. We'll see many differen approaches to conceptualization and operationalization and discuss the strengths and weaknesses of each. In doing so, we'll refer to standards of measurement quality described in Chapter 5.

Chapter 7 concentrates on the general design of a criminal justice research project. A criminal justice research design specifies a strategy for finding out something, for structuring a research project. Chapter 7 describes commonly used strategies; each is adapted in some way from the classical scientific experiment. In the course of describing different strategies, we'll refer to our discussion in Chapter 3 of causal inference and validity.

The last chapter in Part 2 calls your attention to ethical issues in conducting criminal justice research. Ethical problems emerge when the rights of research subjects potentially conflict with a researcher's plan for making measurements or collecting data. We'll see that most ethical questions are rooted in the fundamental principle that research subjects should not be harmed. Although it's not quite that simple, Chapter 8 will help you learn to recognize potential ethical problems and take steps to eliminate or reduce them.

What you learn in Part 2 will bring you to the verge of making controlled observations for criminal justice research. Part 3 will then show you how to take that next step.

4 *General Issues in Research Design*

What You'll Learn in This Chapter

Here you'll learn some fundamental principles about conducting empirical research: variations on who or what is to be studied when, how, and for what purpose. We'll also present a broad overview of the research process.

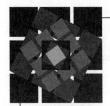

INTRODUCTION

PURPOSES OF RESEARCH
Exploration
Description
Explanation
Application

UNITS OF ANALYSIS
Individuals
Groups
Organizations
Social Artifacts
Units of Analysis in Review
The Ecological Fallacy
Reductionism

THE TIME DIMENSION
Cross-sectional Studies
Longitudinal Studies
Approximating Longitudinal Studies
Retrospective Studies
The Time Dimension Summarized

HOW TO DESIGN A RESEARCH PROJECT
The Research Process
Getting Started
Conceptualization
Choice of Research Method
Operationalization
Population and Sampling
Observations
Data Processing
Analysis
Application
Review

THE RESEARCH PROPOSAL
Elements of a Research Proposal

ANSWERS TO UNITS OF ANALYSIS EXERCISE

MAIN POINTS

REVIEW QUESTIONS AND EXERCISES

ADDITIONAL READINGS

■ *INTRODUCTION*

Science is an enterprise dedicated to "finding out." No matter what you want to find out, though, there are likely to be a great many ways of doing it. Research design, the topic of this chapter, addresses how to plan scientific inquiry—designing a strategy for finding out something. Although the details vary according to what you wish to study, research design has two major aspects: First, you must specify precisely what you want to find out. Second, you must determine the best way to do that. If you can handle the first consideration fully, you'll probably handle the second in the same way. As mathematicians say, a properly framed question contains its own answer.

Let's say you are interested in studying corruption in government. That's certainly a worthy and appropriate topic for criminal justice research. But what *specifically* are you interested in? What do you mean by "corruption"? What kinds of behavior do you have in mind? And what do you mean by "government"? Who do you want to study: all public employees? only sworn police officers? civilian employees? elected officials? Finally, what is your purpose? Do you want to find out *how much* corruption there is? Do you want to learn *why* corruption exists? These are the kinds of questions that need to be answered in research design.

This chapter provides a general introduction to research design, and the other chapters in this part will elaborate on specific aspects. In practice, all aspects of research design are interrelated. We have separated them so that we can explore particular topics in detail. In this chapter, we want to lay out the various possibilities for criminal justice research. In later chapters, the interrelationships among parts will become clearer.

We'll start with a brief examination of some purposes for criminal justice research. Then we'll consider *units of analysis*—the what or whom you want to study. This topic will be elaborated in Chapter 9, which deals with sampling.

Next, we want to draw your attention to alternative ways of handling *time* in criminal justice research. As we'll see, it is sometimes appropriate to examine a static cross section of social life, but other studies follow social processes over time. In this regard, keep in mind our discussion in Chapter 3 about the need to establish the time order of events and processes for making statements about cause.

We then present a brief overview of the whole research process. This serves two purposes: (1) It gives you a map to the remainder of this book, and (2) it gives you a sense of how you might go about designing a study.

We'll conclude this chapter with a summary of guidelines for preparing a *research proposal*. Often the actual conduct of research needs to be preceded by a detailed plan of your intentions—to obtain funding for a major project or perhaps to get an instructor's approval for a class assignment. We'll see that this offers an excellent way to ensure that you have considered all aspects of your research in advance.

■ *PURPOSES OF RESEARCH*

Criminal justice research, of course, serves many purposes. Four of the most common and useful purposes are *exploration, description, explanation,* and *application.* Although a given study can have more than one of these purposes—and most do—it is useful to examine them separately because each has different implications for other aspects of research design.

Exploration

Much research in criminal justice is conducted to explore the nature or frequency of a problem or in some cases a type of policy. A researcher or official may be interested in some crime or criminal justice policy issue about which little is known. Or perhaps some innovative approach to policing, court management, or corrections has been tried in some jurisdiction, and the researcher wishes to determine how common such practices are in other cities or states. An exploratory project might collect data on some measure to establish a baseline with which future changes will be compared.

For example, heightened concern with drug abuse in the late 1980s prompted several attempts to estimate the frequency of drug abuse in the United States. How many people are arrested for drug sales or possession? How many high school seniors report using marijuana in the past week, or in the past month? How many hours per day do drug dealers work, and how much money do they make? These are examples of research questions intended to explore different aspects of the problem of drug use. Exploratory questions may also be formulated in connection with criminal justice responses to drug problems. How many cities have created special police–prosecutor task forces to crack down on drug sales? What sentences are imposed on major dealers or on casual users? How much money is spent on treatment for drug users?

Exploratory studies are also appropriate when some type of policy change is being considered. Stricter enforcement and longer prison sentences were common policy responses to drug abuse in the 1980s and 1990s. Soon jails and prisons began to overflow with newly arrested and sentenced drug dealers and users. Alternatives to incarceration, such as home detention, came to be considered as officials realized that new correctional facilities could not be constructed fast enough. One of the first questions usually asked by public officials when they consider some new policy is, How have other cities (or states) handled this problem?

Exploratory research in criminal justice can be simple or complex, using a variety of methods. For example, a mayor anxious to learn about drug arrests in his or her city might simply phone the police chief and request a report. On the other hand, estimating how many high school seniors have used marijuana requires more sophisticated survey methods. Since the early 1970s, the National Institute of Drug Abuse has questioned nationwide samples of students on drug use. As you might expect, getting accurate responses to such questions is a tricky business, and results from these surveys are by no means definitive.

An exploratory study may also be conducted to develop methods that will be used in a more careful study in the future. For example, researchers and public officials have long been interested in the connection between drug abuse and crime. Over the past 30 years, a number of studies have tried various approaches to investigating this problem, but most require gathering information directly from drug users and dealers. This can be a difficult task. For several years, Bruce Johnson and associates (1985) studied heroin addicts in New York City, trying different ways to contact users and obtain information from them. In a preliminary study, they set up a storefront office in East Harlem, spread word on the street that they would pay subjects for answering a few questions, and then waited for addicts to drop by. The research team soon realized that many drop-in "addicts" were simply street hustlers who seized the chance to make easy money by inventing stories about their careers as heroin users; many even brought in friends and family members. Procedures for recruiting subjects were eventually changed, but the initial interviews were useful to test techniques for questioning subjects.

Description

A major purpose of many criminal justice studies is to describe the scope of crime problems or policy responses to those problems. A researcher or public official observes and then describes what was observed. Criminal justice observation and description use methods grounded in the social sciences and strive to be more accurate than the casual observations people may make about how much crime there is or how teenagers today are much more violent than they used to be. Descriptive studies are often concerned with counting or documenting observations, while exploratory studies focus more on developing a preliminary understanding about a new or unusual problem.

There are many examples of descriptive studies in criminal justice. Uniform Crime Reports (UCR) have been compiled by the FBI since the 1930s. UCR figures are routinely reported in newspapers and widely interpreted as describing crime in the United States. For example, 1993 UCR figures showed that California had the highest rate of auto theft in the nation, while Vermont had the lowest. But, as described more fully in Chapter 6, the UCR fails to take account of crimes not reported to police. Beginning in 1972, the U.S. Census Bureau began conducting the National Crime Victimization Survey (NCVS, formerly known as the National Crime Survey) to provide an alternative measure of crime and more descriptive information about the victims of crime. The NCVS will be described in more detail in Chapter 6.

Because criminal justice policy in the United States is almost exclusively under the control of state and local governments, many descriptive studies seek to obtain and summarize information from local governments. For example, since 1850 the federal government has conducted a census of prisoners in state and local correctional facilities. Like the decennial U.S. census, basic characteristics of the incarcerated population are gathered, in addition to information about persons on probation or parole.

Descriptive studies in criminal justice have many other uses. A researcher may attend meetings of neighborhood anticrime groups and observe their efforts to organize block watch committees. These observations form the basis for a case study that describes the activities of neighborhood crime groups, so that officials and residents of other cities can decide how to promote such organizations themselves. Or, consider research by Richard Wright and Scott Decker (1994), in which they describe in great detail how active burglars search for and select targets, how they gain entry into residences, and how they dispose of the goods they steal.

Of course, there can be great variation in the quality of descriptive research and in the observations on which such descriptions are based. One of the most important dimensions of quality in descriptive criminal justice research is measurement, the subject of Chapter 5. Problems with the quality of measurement are common in criminal justice research and evaluation. For example, the NCVS is conducted in part because measurement problems associated with the UCR undermine its reliability as a record of crime in the United States. The NCVS is itself plagued by different, but no less serious, measurement problems.

The **generalizability** of descriptive research is also important. One way to think about the generalizability of description is to consider how well a study of a particular group of subjects represents other subjects in other locations. Does a descriptive study of neighborhood anticrime groups in one city apply to anticrime groups in a different city? Chapter 9 will describe how sampling and other methods are related to generalizability.

Explanation

A third general purpose of criminal justice research is to explain things. Reporting that urban residents have generally favorable attitudes toward police is a descriptive activity, but reporting why some people feel police are doing a good job while others do not is an explanatory activity. Reporting why California has the highest auto theft rate in the nation is explanation, but simply reporting auto theft rates for different states is description. A researcher has an explanatory purpose if he or she wishes to know why the number of 14-year-olds involved in gangs has increased, as opposed to simply describing changes in gang membership.

Application

With increasing frequency, researchers are conducting criminal justice studies of an applied nature. Applied research stems from a need for specific facts and findings with policy implications. Another purpose for criminal justice research is therefore its application to public policy. Chapter 13 will focus exclusively on applied research, although we will be discussing applied examples and techniques throughout the book. For now, we focus on two major types of applied research.

First, social science research methods are often used to evaluate the effects of specific criminal justice programs. Determining whether or not a program designed to reduce burglary actually had that intended effect is an example of *evaluation*. In its most basic form, evaluation involves comparing the goals of a program to its results. For example, if one goal of increased police foot patrol is to reduce fear of crime, then an evaluation of foot patrol might compare levels of fear before and after increasing the number of police officers who patrol their beats on foot. In most cases, evaluation research uses social science methods to test the results of some program or policy change. Because crime problems persist and seem to change frequently, officials are constantly seeking new approaches, and it is becoming more common for public officials or researchers to conduct evaluations of new programs.

The second type of applied research is *policy analysis.* What would happen to court backlogs if we designated a judge and prosecutor who would handle only drug-dealing cases? How many new police officers would have to be hired if a department shifted to community policing? These are examples of "what if" questions addressed by policy analysis. Answering such questions is sort of a counterpart to program evaluation. Policy analysis is different from other forms of research in criminal justice primarily in its focus on predicting future events. Rather than observing and analyzing current or past behavior, policy analysis is prospective in trying to anticipate the future consequences of alternative actions.

In other ways, conducting research for policy analysis is quite similar to conducting research for other purposes. It is not possible to predict some future event without first conducting research to describe and explain past events. A prison-impact analysis that predicts future prison populations would be based on earlier studies that described, for example, the length of sentences for different offenses and explained how prison population is affected by sentence length.

Our brief discussion of individual research purposes is not intended to imply that research purposes are mutually exclusive. Many criminal justice studies have elements of more than one purpose. For instance, suppose you were interested in evaluating a new program to reduce bicycle theft at your university. You would first want some information that described the problem of bicycle theft on campus. Let's assume your evaluation found that thefts from some campus locations declined, but there was an increase in bikes stolen from racks outside dormitories. Your study might explain these results by finding that bicycles parked outside dorms tended to be unused for longer periods of time. One option for taking further action to reduce thefts would be

to purchase more secure bicycle racks. A policy analysis might compare the costs of installing the racks to the predicted reduction in bike theft.

You will see these different purposes at work in the following discussions of other aspects of research design. We now turn to a consideration of what or whom you want to explore, describe, explain, or evaluate.

■ UNITS OF ANALYSIS

In criminal justice research, there is a great deal of variation in what or who is studied: what are technically called **units of analysis.** Individual people are often units of analysis. You may make observations describing certain characteristics of offenders or crime victims, such as age, gender, or race. You then combine the descriptions of many individuals to provide a descriptive picture of the population that comprises those individuals.

For example, you may note the age and gender of persons convicted of drunk driving in Fort Lauderdale over a certain time period. Aggregating these observations, you might characterize drunk driving offenders as 72 percent men and 28 percent women, with an average age of 26.4 years. This is a descriptive analysis of convicted drunk drivers in Fort Lauderdale. Although the description applies to the group of drunk drivers as a whole, it was based on the characteristics of individual people who had been convicted of drunk driving.

The same situation could exist in an evaluation study. Suppose you wished to determine whether an alcohol education program reduces repeat arrests of first-time drunk driving offenders. You might administer the education program to half the persons convicted of drunk driving in Fort Lauderdale over a period of two months, while the other half does not receive the program. Next, you observe drunk driving arrest records for one year, keeping track of people who had been convicted earlier and of whether or not they had received the alcohol education program. Combining your observations, you find that 5 percent of those who received the program were arrested again, while 20 percent of those who did not receive alcohol education were rearrested within one year. The purpose of the study was to evaluate a program, but individual drunk drivers were still the units of analysis.

Units of analysis in a study are typically also the *units of observation*. Thus, to study what steps people take to protect their homes from burglary, we would observe, perhaps through interviews, individual household residents. Sometimes, however, we "observe" units of analysis indirectly. For example, we might ask individuals about crime prevention measures for the purpose of describing households. We might want to find out whether homes with double-cylinder deadbolt locks are burglarized less often than homes with less substantial protection. In this case, our units of analysis are households, but the units of observation are individual household members who are asked to describe burglaries and home protection to interviewers.

Units of analysis, then, are those units or things we examine in order to create summary descriptions of all such units and to explain differences among them. To clarify this concept further, we will consider a number of common units of analysis.

Individuals

Any variety of individuals may be the units of analysis in criminal justice research. This point is more important than it may seem at first. The norm of *generalized understanding* in social science should suggest that scientific findings are most valuable when they apply to all kinds of people. In practice, however, researchers seldom study all kinds of people. At the very least, studies are typically limited to people who live in a single country, although some comparative studies stretch across national boundaries. For example, the first international crime survey, conducted in 1989, interviewed samples of individuals from several nations in Europe, Asia, North America, and Oceania.

Examples of circumscribed groups whose members may be units of analysis at the individual level are police, victims, defendants in criminal court, correctional inmates, gang members, and active burglars. Note that each of these terms implies some population of individual persons. The term *population* will be considered in some detail in Chapter 9. At this point, it is enough to realize that descriptive studies having individuals as their units of analysis typically aim to describe the population that comprises those individuals.

As the units of analysis, individuals may be considered in the context of their membership in social groupings. An individual may be described as belonging to a rich family or to a poor one, or as living in a high-crime or low-crime neighborhood. A research project might examine whether people who live in high-crime neighborhoods are more likely to have guns at home for protection than are those who live in low-crime areas, or whether children from poor families are more often involved in gangs than children from rich families. In each case, the individual is the unit of analysis—not the neighborhood or the family.

Groups

Social groups may also be the units of analysis for criminal justice research. This is not the same as studying the individuals within a group. If you study the members of a juvenile gang to learn about teenagers who join gangs, the individual (teen gang member) is the unit of analysis. But if you study all the juvenile gangs in a city to learn the differences between big gangs and small ones, between gangs selling drugs and gangs renting rollerblades, and so forth, the unit of analysis is the gang, a social group.

Police beats or patrol districts might be the units of analysis in a study. You might describe a police beat in terms of the total number of people who live within its boundaries, total street mileage, annual crime reports, and whether or not the beat includes a special facility such as a park or high school. You can then determine, for example, whether beats that include a park report more assaults than beats without such facilities, or whether auto thefts are more common in beats with more street mileage. The individual police beat in such a case is the unit of analysis.

Other units of analysis at the group level are households, city blocks, census tracts, cities, counties, and other geographic regions. Each of these terms also implies some population of groups. Street gangs implies some population that includes all street gangs. The population of street gangs could be described, say, in terms of its geographic distribution throughout a city. An explanatory study of street gangs might discover, for example, whether large gangs are more likely than small ones to engage in intergang warfare.

Organizations

Formal political or social organizations may also be the units of analysis in criminal justice research. An example is correctional facilities, which implies, of course, a population of all correctional facilities. Individual facilities might be characterized in terms of their number of employees, whether they are state or federal prisons, security classification, percentage of inmates who are from racial or ethnic minority groups, types of offenses for which inmates are sentenced to each facility, average length of sentence served, and so forth. We might determine whether federal prisons house a larger or smaller percentage of offenders sentenced for white-collar crimes than state prisons. Other examples of formal organizations suitable as units of analysis are police departments, courtrooms, probation offices, drug treatment facilities, and victim services agencies.

When social groups or formal organizations are the units of analysis, their characteristics are often derived from the characteristics of their individual members. Thus a police department might be described in terms of the age, ethnicity, education, and method of selecting its chief. In a descriptive study, we might find the percentage of police departments that have college-educated chiefs. In an explanatory study, we might determine whether departments with college-educated chiefs report, on the average, more or fewer citizen complaints against police use of excessive force. In each example, the police department is the unit of analysis. If we had asked whether college-educated police officers receive more or fewer complaints about excessive use of force, then the individual police officer would be the unit of analysis.

Organizations, social groups, and also individuals may be characterized in other ways—for instance, according to their environments or membership in larger groupings. Community anticrime groups might be characterized in terms of their relationships to other organizations. We might want to determine whether anticrime groups affiliated with schools are more active in organizing neighborhood cleanup campaigns than are anticrime groups associated with churches. The unit of analysis is still the group, even though we are examining group affiliation with other social organizations.

If all this seems unduly complicated, be assured that in most research projects you are likely to undertake, the unit of analysis will be relatively clear to you. When the unit of analysis is not so clear, however, it is absolutely essential to determine what it is. Otherwise, you cannot determine what observations are to be made about whom or what.

Some studies involve making descriptions or explanations about more than one unit of analysis. Consider, for example, an evaluation of community policing programs in selected neighborhoods of a large city. In such an evaluation, you might be interested in how citizens feel about the program (individuals), whether arrests increased in neighborhoods with the new program compared to those without it (groups), and whether the police department's budget increased more than the budget in a similar city (organizations). In such cases it is imperative that researchers anticipate what conclusions they wish to draw with regard to what units of analysis.

Social Artifacts

Another large group of possible units of analysis may be referred to generally as *social artifacts*, or the products of social beings and their behavior. One class of artifacts is such social objects as fictional accounts of crime depicted in mystery books, television dramas, feature films, or country-western songs. "True" crime stories are a similar class of artifacts; they include stories about crime in newspapers and magazines or on television.

Each of these objects implies a population of all such objects: all mass media stories about crime, all newspaper stories about crime, all weekly newsmagazine features about crime, all television news reports about crime, all editorial comments about crime, all letters to the editor about crime. A newspaper story might be characterized by its length, placement on front or later pages, size of headlines, and presence of photographs. The population of all newspaper stories about crime could be analyzed for the purpose of description, explanation, or evaluation.

A researcher could analyze whether television news features or newspaper reports provide the most details about a new police program to increase drug arrests. Or you might examine letters to the editor in a local newspaper to determine whether writers tend to favor or oppose a new program that established roadblocks to deter drunk driving on football weekends at your campus.

Social interactions form another large class of social artifacts suitable for criminal justice research. Police crime reports are an example. At first, you may not think of crime reports as social artifacts, but consider for a moment what they represent. When a crime is reported to the police, officers usually record what happened from a description by a victim or witness. For instance, an assault victim may describe how he suffered an unprovoked attack while innocently enjoying a cold beer after work. However, witnesses to the incident claim the "victim" started a fight by insulting the "offender." The responding police officer must interpret who is telling the truth in trying to sort out the circumstances of a violent social interaction; the officer's report becomes a social artifact that implies the population of all assaults. You might analyze assault reports to find how many involved three or more people, whether assaults tend to involve strangers or people with some prior acquaintance, or whether they more often occurred in public or private locations.

Records of different types of social interactions are common units of analysis in criminal justice research. Criminal history records, meetings of community anticrime groups, presentence investigations, and interactions between police and citizens are examples. Notice that each example requires information about individuals but that social interactions between people are the units of analysis.

Units of Analysis in Review

The purpose of this section has been to stretch your imagination regarding possible units of analysis for criminal justice research. Although individual human beings are often the units of analysis, that is not always the case. Many research questions can more appropriately be answered through the examination of other units of analysis.

The concept of unit of analysis may seem more complicated than it needs to be. It is more important that you grasp the logic of units of analysis than that you be able to repeat a list of the units. It is irrelevant what you call a given unit of analysis: a group, a formal organization, or a social artifact. It is essential, however, that you be able to identify what your unit of analysis is. You must decide whether you are studying assaults or assault victims, police departments or police officers, courtrooms or judges, prisons or prison inmates. Unless you keep this point in mind constantly, you run the risk of making assertions about one unit of analysis based on the examination of another.

To test your grasp of the concept of units of analysis, here are some examples of real research topics. See if you can determine the unit of analysis in each. (The answers are given later in the chapter.)

■ [1] We were also interested in learning whether adolescents perceived drug selling as a possible career. Some 10 percent of the respondents stated that they were at least somewhat likely to sell drugs after finishing school. For those who had never sold, the figures were 4 percent; for current heavy sellers, 63 percent. *individual* (REUTER, MACCOUN, AND MURPHY, 1990:82)

■ [2] Despite the record number of homicides in Chicago in 1974, Chicago's murder rate was actually lower than those in Detroit, Cleveland, Washington, D.C., and Baltimore. *Groups* (WILSON, 1987:22)

■ [3] Communities in which crime constituted a serious problem were very high on fear—in three neighborhoods more than 50 percent of our respondents reported being afraid, and these were our most crime-ridden study areas.   *Group*

(SKOGAN AND MAXFIELD, 1981:111)

■ [4] About 93 percent of all incidents processed by the patrol division in the city of Chicago developed from citizen initiative. Of all dispatched and on-view incidents handled by the Chicago police, only 17 percent involved criminal matters.

Social artifacts   (REISS, 1971:97)

■ [5] There were injuries in about four-fifths of the assault cases, but serious injuries in 42 percent and permanent or disabling injuries in only 4 cases (6 percent). Weapons were used in 78 percent of the cases, but were much more common when the victim and the assailant had a prior relationship (93 percent) than when they were strangers (43 percent).

(VERA INSTITUTE, 1981:24)

■ [6] Australia's ratios of imprisonment to reported robberies are close to those of the United States, while those in Hong Kong, Singapore, New Zealand, and England and Wales are significantly greater than in the United States.

(BLUMSTEIN, 1988:235)

■ [7] Community groups are either almost exclusively white or almost exclusively Latino. None is composed of an ethnic mixture which replicates the population of the neighborhood.

organizations   (PODOLEFSKY, 1983:136)

■ [8] An enormous variation of deviant activities were represented in our sample of 1,485 news items. We categorized these deviant activities into five general types for analysis: violence, economic, political, ideological/cultural, and diversionary.

(ERICSON, BARANEK, AND CHAN, 1991:243–244)

■ [9] Approximately half of the [burglars] (54 percent) admitted to 50 or more lifetime burglaries. . . . Included in this group are 44 offenders who had committed at least 100 such crimes. At the other extreme are 11 individuals who had participated in nine or fewer residential break-ins.

(WRIGHT AND DECKER, 1994:13)

The Ecological Fallacy

At this point, it is appropriate to introduce two important concepts related to units of analysis: the ecological fallacy and reductionism. The first of the concepts, the **ecological fallacy,** means the danger of making assertions about individuals as the unit of analysis based on the examination of groups or other aggregations. Let's consider a hypothetical example of this fallacy.

Suppose we are interested in learning about robbery in different police precincts of a large city. Let's assume that we have information on how many robberies were committed in each police precinct of Chicago for the year 1997. Assume also that we have census data describing some of the characteristics of those precincts. Our analysis of such data might show that a large number of 1997 robberies occurred in the downtown precinct, and that the average family income of persons who live in downtown Chicago (the "Loop") was substantially higher than in other precincts in the city. We might be tempted to conclude that high-income downtown residents were more likely to be robbed than were people who live in other parts of the city—that robbers selected richer victims. In reaching such a conclusion, we run the risk of committing the *ecological fallacy* because lower-income people who did not live in the downtown area were also being robbed there in 1997. Victims might be commuters to jobs in the Loop, people visiting downtown theaters or restaurants, passengers on subway or elevated train platforms, or homeless persons who are not counted by the census. Our problem is that we have examined police *precincts* as our units of analysis, but we wish to draw conclusions about individual *people.*

The same problem would arise if we discovered that incarceration rates were higher in states that have a large proportion of elderly residents. We would not know whether older people were actually imprisoned more often. Or if we found higher suicide rates in cities with large nonwhite populations, we could not be sure whether more nonwhites than whites committed suicide.

Often a criminal justice researcher has no alternative to addressing a particular question through an ecological analysis. Perhaps the most appropriate data are simply not available. For instance, the crime tallies for police precincts and census characteristics mentioned in our example may be easy to obtain, and we may not have the resources to conduct a survey of individual Chicago residents to determine who was being robbed. In such cases, we may reach a tentative conclusion but recognize and note the risk of committing the ecological fallacy.

Don't let these warnings against the ecological fallacy lead you to commit what is called an *individualistic fallacy.* Some students approaching criminal justice research for the first time have trouble reconciling general patterns of attitudes and actions with individual exceptions they know of. If, for example, you read a newspaper story about a Utah resident visiting New York who was murdered on a subway platform, that does not deny the fact that most visitors to New York or most subway riders are not at risk of murder. Similarly, mass media stories and popular films about drug problems in U.S. cities frequently focus on drug use and dealing among African Americans. But that does not mean that most African Americans are drug users, or that drugs are not a problem among whites.

The individualistic fallacy can be especially troublesome for students beginning the study of criminal justice. Newspapers, local television news, and television police dramas often present unusual or highly dramatized versions of crime problems and criminal justice policy. These messages may distort the way many people initially approach research problems in criminal justice.

The ecological fallacy deals with something else altogether—drawing conclusions about individuals based solely on the observation of groups. For example, a recent study examined property crime rates in states that did and did not have state-operated lotteries (Mikesell and Pirog-Good, 1990). Finding that the property crime rate was higher in states with lotteries, the authors concluded that lottery players committed crimes to support their purchase of tickets. Furthermore, finding that the property crime rate was higher in states that had more police officers per resident,

the authors speculated that more police increased the risk of arrest, which increased the "thrills" that lottery-playing thieves enjoyed. Although the patterns observed among variables may be genuine, the danger here lies in drawing unwarranted assumptions about the causes of those patterns— assumptions about individuals who make up the group.

Reductionism

A second concept relating to units of analysis is **reductionism.** Basically, reductionism is an overly strict limitation on the kinds of concepts and variables to be considered as causes in explaining the broad range of human behavior represented by crime and criminal justice policy. Economists may tend to consider only economic variables (marginal value, expected utility); sociologists may consider only sociological variables (values, norms, roles); psychologists may consider only psychological variables (personality types, compulsive personality disorder). For example, why has violent crime by juveniles increased? Is it from a breakdown in traditional family structure? Reduced economic opportunities for teenagers? Exposure to violence in movies and on television? Social scientists from different disciplines tend to look at some explanations for crime problems and ignore the others. Explaining crime solely in terms of economic factors is called *economic reductionism;* explaining crime solely in terms of psychological factors is called *psychological reductionism.* Note how this issue relates to the discussion of theoretical paradigms in Chapter 2.

Reductionism of any type tends to suggest that particular units of analysis or variables are more relevant than others. If we considered the changing family structure as the cause of increased juvenile crime, our unit of analysis would be families. An economist, though, might use the 50 states as the units of analysis and compare juvenile crime rates and economic conditions. A psychologist might choose individual juveniles as the units of analysis to determine how watching violent films affects personality development.

Like the ecological fallacy, reductionism involves the use of inappropriate units of analysis.

The appropriate unit of analysis for a given research question is not always clear, and it is often debated by social scientists, especially across disciplinary boundaries.

■ THE TIME DIMENSION

Time plays different roles in the design and execution of research, aside from the time it takes to do research. For example, we described in Chapter 3 how the time sequence of events and situations is a critical element in determining causation. Time is also involved in the generalizability of research findings. Do the descriptions and explanations that result from a particular study accurately represent the situation of ten years ago or ten years from now, or do they represent only the present state of affairs?

Thus far in this chapter, we have regarded research design as a process for deciding *what aspects* we will observe, *of whom,* and *for what purpose.* Now we will consider a set of time-related options for research designs that cut across each of these earlier considerations. In general, our observations may be made more or less at one time point, or they may be deliberately stretched over a longer period.

Cross-sectional Studies

Many criminal justice research projects are designed to study some phenomenon by taking a cross section of it at one time and analyzing that cross section carefully. Exploratory and descriptive studies are often **cross-sectional.** A single U.S. Census, for instance, is a study aimed at describing the U.S. population at a given time. A single wave of the NCVS is a descriptive cross-sectional study that estimates how many people have been victims of crime in a given time period.

Many exploratory studies are also cross-sectional. For example, a police department may conduct a citywide survey to examine what residents believe are the sources of crime problems in their neighborhood. In all likelihood, the study would ask about crime problems in a single time

frame and might be used to help the department explore various methods of introducing community policing.

Cross-sectional studies for explanatory or evaluation purposes have an inherent problem. Typically their aim is to understand causal processes that occur over time, but their conclusions are based on observations made at only one time. For example, a survey might ask respondents whether their home has been burglarized and whether they have any special locks on their doors, hoping to explain whether or not special locks prevent burglary. Because the questions about burglary victimization and door locks are asked at only one time, it is not possible to determine whether burglary victims installed locks after a burglary, or whether special locks were in place but did not prevent the crime. Some of the ways you can deal with the difficult problem of determining time order will be discussed later.

Longitudinal Studies

Other research projects called **longitudinal studies** are designed to permit observations over an extended period. An example is a researcher who observes the activities of a neighborhood anticrime organization from the time of its inception until its demise. Analysis of newspaper stories about crime or numbers of prison inmates over time are other examples. In the latter instances, it would be irrelevant whether the researcher's observations were made over the course of the actual events under study or at one time, examining a year's worth of newspapers in the library or ten years of annual reports on corrections populations.

Three special types of longitudinal studies should be noted here: trend, cohort, and panel studies; trend and cohort studies will be described more fully in Chapter 7. **Trend studies** look at changes within some general population over time. An example is a comparison of UCR figures over time, showing an increase in reported crime from 1960 through 1995. Or a researcher might want to know whether changes in sentences for certain offenses produced increases in the number of people imprisoned in state institutions. In this case, a trend study might examine annual figures for prison population over time, comparing totals for the years before and after new sentencing laws took effect.

Cohort studies examine more specific populations (cohorts) as they change over time. Typically, a cohort is an age group, such as those people born during the 1940s, but it can also be based on some other time grouping. Cohorts are often defined as a group of people who enter or leave an institution at the same time, such as persons entering a drug treatment center during July, offenders released from custody in 1996, or high school seniors in March 1997.

In one of the best-known cohort studies, Marvin Wolfgang and associates (1972) studied all males born in 1945 who lived in the city of Philadelphia from their tenth birthday through age 18 or older. The researchers examined records from police agencies and public schools to determine how many boys in the cohort had been charged with delinquency or arrested, how old they were when first arrested, and differences in school performance between delinquents and nondelinquents.

Panel studies are similar to trend and cohort studies except that the same set of people is interviewed at two or more times. The NCVS is a good example of a descriptive panel study. A member of each household selected for inclusion in the survey is interviewed seven times at six-month intervals. The survey serves many purposes but was developed initially to estimate how many people were victims of various types of crimes each year. It is designed as a panel study so that persons could be asked about crimes that occurred in the previous six months, and two waves of panel data are combined to estimate the nationwide frequency of victimization over a one-year period.

Panel studies are often used in evaluation research, where the same persons are interviewed both before and after a new program is introduced. For example, an evaluation of policies to reduce fear of crime in the cities of Houston, Texas,

and Newark, New Jersey, used a panel study to test the effectiveness of a crime prevention newsletter (Pate, Wycoff, Skogan, and Sherman, 1986). People who lived in designated neighborhoods were interviewed before and after the newsletter was introduced to determine whether crime prevention tips reduced their fear of crime.

Because the distinctions between trend, cohort, and panel studies are sometimes difficult to grasp at first, let's contrast the three study designs in terms of the same variable: arrests for burglary. A *trend* study might look at shifts in burglary arrests over time, as the UCR does each year. A *cohort* study might follow shifts in burglary arrests among "baby boomers"—say, those who were between ages 18 and 25 in 1968. A sample of 18- to 25-year-olds would be interviewed in 1968, and a new sample of 28- to 35-year-olds would be interviewed in 1978. Persons in each sample would be asked whether they had been arrested for burglary in the previous year. A *panel* study would interview the same specific individuals in 1968 and again in 1978. Notice that only the panel study would give a full picture of changes in burglary arrests. Cohort and trend studies would uncover only net changes, without providing information on changing arrest rates for specific individuals.

Longitudinal studies have an obvious advantage over cross-sectional ones in providing information about processes over time. But often this advantage comes at a heavy cost in both time and money, especially in a large-scale study that follows subjects for many years. Studies of criminal careers may identify a group of subjects at an early age, tracing records of delinquency and adult arrests and perhaps interviewing the subjects as adults.

Panel studies, which offer the most comprehensive data on changes over time, face a special problem: panel attrition. Some of the respondents studied in the first wave of the survey may not participate in later waves. This is comparable to the problem of *experimental mortality* to be discussed in Chapter 7. The danger is that those who drop out of the study may not be typical and may thereby distort the results of the study. For example, let's say you are interested in evaluating the success of a new drug treatment program by conducting weekly drug tests on a panel of participants for a period of 10 months. Regardless of how successful the program appears to be after 10 months, if a substantial number of people drop out of your study, you would expect that treatment was less effective in keeping them off drugs.

Approximating Longitudinal Studies

It may be possible to draw approximate conclusions about processes that take place over time even when only cross-sectional data are available. It is worth noting some of the ways to do that.

Sometimes, cross-sectional data imply processes over time on the basis of simple logic. For example, a study of student drug use was conducted at the University of Hawaii (mentioned in Chapter 2). Students were asked to report whether they had ever tried each of a number of illegal drugs. With regard to marijuana and LSD, it was found that some students had tried both drugs, some had tried only one, and others had not tried either. Because these data were collected at one time, and because some students presumably would experiment with drugs later on, it would seem that the study could not tell the order in which students were likely to experiment with marijuana and LSD: Were students more likely to try marijuana or LSD first?

A closer examination of the data showed, however, that although some students reported having tried marijuana but not LSD, no students in the study had tried only LSD. From this finding it was inferred—as common sense suggested—that marijuana use preceded LSD use. If drug experimentation occurred in the opposite time order, then a study at a given time should have found some students who had tried LSD but not marijuana, and it should have found no students who had tried only marijuana.

Logical inferences may also be made whenever the time order of variables is clear. If we discovered in a cross-sectional study of high school students that men were more likely to smoke marijuana than women, we would conclude that

gender affects the propensity to use marijuana, not the other way around. Thus, even though our observations were made at only one time, we would feel justified in drawing conclusions about processes that take place across time.

Retrospective Studies

Retrospective research, which asks people to recall their pasts, is another common way of approximating observations over time. A study of recidivism, for example, might select a group of prison inmates and analyze their history of delinquency or crime. Or let's say you were interested in whether college students convicted of drunk driving were more likely to have parents with drinking problems compared to college students with no drunk driving record. Such a study would be retrospective because it focuses on the histories of college students who were or were not convicted of drunk driving.

The danger in this technique is evident. Sometimes people have faulty memories; sometimes they lie. Lying is a common problem in criminal justice research that asks people to recall illegal actions. Retrospective recall is one way of approximating observations across time, but it must be used with caution. Retrospective studies that analyze records of past arrests or convictions suffer different problems. Records may be unavailable, incomplete, or inaccurate. We will focus more closely on these issues in Chapter 12.

A more fundamental issue in the retrospective approach hinges on how subjects are selected, and how subject selection affects the kinds of research questions that retrospective studies can address.

Imagine you are a juvenile court judge, and you're troubled by what appears to be a growing number of child abuse cases in your court. Talking with a juvenile caseworker, you wonder whether the parents of these children had been abused or neglected during their own childhood. Together you formulate a hypothesis about the intergenerational transmission of violence: Victims of childhood abuse later abuse their own children. How would you go about investigating that hypothesis?

Given your position as a judge who regularly sees abuse victims, you would probably consider a retrospective approach that examines the backgrounds of families appearing in your court. Let's say you and the caseworker plan to investigate the family backgrounds of 20 abuse victims who appear in your court during the next three months. The caseworker consults with a clinical psychologist from the local university and obtains copies of a questionnaire, or "protocol," that has been used by researchers to study the families of child abuse victims. After interviewing the families of 20 victims, the caseworker reports to you that 18 of the 20 child victims had a mother or father who was abused as a child. It seems safe to conclude that your hypothesis about the intergenerational transmission of violence is strongly supported because 90 percent (18/20) of abuse/neglect victims brought before your court come from families with a history of child abuse.

Think for a moment about how you approached the question of whether child abuse breeds child abuse. You began with abuse victims and retrospectively established that many of their parents had been abused. However, this is different from the question of how many victims of childhood abuse later abuse their own children. That question requires a *prospective* approach, where you begin with childhood victims and then determine how many of them later abuse their own children.

To clarify this point, let's shift from the hypothetical study to actual research that illustrates the difference between prospective and retrospective approaches to the same question. Rosemary Hunter and Nancy Kilstrom (1979) conducted a study of 255 infants and their parents.[1] The researchers began by selecting families of premature infants in a newborn intensive care unit. Interviews with the parents of 255 infants revealed that either the mother or the father in 49 of the families had been the victim of abuse or

neglect; 206 families revealed no history of abuse. In a follow-up study, Hunter and Kilstrom found that within one year, ten of the 255 infants had been abused. Nine of those ten infant victims were from the 49 families with a history of abuse, while one abused infant was from the 206 families with no background of abuse.

Figure 4-1A illustrates these prospective results graphically. Infants in 18 percent (9/49) of families with a history of abuse showed signs of abuse within one year of birth, while less than 1 percent of infants born to parents with no history of abuse were themselves abused within one year. Although that is a sizable difference, notice that the 18 percent figure for continuity of abuse is very similar to the 19 percent rate of abuse discovered in the histories of all 255 families.

Now consider what Hunter and Kilstrom would have found if they had begun with the ten abused infants at time 2 and then checked their family backgrounds. Figure 4-1B illustrates this retrospective approach. A large majority of the ten infant victims (90 percent) had parents with a history of abuse.

You have probably realized by now that the prospective and retrospective approaches address fundamentally different questions, even though the questions may appear similar on the surface:

Prospective: What percent of abuse victims later abuse their children? (18 percent; Figure 4-1A)

Retrospective: What percent of abuse victims have parents who were abused? (90 percent; Figure 4-1B)

More generally, Robert Sampson and John Laub (1993:14) comment on how retrospective and prospective views yield different interpretations about the patterns of criminal offending over time:

■ Looking *back* over the careers of adult criminals exaggerates the prevalence of stability. Looking *forward* from youth reveals the success and failures, including adolescent delinquents who go on to be normal functioning adults. This is the paradox noted [by Lee Robins] earlier: adult criminality seems to be always preceded

[1] This example was suggested by Cathy Spatz Widom (1989c) in a comprehensive review and critique of research on the intergenerational transmission of child abuse.

FIGURE 4-1

Prospective and Retrospective Approaches to a Subject

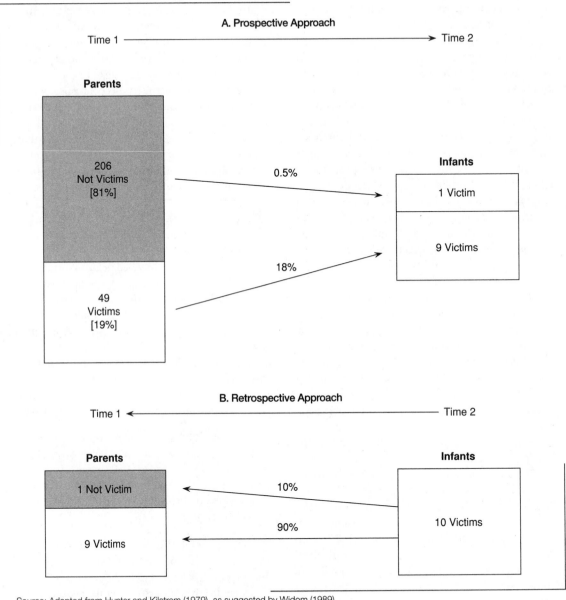

Source: Adapted from Hunter and Kilstrom (1979), as suggested by Widom (1989).

by childhood misconduct, but most conduct-disordered children do not become antisocial or criminal adults (Robins, 1978). [emphasis in original]

Likewise, a retrospective view of child abuse shows that abuse in one generation is almost always preceded by abuse in the prior generation. However, most victims of childhood abuse do not later abuse their own children.

Our intention here is not to suggest that retrospective studies have no value. Rather, we want to sensitize you to how the time dimension is linked to the framing of research questions. A retrospective approach is limited in its ability to reveal how causal processes unfold over time. A retrospective approach is therefore not well suited to answer questions such as, How many childhood victims of abuse or neglect later abuse their own children? A retrospective study could be used, however, to compare whether childhood victims were more likely than nonvictims to have a history of abuse in their family background.

The Time Dimension Summarized

Joel Devine and James Wright (1993:19) describe a clever metaphor that distinguishes longitudinal studies from cross-sectional ones. Think of a cross-sectional study as a snapshot, a trend study as a slide show, and a panel study as a motion picture. A cross-sectional study, like a snapshot, produces an image at one point in time. This can provide useful information about crime— burglary, for example—at a single time, perhaps in a single place. Think of a slide show as a series of snapshots, in sequence over time. By viewing a slide show, we can tell how some indicator— change in burglary rates—varies over time. But a trend study is usually based on aggregate information. It can tell us something about aggregations of burglary over time, but not, for instance, whether the same people are committing burglaries at an increasing or decreasing rate, or whether there are more or fewer burglars with a relatively constant rate of crime commission. A panel study, like a motion picture, can capture moving images of the same individuals and give us information about individual rates of offending over time.

These, then, are some of the ways time figures in criminal justice research and some of the ways researchers have learned to cope with it. In designing any study, you need to look at both the explicit and implicit assumptions you are making about time. Are you interested in describing some process that occurs over time, such as whether mandatory jail sentences reduce drunk driving? Or are you simply going to describe how many people were arrested for drunk driving in the past year? If you want to describe a process that occurs over time, will you be able to make observations at different points in the process, or will you have to approximate such observations—drawing logical inferences from what you can observe now?

■ HOW TO DESIGN A RESEARCH PROJECT

You've now seen some of the options available to criminal justice researchers in designing projects, but what if you were to undertake research? Where would you start? Then where would you go? How would you begin planning your research? These are the topics of this final section of the chapter.

Although research design occurs at the beginning of a research project, it involves all the steps of the subsequent project. The comments to follow, then, should give you some guidance on how to start a research project and will provide an overview of the topics that follow in later chapters of the book. Ultimately, the research process needs to be seen as a whole, and you need to grasp it as a whole in order to create a research design. Unfortunately, however, both textbooks and human cognition operate on the basis of sequential parts.

Every project has a starting point, but it is important to think through later stages even at the beginning. Figure 4-2 presents a schematic view of the social science research process. We present this view reluctantly because it may suggest more of a "cookbook" order to research than is the case in practice. Nonetheless, you should have some overview of the whole process before we launch into the specific details of particular components of research.

The Research Process

At the top of the diagram in Figure 4-2 are interests, ideas, theories, and new programs—the possible beginning points for a line of research. The letters (*A, B, X, Y,* and so forth) represent variables or concepts such as deterrence or child abuse. Thus, you might have a general interest in finding out why the threat of punishment deters some, but not all, people from committing crimes, or you might want to know how burglars select

FIGURE 4-2
The Research Process

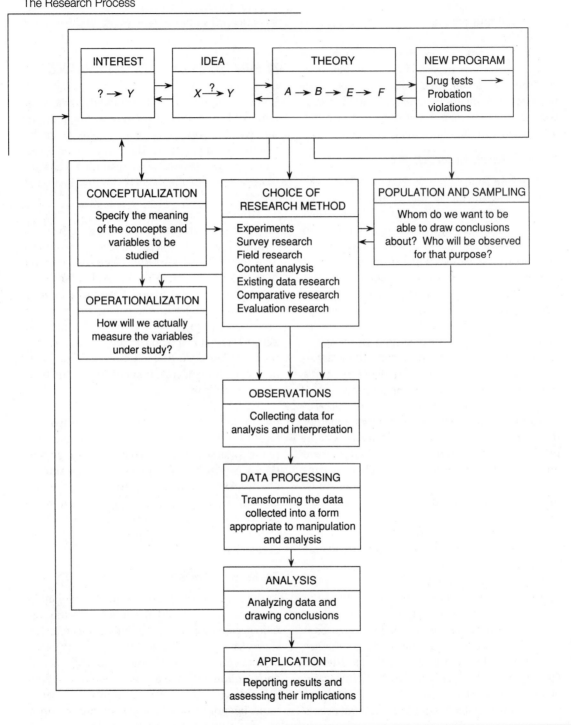

their targets. Alternatively, your inquiry might begin with a specific idea about the way things are. You might have the idea that aggressive arrest policies deter drug use, for example. Question marks in the diagram indicate that you aren't sure things are the way you suspect they are. We have represented a theory as a complex set of relationships among several variables (*A, B, E,* and *F*).

The research process might begin with an idea for a new program. Imagine you are the director of a probation services department, and you want to develop a new program to require weekly drug tests for people on probation. Because you have taken a course on criminal justice research methods, you decide to design an evaluation of the new program before trying it out. The research process begins with your idea for the new drug testing program.

Notice the movement back and forth across these several possible beginnings. An initial interest may lead to the formulation of an idea, which may be fit into a larger theory, and the theory may produce new ideas and create new interests. Or your understanding of some theory may encourage you to consider new policies.

Any or all of these beginnings may suggest the need for empirical research. The purpose of such research can be to explore an interest, test a specific idea, validate a complex theory, or evaluate a new program. Whatever the purpose, a variety of decisions need to be made, as indicated in the remainder of the diagram.

To make this discussion more concrete, let's take a specific research example. Suppose you are concerned about the problem of crime on your campus, and you have a special interest in learning more about how other students view the crime problem and what they think should be done about it. Going a step further, let's say you have the impression that students are especially concerned about violent crimes such as assault and rape, and that many students feel the university should be doing more to prevent violent crime. The source of this idea might be your own interest after being a student for a couple of years. You might develop the idea while reading about

theories of crime in a course you are taking. Perhaps you read recent stories about a "crime wave" on campus. Or maybe some combination of things makes you want to learn more about campus crime problems.

Considering the research purposes discussed earlier in this chapter, your research would be pretty much exploratory. You probably have descriptive and explanatory interests as well: How much of a problem is campus violent crime? Are students especially concerned about crime in certain areas? Why are some students more worried about crime than others? What do students think would be effective changes to reduce campus crime problems?

You should begin to think about units of analysis and the time dimension. Your interest in violent crime might suggest a study of crimes reported to campus police in recent years. In this case, the units of analysis would be social artifacts (crime reports) in a longitudinal study (crime reports in recent years). Or after thinking a bit more, you may be interested in current student attitudes and opinions about violent crime. The units of analysis would then be individuals (college students), and a cross-sectional study would suit your purposes nicely.

Getting Started

To begin pursuing your interest in student concerns about violent crime, you would undoubtedly want to read something about the issue. You might begin by finding out what research has been done on fear of crime and on the sorts of crime that concern people most. Newspaper stories could provide some information on the violent crimes that occurred recently on campus. Appendix A of this book will give you some assistance in using your college library, and Appendixes A and B present some tips on using the Internet to find criminal justice information. In addition, you would probably want to talk to people—other students or campus police officers, for example. These activities will prepare you to handle the various research design decisions we are about to examine. As you review previous research literature, you should make note of the designs used by other researchers, asking whether the same designs would meet your research objective.

What is your objective, by the way? It's important that you are clear about that before you design your study. Do you plan to write a paper based on your research to satisfy a course requirement or as an honors thesis? Is your purpose to gain information that will support an argument for more police protection or better lighting on campus? Do you want to write an article for the campus newspaper or an academic journal?

Usually your objective for undertaking research can be expressed in a report. Appendix C of this book will help you with the organization of research reports, and we recommend that you outline such a report as the first step in the design of any project. Specifically, you should be clear about the kinds of statements you will want to make when the research is complete. Here are two examples of such statements: "*x* percent of State U students believe that sexual assault is a big problem on campus," and "Female students living off campus are more likely than females living in dorms to feel that emergency phones should be installed near buildings where evening classes are held." Although your final report may not look much like your initial image of it, outlining the planned report will help you make better decisions about research design.

Conceptualization

We often talk casually about criminal justice concepts such as deterrence, recidivism, crime prevention, community policing, and child abuse, but it's necessary to specify what we mean by these concepts in order to do research on them. Chapter 5 will examine this process of **conceptualization** in depth. For now, let's see what it might involve in our hypothetical example.

If you are going to study student concerns about violent crime, you must first specify what you mean by "concern about violent crime." This ambiguous phrase can mean different things to different people. Campus police officers are concerned about violent crime because that is part of their job. On one hand, students might be concerned about crime in much the same way they are concerned about other social problems, such as homelessness, unemployment, and global warming—they recognize these things as problems society must deal with, but they don't feel that these issues affect them directly; we could specify this concept as "general concern about violent crime." On the other hand, students may feel that the threat of violent crime does affect them directly, and they express some fear about the possibility of being a victim; let's call this "fear for personal safety."

Obviously, you will need to specify what you mean by the term in your research, but this doesn't necessarily mean you have to settle for a single definition. In fact, you might want to define the concept of "concern about violent crime" in more than one way and see how students feel about each.

You will, of course, need to specify all the concepts you wish to study. If you want to study the possible effect of concern about crime on student behavior, you'll have to decide whether you want to limit your focus to specific precautionary behavior such as keeping doors locked, or general behavior such as going to classes, parties, and football games.

Choice of Research Method

As we'll see in Part 3 of this book, a variety of methods are available to the criminal justice researcher. Each method has strengths and weaknesses, and certain concepts are more appropriately studied by some methods than by others.

In the hypothetical study of concern about crime, a survey might be the most appropriate method for studying both general concern and fear for personal safety. You could either interview students directly or ask them to fill out a questionnaire. As you'll see in Chapter 10, surveys are especially well suited to the study of individuals' attitudes and opinions. Thus, if you wish to examine whether students who are afraid of crime are more likely to believe that campus lighting should be improved than students who are not afraid, a survey is a good method.

This is not to say that you couldn't make good use of other methods presented in Part 3. Through *content analysis* (discussed in Chapter 12), for example, you might examine letters to the editor in your campus newspaper and analyze what letter writers believe should be done to improve campus safety. *Field research* (Chapter 11), where you observed whether students tended to avoid dark areas of the campus compared to well-lighted ones, would help you understand student behavior in avoiding certain areas of the campus at night. Or you might study official complaints made to police and college administrators about crime problems on campus. As you read Part 3, you'll see ways other research methods might be used to study this topic. Usually the best study design is one that uses more than one research method, taking advantage of their different strengths.

Operationalization

Having specified the concepts to be studied and having chosen the research method, you must create concrete measurement techniques. **Operationalization,** discussed in Chapter 5, refers to the concrete steps or operations that will be used to measure specific concepts.

If you have decided to study concern about violent crime by a survey, your operationalization will take the form of questionnaire items. You might operationalize fear for personal safety with the question, "How safe do you feel alone on the campus after dark?" This could be followed by boxes indicating the possible answers "Safe" and "Unsafe." Student attitudes about ways of improving campus safety could be operationalized with the question, "Listed below are different actions that might be taken to reduce violent crime on campus. Beside each description, indicate whether you favor or oppose the actions described." This would be followed by several different actions and "Favor" and "Oppose" boxes beside each.

Population and Sampling

In addition to refining concepts and measurements, decisions must be made about who or what to study. The *population* for a study is that

group (usually of people) about whom we want to be able to draw conclusions. We are almost never able to study all the members of the population that interests us, however. In virtually every case, we must sample subjects for study. Chapter 9 will describe methods for selecting samples that adequately reflect the whole population that interests us. Notice in the diagram in Figure 4-2 that decisions about population and sampling are related to decisions about the research method to be used.

In the study of concern about violent crime, the relevant population is the student population of your college. As you'll discover in Chapter 9, however, selecting a sample requires you to get more specific than that. Will you include part-time as well as full-time students? Only degree candidates or everyone? Students who live on campus, off campus, or both? There are many such questions, and each must be answered in terms of your research purpose. If your purpose is to study concern about sexual assault, you might want to limit your population to female students.

Observations

Having decided what to study among whom by what method, you are ready to make observations—to collect empirical data. The chapters of Part 3, which describe various research methods, will give the different observation methods appropriate to each.

For the survey of concern about violent crime, you might print questionnaires and mail them to a sample selected from the student body, or you could have a team of interviewers conduct the survey over the telephone. The relative advantages and disadvantages of these and other possibilities will be discussed in Chapter 10.

Data Processing

Depending on the research method chosen, you will have amassed a volume of observations in a form that probably isn't easily interpretable. In the case of a survey, the "raw" observations are typically in the form of questionnaires with boxes checked, answers written in spaces, and the like. The data-processing phase for a survey typically involves classifying (coding) the written-in answers and transforming all information to some computer format.

Analysis

Finally, we manipulate the collected data for the purpose of drawing conclusions that reflect on the interests, ideas, and theories that initiated the inquiry. Chapter 14 will describe a few of the many options available to you in analyzing data. Notice that the results of your analyses feed back into your initial interests, ideas, and theories. In practice, this feedback may initiate another cycle of inquiry. In the study of student concern about violent crime, the analysis phase would pursue both descriptive and explanatory purposes. You might begin by calculating the percentages of students who are afraid to be out alone on the campus after dark, together with the percentage who favor or oppose each of the different things that might be done to improve campus safety. Taken together, these percentages would provide a good picture of student opinion on the issue.

Moving beyond simple description, you might describe the opinions of different subsets of the student body: men versus women; freshmen, sophomores, juniors, seniors, graduate students; students who live in dorms or off-campus apartments. You might then conduct some explanatory analysis to make the point that students who are enrolled in classes that meet in the evening hours are most in favor of improved campus lighting.

Application

The final stage of the research process is using the research you've conducted and the conclusions you've reached. To start, you will probably want to communicate your findings so that others will know what you've learned. It may be appropriate to prepare—and even publish—a written report. Perhaps you will make oral presentations in class or at a professional meeting. If you're skilled in computer use, you might prepare a web page that presents your results. Other students will be interested in hearing what you have learned about their concerns about campus violent crime.

Your study might also be useful to actually do something about campus safety. If you find that a large proportion of students you interviewed believe that a parking lot near the library is poorly lighted, university administrators could add more lights or campus police might patrol the area more frequently. Crime prevention programs might be launched in dormitories if residents are more afraid of violent crime than students who live in other types of housing.

Finally, you should consider what your research suggests in regard to further research on your subject. What mistakes should be corrected in future studies? What avenues, opened up slightly in your study, should be pursued further in later investigations?

Review

As this overview shows, research design involves a set of decisions regarding what topic is to be studied among *what population* with *what research methods* for *what purpose*. Whereas the earlier sections of this chapter on research purposes, units of analysis, and the time dimension aimed at broadening your perspective in all these regards, research design is the process of narrowing, of focusing, your perspective for purposes of a particular study.

If you are doing a research project for a course you are taking, many aspects of research design may be specified for you in advance. If you must do a project for a course in experimental methods in criminal justice, the method of research will be specified for you. If the project is for a course in corrections policy, the research topic will be somewhat specified. Because it would not be feasible for us to anticipate all such constraints, the following discussion will assume there are none.

In designing a research project, you will find it useful to begin by assessing three things: your own interests, your abilities, and the resources available to you. Each of these considerations will suggest a large number of possible studies.

What are you interested in understanding? Surely, you have several questions about crime and possible policy responses. Why do some juvenile gangs sell drugs while others steal cars? Why do particular neighborhoods near campus seem to have higher rates of burglary? What types of community groups are more active in neighborhood anticrime programs? Do sentencing policies discriminate against minorities? Do cities with gun control laws have lower murder rates? Are sentences for rape more severe in some states than in others? Are mandatory jail sentences more effective than license suspension in reducing repeat drunk driving offenses? Think for a while about the kinds of questions that interest and concern you.

Once you have a few questions you would be interested in answering, think about the kind of information you need to answer them. What research units of analysis would provide the most relevant information: gangs, burglary victims, households, community groups, police departments, cities, states, drunk drivers? This question should be inseparable from the question of research topics. Then ask which aspects of the units of analysis would provide the information you need to answer your research question.

Your next consideration is how to go about getting that information. Are the relevant data likely to be already available somewhere (say, in a government publication), or would you have to collect them yourself? If you think you would have to collect them, how would you do that? Would it be necessary to observe juvenile gangs, interview a large number of burglary victims, or attend meetings of community crime prevention groups? Or would you have to design an experiment to study sentences for drunk driving?

As you answer these questions, you are well into the process of research design. Keep in mind, however, your own research abilities, the resources available to you, and the time required to complete your research project. Do not design the perfect study if you will be unable to carry it out in a reasonable time. You may want to try a research method you have not used before because research should be a learning experience in many ways, but you should not put yourself at too great a disadvantage.

Once you have a general idea of what you want to study and how, carefully review previous research in journals, books, and government reports to see how other researchers have addressed the topic and what they have learned about it. Your review of the literature may lead you to revise your research design; perhaps you will decide to use another researcher's method or even replicate an earlier study. The independent replication of research projects is a standard procedure in the physical sciences, and it is just as important in criminal justice research. Or you might want to go beyond replication and study some aspect of the topic that you feel other researchers have overlooked.

Here's another approach you might take. Suppose a topic has been studied previously using survey methods. Can you design an experimental study to test the findings of those earlier researchers? Or can you think of how a field study might supplement information gained from a survey? The use of several different research methods to test the same finding is sometimes called *triangulation,* and you should keep it in mind as a valuable research strategy. Because each research method has particular strengths and weaknesses, there is always a danger that research findings will reflect, at least in part, the method of inquiry. In the best of all worlds, your own research design should bring more than one research method to bear on the topic.

■ THE RESEARCH PROPOSAL

The purpose of this chapter has been to give you an overview of the whole research process. That's useful in terms of learning, of course, but this chapter can serve you in another way as well. If you were to undertake a research project—an assignment for this course, perhaps, or even a major study to be funded by the government or a large corporation—you would probably have to provide a research proposal describing what you intend to accomplish and how. We'll conclude this chapter with a discussion of how you might prepare such a proposal.

Elements of a Research Proposal

Some funding agencies have specific requirements for a proposal's elements, structure, or both. For example, in its 1996–1997 Research Plan, the National Institute of Justice (NIJ) describes what should be included in research proposals on such topics as crime prevention and domestic violence (National Institute of Justice, 1996c). Your instructor may have certain requirements for a research proposal you are to prepare in this course. Here are some basic elements that should be discussed in almost any research proposal.

Problem or Objective What exactly do you want to study? Why is it worth studying? Does the proposed study contribute to our general understanding of crime? Does it have practical significance? If your proposal describes an evaluation study, then the problem, objective, or research questions may already be specified for you. For example, the following questions were stated in NIJ's request for an evaluation of a Jackson County, Missouri, antidrug initiative known as "COMBAT":

■ Many elements of COMBAT and associated programs embody a community focus: policing, prosecution, school-based probation counselors, funding for community treatment and prevention service providers. What benefits, if any, can be attributed to this common community focus? Can a similar common focus be produced in other jurisdictions? What, if any, role have central administrative structures of COMBAT played in promoting a common community focus? (National Institute of Justice, 1996d:4)

Literature Review What have others said about this topic? What theories address it, and what do they say? What research has been done? Are the findings consistent, or do past studies disagree? Are there flaws in the body of existing research that you feel you can remedy?

Subjects for Study Who or what will you study in order to collect data? Identify the subjects in general terms and then specifically identify who (or what) is available for study and how you will reach them. Is it appropriate to select a sample? If so, how will you do that? If there is any possibility that your research will have an impact on those you study, how will you ensure that they are not harmed by the research?

Measurement What are the key variables in your study? How will you define and measure them? Do your definitions and measurement methods duplicate (that's okay, incidentally) or differ from those of previous research on this topic? If you have already developed your measurement device (a questionnaire, for example) or if you are using something developed by others, you should include a copy in an appendix to your proposal.

Data-Collection Methods How will you actually collect the data for your study? Will you observe behavior directly or conduct a survey? Will you undertake field research, or are you going to focus on the reanalysis of data already collected by others?

Analysis Give some indication of the kind of analysis you plan to conduct. If you anticipate the use of specific analytic techniques—cross-tabulation, time-series analysis, and so on—you might say that. More important, however, spell out the purpose and logic of your analysis. Are you interested in precise description? Do you intend to explain why things are the way they are? Will you analyze the impact of a new program? What possible explanatory variables will your analysis consider, and how will you know whether you've explained program impact adequately?

Schedule It is often appropriate to provide a schedule for the various stages of research. Even if you don't do this for the proposal, do it for yourself. Unless you have a timeline for accomplishing the several stages of research and keep track of how you're doing, you may end up in trouble.

Budget If you are asking someone to give you money to pay the costs of your research, you will need to provide a budget that specifies where the money will go. Large, expensive projects include budgetary categories such as personnel, equipment, supplies, and expenses like travel and telephones. Even for a more modest project you will pay for yourself, it's a good idea to spend some time anticipating any expenses involved: office supplies, photocopying, computer disks, telephone calls, transportation, and so on.

As you can see, if you were interested in conducting a criminal justice research project, it would be a good idea to prepare a research proposal for your own purposes, even if you weren't required to do so by your instructor or a funding agency. If you are going to invest your time and energy in such a project, you should do what you can to ensure a return on that investment.

■ ANSWERS TO UNITS OF ANALYSIS EXERCISE

(pages 75–76)

1. Individuals (adolescents)
2. Groups (cities)
3. Groups (neighborhoods)
4. Social artifacts (incidents handled by police)
5. Social artifacts (assaults)
6. Groups (countries)
7. Organizations (community groups)
8. Social artifacts (news items)
9. Individuals (burglars)

■ MAIN POINTS

- Exploration is the attempt to develop an initial, rough understanding of some phenomenon.
- Description is the precise measurement and reporting of the characteristics of some population or phenomenon under study.
- Explanation is the discovery and reporting of relationships among different aspects of the phenomenon under study. Whereas descriptive studies answer the question, What's so?, explanatory ones tend to answer the question, Why?
- Application, or applied research, addresses questions about criminal justice policy. Evaluation studies examine the impact of specific programs, while policy analysis estimates the future consequences of some policy action.

- Units of analysis are the people or things whose characteristics researchers observe, describe, and explain. The unit of analysis in criminal justice research is often the individual person, but it may also be a group, organization, or social artifact.
- Cross-sectional studies are those based on observations made at one time. Although such studies are limited by this characteristic, inferences can often be made about processes that occur over time.
- Longitudinal studies are those in which observations are made at many times. Such observations may be made of samples drawn from general populations (trend studies), samples drawn from more specific subpopulations (cohort studies), or the same sample of people each time (panel studies).
- Retrospective studies can sometimes approximate longitudinal studies, but retrospective approaches must be used with care.
- The research process is flexible, involving different steps that are best considered together. The process usually begins with some general interest or idea.
- A research proposal provides a preview of why a study will be undertaken and how it will be conducted. It is a useful device for planning and is required in some circumstances.

■ REVIEW QUESTIONS AND EXERCISES

1. Make up a research example—different from those discussed in the text—that illustrates a researcher falling into the trap of the ecological fallacy. Then describe a modified research project that avoids that trap.
2. Browse through a criminal justice research journal and find examples of at least three different units of analysis. Identify each unit of analysis and present a quotation from the journal in which that unit of analysis is reported.
3. One of the requirements discussed in Chapter 3 for demonstrating causal inference was that the cause must precede the effect in time.

Discuss the relative ability of cross-sectional and longitudinal designs to satisfy this requirement. Describe an example where a cross-sectional study would not be able to establish causal order and an example where a cross-sectional study would be able to meet this requirement.

4. Recall the discussion in Chapter 3 of necessary and sufficient conditions for causal inference. Apply these ideas to interpret the role parents' history of child abuse victimization plays in explaining abuse of their own children as illustrated in Figures 4-1A and 4-1B and the associated discussion.

■ ADDITIONAL READINGS

Chapter 15 of this book will present two examples of criminal justice studies, describing research proposals and published reports. Although the chapter assumes that you have covered other parts of this book, you will benefit from reading through the examples to learn more about the overall research process.

Farrington, David P., Ohlin, Lloyd E., and Wilson, James Q., *Understanding and Controlling Crime: Toward a New Research Strategy* (New York: Springer-Verlag, 1986). Three highly respected criminologists describe the advantages of longitudinal studies and policy experiments for criminal justice research. The book also presents a research agenda for studying the causes of crime and the effectiveness of policy responses.

Gottfredson, Michael R., and Hirschi, Travis, "The Methodological Adequacy of Longitudinal Research on Crime," *Criminology,* Vol. 25 (1987), pp. 581–614. Two other highly respected criminologists point to some of the shortcomings of longitudinal studies. They also describe some contributions of cross-sectional studies.

Miller, Delbert, *Handbook of Research Design and Social Measurement* (New York: Longman, 1983). A useful reference book for introducing or reviewing numerous issues involved in design and measurement. In addition, the book contains a wealth of practical information about foundations, journals, and professional associations.

CHAPTER 5 *Concepts, Operationalization, and Measurement*

What You'll Learn in This Chapter

You'll discover that it's essential to specify exactly what we mean (and don't mean) by the terms we use. This is the first step in the measurement process, which we'll cover here in depth.

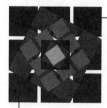

INTRODUCTION

CONCEPTIONS AND CONCEPTS
Conceptualization
Indicators and Dimensions
Confusion over Definitions and Reality
Creating Conceptual Order

OPERATIONALIZATION CHOICES
Measurement
Exhaustive and Exclusive Measurement
Levels of Measurement
Implications of Levels of Measurement

CRITERIA FOR MEASUREMENT QUALITY
Reliability
Validity

COMPOSITE MEASURES
Typologies
An Index of Disorder

MEASUREMENT SUMMARY

MAIN POINTS

REVIEW QUESTIONS AND EXERCISES

ADDITIONAL READINGS

■ *INTRODUCTION*

This chapter describes the progression from having a vague idea about what you want to study to being able to recognize it and measure it in the real world. We will begin with the general issue of conceptualization, which sets up a foundation for our discussion of operationalization and measurement. We'll turn then to different approaches to assessing measurement quality. The chapter concludes with an overview of strategies for combining individual measures into more complex indicators. Our examination of measurement continues into the next chapter, where we will focus on different strategies for measuring crime.

As you read this chapter, keep in mind a central theme: communication. Ultimately, criminal justice and social scientific research seek to communicate findings to an audience—your professor, classmates, readers of a journal, or co-workers in a probation services agency, for example. Moving from vague ideas and interests to a completed research report, as we described in Chapter 4, involves communication at every step. Earlier steps move from vague or general ideas to more precise definitions of critical terms. With more precise definitions, we can begin to develop measures that can be applied in the real world.

■ *CONCEPTIONS AND CONCEPTS*

If you hear the word *recidivism,* what image comes to mind? You might think of someone who served time in prison for burglary and then breaks into a house soon after being released from prison. Or, in contrast to that rather specific image, you might think of the more general image of a habitual criminal. Someone who works in a criminal justice agency might have a different mental image. Police officers might think of an individual they have arrested repeatedly for a variety of offenses, while a judge might think of a defendant who has three prior convictions for theft.

Ultimately, *recidivism* is simply a *term* we use in communication—a name we use to represent a collection of related phenomena that we have ei-ther observed or heard about somewhere. It's as though we have file drawers in our minds containing thousands of sheets of paper, and each sheet of paper has a label in the upper right-hand corner. One sheet of paper in your file drawer has the term *recidivism* on it, and the person who sits next to you in class has one, too.

The technical name for those mental images, those sheets of paper in our file drawers, is *conception.* Each sheet of paper is a conception, a subjective thought about things that we encounter in daily life. Now, those mental images cannot be communicated directly. There is no way we can directly reveal what's written on our mental images. So we use the terms written in the upper right-hand corners as a way of communicating about our conceptions and the things we observe that are related to those conceptions.

For example, the word *crime* represents our conception about certain kinds of behavior. Individuals have different conceptions; they may think of different kinds of behavior when they hear the word *crime.* Tavern owners in Ohio may think of backroom slot machines when they hear this word, but their counterparts in Nevada have different mental images. Or recent burglary victims might recall their own experiences in their conceptions of crime, whereas more fortunate neighbors think of the murder story in yesterday's newspaper.

Because they are subjective and cannot be communicated directly, we use the words, symbols, and phrases of language as a way of communicating about our conceptions and the things we observe that are related to those conceptions.

Concepts are the words or symbols in language that we use to represent these mental images. We use concepts to communicate with one another, to share our mental images. Although a common language enables us to communicate, it is important to recognize that the words and phrases we use represent abstract concepts. This may be a difficult point, but you should recognize that because concepts are abstract, they are independent of the names we assign to them. Crime as a concept is abstract, meaning that the English language assigns this label to represent mental images of illegal acts. Of course, actual crimes are real events, and our mental images of crime may be based on real events (or the stuff of TV drama), but when we talk about crime, without being more specific, we are talking about an abstract concept. Thus, for example, the concept of crime proposed by Gottfredson and Hirschi (1990:15)—using force or fraud in pursuit of self-interest—is abstract. "Crime" is the symbol or label they have assigned to this concept.

Let's discuss a specific example. What is your conception of "serious crime"? What mental images come to mind? Most people agree that airplane hijacking, bank robbery, murder, and rape are serious crimes. What about a physical assault with a club that produces some injury? Many of us would classify that as a serious crime, but we might think twice if the incident took place in a National Hockey League game. Is burglary a serious crime? It doesn't rank up there with gangland slayings, but we would probably agree that it is more serious than shoplifting. How serious is drug use, or drug selling?

Your mental images of serious crime might vary depending on your background and experience. If your home has ever been burglarized, you might be more inclined than someone who has not suffered that experience to rate it as a serious crime. If you have been both burglarized and robbed at gunpoint, you would probably think the burglary was less serious than the robbery. There is quite a bit of disagreement over the seriousness of drug use. Younger people, whether or not they have used drugs, may be less inclined to view drug use as a serious crime, whereas police and other public officials might rank drug use as very serious. In 1996, a majority of California residents approved a state referendum that legalized the use of marijuana for medical purposes, while federal officials in the Department of Justice continued to view marijuana use as a crime.

"Serious crime" is an abstraction, a label we use to represent a concept. However, we must be careful to distinguish the label we use for a concept from the reality that concept represents. There are real robberies, and robbery is a serious crime, but the concept of crime seriousness is not real.

In order to link conceptions, concepts, and measurement, consider Abraham Kaplan's (1964) discussion of three classes of things that scientists measure: direct observables, indirect observables, and constructs. The first class, *direct observables*, includes those things that we can observe simply and directly, like the color of an apple or the words a police officer has written on a crime report. *Indirect observables* require "relatively more subtle, complex, or indirect observations" (1964: 55). We note that a police officer has written "robbery" in the place for "offense type" on a crime report and has indirectly observed what crime has occurred. Newspaper stories, court transcripts, and criminal history records provide indirect observations of past actions. Finally, *constructs* are theoretical creations based on observations that cannot be observed directly or indirectly. IQ is a good example. It is constructed mathematically from observations of the answers given to a large number of questions on an IQ test.

Kaplan (1964:49) defines *concept* as a "family of conceptions." A concept is, as Kaplan notes, a construct. The concept of serious crime, then, is a construct created from your conception of it, our conception of it, and the conceptions of all those who have ever used the term. The concept of serious crime cannot be observed directly or indirectly. We can, however, meaningfully discuss the concept, we can observe examples of serious crime, and we can measure it indirectly.

Conceptualization

Day-to-day communication usually occurs through a system of general but often vague agreements about the use of terms. Usually people do not understand exactly what we wish to communicate, but they get the general drift of our meaning. Although we may not agree completely about the use of the term *serious crime*, it's probably safe to assume that the crime of robbery is more serious than the crime of bicycle theft. A wide range of misunderstandings is the price we pay for our imprecision, but somehow we muddle through. Science, however, aims at more than muddling, and it cannot operate in a context of such imprecision.

Conceptualization is the process by which we specify precisely what we mean when we use particular terms. Suppose we want to find out, for example, whether violent crime is more serious than nonviolent crime. Most of us would probably assume that is true, but it might be interesting to find out whether it's really so. Notice that we can't meaningfully study the issue, let alone agree on the answer, without some precise working agreements about the meanings of the terms we are using. They are working agreements in the sense that they allow us to work on the question.

We begin by clearly differentiating violent and nonviolent crime. In violent crimes, an offender uses force or threatens to use force against a victim. Either nonviolent crimes do not have any direct contact between a victim and an offender, or they may involve contact but no force. For example, pickpocketing involves direct contact but no force. In contrast, robbery offenders at least threaten to use force on a victim. Burglary, auto theft, shoplifting, and the theft of unattended personal property such as bicycles are examples of nonviolent crimes. Assault, rape, robbery, and murder are violent crimes.

Indicators and Dimensions

The end product of the conceptualization process is the specification of a set of indicators of what we have in mind, indicating the presence or absence of the concept we are studying. To illustrate this process, let's discuss the more general concept of *crime seriousness*. This concept is more general than *serious crime* because it implies that some crimes are more serious than others.

One good indicator of crime seriousness is harm to the crime victim. Physical injury is an example of harm, and physical injury is certainly more likely to result from violent crime than from nonviolent crime. What about other kinds of harm? Burglary victims suffer economic harm from property loss and perhaps damage to their homes. Is an economic loss of $800 in a burglary an indicator of more serious crime than a $10 loss in a robbery where the victim was not injured?

Victims of both violent crime and nonviolent crime may suffer psychological harm. Charles Silberman (1978:18–19) describes how people feel a sense of personal violation after discovering that their home has been burglarized. A little more thought may suggest other types of victim harm that can be combined into groups and subgroups.

The technical name for such groupings is **dimension**—some specifiable aspect of a concept. Thus, we might speak of the "victim harm dimension" of crime seriousness. This dimension could include indicators of physical injury, economic loss, or psychological consequences. We could easily think of other indicators and other dimensions related to the general concept of crime seriousness. If we consider the theft of $20 from a poor person to be more serious than the theft of $200 from a wealthy stockbroker, victim wealth might be another dimension. Also consider a victim identity dimension. Killing a burglar in self-defense would not be as serious as threatening to kill the President of the United States.

Thus, it is possible to subdivide the concept of crime seriousness into several sets of dimensions. Specifying dimensions and identifying the various indicators for each of those dimensions are both parts of conceptualization.

Specifying the different dimensions of a concept often paves the way for a more sophisticated understanding of what we are studying. We might observe, for example, that fistfights among high school students produce thousands of injuries per year, but that the annual costs of auto theft produce direct economic harm to hundreds of insurance companies and millions of auto insurance policyholders. Recognizing the many dimensions of crime seriousness, we would not be able to say that violent crime is more serious than nonviolent crime in all cases.

As it happens, defining and measuring crime seriousness are important and puzzling issues in criminal justice policy and research. Domestic violence and acquaintance rape are examples of violent crimes that are often treated differently than physical or sexual violence among strangers.

For instance, the battered woman defense has been used in trials of women who kill a spouse or lover following an extended period of violence (Williams, 1991). Such mitigating circumstances mean that some types of murders are treated differently than others, based in part on motivation and the relationship between victim and offender. Recently, the tendency of courts to punish rape offenders less harshly if they have had some prior relationship with their victims has led to growing protests (Lopez, 1992). Studies have shown that death penalties were more often imposed on blacks convicted of killing whites, which indicates that victim race is related to sentencing and might therefore be considered an indicator of crime seriousness (Baldus, Pulaski, and Woodworth, 1983). Later in this chapter, we will discuss some specific attempts to develop measures of crime seriousness.

Confusion over Definitions and Reality

To review briefly, our concepts are derived from the mental images (conceptions) that summarize collections of seemingly related observations and experiences. Although the observations and experiences are real, our concepts are only mental creations. The terms associated with concepts are merely devices created for communication. The term *crime seriousness* is an example. Ultimately, that phrase is only a collection of letters and has no intrinsic meaning. We could have as easily and meaningfully created the term *crime pettiness* to serve the same purpose.

Often, however, we fall into the trap of believing that terms have real meanings. That danger seems to grow stronger when we begin to take terms seriously and attempt to use them precisely. And the danger is all the greater in the presence of experts who appear to know more than you do about what the terms really mean. It's easy to yield to the authority of experts in such a situation.

Once we have assumed (mistakenly) that terms have real meanings, we begin the tortured task of discovering what those real meanings are and what constitutes a genuine measurement of them.

Figure 5-1 illustrates this process. We make up conceptual summaries of real observations because the summaries are convenient. They prove to be so convenient, however, that we begin to think they are real. The process of regarding as real things that are not is called **reification,** and the reification of concepts in day-to-day life is very common.

Creating Conceptual Order

The design and execution of criminal justice research require clearing away the confusion over concepts and reality. To this end, logicians and scientists have found it useful to distinguish three kinds of definitions: *real, conceptual,* and *operational*. The first of these reflects the reification of terms, and as Carl G. Hempel (1952:6) has cautioned:

■ A "real" definition, according to traditional logic, is not a stipulation determining the meaning of some expression but a statement of the 'essential nature' or the 'essential attributes' of some entity. The notion of essential nature, however, is so vague as to render this characterization useless for the purposes of rigorous inquiry.

The specification of concepts in scientific inquiry depends on conceptual and operational definitions. A **conceptual definition** is a working definition specifically assigned to a term. In the midst of disagreement and confusion over what a term really means, the scientist specifies a working definition for the purposes of the inquiry. Wishing to examine socioeconomic status (SES) in a study, for example, we may simply specify that we are going to treat it as a combination of income and educational attainment. In that definitional decision, we rule out many other possible aspects of SES: occupational status, money in the bank, property, lineage, lifestyle, and so forth.

The specification of conceptual definitions does two important things. First, it serves as a specific working definition a researcher presents so that readers will understand exactly what is meant by a concept. Second, a conceptual definition focuses

FIGURE 5-1
The Process of Conceptual Entrapment

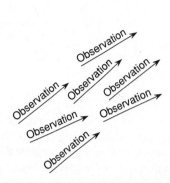

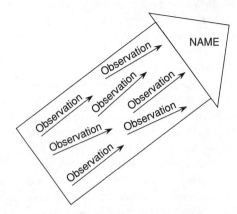

1. Many of our observations in life seem to have something in common. We get the sense that they represent something more general than the simple content of any single observation. We find it useful, moreover, to communicate about the general concept.

2. It is inconvenient to keep describing all the specific observations whenever we want to communicate about the general concept they seem to have in common, so we give a name to the general concept—to stand for whatever it is the specific observations have in commmon.

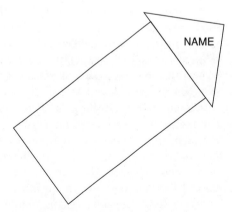

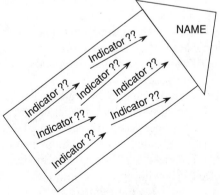

3. As we communicate about the general concept, using its term, we begin to think that the concept is some *thing* that really exists, not just a summary reference for several concrete observations in the world.

4. The belief that the concept itself is real results in irony. We now begin discussing and debating whether specific observations are "really" sufficient indicators of the concept.

our observational strategy. Notice that a conceptual definition does not directly produce observations; rather it channels our efforts to develop actual measures.

As a next step, we must specify exactly what we are going to observe, how we will do it, and what interpretations we are going to place on various possible observations. These further specifications make up the **operational definition** of the concept—a definition that spells out precisely how the concept will be measured. Strictly speaking, an operational definition is a description of the "operations" that will be undertaken in measuring a concept.

Pursuing the definition of SES, we might decide to ask the people we are studying three questions:

1. What was your total household income during the past 12 months?
2. How many persons are in your household?
3. What is the highest level of school you have completed?

We would probably want to specify a system for categorizing the answers people give us. For income, we might use the categories "under $15,000" and "$15,000 to $25,000." Educational attainment might be similarly grouped into categories, and we might simply count the number of people in each household. Finally, we would specify a way to combine a person's responses to these three questions to create a measure of SES. Later material in this chapter will present examples of methods for doing that.

The end result is a working and workable definition of SES. Others might disagree with our conceptualization and operationalization, but the definition has one essential scientific virtue: It is absolutely specific and unambiguous. Even if someone disagreed with our definition, that person would have a good idea how to interpret our research results because what we mean by the term SES—reflected in our analyses and conclusions—would be clear.

Here is a diagram showing the progression of measurement steps from our vague sense of what a term means to specific measurements in a scientific study:

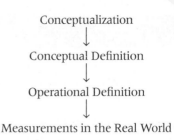

Conceptualization
↓
Conceptual Definition
↓
Operational Definition
↓
Measurements in the Real World

To test your understanding of these measurement steps, return to the beginning of the chapter where we asked you what image comes to mind in connection with the word *recidivism*. Recall your own mental image and compare it with Tony Fabelo's discussion in the box entitled "What Is Recidivism?"

■ *OPERATIONALIZATION CHOICES*

Recall from Chapter 4 that the research process is not usually a set of steps that proceed in order from first to last. This is especially true of **operationalization,** the process of developing operational definitions. Although you begin by conceptualizing what you wish to study, once you start to consider operationalization, you may revise your conceptual definition. Developing an operational definition also moves you closer to measurement, which requires that you think, too, about selecting a data-collection method. In other words, operationalization does not proceed through a systematic checklist.

By way of illustrating this fluid process, let's return to the question of crime seriousness and assume we wish to conduct a descriptive study that shows which crimes are more serious and which crimes are less serious.

Earlier we stated that one obvious dimension of crime seriousness is the penalties that are assigned to different crimes by law. Let's begin with this conceptualization. Our conceptual definition of crime seriousness is therefore the level of punishment that a state criminal code authorizes for different crimes. Notice that this definition has the distinct advantage of being unambiguous, a point noted by Farrell and Swigert (1978:440),

, Texas Criminal Justice Policy Council

The Senate Criminal Justice Committee will be studying the record of the corrections system and the use of recidivism rates as a measure of performance for the system. The first task for the committee should be to clearly define recidivism, understand how it is measured, and determine the implications of adopting recidivism rates as measures of performance.

Defining Recidivism

Recidivism is the reoccurrence of criminal behavior. The rate of recidivism refers to the proportion of a specific group of offenders (for example, those released on parole) who engage in criminal behavior within a given period of time. Indicators of criminal behavior are re-arrests, re-convictions, or re-incarcerations.

Each of these indicators depends on contact with criminal justice officials, and will therefore underestimate the reoccurrence of criminal be-

havior. However, criminal behavior that is unreported and not otherwise known to officials in justice agencies is difficult to measure in a consistent and economically feasible fashion.

In 1991 the Criminal Justice Policy Council recommended to the legislature and state criminal justice agencies that recidivism be measured in the following way:

Recidivism rates should be calculated by counting the number of prison releases or number of offenders placed under community supervision who are reincarcerated for a technical violation or new offense within a uniform period of at-risk street time.

The at-risk street time can be one, two, or three years, but it must be uniform for the group being tracked so that results are not distorted by uneven at-risk periods.

Re-incarceration should be measured using data from the "rap sheets" collected by the Texas Department of Public Safety in their Computerized Criminal History system. A centralized source of information reduces reporting errors.

---

who argue that the legislative maximum sentence is "the most objective determination of the severity of an offense."

We're making progress, which leads us to an operational definition something like this:

■ Consult the *Indiana Criminal Code.* (1) Those crimes that may be punished by death will be judged most serious. (2) Next will be crimes that may be punished by a prison sentence of more than one year. (3) The least serious crimes are those with jail sentences of less than one year and/or fines.

The operations undertaken to measure crime seriousness are specific. Our data-collection strategy is also clear: Go to the library, make a list of

crimes described in the *Indiana Code,* and classify each crime into one of the three groups.

Thinking through these steps should make you quickly realize that we have produced rather narrow conceptual and operational definitions of crime seriousness. We might presume that penalties in the *Indiana Code* take account of additional dimensions like victim harm, offender motivation, and other circumstances of individual crimes. However, the three groups of crimes include very different types of incidents and therefore do not tell us much about crime seriousness.

An alternative conceptualization of crime seriousness might center on what people think of as serious crime. Under this view, crime seriousness is based on people's beliefs, which may reflect

System Wide Recidivism Rates

Recidivism rates can be reported for all offenders in the system—for all offenders released from prison or for all offenders placed on probation. This I call *system wide recidivism rates*. Approximately 48 percent of offenders released from prison on parole or mandatory supervision, or released from county jails on parole, in 1991 were reincarcerated by 1994 for a new offense or a parole violation.

For offenders released from prison in 1991 the reincarceration recidivism rate three years after release from prison by offense of conviction is listed below:

Burglary	56%	Assault	44%
Robbery	54%	Homicide	40%
Theft	52%	Sexual assault	39%
Drugs	43%	Sex offense	34%

For the same group, the reincarceration recidivism rate three years after release by age group is listed below:

17–25	56%
26–30	52%
31–35	48%
36–40	46%
41 or older	35%

The Meaning of System Wide Recidivism Rates

The system wide recidivism rate of prison releases should not be used to measure the performance of institutional programs. There are many socioeconomic factors that can affect system wide recidivism rates.

For example, the system wide recidivism rate of offenders released from prison in 1995 is expected to decrease because of changes in the characteristics of the population released from prison. Offenders are receiving and serving longer sentences, which will raise the average age at release. Therefore, "performance" in terms of system wide recidivism will improve, but not necessarily due to improvements in the delivery of improvements within the prison system.

On the other hand, the system wide recidivism rate of felons released from state jail facilities should be expected to be relatively high, since state jail felons are property and drug offenders who tend to have high recidivism rates.

Source: Adapted from Tony Fabelo, "What Is Recidivism? How Do You Measure It? What Can It Tell Policy Makers?" *Bulletin from the Executive Director,* No. 19, November (Austin, Texas: Criminal Justice Policy Council, 1995).

---

their perceptions of harm to victims, offender motivation, or other dimensions. Conceptualizing crime seriousness in this way suggests a different approach to operationalization: You will present descriptions of crimes to other students in your class and ask them to indicate how serious they believe the different crimes are. If crime seriousness is operationalized in this way, a questionnaire would be the most appropriate data-collection method.

Many other decisions must also be made before you could actually begin taking measurements of crime seriousness. How should crimes be described and how should students indicate whether something is serious or not serious? Will crime descriptions simply be ranked from most to least serious, or will we try to make more precise measurements about how rape compares to smoking marijuana, for example?

Measurement

Operationalization involves describing how actual measurements will be made. The next step is, of course, making the measurements. Singleton, Straits, and Straits (1993:100) define measurement as "the process of assigning numbers or labels to units of analysis in order to represent conceptual properties. This process should be quite familiar to the reader even if the definition is not." You should be able to think of examples of the process. Your instructor assigns number or letter grades to exams and papers to

Jail Stay

RECALL from Chapter 4 that two of the general purposes of research are description and explanation. The distinction between them has important implications for the process of definition and measurement. If you have formed the opinion that description is a simpler task than explanation, you may be surprised to learn that definitions are more problematic for descriptive research than for explanatory research. To illustrate this, we present an example based on an attempt by one of the authors to describe what he thought was a simple concept.

In the course of an evaluation project, Maxfield wished to learn the average number of days people stayed in the Marion County (Indiana) jail. This concept was labeled "jail stay." People can be in the county jail for three reasons: (1) They are serving a sentence of one year or less, (2) they are awaiting trial, or (3) they are held temporarily while waiting to be transferred to another county or state or to prison. The third category includes people who have been

sentenced to prison and are waiting for space to open up, or those who have been arrested and are wanted for some reason in another jurisdiction.

Maxfield vaguely knew these things but did not recognize how they complicated the task of defining and ultimately measuring jail stay. So the original question—"What is the average jail stay?"—was revised to "What is the average jail stay for persons serving sentences, and for persons awaiting trial?"

Just as people can be in jail for different reasons, an individual person can be in jail for more than one reason. For example, let's consider a hypothetical jail resident we'll call Barry. He was convicted of burglary in July 1991 and sentenced to one year in jail. All but 30 days of his sentence were suspended, meaning that he was freed but could be required to serve the remaining 11 months if he got into trouble again. It did not take long. Two months after being released, Barry was arrested for robbery and returned to jail.

---

represent your understanding of course material. You count the number of pages in this week's history assignment to represent how much time you will have to spend studying. The American Bar Association rates nominees to the U.S. Supreme Court as qualified, highly qualified, or not qualified. You might rank last night's date on the proverbial scale of 1 to 10, representing whatever conceptual properties are important to you.

Another way to think of measurement is like scoring. Your instructor scores exams by counting the right answers and assigning some point value to each answer. Referees keep score at basketball games by counting the number of one-point free throws and two-point and three-point field goals for each team. Judges or juries score persons charged with crime by pronouncing "guilty" or "not guilty." City murder rates are scored by counting the number of murder victims and dividing by the number of city residents.

Measurement is distinct from operationalization in that measurement involves actually making observations in the real world and assigning scores—numbers or other labels—to those observations. Making observations, of course, is related to the data-collection method, which is in turn implied by operationalization. However, the measurement process begins much earlier, usually with conceptualization.

Many people consider measurement the most important and difficult phase of criminal justice research. It is difficult, in part, because so many basic concepts in criminal justice are not easy to define as specifically as we would like. Without being able to settle on a conceptual definition, we find operationalizing and measuring things challenging. This is illustrated by the box entitled "Jail Stay."

Even when we can specify unambiguous conceptual definitions, it is often difficult to specify operational definitions that will enable us to make

Now it gets complicated. A judge imposes the remaining nine months of Barry's suspended sentence. Barry is denied bail and must wait for his trial in jail. It is soon learned that Barry is wanted by police in Illinois for passing bad checks. Many people would be delighted to send Barry to Illinois; they tell officials they can have him, pending resolution of the situation in Marion County. Barry is now in jail for three reasons: (1) serving his sentence for the original burglary, (2) awaiting trial on a robbery charge, and (3) waiting for transfer to Illinois.

Is this one jail stay or three? In a sense, it is one jail stay because one person, Barry, is occupying a jail cell. But let's say Barry's trial on the robbery charge is delayed until after he completes his sentence for the burglary. He stays in jail and begins a new jail stay. When he comes up for trial, the prosecutor asks to waive the robbery charges against Barry in hopes of exporting him to the neighboring state, and a new jail stay begins as Barry awaits his free trip to Illinois.

You may recognize this as a problem with units of analysis. Is the unit the person who stays in jail? Or are the separate reasons Barry is in jail—which are social artifacts—the units of analysis? After some thought, Maxfield decided the social artifact was the more appropriate unit because he was interested in whether jail cells are more often occupied by people serving sentences or people awaiting trial. But that produced a new question of how to deal with people like Barry. Do we double-count the overlap in Barry's jail stays, so that he accounts for two jail stays while serving his suspended sentence for burglary and waiting for the robbery trial? This seemed to make sense, but then Barry's two jail stays would count the same as two other people with one jail stay each. In other words, Barry would appear to occupy two jail beds at the same time. This was neither true nor helpful in describing how long people stay in jail for different reasons.

observations and measurements. For example, the fundamental concept of *crime* is virtually impossible to count with any precision. Chapter 6 is devoted entirely to the important but challenging task of measuring crime. Before undertaking that task, we must turn our attention to certain general issues in measurement.

Exhaustive and Exclusive Measurement

An attribute, you'll recall from Chapter 1, is a characteristic or quality of something. "Female" is an example. So are "old" and "student." Variables, on the other hand, are logical sets of attributes. Thus, "gender" is a variable composed of the attributes "female" and "male."

The conceptualization and operationalization processes can be seen as the specification of variables and the attributes composing them. Thus, for instance, "employment status" is a variable that has the attributes "employed" and "unemployed," or the list of attributes could be ex-

panded to include other possibilities such as "employed part-time," "employed full-time," "retired," and so on.

Every variable should have two important qualities. First, the attributes composing it should be *exhaustive*. If the variable is to have any utility in research, you should be able to classify every observation in terms of one of the attributes composing the variable. You will run into trouble if you conceptualize the variable "sentence" in terms of the attributes "prison" and "fine" because some convicted persons are assigned to probation, some have a portion of their prison sentence suspended, and others may receive a mix of prison terms, probation, suspended sentences, or perhaps community service. You could make the list of attributes exhaustive by adding "other" and "combination." Whatever you do, you must be able to classify every observation.

At the same time, attributes composing a variable must be *mutually exclusive*. You must be able to classify every observation in terms of one and only one attribute. Thus, for example, you need to define "prison" and "fine" in such a way that nobody can be both at the same time. That means you must be able to handle the person whose sentence includes both a prison term and a fine. In this case, you might define your attributes more precisely, specifying "prison only," "fine only," and "both prison and fine."

Levels of Measurement

Attributes composing any variable must be mutually exclusive and exhaustive. Attributes may be related in other ways as well, however. Different variables may represent different levels of measurement. We are going to examine four levels of measurement in this section: *nominal, ordinal, interval,* and *ratio.*

Nominal Measures   Variables whose attributes have only the characteristics of exhaustiveness and mutual exclusiveness are **nominal measures.** Examples are gender, race, city of residence, college major, Social Security number, and marital status. Although the attributes composing each of these variables—male and female composing the variable gender—are distinct from one another (and exhaust the possibilities among people), they have none of the additional structures mentioned later. Nominal measures merely offer names or labels for characteristics.

It is useful to imagine a group of people being characterized in terms of a nominal variable and physically grouped by the appropriate attributes. Imagine we are at a convention attended by hundreds of police chiefs. At a social function, we ask them to stand together in groups according to the states in which they live: all those from Vermont in one group, those from California in another, and so forth. (The variable is state of residence; the attributes are live in Vermont, live in California, and so on.) All the people standing in a given group have at least one thing in common; the people in any one group differ from the people in all other groups in that same regard. Where the individual groups are formed, how close they are to one another, and how the groups are arranged in the room would be irrelevant. All that matters

is that all the members of a given group share the same state of residence and that each group has a different shared state of residence.

Ordinal Measures   Variables whose attributes may be logically *rank-ordered* are **ordinal measures.** The different attributes represent relatively more or less of the variable. Examples of variables that can be ordered in some way are opinion of police, occupational status, crime seriousness, and fear of crime.

Let's pursue the earlier example of grouping police chiefs at a social gathering and imagine that we ask all those who had graduated from college to stand in one group, all those with a high school diploma (but who were not also college graduates) to stand in another group, and all those who had not graduated from high school to stand in a third group. This manner of grouping people satisfies the requirements for exhaustiveness and mutual exclusiveness. In addition, however, we might logically arrange the three groups in terms of their amount of formal education (the shared attribute). We might arrange the three groups in a row, ranging from most to least formal education. This arrangement provides a physical representation of an ordinal measure. If we knew which groups two individuals were in, we could determine that one had more, less, or the same formal education as the other.

It is important to note that in this example it is irrelevant how close or far apart the educational groups are from one another. They might stand 5 feet apart or 500 feet apart; the college and high school groups could be 5 feet apart, and the less-than-high-school group might be 500 feet farther down the line. These actual distances have no meaning. The high school group, however, should be between the less-than-high school group and the college group, or else the rank order is incorrect.

Interval Measures   When the actual distance that separates the attributes composing some variables does have meaning, the variables are **interval measures.** The logical distance between attributes can then be expressed in meaningful standard intervals.

About the only interval measures commonly used in social scientific research are constructed measures such as standardized intelligence tests that have been more or less accepted. The interval that separates IQ scores of 100 and 110 is the same as the interval that separates scores of 110 and 120 by virtue of the distribution of observed scores obtained by many thousands of people who have taken the tests over the years.

Ratio Measures Most of the social scientific variables that meet the minimum requirements for interval measures also meet the requirements for ratio measures. In **ratio measures,** the attributes that compose a variable, besides having all the structural characteristics mentioned previously, are based on a true zero point. Examples from criminal justice research are age, dollar value of property loss from burglary, number of prior arrests, blood alcohol content, and length of sentence.

Returning to the illustration of methodological party games at a police chiefs' convention, we might ask the chiefs to group themselves according to years of experience in their present position. All those new to their job would stand together, those with one year of experience together, those with two years on the job together, and so forth. The facts that members of a single group share the same years of experience and that each different group has a different shared length of time on the job satisfy the minimum requirements for a nominal measure. Arranging the several groups in a line from those with the least to those with the most meets the additional requirements of an ordinal measure and permits us to determine whether one person is more experienced, is less experienced, or has the same level of experience as another. If we arrange the groups so there is the same distance between each pair of adjacent groups, we satisfy the additional requirements of an interval measure and then we can say how much more experience one chief has than another. Finally, because one of the attributes included—experience—has a true zero point (police chiefs just appointed to their job), the phalanx of hapless convention goers also meets the requirements for a ratio measure, per-

mitting us to say that one person is twice as experienced as another.

Implications of Levels of Measurement

To review this discussion and to understand why level of measurement may make a difference, consider Table 5-1. It presents information on crime seriousness adapted from a survey of crime severity conducted for the Bureau of Justice Statistics (Wolfgang, Figlio, Tracy, and Singer, 1985). The survey presented brief descriptions of more than 200 different crimes to a sample of 60,000 people. Respondents were asked to assign a score to each crime based on how serious they thought the crime was, compared to bicycle theft (scored at 10).

The first column of Table 5-1 lists some of the crimes depicted in the descriptions. The second column shows a nominal measure that identifies the victim in the crime: home, person, business, or society. Type of victim is an attribute of each crime. The third column lists seriousness scores computed from survey results, ranging from 0.6 for trespassing to 35.7 for murder. These seriousness scores are interval measures because the distance between, for example, auto theft (at 8.0) and accepting a bribe (at 9.0) is the same as that between accepting a bribe (at 9.0) and obstructing justice (at 10.0). Seriousness scores are not ratio measures; there is no absolute zero point and three instances of obstructing justice (at 10.0) do not equal one rape with injury (at 30.0).

The fourth column shows the ranking for each of the 17 crimes in the table; the most serious crime, murder, is ranked 1, followed by rape with injury, and so on. The rankings express only the order of seriousness, however, because the difference between murder (ranked 1) and rape (ranked 2) is smaller than the distance between rape and robbery with injury (ranked 3).

Finally, the crime descriptions presented to respondents indicated the value of property loss for each offense. This is a ratio measure with a true zero point, so that ten burglaries with a loss of $1,000 each have the same property value as one arson offense with a loss of $10,000.

TABLE 5-1
Crime Seriousness and Levels of Measurement

Crime	Victim	Seriousness Score	Rank	Value of Property Loss
Accepting a bribe	Society	9.0	9	0
Arson	Business	12.7	6	$10,000
Auto theft	Home	8.0	10	$12,000
Burglary	Business	15.5	5	$100,000
Burglary	Home	9.6	8	$1,000
Buying stolen property	Society	5.0	12	0
Heroin sales	Society	20.6	4	0
Heroin use	Society	6.5	11	0
Murder	Person	35.7	1	0
Obstructing justice	Society	10.0	7	0
Public intoxication	Society	0.8	15	0
Rape and injury	Person	30.0	2	0
Robbery and injury	Person	21.0	3	$1,000
Robbery attempt	Person	3.3	13	0
Robbery, no injury	Person	8.0	10	$1,000
Shoplifting	Business	2.2	14	$10
Trespassing	Home	0.6	16	0

Source: Adapted from Wolfgang, Figlio, Tracy, and Singer (1985).

Specific analytic techniques require variables that meet certain minimum levels of measurement. For example, you could compute the average property loss from the crimes listed in Table 5-1 by adding up the individual numbers in the fifth column and dividing by the number of crimes listed (17). However, you would not be able to compute the average victim type because that is a nominal variable. You could report the modal—the most common—victim type, which is society in Table 5-1.

You may treat some variables as representing different levels of measurement. Ratio measures are the highest level, progressing down through interval and ordinal to nominal, the lowest level of measurement. A variable that represents a given level of measurement—say, ratio—may also be treated as representing a lower level of measurement—say, ordinal. For example, age is a ratio measure. If you wished to examine only the relationship between age and some ordinal-level variable, such as delinquency involvement (high, medium, and low), you might choose to treat age as an ordinal-level variable as well. You might characterize the subjects of your study as being young, middle-aged, and old, specifying what age range makes up each of those groupings.

Finally, age might be used as a nominal-level variable for certain research purposes. People might be grouped as baby boomers born between 1945 and 1955 or not.

The analytic uses planned for a given variable, then, should determine the level of measurement to be sought, with the realization that some variables are inherently limited to a certain level. If a variable is to be used in a variety of ways that require different levels of measurement, the study should be designed to achieve the highest level possible. Although ratio measures, like number of arrests, can later be reduced to ordinal or nominal ones, it is not possible to convert a nominal or ordinal measure to a ratio one. More generally, you cannot convert a lower-level measure to a higher-level one. That is a one-way street worth remembering.

■ CRITERIA FOR MEASUREMENT QUALITY

Measurements can be made with varying degrees of *precision*, which is the fineness of the distinctions made between the attributes that compose a variable. Saying a woman is "43 years old" is a more precise description than "in her forties." Describing a felony sentence as "18 months" is more precise than "over one year."

As a general rule, precise measurements are superior to imprecise ones, as common sense dictates. Precision is not always necessary or desirable, however. If knowing that a felony sentence is over one year is sufficient for your research purpose, then any additional effort invested in learning the precise sentence would be wasted. The operationalization of concepts, then, must be guided partly by an understanding of the degree of precision required. If your needs are not clear, be more precise rather than less.

But don't confuse precision with accuracy. Describing someone as "born in Stowe, Vermont" is more precise than "born in New England," but suppose the person in question was actually born in Boston? The less precise description, in this instance, is more accurate, a better reflection of the real world.

Precision and accuracy are obviously important qualities in research measurement, and they probably need no further explanation. When criminal justice researchers construct and evaluate measurements, however, they pay special attention to two technical considerations: *reliability* and *validity*.

Reliability

In the abstract, **reliability** is a matter of whether a particular measurement technique, applied repeatedly to the same object, will yield the same result each time. In other words, measurement reliability is roughly the same as measurement consistency or stability. Imagine, for example, a police officer standing on the street and guessing the speed of cars that pass by. The officer's judgment of speed is used to issue speeding tickets. If you received a ticket from this officer and went to court to contest the speeding charge, you would be almost certain to win your case because the judge would no doubt reject this way of measuring speed, regardless of the police officer's experience. The reliability or consistency of this method of measuring vehicle speed is questionable at best. If the same police officer used a portable radar gun, it is doubtful that you would be able to beat

the ticket, however, because the radar device is judged a much more reliable way of measuring speed.

Reliability, though, does not ensure accuracy any more than precision ensures it. The speedometer in your car may be a reliable instrument for measuring speed, but it is common for speedometers to be off by a few miles per hour, especially at higher speeds. If your speedometer shows 55 miles per hour when you are actually traveling at 60, it gives you a consistent but inaccurate reading that might attract the attention of police officers with more accurate radar guns.

Measurement reliability is often a problem with indicators used in criminal justice research. Numerous studies have shown that measures of crime based on police records often suffer reliability problems. For example, McCleary, Nienstedt, and Erven (1982:362) analyzed changes in police records of burglary following a change in how burglary reports were investigated in a large city. Under the new system, detectives formally investigated burglary reports that had been previously examined only by patrol officers. Burglaries declined sharply as soon as the new investigation procedures were implemented. The reason for the decline was that some patrol officers counted some crimes as burglaries that did not meet the official definition of burglary. When a smaller number of detectives began to investigate burglaries, they were more consistent in applying the official definition.

Other examples of reliability problems come up in criminal justice research and policy settings. How consistent are the judgments of probation officers in making presentence investigations used by judges? Berecochea and Gibbs (1991) studied how an inmate security classification system used in California was able to produce more reliable placement of inmates according to security risk. Inconsistency in administering blood alcohol tests in certain states has forced researchers to search for new measures of drunk driving (Heeren, Smith, Morelock, and Hingson, 1985). Drug testing has become an important tool for criminal justice treatment programs, but a study by the Centers for Disease Control found that many laboratories used by government agencies produced unreliable test results (Hansen, Caudill, and Boone, 1985).

Reliability problems crop up in many forms. Reliability is a concern every time a single observer is the source of data because we have no way to guard against that observer's subjectivity. We can't tell for sure how much of what's reported originated in the situation observed and how much in the observer.

Reliability problems may also occur when more than one observer makes measurements. Survey researchers have known for a long time that different interviewers get different answers from respondents as a result of their own attitudes and demeanor. If we were to conduct a study of editorial opinions about work-release centers, we could create a team of coders to read hundreds of editorials and classify them in terms of their position on the issue. Different coders might code the same editorial differently. Or we may want to classify a few hundred community anticrime groups in terms of some standard coding scheme, say, a set of categories created by the National Institute of Justice. A police officer and a neighborhood activist would not code all those groups into the same categories.

These examples illustrate problems of reliability. Similar problems arise whenever we ask people to give us information about themselves. Sometimes we ask questions that people don't know the answers to. (How many times have you seen a police officer in the last month?) Sometimes we ask people about things that are totally irrelevant to them. (Are you satisfied with the FBI's guidelines on the purchase of office supplies?) And sometimes we ask questions that are so complicated that a person who had a clear opinion in the matter might arrive at a different interpretation of the question when asked a second time.

How do you create reliable measures? Because the problem of reliability is a basic one in criminal justice measurement, researchers have developed a number of techniques for dealing with it.

Test–Retest Method   Sometimes it is appropriate to make the same measurement more than once. If

there is no reason to expect the information to change, you should expect the same response both times. If answers vary, however, then the measurement method is, to the extent of that variation, unreliable. Here's an illustration.

In their research on delinquency in England, West and Farrington (1977) interviewed a sample of 411 males from a working-class area of London at age 16 and again at age 18. The subjects were asked to describe a variety of aspects of their lives including educational and work history, leisure pursuits, drinking and smoking habits, delinquent activities, and experience with police and courts.

Because many of these topics involve illegal or at least antisocial activity, West and Farrington were concerned about the accuracy of information obtained in their interviews. They assessed reliability in several ways. One was to compare responses from the later interview at age 18 with those from the first interview at age 16. For example, in each interview the youths were asked at what age they left school. In most cases, there were few discrepancies in stated age from one interview to the next, which led the authors to conclude: "There was therefore no systematic tendency for youths either to increase or lessen their claimed period of school attendance as they grew older, as might have occurred if they had wanted either to exaggerate or to underplay their educational attainments" (1977:76–77). If West and Farrington had found less consistency in answers to this and other items, they would have had good reason to doubt the truthfulness of responses to more sensitive questions. The test–retest method suggested to the authors that memory lapses were the most common source of minor differences.

Although this method can be a useful reliability check, it is limited in some respects. Faulty memory may produce inconsistent responses if there is a long time period between the initial interview and the retest. A different problem can arise in trying to use the test–retest method to check the reliability of attitude or opinion measures. If the test–retest interval is short, then answers given in the second interview may be affected by earlier responses if subjects try to appear to be consistent. This is an example of testing bias, one of the problems that Chapter 7 will describe in connection with research designs.

Interrater Reliability It is also possible for measurement unreliability to be generated by research workers—for example, interviewers and coders. To guard against interviewer unreliability, it is common practice in surveys to have a supervisor call a subsample of the respondents on the telephone and verify selected information. West and Farrington (1977:173) checked interrater reliability in their study of London youths, and they found few significant differences in results obtained from different interviewers.

Comparing measurements from different raters works in other situations as well. For example, Geerken (1994) presents an important discussion of reliability problems that researchers are likely to encounter in measuring prior arrests through police "rap sheets." Duplicate entries, the use of aliases, and the need to transform official crime categories into a smaller number of categories for analysis are among the problems Geerken discusses. One way to increase the consistency of translating official records into research measures, a process often referred to as *coding,* is to have more than one person code a sample of records and then compare the consistency of coding decisions made by each person. This approach was used by Maxfield and Widom (1996) in their analysis of adult arrests of child abuse victims. In Chapter 12, we'll return to the issue of reliability in developing measures from such official records as crime reports.

In general, whenever you are concerned that measures obtained through coding may not be classified reliably, why not have each independently coded by different people? In the hypothetical study of newspaper editorials about a proposed work-release center mentioned above, coding decisions that generate disagreement should be evaluated more carefully and resolved. If you find a great deal of disagreement, your operational definitions of how to code newspaper editorials should be carefully reviewed and made more specific.

Split-Half Method As a general rule, it is always a good idea to make more than one measurement of any subtle or complex social concept, such as prejudice or fear of crime. This procedure lays the groundwork for another check on reliability. Let's say you've created a questionnaire that contains ten items you believe measure prejudicial beliefs about African Americans and delinquency. Using the split-half technique, you would randomly (see Chapter 9) assign those ten items to two sets of five. As we saw in the discussion in Chapter 3 of Lazarsfeld's "interchangeability of indexes," each set should provide a good measure of prejudice, and the sets should agree in the way they classify the respondents. If the two sets of items measure people differently, then that, again, points to a problem in the reliability of how you are measuring the variable.

The reliability of measurements is a fundamental issue in criminal justice research, and we'll return to it in the chapters ahead. For now, however, we hasten to point out that even total reliability doesn't ensure that our measures measure what we think they measure. That brings us to the question of validity.

Validity

In conventional usage, the term **validity** means that an empirical measure adequately reflects the meaning of the concept under consideration. Put another way, measurement validity means: Are you really measuring what you say you are measuring? Recall that an operational definition specifies the operations you will perform to measure a concept. Does your operational definition accurately reflect the concept you are interested in? If the answer is yes, you have a valid measure. A radar gun is a valid measure of vehicle speed, but a wind velocity indicator is not because the volume of air displaced by a slow-moving truck would register higher than that displaced by a fast-moving sports car.

Although methods for assessing reliability are relatively straightforward, it is more difficult to demonstrate that individual measures are valid. Since concepts are not real, but abstract, you cannot directly demonstrate that measures, which are real, are actually measuring an abstract concept. Nevertheless, researchers have some ways of dealing with the issue of validity.

Face validity First, there's something called **face validity.** Particular empirical measures may or may not jibe with our common agreements and our individual mental images about a particular concept. We might quarrel about the adequacy of measuring satisfaction with police services by counting the number of citizen complaints sent to the mayor's office, but we'd surely agree that the number of citizen complaints has something to do with satisfaction. If someone suggested that we measure satisfaction with police by finding out whether or not people like to watch police dramas on TV, we would probably agree that the measure has no face validity; it simply does not make sense.

Second, there are many concrete agreements among researchers about how to measure certain basic concepts. The Bureau of the Census, for example, has created operational definitions of such concepts as family, household, and employment status that seem to have a workable validity in most studies using those concepts.

Content validity This refers to the degree to which a measure covers the range of meanings included within the concept. For instance, this question has frequently been used in surveys to measure fear of crime:

■ How safe do you feel (or would you feel) walking alone in this area after dark? Would you say very safe, fairly safe, fairly unsafe, or very unsafe?

Although this question may be a valid measure of fear of street crime, it is not a good measure of fear of burglary, or auto theft, or bank robbery. The concept of fear of crime is broader than the concept represented in the question.

Criterion-related validity This type of validity compares a measure to some external criterion. A measure can be validated by showing that it predicts scores on another measure that is generally accepted as valid; this is sometimes referred to as *convergent validity.* The validity of College Board

exams, for example, is shown in their ability to predict the success of students in college.

Heeren, Smith, Morelock, and Hingson (1985) offer a good example of criterion-related validity in their efforts to validate a measure of fatal alcohol-related auto accidents. Of course, conducting a blood alcohol laboratory test on everyone killed in auto accidents would be a valid measure. Not all states regularly do this, however, so Heeren and colleagues tested the validity of an alternate measure: single-vehicle fatal accidents involving male drivers occurring between 8:00 P.M. and 3:00 A.M. The validity of this measure was shown by comparing it with the blood alcohol tests for all drivers killed in states that reliably conducted such tests in fatal accidents. Because the two measures agreed closely, Heeren and associates claimed that the proxy or surrogate measure would be valid in other states.

Another approach to criterion-related validity is to show that your measure of a concept is different from measures of similar but distinct concepts. This is called *discriminant validity,* meaning that measures can discriminate different concepts. For example, Skogan and Maxfield (1981:56–57) describe how crime may sometimes be considered a code word for "race" among white Americans. Measures of fear of crime for some people may therefore be contaminated by measuring racist fears about African Americans and crime. They established the discriminant validity of their measure by showing that it was not related to an index of racial intolerance.

Sometimes it is difficult to find behavioral criteria that can be used to validate measures as directly as in the examples above. In those instances, however, we can often approximate such criteria by considering how the variable in question ought, theoretically, to relate to other variables.

Construct validity Construct validity is based on the logical relationships among variables. Let's suppose, for example, that you are interested in studying fear of crime—its sources and consequences. As part of your research, you develop a measure of fear of crime, and you want to assess its validity.

In addition to developing your measure, you will have also developed certain theoretical expectations about the way the variable fear of crime relates to other variables. For instance, you might reasonably conclude that people who are afraid of crime are be less likely to leave their homes at night for entertainment compared to people who are not afraid of crime. If your measure of fear of crime relates to how often people go out at night in the expected fashion, that constitutes evidence of your measure's construct validity. However, if people who are afraid of crime were just as likely to go out at night as people who are not afraid, that challenges the validity of your measure.

Tests of construct validity, then, can offer a weight of evidence that your measure either does or doesn't tap the quality you want it to measure, without providing definitive proof. We have suggested here that tests of construct validity are less compelling than tests of criterion validity. However, you should realize there is room for disagreement about which kind of test is done in a given situation. It is less important that you distinguish these two types than that you understand the logic of validation that they have in common: If we have been successful in measuring some variable, then those measurements should relate to other measures in some logical fashion.

Multiple Measures Another approach to validation of an individual measure is to compare it to alternative measures of the same concept. Although similar to criterion validity, the use of multiple measures does not necessarily assume that the criterion measure is always more accurate. For example, many crimes that are committed never result in an arrest, so arrests are not good measures of how many crimes are committed by individuals. Self-report surveys have often been used to measure delinquency and criminality. But how valid are survey questions that ask people how many crimes they have committed?

The approach used by West and Farrington (and by others) is to ask, for example, how many times someone has committed robbery, and how many times they have been arrested for that crime. Those who admit having been arrested for robbery are asked when and where the arrest occurred. Self-reports can then be validated by checking police arrest records. This works two ways: It is possible to validate individual reports of being arrested for robbery, and researchers can check police records for all persons interviewed to see if there are any records of robbery arrests that subjects do not disclose to interviewers.

Figure 5-2 illustrates the difference between validity and reliability. If you think of measurement as analogous to hitting the bull's-eye on a

FIGURE 5-2
An Analogy to Validity and Reliability

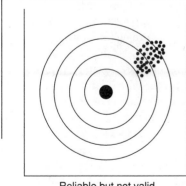 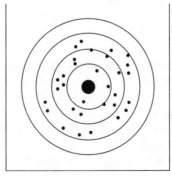 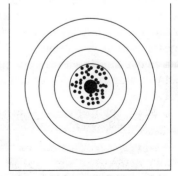

| Reliable but not valid | Valid but not reliable | Valid *and* reliable |

Suggested by an anonymous reviewer.

target, you'll see that reliability looks like a "tight pattern," regardless of where it hits, because reliability is a function of consistency. Validity, on the other hand, relates to the arrangement of shots around the bull's-eye. The failure of reliability in the figure can be seen as a random error; the failure of validity is a systematic error. Notice that neither an unreliable nor an invalid measure is likely to be very useful.

■ COMPOSITE MEASURES

Sometimes it is possible to construct a single measure that captures the variable of interest. Asking auto owners whether their car has been stolen in the previous six months is a straightforward way to measure auto theft victimization. But other variables may be better measured by more than a single indicator. To begin with a simple and well-known example, the FBI crime index is a composite measure of crime that combines police reports for seven different offenses into one indicator.

Composite measures are frequently used in criminal justice research for three reasons. First, despite the care taken in designing studies to provide valid and reliable measurements of variables, the researcher is often unable to develop in advance single indicators of complex concepts. That is especially true with regard to attitudes and opinions that are measured through surveys. For example, we saw earlier in this chapter that measuring fear of crime through a question that asks about feelings of safety on neighborhood streets measures some dimensions of fear but certainly not all of them. This leads us to question the validity of using that single question to measure fear of crime.

Second, you may wish to use a rather refined ordinal measure of a variable, arranging cases in several ordinal categories from very low to very high on a variable such as degree of parental supervision. A single data item might not have enough categories to provide the desired range of variation, but an index or scale formed from several items would.

TABLE 5-2
A Typology of Court Experience

		Serve on Jury?	
		No	Yes
Testify As Witness?	No	A	B
	Yes	C	D

Typology
  A: No experience with court
  B: Experience as juror only
  C: Experience as witness only
  D: Experience as juror and witness

Finally, indexes and scales are *efficient* devices for data analysis. If a single data item gives only a rough indication of a given variable, considering several data items may give us a more comprehensive and more accurate indication. For example, the results of a single drug test would give us some indication of drug use by a probationer. Examining results from several drug tests would give us a better indication, but the manipulation of several data items simultaneously can be very complicated. Composite measures are efficient data-reduction devices. Several indicators may be summarized in a single numerical score, while sometimes very nearly maintaining the specific details of all the individual indicators.

Typologies

Researchers combine variables in different ways to produce different composite measures. The simplest of these is a *typology,* sometimes called a taxonomy. Typologies are produced by the intersection of two or more variables to create a set of categories or types. You may, for example, wish to classify people according to the range of their experience in criminal court. Assume you have asked a sample of people whether they have ever served as a juror and whether they have ever testified as a witness in criminal court. Table 5-2 shows how the yes/no responses to these two questions can be combined into a typology of experience in court.

Typologies can be more complex—combining scores on three or more measures, or combining scores on two measures that take many different values. For an example of a complex typology, consider research by Rolf Loeber and associates (1991) on patterns of delinquency over time. The researchers used a longitudinal design in which a sample of boys was selected from Pittsburgh public schools and interviewed at multiple time points. Extensive interviews were conducted with subjects, including questions that asked about their involvement in delinquency and criminal offending. This approach made it possible to distinguish boys who reported different types of offending at different times.

Loeber and associates first classified delinquent and criminal acts into these ordinal seriousness categories (1991:44):

None: No self-reported delinquency

Minor: Theft of items worth less than $5; vandalism; fare evasion

Moderate: Theft over $5; gang fighting; carrying weapons

Serious: Car theft; breaking and entering; forced sex; selling drugs

Next, to measure change in delinquency over time, the researchers compared reports of delinquency from the first screening interview with reports from later follow-up interviews. These two measures—delinquency at time 1 and delinquency at time 2—formed the typology, which Loeber referred to as a "dynamic classification of offenders" (1991:44). Table 5-3 summarizes this typology.

The first category in the table, "nondelinquent," includes those boys who reported committing no offenses at both the screening and follow-up interviews. "Starters" reported no offenses at screening and then minor, moderate, or serious delinquency at follow-up, while "desistors" were just the opposite. Those who committed the same types of offenses at both times were labeled "stable," and "deescalators" committed less serious offenses at follow-up interviews, and "escalators" moved on to more serious offenses.

Notice the efficiency of this typology. Two variables (delinquency at screening and follow-up) with four categories each are reduced to a single variable with six categories. Furthermore, the two measures of delinquency are themselves

TABLE 5-3

A Typology of Change in Juvenile Offending

	Juvenile Offending*	
Typology	Screening (Time 1)	Follow-up (Time 2)
A. Nondelinquent	0	0
B. Starter	0	1, 2, or 3
C. Desistor	1, 2, or 3	0
D. Stable	1	1
D. Stable	2	2
D. Stable	3	3
E. Deescalator	3	2
E. Deescalator	2 or 3	1
F. Escalator	1	2 or 3
F. Escalator	2	3

*Juvenile offending typology

  0: None
  1: Minor
  2: Moderate
  3: Serious

Source: Adapted from Loeber et al. (1991:43–46).

composite measures, produced by summarizing self-reports from a large number of individual offenses. And notice also how this efficiency is reflected in the meaning of the new composite measure. This dynamic typology summarizes information about time, offending, and offense seriousness in a single measure.

An Index of Disorder

"What is disorder, and what isn't?" asks Wesley Skogan (1990a:4) in his book on the links between crime, fear, and social problems such as public drinking, drug use, litter, prostitution, panhandlers, dilapidated buildings, and groups of boisterous youths. In an influential article, "Broken Windows," James Wilson and George Kelling (1982) describe disorder as signs of crime that may contribute independently to fear and crime itself. The argument goes something like this: Disorder is a symbol of urban decay that people associate with crime. Signs of disorder can produce two related problems. First, disorder may contribute to fear of crime, as urban residents believe that physical decay and "undesirables" are symbols of crime. Second, criminals may interpret evidence of disorder as a signal that informal social control mechanisms in a neighborhood have broken down and that the area is fair game for mayhem and predation.

We suspect that you have a mental image of disorder, but, to paraphrase Skogan's question: How do you measure it? Let's begin by distinguishing two conceptions of disorder. First, we can focus on the *physical presence* of disorder—whether litter, public drinking, public drug use, and the like are actually evident in an urban neighborhood. We might measure the physical presence of disorder through a series of systematic observations, an approach we shall discuss in later chapters.

The second conception focuses on the *perception* of disorder, recognizing that some people might view, for example, public drinking as disorderly, while others (New Orleans residents) consider public drinking to be perfectly acceptable. Questionnaires and survey methods, the topic of Chapter 10, are the best suited for measuring perceived disorder.

Having settled on perceptions of disorder that we will measure through a survey moves us along, but we must make some more decisions. Consider two versions of a question asking about people loitering on the street. The first question is from a series of surveys conducted in three U.S. cities; the second is from a nationwide survey conducted in England and Wales in 1984. Each question is paraphrased from the original questionnaire.

1. Are groups of loiterers hanging out on the streets a big problem, some problem, or almost no problem in your neighborhood? (See Skogan and Maxfield, 1981.)
2. In your area, how common are loiterers hanging around on the street: very common, fairly common, not very common, or not at all common? (See Maxfield, 1987a.)

The first question asks about perceptions of loiterers hanging out as a *problem*, while the second question asks about perceptions of the *frequency* of people hanging out. Notice also that the first question requires two rather different things of respondents: They must perceive loiterers hanging around, *and* they must judge that to be a problem. Skogan uses the first formulation of the

question, reasoning that perception of behavior as a problem is required for it to be perceived as disorder.

Is this a good measure of disorder? The belief that loiterers hanging around is a problem surely has something to do with perceptions of disorder, but there is more to it than that. As it stands we have a measure of one dimension of disorder, but our measure is quite narrow. In order to represent the concept of disorder more completely, we should measure additional behaviors or characteristics that represent other examples of disorder.

Skogan used questions about nine different examples of disorder, and classified them into two groups representing what he calls social and physical disorder (Skogan, 1990:51, 191):

Social Disorder	Physical Disorder
Groups of loiterers	Abandoned buildings
Drug use and sales	Garbage and litter
Vandalism	Junk in vacant lots
Gang activity	
Public drinking	
Street harassment	

Questions corresponding with each of these examples of disorder asked respondents to rate them as big problems (scored 2), some problem (scored 1), or almost no problem (scored 0) in their neighborhood. Together, these nine items measure different types of disorder and appear to have reasonable face validity. However, examining the relationship between each individual item and respondents' fear of crime or experience as a crime victim would be unwieldy at best. So Skogan created two indexes, one for social disorder and one for physical disorder, by adding up the scores for each item and dividing by the number of items in each group. Figure 5-3 shows a hypothetical sample questionnaire for these nine items, together with the scores that would be produced for each index.

This example illustrates how several related variables can be combined to produce an index that has three desirable properties. First, a composite index is a more valid measure of disorder than is an single question. Second, computing

FIGURE 5-3
An Index of Disorder

Introduction:

Now I'm going to read you a list of crime-related problems that may be found in some parts of the city. For each one, please tell me how much of a problem it is in your neighborhood. Is it a big problem, some problem, or almost no problem?

	Big problem	Some problem	No problem
(S) Groups of people loitering	②	1	0
(S) People using or selling drugs	2	①	0
(P) Abandoned buildings	2	1	⓪
(S) Vandalism	2	①	0
(P) Garbage and litter on street	②	1	0
(S) Gangs and gang activity	2	1	⓪
(S) People drinking in public	②	1	0
(P) Junk in vacant lots	2	1	⓪
(S) People making rude or insulting remarks	2	①	0

(S) Social = 2 + 1 + 1 + 0 + 2 + 1 = 7
    Index score = $^7/_6$ = 1.16

(P) Physical = 0 + 2 + 0 = 2
    Index score = $^2/_3$ = 0.67

and averaging across all items in a category create more variation in the index than we could obtain in any single item. Finally, two indexes are more parsimonious than nine individual variables; data analysis and interpretation can be more efficient.

Later chapters will pursue issues of measurement further. Part 3 of this book will describe data collection—how you go about making actual measurements. And the next chapter will focus on different approaches to measuring crime.

■ *MEASUREMENT SUMMARY*

We have covered substantial ground in this chapter but still only introduced the important and often complex issue of measurement in criminal justice research. More than a step in the research process we sketched out in Chapter 4, measurement involves continuous thinking about the conceptual properties you wish to study, how you will operationalize those properties, and how you will develop measures that are reliable and valid. Often, some type of composite measure better represents underlying concepts and thus enhances validity.

■ *MAIN POINTS*

- Concepts are mental images we use as summary devices for bringing together observations and experiences that seem to have something in common.
- Our concepts do not exist in the real world, so they can't be measured directly.
- It is possible to measure the things that our concepts summarize.
- Conceptualization is specifying the vague mental imagery of our concepts, sorting out the kinds of observations and measurements that will be appropriate for our research.

- Operationalization is an extension of the conceptualization process.
- In operationalization, we specify concrete empirical procedures that will result in measurements of variables.
- Operationalization begins in study design and continues throughout the research project, including the analysis of data.
- Nominal measures refer to variables whose attributes are simply different from one another. An example is gender.
- Ordinal measures refer to variables whose attributes may be rank-ordered along some progression from more to less. An example is the variable "worry about burglary," as composed of the attributes "very worried," "somewhat worried," "not very worried," and "not at all worried."
- Interval measures refer to variables whose attributes are not only rank-ordered but are also separated by a uniform distance. An example is the crime seriousness scale developed by Wolfgang, Figlio, Tracy, and Singer (1985).
- Ratio measures are the same as interval measures except that ratio measures are also based on a true zero point. Age is an example of a ratio measure because it contains the attribute zero years old.
- A given variable can sometimes be measured at different levels of measurement. Thus, age, potentially a ratio measure, may also be treated as interval, ordinal, or even nominal. The most appropriate level of measurement used depends on the purpose of the measurement.
- Precision refers to the exactness of the measure used in an observation or description of an attribute. For example, the description of a person as "six feet, one and three-quarters inches tall" is more precise than the description "about six feet tall."
- Reliability refers to the likelihood that a given measurement procedure will yield the same description of a given phenomenon if that measurement is repeated. For example, estimating a person's age by asking his or her friends is less reliable than asking the person directly or checking the birth certificate.

- Validity refers to the extent to which a specific measurement provides data that relate to commonly accepted meanings of a particular concept. There are numerous yardsticks for determining validity: face validity, criterion-related validity, content validity, and construct validity.
- The creation of specific, reliable measures often seems to diminish the richness of meaning our general concepts have. This problem is inevitable. The best solution is to use several different measures, tapping the different aspects of the concept.
- Composite measures, formed by combining two or more variables, are often more valid measures of complex criminal justice concepts.

■ REVIEW QUESTIONS AND EXERCISES

1. Review the box entitled "What Is Recidivism?" From that discussion, write conceptual and operational definitions for recidivism. Summarize how Fabelo proposes to measure the concept. Finally, discuss possible reliability and validity issues associated with Fabelo's proposed measure.

2. Pick a criminal justice concept, perhaps from the list below. Specify that concept so that it could be studied in a research project.

alternative sentencing	child abuse
community corrections	deterrence
discretion	drug-related crime
punishment	rehabilitation
victimless crime	white-collar crime

3. Each year publications such as the "Places Rated Almanac" attract praise from residents of highly rated cities and outraged protest from those who live in lower-rated areas. The 1997 edition rated Orange County, California (where Babbie lives) first and Newark, New Jersey (where Maxfield was a visiting professor) last. Find a recent edition of this or a similar rating guide and discuss the measurement procedures used for developing the ratings. If appropriate, criticize how various dimensions

of the ratings have been operationalized. Can you spot and explain any apparent anomalies in the ratings? For example, the 1997 edition rated Gary, Indiana, higher than Santa Fe, New Mexico.

4. What level of measurement—nominal, ordinal, interval, or ratio—describes each of these variables:

a. Race (white, black, Asian, and so on)

b. Position on the FBI "hierarchy rule"

c. Number of prior arrests

d. Attitudes toward gun control (strongly approve, approve, disapprove, strongly disapprove)

e. Offense type (traffic, misdemeanor, felony)

f. Offense type (violent, nonviolent)

g. Law enforcement agency type (municipal, county, state, federal)

h. Prison security classification (minimum, medium, maximum)

■ ADDITIONAL READINGS

Bureau of Justice Statistics, *Performance Measures for the Criminal Justice System* (Washington, DC: U.S. Department of Justice, Office of Justice Program, Bureau of Justice Statistics, 1993). This collection of essays by prominent criminal justice researchers focuses on developing measures for evaluation uses. The discussion of general measurement issues as encountered in different types of justice agencies is uncommonly thoughtful. You will find this a provocative discussion of how to measure important constructs in corrections, trial courts, and policing. See especially the general essays by John DiIulio and James Q. Wilson.

Carmines, Edward G., and Zeller, Richard A., *Reliability and Validity Assessment* (Thousand Oaks, CA: Sage, 1979). In this chapter, we've examined the basic logic of validity and reliability in social science measurement. Carmines and Zeller explore those issues in more detail and examine some ways of calculating reliability mathematically.

Huizinga, David, and Elliott, Delbert, "Reassessing the Reliability and Validity of Self-report Delinquency Measures," *Journal of Quantitative Criminology*, Vol. 2 (1986), pp. 293–327. Although this article concentrates on self-report measures (a topic we cover in more detail in later chapters), the authors discuss a variety of reliability and validity issues, present examples, and raise some useful points about measurement.

McIver, John P., and Carmines, Edward G., *Unidimensional Scaling* (Thousand Oaks, CA: Sage, 1981). An excellent introduction to some general procedures for developing and testing composite measures.

CHAPTER

6 *Measuring Crime*

What You'll Learn in This Chapter

How do you measure crime? How much crime is there? Researchers and policymakers have developed several different approaches to measuring crime. Nevertheless, there's no definitive answer to the second question. We'll describe a variety of strategies for measuring crime, along with the strengths and weaknesses of each.

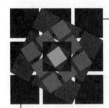

INTRODUCTION

GENERAL ISSUES IN MEASURING CRIME
What Offenses?
What Units of Analysis?
What Purpose?

CRIMES KNOWN TO POLICE
Uniform Crime Reports
UCR and Criteria for Measurement Quality
Incident-Based Police Records
National Incident-Based Reporting System
NIBRS and Criteria for Measurement Quality

MEASURING CRIME THROUGH SURVEYS
National Crime Victimization Survey
NCVS Redesign
Comparing Victim Surveys and Crimes Known
    to Police

SURVEYS OF OFFENDING
National Household Survey on Drug Abuse
Monitoring the Future
Validity and Reliability of Self-report Measures
Self-report Surveys Summarized

DRUG SURVEILLANCE SYSTEMS
Drug Use Forecasting
Drug Abuse Warning Network
Pulse Check

**MEASURING CRIME FOR
SPECIFIC PURPOSES**

MEASURING CRIME: SUMMARY

MAIN POINTS

REVIEW QUESTIONS AND EXERCISES

ADDITIONAL READINGS

■ INTRODUCTION

Having discussed the principles of measurement and measurement quality at some length, our attention now turns to a basic task for criminal justice researchers: measuring crime. Crime is a fundamental dependent variable in criminal justice and criminology. Explanatory studies frequently seek to learn what causes crime, while applied studies often focus on what actions might be effective in reducing crime. Descriptive and exploratory studies may simply wish to count how much crime there is in some specific area, a question of obvious concern to criminal justice officials as well as researchers.

Crime can also be an independent variable—for example, in a study of how crime affects fear or other attitudes, or in determining whether people who live in high-crime areas are more likely than others to favor long prison sentences for drug dealers. Sometimes crime can be both an independent and a dependent variable, as in trying to learn about the relationships between drug use and other offenses.

Whatever your research purpose, and whether you're interested in what causes crime or what crime causes, it should be clear that measuring crime is important. It's also difficult; how to measure crime has long been a central research issue in criminology and criminal justice.

We have three objectives in this chapter. First, we want to sensitize you to how the challenge of measuring crime illustrates the more general measurement issues we discussed in Chapter 5. We'll see that whatever approach you use depends fundamentally on your research purpose and the specific research questions you wish to address. Each approach to measuring crime has its advantages and disadvantages. Our second objective is to introduce you to some available measures of crime and to discuss the strengths and weaknesses of each measure. We will also comment on how different measures satisfy the criteria for measurement quality we discussed in Chapter 5. Finally, we will briefly describe some independent measures of crime developed for specific research or policy purposes.

■ GENERAL ISSUES IN MEASURING CRIME

At the outset, you should be aware of some broad considerations that influence all measures of crime. This section will address three questions: (1) What offenses do you want to measure? (2) What units of analysis should you use? (3) What is the purpose of measuring crime?

What Offenses?

Let's begin by agreeing on a conceptual definition of crime—one that will enable us to decide what specific types of crime we will measure. Recall a definition from Gottfredson and Hirschi (1990:15) mentioned in Chapter 5: "acts of force or fraud undertaken in pursuit of self-interest." This is an interesting definition, but it is better suited to an extended discussion of theories of crime than to our purposes in this chapter. For example, we would have to clarify what was meant by *self-interest,* a term that has engaged philosophers and social scientists for centuries.

Wilson and Herrnstein (1985:22) propose a different definition that should get us started: "A crime is any act committed in violation of a law that prohibits it and authorizes punishment for its commission." Although other criminologists (Gottfredson and Hirschi, for example) might not agree with this conceptual definition, it has the advantage of being reasonably specific. We could be even more specific by consulting a state or federal code and listing the of acts for which the law provides punishment.

Our list would be very long. For example, the *Indiana Code* (IC) includes harvesting ginseng root out of season (IC 14-31-3-16)[1] and selling a switchblade knife (IC 35-47-5-2) as acts punishable by six months' incarceration and a $1,000

---

[1] This citation reflects the standard form of references to a "code"—the body of all laws in effect for a jurisdiction, organized by subject. In this case, "IC" is the abbreviation for *Indiana Code;* the numbers cite title, article, chapter, and section. So this citation refers to Title 14, article 31, chapter 3, section 16 of the *Indiana Code.* "USC" refers to the *United States Code,* that body of federal laws in effect for the United States.

fine. Taking Indiana ginseng out of the state without permission (IC 14-31-3-20) and assault resulting in nonserious bodily injury to an adult (IC 35-42-2-1) are equivalent crimes that could bring one year's incarceration and a fine of $5,000. However we decide to measure crime, we certainly want to distinguish acts of violence and the sale of illegal weapons from irregularities concerning rare herbs.

One of the principal difficulties we encounter when we try to measure crime is that many different types of behaviors and actions are included in our conceptualization of crime as an "act committed in violation of a law that prohibits it and authorizes punishment for its commission." Different measures tend to focus on different types of crime, primarily because not all crimes can be measured the same way with any degree of reliability or validity. So one important step in selecting a measure is deciding what crimes will be included.

What Units of Analysis?

Recall that units of analysis are the specific entities researchers collect information about. Chapter 4 discussed individuals, groups, social artifacts, and other units of analysis. Deciding how to measure crime requires that we once again think about these units.

Crimes involve four elements that are often easier to recognize in the abstract than they are to actually measure. We'll begin with the easiest of these elements, the *offender*. Without an offender, there's no crime, so a crime must at a minimum involve an offender. The offender is therefore one possible unit of analysis. We might decide to study burglars, auto thieves, robbers, child molesters, or people who have committed many different types of offenses.

Crimes also require some sort of *victim*, the second possible unit of analysis. We could study victims of burglary, auto theft, bank robbery, or assault. Notice that this list of victims includes different types of units: households or businesses for burglary, auto owners for auto theft, banks for bank robbery, and individuals for assault. Some of

these units are organizations (banks, businesses), some are individual people, some are abstractions (households), and some are ambiguous (individuals or organizations can own automobiles).

What about so-called victimless crimes like drug use, bookmaking, or prostitution? In a legal sense, there are no victimless crimes because crimes are acts that injure society if not organizations or individuals. But studying crimes in which society only is the victim—prostitution, for example—presents special challenges, and specialized techniques have been developed to measure certain types of victimless crimes. In any event, it's crucial to think about units of analysis in advance. Later we will discuss surveying victims as one approach to counting crime. For now you should recognize that surveying individuals, organizations, and society involve fundamentally different tasks.

The final two elements of crimes are closely intertwined and will be discussed together: *offense* and *incident*. An offense is defined as an individual act of burglary, auto theft, bank robbery, and so on. The Federal Bureau of Investigation (FBI) defines *incident* as "one or more offenses committed by the same offender, or group of offenders *acting in concert*, at the *same time and place*" (Federal Bureau of Investigation, 1988:17; emphasis in original).

Think about the difference between *offense* and *incident* for a moment. A single incident can include multiple offenses, but it's not possible to have one offense and multiple incidents. You should also recognize that a single incident could include multiple victims.

To illustrate the different units of analysis—offenders, victims, offenses, and incidents—consider the examples described in the box entitled "Units of Analysis and Measuring Crime." These examples should help you distinguish units from each other and recognize the links among different units.

Notice that we have said nothing about aggregate units of analysis, a topic we examined in Chapter 4. We have considered only individual units, even though measures of crime are often

Units of Analysis and Measuring Crime

FIGURING out the different units of analysis in counting crimes can seem difficult and confusing at first. Much of the problem comes from the possibility of what database designers call one-to-many and many-to-many relationships. The same incident can have multiple offenses, offenders, and victims, or just one of each. Fortunately, thinking through some examples usually clarifies the matter. Our two examples are adapted from an FBI publication (1988:18).

Example 1

Two males entered a bar. The bartender was forced at gun point to hand over all money from the cash register. The offenders also took money and jewelry from three customers. One of the offenders used his handgun to beat one of the customers, thereby causing serious injury. Both offenders fled on foot.

```
1 incident
    1 robbery offense
        2 offenders
        4 victims (bar cash, three patrons)
    1 aggravated assault offense
        2 offenders
        1 victim
```

Even though only one offender actually assaulted the bar patron, the other offender would be charged with assisting in the offense because he prevented others from coming to the aid of the assault victim.

Example 2

Two males entered a bar. The bartender was forced at gun point to hand over all money from the cash register. The offenders also took money and jewelry from two customers. One of the offenders, in searching for more people to rob, found a female customer in a back room and raped her there, outside of the view of the other offender. When the rapist returned, both offenders fled on foot.

This example includes two incidents because the rape occurred in a different place and the offenders were not acting in concert. And since they were not acting in concert in the same place, only one offender is associated with the rape incident.

```
Incident 1
    1 robbery offense
        2 offenders
        3 victims (bar cash, two patrons)
Incident 2
    1 rape offense
        1 offender
        1 victim
```

based on aggregate units of analysis—neighborhoods, cities, counties, states, and so on.

What Purpose?

Different strategies for measuring crime can be distinguished by their general purpose. Here we emphasize *general purpose* in contrast to the research purposes we described in Chapter 4. Approaches to measuring crime have at least one of three general purposes: (1) monitoring, (2) agency accountability, and (3) research.

We measure crime for the purpose of *monitoring* in much the same way that we measure consumer prices, stock market activity, traffic fatalities, birthrates, population, unemployment, and HIV infection rates. This is more than just a compulsion for counting things, however. We measure a variety of social, economic, demographic, and public health indicators to keep track of social and economic conditions, the size and age distribution of the population, and threats to public health. By the same token, one purpose for measuring crime is to monitor potential threats to public safety and security.

At the national level, two series of crime measures seek to assess "the magnitude, nature, and impact of crime in the Nation" [sic] (U.S. Department of Justice, 1995:1). We shall describe the Uniform Crime Reports (UCR) and the National Crime Victimization Survey (NCVS) in detail later in this chapter. Here we wish to point out that the fundamental purpose for these two measures is monitoring. In the field of public health, this is referred to as *surveillance,* or a *sentinel* system (Mercy et al., 1993). Just as a variety of statistical series administered by the U.S. Public Health Service monitor the incidence of disease and death rates from various causes, the Department of Justice oversees two nationwide surveillance systems for measuring crime.

The second measurement purpose is *agency accountability.* Government agencies are obliged to keep records that document their actions and areas of responsibility. Such accountability is a basic principle of the U.S. version of democratic government and is one reason why individual police departments measure crime. The final purpose is *research;* measures of crime are made for specific research purposes that are distinct from the purpose of surveillance or accountability.

We call these different purposes to your attention for an important reason that we'll encounter throughout this chapter and return to in Chapter 12. Criminal justice research quite often uses measures of crime that are collected for surveillance or accountability purposes, not for research. It's worth keeping that point in mind when you plan a research project that will measure crime with one or more existing series of data.

■ CRIMES KNOWN TO POLICE

It's safe to say that the most widely used measures of crime are based on police records and are commonly referred to as "crimes known to police." We emphasize this phrase because it has important implications for understanding what police records do and do not measure. One thing you

should immediately recognize is that crimes not known to police cannot be measured by consulting police records. We can better understand the significance of this by considering the two ways police come to know about crime: observation and reports from other people.

Certain types of crimes are detected almost exclusively by *observation*—traffic offenses and so-called victimless crimes. Police count drug sales because they observe the transaction; they count incidents of prostitution because they witness soliciting. It is all too obvious to most of us that police detect traffic offenses through observation. Most other crimes, however, are detected and counted because they are *reported to police by other people:* victims or witnesses. Victims report burglaries, robberies, assaults, purse snatchings, and other offenses to police. Witnesses may also report crimes.

If you recognize that police measure crime in these two ways—observation and reports by others—you should be able to think of crimes that are not well measured by police records. Consider shoplifting, for example. Many instances of shoplifting are observed neither by police nor by other people who might report them to police. Those instances are not detected and therefore not measured. Shoplifting certainly is included in our conceptual definition of an act committed in violation of a law that prohibits it and authorizes punishment. However, measuring shoplifting by counting crimes known to police would omit many instances.

Thinking about crime measured almost exclusively by police observation—victimless crimes and traffic offenses—should make you realize that crimes known to police are not a good measure of these types of offenses either. We would be willing to bet that everyone has committed some traffic offense and not been caught. Similarly, most instances of drug sales, not to mention drug possession, are not detected.

The other way police measure crime is also imperfect. Many crimes are not reported to police, especially minor thefts and certain types of assaults. People don't report crimes for several reasons, which tend to vary by type of crime. Attempted thefts may not be reported because no property was lost. Many minor assaults or other personal crimes are considered by victims to be private matters that they will settle themselves without involving the police. Other victims feel that minor losses are not important enough to trouble police, or that reporting a crime would make no difference because police could neither capture the offender nor recover stolen property (Bureau of Justice Statistics, 1996b).

Another problem with police measurement of crime undermines the meaning of the phrase "crimes known to police." Research has shown what some people may have personally experienced: Police do not always make official records of crimes they observe or crimes reported to them. Donald Black (1970) and Albert Reiss (1971) describe a number of factors that influence police decisions on whether or not to officially record crimes they know about. Assaults, for example, between people who know each other well or are related to each other are less likely to be recorded as assaults than are fights between strangers. If a victim urges a police officer not to arrest someone or not to press charges against an offender, the officer is less likely to treat the incident as a crime. Black also found that police more often made official crime reports for incidents that involved victims of higher socioeconomic status. Finally, Richard and Carolyn Rebecca Block (1980) found that robberies in Chicago were less often recorded if no weapon was used, if victims resisted the offender, or if a robbery attempt was unsuccessful. They concluded that robberies are counted by police if they are "based on a stereotypical idea of robbery—a helpless victim attacked by a gun-wielding thug. The more an incident approximates this ideal robbery, the more likely it will become a robbery statistic" (1980:636).

Uniform Crime Reports

Police measures of crime form the basis for the FBI's Uniform Crime Reports, a data series that has been collected since 1930 and has been widely used by criminal justice researchers. We want to alert you to some characteristics of the UCR that affect its suitability as a measure of crime. Most of our comments point to its shortcomings in this regard, but keep in mind that the UCR will continue to be a very useful measure for researchers and public officials.

Because UCR data are based on crimes reported to police, they share the measurement problems mentioned earlier. However, the FBI crime counts include three additional sources of measurement error.

First, the UCR does not even try to count all crimes reported to police. What are referred to as index offenses—also called Part I crimes—are counted if these offenses are reported to police (and recorded by police). Index offenses include murder and nonnegligent manslaughter, forcible rape, robbery, aggravated assault, burglary, larceny-theft, and motor vehicle theft (U.S. Department of Justice, 1995). Other offenses, referred to as Part II crimes, are counted only if a person has been arrested and charged with a crime. The UCR therefore does not include such offenses as shoplifting, drug sales or use, fraud, prostitution, simple assault, vandalism, receiving stolen property, and all other nontraffic offenses unless someone is arrested. This means that a large number of crimes reported to police are not measured in the UCR.

Second, one of the reasons Part II offenses are counted only if an arrest is made is that individual states have varying definitions of crimes. The operational definition of crime can vary from state to state, and this introduces another source of measurement error into the FBI data. For example, the state of Louisiana includes verbal threats in its counts of assaults, while most other states do not (Justice Research and Statistics Association, 1996:20).

The FBI compiles its UCR figures from data submitted by individual states or local law enforcement agencies. In some states, local police and sheriffs' departments send their crime reports to a state agency that forwards crime reports to the FBI. In other states, local law enforcement agencies send crime data directly to the FBI. However, not all local police and sheriffs' departments send complete crime report data to either their state agency or the FBI. Some inconsistency also exists in the quality of data submitted. In other words, individual states, cities, and counties vary in the quality and completeness of crime data sent to the FBI and reported in the annual UCR publication, *Crime in the United States.* Just as the decennial census cannot count everyone who lives in the United States, the FBI is not able to reliably count all crimes—either Part I or Part II offenses—that occur in the United States.

UCR data can also suffer from clerical, data processing, and, in some cases, political problems. For example, Henry Brownstein (1996) describes his experience as a senior analyst in the New York Division of Criminal Justice Services, a state agency that compiles local crime reports for submission under the UCR program. The accuracy of data from cities and counties in New York is affected by staff shortages that undermine efforts to verify local reports, maintenance of an aging computer program that compiles UCR reports, and what Brownstein calls the "New York City reconciliation." Here is how he describes that problem (1996:22–23):

■ As localities and agencies within localities compete amongst themselves for a greater share of State resources, they all compete to show that they are responsible for a greater share of the problem that the resources will be used to solve. Consequently, everyone wants credit for reported crimes and arrests. In New York City, where there are so many competing jurisdictions and agencies, this translates as a problem of duplicate reporting. So every summer a senior data entry clerk conducts the reconciliation, separating out by hand and by assumption the duplicate reports of the same crimes and arrests submitted by different jurisdictions and agencies.

The third source of measurement error in the UCR is produced by the *hierarchy rule* used by police agencies and the FBI to classify crimes. Under the hierarchy rule, if multiple crimes are committed in a single incident, only the most serious is counted in the UCR. For example, if a burglar breaks into a home, rapes one of the occupants, and flees in the homeowner's car, at least three

crimes are committed—burglary, rape, and vehicle theft. Under the FBI hierarchy rule, only the most serious crime, rape, is counted in the UCR, even though if captured, the offender could be charged with all three offenses. In the examples described in the box, "Units of Analysis and Measuring Crime," the UCR would count one offense in each incident: a single robbery in the first example and rape in the second example.

UCR and Criteria for Measurement Quality

Let's now consider how using the UCR to operationalize and measure crime satisfies the criteria for measurement quality we discussed in Chapter 5. Are the UCR data exclusive, exhaustive, valid, and reliable?

First, you should readily see that the UCR is neither an exclusive nor an exhaustive measure. Many crimes are not counted (nonexhaustive), and the hierarchy rule means that crime definitions are not strictly exclusive. Since the rule counts only the most serious crime in an incident where multiple crimes are committed, it does not help us if, for example, we were especially interested in burglary because burglaries are not counted if a rape, robbery, or murder is committed in the same incident.

Since the UCR does not count all crimes, we can rightly question its validity. The UCR does not really measure the concept of crime as we have defined it: any act committed in violation of a law that prohibits it and authorizes punishment for its commission.

Finally, is the UCR a reliable measure? Not all law enforcement agencies submit complete reports to the FBI, and the quality of the data submitted varies. As stated in the 1990 report, "The final responsibility for data submissions rests with the individual contributing law enforcement agency. . . . The statistics' accuracy depends primarily on the adherence of each contributor to the established standards of reporting" (U.S. Department of Justice, 1991:3). You should recognize how inconsistencies in reporting, such as those Brownstein describes for New York, produce problems with the reliability of UCR data.

Also recall the Blocks' study, mentioned earlier, and other research findings that police do not always make records of crimes that come to their attention. When individual police officers exercise discretion in making crime reports, the reliability of measuring crime through the UCR is further undermined.

Before we move on to other approaches to measuring crime, consider how units of analysis figure into UCR data. The UCR system produces what is referred to as a *summary-based* measure of crime. This means that UCR data include summary, or total, crime counts for reporting agencies—cities or counties. UCR data therefore represent groups as units of analysis. Crime reports are available for cities or counties, and these may be aggregated upward to measure crime for states or regions of the United States. But UCR data available from the FBI cannot represent individual crimes, offenders, or victims as units.

Recall that it is possible to aggregate units of analysis to higher levels, but it is not possible to disaggregate grouped data to the individual level. Since UCR data are aggregates, they cannot be used in descriptive or explanatory studies that focus on individual crimes, offenders, or victims. UCR data are therefore restricted to the analysis of such units as cities, counties, states, or regions.

Incident-Based Police Records

The U.S. Department of Justice sponsors two series of crime measures that are based on *incidents* as units of analysis. The first of these, *Supplementary Homicide Reports* (SHR), was begun in 1961 and is actually part of the UCR program, as implied by the word *supplementary.*

Local law enforcement agencies submit detailed information about individual homicide incidents under the SHR program. This includes information about victims and, if known, offenders (age, gender, race), relationship between victim and offender, weapon used, location of incident, and circumstances surrounding the killing. Notice how the SHR relates to our discussion of units of analysis at the beginning of this chapter. Incidents are the basic unit and can include one or more

victims and offenders; since the series is restricted to homicides, offense is held constant.

Because SHR is an incident-based system, investigators can use SHR data to conduct descriptive and explanatory studies that examine individual events. For example, it's possible to compare the relationship between victim and offender for male victims and female victims, or to compare the types of weapons used in killings by strangers and killings by nonstrangers. Such analyses would not be possible if we were studying homicide using UCR summary data. If our unit of analysis was jurisdiction—city or county, for example—we could examine only the aggregate number of homicides in each jurisdiction for a given year; it would not be possible to say anything about individual homicide incidents.

Crime measures based on incidents as units of analysis therefore have several advantages over summary measures. Don't lose sight, however, of the fact that SHR data still represent crimes known to police and recorded by police. It's safe to say that records of homicides will be better represented in police records than will, say, records of shoplifting, but clerical and other errors are still a factor. Brownstein (1996) describes some of these problems, and Maxfield (1989) discusses some validity concerns with respect to the SHR. Most potential errors in the SHR are due to recording and recordkeeping practices, topics we will discuss in Chapter 12.

National Incident-Based Reporting System

The most recent development in police-based measures at the national level is the ongoing effort by the FBI and the Bureau of Justice Statistics (BJS) to convert the UCR to a National Incident-Based Reporting System (NIBRS), pronounced "ny-bers." Planning for the replacement of the UCR began in the mid-1980s, but because NIBRS represents major changes, law enforcement agencies have shifted only gradually to the new system.

Put briefly, NIBRS is a Very Big Deal. We'll first try to put things in perspective by comparing NIBRS and the UCR for a single state, Idaho, that currently reports incident-level measures. Then we will discuss some of the specific features of NIBRS, concluding with comments on progress in implementing the new system.

About 16,000 law enforcement agencies report UCR summary data each year; that's 16,000 annual observations, one for each reporting agency. Idaho has 138 UCR-reporting agencies, so Idaho submits 138 annual observations under UCR reporting. Under NIBRS, Idaho reported just over 100,000 incidents in 1995. So for Idaho, shifting from the summary UCR system for measuring crime to the incident-based NIBRS system meant shifting from 138 units (UCR-reporting jurisdictions) to over 100,000 units. In other words, rather than reporting 138 total crime counts for seven UCR Part I offenses, Idaho reported detailed information on more than 100,000 individual incidents. And this is Idaho, which ranks 41st among the states in 1995 resident population!

This illustrates the main difference between NIBRS and the UCR system: reporting each crime incident rather than reporting the total number of certain crimes for each law enforcement agency. But the significance of shifting from reporting aggregate numbers to reporting individual incidents lies in the type of information that is available about each incident. In essence, NIBRS measures many individual features of each incident, and each of these features is reported individually. Table 6-1 lists most of the "segments" or categories of information recorded for each incident, together with examples of the information recorded within each segment.

Referring back to our earlier discussion of the elements of crime—incidents, offenders, offenses, and victims—you should realize that the information in Table 6-1 is organized around each *incident*. Each incident can include one or more *offenses, offenders,* and *victims,* as we described in the box on units of analysis.

Table 6-1 shows that NIBRS includes much more detailed information about individual incidents, together with the offenses, offenders, and victims within each incident. In addition, NIBRS guidelines call for gathering information about a much broader array of offenses. While the UCR reports information about seven Part I offenses,

TABLE 6-1

Selected Information in National Incident-Based Reporting System Records

Administrative Segment	Offense Segment
Incident date and time	Offense type
Reporting agency ID	Attempted or completed
Other ID numbers	Offender drug/alcohol use
	Location type
	Weapon use

Victim Segment	Offender Segment
Victim ID number	Offender ID number
Offense type	Offender age, gender, race
Victim age, gender, race	
Resident of jurisdiction?	
Type of injury	
Relationship to offender	
Victim type:	
Individual person	
Business	
Government	
Society/public	

Source: Adapted from FBI (1988:6–8, 90).

NIBRS is designed to collect detailed information on 46 "Group A" offenses. NIBRS includes data for additional "Group B" offenses only if a person is arrested. Table 6-2 shows the different scopes of coverage for UCR Part I and NIBRS Group A offenses, using 1994 reports for Idaho.

The first part of Table 6-2 compares NIBRS and UCR totals for the seven UCR Part I offenses. Notice that for each of these offenses NIBRS totals differ from the UCR totals, being higher for all but one of the Part I UCR offenses. Two things account for these differences: revised offense definitions in NIBRS, and the fact that NIBRS does not use the UCR hierarchy rule, which counts only the most serious offense within an incident. Of course, because NIBRS counts all offenses, incident-based totals should be at least slightly higher than UCR totals because more than one offense can be reported for each incident.

The second part of Table 6-2 shows that additional Group A NIBRS offenses just about double the number of crimes "known to police" in Idaho. Simple assault and vandalism are by far the most common of these additional offenses, but drug violations accounted for more than 6,500 offenses in 1994.

TABLE 6-2
Comparing UCR and NIRBS for Idaho, 1994

UCR Part I Offenses	UCR	NIBRS
Murder	40	41
Rape	316	332
Robbery	209	218
Aggregated assault	2,673	2,800
Burglary	8,147	8,143
Larceny	32,597	33,264
MV theft	2,210	2,266
Subtotals	46,192	47,064

Additional NIBRS Group A Offenses	
Arson	359
Simple assault	11,890
Intimidation	1,887
Bribery	1
Counterfeit/forgery	1,399
Vandalism	16,305
Drug violations	3,490
Drug equipment violations	3,122
Embezzlement	243
Extortion/blackmail	17
Fraud	1,317
Gambling	6
Kidnapping/abduction	239
Pornography/obscene material	20
Prostitution	15
Forcible sex offenses	1,025
Nonforcible sex offenses	198
Stolen property	576
Weapons violations	1,335
Subtotal	43,444
NIBRS Group A Total	90,508

Sources: NIBRS: http://www.state.id.us/dle/crimeid/1994/ostate.txt, Idaho Department of Law Enforcement, "Crime in Idaho, 1994." UCR: *Sourcebook of Criminal Justice Statistics, 1995,* Table 3.111, p. 327.

Collecting detailed information on each incident for each offense, victim, and offender, and doing so for a large number of offense types, represent the most significant changes in NIBRS compared to the UCR. Dropping the hierarchy rule is also a major change, but that is a consequence of incident-based reporting. NIBRS incorporates six other revisions, summarized from a publication on NIBRS guidelines (FBI, 1988:12–20):

1. *Victim type.* Table 6-1 lists most categories for victim type; the most notable of these is "society/public," a category that has the effect of annulling the phrase "victimless crime."

2. *Attempted/completed.* UCR summary reports include both attempted and completed offenses, but it's not possible to distinguish them. NIBRS adds a category to indicate whether each offense within each incident was attempted or completed.

3. *Computer-base submission.* UCR reports could be sent to the FBI on paper forms, but NIBRS data must be submitted on computer tape or disks.

4. *Drug-related offenses.* Because the 1980s witnessed a growing public concern with illegal drug use, NIBRS includes provisions to assess offender drug use in nondrug offenses, and to record whether drugs or drug paraphernalia were seized.

5. *Computers and crime.* The 1980s also witnessed an expansion of computer use, including computers as instruments and targets of crime. Categories to record the involvement of computers are included.

6. *Quality control.* Complexity increases the potential for error, but requiring computerized submission makes it easier to check for patterns of problems in NIBRS data. The FBI is also developing audit procedures and standards for reviewing NIBRS data.

NIBRS and Criteria for Measurement Quality

You now have some idea about the potential wealth of information available from NIBRS, and how this new system represents major changes from the UCR. How does incident-based reporting fare on our criteria for measurement quality? After considering NIBRS in light of our earlier comments on the UCR, you will recognize some improvements. Eliminating the hierarchy rule means offense classifications are mutually exclusive. Is NIBRS exhaustive? Table 6-2 lists more offenses compared with the UCR, but because Group B offenses are recorded only for crimes that result in arrest, not all crimes are counted.

In at least one sense, NIBRS data hold the promise of being more reliable. The FBI has produced very thorough documentation on how to record and classify incidents and their component records. Creating auditing standards and requiring submission of data on computer-readable media also enhance reliability. Finally, the FBI requires that state records systems be certified before the state can submit incident-based reports.

The production of NIBRS data is, however, still a selective process: Crimes are selectively reported to police and selectively recorded by police. Chapter 12 will present a detailed examination of sources of measurement error in records produced by police and other public agencies. Here we call your attention to three practical problems researchers are likely to encounter in using NIBRS data to measure crime.

First, pilot NIBRS programs in three small states (Alabama, North Dakota, and South Carolina) produced huge amounts of data for the year 1991. According to Reaves (1993:4), incidents for these three states in 1991 occupy more than 1.3 billion bytes of data (1,300 megabytes). Such voluminous data will challenge the capabilities of most computer systems.

Second, implementing NIBRS requires enormous effort by individual law enforcement agencies to comply with the FBI's detailed specifications on recordkeeping and reporting. Since it is a computer-based system, individual agencies must either develop the necessary data processing capability or adapt existing systems to NIBRS specifications. The FBI and BJS have promoted the shift to NIBRS with technical and financial assistance for state and local agencies. Somewhat paradoxically, this has meant that smaller states and smaller police and sheriff departments within states have been more readily able to develop NIBRS-compliant systems from the ground up with federal assistance. Most larger agencies developed customized records management systems some years ago, and adapting those systems to NIBRS standards has proven to be difficult and costly (MEGG Associates, 1996).

And third, like UCR reporting, NIBRS is voluntary; no agency is required to submit crime reports to the FBI in any form. As a result of the major expense and effort involved in shifting to NIBRS, the conversion process has been slow. In 1988, the FBI published extensive guidelines

on developing and implementing NIBRS. As of December 1995, only nine states had been certified as NIBRS-compliant: Colorado, Idaho, Iowa, Massachusetts, North Dakota, South Carolina, Utah, Vermont, and Virginia. (SEARCH Group, 1995). Of these states, only South Carolina has achieved 100 percent compliance with NIBRS among local law enforcement agencies.

■ MEASURING CRIME THROUGH SURVEYS

Recognizing the shortcomings associated with using measures of crime known to police, we should consider alternative approaches. Conducting a survey that asks people whether or not they have been the victim of a crime is one alternative. Survey research methods will be described in detail in Chapter 10, but for now we assume that you have a general understanding of what a survey involves—presenting a sample of people with carefully worded questions and recording their responses.

In principle, measuring crime through a survey has several advantages. Surveys can obtain information on crimes that were not reported to police. Asking people about victimizations can also measure incidents that police may not have officially recorded as crimes. Finally, asking individual people about crimes that may have happened to them provides data on victims and offenders (individuals) and on the incidents themselves (social artifacts). Like an incident-based reporting system, a survey can therefore provide more disaggregated units of analysis. When conducted in a rigorous, systematic fashion, surveys can result in reliable measures.

National Crime Victimization Survey

Since 1972, the U.S. Census Bureau has conducted the National Crime Victimization Survey (NCVS). The NCVS was launched following pilot studies in the mid-1960s by President Lyndon Johnson's Commission on Law Enforcement and Administration of Justice, known as the President's Crime Commission. One of the primary reasons for conducting crime surveys was to illuminate what came to be referred to as the "dark figure of unreported crime." The NCVS is based on a nationally representative sample of households and uses uniform procedures to select and interview respondents, which enhances the reliability of crime measures. Since individual people living in households are interviewed, the NCVS can be used in studies where individuals or households are the unit of analysis.

The NCVS cannot measure all crimes, however, in part because of the procedures used to select victims. Since the survey is based on a sample of households, it cannot count crimes that have businesses or commercial establishments as victims. Bank robberies, gas station holdups, shoplifting, embezzlement, and securities fraud are examples of crimes that cannot be systematically counted by interviewing household members. Samples of banks, gas stations, retail stores, business establishments, or stockbrokers would be needed to measure those crimes. In much the same fashion, crimes directed at homeless victims cannot be counted by surveys of households.

What about "victimless" crimes? Think for a moment how you would respond to a Census Bureau interviewer who asked whether you had been the victim of a drug sale. If you had bought drugs from a dealer, you might think of yourself as a customer rather than as a victim. Or if you lived near a park where drug sales were common, you might think of yourself as a victim, even though you had not participated in a drug transaction. The point is that victim surveys are not good measures of victimless crimes because the individual survey respondents can't easily be conceived as victims.

Measuring certain forms of delinquency through victim surveys presents similar problems. Status offenses such as truancy and curfew violations do not have identifiable victims that can be included in samples based on households. Homicide and manslaughter are one final type of crime that is not well measured by victim surveys, for obvious reasons.

Since the NCVS, by design, excludes many types of crimes, you should recognize potential validity problems. But what about the reliability of crime surveys in general and the NCVS in particular? Since it is a survey, the NCVS is subject to the errors and shortcomings associated with that method of measuring concepts. The general issues of measurement through surveys will be considered in detail in Chapter 10. Now we will mention some reliability problems that are particularly troublesome in using surveys as a technique to count crime.

For many years, NCVS interviewers began the section of the survey on victimization with the introduction: "Now I'd like to ask some questions about crime. They refer only to the last six months—between [date six months before interview] and [date of interview]. During the last six months, did anyone [crime description]?" (Bureau of Justice Statistics, 1994:122). Respondents were then asked a series of *screening questions* to determine whether they might have been a crime victim in the previous six months. Those who answered yes to screening questions were presented with detailed questions about the incident.

Asking people about crime in this way brings up the possibility of different types of recall error. First, respondents may simply not remember some incidents. This problem is particularly acute for minor crimes, such as theft, and for people who may have been the victim of more than one crime in the six-month recall period.

The second recall problem, called *telescoping*, is that respondents may not accurately recall when an incident occurred. Forward telescoping means that people may respond to questions by mentioning crimes that occurred more than six months ago, thus bringing past incidents forward into the recall period. In contrast, backward telescoping means that respondents inaccurately recall recent crimes as occurring in the more distant past. Since the NCVS tries to count crimes that occur every six months, forward or backward telescoping can produce unreliable counts. However, the NCVS is designed to reduce the possibility of telescoping.

A different type of recall problem affects people who have been victimized several times during the six-month reference period. The Bureau of Justice Statistics (1996b) describes this as a problem with *series victimizations,* which are defined as six or more similar but separate crimes that the respondent cannot describe individually to an interviewer. Series crimes constitute a problem for victimization surveys because it is not clear how they should be counted or combined with individual crimes that the respondent can describe separately. The potential impact of series victimizations is substantial. BJS (1996b) estimates that series crimes in 1993 totaled more than 780,000 personal offenses and about 460,000 property crimes.

Finally, the NCVS underestimates incidents where the victim and offender know each other—domestic violence or other assaults involving friends or acquaintances, for example. Respondents may not tell interviewers about nonstranger crimes for various reasons. Some domestic violence victims view assaults as a personal problem, not as a crime, and may therefore not mention the incidents. Other persons—victims of rape or domestic violence—may feel shame or embarrassment and not wish to talk about their experiences. Finally, respondents who have been victimized by a family member may fear some further assault if they discuss a past incident.

NCVS Redesign

To address these and other concerns about the ability of the NCVS to measure different types of crime, the survey has undergone substantial changes in the last several years. Victimization estimates from interviews conducted in 1993 reflect the full scope of the redesign effort after various changes in survey procedures were gradually incorporated. For the most part, the redesign effort has focused on obtaining better measures of domestic violence and sexual assault, together with steps to help respondents recall a broader range of incidents. Here is a brief summary of major changes (U.S. Bureau of the Census, 1994; Bureau of Justice Statistics, 1996b):

Revised screening questions and added cues throughout the interview to help respondents recall and distinguish minor incidents.

More direct questions on rape and other sexual crimes, reflecting the belief that people's willingness to discuss such incidents has increased in recent years.

Greater attention to measuring victimizations by someone the respondent knows, including incidents of domestic violence.

Gradual increase in the use of telephone interviews to replace in-person interviews.

Increasing the threshold for series victimizations from three to six; this is consistent with other efforts to help respondents distinguish individual victimizations.

Actual crime counts from the major changes in NCVS procedures have only recently become available, and early results indicate that the redesign has measured a greater number of incidents, especially crimes of violence.

Before taking a look at the victimization rates from the redesigned NCVS, consider the changes in survey screening questions summarized in Table 6-3, adapted from Bachman and Saltzman (1995). You should see that the redesigned NCVS presents much more specific questions and cues, in effect encouraging respondents to think about specific types of incidents. Notice in particular the explicit reference to "forced or unwanted sexual acts" in the redesigned survey; the old NCVS made no direct reference to rape or other sexual assaults, implicitly including them in the general categories of "attack you" and "try to attack you." Redesigned NCVS questions also refer more directly to offenses committed by someone known to the respondent:

■ People often don't think of incidents committed by someone they know. Did you have something stolen from you OR were you attacked or threatened by—

    a. Someone at work or at school—

    b. A neighbor or friend—

    c. A relative or family member—

    d. Any other person you've met or known?

TABLE 6-3
Comparison of Old and Redesigned NCVS Screening Questions

General Screening Question	
Old NCVS	Redesigned NCVS
Was anything stolen from you while you were away from home—for instance, at work, in a theater or restaurant, or while traveling?	Were you attacked or threatened OR did you have something stolen from you— a. At home including the yard or porch b. At or near a friend's or neighbor's home c. At work or school d. In a place such as a shopping mall, laundry room, restaurant, bank, or airport e. While riding in any vehicle f. On the street or in a parking lot g. At such places as a party, theater, gym, picnic area, or while fishing or hunting OR h. Did anyone ATTEMPT to attack or attempt to steal anything belonging to you from any of these places?

Screening Questions for Violent Crimes	
Old NCVS	Redesigned NCVS
Did anyone take something from you by using force, such as by a stickup, mugging, or threat? Did anyone TRY to rob you by using force or threatening to harm you? Did anyone beat you up, attack you, or hit you with something such as a rock or bottle? Were you knifed, shot at, or attacked with some other weapon by anyone at all? Did anyone THREATEN to beat you up or threaten you with a knife, gun, or some other weapon, NOT including telephone threats? Did anyone TRY to attack you in some other way?	Has anyone attacked or threatened you in any of these ways— a. With any weapon such as a gun or knife b. With anything like a baseball bat, frying pan, scissors, or stick c. By something thrown, such as a rock d. Include any grabbing, punching, or kicking e. Any rape, attempted rape, or other type of sexual assault f. Any face-to-face threats OR g. Any attack or threat or use of force by anyone at all? Please mention it even if you were not certain it was a crime. Incidents involving forced or unwanted sexual acts are often difficult to talk about. Have you ever been forced or coerced to engage in unwanted sexual activity by— a. Someone you didn't know before b. A casual acquaintance OR c. Someone you know well?

Source: Adapted from Bachman and Saltzman (1995:8).

Table 6-4 compares estimates of victimization rates from the redesigned NCVS with earlier versions of the survey. Panel A, reproduced from a study examining violence against women (Bachman and Saltzman, 1995), shows rates of violent crime victimization by victim/offender relationship for males and females. Notice that the redesigned survey yields higher rates for all categories of relationship but that the increase tends to be greater for nonstranger offenses. The category "intimate" includes married persons as well as those in a quasi-marital or other intimate relationship. Redesigned survey results indicate that just less than 1 percent (9.3 per thousand) of female respondents reported being the victim of a violent offense by an intimate partner or former partner. Changes from previous waves of the NCVS indicate that efforts to uncover more incidents of violence perpetrated by nonstrangers have been successful.

TABLE 6-4

Comparison of Violent Victimization Rate, Old and Redesigned NCVS

Panel A: Average Annual Rate of Violent Victimizations Per 1,000 Persons		
Victim–Offender Relationship	Female	Male
Old NCVS (1987–1991)		
Intimate	5.4	0.5
Other relative	1.1	0.7
Acquaintance/friend	7.6	13.0
Stranger	5.4	12.2
Redesigned NCVS (1992–1993)		
Intimate	9.3	1.4
Other relative	2.8	1.2
Acquaintance/friend	12.9	17.2
Stranger	7.4	19.0

Source: Bachman and Saltzman (1995:8).

Panel B: Rate of Violent Victimizations Per 1,000 Persons		
	Female	Male
1991 NCVS		
Rape	1.4	0.2
Robbery	3.5	7.8
Aggravated assault	4.4	11.5
Simple assault	13.4	20.9
1994 NCVS		
Rape and sexual assault	3.7	0.2
Robbery	4.1	8.1
Aggravated assault	8.1	15.3
Simple assault	26.6	35.9

Source: Bureau of Justice Statistics, 1992b:22 (1991 rates); Bureau of Justice Statistics, 1996a:4 (1994 rates).

Similarly, Panel B in Table 6-4 compares victimization rates for specific violent offenses, showing that estimates of rape and sexual assault victimization rates for females are about 2.5 times higher in 1994 compared with 1991. Notice, however, that the redesigned NCVS includes sexual assault other than rape, so the estimates are not directly comparable. Males are more likely to be victims of both aggravated and simple assault, but you can see that the redesigned NCVS increased estimates of assault victimization rates more for females than for males. This is consistent with redesign efforts to obtain better estimates of violent offenses.

The redesigned NCVS has produced changes in crime counts for other offenses as well. The nature of these will become better known as researchers analyze the new survey data in more detail. At this point, however, we want to underscore two general points about the redesign and the NCVS in general.

First, what you learn about crime from the NCVS or any other survey depends on what you ask and how you ask it. You should always keep in mind that measures of crime are affected in part by the procedures we use to make those measures. Presenting respondents with rather general questions about being attacked by someone discloses fewer crimes of violence than asking questions that describe specific kinds of violence. Likewise, when we specifically ask respondents to think of acts committed by someone they know, we will uncover more offenses than if we do not include such cues and prompts.

The second point is a consequence of the first: Because of the redesigned NCVS, any effort to compare trends and changes in crime over time must take account of changes in measurement. BJS analysts are attentive to this and caution readers of their reports to be aware of changes in survey methods: "Data based on the redesign are not comparable to data before 1993. . . . A number of fundamental changes were introduced when the survey was redesigned. These changes were phased into the sample over several years" (Bureau of Justice Statistics, 1996a:8).

We emphasize these two points because beginning researchers are often less critical users of data such as the NCVS than are more experienced researchers; after all, the survey is sponsored by the U.S. Department of Justice and conducted by the Census Bureau. Examining Table 6-4 without being aware of survey changes would suggest that violent victimization rates had increased sharply from 1991 to 1994, a conclusion that would be misleading.

Comparing Victim Surveys and Crimes Known to Police

Before moving on to the next section, let's briefly compare the different ways of measuring crime we have discussed so far.

Researchers have devoted special attention to comparing data from the UCR and the NCVS in efforts to determine how the two measures differ and the strengths and weaknesses of each method for measuring crime. In fact, Blumstein, Cohen, and Rosenfeld (1991:237) claim that "criminal justice researchers and policy analysts are fortunate in having two independent data series." An early study by Skogan (1974) recognizes that crime surveys and police data take fundamentally different approaches to measuring crime but that UCR and NCVS counts of robbery and auto theft are moderately related. More recently, Blumstein and associates (1991) report that once appropriate statistical adjustments are made, UCR and NCVS data for robbery and burglary exhibit similar trends from 1972 through 1986.

We mentioned that while the UCR provides only summary measures of aggregate units, the NCVS yields more disaggregated data on individual victims, offenders, and incidents. This means that the NCVS is better suited to studies of individual factors in the types of incidents covered by the survey.

SHR and NIBRS data are incident-based systems and can be used to study individual incidents, victims, and offenders. But the SHR measures one type of crime only, and although NIBRS holds great promise for the future, its limited coverage means that it cannot yet serve as a measure of nationwide incidents known to police. For the present, NIBRS data can be used for only those states that currently participate in the program.

By the way, this feature of NIBRS—its availability from only certain local agencies and states—highlights another characteristic of the NCVS worth emphasizing: It is not possible to use survey data to study victimization at the city, state, or regional level. This is because the National Crime Victimization Survey is just that: a *national* survey. It is designed to represent nationwide levels of crime (subject to the limits we have discussed) but cannot provide estimates of crime for cities, counties, or states.

Despite the limited coverage of NIBRS, incident-based measures have great potential for criminal justice research. Like the NCVS, NIBRS will yield details about individual incidents. Unlike the NCVS, NIBRS data can be examined for specific geographic areas at the state and local level.

Another potential strength of NIBRS is highlighted by comparing it with the NCVS. Despite improvements following the survey's redesign, its sampling plan is still restricted to household residents aged 12 and over. We have discussed the significance of a household-based sample. What kinds of offenses might the NCVS miss by not counting victimizations for individuals younger than 12?

Reaves's analysis of 1991 NIBRS data on robbery and rape in Alabama, North Dakota, and South Carolina provides a clue. About 15 percent of female rape victims in those three states were under age 12; that means 397 rape victims would not have been counted by the NCVS (Reaves, 1993:8). Furthermore, the expanded information available under NIBRS revealed that 43 percent of rape victims under age 12 were assaulted by a family member; an additional 46 percent of the offenders were known to the victim. Only 11 percent of female rape victims under age 12 were raped by strangers.

These figures should make you think of child abuse, or at least child sexual abuse, as an offense type not measured by the NCVS. Of course, child abuse is undercounted by UCR and NIBRS data as well because much child abuse is not reported to police. NIBRS data represent new sources of information about this type of crime and other offenses that affect young victims.

■ SURVEYS OF OFFENDING

Just as survey techniques can measure crime by asking people to describe their experiences as victims, people can also be asked about crimes they may have committed. You might initially be skeptical of this technique: How truthful are people when asked about crimes they may have committed? Your concern is justified. Many people may not wish to disclose illegal behavior to interviewers even if they are assured of confidentiality. Others might deliberately lie to interviewers and exaggerate the number of offenses they have committed.

Self-report surveys, however, are probably the best method for trying to measure certain crimes that are poorly measured by other techniques. Thinking back about the other methods we have discussed—crimes known to police and victim surveys—you should be able to imagine several examples. Crimes such as prostitution and drug abuse are excluded from victim surveys and underestimated by police measures of people arrested for these offenses. Public order crimes and delinquency are other examples. A third class of offenses that might be better counted by self-report surveys are crimes that are rarely reported to police or observed by police. We mentioned shoplifting as one example; drunk driving is another.

Think of it this way. As we said earlier, all crimes require an offender. Not all crimes have clearly identifiable victims who can be interviewed, however, and not all crimes are readily observed by police, victims, or witnesses. If we can't observe the offense and can't interview a victim, what's the next logical step?

There are no nationwide efforts to systematically collect self-report measures of all types of crimes. Instead, periodic surveys yield information either on specific types of crime or on crimes committed by a specific target population. We will consider two ongoing self-report surveys here and then make some comments on the validity and reliability of this method for measuring crime.

National Household Survey on Drug Abuse[2]

Like the NCVS, the National Household Survey on Drug Abuse (NHSDA) is based on a national sample of households. Both surveys are designed to monitor nationwide patterns. Unlike the vic-

timization survey, however, the central purpose of the NHSDA is to obtain self-reports of drug use.

The survey has been conducted since 1971 in various forms, although sampling and questioning procedures have been revised a few times. Persons aged 12 and over who live in households are the target population. In 1995, almost 18,000 individuals responded to questions about their use of illegal drugs, alcohol, and tobacco. Given the long series of the NHSDA, it provides information on trends and changes in drug use among respondents.

Think for a moment about what sorts of questions you would ask to learn about people's experience in using illegal drugs. Among other things, you would probably want to distinguish someone who tried marijuana once (but didn't inhale?) from daily users. The drug use survey does this by including questions to distinguish *lifetime* use (ever used) of different drugs from *current* use (used within the last month) and *heavy* use (used within the last week). You may or may not agree that, for example, use in the last month represents current use, but that is the standard used in regular reports on NHSDA results. That's the operational definition of "current use."

You should be able to recognize two potential sources of measurement problems with the NHSDA as we have briefly described the survey. We already raised the first concern: Do people tell the truth when asked about drug use?

The NHSDA incorporates certain procedures to encourage candid responses from individuals. After obtaining basic demographic information about all household residents, interviewers attempt to administer questions to selected respondents in a private place. Interviewers do not directly ask about drug use. Instead, these questions, and questions about other illegal behaviors, are recorded by the respondent on a self-administered questionnaire. Respondents then place their completed questionnaires, with no identifying information recorded on them, into an envelope that is sealed and mailed to a private organization that processes the self-report data anonymously. In addition, the NHSDA, like the

---

[2]Descriptive information about the National Household Survey on Drug Abuse was obtained from Mieczkowski (1996) and Gfroerer (1996).

NCVS, has instituted recent changes in question format and questionnaire design. The 1994 and 1995 waves of the survey are the first to include these changes, made in an effort to improve the validity of self-report measures.

These procedures have been found to produce better measures of drug use than interviews conducted by telephone. Nevertheless, it is assumed that the NHSDA underreports drug use (Gfroerer, 1996). In fact, the circumstances of the NHSDA interview appear to especially affect reporting by adolescents. Gfroerer (1993) found higher reported rates of drug use by youths from surveys administered in school classrooms compared with surveys administered at home. We will discuss an example of school-based surveys shortly, but let's first briefly consider the second source of concern in using the NHSDA as a measure of drug use.

Recall our earlier comments about how the household sample design of the NCVS could measure only victimizations that affected households or household residents. Commercial establishments, people who live in institutional quarters—military housing, college dormitories, or work-release community corrections centers, for example—and homeless people are not eligible for inclusion in a household sample. By the same token, a household survey on drug use excludes people who do not live in traditional households. Think for a moment about the populations we just mentioned and whether you think they are more or less likely to be current or heavy users of illegal drugs.

In an effort to address this problem, beginning in 1991 the NHSDA surveys took special steps to include residents of college dorms, rooming houses, and homeless shelters. Mieczkowski (1996:361) reports that these changes had negligible effects on estimated drug use. But you might wonder about the *combined* effects of the two sources of concern about self-reports. Would residents of rooming houses, college dorms, and homeless shelters be more or less likely to respond truthfully to questions about illegal drug use?

Monitoring the Future[3]

Our second example is different in a couple of respects: It targets a specific population and it asks sampled respondents a broader variety of questions. Since 1975, the National Institute on Drug Abuse has sponsored an annual survey of high school seniors, *Monitoring the Future: A Continuing Study of the Lifestyles and Values of Youth*, or Monitoring the Future (MTF), for short. As its long name implies, the MTF survey is intended to monitor the behaviors, attitudes, and values of young people. In recent years, researchers and policymakers have become especially interested in drug, alcohol, and tobacco use among youth, and the MTF has been used as something of a sentinel to measure such behaviors.

The MTF actually includes several samples of high school students and others, totaling about 50,000 respondents each year (National Institute on Drug Abuse, 1996). We'll begin by describing the high school sample and then briefly mention others.

Each spring, high schools are sampled within particular geographic areas. In larger high schools, samples of up to 350 individual seniors are selected, while all seniors may participate in smaller schools. Sampled students fill out computer scan sheets in response to batteries of questions that include self-reported use of alcohol, tobacco, and illegal drugs. Respondents also report on involvement in delinquency and certain other illegal acts. In most cases, students record their answers in classrooms during normal school hours, although in some circumstances students complete the questionnaires in larger groups.

The core sample of MTF—surveys of high school seniors—thus provides an annual cross section for measuring drug use and other illegal acts. In addition, the MTF has expanded its samples over the years to include public school

---

[3] Descriptive information about the Monitoring the Future study is drawn primarily from three sources: Johnston, O'Malley, and Bachman (1996); Mieczkowski (1996); and the National Institute on Drug Abuse (1996).

students in eighth and tenth grades (since 1991). A subset of about 2,400 MTF respondents from the high school samples is selected each year to receive a follow-up mail questionnaire. The follow-up samples provide MTF data from college students—those high school seniors who went on to college—as well as adults. Data from the oldest follow-up group were first collected in 1976, so assuming most high school seniors are age 18, respondents in the 1996 follow-up sample could have been up to 38 years old.

Now recall our discussion of the time dimension in Chapter 4. Each year, both MTF and the NHSDA measure drug use for a *cross section* of high school seniors and adults in households, thus providing a snapshot of annual rates of self-reported drug use. Examining annual results from MTF and the NHSDA over time provides a *time series* or trend study that enables researchers and policymakers to detect changes in drug use among high school seniors, college students, and adults. Finally, the follow-up samples of MTF respondents constitute a series of *panel studies* where changes in drug use among individual respondents can be studied over time. Thomas Mieczkowski (1996) presents an excellent discussion of these two surveys and compares self-reported drug use from each series over time.

Since MTF measures for all samples are collected through self-reports, this source of data shares the potential problems we mentioned in connection with the NHSDA. We noted that at least one study (Gfroerer, 1993) suggests that young people self-report drug use more frequently in school settings than in their homes. However, Mieczkowski (1996:378) points out that students are asked to provide their names to survey staff, something that's necessary for later follow-ups but might undermine the truthfulness of their responses.

What about sampling procedures for MTF? In one sense, selecting schools and then students within schools is a sound procedure for sampling high school seniors. But you should be able to think of at least one problem with this approach. Students who are absent on the day the survey is administered are not included and are not eligible for the follow-up sample. We might reasonably expect that students with poor attendance records are absent more often and thus less represented in the sample. And since our interest in the MTF is as a measure of drug use and offending, we might suspect that students with poor attendance records might have higher rates of drug use and offending.

Validity and Reliability of Self-report Measures

This chapter cannot supply the final word on efforts to validate self-report measures. On the one hand, the final word has not yet been written; but on the other hand, a small number of researchers have examined the issue in some detail. In most cases, the latter studies compare self-reported offending to other measures, usually records of offending from law enforcement and juvenile justice agencies. You may recognize this as an example of *convergent validity*, a topic from Chapter 5.

For example, in their study of London delinquents (mentioned in Chapter 5), Donald West and David Farrington (1977:22) compared official criminal records to self-reported delinquent convictions disclosed in interviews with their subjects. Only a small proportion of subjects failed to mention one or more delinquent acts that appeared in criminal records. After further study, West and Farrington concluded that these omissions were due more to memory lapses than to untruthful responses because most inconsistencies between the sources occurred for high-rate delinquents.

In a more recent longitudinal study of a sample of Pittsburgh youths, Farrington and associates (1996) examine convergent validity by again comparing self-reported offending and arrests to official records of arrests and juvenile petitions. Because it is a longitudinal panel study, interviewing the sample at multiple time points, the authors are able to estimate *predictive validity* by comparing self-reported delinquency at one time period to arrests and juvenile petitions at later times. As you might expect, the relationship is imperfect, but the researchers did find that subjects who self-reported higher levels of more serious offenses at time 1 were much more likely to have official arrest or delinquency records at time 2.

We call two additional studies of self-report validity to your attention before summing up this method of measuring crime. Joseph Weis (1986) presents a very thorough discussion of the strengths and weaknesses of self-report and official arrest records as measures of offending. Validity and reliability of self-reports are discussed in unusual detail by David Huizinga and Delbert Elliott (1986) as they draw on data from a long-term panel study. Among other things, Huizinga and Elliott make some important comments about the self-interests of researchers in too readily accepting the validity of whatever measure of crime they happen to be using.

Self-report Surveys Summarized

Researchers and policymakers are best advised to be *critical users* of measures obtained from self-report surveys. We emphasize both "critical" and "users," meaning that self-reports can and should be used to measure offending but that researchers, public officials, and others who use such measures should be aware of their strengths and limitations. For example, since MTF and NHSDA sampling and interviewing procedures have remained relatively constant, the surveys provide reasonably consistent information on trends in drug use or offending over time. These two surveys are better as measures of change than as measures of absolute levels.

Our discussion of these two surveys also highlighted the importance of sampling procedures. We will discuss sampling in detail in later chapters, but now you should realize that it's important to consider how self-report subjects were selected. Samples based on households may not be readily generalized to other populations, and results obtained from high school seniors in class may be different from data obtained from dropouts or chronic truants.

Also consider that alternative measures of offenses such as drug use and delinquency are not readily available. This leaves three alternatives: (1) carefully using imperfect measures, (2) having no measures of certain types of offenses, or (3) developing new measures. Our strong preference is to pursue both the first and third alternatives. Having read Chapter 5 and worked your way through most of this chapter, you are becoming better equipped to carefully interpret measures of all kinds. We now consider some different measures of drug use that have been less widely used in criminal justice research.

■ DRUG SURVEILLANCE SYSTEMS

The challenge of developing reliable and valid measures of such offenses as drug use has prompted researchers and policymakers to search for alternative approaches. We will briefly discuss examples of focused efforts to monitor drug use and its consequences among specialized populations.

Drug Use Forecasting

The National Institute of Justice (NIJ) has conducted the Drug Use Forecasting (DUF) program since 1987. Four times per year, cities that participate in DUF select samples of persons arrested for a variety of offenses. Anonymous interviews and urine specimens are obtained from those who agree to take part in the voluntary study. In 1995, about 225 adult males were selected in each of 23 participating cities; about 100 adult females were also selected in most sites, and samples of juvenile detainees were obtained from 12 cities (National Institute of Justice, 1996a : 11).

The main purpose of DUF is to provide an ongoing assessment of the prevalence of drug use among persons arrested for criminal offenses. Results for 1995 showed that a majority of male and female arrestees in virtually all sites tested positive for one or more illegal drugs; close to 80 percent of men tested positive in Chicago (National Institute of Justice, 1996a : 18).

Annual DUF results are widely distributed by NIJ and have come to be viewed as a rough and ready indicator of drug use among criminal offenders. More important, DUF samples have been collected four times per year since 1987 and can therefore indicate trends in drug use among arrestees. Trends vary by city, but rates of positive tests for any drug have remained fairly high, showing some fluctuation in different cities. Greater changes are exhibited for specific drugs, and these series reveal fluctuations in the use of cocaine, opiates, and methamphetamine.

For our purposes in this chapter, the most interesting aspect of DUF is that it combines urinalysis and self-report measures of drug use. Interviews with arrestees include self-report items, so responses can be compared with urine test results. Unfortunately, few comparisons of these two measures have been made, and researchers reach different conclusions about how well self-reports stand up to urinalysis results. Rosenfeld and Decker (1993) conclude that DUF subjects substantially underreport drug use. Mieczkowski (1990a) reports some correspondence between self-reports and urine tests but argues convincingly that arrestees who may have recently used multiple drugs are not the best persons to verify the truthfulness of self-reports. This quote from the 1995 annual DUF report illustrates this point clearly:

■ At times, obtaining valid self-reported data in a jail or lockup [where interviews are conducted] can be difficult. The sensitivity of the topic, the proximity of jail staff, the confidence arrestees have in the guarantee of anonymity, and the lucidness of respondents all affect the data collection process. (National Institute of Justice, 1996a:9)

Any measure of crime is selective; neither all crimes nor all people are included. In what ways is the DUF program selective as a measure of drug use? From what we have said so far you should see three ways rather clearly. First, DUF operates in only 23 cities. Because participation requires a substantial effort from police departments, we can't assume that participating cities are representative of other cities. Second, and perhaps most important, DUF includes only arrested persons. It's obvious that we cannot generalize from people who are arrested to the population at large. It's less obvious that arrest is a selective process.

Police exercise discretion in deciding whether or not to make an arrest, and their priorities can change over time. Third, DUF interviews and testing are voluntary. It is perhaps surprising that a large proportion of 1995 arrestees agreed to participate: More than 90 percent consented to the interview and more than 80 percent provided a urine specimen (National Institute of Justice, 1996a:11).

DUF is selective in one other important way: Individual cities receive detailed guidelines on selecting participants, but selection procedures are neither random nor regularly monitored. This means that inconsistencies can, and probably do, exist across sites and within sites over time.

Even though DUF exhibits a number of shortcomings as a measure of drug use, it is an imaginative attempt to obtain a different type of measure. Data from DUF can provide information about gross trends in drug use among arrested persons. Additional data collected through the interview may be used to analyze drug use by arrested offense, age, gender, and other variables.

Drug Abuse Warning Network

The DUF system implicitly assumes that at least some drug users will be involved in other offenses. Our next specialized measure assumes that drug use can produce acute health problems that cause users to seek treatment in hospital emergency rooms. The Drug Abuse Warning Network (DAWN) collects emergency medical treatment reports for "drug episodes" from a sample of more than 500 hospitals and about 150 medical examiners nationwide (McCaig and Greenblatt, 1996).

Drug episodes are defined as visits to a hospital emergency room that are produced by or directly related to use of illegal drugs or nonmedical use of legal drugs. Included under this definition are direct effects of drug ingestion (overdoses, other physical or psychic reactions) as well as injuries or deaths where drug intoxication was a contributing factor. Nonfatal episodes are drawn from emergency rooms, while drug-related deaths are recorded by medical examiners. Notice that DAWN is based on units of analysis that are only indirectly linked to criminal offenses. The concept of drug episodes is most relevant for studies of public health, and in fact DAWN was designed as a data system for health surveillance.

Since it was begun in the early 1970s, DAWN affords a comparatively long-term time series that monitors the most serious medical consequences of drug use. Like DUF, DAWN is best suited to measuring trends. For example, learning that the participating hospitals in Baltimore mentioned opiates (heroin or morphine) in 1,667 drug episodes for 1990 is not especially meaningful. Comparing Baltimore to San Francisco, a city with about the same population in 1990, helps a little. San Francisco had 3,954 opiate drug episodes in 1990, which suggests that heroin and morphine presented a greater medical problem in that California city. In 1994, however, DAWN recorded 3,123 opiate drug episodes for San Francisco and 8,882 for Baltimore.[4]

Like DUF, DAWN records include demographic and other information about the individuals whose drug episodes bring them to hospitals and morgues. But the unusual unit of analysis for DAWN means that one individual can account for multiple drug episodes. This makes it difficult to use DAWN data for research where individual people are the unit of analysis.

Mieczkowski (1996:387) points out that DAWN data for a single metropolitan area might serve as indicators of the impact of antidrug programs. For example, examining trends in drug episodes involving teenagers might be used in an evaluation of high school education and prevention programs. Or measures of police cocaine seizures might be compared to changes in cocaine drug emergencies.

Pulse Check

Our discussion of different measures has so far described systematic attempts to count crime and drug use through surveys, tabulations of crime reports, arrests, and emergency room episodes. A recent addition to the battery of systems that

monitor drug problems is completely different. Since 1992, the Office of National Drug Control Policy (ONDCP) has published a quarterly or semiannual report based on qualitative information obtained from selected cities.

Pulse Check reports efforts by researchers to collect information from three sources: ethnographers, local and federal law enforcement officers, and drug treatment service providers (ONDCP, 1996). All sources are in or near the cities for which they provide information. Researchers conduct semistructured interviews by telephone, asking about trends in the availability and use of different types of drugs.

Ethnographers are usually local researchers who have extensive experience in qualitative field methods, a topic we will examine in Chapter 11. The basic premise of ethnographic research is that researchers can learn much about social phenomena by immersing themselves in the field: "The ethnographer, who is fully revealed as a social science researcher, enters the drug user's world to record and describe it" (ONDCP, 1996:3). By the same token, Wright and Decker (1994) studied burglars in the field, Terry Williams (1989) entered the world of cocaine dealers, and Tracey Bush reported on domestic violence in a London public housing project after living there for five years (Hood-Williams and Bush, 1995). Other criminal justice researchers have studied other dimensions of crime and criminal justice agencies through ethnographic research.

Semistructured telephone interviews are also conducted with police officers who are active in drug enforcement. You may realize that police know quite a bit about what goes on in the streets, knowledge that is not reflected in crime or arrest reports. Because drug enforcement requires a great deal of information gathering, police who work on special drug squads or task forces have considerable qualitative information about the drug scene in their jurisdiction.

By the same token, drug treatment professionals have regular contact with drug users and former users. They are in a position to learn about new drugs on the street, the strength or purity of

---

[4]Data from *Advance Report Number 17.* Supporting tables available at: ftp://ftp.samhsa.gov/pub/dawn/. See McCaig and Greenblatt (1996).

TABLE 6-5
Pulse Check: Heroin

	Incidence	Who's using?	Change in users	Price and purity	Emerging drugs
Ethnographers					
Washington, D.C.	Stable	Wide range: teens to aged 50s; all ethnicities	More young users; more women	$5–$10/bag; high purity	Inhalants, LSD, clonidine
Miami	Up	Older users	Increase in deaths due to use	$10/bag; low purity (15%), but improving	Rohypnol, ketamine
Police					
Washington, D.C.	Up	Primarily aged 25–40; club-goers	Younger; more middle and upper class	$25–$40/bag; 14–90% pure	PCP, rohypnol, methamphetamine
Miami	Stable	Traditional older users	None	$125,000/kilo; 90% wholesale, 2–4% retail	Rohypnol

Source: Adapted from Office of National Drug Control Policy (1996, Tables 1 and 2).

different drugs, and the emergence or decline of particular dealing networks.

Table 6-5 gives you an idea of what sort of information is available from *Pulse Check*. Ethnographers and police are asked similar types of questions about drug users, sellers, prices, and so on. Table 6-5 shows how these two sources of qualitative information responded to questions about heroin in two cities. You will see some differences in ratings by the two types of observers in each city, but notice the general agreement on user profiles.

Information from treatment providers cannot be compared with police and ethnographer sources quite so easily. Treatment provider responses are organized by region, not by individual city, and records on treatment clients are tabulated by age, gender, race, and type of drug use.

■ *MEASURING CRIME FOR SPECIFIC PURPOSES*

Each of the crime measures discussed so far can be used for a variety of research purposes—exploration, description, explanation, and applied research. However, each has the primary purpose of providing some type of crime count—crimes known to police, victimizations of households and

people who live in households, self-reported drug use and other offending, drug use among arrestees and emergency room patients, or qualitative assessments of drug use and availability in specific urban areas. Such measures are useful for criminal justice and public health professionals. Researchers have also made extensive use of data from standard series such as the UCR, SHR, and NCVS.

Often, however, none of these regular series of crime measures meets the needs of researchers, public officials, or others who are looking for specialized information about crime. Part 3 of this book is devoted entirely to methods of making measurements and collecting data. At this point, we want to call your attention to examples of crime measures developed for specific research and policy purposes.

Crime Surveys   We have seen that victim surveys have certain advantages over other measures of crime. Surveys are especially useful for learning about crimes not reported to police. Because the NCVS is a national survey, one drawback is that it cannot be used to estimate victimizations for individual cities or states. Because of their potential strengths, victim surveys are more often being conducted in specific states, cities, or even neighborhoods. Sometimes local surveys are conducted by researchers, but survey methods are also used by local governments, police departments, and even community organizations. Cities or counties that have shifted to community policing often conduct victim surveys to learn more about crime problems that affect people in particular areas.

For example, the Kansas City, Missouri, Police Department conducts community safety surveys before implementing new programs in a specific area. Questions ask about crime problems, victimization experience, and feelings of neighborhood safety. After neighborhood initiatives have been in effect for approximately one year, police conduct another survey to assess change. Similarly, certain community groups in Kansas City periodically survey neighborhood residents about local crime problems. Results are shared with police officers assigned to the community and used to direct targeted anticrime initiatives.

Such surveys are rarely up to the standards required by researchers, or those that guide such efforts as the NCVS. They usually do not employ probability samples (we'll discuss these in Chapter 9), and questionnaires are sometimes casual affairs at best. Nevertheless, local crime surveys are useful tools for public officials and citizens in many communities. In recent years, a variety of publications have been issued to guide such survey applications. See the book by John Eck and Nancy LaVigne (1994) and an excellent handbook by the Bureau of Justice Assistance (1993) for examples of publications prepared for use by law enforcement agencies.

What about self-report surveys? The Kansas City-based Kauffman Foundation sponsors an annual survey of students in local high schools that is modeled after the MTF surveys. Information about drug and alcohol use by Kansas City youths helps local officials plan and evaluate programs to reduce substance abuse.

Incident-based Crime Records   We mentioned earlier that larger jurisdictions have been slow to convert from UCR reporting to the NIBRS system, largely because police departments in large cities have tailored data management systems to their own particular needs. Advances in geographic information systems coupled with computer software to produce maps of crime patterns have spurred the development of very sophisti-

cated incident-based crime data systems in some agencies.

Chicago offers one of the best examples among U.S. cities. Under the leadership of researchers at the Illinois Criminal Justice Information Authority and Loyola University of Chicago, detailed information about crimes reported to police can be linked to a variety of other information to reveal space-based patterns of crime (C. Block, 1995; R. Block, 1995). Chicago's system has been developed to be powerful, timely (updated daily), and easy to use. Community police officers in the city regularly produce maps of crime patterns for their own use and to share with neighborhood residents. Researchers have also used these data to examine, for example, the clustering of violent crime around taverns and liquor stores (Block and Block, 1995).

Cities and other jurisdictions vary in the quality of their records systems, but many departments are making rapid advances. In Chapter 12 we will discuss the availability and suitability of locally maintained crime records for research purposes. For now, keep in mind that local measures of crimes known to police may be more current, complete, and detailed than measures submitted to the FBI under its UCR, SHR, or NIBRS data series.

Observing Crime   We have mentioned that police learn about certain types of crime primarily through observation. Drug use and sales, prostitution, public order offenses, and drunk driving are examples. Researchers may face situations where they need to make independent observations of crime.

For example, we have pointed out that shoplifting is poorly measured by police records. Victim surveys could reveal some instances of shoplifting, but only if we sampled shops, and then we would learn about only those incidents detected by shop staff. Self-report surveys could tell us something about *shoplifters,* but it would be difficult to use this method to measure *shoplifting incidents.* Terry Baumer and Dennis Rosenbaum (1982) conducted systematic observations of a large department store in Chicago for descriptive and applied purposes. Using ingenious methods we will discuss in Chapter 11, they sought to estimate the frequency of shoplifting and to evaluate the effectiveness of different store security measures.

What about assault? Again, police measure assaults that are reported to them, usually by victims or witnesses. The NCVS was redesigned in part to get better counts of assault, but for some research purposes, independent observations may yield better measures.

Homel and associates (1992, 1994) were interested in the links between drinking and violence in bars and nightclubs. Specifically, they sought to learn what sorts of physical features and situations in bars tended to either discourage or facilitate violence. Their explanatory study required selecting samples of public drinking establishments in Sydney, Australia, and dispatching pairs of observers to each site. Observers recorded information about violent incidents they witnessed, together with details about each bar's physical layout, entertainment, and procedures for controlling access and regulating conduct. Researchers were able to make general explanatory statements about how the physical environment and management practices were related to violence.

Police normally learn about drug use or sales only if they witness the acts. Constraints on the ability of police to make such observations are often cited as obstacles to the enforcement of drug laws. In many communities, however, neighborhood organizations supplement law enforcement through patrols and targeted surveillance of drug activity in specific neighborhoods. If such citizen patrols witness suspected drug activity, they inform police, community prosecutors, or other justice officials who may launch further investigations. Neighborhood organizations in Kansas City, Albuquerque, Philadelphia, and many other cities use directed observations in this way.

These examples of directed observation have three common characteristics. First, each has a fairly specific research or policy purpose. Baumer and Rosenbaum wanted to obtain estimates of shoplifting frequency and to evaluate the effects of certain security measures; Homel and associ-

ates wished to learn more about the association between public drinking and violence; members of community organizations participate in neighborhood surveillance to take action against local drug and other problems. Second, the three examples focus on relatively small areas—a single department store, a sample of bars in Sydney, or a specific neighborhood. Finally, the expected density of incidents made observation an appropriate way to measure crime. Shoplifting happens in shops, and large department stores offer opportunities to observe many incidents; it's well known that public violence is relatively common in bars, and police records can be used to select bars with a history of violence; finally, citizen patrols and neighborhood surveillance programs are launched *because* residents are troubled by local drug problems.

■ *MEASURING CRIME: SUMMARY*

Table 6-6 summarizes some of what we have considered in this chapter by comparing the different measures of crime. Each method has its own strengths and weaknesses. The UCR and SHR provide the best counts for murder and crimes where the victim is either a business or a commercial establishment. Crimes against persons or households that are not reported to police are best counted by the NCVS. Usually these are less serious crimes, many of them UCR Part II incidents that are counted only if a suspect is arrested. Recent changes in NCVS procedures have increased the counts of sexual assault and other violent victimizations. Compared with the UCR, NIBRS potentially adds much greater detail to a broader range of offenses. NIBRS complements the NCVS by including disaggregated incident-based reports for state and local areas, and recording detailed information on crimes against children under age 12.

Self-report surveys are best at measuring crimes that do not have readily identifiable victims and those that are less often observed by or reported to police. The two self-report surveys

TABLE 6-6
Summary of Measures of Crime

	Units	Target population	Crime coverage	Best count for
Known to Police				
UCR	Aggregate: reporting agency	All law enforcement agencies; 98% reporting	Limited number of reported and recorded crimes	Commercial and business victims
SHR	Incident	All law enforcement agencies; 98% reporting	Homicides only	Homicides
NIBRS	Incident	All law enforcement agencies; limited reporting	Extensive	Details on local incidents; victims under age 12
Surveys				
NCVS	Victimization, individuals, and households	Individuals in households	Household and personal crimes	Household and personal crimes not reported to police
NHSDA	Individual respondent, offender	Individuals in households	Drug use	Drug use by adults in households
MTF	Individual respondent, offender	High school seniors; follow-up on sample	Substance use, delinquency, offending	Drug use by high school seniors
Sentinel				
DUF	Arrested offenders	Quarterly samples of arrestees, 23 cities	Drug use	Changes in drug use among arrestees
DAWN	Medical emergency: drug episodes	National sample of hospitals	Drug-related medical emergencies	Changes in acute drug use problems
Pulse Check	Aggregate: ethnographer, police, treatment report	Selected cities (number varies)	Qualitative assessments of drug use, price, user profiles	Comparative profile of drug use, price, use patterns

listed in Table 6-6 sample different populations and use different interview procedures.

Sentinel measures target more narrowly defined populations for the purposes of monitoring and are best seen as measures of change. The two quantitative series in Table 6-6 measure drug use in the context of medical and legal crises, while the qualitative *Pulse Check* depends on judgments from street-level experts.

Be aware that Table 6-6 and our discussions throughout this chapter include only a partial listing of crime measures used by researchers and public officials. Each local and state law enforcement agency maintains its own records, which often provide the best measures for research in specific geographic areas. Finally, a specific research purpose may require collecting independent measures of crime.

Don't forget that all crime measures are selective, so you must understand the selection process. Despite their various flaws, the measures of crime available to you can serve many research purposes. You are best advised to be a critical and careful user of whatever measure of crime best suits your research purpose.

■ MAIN POINTS

- Crime is a fundamental concept in criminal justice research. Different approaches to measuring crime illustrate general principles of conceptualization, operationalization, and measurement.
- Before using any measure of crime, you should understand what types of offenses it does and does not include.
- Different measures of crime are based on different units of analysis. Uniform crime reports are summary measures that report totals for

individual agencies. Other measures use of-fenders, victims, incidents, or offenses as the units of analysis.

- Crime data are collected for one or more general purposes: monitoring, agency accountability, and research.

- Crimes known to police have been the most widely used measures. UCR data are available for most of the 20th century; more detailed information about homicides was added to the UCR in 1961. Most recently, the FBI has developed an incident-based reporting system that is gradually being adopted.

- Surveys of victims reveal information about crimes that are not reported to police. The NCVS includes very detailed information about personal and household incidents but does not count crimes against businesses or individual victims under age 12. Although the NCVS is a nationally representative measure, it cannot estimate victimizations for state or local areas.

- Self-report surveys were developed to measure crimes with unclear victims that are less often detected by police. Two surveys estimate drug use among high school seniors and adults.

- Self-report surveys do not measure all drug use because of incomplete reporting by respondents and procedures for selecting survey respondents.

- DUF and DAWN provide measures of drug use among special populations but are best suited to monitoring change in drug use. A qualitative monitoring system reflects the perceptions and judgments of selected experts in specific cities.

- We have many different measures of crime because each measure is imperfect. Each measure has its strengths and weaknesses.

■ REVIEW QUESTIONS AND EXERCISES

1. Los Angeles police consider a murder to be gang-related if either the victim or the of-fender is known to be a gang member, whereas Chicago police record a murder as gang-related only if the killing is directly related to gang activities (Spergel, 1990). Describe how these different operational definitions illustrate general points about measuring crime discussed in this chapter.

2. How would you measure crime if you wanted to evaluate a community policing program that encourages neighborhood residents to report incidents to police?

3. A very high proportion of auto thefts and household burglaries of owner-occupied homes are reported to police. Why do you think that is true?

4. Published reports and actual data from various measures of crime we have discussed are increasingly available on the World Wide Web. For example, you can find 1995 DAWN reports at the following address, enclosed in square brackets: [http://www.health.org.pubs/96DAWN/]. Check this site, or some other site of interest to you, and download or record data on at least two offenses (or indicators of two drugs) in two cities over a five-year period. Bring your data to class and discuss what you have found.

■ ADDITIONAL READINGS

Blumstein, Alfred, Cohen, Jacqueline, and Rosenfeld, Richard, "Trend and Deviation in Crime Rates: A Comparison of UCR and NCS Data for Burglary and Robbery," *Criminology*, Vol. 29 (1991), pp. 237–63. An excellent discussion of how the UCR and NCVS yield similar counts for these two offenses after taking account of the different designs of the two measuring systems.

Huizinga, David, and Elliott, Delbert S., "Reassessing the Reliability and Validity of Self-report Delinquency Measures," *Journal of Quantitative Criminology*, Vol. 2, no. 4 (1986), pp. 293–327; and Weis, Joseph G., "Issues in the Measurement of Criminal Careers," Chap. 1, In Alfred Blumstein, Jacqueline Cohen, Jeffrey A. Roth, and Christy A. Visher (eds.), *Criminal Careers and "Career Criminals,"* Vol. 2 (Washington, DC: National Academy Press, 1986), pp. 1–51. These are very thorough discussions of the advantages and disadvantages of self-reports and police records. Each addresses important validity and reliability issues.

MacKenzie, Doris L., Baunach, P. J., and Roberg, Roy R. (eds.), *Measuring Crime: Large-Scale, Long-Range Efforts* (Albany, NY: State University of New York Press, 1990); and O'Brien, Robert M., *Crime and Victimization Data* (Newbury Park, CA: Sage, 1985). Together, these two books cover many issues in the measurement of crime and other central concepts. O'Brien's book is the better treatment of reliability and validity. Selections in the MacKenzie, Baunach, and Roberg volume describe the NCVS, UCR, and standard measures of incarcerated persons, together with ongoing revisions of these measures.

Mieczkowski, Thomas M., "The Prevalence of Drug Use in the United States." In Michael Tonry (ed.), *Crime and Justice: An Annual Review of Research* (Chicago: University of Chicago Press, 1996), pp. 349–414. A very good source of information about measures of drug use. Mieczkowski discusses self-report surveys, DAWN, and DUF and compares results from each series.

Snyder, Howard N., and Sickmund, Melissa, *Juvenile Offenders and Victims: A National Report* (Washington, DC: Office of Juvenile Justice and Delinquency Prevention, 1995). This report presents extensive descriptive information on juvenile crime and is unusual in two respects. It combines crime measures from several sources, and it is one of the few recent reports to include information from NIBRS. Examining this report illustrates why it is important and necessary to use multiple measures of crime.

7 Experimental and Quasi-experimental Designs

What You'll Learn in This Chapter

Here you'll learn the experimental approach to social science research. We'll examine a wide variety of experimental and other designs available to criminal justice researchers.

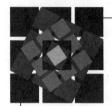

INTRODUCTION

TOPICS APPROPRIATE TO EXPERIMENTS

THE CLASSICAL EXPERIMENT
Independent and Dependent Variables
Pretesting and Posttesting
Experimental and Control Groups
Double-Blind Experiment
Selecting Subjects
Randomization

EXPERIMENTS AND CAUSAL INFERENCE
Experiments and Threats to Validity
Threats to Internal Validity
Ruling Out Threats to Internal Validity
Generalizability
Threats to Construct Validity
Threats to External Validity
Threats to Statistical Conclusion Validity

VARIATIONS IN THE CLASSICAL EXPERIMENTAL DESIGN

QUASI-EXPERIMENTAL DESIGNS
Nonequivalent-Groups Designs
Cohort Designs
Time-Series Designs
Variations in Time-Series Designs
Gun Control, Homicide, and Suicide

EXPERIMENTAL AND QUASI-EXPERIMENTAL DESIGNS SUMMARIZED

MAIN POINTS

REVIEW QUESTIONS AND EXERCISES

ADDITIONAL READINGS

■ *INTRODUCTION*

This chapter focuses more closely on actual research designs. Chapter 4 introduced the basic principles and steps we will cover here in some detail. Recall that research design in the most general sense involves planning a strategy for finding out something. Here our attention turns to specific strategies for structuring a research project.

We'll first discuss the *experiment* as a mode of scientific observation in criminal justice research. Abraham Kaplan (1964:144) describes experimentation as "a process of observation, to be carried out in a situation expressly brought about for that purpose." At base, experiments involve (1) taking action and (2) observing the consequences of that action. Social scientific researchers typically select a group of subjects, do something to them, and observe the effect of what was done. In this chapter, we'll examine both the logic and the various techniques involved in criminal justice experiments.

It is worth noting at the outset that experiments are often used in nonscientific human inquiry as well. We experiment copiously in our attempt to develop a more generalized understanding about the world we live in. Many adult skills are learned through experimentation: riding a bicycle, driving a car, swimming, and so forth. Students discover how much studying is required for academic success through experimentation. Professors learn how much preparation is required for successful lectures through experimentation. This chapter will discuss some ways in which experiments are used to develop generalized understandings in criminal justice. We'll see that, like other methods available to the criminal justice researcher, experiments and other designs have their own special strengths and weaknesses.

■ *TOPICS APPROPRIATE TO EXPERIMENTS*

Experiments are especially well suited to research projects that involve relatively well-defined concepts and propositions. A further requirement is being able to control the conditions under which research is conducted. The traditional model of science, discussed at length in Chapter 2, and the experimental model are closely related.

Experimentation, then, is especially appropriate for hypothesis testing. It is better suited to explanation and evaluation than to descriptive purposes. Let's assume, for example, that we are interested in studying alcohol abuse among college students and in discovering ways to reduce it. We might hypothesize that acquiring an understanding about the health *consequences* of binge drinking and long-term alcohol use will have the effect of reducing alcohol abuse. We can test this hypothesis experimentally. To begin, we might ask a group of experimental subjects how much beer, wine, or spirits they drank on the previous day and how frequently, in an average week, they consume alcohol for the specific purpose of getting drunk. Next, we would show these subjects a video depicting the various physiological effects of chronic drinking and binge drinking. Finally—say, one month later—we would again ask the subjects about their use of alcohol in the previous week to determine whether watching the video has actually reduced alcohol use.

Because experiments are best suited for hypothesis testing, they may also be appropriate in the study of criminal justice policy. In Chapter 2, we discussed the logical similarity between hypotheses and criminal justice policies, noting that evaluation research is conceptually equivalent to testing hypotheses. The experimental model therefore can be a useful design for evaluating criminal justice policy.

You might typically think of experiments being conducted in laboratories under carefully controlled conditions. Although this may be true in the natural sciences, few social scientific experiments can be staged in laboratory settings. The most notable exception to this occurs in the discipline of psychology, where laboratory experiments are common. Criminal justice experiments are almost always conducted in field settings outside the laboratory.

■ *THE CLASSICAL EXPERIMENT*

Like much of the vocabulary of research, the word *experiment* has acquired both a general and a specialized meaning. So far, we have referred to the general use, defined by Farrington, Ohlin, and Wilson (1986:65) as "a systematic attempt to test a causal hypothesis about the effect of variations in one factor (the independent variable) on another (the dependent variable). . . . The defining feature of an experiment lies in the control of the independent variable by the experimenter." In a narrower sense, the term *experiment* refers to a specific way of structuring research, usually called the *classical experiment*. This section will present the requirements and components of the classical experiment. Later in the chapter, we will turn to designs that can be used when some of the requirements for classical experiments cannot be met.

The most conventional type of experiment, in the natural as well as the social sciences, involves three major pairs of components: (1) independent and dependent variables, (2) pretesting and posttesting, and (3) experimental and control groups. We will now deal with each of those components and the way they are put together in the execution of an experiment.

Independent and Dependent Variables

Essentially, an experiment examines the effect of an **independent variable** on a **dependent variable.** Typically, the independent variable takes the form of an experimental stimulus, which is either present or absent—that is, a *dichotomous* variable, having two attributes. (That need not be the case, however, as later sections of this chapter will indicate.) In the example concerning alcohol abuse, how often subjects used alcohol is the dependent variable, and exposure to a video about alcohol's effects is the independent variable. The researcher's hypothesis suggests that alcohol use depends, in part, on understanding its physiological and health effects. The purpose of the experiment is to test the validity of this hypothesis.

The independent and dependent variables appropriate to experimentation are nearly limitless.

It should be noted, moreover, that a given variable might serve as an independent variable in one experiment and as a dependent variable in another. For example, alcohol abuse is the dependent variable in our example, but it might be the independent variable in an experiment that examines the effect of alcohol abuse on academic performance.

In the terms of our earlier discussion of cause and effect, the independent variable is the cause and the dependent variable is the effect. Thus, we might say that watching the video *causes* a change in alcohol use or that reduced alcohol use is an *effect* of watching the video.

It is essential that both independent and dependent variables be operationally defined for the purposes of experimentation. Such operational definitions might involve a variety of observation methods. Responses to a questionnaire, for example, might be the basis for defining self-reported alcohol use on the previous day. Alternatively, alcohol use by subjects could be measured with Breathalyzer or blood alcohol tests.

Conventionally, in the experimental model, the dependent and independent variables must be operationally defined before the experiment begins. However, as we will see in connection with survey research and other methods, it is sometimes appropriate to first make a wide variety of observations during data collection and then determine the most useful operational definitions of variables during later analyses. Ultimately, however, experimentation requires specific and standardized measurements and observations.

Pretesting and Posttesting

In the simplest experimental design, subjects are measured in terms of a dependent variable (pretested), exposed to a stimulus that represents an independent variable, and then remeasured in terms of the dependent variable (posttested). Differences noted between the first and second measurements on the dependent variable are then attributed to the influence of the independent variable.

In the example of alcohol use, we would begin by pretesting the extent of alcohol use among our

FIGURE 7-1
Diagram of Basic Experimental Design

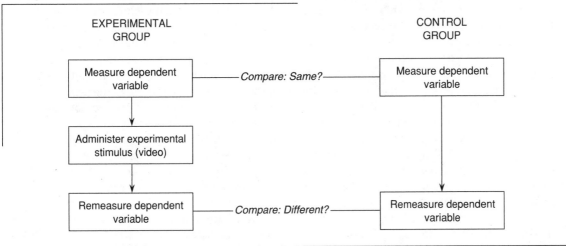

experimental subjects. Using a questionnaire, we could measure the extent of alcohol use reported by each individual subject and the average level of alcohol use for the whole group. After showing subjects the video that described the effects of alcohol, we could administer the same questionnaire again. Responses given in this posttest would permit us to measure the later extent of alcohol use by each subject and the average level of alcohol use of the group as a whole. If we discovered a lower level of alcohol use on the second administration of the questionnaire, we might conclude that the video had indeed reduced the use of alcohol among the subjects.

In the experimental examination of behaviors such as alcohol use, we face a special practical problem relating to validity. As you may have imagined, the subjects might respond differently to the questionnaires the second time, even if their level of drinking remained unchanged. During the first administration of the questionnaire, the subjects may have been unaware of its purpose. By the time of the second measurement, they might have figured out the purpose of the experiment, become sensitized to the questions about drinking, and changed their answers. Thus, the video would seem to have reduced alcohol abuse, although, in fact, it had not.

This is an example of a more general problem that plagues many forms of criminal justice research. The very act of studying something may change it. The techniques for dealing with this problem in the context of experimentation will be discussed in various places throughout the chapter.

Experimental and Control Groups

The foremost way to offset the effects of the experiment itself is to use a **control group.** Laboratory experiments seldom, if ever, involve only the observation of an experimental group to which a stimulus has been administered. The researchers also observe a control group to which the experimental stimulus has not been administered.

In the example of alcohol abuse, two groups of subjects might be examined. To begin, each group is administered a questionnaire designed to measure their alcohol use in general and binge drinking in particular. Then only one of the groups—the experimental group—is shown the video. Later, the researcher administers a posttest of alcohol use to both groups. Figure 7-1 illustrates this basic experimental design.

Using a control group allows the researcher to control for the effects of the experiment itself. If participation in the experiment were to lead the subjects to report less alcohol use, that should occur in both experimental and control groups. If the overall level of drinking exhibited by the control group decreases between the pretest and posttest as much as for the experimental group, then the apparent reduction in alcohol use must be a function of the experiment or of some external factor rather than a function of watching the video specifically. If, on the other hand, drinking decreases only in the experimental group, then the reduction would seem to be a consequence of exposure to the video (because that's the only difference between the two groups). Or, alternatively, if drinking decreases more in the experimental group than in the control group, then that, too, is grounds for assuming that watching the video reduced alcohol use.

The need for control groups in social research became clear in a series of employee satisfaction studies conducted by F. J. Roethlisberger and W. J. Dickson (1939) in the late 1920s and early 1930s. They studied working conditions in the telephone "bank wiring room" of the Western Electric Works in Chicago, attempting to discover what changes in working conditions would improve employee satisfaction and productivity.

To the researchers' great satisfaction, they discovered that making working conditions better consistently increased satisfaction and productivity. When the workroom was brightened by better lighting, for example, productivity went up. Lighting was further improved, and productivity went up again. To substantiate their scientific conclusion, the researchers then dimmed the lights: *Productivity again improved!*

It became evident then that the wiring room workers were responding more to the attention given them by the researchers than to improved working conditions. As a result of this phenomenon, often called the *Hawthorne effect*, social researchers have become more sensitive to and cautious about the possible effects of experiments themselves. The use of a proper control group—studied intensively without any of the working conditions changed otherwise—would have found this effect in the wiring room study.

The need for control groups in experimentation has been most evident in medical research. Time and again, patients who participate in medical experiments have appeared to improve, and it has been unclear how much of the improvement has come from the experimental treatment and how much from the experiment. Now, in testing the effects of new drugs, medical researchers frequently administer a placebo (for example, sugar pills) to a control group. Thus, the control-group patients believe they, like the experimental group, are receiving an experimental drug. Often they improve. If the new drug is effective, however, those who receive that drug will improve more than those who received the placebo.

In criminal justice experiments, control groups are important as a guard not only against the effects of the experiments themselves but also against the effects of events that may occur outside the laboratory during the course of experiments. Suppose that the alcohol use experiment was being conducted on your campus, and at that time a popular athlete was hospitalized for acute alcohol poisoning after drinking a liter of rum. This event might shock the experimental subjects and thereby decrease their reported drinking. Because such an effect should happen about equally for members of the control and experimental groups, lesser levels of reported alcohol use in the experimental group than in the control group would again demonstrate the impact of the experimental stimulus: watching the video that describes the health effects of alcohol abuse.

Sometimes an experimental design requires more than one experimental or control group. In the case of the alcohol video, for example, you might also want to examine the impact of participating in group discussions about why college students drink alcohol, with the intent of demonstrating that peer pressure may promote drinking by people who would otherwise abstain. You might have one group see the video and participate in the group discussions; another group would only see the video; still another group would only participate in group discussions; and the control group would do neither. With this kind of design, you could determine the impact of each stimulus separately, as well as their combined effect.

Double-Blind Experiment

Mention was made earlier of the problem in medical experimentation of patients improving when they think they are receiving a new drug; thus, it is often necessary to administer a placebo to a control group.

Sometimes experimenters have this same tendency to prejudge results. In medical research, the experimenters may be more likely to "observe" improvements among patients who receive the experimental drug than among those receiving the placebo. (That would be most likely, perhaps, for the researcher who developed the drug.) A *double-blind experiment* eliminates the possibility because neither the subjects nor the experimenters know which is the experimental group and which is the control. In medical experiments, those researchers who are responsible for administering the drug and for noting improvements are not told which subjects receive the drug and which receive the placebo. Conversely, the researcher who knows which subjects are in which group is not responsible for administering the experiment.

A good example of a double-blind experiment is the study of roadside sobriety checkpoints by Voas, Rhodenizer, and Lynn (1985). The researchers sought to evaluate a training program designed to help police officers decide which drivers stopped at roadside checkpoints should be asked to take Breathalyzer tests. Asking sober drivers to take a Breathalyzer test wastes time and money, not to mention annoying innocent people. On the other hand, failing to screen drunk drivers defeats the purpose of the checkpoint program.

In the experiment to evaluate this program, subjects were given varying doses of alcohol (or no alcohol) mixed with grapefruit juice to mask the taste so that they could not know how much alcohol (if any) they had been given. Subjects were then instructed to drive down a road (closed to other traffic for the purpose of this experi-

ment), where they met the police roadblock. Some police had received the training course (the experimental group), while others had not (the control group). Neither the experimental nor the control group, nor researchers at the checkpoint, knew which drivers had been given alcohol and which had not until after the experiment. This double-blind experiment was therefore able to test the effects of a training program without being contaminated by the prejudgments of police officers or researchers.

In social scientific experiments, as in medical experiments, the danger of experimenter bias is further reduced to the extent that the operational definitions of the dependent variables are clear and precise. Thus, researchers are less likely to unconsciously bias their interpretation of a blood alcohol test than they are to unconsciously bias their subjective assessment of how intoxicated a driver is. Since the purpose of the experiment described above was to evaluate subjective assessments, the double-blind procedure provided an appropriate safeguard.

Selecting Subjects

Before beginning an experiment, you must make two basic decisions about who will participate. First, you must decide on the target population— the group to which the results of your experiment will apply. If your experiment is designed to determine whether restitution is more effective than probation in reducing recidivism, your target population is some group of persons who are convicted of crimes. In our hypothetical experiment about the effects of watching a video on the health consequences of alcohol abuse, your target population might be college students.

Selecting a target population is a fundamental step in conceptualizing and designing a research project. Chapter 9 will describe various ways of representing a target population through sampling. At this point, you should simply recognize that deciding to whom or to what your research will apply is an essential first step.

The second decision is how particular members of the target population will be selected for your experiment. In most cases, the methods used to select subjects must meet the scientific norm of generalizability; it should be possible to generalize from the subjects actually studied to the population those subjects represent.

Aside from the question of generalizability, the cardinal rule of subject selection and experimentation is the comparability of experimental and control groups. Ideally, the control group represents what the experimental group would have been like if it had not been exposed to the experimental stimulus. It is essential, therefore, that experimental and control groups be as similar as possible.

Randomization

Having recruited, by whatever means, a group of subjects, the experimenter randomly assigns those subjects to either the experimental or the control group. That might be accomplished by numbering all the subjects serially and selecting numbers by means of a random-number table, or the experimenter might assign the odd-numbered subjects to the experimental group and the even-numbered subjects to the control group.

Randomization is a central feature of the classical experiment. The most important characteristic of randomization is that it produces experimental and control groups that are *equivalent.* Put another way, randomization reduces possible sources of systematic bias in assigning subjects to groups. The basic principle is simple: If subjects are assigned to experimental and control groups through a random process, such as flipping a coin, the assignment process is said to be *unbiased* and the resultant groups are equivalent.

Although the rationale underlying this principle is a bit complex, understanding how randomization produces equivalent groups is a key point. David Farrington and associates (1986:66) compare randomization in criminal justice research to laboratory controls in the natural sciences: "The control of extraneous variables by randomization is similar to the control of extraneous variables in the physical sciences by holding physical conditions (e.g., temperature, pressure) constant. Randomization insures that the average unit in [the] treatment group is approximately equivalent to the average unit in another [group] before the treatment is applied." To put it another way, you've surely heard the expression, "All other things being equal." Randomization makes it possible to assume that all other things *are* equal.

■ EXPERIMENTS AND CAUSAL INFERENCE

The central features of the classical experiment are independent and dependent variables, pretesting and posttesting, and experimental and control groups created through random assignment. Think of these features as building blocks of a research design to demonstrate a cause-and-effect relationship. This point will become clearer when you compare the criteria for causality, discussed in Chapter 3, to the features of the classical experiment (see Figure 7-2).

FIGURE 7-2
Another Look at the Classical Experiment

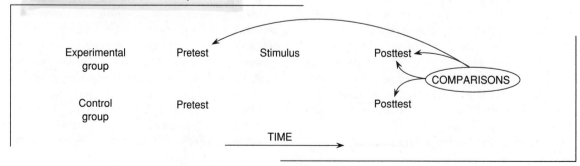

The experimental design ensures that the *cause precedes the effect in time* by taking posttest measurements of the dependent variable after introducing the experimental stimulus. The second criterion for causation, an *empirical correlation between the cause-and-effect variables,* is determined by comparing the pretest (where the experimental stimulus is not present) to the posttest for the experimental group (after the experimental stimulus is administered). A change from pretest to posttest measures demonstrates correlation.

The final requirement is to show that the *observed correlation between cause and effect is not due to the influence of some third variable.* This is satisfied in two ways. First, compare the posttest measures for the experimental group (stimulus present) and control group (stimulus not present). If the observed correlation between the stimulus and the dependent variable is due to some other factor, then the two posttest scores will be similar. Second, random assignment ensures that the experimental and control groups are equivalent and that they will not differ on some other variable that could account for the empirical correlation between cause and effect.

Experiments and Threats to Validity

The classical experiment is designed to satisfy the three requirements for demonstrating cause-and-effect relationships. But what about threats to the validity of causal inference discussed in Chapter 3? Now we want to review those threats, consider each in more detail, and describe how the classical experiment reduces many of them. A book by Campbell and Stanley (1966) is the most frequently cited authority on validity threats. For a fuller discussion, on which we draw heavily, see the book by Cook and Campbell (1979). We will present these threats in a slightly different order, beginning with threats to internal validity.

Threats to Internal Validity

The problem of internal invalidity refers to the possibility that the conclusions drawn from experimental results may not accurately reflect what has gone on in the experiment itself. As we stated in Chapter 3, conclusions about cause and effect may be biased in some systematic way. Campbell and Stanley (1966:5–6) and Cook and Campbell (1979:51–55) point to several sources of the problem.

1. *History.* Historical events may occur during the course of the experiment that will confound the experimental results. The hospitalization of a popular athlete for acute alcohol poisoning during an experiment on reducing alcohol use is an example.

2. *Maturation.* People are continually growing and changing, whether in an experiment or not, and those changes affect the results of the experiment. In a long-term experiment, the fact that the subjects grow older (and wiser?) may have an effect. In shorter experiments, they may become tired, sleepy, bored, or hungry, or change in other ways that affect their behavior in the experiment. A long-term study of alcohol abuse might reveal a decline in binge drinking as the subjects mature.

   History and maturation are similar in that they represent a correlation between cause and effect that is due to something other than the independent variable. They're different in that history represents something that's outside the experiment altogether, whereas maturation refers to change within the subjects themselves.

3. *Testing.* Often the process of testing and retesting influences people's behavior and thereby confounds the experimental results. Suppose we administer a questionnaire to a group as a way of measuring their alcohol use. Then we administer an experimental stimulus and remeasure their alcohol use. By the time we conduct the posttest, the subjects may have gotten more sensitive to the issue of alcohol use and provide different answers. In fact, they may have figured out that we are trying to determine whether they drink too much. Since excessive drinking is frowned on by university authorities, our subjects will be on their best behavior and give answers that they think we want or that will make them look good.

4. *Instrumentation.* Thus far, we haven't said much about the process of measurement in pretesting and posttesting, and it's appropriate to remind you of the problems of conceptualization and operationalization discussed in Chapter 5. If we use different measures of the dependent variable (say, different questionnaires about alcohol use), how can we be sure that they are comparable? Perhaps alcohol use seems to have decreased simply because the pretest measure was more sensitive than the posttest measure. Or if the measurements are being made by the experimenters, their standards or abilities may change over the course of the experiment. This is a problem of reliability.

Instrumentation is always a potential problem in criminal justice research that uses secondary sources of information, such as police records about crime or court records about probation violations. There may be changes in how probation violations are defined or changes in the recordkeeping practices of police departments. We will have more to say about the nature of instrumentation problems, together with ways to detect and minimize them, in Chapter 12.

You may be confused about the differences between testing and instrumentation threats to internal validity. In general, testing refers to changes in how subjects respond to measurement, while instrumentation is concerned with changes in the measurement process itself. If police officers respond differently to pretest and posttest questionnaires about prejudice, for example, that is a testing problem. However, if different questionnaires about prejudice are used in pretest and posttest measurements, instrumentation is a potential threat.

5. *Statistical regression.* Sometimes it's appropriate to conduct experiments on subjects who start out with extreme scores on the dependent variable. For example, Murray and Cox (1979) examined a program to incarcerate high-rate male juvenile offenders. They found that rearrest rates for subjects who had served sentences averaging 11 months were substantially lower than those for other offenders who were not incarcerated. These findings were questioned by Maltz, Gordon, McDowall, and McCleary (1980), who pointed out that the number of crimes committed by any given offender fluctuates over time. They argued that subjects in the experimental group—chronic offenders—were jailed following a period when their offense rates were abnormally high and that the decline in posttest arrests simply reflected a natural return to less extreme rates of offending. Even without any experimental stimulus, then, the group as a whole was likely to show some improvement over time.

Commonly referred to as "regression to the mean," this validity threat can emerge whenever researchers are interested in cases that have extreme scores on some variable. As a simple example, statisticians often point out that extremely tall people as a group are likely to have children shorter than themselves, and extremely short people as a group are likely to have children taller than themselves. The danger, then, is that changes occurring by virtue of subjects starting out in extreme positions will be attributed erroneously to the effects of the experimental stimulus.

6. *Selection biases.* Randomization eliminates the potential for systematic bias in selecting subjects, but subjects may be chosen in other ways that can threaten validity. Volunteers are often solicited for experiments conducted on college campuses. Students who volunteer for an experiment may not be typical of students as a whole, however. Volunteers may be more interested in the subject of the experiment and more likely to respond to a stimulus. Or if experimental subjects are paid some fee, students in greater financial need may participate, although they may not be representative of other students.

A common type of selection bias in applied criminal justice studies is produced by the natural caution of public officials. Let's say you are a bail commissioner in a large city and the mayor wants to try a new program to increase the number of arrested persons who are released on bail. The mayor asks you to decide what kinds of defendants should be eligible for release and informs you that staff from the city's criminal justice services agency will be evaluating the program. In establishing eligibility criteria, you will probably try to select defendants who will not be arrested again while on bail and defendants who will most likely show up for scheduled court appearances. In other words, you will try to select participants who are least likely to fail. This common and understandable caution is sometimes referred to as *creaming*—skimming the best risks off the top. Creaming is a threat to validity because the low-risk persons selected for release may be most likely to succeed, yet they do not represent the jail population as a whole.

7. *Experimental mortality.* Experimental subjects often drop out of an experiment before it is completed, and that can affect statistical comparisons and conclusions. This is termed experimental mortality. In the classical experiment involving an experimental and a control group, each with a pretest and a posttest, suppose that the heavy drinkers in the experimental group are so alienated by the video on the health effects of binge drinking that they tell the experimenter to forget it and leave. Those subjects who stick around for the posttest were less heavy drinkers to start with, and the group results will thus reflect a substantial "decrease" in alcohol use.

In this example, mortality is related to the experimental stimulus itself: Subjects who score highest on the pretest are the most likely to drop out after viewing the video. Mortality may also be a problem in experiments that take place over a long period of time (people may move away) or in experiments that require a substantial commitment of effort or time by subjects; they may become bored with the study or simply decide it's not worth the effort.

8. *Causal time order.* In criminal justice research, there may be ambiguity about the time order of the experimental stimulus and the dependent variable. Whenever this occurs, the research conclusion that the stimulus *caused* the dependent variable can be challenged with the explanation that the "dependent" variable actually caused changes in the stimulus. Many early studies of the relationship between different types of punishments and rates of offending exhibited this threat to validity by relying on single interviews with subjects who were asked how they viewed alternative punishments and whether or not they had committed any crimes. As you'll recall, Chapter 3 examined the issue of causal time order in depth.

9. *Diffusion or imitation of treatments.* In the event that experimental and control-group subjects are in communication with each other, it's possible that experimental subjects will pass on some elements of the experimental stimulus to the control group. In their study of policies to reduce fear of crime, Pate, Wycoff, Skogan, and Sherman (1986) distributed different types of crime prevention newsletters to selected households in Newark, New Jersey, and Houston, Texas. Treatment households received a newsletter, and control households did not. Posttest measures of fear and other attitudes sought to determine whether scores on these dependent variables were lower among those who received the newsletters than among those who had not. Pate and associates acknowledge the possibility that some control households could have seen newsletters received by their neighbors—an example of treatment diffusion. In that case, the control group becomes affected by the stimulus and is not a real control. Sometimes we speak of the control group having been "contaminated."

10. *Compensatory treatment.* As we'll see in Chapter 13, in experiments in real-life situations—such as a special job training program for incarcerated felons—subjects in

the control group are often deprived of something considered to be of value. In such cases, there may be pressures to offer some form of compensation. Recall the discussion in Chapter 3 of how police in the Kansas City Preventive Patrol Experiment patrolled the perimeter of reactive beats—those with no preventive patrol. As we noted, they more often used lights and sirens when responding to calls for service in the reactive beats. Some police officers compensated for the absence of preventive patrol in a way that reduced the differences among proactive, reactive, and control beats.

You may find it helpful to think of treatment diffusion as the accidental spillover of an experimental stimulus, in contrast to the more intentional compensatory treatment by public officials that occurred in the Kansas City case. In applied criminal justice research, compensation is probably more common, and researchers often take steps to prevent it. For example, in an evaluation of intensive supervision probation (ISP) programs in 11 sites, researchers from the RAND Corporation recognized that probation officers might provide enhanced supervision to clients in the control group, under the assumption that the experimental program (ISP) was better than traditional probation (Petersilia, 1989). This potential for compensation was reduced in two ways. First, researchers explained to program staff why the experimental and control groups should receive different types of services. Second, a type of double-blind procedure was used where researchers tried to disguise the records of subjects in the control group so probation staff could not distinguish subjects who were participating in the experiment from their regular probation caseload.

11. *Compensatory rivalry.* In real-life experiments, subjects deprived of the experimental stimulus may try to compensate by working harder. Suppose an experimental career development program for corrections officers is the experimental stimulus; the control group may work harder than before in an attempt to keep pace with the "special" experimental subjects.

12. *Demoralization.* On the other hand, feelings of deprivation among the control group may result in their giving up. A career development program for corrections officers may prompt demoralization among control-group subjects who believe their opportunities for advancement will suffer. As a result, it may not be clear whether posttest differences between experimental and control groups in, say, job performance actually reflected program impacts or were due to demoralization among the control group.

Notice that the possibilities of compensatory rivalry and demoralization are based on subjects' reactions to the experiment, while diffusion and compensatory treatment are accidental or intentional extensions of the experimental stimulus to the control group. In studies where agency staff, not researchers, administer an experimental treatment to subjects, there is a greater potential for intentional compensation. In studies where subjects in a control group are aware that other subjects are receiving a desirable treatment, compensatory rivalry or demoralization is possible.

Ruling Out Threats to Internal Validity

These, then, are the threats to internal validity cited by Campbell, Stanley, and Cook. The classical experiment, coupled with proper subject selection and assignment, can *potentially* handle each of the 12 threats to internal validity.

How do you determine whether a particular design rules out threats to internal validity? Cook and Campbell (1979: 55) provide an excellent rule of thumb: "Estimating the internal validity of a relationship is a deductive process in which the investigator has to systematically think through how each of the internal validity threats can be ruled out." Let's look again at the classical experiment, presented graphically in Figure 7-2.

Pursuing the example of the educational video as an attempt to reduce alcohol abuse, if we use the experimental design shown in Figure 7-2, we should expect two findings. For the experimental group, the frequency of drinking measured in their posttest should be less than in their pretest. In addition, when the two posttests are compared, the experimental group should have less drinking than the control group.

This design guards against the problem of history because anything occurring outside the experiment that might affect the experimental group should also affect the control group. There should still be a difference in the two posttest results. The same comparison guards against problems of maturation as long as the subjects have been randomly assigned to the two groups. Testing and instrumentation should not be problems because both the experimental and control groups are subject to the same tests and experimenter effects. If the subjects have been assigned to the two groups randomly, statistical regression should affect both equally, even if people with extreme scores on drinking (or whatever the dependent variable is) are being studied. Selection bias is ruled out by the random assignment of subjects.

Experimental mortality can be more complicated to handle because dropout rates may be different between the experimental and control groups. The experimental treatment itself may increase mortality in the group exposed to the video. As a result, the group of experimental subjects that received the posttest will be different from the group that received the pretest. In our example of the alcohol video, it would probably not be possible to handle this problem by administering a placebo, for instance. In general, however, the potential for mortality can be reduced by shortening the time between pretest and posttest, by emphasizing to subjects the importance of completing the posttest, or perhaps by offering cash payments for participating in all phases of the experiment.

The remaining problems of internal invalidity can be avoided through the careful administration of a controlled experimental design. The experimental design we've been discussing facilitates the clear specification of independent and dependent variables. Experimental and control subjects can be kept separate to reduce the possibility of diffusion or imitation of treatments. Administrative controls can avoid compensations given to the control group, and compensatory rivalry can be watched for and taken into account in evaluating the results of the experiment, as can the problem of demoralization.

We emphasize careful administration here. Random assignment, pretest and posttest measures, or using control and experimental groups do not automatically rule out threats to validity. This caution is especially true in field studies and evaluation research, where subjects participate in natural settings and uncontrolled variation in the experimental stimulus may be present. Control over experimental conditions is the hallmark of this approach, but conditions in field settings are usually more difficult to control.

Compare, for example, our hypothetical study of alcohol use among college students to the field experiment on ISP described by Petersilia (1989). In Petersilia's study, more intensive probation is the independent variable and recidivism is the dependent variable. Subjects were randomly assigned to the experimental group (ISP) or the control group (regular probation).

The alcohol use study could conceivably be completed in about one week, using subjects from a class, dormitory, or house on a single campus. ISP programs were evaluated in 11 sites over four years, using probation clients as subjects. The video on the health effects of alcohol use is a well-defined treatment that is readily standardized and can easily be controlled by researchers. The experimental treatment in the ISP programs is a reduced caseload for probation workers, together with an increased number of regular contacts with each probation client; program staff, not researchers, administer the experimental treatment. There is a great potential for uncontrolled variation in the delivery of ISP treatments; ISP is not a simple dichotomous treatment as is the video/no-video treatment in the alcohol use experiment.

Finally, the alcohol use questionnaire could easily be administered by researchers, providing reliable measures of alcohol use. Data on recidivism for the ISP study were collected by probation staff in each of 11 sites. Although recidivism can be readily defined as the number of new arrests after beginning probation, there may be wide variation in the ability of staff in the 11 sites to reliably detect new arrests.

These remarks are not intended to criticize the ISP study. In her description of the evaluation, Petersilia (1989) documents the extensive steps taken by RAND Corporation researchers to control possible validity threats. Our point is that field experiments and evaluations can present many obstacles that are not eliminated by simply adopting a randomized experimental design. Careful administration and control throughout the experiment are necessary to reduce potential threats to internal validity. In Chapter 13, we will consider the problems of administering field experiments in more detail.

Generalizability

The problems of internal invalidity are only some of the complications faced by experimenters. They also have the problem of generalizing from experimental findings to the real world. Even if the results of an experiment are an accurate gauge of what happened during that experiment, do they really tell us anything about life in the wilds of society? Following our discussion of cause and effect in Chapter 3, we will consider two dimensions of generalizability: construct validity and external validity.

Threats to Construct Validity

In the language of experimentation, *construct validity* is the correspondence between the empirical test of a hypothesis and the underlying causal process that the experiment is intended to represent. As stated in Chapter 3, construct validity is concerned with generalizing from what we observe in an experiment to actual causal processes in the real world. In our hypothetical example, the educational video is how we operationalize the construct of understanding the health effects of alcohol abuse. Our questionnaire represents the dependent construct of actual alcohol use.

Are these reasonable ways to represent the underlying causal process in which understanding the effects of alcohol use causes people to reduce excessive or abusive drinking? If you think this is a reasonable representation but one that is certainly incomplete, you're on the right track. People develop an understanding of the health effects of alcohol use in many ways. Watching an educational video is one way; having personal experience, talking to friends and parents, taking other courses, and reading books and articles are other ways. Our video may do a good job of representing the health effects of alcohol use, but it is an incomplete representation of that construct. Alternatively, the video may be poorly produced, too technical, or incomplete. Then the experimental stimulus may not adequately represent the construct we are interested in—educating students about the health effects of alcohol use. There may also be problems with our measure of the dependent variable: questionnaire items on self-reported alcohol use.

By this time, you should recognize a similarity between construct validity and some of the measurement issues presented in Chapter 5. Almost any empirical example or measure of a construct is incomplete. Part of construct validity refers to how completely an empirical measure can represent a construct, or how well you can generalize from a measure to a construct.

A related issue in construct validity is whether a given level of treatment is sufficient. Perhaps showing a single video to a group of subjects would have little effect on alcohol use, but administering a series of videos over several weeks would produce a greater impact. We could test this experimentally by having more than one experimental group and varying the number of videos seen by different groups.

Threats to construct validity are difficult problems in criminal justice experiments, often because researchers do not clearly specify precisely what constructs are to be represented by particular measures or experimental treatments. For example, Anne Schneider (1990) points out that many studies of probation policies do not specify whether an innovative probation program represents a punishment or an attempt to reform offenders through counseling or other treatments. As a consequence, it is not clear what specific components of an effective probation program might be. Do the punitive components of probation reduce subsequent offending, or does enhanced counseling have a greater impact?

David Farrington and associates (1986:92) make a related point: "Most treatments in existing experiments are not based on a well-developed theory but on a vague idea about what might influence offending. The treatments given are often heterogeneous, making it difficult to know which element was responsible for any observed effect." These authors also point to the importance of thinking about levels of constructs. The RAND Corporation evaluation of intensive supervision again provides a good example of why this is important. The ISP program explicitly defined enhanced probation as punitive. This leads to another question of how enhanced probation must be. If a typical probation officer carries an average caseload of 100 clients and sees each an average of twice per month, what workload and contact level are sufficiently intensive to reduce recidivism? Cutting the workload in half and doubling the number of contacts would be more intensive, but would it be intensive enough to produce a decline in recidivism? Again, an experiment could test this question by including more than one experimental group and giving each a different level of probation supervision.

Three elements of enhancing construct validity, therefore, are: (1) linking constructs and measures to theory, (2) clearly indicating what constructs are represented by specific measures, and (3) thinking carefully about what levels of treatment may be necessary to produce some level of change in the dependent measure.

Threats to External Validity

Will an experimental study, conducted with the kind of control we have emphasized here, produce results that would also be found in more natural settings? Can an intensive probation program shown to be successful in Minneapolis achieve similar results in Miami? External validity represents a slightly different form of generalizability, one where the question is whether results from experiments in one setting (time and place) would be obtained in other settings, or whether a treatment found to be effective for one population will have similar effects on a different group.

Threats to external validity are greater for experiments conducted under carefully controlled conditions. If the alcohol education experiment revealed that drinking decreased among students in the experimental group, then we could be confident that the video actually reduced alcohol use among our experimental subjects. But will the video have the same effect on high school students or adults if it is broadcast on television? We can not be certain because the carefully controlled conditions of the experiment might have had something to do with the video's effectiveness.

In contrast, criminal justice field experiments are conducted in more natural settings. Real probation officers in 11 different local jurisdictions delivered intensive supervision to real probationers in the RAND experiment. Because of the real-world conditions and multiple sites, there were fewer potential threats to external validity. This is not to say that external validity is never a problem in field experiments. The 11 probation agencies that participated in this evaluation may not be typical of probation agencies in other areas. The simple fact that they were willing to participate in the study suggests that staff could be more dedicated or more amenable to trying new approaches to probation. One of the advantages of field experiments in criminal justice is that because they take place under more real-world conditions, results are more likely to be valid in other real-world settings.

There are no free lunches. You may have detected a fundamental conflict between internal and external validity. Threats to internal validity are reduced by conducting experiments under carefully controlled conditions, which may restrict our ability to generalize results to real-world settings. Field experiments generally have greater external validity, but their internal validity may suffer because such studies are more difficult to monitor than those taking place in more controlled settings.

Cook and Campbell (1979:83) offer some useful advice for resolving the potential for conflict between internal and external validity. Explanatory studies that test cause-and-effect theories should place greater emphasis on internal validity, while applied studies should be more concerned with external validity. This is not a hard and fast rule because internal validity must be established before external validity becomes an issue. That is, applied researchers must have confidence in the internal validity of their cause-and-effect relationships before they ask whether similar relationships would be found in other settings.

Threats to Statistical Conclusion Validity

Our discussion of statistical conclusion validity will be brief, but not because it is unimportant. Rather, a full comprehension of statistical conclusion validity requires an understanding of sampling and statistical analysis methods, particularly inferential statistics. Chapters 9 and 14 will introduce some of these concepts, but an adequate treatment requires one or more specialized courses in statistics.

Fortunately, the basic principle is simple. Virtually all experimental research in criminal justice is based on samples of subjects that represent a target population. Larger samples of subjects, up to a point, are more representative of the target population than are smaller samples. Statistical conclusion validity becomes an issue when findings are based on small samples of cases. Because experiments are often costly and time-consuming, they are frequently conducted with relatively small numbers of subjects. In such cases, only large differences between experimental and control groups on posttest measures can be detected with any degree of confidence.

In practice, this means that finding cause-and-effect relationships through experiments depends on two related factors: the number of subjects and the magnitude of posttest differences between the experimental and control groups. Experiments with large numbers of cases may be able to reliably detect small differences, but experiments with smaller numbers can detect only large differences.

Threats to statistical conclusion validity can be magnified by other difficulties in field experiments. If treatment spillover or compensation is a problem, then smaller differences in the experimental stimulus will be delivered to each group. More generally, David Weisburd and associates (1993) concluded, after reviewing a large number of criminal justice experiments, that failure to maintain control over experimental conditions reduced statistical conclusion validity even for studies with large numbers of subjects. We will revisit such issues in Chapter 13.

■ VARIATIONS IN THE CLASSICAL EXPERIMENTAL DESIGN

In describing the classical experiment, we mentioned that it could be modified to reduce threats to validity. We now turn to a more systematic consideration of variations on the classical experiment that can be produced by manipulating the building blocks of experiments.

Slightly restating our earlier remarks, there are four basic building blocks in experimental designs: (1) the number of experimental and control groups, (2) the number and variation of experimental stimuli, (3) the number of pretest and posttest measurements, and (4) the procedures used to select subjects and assign them to groups. By way of illustrating these building blocks and how they are used to produce different designs, we adopt the system of notation used by Campbell and Stanley (1966). Figure 7-3 presents this notation and shows how it is used to represent the classical experiment and examples of variations on this design.

In Figure 7-3, the symbol O represents observations or measurements, and X represents an experimental stimulus or treatment. Different

FIGURE 7-3

Variations in the Experimental Design

	Classical Experiment		
Experimental group	O	X	O
Control group	O		O
	t_1	t_2	t_3
		Time	

O = observation or measurement
X = experimental stimulus
t = time point

	Posttest Only	
Experimental group	X	O
Control group		O
	t_1	t_2

	Factorial		
Experimental treatment 1	O	X_1	O
Experimental treatment 2	O	X_2	O
Control	O		O
	t_1	t_2	t_3

time points are displayed as t with a subscript to represent time order. Thus, for the classical experiment shown in Figure 7-3, O at t_1 is the pretest, O at t_3 is the posttest, and the experimental stimulus, X, is administered to the experimental group at t_2, between the pretest and posttest. Measures are taken for the control group at times t_1 and t_3, but the experimental stimulus is not administered to the control group.

Now consider the design labeled "Posttest Only." As implied by its name, no pretest measures are made on either the experimental or control group. If you think for a moment about the threats to internal validity, you may imagine situations where a posttest-only design is appropriate. Testing and retesting might especially influence subjects' behavior if measurements are made by administering a questionnaire, where subjects' responses to the posttest might be affected by their experience in the pretest. A posttest-only design can reduce the possibility of

testing as a threat to validity by eliminating the pretest.

Without a pretest, it is obviously not possible to detect *change* in measures of the dependent variable, but we can still test the effects of the experimental stimulus by comparing posttest measures for the experimental group to posttest measures for the control group. For example, if we were concerned about the possibility of sensitizing subjects in a study of an alcohol education video, we could eliminate the pretest and examine the posttest differences between experimental and control groups. Randomization is the key to the posttest-only design. If subjects are randomly assigned to experimental and control groups, we expect them to be equivalent. Any posttest differences between the two groups on the dependent variable can then be attributed to the influence of the video.

In general, posttest-only designs are appropriate when researchers suspect that the process of measurement may bias subjects' responses to a questionnaire or other instrument. This is more likely when only a short time elapses between pretest and posttest measurements. The number of observations made on subjects is a design building block that may be varied as needed. We emphasize here that random assignment is essential in a posttest-only design.

Figure 7-3 also shows a factorial design, which has two experimental groups that receive different treatments, or different levels of a single treatment, and one control group. This design is useful for comparing the effects of different interventions, or different amounts of a single treatment. In evaluating an ISP program, we might wish to compare how different levels of contact between probation officers and probation clients affected recidivism. In this case, subjects in one experimental group might receive weekly contact (X_1), the other experimental group would be seen by probation officers twice each week (X_2), and control group subjects would have normal contact (say, monthly) with probation officers. Since more contact is more expensive than less contact, we would be interested in seeing how much difference in recidivism was produced by monthly, weekly, and twice-weekly contacts.

Thus, an experimental design may have more than one group receiving different versions or levels of experimental treatment. We can also vary the number of measurements made on dependent variables. No hard and fast rules exist for using these building blocks to design any given experiment. A useful rule of thumb, however, is to keep a design as simple as possible to control plausible threats to validity. The specific design for any particular study will depend on your research purpose, available resources, and unavoidable constraints in designing and actually carrying out the experiment.

One very common constraint is how subjects or units of analysis are selected and assigned to experimental or control groups. This building block now brings us to the subject of quasi-experimental designs.

■ QUASI-EXPERIMENTAL DESIGNS

By now you should recognize the value of random assignment in controlling threats to validity. However, it is often impossible to randomly select subjects for experimental and control groups. There may be legal or ethical reasons why randomization cannot be used in criminal justice experiments; we will examine these problems in Chapter 8. More often, there may be practical or administrative obstacles, as discussed in Chapters 9 and 13.

When randomization is not possible, the next best choice is often a *quasi-experimental design*. The prefix *quasi-* is significant, meaning "to a certain degree." A quasi-experiment is, to a certain degree, an experiment. In most cases, quasi-experiments do not randomly assign subjects, and therefore they may suffer from the internal validity threats that are so well controlled in true experiments. Without random assignment, the other building blocks of experimental design must be used creatively to reduce validity threats. Following Cook and Campbell, we will group

quasi-experimental designs into two categories: nonequivalent-groups designs and time-series designs. Each can be represented with the *O, X,* and *t* notation used in Figure 7-3.

Nonequivalent-Groups Designs

Again, the name for this family of designs is meaningful. We assume that random assignment produces equivalent experimental and control groups. When it is not possible to create groups through randomization, we must use some other procedure, one that is not random. If we construct groups through some nonrandom procedure, however, we cannot assume that the groups are equivalent—hence, the label *nonequivalent-groups design*.

Whenever experimental and control groups are not equivalent, we should select subjects in some way that makes the two groups as comparable as possible. Often the best way to achieve comparability is through a matching process in which subjects in the experimental group are matched with subjects in a comparison group. The term *comparison group* is commonly used, rather than *control group*, to highlight the nonequivalence of groups in quasi-experimental designs. A comparison group does, however, serve the same function as a control group.

Some examples of research that use nonequivalent-control-group designs illustrate various approaches to matching and the creative use of experimental design building blocks. Examples include studies of child abuse (Widom, 1989b), obscene phone calls (Clarke, 1992a), and an instrument to predict parole risk (Bonta and Motiuk, 1990). Refer to Figure 7-4 for a diagram of each design with the *X, O,* and *t* notation. The solid line that separates treatment and comparison groups in the figure signifies that subjects have been placed in groups through some nonrandom procedure.

Child Abuse and Later Arrest Cathy Spatz Widom (1989b) studied the long-term effects of child abuse, addressing whether abused children are more likely to be charged with delinquent or adult criminal offenses than children who were

FIGURE 7-4
Quasi-Experimental Design Examples

Widom (1989b)

Treatment group	X	O
Comparison group		O
	t_1	t_2

X = official record of child abuse
O = counts of juvenile or adult arrest

Clarke (1992a)

Treatment group	O	X	O
Comparison group	O		O
	t_1	t_2	t_3

X = caller identification and call tracing
O = customer complaints of obscene calls

Bonta and Motiuk (1990)

Treatment group	X	O_a	O_b (hi LSI)
			O_b (lo LSI)
Comparison group		O_a	O_b (hi LSI)
			O_b (lo LSI)
	t_1	t_2	t_3

X = exposure to LSI results
O_a = released, not released
O_b = parole violations, arrests

not abused. Child abuse was the experimental stimulus, and the number of subsequent arrests was the dependent variable.

Of course, it is not possible to assign children randomly to groups where some are abused and others are not. Widom's design called for selecting a sample of children who, according to court records, had been abused. She then matched each abused subject with a comparison subject—of the same gender, race, age, and approximate socioeconomic status—who had not been abused. These matching criteria assumed that age at the time of abuse, gender, race, and socioeconomic status differences might confound any observed relationship between abuse and later arrests.

You may be wondering how a researcher selects important variables to use in matching experimental and comparison subjects. We cannot

give you a definitive answer to that question, any more than we could specify what particular variables should be used in any given experiment. The answer ultimately depends on the nature and purpose of the experiment. As a general rule, however, the two groups should be comparable in terms of variables that are likely to be related to the dependent variable under study. Widom matched on gender, race, and socioeconomic status because these variables are correlated with juvenile and adult arrest rates. Age at the time of reported abuse was also an important variable because children abused at a younger age had a longer "at-risk" period for delinquent arrests.

Widom produced experimental and comparison groups by matching individual subjects, referred to as *individual matching*. It is also possible to construct experimental and comparison groups through *aggregate matching*, where the average characteristics of each group are comparable. This is illustrated in our next example.

Predicting Parole Risk Deciding which inmates should be paroled and which present too great a risk for parole is a fundamental problem in corrections policy. Two corrections officials in Canada tested a prediction tool, the Level of Supervision Inventory (LSI), as an aid in deciding which inmates could be released to parole and halfway houses (Bonta and Motiuk, 1990). Low scores on the LSI were intended to indicate that the inmate presented a low risk for parole or release to a halfway house.

Bonta and Motiuk were interested in the answers to two questions: (1) Do inmates who score low on the LSI have fewer parole violations and rearrests than inmates who score high? and (2) Does the use of the LSI increase the number of inmates released to parole and halfway houses? The first question is relatively straightforward; a prediction instrument is not helpful if it cannot discriminate between inmates who present greater or lesser risks on release.

The second question requires a bit more explanation. Recall our earlier discussion of "creaming" as a selection bias—the natural tendency of public officials to choose experimental subjects who are least likely to fail. Parole boards are understandably cautious in deciding whom to release or place in some experimental program. A measure such as the LSI can provide a more objective indicator of an inmate's risk and might result in parole for more people. Bonta and Motiuk developed an ingenious double-blind procedure to test both whether the LSI was a good measure of parole risk and whether officials who used the LSI released more inmates than officials who did not use it.

The corrections staff administered the LSI to all inmates who were serving sentences of four months or more in three Canadian jails. But the LSI was used to make release decisions in only two of the jails; inmates released from those facilities were in the treatment group. Staff in the third jail were not informed of LSI scores; they selected inmates for release using existing procedures. Persons released from the third jail made up the comparison group. This design made it possible for the researchers to address their two questions directly.

First, the two jails using the LSI did in fact release more inmates to parole and halfway houses compared to the jail where the LSI was not used. Since LSI scores on inmates in all three jails were known to researchers, they were able to determine that many low-scoring inmates from the blind jail were not released. Comparing measures of misconduct while incarcerated, Bonta and Motiuk found that the low-LSI group encountered fewer problems than the high-LSI group did.

All inmates were eventually released, which enabled the researchers to compare postparole performance for the low- and high-LSI inmates. Those inmates who scored low on the LSI, whether they were released early or stayed in jail, had fewer parole violations and fewer arrests than did inmates who scored higher on the LSI. Bonta and Motiuk were therefore able to conclude that: (1) the LSI was a good predictor of parole risk, and (2) officials who used the LSI approved more inmates for release compared to officials who did not use the LSI. Notice how these two findings go together to indicate that the LSI helped corrections officials make better decisions: Low-scoring

inmates performed better on release, and more low-risk inmates were released.

Let's briefly summarize how this study used the building blocks of experimental design. First, officials' exposure to LSI results was the experimental treatment. Second, the treatment was administered to officials who rated the inmates in two jails, the experimental group, but not to officials in the third jail, the comparison group. Third, it was not practical to randomly assign corrections officials to treatment and comparison groups because a single board in each jail made release decisions. Because of this, Bonta and Motiuk created treatment and comparison groups through aggregate matching. Aggregate characteristics of inmates in the two treatment jails were matched against the same characteristics of inmates in the comparison jail. Although the two groups were not technically equivalent, since they had not been created through random assignment, aggregate indicators of prior and current offenses, average sentence length, and LSI score were very similar for the two groups (Bonta and Motiuk, 1990:501).

Finally, two different dependent variables were measured: whether or not inmates were released to parole or halfway houses, and the performance of all inmates after release. Release/no release, measured at t_2, addressed whether using the LSI increased the number of inmates paroled and placed in halfway houses. Frequency counts of parole violations and arrests one year after release—at t_3—measured the predictive accuracy of the LSI.

Deterring Obscene Phone Calls In 1988, the New Jersey Bell telephone company introduced caller identification and instant call tracing in a small number of telephone exchange areas. Caller identification displays the phone number of the person who is placing a call on the telephone of the call recipient. Instant call tracing allows the recipient of an obscene or threatening call to automatically initiate a procedure to trace the source of the call.

Ronald Clarke (1992a) studied the effects of these new technologies in deterring obscene phone calls. Clarke expected that obscene calls would decrease in areas where the new services were available. To test this, he compared records of formal customer complaints about annoying calls in the New Jersey areas that had the new services to formal complaints in other New Jersey areas where caller identification and call tracing were not available. One year later, the number of formal complaints had dropped sharply in areas serviced by the new technology, and no decline was found in other New Jersey Bell areas.

In this study, telephone service areas with new services were the treatment group, and areas without the services were the comparison group. Clarke's matching criterion was a simple one: telephone service by New Jersey Bell, assuming the volume of obscene phone calls was relatively constant within a single phone service area. Of course, matching on telephone service area cannot eliminate the possibility that the volume of obscene phone calls varies from one part of New Jersey to another, but Clarke's choice of a comparison group is straightforward and certainly more plausible than comparing New Jersey to, say, Nebraska.

Clarke's study is a good example of a natural field experiment. The experimental stimulus— caller identification and call tracing—was not specifically introduced by Clarke, but he was able to obtain measures for the dependent variable before and after the experimental stimulus was introduced. He then compared the levels of change from pretest to posttest measures between the treatment and comparison groups. Randomization could not be used, but Clarke's design made it possible to infer with reasonable confidence that caller identification and call tracing reduced the number of formal complaints about obscene phone calls.

Together, these three studies illustrate different approaches to research design when it is not possible to randomly assign subjects to treatment and control groups. Lacking random assignment, researchers must use creative procedures for selecting subjects, constructing treatment and comparison groups, measuring dependent variables, and exercising other controls to reduce possible threats to validity.

Cohort Designs

Chapter 4 introduced cohort studies as examples of longitudinal designs. We can also view cohort studies as nonequivalent-control-group designs. Recall from Chapter 4 that a cohort may be defined as a group of subjects who enter or leave an institution at the same time. For example, a class of police officers who graduate from a training academy at the same time could be considered a cohort. Or we might view all persons who were sentenced to probation in May as a cohort.

Now think of a cohort that is exposed to some experimental stimulus. The May probation cohort might be required to complete 100 hours of community service in addition to meeting other conditions of probation. If we were interested in whether probationers who received community service sentences were charged with fewer probation violations, we could compare the performance of subjects in the May cohort with the performance of the April cohort, or the June cohort, or some other cohort that was not sentenced to community service. Cohorts that did not receive community service sentences would serve as comparison groups. The groups would not be equivalent because they were not created by random assignment, but if we could assume that a comparison cohort did not systematically differ from a treatment cohort on important variables, we would be able to use this design to determine whether community service sentences reduce probation violations.

That last assumption is very important and may not be viable. Perhaps a criminal court docket is organized to schedule certain types of cases at the same time, so a May cohort would be systematically different from a June cohort. But if the assumption of comparability can be met, cohorts may be used to construct nonequivalent comparison and experimental groups by taking advantage of the natural flow of cases through some institutional process.

Terance Miethe's (1987) study of determinant sentencing guidelines in Minnesota is a good example of a cohort design. Determinant sentencing laws seek to produce more uniform sanctions for similar types of offenses by reducing a judge's discretion. Under the Minnesota guidelines, judges were instructed to impose specific sentences after considering only the severity of the offense and an offender's prior record (Miethe, 1987: 158). Miethe was interested in how prosecutors adapted to the new law. Specifically, he hypothesized that prosecutors would engage in more charge bargaining in an effort to influence what offense defendants would face and, therefore, what sanction a judge would impose under sentencing guidelines.

The Minnesota law—the experimental stimulus—became effective in 1980. Three samples of convicted felons were studied: one preintervention cohort (those convicted in 1978) and two postintervention cohorts (felons convicted in 1980–81 and in 1981–82). Data on case and defendant characteristics were gathered from court records. Information from the 1978 cohort served as pretest observations, and data from the 1980–81 and 1981–82 cohorts were posttest observations. Similarly, the two post-1980 cohorts served as treatment groups because they were convicted after the guidelines became effective, and the 1978 cohort served as a comparison group.

These three groups of offenders could not be considered equivalent because they were not produced by random assignment. However, Miethe examined summary statistics for all three samples and found few aggregate differences across the three groups. Testing his hypothesis, Miethe found no systematic change in charge bargaining, concluding that sentencing guidelines appeared to reduce discretion by prosecutors. Because of the regular flow of cases through an institution—criminal courts in this example— it was possible to use a cohort design that compared case processing for defendants convicted before and after sentencing guidelines became effective.

Time-Series Designs

We introduced the concept of longitudinal studies in Chapter 4. Time-series designs are common examples of longitudinal studies in criminal justice research. As the name implies, a time-series design involves examining a series of observations on some variable over time. A simple example is examining trends in arrests for drunk driving over time to see whether the number of arrests is increasing, decreasing, or staying about the same. A police executive might be interested in keeping track of arrests for drunk driving, or arrests for other offenses, as a way of monitoring the performance of patrol officers. Or state corrections officials might want to study trends in prison admissions as a way of predicting future needs for correctional facilities.

An *interrupted time series* is a special type of time-series design that can be used in cause-and-effect studies. A series of observations is compared before and after some intervention is introduced. For example, a researcher might want to know whether roadside sobriety checkpoints caused a decrease in fatal automobile accidents. Trends in accidents could be compared before and after the roadside checkpoints are established.

Interrupted time-series designs can be very useful in criminal justice research, especially in applied studies. They do have some limitations, however, just like other ways of structuring research. Cook and Campbell (1979) describe the strengths and limitations of different approaches to time-series designs. We will introduce these approaches and their flaws with a hypothetical example and then describe some specific criminal justice applications.

We continue with the example of sobriety checkpoints. Figure 7-5 presents four possible patterns of alcohol-related automobile accidents. The vertical line in each pattern shows the time when the roadside checkpoint program is introduced. Which of these patterns indicates that the new program caused a reduction in car accidents?

If the time-series results looked like pattern 1 in Figure 7-5, you might think *initially* that the checkpoints caused a reduction in alcohol-related accidents, but there seems to be a general downward trend in accidents that continues after the intervention. It's safer to conclude that the decline would have continued even without the roadside checkpoints.

Pattern 2 shows that an increasing trend in auto accidents has been reversed after the intervention, but this appears to be due to a regular pattern in which accidents have been bouncing up and down. The intervention was introduced at the peak of an upward trend, and the later decline may be an artifact of the underlying pattern rather than of the new program.

Patterns 1 and 2 illustrate some outside trend, rather than an intervention, that may account for a pattern observed over time. You should recognize this as an example of *history* as a validity threat to the inference that the new checkpoint program caused a change in auto accidents. The general decline in pattern 1 may be due to reduced drunk driving that has nothing to do with sobriety checkpoints. Pattern 2 illustrates what is referred to as *seasonality* in a time series—a regular pattern of change over time. Cook and Campbell describe seasonality as a special case of history. In our example, the data might reflect seasonal variation in alcohol-related accidents that occurs around holidays or maybe on football weekends near a college campus.

Patterns 3 and 4 lend more support to the inference that sobriety checkpoints caused a decline in alcohol-related accidents, but the two patterns are different in a subtle way. In pattern 3, accidents decline more sharply from a general downward trend immediately after the checkpoint program, while pattern 4 displays a sharper decline some time after the new program is established. Which pattern provides stronger support for the inference?

In considering your answer, recall what we have said about construct validity; think about the underlying causal process these two patterns represent. Pattern 3 suggests that the program was immediately effective and supports what we might call an incapacitation effect: Roadside checkpoints enabled police to identify and arrest drunk drivers, thereby getting them off the road and reducing accidents. Pattern 4 suggests a deterrent effect: As drivers learned about the checkpoints, they less often drove after drinking and accidents eventually declined. Either explanation is possible. This illustrates an important limitation of interrupted time-series designs: They operationalize complex causal constructs in simple ways. Your interpretation depends in large part on how you understand this causal process.

Research by Richard McCleary and associates (McCleary, Neinstedt, and Erven, 1982), mentioned in Chapter 5, illustrates the need to think carefully about how well time-series results reflect underlying causal patterns. Recall that McCleary and colleagues found a sharp decline in burglaries immediately after a special burglary investigation unit was established in a western city. This finding was at odds with their understanding of how police investigations could reasonably be expected to reduce burglary. A special unit might eventually be able to reduce the number of burglaries after investigating incidents over a period of time and making arrests. But it is highly unlikely that changing investigative procedures would have an immediate impact. This discrepancy prompted McCleary and associates to look more closely at the policy change and led to their conclusion that the apparent decline in burglaries was produced by changes in recordkeeping practices. No evidence existed of any decline in the actual number of burglaries.

This example should remind you of our discussion of *instrumentation* earlier in this chapter. Changes in the way police counted burglaries produced what appeared to be a reduction in burglary. Instrumentation can be a particular problem in time-series designs for two reasons. First, observations are usually made over a relatively long time period, which increases the likelihood of changes in measurement instruments. Second, time-series designs often use measures that are produced by an organization such as a police department, criminal court, probation office, or corrections department. There may be changes or irregularities in the way data are collected by these agencies that are not readily apparent to researchers, and that are in any case not subject to their control.

Chapter 12 will consider in detail the problems of instrumentation and reliability that researchers often encounter when using agency records. We

FIGURE 7-5
Four Patterns of Change in Fatal Automobile Accidents (Hypothetical Data)

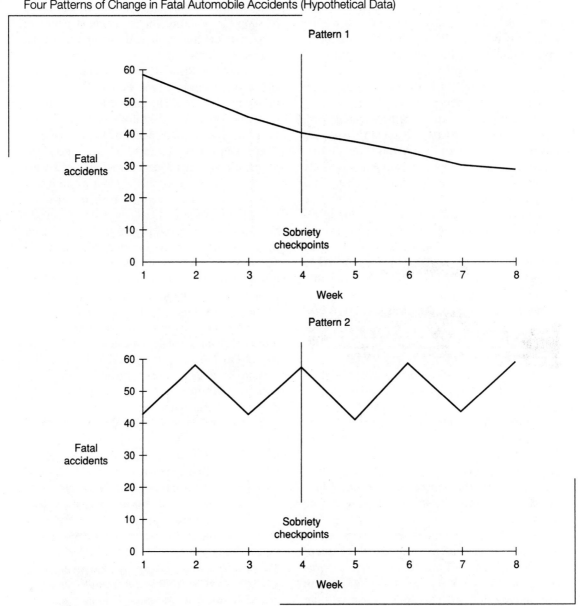

raise the issue here because such problems can be especially troublesome in time-series designs.

Variations in Time-Series Designs

If we view the basic interrupted time-series design as an adaptation of basic design building blocks, we can consider how modifications can help control many validity problems. The simplest time-series design studies one group, the treatment group, over time. Rather than making one pretest and one posttest observation, the interrupted time-series design makes a longer series of observations before and after introducing an experimental treatment.

FIGURE 7-5
(continued)

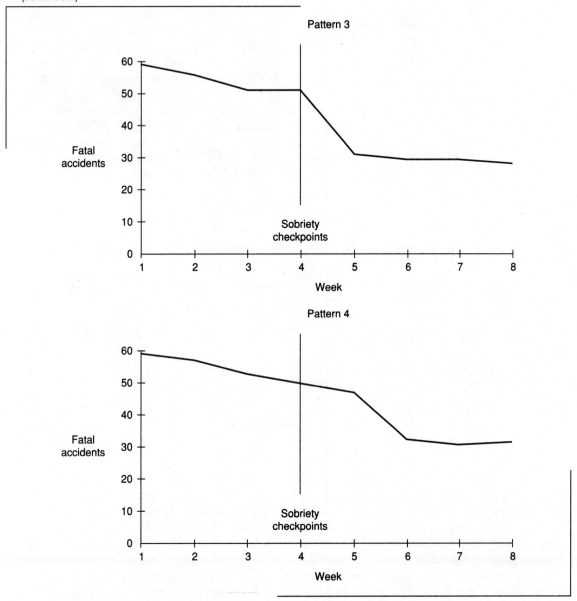

What if we considered the other building blocks of experimental design? Figure 7-6 presents the basic design and some variations using the familiar *O, X,* and *t* notation. The basic design is shown at the top of Figure 7-6, where many pretest and posttest observations are made on a single group that receives some treatment.

We could strengthen this design by adding a comparison series of observations on some group that does not receive the treatment. If, for example, roadside sobriety checkpoints were introduced all over the state of Ohio but were not used at all in Michigan, then we could compare auto accidents in Ohio (the treatment series) with auto

FIGURE 7-6
Interrupted Time-Series Designs

Simple Interrupted Time Series

O	O	O	O	X	O	O	O	O
t_1	t_2	t_3	t_4		t_5	t_6	t_7	t_8

Interrupted Time Series with
Nonequivalent Comparison Group

O	O	O	O	X	O	O	O	O
O	O	O	O		O	O	O	O
t_1	t_2	t_3	t_4		t_5	t_6	t_7	t_8

Interrupted Time Series
with Removed Treatment

O	O	X	O	O	O	$-X$	O	O	O
t_1	t_2		t_3	t_4	t_5		t_6	t_7	t_8

Interrupted Time Series
with Switching Replications

O	O	O	X	O	O	O	O	O
O	O	O	O	O	X	O	O	O
t_1	t_2	t_3	t_4		t_5	t_6	t_7	t_8

accidents in Michigan (the comparison series). If checkpoints caused a reduction in alcohol-related accidents, we would expect to see a decline in Ohio following the intervention, but there should be no change or a lesser decline in Michigan over the same time period. The second panel of Figure 7-6 shows this design—an interrupted time series with a nonequivalent comparison group. The two series are not equivalent because we did not randomly assign drivers to Ohio or Michigan.

A single-series design may be modified by introducing and then removing the intervention, as shown in the third panel of Figure 7-6. We might test sobriety checkpoints by setting them up every weekend for a month and then not setting them up for the next few months. If the checkpoints caused a reduction in alcohol-related accidents, we might expect an increase after they were removed. On the other hand, the effects of weekend checkpoints might persist even after we removed them.

Since different states or cities sometimes introduce new drunk driving programs at different times, we might be able to use what Cook and Campbell (1979:223) call a *time-series design with switching replications.* The bottom of Figure 7-6 illustrates this design. For example, assume that Ohio begins using checkpoints in May 1992 and Michigan introduces them in July of the same year. A switching replications design could strengthen our conclusion that checkpoints reduce accidents if we saw that a decline in Ohio began in June and a similar pattern was found in Michigan beginning in August. The fact that similar changes occurred in the dependent variable in different states at different times, corresponding to when the program was introduced, would add to our confidence in stating that sobriety checkpoints actually reduced auto accidents.

Gun Control, Homicide, and Suicide

We conclude our discussion of quasi-experimental designs by presenting a study that incorporated both nonequivalent groups and interrupted time-series designs. Colin Loftin and associates (1991) examined the impact of a 1976 law that restricted handgun ownership in Washington, D.C. It was hoped that the law would reduce violent crime in general, but Loftin and colleagues were interested primarily in its effects on gun-related deaths. They examined two dependent variables, homicides and suicides by firearms, using data collected by the National Center for Health Statistics (NCHS) on the cause and mode of death.

Because the law applied to only the District of Columbia and not to other cities in the Washington metropolitan area, the researchers were able to construct a comparison group from adjacent areas in Maryland and Virginia. If the new law reduced the number of deaths by firearms, there should be a greater decline (or lesser increase) in Washington than in nearby Maryland and Virginia cities.

Loftin and associates took advantage of the specific focus of the law to create another type of comparison. Restrictive handgun legislation could be expected to affect violent death by firearms only; the law could not be expected to reduce homicides or suicides that involved other weapons. So changes in gun-related homicides

FIGURE 7-7
Designs Used in Gun Control Evaluation by Loftin, McDowall, Wiersma, and Cottey (1991)

Nonequivalent Groups

				Results
District of Columbia gun-related homicides, suicides	O	X	O	$-25\%, -23\%$
District of Columbia nongun homicides, suicides	O	(X)	O	$-4\%, -9\%$
Maryland and Virginia gun-related homicides, suicides	O		O	$-7\%, +12\%$
Maryland and Virginia nongun homicides, suicides	O		O	$+23\%, -2\%$
	t_1	t_2	t_3	

Time

Time Series

District of Columbia gun-related homicides, suicides	O	O	O	O	X	O	O	O	O
District of Columbia nongun homicides, suicides	O	O	O	O	(X)	O	O	O	O
Maryland and Virginia gun-related homicides, suicides	O	O	O	O		O	O	O	O
Maryland and Virginia nongun homicides, suicides	O	O	O	O		O	O	O	O
	t_1	t_2	t_3	t_4		t_5	t_6	t_7	t_8

and suicides were compared to changes in homicides and suicides involving other weapons.

Cook and Campbell (1979:118, 218) refer to this second type of comparison as a *design with nonequivalent dependent variables*. Gun-related homicide and suicide were specific targets of the law and could be expected to change, but other homicides and suicides should not be affected. Since the two classes of dependent variables were not equivalent, they served as additional controls in testing the cause-and-effect relationship between gun legislation and deaths by firearms.

NCHS data from 1968 through September 1976 (when the law became effective) were the pretest observations, and deaths from October 1976 through 1987 were the posttest observations. For the time-series analysis, monthly totals were used: 105 monthly observations for the pretest and 135 for the posttest. Loftin and colleagues also compared average monthly deaths before and after the gun control law in each category (gun-related, nongun-related, District of Columbia, Maryland, and Virginia).

Comparing pre- and postintervention average deaths per month, Loftin and associates found that the average number of gun-related homicides and suicides per month declined by 25 percent and 23 percent, respectively, in the District of Columbia. Suicides and homicides by other means also declined in the District, but the reduction was much smaller. Figures for Maryland and Virginia showed an increase in gun-related suicides and nongun homicides, while gun-related homicides and nongun suicides declined slightly. Analysis of time-series data, the 105 pretest and 135 posttest monthly observations, found similar results.

Figure 7-7 illustrates the designs used in this study, where X signifies the introduction of a treatment, or independent variable (the gun control law). The nonequivalent dependent variables designs show X in parentheses (X) to signify that the treatment is present but it is not expected to affect the dependent variable—nongun homicides and suicides. Notice the two types of comparisons: Virginia and Maryland served as nonequivalent comparison sites, and nongun homicides and suicides were nonequivalent control variables. Neither the comparison sites nor the comparison variables showed as much change in the expected direction as the decline in gun-related homicides and suicides in the District of Columbia.

Loftin and associates used the central features of experimental design to test the effects of a gun control law. Observations were made for groups and variables that could reasonably be expected to change (gun-related deaths in Washington) and for groups and variables that should not have been affected by the law (all suicides and homicides in Maryland and Virginia, nongun deaths in Washington). The pattern of findings lends considerable support to their conclusion that the District of Columbia law did reduce deaths due to firearms. Let's now examine how this study deals with threats to validity.

The same historical factors would have affected all groups and variables, but a significantly greater decline in gun-related deaths still occurred in Washington. The pattern of findings eliminates possible selection problems, unless one assumes that lethal-minded gun owners fled Washington to Maryland and Virginia suburbs after 1976. Maturation, regression, testing, and diffusion of treatment are not problems. Instrumentation would be a problem only if there were changes in how the NCHS determined cause and mode of death, but even then, it would have similarly affected all groups and all variables.

The researchers used a sufficient number of cases and appropriate methods of analysis to rule out problems with statistical conclusion validity. Construct validity is enhanced by the careful selection of dependent variables and by clear specification of what the District of Columbia law could and could not be expected to change. The external validity of these findings is more difficult to evaluate. It is not clear that a similar law would have similar impacts in another metropolitan area. This can best be established through replication.

Note how Loftin and associates adapted design building blocks to strengthen their conclusions. And consider how a simple interrupted time-series study of gun-related homicides and sui-

cides—no comparison groups or nonequivalent variables—would have produced ambiguous results. Without the comparisons, it would not be possible to know whether declines in gun-related deaths were due to the law or to some outside factors. Adding a nonequivalent comparison group as well as nonequivalent dependent variables enabled Loftin and colleagues to control for alternative explanations of their findings.

■ EXPERIMENTAL AND QUASI-EXPERIMENTAL DESIGNS SUMMARIZED

By now, we hope you recognize that there are no magic formulas or cookbooks for designing an experimental or quasi-experimental study. Researchers have an almost infinite variety of ways of varying the number and composition of groups of subjects, selecting subjects, determining how many observations to make, and deciding what types of experimental stimuli to introduce or study.

This chapter has focused on variations in experimental and quasi-experimental designs, but there are other ways to structure research as well. Some of these were mentioned in Chapter 4; we will describe others in later chapters. Variations on the classical experimental designs are especially useful for explanatory research and in evaluation studies, but exploratory and descriptive studies usually use other methods. Surveys conducted at one point in time, for example, may be used to explore or describe such phenomena as fear of crime or public attitudes toward punishment. Longitudinal studies of age cohorts are often the best ways to examine criminal careers or developmental causes of delinquency.

Even when experimental designs would be the best choice, it is not always possible to construct treatment and control groups, to use random assignment, or even to analyze a series of observations over time. For instance, Rosenbaum and others (1992) conducted an extensive study of community organizations and their potential for addressing problems of drug abuse. Researchers conducted community surveys, interviewed members of neighborhood groups, observed group meetings, participated in planning sessions, and made observations of physical and social conditions in project neighborhoods. Antidrug activity by groups in eight sites was the experimental treatment, but this treatment was neither introduced nor controlled by the researchers. The large and varying scope of group activities, combined with limited funding for research, made it impossible to construct anything like comparison groups. Nevertheless, Rosenbaum and associates were able to conduct what amounted to eight case studies and to provide valuable insights about the kinds of group actions that were more or less effective in combating neighborhood drug problems.

As we stated early in this chapter, experiments are best suited to topics that involve well-defined concepts and propositions. Experiments and quasi-experiments also require that researchers be able to exercise, or at least approximate, some degree of control over an experimental stimulus. Finally, these designs depend on being able to unambiguously establish the time order of experimental treatments and observations on the dependent variable. Often it is not possible to achieve the necessary degree of control.

In designing a research project, you should be alert to opportunities for using an experimental design. You should also be aware of how quasi-experimental designs can be developed when randomization is not possible. Experiments and quasi-experiments lend themselves to a logical rigor that is often much more difficult to achieve in other modes of observation. The building blocks of research design can be used in creative ways to address a variety of criminal justice research questions. Careful attention to design issues, and to how design elements can reduce validity threats, is essential to the research process.

■ *MAIN POINTS*

- Experiments are an excellent vehicle for the controlled testing of causal processes. Experiments may also be appropriate for evaluation studies.

- The classical experiment tests the effect of an experimental stimulus on some dependent variable through the pretesting and posttesting of experimental and control groups.

- It is generally less important that a group of experimental subjects be representative of some larger population than that experimental and control groups be similar to each other.

- Randomization is the best way to achieve comparability in the experimental and control groups.

- There are 12 sources of internal invalidity in experimental design:

History	Causal time order
Maturation	Diffusion or imitation
Testing	of treatments
Instrumentation	Compensatory
Regression	treatment
Selection biases	Compensatory rivalry
Mortality	Demoralization

- The classical experiment with random assignment of subject guards against most of the threats to internal invalidity.

- Experiments also face problems of generalizability. Because experiments often take place under controlled conditions, results may not be generalizable to real-world constructs. Or findings from an experiment in one setting may not apply to other settings.

- The classical experiment may be modified to suit specific research purposes by changing the number of experimental and control groups, the number and types of experimental stimuli, and the number of pretest or posttest measurements.

- Quasi-experiments may be conducted when it is not possible or desirable to use an experimental design.

- Nonequivalent-groups and time-series designs are two general types of quasi-experiments.

- Both experiments and quasi-experiments may be customized by using design building blocks to suit particular research purposes.

- Not all research purposes and questions are amenable to experimental or quasi-experimental designs because researchers may not be able to exercise the required degree of control.

■ REVIEW QUESTIONS AND EXERCISES

1. You have no doubt heard about shock incarceration, or "boot camp," programs. Describe an experimental design to test the causal hypothesis that shock incarceration programs reduce recidivism. Is your experimental design feasible? Why or why not?

2. We have described how experiments are well suited to controlling validity threats. What about quasi-experiments? Find an example of a quasi-experiment and discuss possible threats to internal, construct, and external validity.

3. Experiments are often conducted in public health research, where a distinction is made between an *efficacy experiment* and an *effectiveness experiment*. Efficacy experiments focus on whether some new health program works under ideal conditions, whereas effectiveness experiments test the program under typical conditions that health professionals encounter in their day-to-day work. Discuss how efficacy experiments and effectiveness experiments reflect concerns about internal validity threats on the one hand and generalizability on the other hand.

■ ADDITIONAL READINGS

Campbell, Donald T., and Stanley, Julian, *Experimental and Quasi-experimental Designs for Research* (Chicago: Rand McNally, 1966). An excellent analysis of the logic and methods of experimentation in social research. This short book is widely cited as the classic discussion of validity threats.

Cook, Thomas D., and Campbell, Donald T., *Quasi-experimentation: Design and Analysis Issues for Field Settings* (Boston: Houghton Mifflin, 1979). The authors update and substantially expand issues introduced in Campbell and Stanley. Although Cook and Campbell can be difficult reading, this book remains the definitive treatment of the principles of experimental and quasi-experimental designs for social science.

Farrington, David P., Ohlin, Lloyd E., and Wilson, James Q., *Understanding and Controlling Crime: Toward a New Research Strategy* (New York: Springer-Verlag, 1986). We mentioned this book at the end of Chapter 4 as a source of information on longitudinal research. Additionally, the authors describe the strengths of experiments in criminal justice research.

Lempert, Richard O., and Visher, Christy A., *Randomized Field Experiments in Criminal Justice Agencies* (Washington, DC: U.S. Department of Justice, Office of Justice Programs, National Institute of Justice, 1988). The authors describe policy experiments in nontechnical language. This publication presents a good overview of basic topics in experimental design. It is especially useful for beginning researchers and public officials who will work with researchers in conducting field experiments.

Sherman, Lawrence W., *Policing Domestic Violence: Experiments and Dilemmas* (New York: Free Press, 1992). This book summarizes many of the complex issues that confront recent field experiments on police responses to domestic violence. Sherman describes domestic violence programs and experiments in a readable, almost breezy style. In addition, there are references to detailed reports of individual field experiments conducted in several cities.

Wright, Richard, Logie, Robert H., and Decker, Scott H., "Criminal Expertise and Offender Decision Making: An Experimental Study of the Target Selection Process in Residential Burglary," *Journal of Research in Crime and Delinquency*, Vol. 32 (1995), pp. 39–55. An interesting application of experimental design to learn how residential burglars decide which targets are promising.

8 CHAPTER

Ethics and Criminal Justice Research

What You'll Learn in This Chapter

You'll see some of the ethical considerations that must be taken into account along with the scientific ones in the design and execution of research. We'll describe different types of ethical issues and ways of handling them.

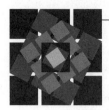

INTRODUCTION

ETHICAL ISSUES IN CRIMINAL JUSTICE RESEARCH
No Harm to Participants
Voluntary Participation
Anonymity and Confidentiality
Deceiving Subjects
Analysis and Reporting
Legal Liability
Special Problems

PROMOTING COMPLIANCE WITH ETHICAL PRINCIPLES
Institutional Review Boards
Institutional Review Board Requirements
   and Researcher Rights

TWO ETHICAL CONTROVERSIES
Trouble in the Tearoom
Simulating a Prison

DISCUSSION EXAMPLES

MAIN POINTS

REVIEW QUESTIONS AND EXERCISES

ADDITIONAL READINGS

■ *INTRODUCTION*

So far, we have described various research procedures and constraints on them. We've seen that the logic of science suggests certain research procedures, but we've also seen that some scientifically appropriate designs aren't administratively feasible, since some "perfect" study designs would be too expensive, would take too long to execute, or would not yield useful results. We have also come to recognize constraints on measurement. Throughout the book, we've dealt with workable compromises.

Ethical considerations represent another compromise in criminal justice research, somewhat subtle and less obvious, but nonetheless extremely important. Just as you wouldn't use certain procedures because they are impractical or too expensive, there are some procedures you couldn't use because of ethical considerations.

We introduce the issue of ethics by relating a story from Earl Babbie's book, *The Practice of Social Research* (1995:447):

■ Several years ago, I was invited to sit in on a planning session to design a study of legal education in California. The joint project was to be conducted by a university research center and the state bar association. The purpose of the project was to improve legal education by learning which aspects of the law school experience were related to success on the bar exam. Essentially, the plan was to prepare a questionnaire that would get detailed information about the law school experiences of individuals. People would be required to answer the questionnaire when they took the bar exam. By analyzing how people with different kinds of law school experiences did on the bar exam, it would be possible to find out what sorts of things worked and what didn't. The findings of the research could be made available to law schools, and ultimately legal education could be improved.

The exciting thing about collaborating with the bar association was that all the normally aggravating logistical hassles would be handled. There would be no problem getting permission to administer questionnaires in conjunction with the exam, for example, and the problem of nonresponse could be eliminated altogether.

I left the meeting excited about the prospects for the study. When I told a colleague about it, I glowed about the absolute handling of the nonresponse problem. Her immediate comment turned everything around completely. "That's unethical. There's no law requiring the questionnaire, and participation in research has to be voluntary." The study wasn't done.

It now seems obvious that requiring participation would have been inappropriate. You may have seen that before you read the comment by Babbie's colleague.

All of us consider ourselves ethical—not perfect perhaps, but more ethical than most of humanity. The problem in criminal justice research—and probably in life—is that ethical considerations are not always apparent to us. As a result, we often plunge into things without seeing ethical issues that may be apparent to others and may even be obvious to us when they are pointed out. Our excitement at the prospect of a new research project may blind us to obstacles that ethical considerations present.

Any of us can immediately see that a study that requires juvenile gang members to demonstrate drive-by shooting techniques is unethical. You'd speak out immediately if it were suggested that we interview people about drug use and then publish what they said in the local newspaper. But, as ethical as you are, you might totally miss the ethical issues in other situations—not because you're bad, but because we all do that.

■ *ETHICAL ISSUES IN CRIMINAL JUSTICE RESEARCH*

In most dictionaries and in common usage, ethics is typically associated with morality, and both deal with matters of right and wrong. But what is right and what wrong? What is the source of the distinction? For individuals, the sources vary from religion to political ideology to the pragmatic observation of what seems to work and what doesn't.

Webster's New World Dictionary is typical among dictionaries in defining *ethical* as "conforming to the standards of conduct of a given profession or group." Although the idea may frustrate those in search of moral absolutes, what we regard as moral and ethical in day-to-day life is merely a matter of agreement among members of a group. And it is not surprising that different groups have agreed on different codes of conduct. If you are going to live in a particular society, then, it is extremely useful for you to know what that society considers ethical and unethical. The same holds true for the criminal justice research "community."

If you are going to do criminal justice research, you should be aware of the general agreements shared by researchers about what's proper and improper in the conduct of scientific inquiry. Ethical issues in criminal justice can be especially challenging because research questions frequently address illegal behavior that people are anxious to conceal.

The sections that follow will summarize some of the more important ethical issues and agreements in criminal justice research. Our discussion is restricted to ethical issues in criminal justice *research,* not ethics in criminal justice policy and practice. We will not consider such questions as the morality of the death penalty, acceptable police practices, the ethics of punishment, or codes of conduct for attorneys and judges. If you are interested in substantive ethical issues in criminal justice policy, consult Elliston and Bowie (1982) for an introduction, Schmalleger (1991) for an annotated bibliography of readings, or the journal *Criminal Justice Ethics* for a wide range of articles.

No Harm to Participants

Balancing the potential benefits from doing research against the possibility of harm to the people being studied—or harm to others—is a fundamental ethical dilemma in all research. Biomedical research presents potential harm to the health of people or animals. Social research may produce psychological harm or embarrassment to people who are asked to reveal information about themselves. Criminal justice research has the potential to produce both physical and psychological harm as well as embarrassment. Although the likelihood of physical harm may seem remote, it is worthwhile to consider possible ways this might occur.

Harm to subjects, researchers, or third parties is a potential threat in field studies that collect information from or about persons engaged in criminal activity; this is especially true for field research. Several studies of drug crimes involve locating and interviewing active users and dealers. For example, Bruce Johnson and associates (1985) studied heroin users in New York, recruiting subjects by spreading the word through various means. Other researchers have studied dealers in Detroit (Mieczkowski, 1990b), New York (Williams, 1989), and St. Louis (Jacobs, 1996). Collecting information from active criminals presents at least the possibility of violence against research subjects by other drug dealers.

Potential danger to field researchers should also be considered. For instance, Reuter, Mac-Coun, and Murphy (1990) selected their drug dealer subjects by consulting probation department records. The researchers recognized that sampling persons from different Washington, D.C., neighborhoods would have produced a more generalizable group of subjects, but they rejected that approach because mass media reports of widespread drug-related violence generated concern about the safety of research staff (1990:119).

A series of experimental studies of bystander intervention by Latané and Darley (1970) staged crimes that, in some instances, could have produced harm to either subjects or research staff. They were interested in circumstances when witnesses to a "crime" would or would not intervene. In one experiment, staging a liquor store holdup, a bystander called police, who responded with drawn guns.

More generally, John Monahan and associates (1993) distinguish three different groups at potential risk of physical harm in their research on violence. First are research subjects themselves. Women at risk of domestic violence, for example, may be exposed to greater danger if assailants learn they have disclosed past victimizations to researchers. Second, researchers might trigger attacks on themselves when they interview subjects who have a history of violent offending. Third, and most difficult, is the possibility that collecting information from unstable individuals might increase the risk of harm to third parties. The last category presents a new dilemma if researchers learn that subjects intend to attack some third party. Should researchers honor a promise of confidentiality to subjects or intervene to prevent harm to third parties?

Some potential for psychological harm to subjects exists when interviews are used to collect information. Crime surveys that ask respondents about their experiences as victims of crime may remind them of a traumatic, or at least an unpleasant, experience. Studies of the National Crime Victimization Survey (NCVS) show that victims of assault, identified from police records, do not always disclose their victimization to interviewers (Murphy and Dodge, 1981; Turner, 1972). Victims may be especially reluctant to describe attacks by family members because they feel embarrassed or at risk of further assault (O'Brien, 1985). The redesigned NCVS, as we saw in Chapter 6, incorporates new questioning procedures to reduce the potential for embarrassment and risk to respondents. Surveys may also ask respondents about illegal behaviors such as drug use or crimes they have committed. Talking about such actions to interviewers can be embarrassing.

Although the fact often goes unrecognized, subjects can also be harmed by the analysis and reporting of data. Every now and then, research subjects read the books published about the studies they participated in. Reasonably sophisticated subjects will be able to locate themselves in the various indexes and tables. Having done so, they may find themselves characterized—though not identified by name—as criminals, deviants, probation violators, and so forth.

Largely for this reason, NCVS information on respondents' city of residence is not available to researchers or the public. The relative rarity of some types of crime means that if crime victimization were reported by city of residence, individual victims might recognize the portrayal of their experience or might be identified by third parties.

By now, you should realize that just about any research runs some risk of injuring other people somehow. A researcher can never completely guard against all these possible injuries, yet some study designs make injuries more likely than others. If a particular research procedure seems likely to produce unpleasant effects for subjects—asking survey respondents to report deviant behavior, for example—the researcher should have the firmest scientific grounds for doing it. If the research design is essential and also likely to be unpleasant for subjects, you will find yourself in an ethical netherworld, forced to do some personal agonizing. Although agonizing has little value in itself, it may be a healthy sign that you have become sensitive to the problem.

As a general principle, possible harm to subjects may be justified if the potential benefits of the study outweigh the harm. Of course, this raises a further question of how you determine whether possible benefits offset possible harms. There is no simple answer, but as we will see, the research community has adopted other safeguards that enable subjects to help make such determinations themselves.

Not harming people is an easy norm to accept in theory, but it is often difficult to ensure in practice. Sensitivity to the issue and experience with its applications, however, should improve the researcher's tact in delicate areas of research.

Voluntary Participation

Criminal justice research often, though not always, intrudes into people's lives. The interviewer's knock on the door or the arrival of a questionnaire in the mail signals the beginning of an activity that the respondent has not requested and one that may require a significant portion of his or her time and energy. Being selected to participate in an experiment disrupts the subject's regular activities.

Moreover, criminal justice research often requires that people reveal personal information about themselves—information that may be unknown to their friends and associates. Other professionals, such as physicians and lawyers, also require such information. Their requests may be justified, however, because the information helps them to serve the personal interests of the respondent. The criminal justice researcher can seldom make this claim. Like medical scientists, we can argue only that the research effort may ultimately help all humanity.

A major tenet of medical research ethics is that experimental participation must be *voluntary.* The same norm applies to research in criminal justice. No one should be forced to participate. But this norm is far easier to accept in theory than to apply in practice.

For example, prisoners are sometimes used as subjects in experimental studies. In the most rigorously ethical cases, the prisoners are told the nature—and the possible dangers—of the experiment; they are told that participation is completely voluntary; and they are further instructed that they can expect no special rewards (such as early parole) for participation. Even under these conditions, it is often clear that volunteers are motivated by the belief that they will personally benefit from their cooperation. In other cases, prisoners—or other subjects—may be offered small cash payments in exchange for participation. To people with very low incomes, small payments may be an incentive to participate in a study they would not otherwise endure.

When the instructor in an introductory criminal justice class asks students to fill out a questionnaire that she or he hopes to analyze and publish, students should always be told that their participation in the survey is completely voluntary. Even so, students might fear that nonparticipation will somehow affect their grade. The instructor should therefore be especially sensitive to the implied sanctions and make provisions to obviate them. For example, students could be asked to return the questionnaires by mail or to drop them in a box near the door just before the next course meeting.

You should be clear that this norm of voluntary participation works against a number of scientific concerns. In the most general terms, the scientific goal of generalizability is threatened if experimental subjects or survey respondents are only the people who willingly participate in such things. This orientation may reflect more general personality traits; possibly, then, the results of the research will not be generalizable to all kinds of people. Most clearly, in the case of a descriptive survey, a researcher cannot generalize the sample survey findings to an entire population unless a substantial majority of the scientifically selected sample actually participates—both the willing respondents and the somewhat unwilling.

As we will see in Chapter 11, field research has its own ethical dilemmas in this regard. Often a researcher who conducts observations in the field cannot even reveal that a study is being done, for fear that that revelation might significantly affect what is being studied. Imagine, for example, that you are interested in whether or not the way stereo headphones are displayed in a discount store reduces shoplifting, and you plan a field study in which you will make observations of store displays and shoplifting. You cannot very well ask all shoppers whether they agree to participate in your study.

The norm of voluntary participation is an important one, but it is sometimes impossible to follow. In cases where you feel ultimately justified in violating it, it is all the more important that you observe the other ethical norms of scientific research.

Anonymity and Confidentiality

The clearest concern in the protection of the subjects' interests and well-being is the protection of their identity. If revealing their behavior or responses to survey questions would injure them in any way, adherence to this norm becomes crucial. Two techniques—anonymity and confidentiality—assist you in this regard, although the two are often confused.

Anonymity A survey respondent or any person being studied is considered *anonymous* when the researcher cannot associate a given piece of information with a given person. Anonymity counteracts many potential ethical difficulties. Studies that use field observation techniques are often able to ensure that research subjects cannot be identified. Researchers may also gain access to nonpublic records from courts, corrections departments, or other criminal justice agencies in which the names of persons have been removed.

One example of anonymity would be a mail survey in which no identification numbers are put on the questionnaires before their return to the research office. Likewise, a telephone survey is anonymous if residential phone numbers are selected at random and respondents are not asked for identifying information.

As we will see in Chapter 10 on survey research, assuring anonymity makes it difficult to keep track of completed interviews with sampled respondents. Nevertheless, in some situations, you may be advised to pay the necessary price to gain anonymity. In a survey of drug use, for example, you may decide that the likelihood and accuracy of responses will be enhanced by guaranteeing anonymity.

Respondents in many surveys cannot be considered anonymous because an interviewer collects the information from a person whose name and address may be known. Other means of data collection may similarly make it impossible to guarantee anonymity for subjects. If you wished to examine juvenile arrest records for a sample of seventh-grade students, for example, you would need to know their names even though you might not be interviewing them or having them fill out a questionnaire.

Confidentiality *Confidentiality* means that a researcher is able to link information with a given person's identity but essentially promises not to do so publicly. In a survey of self-reported drug use, for example, the researcher would be in a position to make public the use of illegal drugs by a given respondent, but the respondent is assured that this will not be done. Similarly, if field interviews are conducted with juvenile gang members, researchers certify that information will not be disclosed to police or other officials. Studies using court or police records that include individuals' names may protect confidentiality by not reporting any identifying information.

Some techniques ensure better performance on this guarantee. To begin, field or survey interviewers who have access to respondent identifications should be trained in their ethical responsibilities. As soon as possible, all names and addresses should be removed from data-collection forms and replaced by identification numbers. A master identification file should be created linking numbers to names to permit the later correction of missing or contradictory information. This file should be kept under lock and key and should be available only for legitimate purposes.

Whenever a survey is confidential rather than anonymous, it is the researcher's responsibility to make that fact clear to the respondent. Never use the term *anonymous* to mean *confidential*. Note, however, that research subjects may not clearly understand the difference. In any event, subjects should be assured that the information they provide will be used for research purposes only and not be disclosed to third parties.

Deceiving Subjects

We've seen that the handling of subjects' identities is an important ethical consideration. Handling your own identity as a researcher can be tricky also. Sometimes it's useful and even necessary to identify yourself as a researcher to those you want to study. You'd have to be a master con artist to get people to participate in a laboratory experiment or complete a lengthy questionnaire without letting on that you are conducting research.

Even when it's possible and important to conceal your research identity, an important ethical dimension must be considered. Deceiving people is unethical, and in criminal justice research, deception needs to be justified by compelling scientific or administrative concerns. Even then, the justification will be arguable.

Sometimes researchers admit that they are doing research but fudge about why they are doing it or for whom. For example, Cathy Spatz Widom interviewed victims of child abuse some 15 years after their cases had been heard in criminal or juvenile courts (Luntz and Widom, 1994). She was interested in whether child abuse victims were more likely than a comparison group of nonvictims to have been arrested, attempted suicide, or developed various psychological problems. Interviewers could not describe the purpose of the study without potentially biasing responses. Still, it was necessary to provide a plausible explanation for asking detailed questions about personal and family experiences. Widom's solution was to inform subjects that they had been selected to participate in a study of human development. Doing that improved the scientific quality of her study, but it raised the potential ethical issue of deception in the process.

Although you might initially think that concealing your research purpose by deception would be particularly useful in studying active offenders, James Inciardi (1993), in describing methods for studying "crack houses," makes a convincing case that this is inadvisable. In the first place, concealing your research role when associating with drug dealers and users implies that you are associating with them for the purpose of obtaining illegal drugs. Faced with this situation, you would have the choice of engaging in illegal behavior yourself or offering a convincing explanation for declining. In the second case, in Inciardi's case, masquerading as a crack-house patron would have exposed the researcher to the considerable danger of violence that is common in such places. Since the choice of committing illegal acts or becoming a victim of violence is really no choice at all, Inciardi advises researchers who study active offenders in field settings: ". . . don't go undercover" (1993:152).

Analysis and Reporting

As a criminal justice researcher, then, you have ethical obligations to your subjects of study. At the same time, you have ethical obligations to your colleagues in the scientific community; a few comments on those obligations are in order.

In any rigorous study, the researcher should be more familiar than anyone else with the technical shortcomings and failures of the study. You have an obligation to make those shortcomings known to your readers. Even though you may feel foolish admitting mistakes, you should do it anyway.

Negative findings should be reported if they are at all related to your analysis. There is an unfortunate myth in social scientific reporting that only positive discoveries are worth reporting (and journal editors are sometimes guilty of believing that as well). In social science, however, it is often

as important to know that two variables are not related as to know that they are.

Similarly, you should avoid the temptation to save face by describing your findings as the product of a carefully preplanned analytic strategy when that is not the case. Many findings arrive unexpectedly, even though they may seem obvious in retrospect. So you uncovered an interesting relationship by accident—so what? Embroidering such situations with descriptions of fictitious hypotheses is dishonest and tends to mislead inexperienced researchers into thinking that all scientific inquiry is rigorously preplanned and organized.

In general, science progresses through honesty and openness, and it is retarded by ego defenses and deception. You can serve your fellow researchers—and scientific discovery as a whole—by telling the truth about all the pitfalls and problems you have experienced in a particular line of inquiry. Perhaps you'll save them from the same problems.

Legal Liability

Two types of ethical problems expose researchers to potential legal liability. First, assume you are making field observations of criminal activity, such as street prostitution, that is not reported to police. Under criminal law in many states, you might be arrested for obstruction of justice or being an accessory to a crime. Potentially more troublesome is the situation when participant observation of crime or deviance draws researchers into criminal or deviant roles themselves. For example, in his study of impersonal sex in public places, Laud Humphreys (1975) posed as a lookout for men who engaged in homosexual acts in public rest rooms. We will discuss the ethical problems raised by this study later in the chapter.

The second and more common potential source of legal problems is having knowledge that research subjects have committed illegal acts. Self-report surveys or field interviews may ask subjects about crimes they have committed. If respondents report committing offenses they have never been arrested for or charged with, a researcher's knowledge of them might be construed as obstruction of justice. Or research data may be subject to subpoena by a criminal court. Since disclosure of research data that could be traced to individual subjects violates the ethical principle of confidentiality, a new dilemma emerges.

Fortunately, federal law protects researchers from legal action in most circumstances, provided that appropriate safeguards are used to protect research data. The 1996 research plan published by the National Institute of Justice summarizes this protection: "[Research] information and copies thereof shall be immune from legal process, and shall not, without the consent of the person furnishing such information, be admitted as evidence or used for any purpose in any action, suit, or other judicial, legislative, or administrative proceedings" (42 U.S. Code 3789g). This not only protects researchers from legal action but can also be extremely valuable in assuring subjects that they cannot be prosecuted for crimes they describe to an interviewer or field worker. For example, Bruce Johnson and associates (1985:219) prominently displayed a Federal Certificate of Confidentiality at their research office to assure heroin dealers that they could not be prosecuted for crimes disclosed to interviewers. More savvy than many people about such matters, heroin users were duly impressed.

Note that such immunity requires confidential information to be protected. We have already discussed the principle of confidentiality, so this bargain should be an easy one to keep.

Somewhere between legal liability and physical danger lies the potential risk to field researchers from law enforcement. Despite being up-front with crack users about his role as a researcher, Inciardi (1993) points out that police could not be expected to distinguish him from his subjects. Visibly associating with offenders in natural settings brings some risk of being arrested or inadvertently being an accessory to crime. See Inciardi's description of his experiences in fleeing the scene of a robbery and being caught up in a crack-house raid.

Special Problems

Certain types of criminal justice studies present special ethical problems in addition to those we

have mentioned. Applied research, for example, may evaluate some existing or new program. As we will describe in Chapter 13, evaluations frequently have the potential to disrupt the routine operations of agencies being studied. Obviously, it is best to minimize such interferences whenever possible.

Staff Misbehavior While conducting applied research, you may become aware of irregular or illegal practices by staff in public agencies. You are then faced with the ethical question of whether or not to report such information. For example, investigators conducting an evaluation of an innovative probation program learned that police visits to the residences of subjects were not taking place as planned. Instead, it appeared that police assigned to the program had been submitting falsified log sheets and had not actually checked on probationers.[1]

What is the ethical dilemma in this case? On the one hand, researchers were evaluating the probation program and therefore obliged to report reasons it did or did not operate as planned. Failure to deliver program treatments (home visits) is an example of a program not operating as planned. Investigators had guaranteed confidentiality to program clients, the persons assigned to probation, but no such agreement had been struck with program staff. On the other hand, researchers had assured agency personnel that their purpose was to evaluate the probation program, not how well individuals were or were not doing their jobs. If researchers disclosed their knowledge that police were falsifying reports, they would have violated this implied trust.

What would you have done in this situation? We will tell you what the researchers decided at the end of this chapter. You should recognize, however, how applied research in criminal justice agencies can produce a variety of ethical issues.

Research Causes Crime Because criminal acts and their circumstances are complex and imperfectly understood, there is sometimes a potential for a research project to produce crime or influence its

---

[1]Information about this example was provided through personal communication between researchers and one of the authors.

location or target. Needless to say, this is a potentially serious ethical issue for researchers.

Just about everyone agrees that it is unethical to encourage someone to commit an offense solely for the purpose of a research project. What's more difficult is recognizing situations where research might indirectly promote offending. Scott Decker and Barrik Van Winkle (1996) discuss such a possibility in their research on gang members. Some gang members offered to illustrate their willingness to use violence by inviting researchers to witness a drive-by shooting. Researchers declined all such invitations (1996:46). More difficult was the question of how subjects used the $20 cash payments they received in exchange for being interviewed (1996:51):

■ We set the fee low enough that we were confident that it would not have a criminogenic effect. While twenty dollars is not a small amount of money, it is not sufficient to purchase a gun or bankroll a large drug buy. We are sure that some of our subjects used the money for illegal purposes. But, after all, these were individuals who were regularly engaged in delinquent and criminal acts.

You may or may not agree with the authors' reasoning in the last sentence. But their consideration of how cash payments would be used by active offenders represents an unusually careful recognition of the ethical dilemmas that emerge in studying active offenders.

A different type of ethical problem is the possibility of crime displacement in studies of crime prevention programs. For example, consider an experimental program to reduce street prostitution in one area of a city. Researchers studying such a program might designate experimental target areas for enhanced enforcement as well as nearby comparison areas that would not receive an intervention. If prostitution is displaced from target areas to adjacent neighborhoods, the evaluation study contributes to an increase in prostitution in the comparison areas.

In a review of more than 50 evaluations of crime prevention projects, René Hesseling (1994) concluded that displacement tended to accompany programs that targeted street prostitution, bank robbery, and certain combinations of offenses. The type of crime prevention action also made a difference. Displacement was more common for target-hardening programs. For example, installing security screens on ground floor windows in some buildings seemed to displace burglary to less protected structures.

Researchers cannot be expected to control actions by criminal justice officials that may benefit some people at the expense of others. However, it is reasonable to expect that researchers involved in planning an evaluation study should anticipate the possibility of such things as displacement and bring them to the attention of program staff.

Withholding Desirable Treatments Experimental designs in criminal justice research can produce different kinds of ethical questions. Recall our discussion in Chapter 7 of compensatory threats to validity when a desirable treatment is provided to an experimental group and withheld from a control group. Suppose, for example, it is believed that diverting domestic violence offenders from prosecution to counseling reduces the possibility of repeat violence. Is it ethical to conduct an experiment in which some offenders are prosecuted but others are not?

You may recognize the similarity between this question and those faced by medical researchers who test the effectiveness of experimental drugs. Physicians typically respond to such questions by pointing out that the effectiveness of a drug cannot be demonstrated without such experiments. Failure to conduct research, even at the potential expense of control group subjects, would therefore make it impossible to develop new drugs or distinguish beneficial treatments from those that are ineffective or might actually be harmful.

One solution to this dilemma is to interrupt an experiment if preliminary results indicate that a new policy, or drug, does in fact produce improvements in a treatment group. For example, Michael Dennis (1990) describes how such plans were incorporated into a long-term evaluation of enhanced drug treatment counseling. If preliminary results indicated that the new counseling program reduced drug use, researchers and program staff were prepared to expand enhanced counseling to subjects in the control group. Dennis recognized this potential ethical issue and planned his elaborate research design to accommodate such midstream changes.

Random Assignment The use of random assignment in experimental studies raises similar questions. If a desirable or beneficial policy is being tested, is it ethical to assign the treatment randomly to some people and not to others? Such questions are more often raised by officials and the general public than by researchers. For instance, Erez (1985) surveyed prisoners on their perceptions of how 100 spaces in a special rehabilitation program should be allocated among 500 inmates. Randomly drawing names was rated least fair, behind merit, "first-come first-served," and need, which was the procedure most preferred by prisoners. Prisoners are not alone in their skepticism. Joan Petersilia (1989:446) speculates that "to some lawyers, the word 'random' is apparently synonymous with arbitrary and capricious."

Researchers, however, generally view random assignment as an ethical procedure for deciding how potentially beneficial (or harmful) experimental treatments should be allocated among subjects. Lempert and Visher (1988) recommend that researchers work closely with program staff to explain that random selection is not arbitrary or biased, and that federal regulations and case law have upheld its legitimacy in policy experiments. The key is for researchers to explain that random assignment assures each subject an equal chance of participating in an experimental program, and that this is a fair and ethical procedure for allocating limited resources.

Research in criminal justice, especially applied research, can pose a variety of ethical dilemmas, only some of which we have mentioned here. See the additional readings listed at the end of this chapter for a more complete discussion.

■ PROMOTING COMPLIANCE WITH ETHICAL PRINCIPLES

No matter how sensitive they might be to the rights of individuals and possible ways subjects might be harmed, researchers are not always the best judges of whether or not adequate safeguards are used. Recall Babbie's excitement about a project that would require attorneys to complete a questionnaire. He immediately recognized the research benefits for increasing response rates but lost sight of the ethical problems such a requirement would raise.

If the professionals who design and conduct a research project can fail to consider ethical problems, how can such problems be avoided? One approach is for researchers to consult one of the codes of ethics produced by professional associations. Formal codes of conduct describe what is considered acceptable and unacceptable professional behavior. The American Psychological Association (1995) code of ethics is quite detailed, reflecting the different professional roles of psychologists in research, clinical treatment, and education. Many of the ethical questions criminal justice researchers are likely to encounter are addressed in the ethics code of the American Sociological Association (1996). Paul Reynolds (1979: 442–449) has created a composite code for the use of human subjects in research, drawing on 24 codes of ethics published by national associations of social scientists.

Professional codes of ethics for social scientists cannot, however, be expected to prevent unethical practices in criminal justice research any more than the American Bar Association's Code of Professional Responsibility eliminates breaches of ethics by attorneys. For this reason, and in reaction to some controversial medical and social science research, the U.S. Department of Health and Human Services (HHS) has established regulations concerning the protection of human research subjects. These regulations do not apply to all social science or criminal justice research. It is, however, worthwhile to understand some of their general provisions. Material in the following section is based on the 1992 *Code of Federal Regulations*, Title 45, Chapter 46.

Institutional Review Boards

Government agencies and nongovernment organizations (including universities) that conduct research involving human subjects must establish review committees, known as institutional review boards (IRBs). These IRBs have two general purposes. First, board members make judgments about the overall risks to human subjects and whether these risks are acceptable, given the expected benefits from actually doing the research. Second, the IRB determines whether procedures to be used by the project include adequate safeguards to protect the safety, confidentiality, and general welfare of human subjects.

Under HHS regulations, virtually all research that uses human subjects in any way, including simply asking people questions, is subject to IRB review. The few exceptions potentially include research conducted for educational purposes and studies that collect anonymous information only. But even those studies may be subject to review if they use certain special populations (discussed below) or procedures that might conceivably harm participants. In other words, it's safe to assume that most research is subject to IRB review if original data will be collected from individuals whose identities will be known. If you think about the various ways subjects might be harmed and the difficulty of conducting anonymous studies, you can understand why this is the case.

Federal regulations and IRB guidelines address other potential ethical issues in social research. Foremost among these is the typical IRB requirement for dealing with the ethical principle of voluntary participation.

Informed Consent   The norm of voluntary participation is usually satisfied by informing subjects about research procedures and then obtaining their consent to participate. Although this may seem like a simple requirement, obtaining informed consent may present several practical difficulties. It requires that subjects understand the purpose of the research, possible risks and side effects, possible benefits to subjects, and the procedures that will be used.

If you recall that deception may sometimes be necessary, you will realize how the requirement to inform subjects about research procedures and so on can present something of a dilemma. Researchers usually address this problem by telling subjects at least part of the truth, or a slightly revised version of why the research is being conducted. In Widom's study of child abuse, subjects were partially informed about the purpose of research—human development—one component of which is being a victim of child abuse, which the subjects were not told.

Another potential problem with obtaining informed consent is ensuring that subjects have the capacity to understand your description of risks, benefits, procedures, and so forth. You may have to provide oral descriptions to participants who are unable to read. For subjects who do not speak English, be prepared to describe procedures in their native language. If you use specialized terms or language common in criminal justice research, participants may not understand your meaning and thus may be unable to grant informed consent. For example, consider this statement: "The purpose of this study is to determine whether less restrictive sanctions such as restitution produce heightened sensitivity to social responsibility among persistent juvenile offenders and a decline in long-term recidivism." Can you think of a better way to describe this study to delinquent 14-year-olds? Figure 8-1 presents a good example of an informed consent statement that was used in an experimental study of home detention for juvenile burglars. Notice how the statement describes research procedures clearly, and unambiguously tells subjects that participation is voluntary.

Other guidelines for obtaining informed consent include explicitly telling people that their participation is voluntary and assuring them of confidentiality. However, it is more important that you understand how informed consent addresses a variety of ethical issues in conducting criminal justice research. First of all, it ensures that participation is voluntary. Second, by informing subjects of procedures, risks, and benefits, you are empowering them to resolve the fundamental ethical dilemma of whether the possible benefits of the research offset the possible risks of participation.

Special Populations   Federal regulations on human subjects include special provisions for certain types of subjects, and two of these are particularly important in criminal justice research—juveniles and prisoners. Juveniles, of course, are treated differently from adults in most aspects of the law. Their status as a special population of human

FIGURE 8-1
Informed Consent Statement for Evaluation of Marion County Juvenile Monitoring Program

You and your parents or guardian are invited to participate in a research study of the monitoring program that you were assigned to by the Juvenile Court. The purpose of this research is to study the program and your reactions to it. In order to do this a member of the research team will need to review you and your parents/guardians when you complete the monitoring program. These interviews will take about 15 minutes and will focus on your experiences with the court and monitoring program, the things you do, things that have happened to you, and what you think. In addition, we will record from the court records information about the case for which you were placed in the monitoring program, prior cases, and other information that is put in the records after you are released from the monitoring program.

Anything you or your parents or guardian tell us will be strictly confidential. This means that only the researchers will have your answers. They *will not* under any conditions (except at your request) be given to the court, the police, probation officers, your parents, or your child!

Your participation in this research is voluntary. If you don't want to take part, you don't have to! If you decide to participate, you can change your mind at any time. Whether you participate or not will have no effect on the program, probation, or your relationship with the court.

The research is being directed by Dr. Terry Baumer and Dr. Robert Mendelsohn from the Indiana University School of Public and Environmental Affairs here in Indianapolis. If you ever have any questions about the research or comments about the monitoring program that you think we should know about, please call one of us at 274-0531.

Consent Statement

We agree to participate in this study of the Marion County Juvenile Monitoring Program. We have read the above statement and understand what will be required and that all information will be confidential. We also understand that we can withdraw from the study at any time without penalty.

Juvenile _____ Date: _____

Parent/Guardian _____

Parent/Guardian _____

Researcher _____

subjects reflects the legal status of juveniles, as well as their capacity to grant informed consent. In most studies that involve juveniles, consent must be obtained both from parents or guardians and from the juvenile subjects themselves.

In some studies, however, such as those that focus on abused children, it is obviously not desirable to obtain parental consent. Scott Decker and Barrik Van Winkle (1996) faced this problem in their study of St. Louis gang members. See the box "Ethics and Juvenile Gang Members" on p. 188 for their discussion of how they reconciled the conflict between two ethical principles and satisfied the concerns of their university's IRB.

Prisoners are treated as a special population for somewhat different reasons. Because of their ready accessibility for experiments and inter-

views, prisoners have frequently been used in biomedical experiments that produced serious harm (Mitford, 1973). Recognizing this, HHS regulations specify that prisoner subjects may not be exposed to risks that would be considered excessive for nonprison subjects. Furthermore, undue influence or coercion cannot be used in recruiting prisoner subjects. Informed consent statements presented to prospective subjects must indicate that a decision not to participate in a study will have no influence on work assignments, privileges, or parole decisions. To help ensure that these ethical issues are recognized, if an IRB reviews a project where prisoners will be subjects, at least one member of that IRB must be either a prisoner or someone specifically designated to represent the interests of prisoners.

We mentioned earlier that random assignment is generally recognized as an ethical procedure for selecting subjects or deciding which subjects will receive an experimental treatment. HHS regulations emphasize this in describing special provisions for using prison subjects: "Unless the principal investigator provides to the [IRB] justification in writing for following some other procedures, control subjects must be selected randomly from the group of available prisoners who meet the characteristics needed for that particular research project" (45 CFR 46.304 (4)). Thus, federal regulations recognize random selection as the most equitable procedure for choosing subjects.

See Chapter 15 for an example of an informed consent statement in research with incarcerated subjects.

Institutional Review Board Requirements and Researcher Rights

Federal regulations contain many more provisions for institutional review boards and other protections for human subjects. Some researchers may feel that such regulations actually *create* ethical problems by setting constraints on their freedom and professional judgments in conducting research. Recall that potential conflict between the rights of researchers to discover new knowledge and the rights of subjects to be free from unnecessary harm is a fundamental ethical dilemma. It is at least inconvenient to have outsiders review a research proposal. Or you may feel insulted by the implication that the potential benefits of your research will not outweigh the potential harm or inconvenience to human subjects.

There is some merit in such concerns; however, you should not lose sight of the reasons IRB requirements and other regulations were created. Researchers are not always the best judges of the potential for their work to harm individuals. In designing and conducting criminal justice research, we may become excited about discovering something new about why people commit crimes or what new approaches to criminal sentencing hold promise. That excitement and commitment to scientific advancement may lead researchers to overlook possible harms to individual rights or well-being. You may recognize this as another way of asking whether the ends justify the means. Since researchers are not always disinterested parties in answering such questions, IRBs are established to provide outside judgments.

Also recognize that IRBs can be sources of expert advice on how to resolve ethical dilemmas. Decker and Van Winkle shared their university's concern about balancing confidentiality against informed consent from juvenile subjects; together they were able to fashion a workable compromise.

Another reason for creating regulations to protect human subjects, and IRBs to monitor compliance with those regulations, is the perceived failure of other means, together with ethical controversies raised by some actual studies (Homan, 1991; Reynolds, 1979). In the next section, we will describe briefly two research projects that provoked widespread ethical controversy and discussion. These are not the only two controversial projects that have been done; they simply illustrate ethical issues in the real world.

■ TWO ETHICAL CONTROVERSIES

The first project studied homosexual behavior in public rest rooms, and the second examined how "prisoners" and "guards" reacted in a simulated prison setting.

Trouble in the Tearoom

As a graduate student, Laud Humphreys became interested in studying homosexuality. He developed a special interest in the casual and fleeting homosexual acts engaged in by some nonhomosexuals. In particular, his research interest focused on homosexual acts between strangers who meet in the public rest rooms in parks, called "tearooms" among homosexuals. The result was the publication of *The Tearoom Trade* (Humphreys, 1975).

What particularly interested Humphreys about the tearoom activity was that the participants seemed to live "normal" lives otherwise, as family men and accepted members of the community. They did nothing else that might qualify them as

Ethics and Juvenile Gang Members

SCOTT Decker and Barrik Van Winkle faced a range of ethical issues in their study of gang members. Many of these should be obvious given what has been said so far in this chapter. Violence was common among subjects and presented a real risk to researchers. Writing in 1996, Decker (1996:252) reported that 11 of the 99 members of the original sample had been killed since the project began in 1990. There was also the obvious need to assure confidentiality to subjects.

Their project was supported by a federal agency and administered through a university, so Decker and Van Winkle had to comply with federal human subjects guidelines as administered by the university institutional review board (IRB). And because many of the subjects were juveniles, they had to address federal regulations concerning that special population. Foremost among these was the normal requirement that informed consent for juveniles include parental notification and approval.

You may immediately recognize the conflicting ethical principles at work here, together with the potential for conflict. The promise of confidentiality to gang members is one such principle that was essential for researchers to obtain candid reports of violence and other law-breaking behavior. But the need for confidentiality conflicted with initial IRB requirements to obtain parental consent for their children to participate in the research.

■ This would have violated our commitment to maintain the confidentiality of each subject, not to mention the ethical and practical difficulties of finding and informing each parent. We told the Human Subjects Committee that we would not, in effect, tell par-

homosexuals. Thus, it was important to them that they remain anonymous in their tearoom visits. How would you study something like that?

Humphreys decided to take advantage of the social structure of the situation. Typically, the tearoom encounter involved three people: the two men actually engaged in the homosexual act and a lookout, called the "watchqueen." Thus, Humphreys began to show up at public rest rooms, offering to serve as watchqueen whenever it seemed appropriate. Since the watchqueen's payoff was the chance to watch the action, Humphreys was able to conduct field observations, just as he would if he were studying drug dealers or jaywalking at intersections.

To round out his understanding of the tearoom trade, Humphreys needed to know something more about the people who participated. Since the men probably would not have been thrilled about being interviewed, Humphreys developed a different solution. Whenever possible, he noted the license plate numbers of participants' cars and then tracked down their names and addresses through the police. Humphreys then visited the men at their homes, disguising himself enough to avoid recognition, and announced that he was conducting a survey. In that fashion, he collected the personal information he was unable to get in the rest rooms.

Humphreys's research provoked considerable controversy, both within and outside the social scientific community. Some critics charged Humphreys with a gross invasion of privacy in the name of science. What men did in public rest rooms was their own business and not Humphreys's. Others were concerned about the deceit involved; Humphreys had lied to the participants by leading them to believe he was only a voyeur-participant. People who felt that the tearoom participants, because they were in a public facility, were fair game for observation nonetheless protested the follow-up survey. They felt it was unethical for Humphreys to trace the participants to their homes and to interview them under false pretenses. Still others justified Humphreys's research. The topic, they said, was worth study. It

ents that their child was being interviewed because they were an active gang member, knowledge that the parents may not have had. (Decker and Van Winkle, 1996:52)

You might think deception would be a possibility—informing parents that their child was selected for a youth development study, for example. This would not, however, solve the logistical difficulty of locating parents or guardians, some of whom had lost contact with their children. Furthermore, it was likely that even if parents or guardians could be located, suspicions about the research project and the reasons their children were selected would prevent many parents from granting consent. Loss of juvenile subjects in this way would compromise the norm of generality as we have described it in this chapter and elsewhere.

Finally, waiving the requirement for parental consent would have undermined the legal principle that the interests of juveniles must be protected by a supervising adult. Remember that researchers are not always the best judges of whether sufficient precautions have been taken to protect subjects. Here is how Decker and Van Winkle (1996:52) resolved the issue with their IRB:

■ We reached a compromise in which we found an advocate for each juvenile member of our sample; this person—a university employee—was responsible for making sure that the subject understood (1) their rights to refuse or quit the interview at any time without penalty and (2) the confidential nature of the project. All subjects signed the consent form.

Source: Adapted from Decker and Van Winkle (1996).

couldn't be studied any other way, and they regarded the deceit as essentially harmless, noting that Humphreys was careful not to harm his subjects by disclosing their tearoom activities.

The tearoom trade controversy, as you might imagine, has never been resolved. It is still debated, and it probably always will be because it stirs emotions and contains ethical issues people disagree about. What do you think? Was Humphreys ethical in doing what he did? Are there parts of the research you feel were acceptable and other parts that were not? Whatever your opinion, you are sure to find others who disagree with you.

Simulating a Prison

The second illustration differs from the first in many ways. Whereas Humphreys's study involved participant observation, this study setting was in the laboratory. Where the first examined a form of human deviance, the study we're going to look at now examined how people behave in formal institutions.

Few people would disagree that prisons are dehumanizing. Inmates forfeit freedom, of course, but their incarceration is also accompanied by a loss of privacy and individual identity. Violence and forced homosexuality are among the realities of prison life that many people point to as evidence of the failure of prisons to rehabilitate inmates.

Although the problems of prisons have many sources, psychologists Haney, Banks, and Zimbardo (1973) were interested in two general explanations. One they referred to as the *dispositional hypothesis*—prisons are brutal and dehumanizing because of the types of people who run them and are incarcerated in them. Inmates have demonstrated their disrespect for legal order and their willingness to use deceit and violence; persons who work as prison guards may be disproportionately authoritarian and sadistic. On the other hand is the *situational hypothesis*—the prison environment itself creates brutal, dehumanizing conditions independent of the kinds of people who live and work in the institutions.

Haney and associates set out to test the situational hypothesis by creating a functional prison simulation in which healthy, psychologically normal male college students were assigned to roles as prisoners and guards. The "prison" was constructed in the basement of a psychology building: three 6 × 9 foot "cells" furnished with only a cot, a prison "yard" in a corridor, and a 2 × 2 × 7-foot solitary confinement cell. Twenty-one subjects were selected from 75 volunteers after screening to eliminate those with physical or psychological problems, and they were offered $15 per day for their participation. These subjects were randomly assigned to be either guards or prisoners.

All subjects signed contracts that included instructions about prisoner and guard roles for the planned two-week experiment. "Prisoners" were told that they would be confined throughout the experiment, they would be under constant surveillance, and their civil rights would be suspended; they were, however, guaranteed that they would not be subject to physical abuse. "Guards" were given minimal instructions, most notably that physical aggression or physical punishment of "prisoners" was prohibited. Together with a "warden," they were generally free to develop prison rules and procedures. Although the researchers planned to study how both guards and prisoners reacted to their roles, guards were led to believe that the main purpose of the experiment was to study prisoners.

If you had been a prisoner in this experiment, you would have experienced something like the following after signing your contract: First, you would have been arrested without notice at your home by a real police officer, perhaps with the neighbors looking on. After being searched and taken to the (real) police station in handcuffs, you would have been booked, fingerprinted, and been placed in a police detention facility. Next, you would be blindfolded and driven to "prison," where you would be stripped, sprayed with a delousing solution, and left to stand naked for a period of time in the prison "yard." Eventually, you would be issued a prison uniform (a loose overshirt stamped with your ID number), fitted with

an ankle chain, led to your cell, and ordered to remain silent. Your prison term would then be totally controlled by the guards.

Wearing mirrored sunglasses, khaki uniforms, badges, and nightsticks, guards supervised prisoner work assignments and held lineups three times per day. Although lineups initially lasted only a few minutes, guards later extended them to several hours. Prisoners were fed bland meals and accompanied by guards on three authorized toilet visits per day.

The behavior of all subjects in the prison yard and other open areas was videotaped; audiotapes were made continuously while prisoners were in their cells. Researchers administered brief questionnaires throughout the experiment to assess emotional changes in prisoners and guards. About one month after the experiment was concluded, interviews were conducted with all subjects to assess their reactions.

Haney and associates (1973:88) had planned to run the prison experiment for two weeks, but they halted the study after six days because subjects displayed "unexpectedly intense reactions." Five prisoners had to be released even before that time because they showed signs of acute depression or anxiety.

Subjects in each group accepted their roles all too readily. Prisoners and guards could interact with each other in friendly ways because guards had the power to make prison rules. But interactions turned out to be overwhelmingly hostile and negative. Guards had become aggressive, while the prisoners became passive. When the experiment ended prematurely, prisoners were happy about their early "parole," but guards were disappointed that the study would not continue.

Haney and colleagues justify the prison simulation study in part by claiming that the dispositional/situational hypotheses could not be evaluated by using other research designs. It is clear that the researchers were sensitive to ethical issues. They obtained subjects' consent to the experiment through signed contracts. Prisoners who developed signs of acute distress were released early. The entire study was terminated after less than half of the planned two weeks had elapsed when its unexpectedly harsh impact on subjects became evident. Finally, researchers conducted group therapy debriefing sessions with prisoners and guards, together with follow-up contacts for one year to ensure that subjects' negative experiences were temporary.

Two related features of this experiment raise ethical questions, however. First, subjects were not fully informed of the procedures. Although we have seen that deception, including something less than full disclosure, can often be justified, in this case deception was partially due to the researchers' uncertainty about how the prison simulation would proceed. This is the second and more important ethical problem: Guards were granted the power to make up and modify rules as the study progressed, and their behavior became increasingly authoritarian. Comments by guards illustrate their reactions as the experiment unfolded (Haney, Banks, and Zimbardo, 1973:88):

■ "They [the prisoners] didn't see it as an experiment. It was real and they were fighting to keep their identity. But we were always there to show them just who was boss."

"During the inspection, I went to cell 2 to mess up a bed which the prisoner had made and he grabbed me, screaming that he had just made it. . . . He grabbed my throat, and although he was laughing, I was pretty scared. I lashed out with my stick and hit him in the chin (although not very hard), and when I freed myself I became angry."

"Acting authoritatively can be fun. Power can be a great pleasure."

How do you feel about this experiment? On the one hand, it provided valuable insights into how otherwise normal people react in a simulated prison environment. Subjects appeared to suffer no long-term harm, in part because of precautions taken by researchers. Paul Reynolds (1979:139) cites a certain irony in the short-term discomforts endured by the college student subjects: "There is evidence that the major burdens were borne by individuals from advantaged social

categories and that the major benefactors would be individuals from less advantaged social categories [actual prisoners], an uneven distribution of costs and benefits that many nevertheless consider equitable." On the other hand, researchers did not anticipate how much and how quickly subjects would accept their roles. The experiment had to be halted prematurely. In discussing their findings, Haney and associates (1973:90) note: "Our results are . . . congruent with those of Milgram[2] who most convincingly demonstrated the proposition that evil acts are not necessarily the deeds of evil men, but may be attributable to the operation of powerful social forces." This quote illustrates the fundamental dilemma—balancing the right to conduct research against the rights of subjects. Is it ethical to create powerful social forces that instigate evil acts?

■ DISCUSSION EXAMPLES

Research ethics, then, is an important and ambiguous topic. The difficulty of resolving ethical issues should not be an excuse for ignoring them, however. You should keep ethics in mind as you read other chapters in this book and whenever you plan some research project.

To further sensitize you to the ethical component of social research, we've prepared ten brief descriptions of real and hypothetical research situations. Can you see the ethical issue in each? How do you feel about it? Are the procedures described ultimately acceptable or unacceptable? It would be very useful to discuss these examples with other students in your class.

1. A researcher studies speeding on urban expressways by using a small radar gun to detect speeders, while an assistant records the license numbers of cars traveling more than 10 miles per hour over the posted limit. The speeders' addresses are traced and they

---

[2] Here the authors are referring to controversial research on obedience to authority by Lester Milgram (1965).

receive a mailed questionnaire with a cover letter beginning: "You were observed traveling more than 10 miles per hour over the speed limit on [date and location]. . . ."

2. After a field study of deviant behavior during a riot, law enforcement officials demand that the researcher identify those people who were observed looting. Rather than risk arrest as an accomplice after the fact, the researcher complies.

3. In a federally funded study of a probation program, a researcher discovers that one participant was involved in a murder while on probation. Public disclosure of this incident might threaten the program that the researcher believes, from all evidence, is beneficial. Judging the murder to be an anomaly, researchers do not disclose it to federal sponsors or describe it in published reports.

4. As part of a course on domestic violence, a professor requires students to telephone a domestic violence hotline, pretend to be a victim, and request help. Students then write up a description of the assistance offered by hotline staff and turn it in to the professor.

5. After completing the final draft of a book about a research project, the researcher–author discovers that 25 of the 2,000 survey interviews were falsified by interviewers. He chooses to ignore that fact and publish the book anyway.

6. This quote is from a report on crack dealers by Bruce Jacobs (1996:364–365, note 5):

■ I informed police of my research, realizing that I could not withhold information from authorities if they should subpoena it. This never happened, perhaps because I told police that the research was about street life and urbanism rather than about gangs and crack distribution per se. Although technically this was a violation of the law, many other sociologists studying deviant populations have done the same thing to acquire valid observational data. . . . In addition,

my university's Human Subject Review committee approved this research because I obtained written informed consent from all respondents and included safeguards to protect their anonymity and confidentiality.

7. A criminal justice professor asks students in an introductory class to complete questionnaires that the professor will analyze and use in preparing a journal article for publication.

8. While observing police officers on patrol, a researcher accompanies a uniformed officer to a restaurant, where both are told that whatever they order will be "on the house."

9. A researcher studying juvenile gangs is asked by a federal funding agency not to publish findings indicating that gang members are less often involved in illegal drug sales than are nongang members.

10. In the example mentioned on page 182, the researchers disclosed to public officials that police were not making visits to probationers as called for in the program intervention. The published reports describe the problem as "irregularities in program delivery."

■ MAIN POINTS

- In addition to technical, scientific considerations, criminal justice research projects are shaped by ethical considerations.
- What's ethically "right" and "wrong" in research is ultimately a matter of what people agree is right and wrong.
- Researchers tend not to be the best judges of whether or not their own work adequately addresses ethical questions.
- Most ethical questions involve weighing the possible benefits of research against the potential for harm to research subjects.
- Criminal justice research may generate special ethical questions, including the potential for legal liability and physical harm.
- Scientists agree that participation in research should, as a general norm, be voluntary. This

norm, however, can conflict with the scientific need for generalizability.

- Probably all scientists agree that research should not harm those who participate in it, unless they willingly and knowingly accept the risks of harm.
- Anonymity refers to the situation in which even the researchers cannot identify specific information with the individuals it describes.
- Confidentiality refers to the situation in which the researcher—though knowing which data describe which subjects—agrees to keep that information confidential.
- Compliance with ethical principles is promoted by professional associations and by regulations issued by the Department of Health and Human Services (HHS).
- HHS regulations include special provisions for two types of subjects of particular interest to criminal justice researchers: prisoners and juveniles.
- Institutional review boards (IRBs) play an important role in ensuring that the rights and interests of human subjects are protected.

■ REVIEW QUESTIONS AND EXERCISES

1. Review the discussion of Laud Humphreys's tearoom research. See if you can design a study that addresses the same research questions but avoids the ethical criticisms leveled at Humphreys.
2. Discuss the general trade-offs between the requirements of sound scientific methods and the need to protect human subjects. Where do tensions exist? You may find it helpful to review Chapter 7, paying particular attention to validity threats and how experiments strive to reduce those threats.
3. Review the box, "Ethics and Juvenile Gang Members," noting that Decker and Van

Winkle developed an informed consent form for their subjects. Try your hand at preparing such a form, keeping in mind the various ethical principles discussed in this chapter.

■ ADDITIONAL READINGS

Homan, Roger, *The Ethics of Social Research* (New York: Longman, 1991). A thoughtful analysis of the ethical issues of social science research.

Inciardi, James A., "Some Considerations on the Methods, Dangers, and Ethics of Crack-house Research," Appendix A in James A. Inciardi, Dorothy Lockwood, and Anne E. Pettieger, *Women and Crack Cocaine* (New York: Macmillan, 1993), pp. 147–157. In this thoughtful essay, Inciardi describes the dangers and depressing realities of field research in a crack house. Should a field researcher intervene when witnessing a gang rape in a crack house? Read this selection for Inciardi's answer.

Lee, Raymond, *Doing Research on Sensitive Topics* (Thousand Oaks, CA: Sage, 1993). This book examines the conflicts between scientific research needs and the rights of the humans involved, together with guidelines for dealing with those conflicts.

Reynolds, Paul D., *Ethical Dilemmas and Social Research* (San Francisco: Jossey-Bass, 1979). This book compares codes of ethics issued by several professional societies and concludes with a composite code that is especially valuable for criminal justice researchers.

Wexler, Sandra, "Ethical Obligations and Social Research," in Kimberly L. Kempf (ed.), *Measurement Issues in Criminology* (New York: Springer-Verlag, 1990). A good, brief summary of ethical issues in criminal justice research. Informed consent is discussed in some detail. Wexler presents several guidelines on complying with ethical principles.

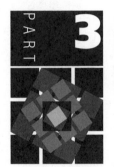

3 *Modes of Observation*

WE have a hunch that you may have grown impatient. If you began this book with a view that doing research means making observations and analyzing what you've observed, the preliminary discussions of various aspects of research design may have seemed too long. It bears repeating, however, that the structuring of inquiry is an integral part of research. With that point firmly in mind, let's dive into the various observational techniques available for criminal justice research.

We'll begin with an overview of the three basic ways criminal justice researchers collect data for measurement. Chapter 9 then examines how social scientists go about selecting people or things for observation. Our discussion of sampling addresses the fundamental scientific issue of generalizability. As we'll see, it is possible for us to select a few people or things for observation and then apply what we observe to a much larger group of people or things than we actually observed. It is possible, for example, to ask 1,000 Americans how they feel about "three strikes and you're out" laws and then accurately predict how tens of millions of people feel about it.

Chapter 10 describes survey research and other techniques for collecting data by asking people questions. We'll cover different ways of asking people questions and discuss the various uses of surveys and related techniques in criminal justice research.

Chapter 11, on field research, examines what is perhaps the most natural form of data collection: the direct observation of phenomena in natural settings. As we will see, observations can be highly structured and systematic (such as counting pedestrians who walk by some specified point) or less structured and more flexible.

Chapter 12 discusses three forms of data collection that take advantage of some of the data available all around us. Criminal justice researchers often examine data collected by public agencies; the Uniform Crime Reports and National Crime Victimization Survey are examples. Content analysis is a method of collecting data through carefully specifying and counting communications such as news stories, court opinions, or even recorded visual images. Criminal justice researchers may also conduct secondary analysis of data collected by others.

CHAPTER 9 Overview of Data Collection and Sampling

What You'll Learn in This Chapter

We will begin with a broad look at different ways of collecting data for criminal justice research. Then we'll see how sampling makes it possible to select a few hundred or thousand people for study—and discover things that apply to hundreds of millions of people not studied.

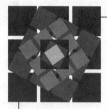

INTRODUCTION

THREE SOURCES OF DATA
Asking Questions
Making Observations
Examining Written Records
Sources of Data Compared

GENERAL ISSUES IN DATA COLLECTION
Measurement Validity and Reliability
Obtrusive and Unobtrusive Measures
Be Careful, But Be Creative

SAMPLING

THE LOGIC OF PROBABILITY SAMPLING
Conscious and Unconscious Sampling Bias
Representativeness and Probability of Selection

SAMPLING CONCEPTS AND TERMINOLOGY

**PROBABILITY SAMPLING THEORY
AND SAMPLING DISTRIBUTION**
Probability Sampling Theory
The Sampling Distribution of Ten Cases
Binomial Sampling Distribution

POPULATIONS AND SAMPLING FRAMES

TYPES OF SAMPLING DESIGNS
Simple Random Sampling
Systematic Sampling
Stratified Sampling
Disproportionate Stratified Sampling
Multistage Cluster Sampling
Multistage Cluster Sampling with Stratification

**ILLUSTRATION: TWO NATIONAL
CRIME SURVEYS**
National Crime Victimization Survey
British Crime Survey

PROBABILITY SAMPLING IN REVIEW

NONPROBABILITY SAMPLING
Purposive or Judgmental Sampling
Quota Sampling
Reliance on Available Subjects
Snowball Sampling

MAIN POINTS

REVIEW QUESTIONS AND EXERCISES

ADDITIONAL READINGS

■ *INTRODUCTION*

We have two purposes in this chapter: first to call your attention to some general issues in actual data collection, and second to discuss the logic and fundamental principles of sampling. Along the way, we will introduce you to three basic ways of collecting information and consider how they can be modified to suit different research purposes.

As with most aspects of designing and executing criminal justice research, the choices you make about data collection and sampling depend on your particular research purpose. And, as we saw in Chapter 5, data collection is closely linked to measurement choices, which in turn depend on how you define particular concepts.

It is often necessary to make compromises. For example, if you were interested in whether or not mandatory jail sentences reduced highway deaths due to drunk driving, collecting blood samples from all drivers in fatal automobile accidents would be an ideal way to produce a measure of drunk driving. But since police in many states do not routinely collect blood samples, you might have to develop an alternative measure that would require you to collect data in some other way. In this case, specifying measures of drunk driving and traffic deaths are relatively straightforward; the difficulty arises in actually collecting the data.

We have talked a lot about observation, and we will do so even more in the next four chapters. A criminal justice researcher has a whole world of potential observations, yet nobody can observe everything. A critical part of criminal justice research, then, is deciding what will be observed and what won't. If you want to study drug users, for example, which drug users should you study?

Sampling is the process of selecting observations. In the second part of this chapter, we will examine different sampling techniques. Sampling is ordinarily used to select observations for one of two related reasons. First, it is often not possible to collect information from all persons or other units you wish to study. You may wish to know what proportion of all persons arrested in U.S. cities have recently used drugs, but collecting all that data would be virtually impossible. You have to look at a sample of observations.

The second reason for sampling is that it is often not necessary to collect data from all persons or other units. As we'll see, probability sampling techniques—those that involve random sampling—allow a researcher to make relatively few observations and then generalize from those observations to a much wider population. If you were interested in what proportion of high school students have used marijuana, collecting data from a probability sample of a few thousand students would serve just as well as studying every high school student in the country.

Although probability sampling is central to criminal justice research, we'll take some time to examine a variety of nonprobability methods as well. Though not based on random selection, these methods have their own logic and can provide useful samples for criminal justice inquiry. We'll examine both the advantages and the shortcomings of such methods, and we'll see where they fit in the larger picture of sampling and collecting data.

■ *THREE SOURCES OF DATA* ✓

Thinking back to our examination of different ways to measure crime from Chapter 6, you should recognize three general approaches. We can measure crime by asking people questions about victimization or about offenses they have committed, by observing actual behavior, or by using existing data. These approaches to measuring crime illustrate the three basic ways of collecting data for criminal justice research: asking questions, making observations, and examining written records.

Chapters 10–12 examine each of these techniques in turn. Now, however, we want to take a broad view of different ways to collect data.

Asking Questions √

In criminal justice and other types of social science research, when we collect data by asking people questions, we often use the survey method. The National Crime Victimization Survey (NCVS) and the Monitoring the Future Survey, mentioned in Chapter 6, are examples. A formal questionnaire that embodies operationalizations of concepts is a key element in these and other surveys.

There are also other ways of making observations by asking people questions that we may not normally associate with survey methods. If you were studying the decision-making processes of a parole board, for example, you might interview members of the board and other persons who have input into the decision-making process. Although you would probably ask the same questions of everyone you interviewed, you might interject some specific questions that are unique for each individual, based on their answers to standard questions.

Sometimes small groups of subjects, called **focus groups,** are brought together for a structured discussion of some research question. This technique was developed as a market research tool to explore how targeted consumers might respond to some new product or advertising campaign (Krueger, 1994). Groups of 12 to 15 subjects are selected according to some criteria—subscribers to *Beer World,* for example, to assess how literate beer drinkers would react to a new brew—and engaged in a focused discussion of the new product and various things that contribute to beer-buying decisions.

Focus groups are used increasingly in criminal justice research. For instance, one of the goals of community policing is to develop law enforcement services that are more responsive to crime and other problems that trouble specific neighborhoods. Focus groups have been adopted in recent years by many police departments to explore and more precisely define the concerns of residents. This is something like market research for police—learning what consumers want.

Ways to collect data by asking people questions will be examined in Chapter 10, including survey methods, focus groups, and other types of interviewing techniques.

Making Observations √

Let's say you are interested in the relationship between street lighting and fear of crime on your campus, and you hypothesize that poor lighting in certain areas increases fear. How would you measure lighting? Since you would probably conduct a survey to measure fear, you might include a question that asked people to rate the quality of lighting on campus. Alternatively, you could directly observe levels of lighting in specific areas, perhaps rating each area on a five-point scale ranging from very good to very poor. Or you could use a light meter to obtain standard measurements of light levels (expressed in lumens for the technically inclined) by holding the device at some standard distance from each streetlight and recording the meter's reading. Through observation, you could also note the presence of shadows or physical features that impaired visibility near streetlights.

Direct observation encompasses a broad range of methods for gathering data—from counting the number of participants who attend a community crime prevention meeting to urinalysis tests for drug use. The defining characteristic of direct observation is obtaining measurements by observing behavior, traces of behavior, or physical objects without interacting with research subjects. When you ask people questions, either in a face-to-face interview or by having subjects complete a self-administered questionnaire, you interact with them. In contrast, direct observation does not involve verbal interaction. Thus, for example, you could measure cocaine use among a group of probationers by administering a questionnaire that asked them whether or not they had used cocaine in the past 48 hours, or you could administer a urinalysis test for cocaine use.

You might think that direct observation of cocaine use through urinalysis would be superior to asking people whether or not they used cocaine.

Practical difficulties often prevent the use of such methods, however. Consider, for example, the ethical issues that might be involved in conducting urinalysis tests on a national sample of high school seniors.

Forms of direct observation other than conducting laboratory tests of drug use present other types of problems. If, for example, you were interested in community crime prevention groups, you might attend a group meeting and observe not only how many people attended but also what types of concerns were expressed and how attendees felt about some particular issue—say, neighborhood watch—that was discussed at the meeting. Although you would not be asking people about their views of neighborhood watch, your observations would require making judgments about particular comments. Were they positive, negative, or mixed? Did they raise questions about some particular aspect of neighborhood watch?

We will consider direct observation in detail in Chapter 11, which is entitled "Field Research" to reflect that observations are normally made in more natural settings, outside the laboratory.

Examining Written Records ✓

Many measurements are made by consulting written documents or other types of records. The concept of criminal history, for example, may be measured by consulting records maintained by police, juvenile authorities, or criminal courts. Rather than directly observing criminal behavior or asking subjects about arrests or convictions, researchers commonly examine records maintained by public agencies as sources for measures of something like criminal history.

As with other methods of collecting data, written records are used in a variety of ways, corresponding roughly to different types of written records. Criminal justice researchers frequently make use of information routinely collected by government agencies and made available to the general public. Uniform Crime Reports (UCR), published by the FBI, and reports from the decennial census of the U.S. population are ex-

amples. Such written records are compiled by the FBI and the Census Bureau for the specific purpose of sharing information with researchers, government officials, and the general public.

Virtually all public agencies maintain other types of records for their own use that are not normally released to the general public but that may be accessible to researchers. Records of juvenile offenses, for instance, are not disclosed to third parties, but criminal justice researchers commonly obtain access. Budget documents, information on inmate populations in correctional institutions, the number of monthly contacts between probation officers and clients, and the number of traffic tickets written by police officers are other examples of written records that may be sources of criminal justice data.

Court decisions form another type of written record that is fundamental to conducting legal research. Judicial opinions express principles of law that attorneys and legal scholars consult regularly. Court decisions may be used by criminal justice researchers in slightly different ways. For example, you might be interested in how frequently the "battered spouse" defense has been cited in homicide cases over some period of time. To address that question, you could review trial court transcripts or the texts of appellate court opinions in homicide cases.

Analyzing court decisions is a specialized example of content analysis, where information from documents, normally text, is systematically examined by researchers. For instance, if you wanted to know whether the editorial staffs of daily newspapers in the nation's 100 largest cities were for or against gun control, you could examine editorials published in those newspapers and record whether the writer favored or opposed gun control.

Chapter 12 will consider in detail the various ways written records can serve as sources of data in criminal justice research. However, we wish to make one more point—perhaps one that has already occurred to you—before moving on. Even though you may gather data from written records, someone else originally gathered the data by direct observation or by asking people questions.

For example, we described UCR data as written records published by the FBI. But how does the FBI get such data? In Chapter 6, we mentioned that UCR data are compiled from reports submitted from each state. In some states, individual law enforcement agencies send crime reports directly to the FBI; in others, state-level departments obtain data from local agencies and then forward the crime reports to the FBI. In each case, crimes were first recorded by police, who observed crimes in progress or, more commonly, took reports from victims. So the UCR crime data that a researcher might obtain from written records were originally collected by direct observation or by asking people—victims and witnesses—questions.

That data from written records were originally collected either through observation or by asking people questions raises an important issue: If you will use data from written records in your research, it is essential that you understand how those data were originally collected. We'll expand on this point in Chapter 12.

Sources of Data Compared

As you design a research or evaluation project, you will have to make choices about measurement and data collection together. Such choices are ultimately linked to your purposes for conducting research, subject to constraints on what is possible and, as we saw in Chapter 8, what is ethical. You may find that multiple measures of some concept are needed; Chapter 5 noted how multiple measures can be incorporated into a research design. By the same token, criminal justice research frequently uses multiple sources of data collected through different methods of observation.

Let's consider an example, one we introduced in Chapter 5, where different ways of collecting data might be used. In a widely cited article, James Q. Wilson and George Kelling (1982) argue that broken windows, graffiti, abandoned buildings, junk cars, and the like are symbols of urban decay that people associate with crime

problems. Other researchers have referred to such urban problems as "incivilities," which also include social signs of disorder like the presence of homeless persons, drunks, or teenage gangs on city streets (Skogan, 1990a). As we mentioned in Chapter 5, incivilities can be the source of two related problems: They may facilitate crime directly, or they may contribute to the fear of crime.

How would you measure and collect data on incivilities? As you might expect after a bit of thought, incivilities can be assessed using each of the three ways of collecting data. A survey could show whether urban residents believe incivilities are present in their neighborhoods or perceive them to be problems. Direct observation of neighborhood conditions would reveal the presence of broken windows, graffiti, and people loitering in the street. Observers might also develop measures that rate the conditions of buildings in a neighborhood, ranging from good through fair to poor, or some similar scale. Or, if litter is viewed as an incivility or a sign that people don't care about neighborhood conditions, direct observation could produce a litter index by counting discarded wine bottles, burger wrappers, and the like. Written records could also be sources of data for incivility measures. Records of arrests for loitering, disturbing the peace, or public indecency are possible candidates. Transportation authorities in large cities might keep records of the number of subway cars taken out of service because of graffiti. Or housing department records could be consulted to develop a measure of abandoned or substandard buildings.

The box on p. 202 entitled "Multiple Measures in Home Detention" provides a different example of how information obtained through each of the three methods of data collection was used to address research questions.

■ GENERAL ISSUES IN DATA COLLECTION

Now we will touch on some more general issues to think about as you consider what data-collection approach is best for some specific research application. We will also link our previous discussion of measurement principles to the nuts and bolts of making actual measurements.

Measurement Validity and Reliability

Of course, in making plans to collect data, you'll be attentive to the validity and reliability of your measures. We devoted considerable attention to these two criteria for measurement quality in Chapter 5, and we wish to reinforce their importance before moving on.

When you begin to think more specifically about actually making measurements and when you actually begin to collect data, you often think of validity and reliability questions that you might have overlooked in the design stage. For example, in their study of electronically monitored home detention (ELMO), Baumer and Mendelsohn (1990) initially thought that measuring successful computer contacts with people assigned to ELMO would be straightforward; the computer would automatically keep track of calls and their outcomes. This should produce a valid and reliable measure of computer contact; the researchers would simply copy data from computer disks.

After beginning their research, however, Baumer and Mendelsohn encountered three types of problems in using the computer contact data. First was the problem of translating the manufacturer's computer codes into symbols the researchers could understand. This was eventually solved, but only after extremely laborious translation of computer codes.

Second, attempting to contact someone on home detention could be unsuccessful in a surprising variety of ways. Of course, if no one answered the phone after several rings, that was an unsuccessful contact attempt. If the phone was answered but no contact was made between the base unit and the wristlet or anklet, the computer recorded an "unsuccessful." Getting a busy signal, an answering machine, or a voice mail system was also an unsuccessful computer call.

The third problem was most interesting and troublesome. People assigned to ELMO and manual home detention could legitimately be away from home while working at their job. Normally, the computer would be programmed not to call

people during their scheduled working hours. Schedules frequently changed, however, sometimes on short notice. Baumer and Mendelsohn found that ELMO subjects spent more time on the job, often seeking overtime, just to get out of the house. Problems emerged because community corrections staff were not always able to reprogram the computer's calling schedule to accommodate work schedule changes. Furthermore, when the computer got one unsuccessful call outcome, it was programmed to accelerate the number of repeat calls, in something like a frantic attempt to make contact. This, of course, had the effect of multiplying the number of unsuccessful calls, even if the person to whom the computer was "reaching out" was legitimately absent from home.

Our purpose in this example is to show that what appears at first to be a valid measure, reliably recorded by a computer, was in fact far from perfect and required careful interpretation. So, in making decisions about measurement and data collection, be prepared to make some adjustments in case you encounter unexpected difficulty or ambiguity. After you begin to make actual observations, deficiencies may become evident in what initially appeared to be a valid measure. More commonly, collecting data will reveal potential reliability problems that are difficult to anticipate in the design stages of a research project. The chapters that follow will describe how to identify and deal with reliability problems in each mode of data collection.

In any event, being attentive to measurement quality is not merely a pro forma exercise that is easily taken care of in a research office. Unless you are using measures and data-collecting techniques that have been widely adopted and accepted by others, you are well advised to continually evaluate measurement and data-collection procedures.

Obtrusive and Unobtrusive Measures

A distinction is often made between obtrusive and unobtrusive measurement. In obtrusive or reactive measurement, research subjects are aware that they are being studied. Unobtrusive mea-

Multiple Measures in Home Detention

TERRY BAUMER and Robert Mendelsohn (1990) conducted an experimental evaluation of electronic monitoring (ELMO) as a supplement to home detention. People convicted of misdemeanors or minor nonviolent felonies were randomly assigned to home detention with ELMO (the experimental group) or home detention with manual monitoring (the control group). Subjects in the control group were monitored through phone calls and personal visits to homes and workplaces by staff in the implementing agency, a county community corrections department.

ELMO is intended to enhance the supervision of persons sentenced to home detention while conserving agency staff resources. ELMO subjects were fitted with electronic devices worn on a wrist or ankle; a base unit was attached to their home telephone. Several times per day (and night), a centrally located computer dialed the home of each ELMO subject, announcing that the "On Guard" system was calling and instructing whoever answered the phone to place the electronic bracelet or wristlet in the base unit. When done correctly, this completed an electronic circuit and the computer recorded a successful telephone contact.

The evaluation sought to determine whether ELMO reduced misconduct by people while they were on home detention, as well as subsequent arrests up to one year after they completed their home detention sentence. In addition, Baumer and Mendelsohn were interested in the program's day-to-day operation in a community corrections agency, and in how ELMO affected the lives of those who wore the bracelets. More specifically, their research addressed these questions:

1. How many people in the experimental and control groups were rearrested within one year of their release?
2. Were ELMO subjects more or less frequently cited for misbehavior than subjects on home detention with manual monitoring?
3. Did the implementing agency understand the ELMO technology? Was the ELMO equipment readily integrated into routine agency operations, or did it disrupt normal agency activities?
4. For the experimental group, how did ELMO affect their daily lives? Was wearing the bracelet inconvenient, embarrassing, or uncomfortable? Was being subject to a call at any time of the day or night stressful or annoying?

surement does not involve direct interaction between researchers and subjects, and subjects are not aware that they are being studied. For example, asking people whether they have ever stolen some article from a shop is obtrusive, while covertly observing people in a shop and then counting how many people steal something is unobtrusive.

Unobtrusive measures are often preferred because they may reduce or eliminate the possibility of validity threats due to testing bias. By not interacting directly with subjects, researchers can obtain measures that are uncontaminated by subjects' reactions to the measurement process.

You should carefully consider what kinds of measurement are obtrusive and unobtrusive.

Some textbooks obscure the distinguishing characteristic—Are subjects aware they are being measured?—by stating that direct observation and written records are unobtrusive measures. In many situations this is true, but not always. Let's consider a hypothetical example.

Assume you are interested in whether or not restricting the sale of paint in aerosol cans reduces the incidence of graffiti. That's certainly a reasonable expectation, and a city ordinance that prohibited the sale of spray paint to persons under 18 years of age might be a reasonable approach to trying to reduce graffiti. You might test your hypothesis with a quasi-experimental design in which you obtained pretest and posttest measures before and after the ordinance went into effect.

To address these questions, Baumer and Mendelsohn collected data by consulting written records, asking questions, and making direct observations. Police arrest records were used to assess recidivism by persons in the treatment and control groups. To answer the second question, researchers examined records of misconduct that were maintained by the implementing agency. ELMO computer technology afforded another source of information about misconduct, one that was also used by the implementing agency. Results from each computer-generated call to ELMO subjects were automatically recorded, producing a form of direct observation.

Baumer and Mendelsohn conducted extensive observations of day-to-day operations at the community corrections department. From these observations, they concluded that the ELMO technology did initially disrupt other routine tasks. But after some initial difficulties, a staff member was dedicated to the experimental program and soon integrated the computer-generated data into other information on subject performance that was regularly consulted by agency staff and administrators.

Each experimental and control subject was interviewed before beginning home detention and after completing their sentence. The interview schedule included several questions about personal and family reactions to being constantly subject to a phone call and to having to wear the ELMO wristlet or anklet.

In one sense, the reactions of persons sentenced to ELMO-enhanced home detention could be obtained only by asking questions about their experience. However, Baumer and Mendelsohn took this one step further through participant observation: Each researcher "sentenced" himself to ELMO for two weeks, alternating the wristlet and anklet devices. This form of direct observation enabled the investigators to verify subject claims about the punitive aspects of home detention and provided rich detail about discomfort, inconvenience, and annoyance. The researchers, and their spouses, were awakened by 2:00 A.M. greetings from the tireless and tiresome "On Guard" system. Showering was difficult and stressful with one ear listening for the phone. These two male researchers devoted some additional thought to selecting each day's wardrobe; they also realized that the anklet-mounted device would present challenges to women who wore pantyhose or to persons of either gender partial to boots.

Now consider some possible unobtrusive measures of the dependent variable, graffiti. An obvious one is direct observation. You could observe buildings, fences, and other structures or surfaces, counting the number that exhibited graffiti or perhaps measuring the total surface area covered by paint. However, this would work only if you actually made pretest observations before the law went into effect. If you decided to test your hypothesis some time after the law had become effective, you obviously could not make pretest observations.

An alternative measure is to consult police records of arrests for vandalism. You could first check all vandalism arrests before and after the law became effective and then screen the arrests for cases involving graffiti. A decrease might be attributable to the ordinance banning spray paint sales to minors, subject to a careful assessment of possible threats to the validity of that inference.

But are police records of arrests for vandalism really an unobtrusive measure? If you went to the police station to get copies of arrest records, you would not be interacting with subjects, and the subjects themselves—people arrested for vandalism—would not be aware of their role in your research. But such subjects were aware of their role as persons arrested for vandalism, and they did interact with police officers. Although your secondary measurement—getting copies from the police—is clearly unobtrusive, the primary measurement—arrest by police—was anything but unobtrusive. Subjects may not have been aware of their participation in your research, but they were certainly aware of their participation in data collection by the arresting police officers.

Our point here is similar to one mentioned earlier in this chapter: A researcher may collect data from written records, but some previous measurement process actually produced the written records. Describing written records, or secondary sources of data, as unobtrusive measures can be misleading and suggests that the researcher has not considered how written records were originally produced. It is more accurate to consider the extent to which the measurement process involves direct interaction with research subjects. This could include interaction between researchers and subjects through a questionnaire, or interaction between subjects and some other person who originally collected data that researchers will later use.

If you are thinking that the issue of subjects being aware of measurement is similar to our discussion in Chapter 7 of testing as a validity threat, you're on the right track. Rather than distinguishing between obtrusive and unobtrusive measurement, it is more useful to focus on reducing bias or threats to validity in the measurement process generally. If you suspect that interactive data collection such as a survey will produce biased measures, you should try to develop some noninteractive measures or other procedures that will reduce the potential bias.

Be Careful, But Be Creative

These are our final introductory words of wisdom before we move to the topic of sampling. In the chapters that follow, we urge you to be cautious in formulating questionnaire items, making direct observations, or using data that were originally collected by someone else. Being attentive to questions of validity and reliability is a critical first step in careful measurement and data collection.

If you use written records, learn how they were produced. For example, you might assume, as Maxfield once did, that prison population figures produced by your state department of correction are accurate; counting and keeping track of incarcerated persons should be a pretty straightforward exercise. Digging a little deeper, Maxfield learned that the Indiana Department of Correction "loses" about 10 percent of its prison population each year (Indiana Department of Correction, staff from statistical analysis section, personal communication, 1990). Roughly equivalent to inventory shrinkage in a retail store, the department loses track of inmates in various ways, and summary statistics are adjusted to reflect such losses.[1]

Being careful is important, but so is being creative. Because measurement is so important but often so difficult in criminal justice research, it is frequently necessary to devise creative substitutes for direct measures. Chapters 10–12 will present several examples of creative approaches to measurement and data collection.

■ SAMPLING ✓

Sampling in general refers to selecting some part of a population. **Probability sampling** is a method of selection in which each member of a population has a *known* chance or probability of being selected. Because probability sampling has foundations in statistics, you will find it more rigorous and precise than earlier topics in this book. Where criminal justice research as a whole is both art and science, sampling, as practiced in social science research, generally leans more in the direction of science. As a result, some students find sampling more difficult than other aspects of research methods because it is more "technical." At the same time, other students say the logical neatness of sampling actually makes it easier for

---

[1] For example, an inmate's lawyer might arrange for a hearing in a county court, perhaps to review the inmate's sentence. The inmate is physically moved from a state correctional facility to a county jail, which may be hundreds of miles away. At the hearing, a judge suspends the balance of the inmate's sentence. The happy person is immediately set free, but no one bothers to inform the correctional facility, where the inmate is eventually recorded as lost.

them to comprehend than, say, conceptualization or causation. We can't predict your reaction, of course, but we can report that even students who normally don't do well with technical topics have been able to master the logic of probability sampling.

Throughout this chapter, we will frequently refer to sampling applications in social research in general and present criminal justice examples to illustrate basic sampling principles. We'll begin our discussion with a description of the logic of probability sampling and a brief glossary of sampling concepts and terminology. Then we'll look at the concept of sampling distribution: the basis of estimating the accuracy of findings based on samples. Following these theoretical discussions, we'll consider populations and sampling frames, focusing on practical problems of determining the target group of the study and the way to begin selecting a sample. Next, we'll examine the ba-

sic sample designs: simple random samples, systematic samples, stratified samples, and cluster samples. Finally, we will discuss different types and applications of nonprobability sampling.

■ *THE LOGIC OF PROBABILITY SAMPLING*

If all members of a population were identical in all respects— all demographic characteristics, attitudes, experiences, behaviors, and so on—there would be no need for careful sampling procedures. Any sample would be sufficient. In this extreme case of homogeneity, in fact, one case would be sufficient as a sample to study characteristics of the whole population.

In fact, of course, the human beings who make up any real population are heterogeneous, varying in many ways. Figure 9-1 offers a simplified illustration of a heterogeneous population: The 100

FIGURE 9-1
A Population of 100 Folks

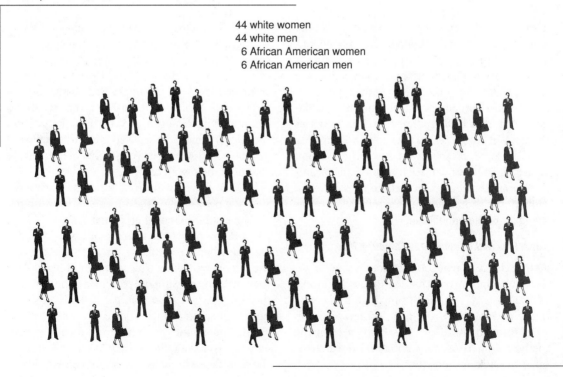

44 white women
44 white men
 6 African American women
 6 African American men

FIGURE 9-2
A Sample of Convenience: Easy, But Not Representative

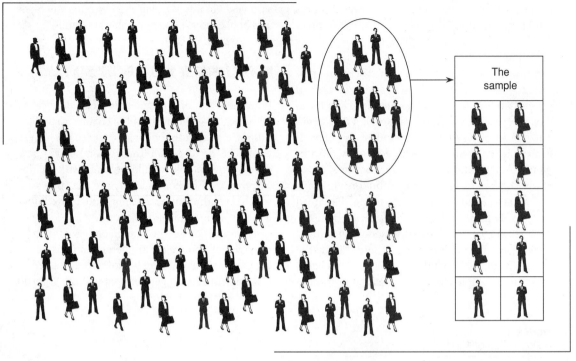

members of this small population differ by gender and race. We'll use this hypothetical micropopulation to illustrate various aspects of sampling.

A sample of individuals from a population, if it is to provide useful descriptions of the total population, must contain essentially the same variations that exist in the population. This is not as simple as it might seem. Let's take a minute to look at some of the ways researchers might go astray. Then we will see how probability sampling provides an efficient method for selecting a sample that should adequately reflect variations that exist in the population.

Conscious and Unconscious Sampling Bias

At first glance, it may look as though sampling is a pretty straightforward matter. To select a sample of 100 lawyers, you might simply go to a courthouse and interview the first 100 lawyers who walk through the door. This kind of sampling method is often used by untrained researchers, but it has serious problems.

Figure 9-2 illustrates what can happen when you simply select people who are convenient for study. Although women make up only 50 percent of our micropopulation, those closest to the researcher (people in the upper right-hand corner of Figure 9-2) happen to be 70 percent women. Although the population is 12 percent African American, none were selected into this sample of people who happened to be conveniently situated near the researcher.

Moving beyond the risks inherent in simply studying people who are convenient, we need to consider other potential problems as well. To begin, your own personal leanings or biases may affect the sample selected in this manner; hence, the sample would not truly represent the population of lawyers. Suppose you're a little intimidated by lawyers who look particularly prosperous, feeling they might ridicule your research effort. You might consciously or unconsciously avoid interviewing them. Or you might feel that the attitudes of "establishment" lawyers would be irrelevant to your research purposes, and you avoid interviewing them.

Even if you sought to interview a "balanced" group of lawyers, you wouldn't know the exact proportions of different types of lawyers who make up such a balance, and you wouldn't always be able to identify the different types just by watching them walk by.

You could make a conscientious effort to interview every tenth lawyer who enters the courthouse, but you still could not be sure of a representative sample because different types of lawyers visit the courthouse with different frequencies, and some never go to the courthouse at all. Your sample would overrepresent lawyers who visit the courthouse more often.

When we speak of *bias* in connection with sampling, this simply means those selected are not "typical" or "representative" of the larger populations they have been chosen from. This kind of bias is virtually inevitable when you pick people by the seat of your pants.

Similarly, "public opinion call-in polls"—in which radio stations or newspapers ask people to call specified telephone numbers to register their opinions—cannot be trusted to represent the general population. At the very least, not everyone in the population is even aware of the poll. This problem also invalidates polls by magazines and newspapers that publish coupons for readers to complete and mail in. Even among those who are aware of such polls, not all will express an opinion, especially if doing so will cost them a stamp, an envelope, or a telephone charge.

The possibilities for inadvertent sampling bias are endless and not always obvious. Fortunately, some techniques help us avoid bias.

Representativeness and Probability of Selection

Although the term **representativeness** has no precise, scientific meaning, it carries a common-sense meaning that makes it useful in the discussion of sampling. As we'll use the term here, a sample is *representative* of the population from which it is selected if the aggregate characteristics of the sample closely approximate those same aggregate characteristics in the population.

If the population, for example, contains 50 percent women, a representative sample will also contain "close to" 50 percent women. Later in this chapter, we'll discuss "how close" in detail. Notice that samples need not be representative in all respects; representativeness is limited to those characteristics that are relevant to the substantive interests of the study.

A basic principle of probability sampling is that a sample will be representative of the population from which it is selected if all members of the population have an equal chance of being selected in the sample. Samples that have this quality are often labeled *EPSEM samples* (**equal probability of selection method**). This principle forms the basis of probability sampling. Moving beyond it, we must realize that samples—even carefully selected EPSEM samples—are seldom, if ever, perfectly representative of the populations from which they are drawn. Nevertheless, probability sampling offers two special advantages.

First, probability samples, though never perfectly representative, are typically more representative than other types of samples because they avoid the biases discussed in the preceding section. In practice, there is a greater likelihood that a probability sample will be representative of the population from which it is drawn than that a nonprobability sample will be.

Second and more important, probability theory permits us to estimate the accuracy or representativeness of the sample. Conceivably, an uninformed researcher might, through wholly haphazard means, select a sample that nearly perfectly represents the larger population. The odds are against doing so, however, and we could not estimate the likelihood that a haphazard sample achieves representativeness. The probability sample, on the other hand, can provide an accurate estimate of success or failure.

■ SAMPLING CONCEPTS AND TERMINOLOGY

Our discussions of sampling theory and practice use a number of technical terms that we will quickly define now. For the most part, we'll employ terms commonly used in sampling and statistical textbooks so that you can understand those other sources better.

In presenting this glossary of sampling concepts and terminology, we would like to acknowledge a debt to Leslie Kish (1965) and his excellent textbook, *Survey Sampling*. Although we have modified some of the conventions used by Kish, his presentation is the most important source of this discussion.

Element   An element is that unit about which information is collected and that provides the basis of analysis. Typically, in survey research, elements are people or certain types of people. However, other kinds of units can be the elements for criminal justice research—correctional facilities, gangs, police beats, or court cases, for example. Elements and units of analysis are often the same in a given study, although the former refers to sample selection and the latter refers to data analysis.

Population   A *population* is the theoretically specified grouping of study elements. Whereas the vague term *delinquents* might be the target for a study, the delineation of the population includes the definition of the element *delinquents* (for example, being charged with a delinquent offense) and the time referent for the study (delinquents as of when?). Translating the abstract *adult drug addicts* into a workable population requires specifying the age that defines *adult* and the level of drug use that constitutes an *addict*. Specifying the term *college student* includes a consideration of full-time and part-time students, degree candidates and nondegree candidates, undergraduate and graduate students, and similar issues.

Although researchers must begin with a careful specification of their population, poetic license usually permits them to phrase their reports in terms of the hypothetical universe. For ease of presentation, even the most conscientious researcher normally speaks of "delinquents" rather than "males and females between the ages of 6 and 18 who have been arrested for an offense described in 46.12.02 §6 of the California Code." The primary guide in this matter, as in most others, is that you should not mislead or deceive your readers.

Study Population   A study population is that aggregation of elements from which the sample is actually selected. As a practical matter, you are seldom in a position to guarantee that every element meeting the theoretical definitions laid down actually has a chance of being selected in the sample. Even where lists of elements exist for sampling purposes, they are usually somewhat incomplete. Some students are always omitted, inadvertently, from student rosters. Some telephone subscribers request that their names and numbers be unlisted. The study population, then, is the aggregation of elements from which the sample is selected.

Often researchers decide to limit their study populations more severely than indicated in the preceding examples. National polling firms may limit their samples to the 48 adjacent states, omitting Alaska and Hawaii for practical reasons. A researcher who wants to sample criminal court judges may limit the study population to those who serve in courts with felony jurisdiction, omitting those who serve in misdemeanor courts. In a sense, we might say that these researchers have redefined their universes and populations, and then they must make the revisions clear to their readers.

Sampling Unit   A *sampling unit* is that element or set of elements considered for selection in some stage of sampling. In the simplest case, called a *single-stage sample*, the sampling units are the same as the elements. In more complex samples, different levels of sampling units may be used. For instance, you might select a sample of federal correctional facilities, then select a sample of cell blocks within the selected facilities, and finally select a sample of inmates from the selected cell blocks. This is an example of a *multistage sample*. The sampling units for these three stages of sampling are, respectively, federal correctional institutions, cell blocks, and inmates; only the last are the elements. More specifically, the terms *primary sampling units*, *secondary sampling units*, and *final sampling units* are used to designate the successive stages.

Sampling Frame   A sampling frame is the actual list of sampling units from which the sample, or some stage of the sample, is selected. In single-stage sampling designs, the sampling frame is simply a list of the elements in the study population. If a simple sample of prison inmates is selected from a roster in a single facility, the roster is the sampling frame. If the primary sampling unit for a multistage sample of prison inmates is the prison facility, then the list of prison facilities is the sampling frame.

In practice, existing sampling frames often define the study population rather than the other way around. We often begin with a population in mind for our study and then we search for possible sampling frames. The frames available for our use are examined and evaluated, and we decide which frame presents a study population most appropriate to our needs. For example, since there is no nationwide list of prison inmates, some alternative sampling frame, such as a list of facilities, must be used.

Observation Unit An *observation unit*, or a unit of data collection, is an element or aggregation of elements from which information is collected. Again, unit of analysis and unit of observation are often the same, but that need not be the case. Thus, the researcher may interview heads of households (the observation units) to collect information about all members of the households (the units of analysis).

Our task is simplified when the unit of analysis and the observation unit are the same. Often that is not possible or feasible, however, and in such situations we need to exercise some ingenuity in collecting data relevant to our units of analysis without actually observing those units.

Variable As discussed earlier, a **variable** is a set of mutually exclusive attributes: gender, age, employment status, and so forth. The elements of a given population may be described in terms of their individual attributes on a given variable. Often criminal justice research aims to describe the distribution of attributes that make up a variable in a population. Thus, a researcher may describe the distribution of assault victimization in a population by examining the relative frequency of assault among members of the population.

A variable, by definition, must possess variation—it must vary. If all elements in the population have the same attribute, then that attribute is a constant in the population, rather than part of a variable.

Parameter A *parameter* is the summary description of a given variable in a population. The mean income of all families in a city and the age distribution of the city's population are parameters. An important portion of criminal justice research involves estimating population parameters on the basis of sample observations.

Statistic A *statistic* is the summary description of a given variable in a sample. Sample statistics are used to make estimates of population parameters. Thus, the mean income computed from a sample and the age distribution of that sample are statistics, and those statistics are used to estimate income and age parameters in a population.

Sampling Error Probability sampling methods seldom, if ever, provide statistics exactly equal to the parameters that they are used to estimate. Probability theory, however, permits us to estimate the degree of error to be expected for a given sample design. *Sampling error* is a fundamental concept we will discuss in more detail later.

Confidence Levels and Confidence Intervals The two key components of sampling error estimates are **confidence levels** and **confidence intervals.** We express the accuracy of our sample statistics in terms of a level of confidence that the statistics fall within a specified interval from the parameter. To illustrate, we may say we are 95 percent confident that our sample statistics (for example, 50 percent favor longer prison terms for sexual assault offenders) are within plus or minus 5 percentage points of the population parameter. As the confidence interval is expanded for a given statistic, our confidence increases, and we may say we are 99.9 percent confident that our statistic falls within 7.5 percentage points of the parameter. We'll describe how sampling intervals and levels are calculated in the next section, making these two concepts even clearer.

■ *PROBABILITY SAMPLING THEORY AND SAMPLING DISTRIBUTION*

With definitions in hand, we can now examine the basic theory of probability sampling as it applies to criminal justice research. We'll also consider the logic of sampling distribution and sampling

FIGURE 9-3
A Population of Ten People with $0–$9

error with regard to a **binomial variable**—that is, a variable composed of two attributes.

Probability Sampling Theory

The ultimate purpose of sampling is to select a set of elements from a population in such a way that descriptions of those elements (statistics) accurately portray the parameters of the total population from which the elements are selected. Probability sampling enhances the likelihood of accomplishing this aim and also provides methods for estimating the degree of probable success.

Random selection is the key to this process. In random selection, each element has an equal chance of selection independent of any other event in the selection process. Flipping a coin is the most frequently cited example: The "selection" of a head or a tail is independent of previous selections of heads or tails.

There are two reasons for using random selection methods. First, this procedure serves as a check on conscious or unconscious bias on the part of the researcher. The researcher who selects cases on an intuitive basis might choose cases that would support his or her research expectations or

hypotheses. Random selection erases this danger. Second, and more important, random selection offers access to the body of probability theory, which provides the basis for estimates of population parameters and estimates of error.

The Sampling Distribution of Ten Cases

To introduce the statistics of probability sampling, let's begin with a simple example of only ten cases.[2] Suppose there are ten people in a group, and each has a certain amount of money in his or her pocket. To simplify, let's assume that one person has no money, another has $1, another has $2, and so forth up to the person who has $9. Figure 9-3 illustrates the population of ten people.

Our task is to determine the average amount of money one person has—specifically, the mean number of dollars. If you simply add up the money shown in Figure 9-3, the total is $45, so the mean is $4.50 ($45 ÷ 10). Our purpose in the rest of this exercise is to estimate that mean without actually observing all ten individuals. We'll do

---

[2]We thank Hanan Selvin for suggesting this way of introducing probability sampling.

that by selecting random samples from the population and using the means of those samples to estimate the mean of the whole population.

To start, suppose we were to select—at random—a sample of only one person from the ten. Depending on which person we selected, we would estimate the group's mean as anywhere from $0 to $9. Figure 9-4 shows a display of those ten possible samples. The ten dots shown on the graph represent the ten "sample" means we would get as estimates of the population. The distribution of the dots on the graph is called the *sampling distribution.* Obviously, it is not a good idea to select a sample of only one because we stand a good chance of missing the true mean of $4.50 by quite a bit.

What if we take samples of two each? As you can see from Figure 9-5, increasing the sample size improves our estimations. There are now 45 possible samples: $0/$1, $0/$2, . . . , $7/$8, $8/$9. Moreover, some of those samples produce the same means. For example, $0/$6, $1/$5, and $2/$4 all produce means of $3. In Figure 9-5, the three dots shown above the $3 mean represent those three samples.

The 45 sample means are not evenly distributed, as you can see. Rather, they are somewhat clustered around the true value of $4.50. Only two samples deviate by as much as $4 from the true value ($0/$1 and $8/$9), whereas five of the samples give the true estimate of $4.50; another eight samples miss the mark by only $.50 (plus or minus).

Now suppose we select even larger samples. What do you suppose that will do to our estimates of the mean? Figure 9-6 presents the sampling distributions of samples of 3, 4, 5, and 6. The progression of the sampling distributions is clear. Every increase in sample size improves the distribution of estimates of the mean in two related ways. First, in the distribution for samples of five, for example, no sample means are at the extreme ends of the distribution. You should understand the reason: It is not possible to select five elements from our population and obtain an average of less than $2 or greater than $7. The second way sampling distributions improve with larger samples is that sample means cluster around the

true population mean of $4.50. Figure 9-6 clearly shows this tendency.

The limiting case in this procedure, of course, is to select a sample of ten. Then there is only one possible sample (everyone), and it gives the true mean of $4.50.

Binomial Sampling Distribution

Let's turn now to a more realistic sampling situation and see how the notion of sampling distribution applies. This simple example involves a population much larger than ten. Let's assume for the moment that we wish to study the population of Placid Coast, California, to assess the approval or disapproval of a proposed law to ban possession of handguns within the city limits. The study population is that aggregation of, say, 20,000 registered voters whose names and addresses appear on registration lists: the sampling frame. The elements are the individual registered voters. The variable under consideration is attitudes toward the proposed law: approve and disapprove. Measured in this way, attitude toward the law is a binomial variable; it can have only two values. We'll select a random sample of, say, 100 persons for the purpose of estimating the entire population of registered voters.

Figure 9-7 presents all the possible values of this parameter in the population—from 0 percent approval to 100 percent approval. The midpoint of the line—50 percent—represents half the voters approving of the handgun ban and the other half disapproving.

To choose our sample, we give each person on the voter registration list a number and use a computer program to generate 100 random numbers. Then we interview the 100 people whose numbers have been selected and ask for their attitudes toward the handgun ban: whether they approve or disapprove. Suppose this operation gives us 48 people who approve of the law and 52 who disapprove. We present this statistic by placing a dot at the point representing 48 percent, as shown in Figure 9-8.

Now suppose we select another sample of 100 people in exactly the same fashion and measure their approval or disapproval of the proposed law. Perhaps 51 people in the second sample

FIGURE 9-4
The Sampling Distribution of Samples of 1

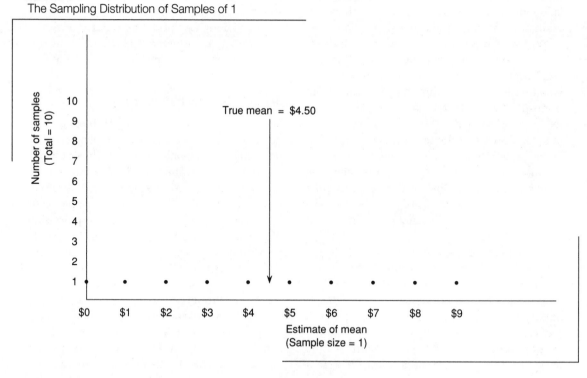

FIGURE 9-5
The Sampling Distribution of Samples of 2

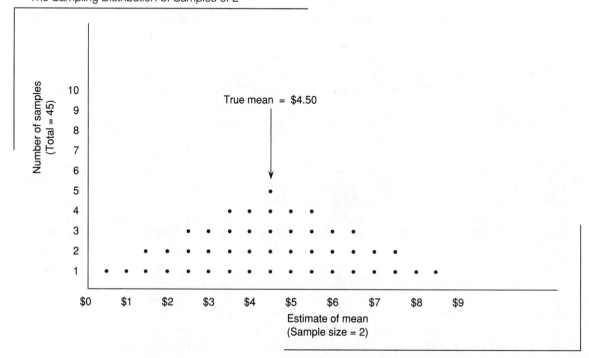

FIGURE 9-6
The Sampling Distribution of Samples of 3, 4, 5, and 6

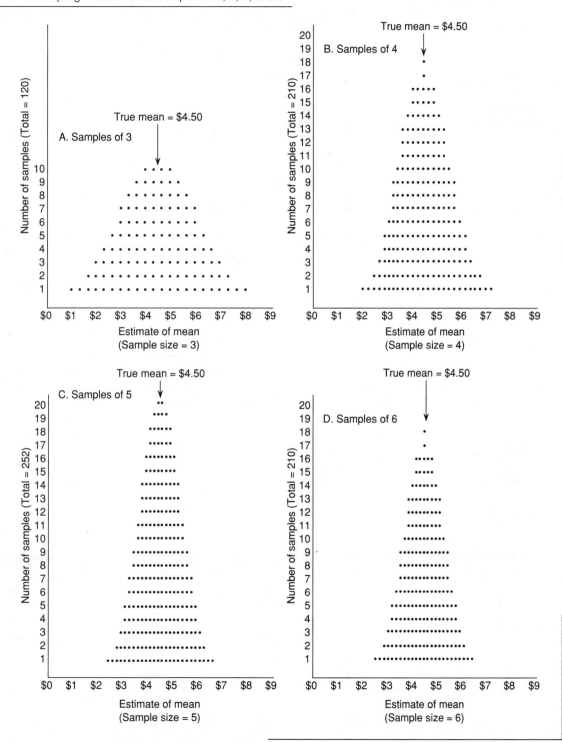

FIGURE 9-7
Range of Possible Sample Study Results

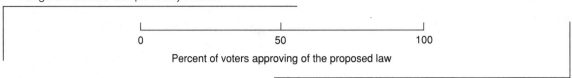

FIGURE 9-8
Results Produced by Three Hypothetical Samples

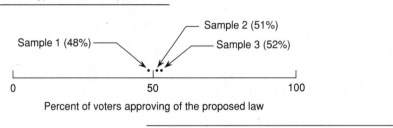

approve of the law. We place another dot in the appropriate place on the line in Figure 9-8. Repeating this process once more, we may discover that 52 people in the third sample approve of the handgun ban.

Figure 9-8 presents the three different sample statistics that represent the percentages of people in each of the three random samples who approved of the proposed law. Each of the random samples, then, gives us an estimate of the percentage of people in the total population of registered voters who approve of the handgun law. Unfortunately, we now have three separate estimates.

To rescue ourselves from this dilemma, let's draw more and more samples of 100 registered voters each, question each of the samples concerning their approval or disapproval, and plot the new sample statistics on our summary graph. In drawing many such samples, we discover that some of the new samples provide duplicate estimates, as in our earlier illustration with ten cases. Figure 9-9 shows the sampling distribution of hundreds of samples. This is often referred to as a normal or bell shaped curve.

Note that by increasing the number of samples selected and interviewed, we have also increased

FIGURE 9-9
The Sampling Distribution

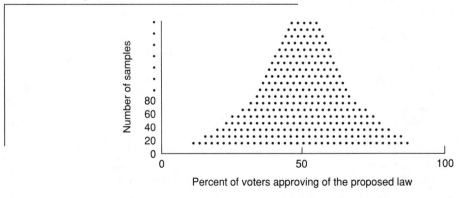

the range of estimates provided by the sampling operation. In one sense, we have increased our dilemma in attempting to find the parameter in the population. Probability theory, however, provides certain important rules about the sampling distribution presented in Figure 9-9.

First, if many independent random samples are selected from a population, then the sample statistics provided by those samples will be distributed around the population parameter in a known way. Thus, although Figure 9-9 shows a wide range of estimates, more of them are in the vicinity of 50 percent than elsewhere in the graph. Probability theory tells us, then, that the true value is in the vicinity of 50 percent.

Second, probability theory gives us a formula for estimating how closely the sample statistics are clustered around the true value:

$$s = \sqrt{\frac{P \times Q}{n}}$$

where s is the standard error (a measure of the sampling error), n is the number of cases in each sample, and P and Q are the population parameters for the binomial. If 60 percent of registered voters approve of the ban on handguns and 40 percent disapprove, then P and Q are 60 percent and 40 percent, or .6 and .4, respectively. Note that $Q = 1 - P$ and $P = 1 - Q$.

Let's assume that the population parameter in the example is 50 percent approval of the proposed law and 50 percent disapproval. Recall that we have been selecting samples of 100 cases each. When these numbers are put into the formula, we get

$$s = \sqrt{\frac{.5 \times .5}{100}} = .05$$

The standard error equals .05, or 5 percent.

In probability theory, the standard error is a valuable piece of information because it indicates the extent to which the sample estimates will be distributed around the population parameter. If you are familiar with the standard deviation in statistics, you may recognize that the standard error in this case is the standard deviation of the sampling distribution.

Specifically, probability theory indicates that certain proportions of the sample estimates will fall within specified increments—each equal to one standard error—from the population parameter. Approximately 34 percent (.3413) of the sample estimates will fall within one standard error increment above the population parameter, and another 34 percent will fall within one standard error increment below the parameter. In our example, the standard error increment is 5 percent, so we know that 34 percent of our samples will give estimates of approval between 50 percent (the parameter) and 55 percent (one standard error above); another 34 percent of the samples will give estimates between 50 percent and 45 percent (one standard error below the parameter). Taken together, then, we know that roughly two-thirds (68 percent) of the samples will give estimates between 45 and 55 percent, which is within 5 percent of the parameter.

The standard error is also a function of the sample size—an inverse function. As the sample size increases, the standard error decreases. As the sample size increases, the several samples will be clustered nearer to the true value (Figures 9-5 and 9-6 illustrate this graphically). Another rule of thumb is evident in the formula: Because of the square root operation, the standard error is reduced by half if the sample size is quadrupled. In our example, samples of 100 produce a standard error of 5 percent; to reduce the standard error to 2.5 percent, we would have to increase the sample size to 400.

All of this information is provided by established probability theory in reference to the selection of large numbers of random samples. If the population parameter is known and many random samples are selected, we are able to predict how many of the samples will fall within specified intervals from the parameter. Be clear that this discussion only illustrates the logic of probability sampling. It does not describe the way research is actually conducted. Usually we do not know the parameter; we conduct a sample survey to estimate that value. Moreover, we don't actually select large numbers of samples; we select only one sample. Nevertheless, this discussion of probability theory provides the basis for making inferences about the typical research situation. Knowing what it would be like to select thousands of samples allows us to make assumptions about the one sample we do select and study.

Whereas probability theory specifies that 68 percent of that fictitious large number of samples would produce estimates that fall within one standard error of the parameter, we can turn the logic around and infer that any single random sample has a 68 percent chance of falling within that range. In this regard, we speak of *confidence levels:* We are 68 percent confident that our sample estimate is within one standard error of the parameter. Or we may say that we are 95 percent confident that the sample statistic is within two standard errors of the parameter, and so forth. Quite reasonably, our confidence increases as the margin for error is extended. We are virtually positive (99.9 percent) that our statistic is within three standard errors of the true value.

Although we may be confident (at some level) of being within a certain range of the parameter, we seldom know what the parameter is. To resolve this dilemma, we substitute our sample estimate for the parameter in the formula; lacking the true value, we substitute the best available guess.

The result of these inferences and estimations is that we are able to estimate a population parameter and also the expected degree of error on the basis of one sample drawn from a population. Beginning with the question: What percentage of the registered voters in Placid Coast approve of the proposed handgun ban?, you could select a random sample of 100 registered voters and interview them. You might then report that your best estimate is that 50 percent of registered voters approve of the gun ban and that you are 95 percent confident that between 40 and 60 percent (plus or minus two standard errors) approve. The range from 40 to 60 percent is called the *confidence interval.* (At the 68 percent confidence level, the confidence interval is 45–55 percent.)

The logic of confidence levels and confidence intervals also provides the basis for determining the appropriate sample size for a study. Once you have decided on the sampling error you can tolerate, you can calculate the number of cases needed in your sample.

This, then, is the basic logic of probability sampling. Random selection permits the researcher to link findings from a sample to the body of probability theory so as to estimate the accuracy of those findings. All statements of accuracy in sampling must specify both a confidence level and a confidence interval. Researchers may report that they are x percent confident that the population parameter is between two specific values.

This discussion has considered only one type of statistic: the percentages produced by a binomial or dichotomous variable. The same logic, however, applies to the examination of other statistics, such as mean income. Because those computations are somewhat more complicated, we chose to consider only binomials in this introduction.

You should be cautioned that the survey uses of probability theory as discussed previously are not wholly justified technically. The theory of sampling distribution makes assumptions that almost never apply in survey conditions. Finding the number of samples contained within specified increments of standard errors, for example, assumes an infinitely large population and an infinite number of samples among other things. Moreover, the inferential jump from the distribution of several samples to the probable characteristics of one sample has been grossly oversimplified in our discussion.

These cautions are offered to give you perspective. Researchers often appear to overestimate the precision of estimates produced by use of probability theory in connection with criminal justice and other social research. As will be mentioned throughout the book, variations in sampling techniques and nonsampling factors may further reduce the legitimacy of such estimates. Nevertheless, the calculations discussed in this section can be extremely valuable to you in understanding and evaluating your data. Although the calculations do not provide as precise estimates as some researchers might assume, they can be quite valid for practical purposes. They are unquestionably more valid than less rigorously derived estimates based on less rigorous sampling methods.

Most important, you should be familiar with the basic logic underlying the calculations. If you are so informed, you will be able to react sensibly to your own data and to those reported by others.

■ *POPULATIONS AND SAMPLING FRAMES*

Although it is necessary for the research consumer, student, and researcher to understand the theoretical foundations of sampling, it is no less important that they appreciate the less-than-perfect conditions that exist in the field. This section is devoted to a discussion of one aspect of field conditions that requires a compromise with regard to theoretical conditions and assumptions. We'll consider the congruence of or disparity between populations and sampling frames.

Simply put, a sampling frame is the list or quasi-list of elements from which a probability sample is selected. Properly drawn samples provide information appropriate for describing the population of elements that compose the sampling frame—nothing more. It is necessary to make this point in view of the common tendency for researchers to select samples from a given sampling frame and then make assertions about a population that is similar, but not identical, to the study population defined by the sampling frame.

For example, if you wished to study the attitudes of corrections administrators toward determinant sentencing policies, you might select a sample by consulting the membership roster of the American Correctional Association. In this case, the membership roster is your sampling frame, and corrections administrators are the population you wish to describe. However, unless all corrections administrators are members of the American Correctional Association, and all members are listed in the roster, you are incorrect in generalizing your results to all corrections administrators.

Studies of organizations are often the simplest from a sampling standpoint because organizations typically have membership lists. In such cases, the list of members may be an acceptable sampling frame. If a random sample is selected from a membership list, then the data collected from that sample may be taken as representative of all members—if all members are included in the list. It is, however, imperative that researchers learn

how complete or incomplete such lists might be, and limit their generalizations to listed sample elements rather than to an entire population.

Other lists of individuals may be especially relevant to the research needs of a particular study. Lists of licensed drivers, automobile owners, welfare recipients, taxpayers, holders of weapons permits, and licensed professionals are just a few examples. Although it may be difficult to gain access to some of these lists, they provide excellent sampling frames for specialized research purposes.

Telephone directories are frequently used for "quick and dirty" public opinion polls. Undeniably they are easy and inexpensive to use, and that is no doubt the reason for their popularity. Of course, a given directory will not include new subscribers or those who have requested unlisted numbers. Sampling is further complicated by the inclusion of nonresidential listings in directories. Unfortunately, telephone directories are all too often taken to be a listing of a city's population. There are many defects in this reasoning. Poor people are less likely to have telephones; rich people may have more than one line. Telephone companies may not publish listings for temporary residents, such as students. And persons who live in institutions or group quarters—dormitories, nursing homes, rooming houses, and the like—are not listed in phone directories.

Street directories and tax maps are often used for easy samples of households, but they may also suffer from incompleteness and possible bias. For example, in strictly zoned urban regions, illegal housing units are unlikely to appear on official records. As a result, such units would have no chance for selection and sample findings could not be representative of those units, which are often poorer and more overcrowded than the average.

■ *TYPES OF SAMPLING DESIGNS*

So far, we have focused on simple random sampling. And, indeed, the body of statistics typically used by criminal justice researchers assumes such a sample. As we will see shortly, however, you have a number of options in choosing your sampling method, and you will seldom (if ever) choose simple random sampling. There are two reasons for that. First, with all but the simplest sampling frame, simple random sampling is not feasible. Second, simple random sampling may not be the most accurate method available. Let's turn now to a discussion of simple random sampling and the other options available.

Simple Random Sampling

As noted, **simple random sampling** is the basic sampling method assumed in the statistical computations of social research. The mathematics of random sampling are especially complex, so we'll detour around them in favor of describing the ways this method is used in the field.

Once a sampling frame has been established in keeping with the guidelines we presented, to use simple random sampling the researcher assigns a single number to each element in the list, not skipping any number in the process. A table of random numbers, or a computer program for generating them, is then used to select elements for the sample.

If your sampling frame is a computerized database or some other form of machine-readable data, a simple random sample can be selected automatically by computer. In effect, the computer program numbers the elements in the sampling frame, generates its own series of random numbers, and prints out the list of elements selected.

Systematic Sampling

Simple random sampling is seldom used in practice, primarily because it is not usually the most efficient method, and it can be laborious if done manually. It typically requires a list of elements. When such a list is available, however, researchers usually use **systematic sampling** rather than simple random sampling.

In systematic sampling, all the elements in the list are chosen (systematically) for inclusion in the sample. If the list contains 10,000 elements and you want a sample of 1,000, you select every tenth element for your sample. To ensure against any possible human bias, you should select the first element at random. Thus, to systematically select 1,000 from a list of 10,000 elements, you would

begin by selecting a random number between one and ten. The element having that number, plus every tenth element following it, is included in the sample. This method is technically referred to as a systematic sample with a random start.

In practice, systematic sampling is virtually identical to simple random sampling. If the list of elements is indeed randomized before sampling, one might argue that a systematic sample drawn from that list is in fact a simple random sample. By now, debates over the relative merits of simple random sampling and systematic sampling have been resolved largely in favor of the simpler method: systematic sampling. Empirically, the results are virtually identical.

Systematic sampling has one danger. A periodic arrangement of elements in the list can make systematic sampling unwise; this arrangement is usually called *periodicity*. If the list of elements is arranged in a cyclical pattern that coincides with the sampling interval, a grossly biased sample may be drawn. For example, suppose we select a sample of apartments in an apartment building. If the sample is drawn from a list of apartments arranged in numerical order (for example, 101, 102, 103, 104, 201, 202, and so on), there is a danger of the sampling interval coinciding with the number of apartments on a floor or some multiple of it. Then the samples might include only northwest-corner apartments or only apartments near the elevator. If these types of apartments have some other particular characteristic in common (for example, higher rent), the sample will be biased. The same danger would appear in a systematic sample of houses in a subdivision arranged with the same number of houses on a block.

In considering a systematic sample from a list, then, you should carefully examine the nature of that list. If the elements are arranged in any particular order, you should figure out whether that order will bias the sample to be selected and take steps to counteract any possible bias.

In summary, however, systematic sampling is usually superior to simple random sampling, in convenience if nothing else. Problems in the ordering of elements in the sampling frame can usually be remedied quite easily.

Stratified Sampling

We have discussed two methods of selecting a sample from a list: random and systematic. **Stratification** is not an alternative to these methods, but it represents a possible modification in their use. Simple random sampling and systematic sampling both ensure a degree of representativeness and permit an estimate of the error present. Stratified sampling is a method for obtaining a greater degree of representativeness—decreasing the probable sampling error. To understand why that is the case, we must return briefly to the basic theory of sampling distribution.

Recall that sampling error is reduced by two factors in the sample design: (1) A large sample produces a smaller sampling error than a small sample, and (2) a homogeneous population produces samples with smaller sampling errors than a heterogeneous population does. If 99 percent of the population agrees with a certain statement, it is extremely unlikely that any probability sample will greatly misrepresent the extent of agreement. If the population is split 50–50 on the statement, then the sampling error will be much greater.

Stratified sampling is based on this second factor in sampling theory. Rather than selecting your sample from the total population at large, you ensure that appropriate numbers of elements are drawn from homogeneous subsets of that population. To get a stratified sample of university students, for example, you would first organize your population by college class and then draw appropriate numbers of freshmen, sophomores, juniors, and seniors. In a nonstratified sample, representation by class would be subject to the same sampling error as other variables. In a sample stratified by class, the sampling error on this variable is reduced to zero.

Even more complex stratification methods are possible. In addition to stratifying by class, you might also stratify by gender, by grade-point average, and so forth. In this fashion, you could ensure that your sample contains the proper numbers of freshman men with a 4.0 average, freshman women with a 4.0 average, and so forth.

The ultimate function of stratification, then, is to organize the population into homogeneous subsets (with heterogeneity between subsets) and to select the appropriate number of elements from each. To the extent that the subsets are homogeneous on the stratification variables, they may be homogeneous on other variables as well. Because age is related to college class, a sample stratified by class will be more representative in terms of age as well.

The choice of stratification variables typically depends on what variables are available. Gender can often be determined in a list of names. Many local government sources of information on housing units are arranged geographically. Age, race, education, some measure of occupation, and other variables are often included on lists of persons who have had some contact with criminal justice officials.

In selecting stratification variables, however, you should be concerned primarily with those that are presumably related to the variables that you want to represent accurately. Because gender is related to many variables and is often available for stratification, it is frequently used. Age and race are related to many variables of interest in criminal justice research. Income is also related to many variables, but it is often not available for stratification. Geographic location within a city, state, or nation is related to many things. Within a city, stratification by geographic location usually increases representativeness in social class, ethnic group, and so forth.

Stratified sampling ensures the proper representation of the stratification variables to enhance representation of other variables related to them. Taken as a whole, then, a stratified sample is likely to be more representative on a number of variables than a simple random sample. Although the simple random sample is still regarded as somewhat sacred, it should now be clear that you can often do better.

Disproportionate Stratified Sampling

Another use of stratification is to purposively produce samples that are not representative of a population on some variable. Since the purpose of sampling we have been discussing so far is to represent a larger population, you may wonder why anyone would want to intentionally produce a sample that was not representative.

To understand the logic of disproportionate stratification, consider again the role of population homogeneity in determining sample size. If members of a population vary widely on some variable of interest, then larger samples must be drawn to adequately represent that population. Similarly, if only a small number of people in a population exhibit some attribute or characteristic of interest, then a large sample must be drawn to produce adequate numbers of elements that exhibit the uncommon condition. Disproportionate stratification is a way of obtaining sufficient numbers of these "rare" cases by selecting a disproportionate number.

The best example of disproportionate sampling in criminal justice is a national crime survey where one goal is to obtain some minimum number of crime victims in a sample. Because crime victimization for certain offenses—such as robbery or aggravated assault—is relatively rare on a national scale, persons who live in large urban areas, where serious crime is more common, are disproportionately sampled.

The British Crime Survey (BCS) is a nationwide survey of people aged 16 and over in England and Wales. Conducted approximately every other year since 1982, the BCS oversamples persons who live in inner-city areas. This produces a larger number of survey respondents who are crime victims than would result from proportionate random samples drawn from the population of England and Wales.

Multistage Cluster Sampling

The preceding sections have described reasonably simple procedures for sampling from lists of elements. This situation is ideal. Unfortunately, however, many interesting research problems require the selection of samples from populations that cannot easily be listed for sampling purposes; that is, sampling frames are not readily available. Examples are the population of a city, state, or nation; all police officers in the United States; and

so forth. In such cases, the sample design must be much more complex. Such a design typically involves the initial sampling of groups of elements—clusters—followed by the selection of elements within each of the selected clusters.

Cluster sampling may be used when it is either impossible or impractical to compile an exhaustive list of the elements that compose the target population. All law enforcement officers in the United States are an example of such a population. It is often the case, however, that the population elements are already grouped into subpopulations, and a list of those subpopulations either exists or can be created. Thus, U.S. law enforcement officers are employed by individual cities, counties, or states, and it would be possible to create lists of those political units. For cluster sampling, then, you could sample the list of cities, counties, and states in some manner as discussed previously (for example, a systematic sample stratified by population). Next, you could obtain lists of law enforcement officers from agencies in each of the selected jurisdictions. Each of the lists would then be sampled to provide samples of police officers for study.

Another typical situation concerns sampling among population areas such as a city. Although there is no single list of a city's population, citizens reside on discrete city blocks or census blocks. It is possible, therefore, to select a sample of blocks initially, create a list of persons who live on each of the selected blocks, and then sample persons from that list.

In a more complex design, you might sample blocks, list the households on each selected block, sample the households, list the persons who reside in each household, and finally sample persons within each selected household. This multistage sample design would lead to the ultimate selection of a sample of individuals without requiring the initial listing of all individuals in the city's population.

Multistage cluster sampling, then, involves the repetition of two basic steps: listing and sampling. The list of primary sampling units (city blocks) is compiled and perhaps stratified for sampling. Then a sample of those units is selected. The list of secondary sampling units is then sampled, and the process continues.

Cluster sampling is highly recommended for its efficiency, but the price of that efficiency is a less accurate sample. A simple random sample drawn from a population list is subject to a single sampling error, but a two-stage cluster sample is subject to two sampling errors. First, the initial sample of clusters represents the population of clusters only within a range of sampling error. Second, the sample of elements selected within a given cluster represents all the elements in that cluster only within a range of sampling error. Thus, for example, you run a certain risk of selecting a sample of disproportionately wealthy city blocks, plus a sample of disproportionately wealthy households within those blocks. The best solution to this problem lies in the number of clusters selected initially and the number of elements selected within each cluster.

Recall that sampling error is reduced by two factors: an increase in the sample size and increased homogeneity of the elements being sampled. These factors operate at each level of a multistage sample design. A sample of clusters will best represent all clusters if a large number are selected and if all clusters are very much alike. A sample of elements will best represent all elements in a given cluster if a large number are selected from the cluster and if all the elements in the cluster are very much alike.

A good general guideline for cluster design is to maximize the number of clusters selected while decreasing the number of elements within each cluster. But this scientific guideline must be balanced against an administrative constraint. The efficiency of cluster sampling is based on the ability to minimize the list of population elements. By initially selecting clusters, you need only list the elements that make up the selected clusters, not all elements in the entire population. Increasing the number of clusters, however, goes directly against this efficiency in cluster sampling. A small number of clusters may be listed more quickly and more cheaply than a large number. Remember that all the elements in a selected cluster must be listed even if only a few are to be chosen in the sample.

The final sample design will reflect these two constraints. In effect, you will probably select as many clusters as you can afford. Lest this issue be left too open-ended, we present one rule of thumb. Population researchers conventionally aim for the selection of 5 households per census block. If a total of 2,000 households are to be interviewed, researchers aim at 400 blocks with 5 household interviews on each. Figure 9-10 presents a graphic overview of this process.

Before turning to more detailed procedures available to cluster sampling, we repeat that this method almost inevitably involves a loss of accuracy. The manner in which this loss of accuracy appears, however, is somewhat complex. First, as noted earlier, a multistage sample design is subject to a sampling error at each stage. Because the sample size is necessarily smaller at each stage than the total sample size, the sampling error at each stage will be greater than would be the case for a single-stage random sample of elements. Second, sampling error is estimated on the basis of observed variance among the sample elements. When those elements are drawn from relatively homogeneous clusters, the estimated sampling error will be too optimistic and must be corrected in light of the cluster sample design.

Multistage Cluster Sampling with Stratification

Thus far, we have looked at cluster sampling as though a simple random sample were selected at each stage of the design. In fact, stratification techniques can be used to refine and improve the sample being selected. The basic options available are essentially the same as those possible in single-stage sampling from a list. In selecting a national sample of law enforcement officers, for example, you might initially stratify your list of agencies by type (state, county, municipal), geographic region, size, and rural or urban location.

Once the primary sampling units (law enforcement agencies) have been grouped according to the relevant, available stratification variables, either simple random or systematic sampling techniques can be used to select the sample. You might select a specified number of units from

FIGURE 9-10
Multistage Cluster Sampling

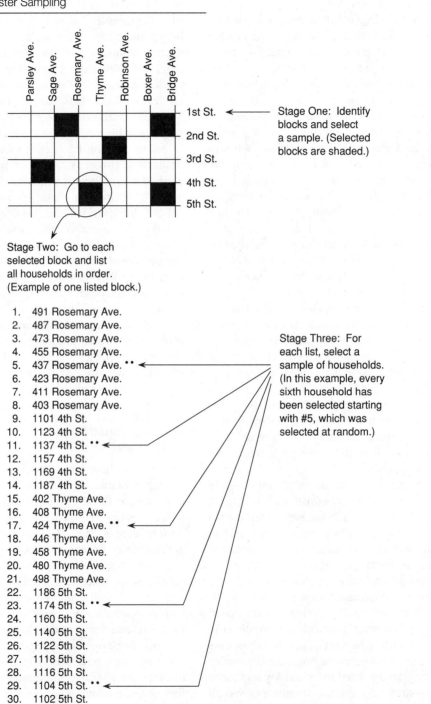

Stage One: Identify blocks and select a sample. (Selected blocks are shaded.)

Stage Two: Go to each selected block and list all households in order. (Example of one listed block.)

1.   491 Rosemary Ave.
2.   487 Rosemary Ave.
3.   473 Rosemary Ave.
4.   455 Rosemary Ave.
5.   437 Rosemary Ave. ••
6.   423 Rosemary Ave.
7.   411 Rosemary Ave.
8.   403 Rosemary Ave.
9.   1101 4th St.
10. 1123 4th St.
11. 1137 4th St. ••
12. 1157 4th St.
13. 1169 4th St.
14. 1187 4th St.
15. 402 Thyme Ave.
16. 408 Thyme Ave.
17. 424 Thyme Ave. ••
18. 446 Thyme Ave.
19. 458 Thyme Ave.
20. 480 Thyme Ave.
21. 498 Thyme Ave.
22. 1186 5th St.
23. 1174 5th St. ••
24. 1160 5th St.
25. 1140 5th St.
26. 1122 5th St.
27. 1118 5th St.
28. 1116 5th St.
29. 1104 5th St. ••
30. 1102 5th St.

Stage Three: For each list, select a sample of households. (In this example, every sixth household has been selected starting with #5, which was selected at random.)

each group or stratum, or you might arrange the stratified clusters in a continuous list and systematically sample that list.

To the extent that clusters are combined into homogeneous strata, the sampling error at this stage will be reduced. The primary goal of stratification, as before, is homogeneity.

There is no reason stratification could not take place at each level of sampling. The elements listed within a selected cluster might be stratified before the next stage of sampling. Typically, however, that is not done. (Recall the assumption of relative homogeneity within clusters.)

■ ILLUSTRATION: TWO NATIONAL CRIME SURVEYS

By now, it may have occurred to you that many different techniques of sampling and their various components can be combined in different ways to suit various needs. In this regard, the different components of sampling can be tailored to specific purposes in much the same way research design principles can be modified to suit various needs. Since sample frames suitable for simple random sampling are often unavailable, multistage cluster sampling is used to move from aggregate sample units to actual sample elements. Stratification can be added to ensure that samples are representative of important variables. And samples may be designed to produce elements that are proportionate or disproportionate to the population.

To illustrate how these various building blocks may be combined in complex ways, we will briefly describe the sampling procedures for two national crime surveys: the NCVS, conducted by the Census Bureau, and the BCS. Each is a multistage cluster sample, but the two surveys use different strategies to produce sufficient numbers of cases that exhibit one important attribute of interest, victimization. Our summary description is adapted from the Bureau of Justice Statistics (1996b) for the NCVS and from Mayhew, Maung, and Mirrlees-Black (1993) for the BCS.

National Crime Victimization Survey

Although various parts of the NCVS have been modified since the surveys were begun in 1972, the basic sampling strategies have remained relatively unchanged. The survey seeks to represent the nationwide population of persons aged 12 and over who are living in households. The phrase "living in households" is significant, as we noted in Chapter 6. NCVS procedures are not designed to sample homeless persons or people who live in institutional settings such as military group housing, temporary housing, or correctional facilities. Also, since the sample targets persons who live in households, it cannot provide estimates of crimes where a commercial establishment or business is the victim.

Since there is no national list of households in the United States, multistage sampling must be used to get from larger units to households and their residents. The national sampling frame used in the first stage defines primary sampling units (PSUs) as large metropolitan areas, nonmetropolitan counties, or a group of contiguous counties (to represent rural areas).

The largest PSUs are specified as "self-representing" and are automatically included in the first stage of sampling. The remaining PSUs are stratified by size, population density, reported crimes, and other variables into about 150 strata. One PSU is then selected from each stratum, with a probability proportionate to the population of the PSU. Thus, for example, if one stratum included Bugtussle, Arkansas (population 7,000), Punkinseed, Ohio (5,000), and Rancid, California (3,000), the probability that each PSU will be selected is: 7/15 for Bugtussle, 5/15 for Punkinseed, and 3/15 for Rancid.

Subsequent stages first select census enumeration districts (defined in each decennial census) through systematic sampling, again with a probability proportionate to size. Next, clusters of approximately four housing units are selected from each enumeration district. Since lists of housing units within each enumeration district become outdated over the ten years between census counts, various procedures are used to include newly constructed housing units.

For the 1994 NCVS, these procedures yielded a sample of approximately 56,000 housing units. Completed interviews were obtained from about 120,000 household occupants.

The sample design for the NCVS is an excellent illustration of the relationship between sample size and variation in the target population. Since serious crime is a relatively rare event when averaged across the entire U.S. population, very large samples must be drawn. The NCVS is an extremely complex survey that uses equally complex sampling methods. For further information, consult annual reports issued by the Bureau of Justice Statistics entitled *Criminal Victimization in the United States*.

British Crime Survey

Sampling procedures were changed in the 1992 BCS and remain essentially similar for the most current survey (1996 at this writing). While NCVS respondents are interviewed every six months to provide annual estimates of victimization, the BCS has been conducted six times at irregular intervals since 1982. In part, this reflects the intent of the BCS to support research and policy development in addition to estimating crime. While NCVS sampling procedures begin with demographic units and work down to selecting housing units, the BCS begins with electoral districts and eventually selects households that are recorded on lists of addresses organized by post office codes, similar to U.S. zip codes. Other differences between the two crime surveys illustrate the flexibility of multistage cluster sampling. Table 9-1 summarizes the stages and clusters used to draw a sample of 14,890 households for the 1992 BCS.

The first stage of sampling for the 1992 BCS drew 289 parliamentary constituencies, or districts from which members of the House of Commons are elected. These are roughly equivalent to U.S. congressional districts but are much more numerous relative to the smaller area and population of England and Wales. Parliamentary constituencies were stratified by geographic area and

TABLE 9-1

Multistage Cluster Sampling in the 1992 British Crime Survey

Stage	Unit	Sample
1	Parliamentary constituency	289 total 70 inner city 219 other areas
2	Postcode sector	2 each constituency
3	Postcode segment	1 each sector
4	Household address	28 or 29 each segment for inner cities 25 each district for other areas
5	Respondent	1 per household

Stage	Cumulative sample size, N
1	289 constituencies 70 inner city 219 other areas
2	578 postcode sectors (289×2)
3	578 postcode segments
4	3,990 inner-city addresses (average 28.5 addresses each segment) ($3,990 = 70 \times 2 \times 28.5$) 10,900 other area addresses (average 24.88 addresses each segment) ($10,950 = 219 \times 2 \times 25$) 14,890 total addresses −1,773 empty, demolished addresses −3,058 refusals, no contact
5	10,059 completed interviews

Source: Adapted from Mayhew, Maung, and Mirrlees-Black (1993:149–154).

population density. Within constituencies, two sample points were then selected from a listing of postal code prefixes. Again, think of U.S. zip codes, where the first three digits of a five-digit zip code represent metropolitan area regions within a state; if you sample from a list of the first three digits, you'll get a sample of postal delivery areas. Although this simplifies the BCS procedure a bit, you should see how a list of postal code prefixes served as a sampling frame for the second stage.

Stage 3 involved dividing each sample point into four segments with approximately equal numbers of mail delivery addresses. One of these four segments was selected at random, and a starting point for systematic sampling was then randomly selected. In stage 4, about every 30th address on the list, within selected segments, was included.

Each segment yielded about 29 addresses for inner-city areas and 25 addresses for areas outside inner cities. As mentioned earlier, this oversample of urban areas produced a larger number of crime victims than might be obtained through strictly proportionate sampling procedures, such as those used in the NCVS.

In most cases, one dwelling unit was found per listed address; where this was not true, BCS researchers used a random procedure to select one dwelling unit to be included in the final stage of the sample, the actual selection of household respondents. Household residents aged 16 and over were listed, and one was randomly selected by interviewers.

Sampling designs for both the BCS and NCVS are more complex than we have represented here but you should have a general understanding of how multistage cluster sampling was used in each. There are two principal differences between the samples. The NCVS uses *proportionate* sampling to select a large number of respondents who may then represent the relatively rare attribute of victimization. The BCS sampled a *disproportionate* number of inner-city respondents who were more likely to be victims of crime, and it was able to represent the relatively rare attribute with a sample less than one-tenth the size of that used in the NCVS. This was possible, in large part, because of another primary difference between the two samples: A suitable sampling frame of addresses was available for England and Wales, but not for the United States.

■ *PROBABILITY SAMPLING IN REVIEW*

Depending on the field situation, probability sampling can be very simple or it can be extremely difficult, time-consuming, and expensive. Whatever the situation, however, it is usually the preferred method for selecting study elements. It's worth restating the two main reasons for this.

First, probability sampling avoids conscious or unconscious biases in element selection on the part of the researcher. If all elements in the population have an equal (or unequal and subsequently weighted) chance of selection, there is an excellent chance that the sample so selected will closely represent the population of all elements.

Second, probability sampling permits estimates of sampling error. Although no probability sample will be perfectly representative in all respects, controlled selection methods permit the researcher to estimate the degree of expected error in that regard.

In spite of the preceding comments, it is sometimes not possible to use standard probability sampling methods. Sometimes it isn't even appropriate to do so. In those cases, nonprobability sampling is used.

■ *NONPROBABILITY SAMPLING*

You can no doubt envision situations in which it would be either impossible or unfeasible to select the kinds of probability samples we have described. Suppose you wanted to study auto thieves. There is no list of all auto thieves nor are you likely to create such a list. Moreover, as we'll see, there are times when probability sampling wouldn't be appropriate even if it were possible. In many such situations, **nonprobability sampling** procedures are called for. We'll examine four types in this section: purposive or judgmental sampling, quota sampling, the reliance on available subjects, and snowball sampling.

Purposive or Judgmental Sampling

Occasionally it may be appropriate to select a sample on the basis of your own knowledge of the population, its elements, and the nature of your research aims—in short, based on your judgment and the purpose of the study. Such a sample is called a **purposive sample.**

You may wish to study a small subset of a larger population in which many members of the subset are easily identified but the enumeration of all of them would be nearly impossible. For example, you might want to study members of community crime prevention groups; many members are easily visible, but it would not be feasible to define and sample all members of community crime prevention organizations. In studying a sample of the most visible members, you may collect data sufficient for your purposes.

Criminal justice research often compares practices in different jurisdictions—cities or states, for example. In such cases, study elements may be selected because they exhibit some particular attribute. For instance, Spohn and Horney (1991) were interested in how differences among states in rape shield laws affected the use of evidence in sexual assault cases. Strong rape shield laws restricted the use of evidence or testimony about a rape victim's sexual behavior, whereas weak laws routinely permitted such testimony. Spohn and Horney selected a purposive sample of six states for analysis based on the strength of their rape shield laws. Similarly, LaFree (1985) studied the link between prosecutorial discretion and race differences in sentencing by selecting three jurisdictions where prosecutors maintained a high degree of control over assistants and three jurisdictions where prosecutor control was weaker. After selecting the six sites, LaFree sampled more than 3,000 burglary and robbery cases for analysis across all sites.

Purposive or judgmental sampling may also be used to represent patterns of complex variation. In their study of fear of crime, Skogan and Maxfield (1981) analyzed survey data from several neighborhoods in three cities. Within each city, three types of neighborhoods were selected: stable, working-class; low-income, high-transition; and middle-class with a high proportion of owner-occupied homes. Within each neighborhood, probability samples of residents were drawn for telephone interviews. By combining purposive and probability sampling techniques, Skogan and Maxfield obtained homogeneous samples within neighborhoods and also represented the considerable heterogeneity across neighborhoods.

One of the best known social science applications of judgmental sampling is the selection of voting precincts for exit polls on election days. On the basis of previous voting results in a given area (city, state, nation), TV networks select voting precincts that, in combination, produce results similar to those of the entire area. The theory is that the selected precincts are a cross section of the entire electorate. Each time an election is held, analysts evaluate the adequacy of selected precincts and make revisions, additions, or deletions. The goal is to update the group of precincts to ensure that it provides a good representation of all precincts.

Pretesting a questionnaire is another situation where purposive sampling is common. If, for example, you planned to study peoples' attitudes about court-ordered restitution for crime victims, you might want to test the questionnaire on a sample of crime victims. Instead of selecting a probability sample of the general population, you might select some number of known crime victims, perhaps from court records.

Quota Sampling

Like probability sampling, **quota sampling** addresses the issue of representativeness, although the two methods approach the issue quite differently. Quota sampling begins with a matrix that describes the characteristics of the target population you wish to represent. To do this, you need to know what proportion of the population is male or female, for example, and what proportions fall into various age categories, education levels, ethnic groups, and so forth. In establishing a national quota sample, you would need to know what proportion of the national population is urban, eastern, male, under 25, white, working-class, and all the other permutations of such a matrix.

Once such a matrix has been created and a relative proportion assigned to each cell in the matrix, you collect data from people who have all the characteristics of a given cell. All the persons in a given cell are then assigned a weight appropriate to their portion of the total population. When all the sample elements are so weighted, the overall data should provide a reasonable representation of the total population.

Quota sampling has two inherent problems. First, the quota frame (the proportions that different cells represent) must be accurate, and it is often difficult to get up-to-date information for this purpose. A quota sample of auto thieves or teenage vandals would obviously suffer from this difficulty. Second, biases may exist in the selection of sample elements within a given cell—even though its proportion of the population is accurately estimated. An interviewer, instructed to interview five persons who meet a given complex set of characteristics, may still avoid people who live at the top of seven-story walk-ups, have particularly run-down homes, or own vicious dogs.

On the other hand, quota and purposive sampling may be combined to produce samples that are intuitively, if not statistically, representative. For example, Horney and Marshall (1992a) designed an experimental study to compare different ways of obtaining data on self-reported offending. They wished to represent the population of convicted offenders. A probability sample of prison residents was rejected because it would be biased by length of sentence; persons with long sentences would be overrepresented. Instead, Horney and Marshall interviewed all males admitted to the Nebraska Department of Correction screening unit until they obtained 700 interviews. By default, this procedure represented an entire intake cohort, which arguably represented the population of convicted offenders sentenced to prison.

Reliance on Available Subjects

Relying on available subjects—that is, stopping people at a street corner or some other location—is sometimes called *convenience sampling.* University researchers frequently conduct surveys among the students enrolled in large lecture classes. The ease and economy of such a method explain its popularity; however, it seldom produces data of any general value. It may be useful to pretest a questionnaire, but it should not be used for a study purportedly describing students as a whole.

Reliance on available subjects can be an appropriate sampling method in some applications. In general, however, it is justified only if the researcher wants to study the characteristics of people who are passing the sampling point at some specified time. For example, in her study of street lighting as a crime prevention strategy, Kate Painter (1991) interviewed samples of pedestrians as they walked through an area of London before and after improvements in lighting conditions. Painter clearly understood the scope and limits of this sampling technique: "The aim of the pedestrian survey was to examine the impact of enhanced lighting on the local population who used the street after dark. It was envisaged that this population would be characteristically different from the majority of householders who lived in Landor Walk" (1991:28). In other words, interviewing a sample of available evening pedestrians is an appropriate sampling technique for generalizing to the population of evening pedestrians, and the population of pedestrians will not be the same as the population of residents.

In a more general sense, samples like Painter's select elements of a process—the process that generates evening pedestrians—rather than elements of a population. If you can safely assume that no systematic pattern generates elements of a process, then a sample of available elements as they happen to pass by can be considered to be representative. The technical term for this is a *Poisson process.* So, for example, if you are interested in studying crimes reported to police, then selecting a sample of, say, every seventh crime report over a two-month period would be representative of the general population of crime reports over that two-month period.

Baumer and Rosenbaum (1982) provide another good example of the appropriate use of samples of available subjects. They were interested in two general questions about shoplifting: (1) What proportion of shoppers in a store steal something? (2) How effective is store security in detecting shoplifters?

Their approach was to observe a sample of people from the time they entered a large department store until the time they left. Assuming that persons who enter a store represent a Poisson process, Baumer and Rosenbaum could generalize from their sample—observing every 20th person to enter—to the larger population of shoppers at that store. We will describe this study in more detail in Chapter 11 on direct observation because Baumer and Rosenbaum used clever techniques to actually conduct their observations.

Finally, Marcus Felson and associates (1996) report on efforts to reduce crime and disorder in New York's Port Authority bus terminal, the world's busiest bus station. Among the most important objectives were to reduce perceptions of crime problems and to improve how travelers felt about the Port Authority terminal; you will recognize these as research questions appropriate to some sort of survey. Since more than 170,000 passengers pass through the bus station on an average spring day, there should be no difficulty obtaining a sufficiently large sample of users. But how would you go about selecting a sample? Felson and associates point out that stopping passengers on their way to or from a bus was out of the question. Most passengers are commuters whose New York journey to and from work is timed to the minute, with none to spare for an interviewer's questions. Here's how Felson and associates describe the solution and the sampling strategy it embodied (1996:90–91):

■ Response rates would have been low if the Port Authority had tried to interview rushing customers or to hand out questionnaires to be returned later. Their solution was ingenious. The Port Authority drew a sample of outgoing buses . . . and placed representatives aboard. After the bus had departed, he or she would hand out a questionnaire to be completed during the trip . . . [and] collect these questionnaires as each customer arrived at the destination. This procedure produced a very high response rate and high completion rate for each item.

Snowball Sampling

Another type of nonprobability sampling that closely resembles the available subjects approach is called **snowball sampling.** Most commonly used in field observation studies or specialized interviewing, snowball sampling begins by identifying a single or small number of subjects and then asks that subject to identify others like him or her who might be willing to participate in a study.

Criminal justice research on active criminals or deviants frequently uses snowball sampling techniques. An initial contact is often made by consulting criminal justice agency records to identify, say, someone convicted of auto theft and placed on probation. That person is interviewed and asked to suggest other auto thieves whom

researchers could contact. Johnson and others (1985) identified their sample of heroin users through snowball sampling techniques. Inciardi and others (1991) studied high-risk behaviors for HIV infection among a snowball sample of serious delinquent offenders.

Contacting an initial subject or informant who will then refer you to other subjects can be especially difficult in studies of active offenders. As in most aspects of criminal justice research, different approaches to initiating contacts for snowball sampling have their own advantages and disadvantages. Beginning with subjects who have a previous arrest or conviction is usually the easiest method for researchers, but it suffers potential bias by depending on offenders who are known to police or other officials (McCall, 1978).

Snowball samples are essentially variations on purposive samples (you want to sample juvenile gang members) and on samples of available subjects (sample elements identify other sample elements for you). And like other types of nonprobability samples, snowball samples are most appropriate when it is impossible to determine the probability that any given element will be selected in a sample. Furthermore, snowball techniques may be necessary when the target population is difficult to locate or even identify. Approaching pedestrians who happen to pass by, for example, is not an efficient technique for selecting a sample of prostitutes or juvenile gang members.

Because snowball samples are used most commonly in field research, we'll have more to say about this method of selecting subjects in Chapter 11 on field methods and observation. In the meantime, for recent examples of different approaches to sampling active offenders, see the study of burglars by Wright and Decker (1994), research on drug dealers by Jacobs (1996), or Decker and Van Winkle (1996) on gang members.

■ MAIN POINTS

• Asking questions, making observations, and examining written records are three ways to collect criminal justice data. Each source of data is widely used in criminal justice research; each has its own advantages and disadvantages.

- Regardless of which data-collection methods are used, researchers must carefully consider measurement reliability and validity and the extent to which subjects are aware of the data-collection process.

- In selecting from among the several options for data collection and sampling, criminal justice researchers are best advised to be careful and creative.

- A sample is a special subset of a population observed for purposes of making inferences about the nature of the total population itself.

- The chief criterion of a sample's quality is the degree to which it is representative—the extent to which the characteristics of the sample are the same as those of the population from which it was selected.

- The most carefully selected sample is almost never a perfect representation of the population from which it was selected. Some degree of sampling error always exists.

- Probability sampling methods provide one excellent way of selecting samples that will be quite representative. They make it possible for you to estimate the amount of sampling error that should be expected in a given sample.

- The chief principle of probability sampling is that every member of the total population must have some known nonzero probability of being selected into the sample.

- An EPSEM sample is one in which every member of a population has the same probability of being selected.

- A sampling frame is a list or quasi-list of the members of a population. It is the resource used in the selection of a sample. A sample's representativeness depends directly on the extent to which a sampling frame contains all the members of the total population that the sample is intended to represent.

- Simple random sampling is logically the most fundamental technique in probability sampling, although it is seldom used in practice.

- Systematic sampling involves using a sampling frame to select units that appear at some specified interval—for example, every 8th, or 15th, or 1,023rd unit. This method is functionally equivalent to simple random sampling, with a few exceptions, and it is more practical.

- Stratification is the process of grouping the members of a population into relatively homogeneous strata before sampling. It improves the representativeness of a sample by reducing the sampling error.

- Multistage cluster sampling is a more complex sampling technique that is frequently used when there is no list of all the members of a population. An initial sample of groups of members (clusters) is selected first. Then all the members of the selected cluster are listed, often through direct observation in the field. Finally, the members listed in each of the selected clusters are subsampled to provide the final sample of members.

- The NCVS and BCS are national crime surveys based on multistage cluster samples. Sampling methods for each survey illustrate different approaches to representing relatively rare events.

- Purposive sampling is a nonprobability sampling method in which the researcher uses his or her own judgment to select sample members. It is sometimes called a judgmental sample.

- Quota sampling is another nonprobability sampling method. You begin with a detailed description of the characteristics of the total population (quota matrix) and then select your sample members in a way that includes the different composite profiles that exist in the population. The representativeness of quota sampling depends in large part on the accuracy of the quota matrix as a reflection of the characteristics of the population.

- In general, nonprobability sampling methods are regarded as less reliable than probability sampling methods. On the other hand, they are often easier and cheaper to use. Nonprobability samples are often useful for specialized applications in criminal justice research.

- Snowball samples accumulate subjects through chains of referrals and are most commonly used in field research.

■ *REVIEW QUESTIONS AND EXERCISES*

1. Review our summary of the National Institute of Justice Drug Use Forecasting (DUF) program in Chapter 6. Specify the target population, study population, sampling frame, and elements used in the DUF program. Describe what type of sample DUF uses and discuss the advantages and disadvantages of DUF sampling procedures.

2. Discuss possible study populations, elements, sampling units, and sampling frames for drawing a sample to represent the populations listed here. You may wish to limit your discussion to populations in a specific state or other jurisdiction.
   a. Municipal police officers
   b. Felony court judges
   c. Burglars
   d. Licensed automobile drivers
   e. State police superintendents
   f. Persons incarcerated in county jails

3. Assume you were interested in traffic safety around your campus, specifically in speeding on one of the main streets that border your campus. Describe how you might collect data on speeding by asking questions, making observations, or examining written records. What study population would be represented by data collected in each manner?

■ *ADDITIONAL READINGS*

Caudle, Sharon, "Using Qualitative Approaches," in Joseph S. Wholey, Harry P. Hatry, and Kathryn E. Newcomer (eds.), *Handbook of Practical Program Evaluation* (San Francisco: Jossey Bass, 1994). As we will see in Chapter 13, nonprobability samples are often used to evaluate criminal justice programs. Caudle's essay describes different approaches to drawing such samples.

General Accounting Office, *Using Statistical Sampling* (Washington, DC: U.S. General Accounting Office, 1992). One of a series of handbooks on evaluation methods, this is a rich source of practical information on how to draw probability samples. You will also find suggestions on how to work around various difficulties in actually selecting samples, together with illustrations of sampling people and other types of elements.

Jacob, Herbert, *Using Published Data: Errors and Remedies* (Newbury Park, CA: Sage, 1984). Although Jacob focuses on written records (the subject of Chapter 12 in this text), his discussion of general issues in measurement is excellent. The book is a model of clarity and common sense; read it carefully and save it for future reference.

Kish, Leslie, *Survey Sampling* (New York: Wiley, 1965). Unquestionably the definitive work on sampling in social research. Kish's coverage ranges from the simplest matters to the most complex and mathematical. He is both highly theoretical and downright practical. Easily readable and difficult passages intermingle as Kish exhausts everything you could want or need to know about each aspect of sampling.

Sudman, Seymour, "Applied Sampling," in Peter H. Rossi, James D. Wright, and Andy B. Anderson (eds.), *Handbook of Survey Research* (New York: Academic Press, 1983). An excellent practical guide to survey sampling.

10 *Survey Research and Other Ways of Asking Questions*

What You'll Learn in This Chapter

Here you'll learn how mail, interview, and telephone surveys can be used in criminal justice research. You'll also learn about ways of collecting data by asking people questions.

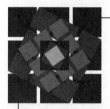

INTRODUCTION

TOPICS APPROPRIATE TO SURVEY RESEARCH
Counting Crime
Self-reports
Perceptions and Attitudes
Policy Proposals
Targeted Victim Surveys
Other Evaluation Uses
General-Purpose Crime Surveys

GUIDELINES FOR ASKING QUESTIONS
Open-Ended and Closed-Ended Questions
Questions and Statements
Make Items Clear
Short Items Are Best
Avoid Negative Items
Avoid Biased Items and Terms
Tips on Self-report Items

QUESTIONNAIRE CONSTRUCTION
General Questionnaire Format
Contingency Questions
Matrix Questions
Ordering Questions in a Questionnaire

SELF-ADMINISTERED QUESTIONNAIRES
Mail Distribution and Return
Warning Mailings, Cover Letters
Monitoring Returns
Follow-up Mailings
Acceptable Response Rates

IN-PERSON INTERVIEW SURVEYS
The Role of the Interviewer
General Rules for Interviewing
Coordination and Control

TELEPHONE SURVEYS
Computer-Assisted Interviewing

COMPARISON OF THE THREE METHODS

STRENGTHS AND WEAKNESSES OF SURVEY RESEARCH

OTHER WAYS OF ASKING QUESTIONS
Specialized Interviewing
Focus Groups

SHOULD YOU DO IT YOURSELF?

MAIN POINTS

REVIEW QUESTIONS AND EXERCISES

ADDITIONAL READINGS

■ *INTRODUCTION*

Survey research is a very old research technique. We find this passage in the Old Testament: "After the plague the Lord said to Moses and to Eleazar the son of Aaron, the priest, 'Take a census of all the congregation of the people of Israel, from twenty old and upward'" (Numbers 26:1–2). Ancient Egyptian rulers conducted censuses for the purpose of administering their domains. And Jesus was born away from home because Joseph and Mary were journeying to Joseph's ancestral home for a Roman census.

A little-known survey was attempted among French workers in 1880. A German political sociologist mailed some 25,000 questionnaires to workers to determine the extent of their exploitation by employers. The rather lengthy questionnaire included items such as these: "Does your employer or his representative resort to trickery in order to defraud you of a part of your earnings? If you are paid piece rates, is the quality of the article made a pretext for fraudulent deductions from your wages?" The survey researcher in this case was not George Gallup but Karl Marx (1880:208). Although 25,000 questionnaires were mailed out, there is no record of any being returned. And you need not know much about survey methods to recognize the loaded questions posed by Marx.

Survey research is perhaps the most frequently used mode of observation in sociology and political science, and surveys are often used in criminal justice research as well. You have no doubt been a respondent in a survey more than once, and you may have conducted a survey of your own.

We have already mentioned several of the fundamental elements of survey research in this book, so you are familiar with many aspects of this important data-collection method. Chapter 9 covered the topic of sampling and referred most often to survey situations. We have mentioned the National Crime Victim Survey (NCVS) in several chapters, and Chapter 6 described how other surveys produce measures of crime through self-reports.

We will begin this chapter by discussing the criminal justice topics that are most appropriate for survey methods. Next, we will cover the basic principles of how to ask people questions for research purposes, including some of the details of questionnaire construction. We'll describe the three basic ways of administering questionnaires—self-administration, face-to-face interviews, and telephone interviews—and summarize the strengths and weaknesses of each method. After discussing more specialized interviewing techniques, such as focus groups, we will conclude the chapter with some advice on the promise and pitfalls of conducting your own survey.

■ *TOPICS APPROPRIATE TO SURVEY RESEARCH*

Surveys may be used for descriptive, explanatory, exploratory, and applied research. They are chiefly used in studies that have individual people as the units of analysis. However, this method can be used for other units of analysis, such as households or organizations, but it is still necessary that some individual persons act as respondents or informants.

For example, researchers sometimes use victimization incidents as units of analysis in examining data from crime surveys. The fact that some persons may be victimized more than once and others not at all means that victimization incidents are not the same units as individual people. However, a survey questionnaire must still be administered to people who provide information about victimization incidents. In a similar fashion, the National Jail Census, conducted about every five years by the Census Bureau, collects information about local detention facilities. Jails are the units of analysis, but information about each jail is provided by an individual person.

In earlier chapters, we mentioned some topics in criminal justice research that are especially well suited for survey methods. In this section, we will organize these topics into broad categories of research applications where survey methods can be used.

Counting Crime

Chapter 6 covered this use of surveys in detail. Asking people about victimizations is a measure of crime that adjusts for some of the problems found in data collected by police. Of course, survey measures have their own problems. Most of these difficulties, such as recall error and reluctance to discuss victimization with interviewers, are inherent in survey methods. Nevertheless, with continued efforts to reduce such problems victim surveys have become important sources of data about the volume of crime in the United States and in other countries.

Self-reports

Surveys that ask people about crimes they may have committed were also discussed in Chapter 6. Robert O'Brien (1985:65) has described self-report surveys as "the dominant method in criminology for studying the etiology of crime." For research topics that seek to explore or explain why people commit criminal, delinquent, or deviant acts, asking questions is the best method available.

Within the general category of self-report surveys, two different applications are distinguished by their target population and sampling methods. Studies of offenders select samples of respondents known to have committed crimes, often prisoners. Typically, the focus is on the *frequency* of offending, or how many crimes of various types are committed by active offenders over a period of time. A study of incarcerated felons by Chaiken and Chaiken (1982) is among the best-known self-report surveys of offenders. John Ball and associates (1982) studied a sample of heroin addicts, documenting the crimes they committed over several years.

The other type of self-report survey focuses on the *prevalence* of offending, or how many people commit crimes, in contrast to the number of crimes committed by a target population of offenders. Such surveys typically use samples that

represent a broader population, such as U.S. households, adult males, or high school seniors. The National Youth Survey (NYS), sponsored by the National Institute for Mental Health and the Office of Juvenile Justice and Delinquency Prevention, was conducted eight times from 1976 through 1989. The NYS is a panel study (described in Chapter 4) that began in 1976 with a national probability sample of children who were then aged 11–17. Since the survey's first wave, data from the NYS have been used to make estimates of the prevalence of criminal and delinquent acts. Delbert Elliott and associates (1989) present comprehensive results from the NYS, and Finn Esbensen and Delbert Elliott (1994) describe patterns of drug use over eight waves of the survey. Other examples of self-report surveys were described in Chapter 6.

Chapter 6 also mentioned some of the problems that emerge in self-report surveys—most notably, validity and reliability. General population surveys and surveys of offenders tend to present different types of difficulties. Recall error and the reporting of fabricated offenses may be problems in a survey of high-rate offenders (Horney and Marshall, 1992a), while respondents in general-population self-report surveys may be reluctant to disclose illegal behavior. When we discuss questionnaire construction later in this chapter, we will present some examples and suggestions on creating self-report items.

Perceptions and Attitudes

Another application of surveys in criminal justice is to learn how people feel about crime and criminal justice policy. Public views about sentencing policies, gun control, police performance, and drug abuse are often solicited in opinion polls. The General Social Survey has been an ongoing survey of social indicators in the United States since 1972. Questions about fear of crime and about other perceptions of crime problems are regularly included. Since the mid-1970s, a growing number of explanatory studies have been conducted on public perceptions about crime and crime problems. A large body of research on fear of crime has grown, in part, from the realization that fear and its behavioral consequences were much more widespread among the population than was actual criminal victimization (Skogan and Maxfield, 1981).

Policy Proposals

The intractability of crime prompts a continuous search for policy responses, and many of these responses require participation, or at least approval, by the general public. Surveys are well suited to gauge public reaction to proposals like community policing or neighborhood watch. For instance, the 1984 British Crime Survey (BCS) included a series of items describing neighborhood watch programs and asked respondents whether they would be willing to participate in such a program in their community. Although most people expressed general support, only about a third of respondents indicated that they would be willing to join a neighborhood watch organization. As a result, officials in the British Home Office began to rethink the viability of neighborhood watch programs (Hough and Mayhew, 1985:48–49).

Community policing links police and neighborhood residents in a joint effort to address urban crime problems. One crucial element of community policing is that police officers learn more about crime and public order problems that most concern the public. Rather than simply reacting to citizen crime reports, police are expected to become more proactive in identifying neighborhood problems that contribute to crime. Neighborhood surveys, conducted for or by police, can be helpful in sorting out the types of problems that trouble residents.

Targeted Victim Surveys

Victim surveys that target individual cities or neighborhoods are important tools for evaluating policy innovations. Many criminal justice programs seek to prevent or reduce crime in some specific area, but crimes reported to police cannot be used to evaluate many types of programs.

To see why this is so, consider a hypothetical community policing program that encouraged neighborhood residents to report all suspected crimes to the police. We saw in Chapter 6 that many minor incidents are not reported because victims believe the police would not want to be bothered. But if a new program stresses that police want to be bothered, the proportion of crimes reported may increase and produce what appears to be an increase in crime.

The solution is to conduct targeted victim surveys before and after introducing some policy change. Such victim surveys are especially appropriate for evaluating any policy that may increase crime reporting as a side effect.

Notice that large-scale surveys such as the NCVS cannot be used to evaluate local crime prevention programs. This is because, as we have seen, the NCVS is designed to represent the national population of persons who live in households. The NCVS is not representative of any particular jurisdiction, and indeed it is not possible to identify the specific location of victimizations from NCVS data.

Other Evaluation Uses

Other types of surveys may be appropriate for applied studies. For example, a continuing series of neighborhood surveys is part of multiyear research to evaluate community policing in Chicago. Here's an example of how the researchers link their information needs to surveys (Chicago Community Policing Evaluation Consortium, 1996:9):

■ A key aspect of community policing is enhanced communication between police and city residents to facilitate problem solving. As such, the extent to which residents *are aware* of Chicago's community policing program is important to [its] success. [emphasis added]

In general, surveys can be used to evaluate policy that seeks to change attitudes, beliefs, or other perceptions. For example, consider a program designed to promote victim and witness cooperation in criminal court by reducing case processing time. At first, you might consider direct measures of case processing time as indicators of program success. If the program goal is to increase cooperation, however, a survey that asks how victims and witnesses *perceived* case processing time would be more appropriate.

General-Purpose Crime Surveys

As the name implies, these surveys are designed for more than one of the purposes we have mentioned. The 1982 BCS, for example, included questions to estimate victimization, a small number of self-report items, and numerous questions to support explanatory research on the etiology of victimization. In other years, the BCS has included special batteries of questions about fear of crime (1984), contacts with the police (1988 and 1996), self-reported drug use (1994), and security measures used to protect households and vehicles (1996).

The NCVS has traditionally focused on counting crime. In recent years, however, efforts have been devoted to incrementally redesigning the survey to broaden its scope (Lynch, 1990; Bachman and Taylor, 1994). For instance, supplementary items on fear and respondent behavior were added to the 1983 National Crime Survey, and special questions were added to a 1989 NCVS supplement to study crime in schools.

■ GUIDELINES FOR ASKING QUESTIONS

A defining feature of survey methods is that research concepts are operationalized by asking people questions. Several general guidelines can assist you in framing and asking questions that serve as excellent operationalizations of variables. You should also be aware of pitfalls that can result in useless and even misleading information. We'll begin with some of the options available to you in creating questionnaires.

Open-Ended and Closed-Ended Questions

In asking questions, researchers have two basic options and each can accommodate certain variations. The first case is *open-ended questions,* in which the respondent is asked to provide his or her own answers. For example, the respondent may be asked, "What do you feel is the most important crime problem facing the police in your city today?" and be provided with a space to write in the answer (or be asked to report it orally to an interviewer).

In the other case—*closed-ended questions*—the respondent is asked to select an answer from among a list provided by the researcher. Closed-ended questions are very popular because they provide more uniform responses and are more easily processed.

Open-ended responses must be coded before they can be processed for computer analysis. This coding process often requires that the researcher interpret the meaning of responses, which opens up the possibility of misunderstanding and researcher bias. Also, some respondents may give answers that are essentially irrelevant to the researcher's intent. Closed-ended responses, on the other hand, can often be transferred directly into a computer format.

The chief shortcoming of closed-ended questions lies in the researcher's structuring of responses. When the relevant answers to a given question are relatively clear, there should be no problem. In other cases, however, the researcher's list of responses may overlook some important answers. When you ask about "the most important crime problem facing the police in your city today," for example, your checklist might omit certain crime problems that respondents consider important.

In constructing closed-ended questions, you should be guided by two of the requirements for operationalizing variables stated in Chapter 5. First, the response categories provided should be *exhaustive:* They should include all the possible responses that might be expected. Often researchers ensure this by adding a category labeled something like "Other (Please specify: _____)."

Second, the answer categories must be *mutually exclusive:* The respondent should not feel compelled to select more than one. (In some cases, you may wish to solicit multiple answers, but these may create difficulties in data processing and later analysis.) To ensure that your categories are mutually exclusive, you should carefully consider each combination of categories, asking yourself whether a person could reasonably choose more than one answer. In addition, it is useful to add an instruction that the respondent select the one best answer. This technique is still not a satisfactory substitute for a carefully constructed set of responses.

Questions and Statements

The term **questionnaire** suggests a collection of questions, but a typical questionnaire probably has as many statements as questions. This is because the researcher is often interested in determining the extent to which respondents hold a particular attitude or perspective. If you are able to summarize the attitude in a fairly brief statement, you will often present that statement and ask respondents whether they agree or disagree with it. Rensis Likert has formalized this procedure through the creation of the Likert scale, a format in which respondents are asked to strongly agree, agree, disagree, or strongly disagree, or perhaps strongly approve, approve, and so forth.

Both questions and statements may be used profitably. Using both in a questionnaire allows you more flexibility in the design of items and can make the questionnaire more interesting as well.

Make Items Clear

It should go without saying that questionnaire items should be clear and unambiguous, but the broad proliferation of unclear and ambiguous questions in surveys makes the point worth stressing here. You can become so deeply involved in the topic that opinions and perspectives are clear to you but will not be clear to your respondents, many of whom have given little or no attention to the topic. Or if you have only a superficial understanding of the topic, you may fail to specify the intent of your question sufficiently. The question "What do you think about the governor's decision about prison furloughs?" may evoke in the respondent a counterquestion or two: "Which governor's decision?" "What are prison furloughs?" Questionnaire items should be precise so that the respondent knows exactly what the researcher wants an answer to.

Frequently, researchers ask respondents for a single answer to a combination question. Such "double-barreled" questions seem to occur most often when the researcher has personally identified with a complex question. For example, you might ask respondents to agree or disagree with the statement "The Department of Correction should stop releasing inmates for weekend furloughs and concentrate on rehabilitating criminals." Although many people would unequivocally agree with the statement and others would unequivocally disagree, still others would be unable to answer. Some might want to terminate the furlough program and punish—not rehabilitate—prisoners. Others may want to expand rehabilitation efforts while maintaining weekend furloughs; they could neither agree nor disagree without misleading you.

Short Items Are Best

In the interest of being unambiguous and precise and pointing to the relevance of an issue, the researcher is often led to use long and complicated items. That should be avoided. In the case of questionnaires respondents complete themselves, people are often unwilling to study an item in order to understand it. The respondent should be able to read an item quickly, understand its intent, and select or provide an answer without difficulty. In general, you should assume that respondents will read items quickly and give quick answers; therefore, you should provide clear, short items that will not be misinterpreted under those conditions. Questions read to respondents in person or over the phone should be similarly brief.

Avoid Negative Items

A negation in a questionnaire item paves the way for easy misinterpretation. Asked to agree or disagree with the statement "Drugs such as marijuana should not be legalized," many respondents will overlook the word *not* and answer on that basis. Thus, some will agree with the statement when they are in favor of legalizing marijuana and others will agree when they oppose it. And you may never know which is which.

Avoid Biased Items and Terms

Recall from the earlier discussion of conceptualization and operationalization that there are no ultimately true meanings for any of the concepts we typically study in social science. This same general principle applies to the responses we get from persons in a survey.

The meaning of someone's response to a question depends in large part on the wording of the question. That is true of every question and answer. Some questions seem to encourage particular responses more than other questions. Questions that encourage respondents to answer in a particular way are called *biased*.

Most researchers recognize the likely effect of a question that begins "Don't you agree with the President of the United States that . . . ," and no reputable researcher would use such an item. The biasing effect of items and terms is far subtler than this example suggests, however.

The mere identification of an attitude or position with a prestigious (or unpopular) person or agency can bias responses. An item that starts with "Do you agree or disagree with the recent Supreme Court decision that . . ." would have a similar effect. We are not suggesting that such wording will necessarily produce consensus or even a majority in support of the position identified with the prestigious person or agency, only that support will likely be increased over what would have been obtained without such identification.

Sometimes the impact of different forms of question wording is relatively subtle. For example, Kenneth Rasinski (1989) analyzed the results of several General Social Survey studies of attitudes toward government spending, and he found that the way programs were identified had an impact on the amount of public support they received. Here are some comparisons:

More Support	**Less Support**
"Assistance to the poor"	"Welfare"
"Halting rising crime rate"	"Law enforcement"
"Dealing with drug addiction"	"Drug rehabilitation"

In 1986, for example, 62.8 percent of the respondents said too little money was being spent on "assistance to the poor," while in a matched survey that year, only 23.1 percent said we were spending too little on "welfare."

In this context, you need to be generally wary of what researchers call the social desirability of questions and answers. Whenever you ask people for information, they answer through a filter of what will make them look good. That is especially true if they are being interviewed in a face-to-face situation.

The main guidance we offer is that you imagine how you would feel giving each of the answers you offer to respondents. If you'd feel embarrassed, perverted, inhumane, stupid, irresponsible, or anything like that, then you should give some serious thought to whether others will be willing to give those answers. You must carefully examine the purpose of your inquiry and construct items that will be most useful to it.

Tips on Self-report Items

Social desirability is one of the problems that plagues self-report crime questions in general-population surveys. Adhering to the ethical principles of confidentiality and anonymity, as well as convincing respondents that you are doing so, is one way of getting more truthful responses to self-report items. Other techniques help avoid or reduce problems with self-report items.

One method, used in the BCS, is to introduce a group of self-report items with a disclaimer and to sanitize the presentation of offenses. The self-report section of the 1984 BCS began with this introduction: "There are lots of things which are actually crimes, but which are done by lots of people, and which many people do not think of as crimes. On this card [printed card handed to respondents] are a list of eight of them. For each one can you tell me how many people you think do it—most people, a lot of people, or no one." Respondents then read a card, shown in Figure 10-1, that presented descriptions of various offenses. Interviewers first asked respondents how many people they thought ever did X, where X corresponded to the letter for an offense shown in Figure 10-1. Next, respondents were asked whether they had ever done X. Interviewers then moved on down the list of letters for each offense on the showcard.

This procedure incorporates three techniques for overcoming the socially desirable response of

FIGURE 10-1
Showcard for Self-report Items,
1984 British Crime Survey

A. Taken office supplies from work (such as stationery, envelopes and pens) when not supposed to.

B. Taken things other than office supplies from work
   (such as tools, money or other goods) when not
   supposed to.

C. Fiddled expenses [*fiddled* is the Queen's English
   equivalent of *fudged*].

D. Deliberately traveled [on a train] without a ticket or
   paid too low a fare.

E. Failed to declare something at customs on which
   duty was payable.

F. Cheated on tax.

G. Used cannabis (hashish, marijuana, ganga, grass).

H. Regularly driven a car when they know they have
   drunk enough to be well above the legal limit.

Source: Adapted from the 1984 British Crime Survey (NOP
Market Research Limited, 1985).

not admitting to having committed a crime. First is the disclaimer, which is intended to reassure respondents that "many people" do not really think of various acts as crimes. Second, respondents are asked how many people they think commit each offense before being asked whether they have done so themselves. This takes advantage of a common human justification for engaging in certain kinds of behavior—other people do it. Third, asking whether they "have ever done *X*" is less confrontational than asking whether they "have ever cheated on an expense account." Again, the foibles of human behavior are at work here, in much the same way that people use euphemisms such as "rest room" or "sleep together" rather than "toilet" or "have sexual intercourse."

It is, of course, entirely unrealistic to expect that such ploys will reassure all respondents. Furthermore, disclaimers about serious offenses such as rape or bank robbery would be ludicrous. But such techniques illustrate how thoughtful wording and introductions can be incorporated into sensitive questions.

Self-report surveys of known offenders encounter different problems. Incarcerated persons may be reluctant to admit committing crimes because of the legal consequences. High-rate offenders may have difficulty distinguishing among their large number of different crimes or remembering even approximate dates. Our discussion in Chapter 8 of immunity from prosecution for offenses revealed in certain forms of sponsored research can allay the fears of many active criminals. Sorting out dates and details of individual crimes among high-rate offenders requires different strategies.

One technique that is useful in surveys of active criminals is to interview subjects several times at regular intervals. For example, Johnson and others (1985:198–220) interviewed their sample of heroin users daily over an extended time. Each subject was asked to provide details about drug use, drug sales, and other criminal activity. After subjects had become accustomed to thinking about and reporting their daily activities to researchers, they began to complete self-administered questionnaires once per week in which they recorded what they had been doing in the past seven days.

A similar approach was used by Horney and Marshall (1992a), who questioned methods used by RAND Corporation researchers to obtain self-report data from prisoners. In the RAND study (Chaiken and Chaiken, 1982), high-rate offenders were asked to estimate their usual level of criminal activity, a procedure that Horney and Marshall believed might produce inflated estimates of crimes committed. Their solution was to present inmates with a "crime calendar," on which subjects recorded month-by-month lists of offenses. In an experimental comparison of the crime calendar approach with the RAND method, Horney and Marshall found no differences in the numbers of crimes recalled by subjects. It is likely, however, that a monthly diary format helped subjects more accurately recall the numbers and characteristics of crimes they had committed.

Obtaining valid and reliable results from self-report items is challenging, but self-report survey techniques are important tools for addressing certain types of criminal justice research questions. Because of this, researchers are constantly striving to improve self-report items. See the collection of essays by Charles Turner and associates (1992) for a detailed discussion of issues involved in measuring drug use through self-reports, with particular attention to methods used in the National Household Survey on Drug Abuse.

A recent fascinating development in self-report surveys comes from efforts to measure drug use in the 1994 BCS. Previous waves of the BCS, a face-to-face interview survey, asked respondents to complete a self-administered questionnaire about drug use, printed as a small booklet that was prominently marked *Confidential*. For the 1994 survey, respondents answered self-report questions on laptop computers. This novel approach is an example of *computer-assisted personal interviewing* (CAPI), where interviewers read questions from computer screens and then type in respondents' answers. For self-report drug items, interviewers handed their computers to subjects, who then keyed in the responses themselves. Ramsay and Percy (1996) report that CAPI appeared to produce at least two benefits. First, respondents seemed to sense a greater degree of confidentiality when they responded to questions on a computer screen, compared to questions on a written form. Second, the laptop computers were something of a novelty that stimulated respondents' interests; this was especially true for younger respondents.

Results from the 1994 BCS also suggest that CAPI techniques produced higher estimates of illegal drug use compared to those revealed in previous surveys. Table 10–1 compares self-reported drug use from the 1994 BCS (Ramsay and Percy, 1996) to results from the 1992 BCS (Mott and Mirrlees-Black, 1995) where respondents answered questions in printed booklets. We present results for only three drugs here, together with tabulations about the illegal use of any drug. For each drug, the survey measured "lifetime use" (Ever used?) and use in the last 12 months. Notice that rates of self-reported use are substantially higher in 1994 than in 1992, with the exception of "semeron" use, reported by very

TABLE 10-1

Self-reported Drug Use, 1992 and 1994 BCS

	Percent of respondents aged 16–29 who report use	
	1992	1994
Marijuana or cannabis		
Ever used?	24	34
Used in previous 12 months?	12	20
Amphetamines		
Ever used?	9	15
Used in previous 12 months?	4	7
Semeron		
Ever used?	.3	.0
Used in previous 12 months?	.1	.0
Any drug		
Ever used?	28	43
Used in previous 12 months?	14	23

Source: 1992 data adapted from Mott and Mirrlees-Black (1995:41–42); 1994 data adapted from Ramsay and Percy (1996:84–87).

few respondents in 1992 and none in 1994. If you've never heard of semeron, you're not alone. It's a fictitious drug, included in the list of real drugs to detect untruthful or exaggerated responses. If someone confessed to using semeron, his or her responses to other self-reported items would be suspect. Notice from Table 10-1 that CAPI use in 1994 reduced the number of respondents who admitted using a drug that doesn't exist.

With this example, it's appropriate to repeat (from Chapter 9) our general advice on data collection: Be careful, but be creative. Use care in developing and interpreting items on self-reported offending, but also be creative in thinking about ways to get better measures. Computer-assisted personal interviewing is a recent innovation that holds promise for measuring hard-to-measure concepts. And there's always room for additional creativity in devising survey questions and techniques for criminal justice research.

■ *QUESTIONNAIRE CONSTRUCTION*

Since questionnaires are the fundamental instruments of survey research, we'll now turn our attention to some of the established techniques for constructing questionnaires. You should read the following sections as a continuation of our theoretical discussions (in Chapter 5) of conceptualization and measurement and also to learn a concrete practical skill.

Of course, how a questionnaire is constructed depends on how the questionnaire will be administered to respondents. Later in this chapter, we will consider the three modes of administration: self-administered, in-person interview, and telephone interview. For now, we will simply point out that a rough continuum of questionnaire complexity is associated with the three modes of administration. In general, questionnaires administered through in-person interviews are the most complex. Self-administered questionnaires are usually the least complex and must be more carefully formatted than questionnaires administered by trained interviewers, either in person or by telephone.

General Questionnaire Format

The format of a questionnaire is just as important as the nature and wording of the questions. An improperly laid-out questionnaire can cause respondents to miss questions, confuse them about the nature of the data desired, and in the extreme, lead them to throw the questionnaire away.

As a general rule, the questionnaire should be spread out and uncluttered. Inexperienced researchers tend to fear that their questionnaire will look too long, so they squeeze several questions onto a single line, abbreviate questions, and try to use as few pages as possible. Such efforts are ill-advised and even dangerous. Putting more than one question on a line will cause some respondents to miss the second question altogether. Some respondents will misinterpret abbreviated questions. And, more generally, respondents who have spent considerable time on the first page of what seemed a short questionnaire will be more demoralized than respondents who quickly completed the first several pages of what initially seemed a long form. Moreover, the latter will have made fewer errors and will not have been forced to reread confusing, abbreviated questions.

Nor will they have been forced to write a long answer in a tiny space.

The desirability of spreading questions out in the questionnaire cannot be overemphasized. Squeezed-together questionnaires are disastrous, whether they are to be completed by the respondents themselves or administered by trained interviewers. And the processing of such questionnaires, with feeble check marks and tiny words scrawled in blanks, can be another nightmare.

Contingency Questions

Quite often in questionnaires, certain questions are clearly relevant to only some of the respondents and irrelevant to others. A victimization survey, for example, presents batteries of questions about victimization incidents that are meaningful to only crime victims.

Frequently, this situation—realizing that the topic is relevant to only some respondents—arises when you wish to ask a series of questions about a certain topic. You may want to ask whether your respondents belong to a particular organization and, if so, how often they attend meetings, whether they have held office in the organization, and so forth. Or you might want to ask whether respondents have heard anything about a certain policy proposal, such as opening a youth shelter in the neighborhood, and then learn the attitudes of those who have heard of it.

The subsequent questions in series such as these are called *contingency questions;* whether they are to be asked and answered is contingent on the response to the first question in the series. The proper use of contingency questions can make the respondents' task easier in completing the questionnaire because they do not have to answer questions that are irrelevant to them.

There are several formats for contingency questions. The one shown in Figure 10-2 is probably the clearest and most effective. Note that the questions shown in the figure could have been dealt with in a single question: "How many times, if any, have you smoked marijuana?" The response categories then would be: "Never," "Once," "2 to 5 times," and so forth. This single

FIGURE 10-2
Contingency Question Format

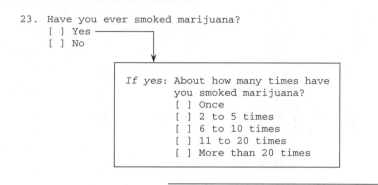

```
23. Have you ever smoked marijuana?
    [ ] Yes
    [ ] No

              If yes: About how many times have
                      you smoked marijuana?
                      [ ] Once
                      [ ] 2 to 5 times
                      [ ] 6 to 10 times
                      [ ] 11 to 20 times
                      [ ] More than 20 times
```

question would apply to all respondents, and each would find an appropriate answer category. Such a question, however, might put pressure on some respondents to report having smoked marijuana, since the main question asks how many times they have smoked it. The contingency question format illustrated in Figure 10-2 reduces the subtle pressure on respondents to report having smoked marijuana. This discussion shows how seemingly theoretical issues of validity and reliability are involved in so mundane a matter as how to put questions on a piece of paper.

Used properly, complex sets of contingency questions can even be constructed without confusing the respondent. Sometimes a set of contingency questions is long enough to extend over several pages.

Victim surveys are good examples of contingency questions. Figure 10-3 presents a few questions from the NCVS questionnaire used in 1993, incorporating changes made as a result of the survey's redesign. All respondents are asked a series of screening questions to reveal possible victimizations. Persons who answer yes to any of the screening questions then complete a crime incident report that presents a large number of items designed to measure details of the victimization incident.

As you can see in Figure 10-3, the crime incident report itself contains contingency questions. You might also notice that even this brief adaptation from the NCVS screening and crime incident report questionnaires is rather complex. NCVS questionnaires are administered through in-person or telephone interviews. It would be difficult to construct a self-administered victimization questionnaire with such complicated contingency questions.

Matrix Questions

Often you will want to ask several questions that have the same set of answer categories. This happens whenever the Likert response categories are used. Then it is often possible to construct a matrix of items and answers, as illustrated in Figure 10-4.

This format has three advantages. First, it uses space efficiently. Second, respondents probably find it faster to complete a set of questions presented in this fashion. In addition, this format may increase the comparability of responses given to different questions for the respondent as well as for the researcher. Because respondents can quickly review their answers to earlier items in the set, they might choose between, say, "strongly agree" and "agree" on a given statement by comparing their strength of agreement with their earlier responses in the set.

Some dangers are inherent in using this format as well. Its advantages may encourage you to structure an item so that the responses fit into the matrix format when a different, more

FIGURE 10-3
NCVS Screening Questions and Crime Incident Report

Screening Question:

36a. I'm going to read you some examples that will give you an idea of the kinds of crimes this study covers. As I go through them, tell me if any of these happened to you in the last six months—that is, since [date].

Was something belonging to you stolen, such as—

(a)   Things that you carry, like a wallet, briefcase, or purse?
(b)   Clothing, jewelry, or calculator?
(c)   Bicycle or sports equipment?
(d)   Things in your home, like a TV, stereo, or tools?

Crime Incident Report:

20a. Were you or any other member of this household present when this incident occurred?

_____ Yes [ask item 20b]

_____ No   [skip to 56, page 8]

20b. Which household members were present?

_____ Respondent only [ask item 21]

_____ Respondent and other household member(s) [ask item 21]

_____ Only other household member(s) [skip to 56, page 8]

21. Did you personally see an offender?

_____ Yes

_____ No

. . . .

56. Do you know or have you learned anything about the offender(s)—for instance, whether there was one or more than one offender involved, whether it was someone young or old, or male or female?

_____ Yes [ask item 57]

_____ No   [skip to 88, page 11]

Source: Adapted from Bureau of Justice Statistics 1996b:124–135.

FIGURE 10-4
Matrix Question Format

17. Beside each of the statements presented below, please indicate whether you Strongly Agree (SA), Agree (A), Disagree (D), Strongly Disagree (SD), or are Undecided (U).

	·SA	A	D	SD	U
a. What this country needs is more law and order	[ ]	[ ]	[ ]	[ ]	[ ]
b. Police in America should not carry guns	[ ]	[ ]	[ ]	[ ]	[ ]
c. Repeat drug dealers should receive life sentences	[ ]	[ ]	[ ]	[ ]	[ ]

idiosyncratic, set of responses might be more appropriate. Also, the matrix question format can generate a response set among some respondents. This means that respondents may develop a pat-tern of, say, agreeing with all the statements, with-out really thinking about what the statements mean. That is especially likely if the set of state-ments begins with several that indicate a particular orientation (for example, a conservative political perspective) and then only a few later ones represent the opposite orientation. Respondents might assume that all the statements represent the same orientation and, reading quickly, misread some of them, thereby giving the wrong answers. This problem can be reduced somewhat by alternating statements that represent different orientations and by making all statements short and clear.

A more difficult problem is when a response is generated through respondent boredom or fatigue. This can be avoided by keeping matrix questions and the entire questionnaire as short as possible. Later in this chapter, in the section on comparing different methods of questionnaire administration, we will describe a useful technique for avoiding response sets generated by respondent fatigue.

Ordering Questions in a Questionnaire

The order in which questions are asked can also affect the answers given. The appearance of one question can affect the answers given to later ones. For example, if several questions have been asked about the dangers of illegal drug use and then a question asks respondents to volunteer (open-ended) what they believe to be the most serious crime problems in U.S. cities, drug use will receive more citations than would otherwise be the case. In this situation, it is preferable to ask the open-ended question first.

If respondents are asked to rate the overall effectiveness of corrections policy, they will answer later questions about specific aspects of correctional institutions in a way that is consistent with their initial assessment. The converse is true as well. If respondents are first asked specific questions about prisons and other correctional facilities, their subsequent overall assessment will be influenced by the earlier answer.

The safest solution is sensitivity to the problem. Although you cannot avoid the effect of question order, you should attempt to estimate what that effect will be. Then you will be able to interpret results in a meaningful fashion. If the order of questions seems an especially important issue in a given study, you might construct several versions of the questionnaire that contain the different possible orderings of questions. You could then determine the effects of ordering. At the very least, you should pretest your questionnaire in the different forms.

The desired ordering of questions differs somewhat between self-administered questionnaires and interviews. In the former, it is usually best to begin the questionnaire with the most interesting set of questions. The potential respondents who glance casually at the first few questions should want to answer them. Perhaps the questions will ask for attitudes that they are aching to express. At the same time, however, the initial questions should be neither threatening nor sensitive. It might be a bad idea to begin with questions about sexual behavior or drug use. Requests for duller demographic data (age, gender, and the like) should generally be placed at the end of a self-administered questionnaire. Placing these questions at the beginning, as many inexperienced researchers are tempted to do, gives the questionnaire the initial appearance of a routine form, and the person who receives it may not be motivated to complete it.

Just the opposite is generally true for in-person interview and telephone surveys. When the potential respondent's door first opens, the interviewer must begin to establish rapport quickly. After a short introduction to the study, the interviewer can best begin by enumerating the members of the household, getting demographic data about each. Such questions are easily answered and generally nonthreatening. Once the initial rapport has been established, the interviewer can move into the area of attitudes and more sensitive matters. An interview that began with the question "Do you ever worry about strangers appearing at your doorstep?" would probably end rather quickly.

■ SELF-ADMINISTERED QUESTIONNAIRES

We will now turn our attention to different ways of actually presenting questions to respondents. We will begin by describing self-administered questionnaires—forms respondents complete themselves. This is followed by a discussion of in-person interview and telephone surveys.

Although the mail survey is the typical method used in self-administered studies, several other methods are also common. In some cases, it may be appropriate to administer the questionnaire to a group of respondents gathered at the same place at the same time, such as police officers at roll call or prison inmates at some specially arranged assembly. Or probationers might complete a questionnaire when they report for a meeting with their probation supervisor. You may recall from Chapter 6 that the Monitoring the Future survey has high school seniors complete self-administered questionnaires in class.

Some recent experimentation has been conducted on the home delivery of questionnaires. A research worker delivers the questionnaire to the home of sample respondents and explains the study. Then the questionnaire is left for the respondent to complete, and the researcher picks it up later.

Home delivery and the mail can be used in combination as well. Questionnaires can be mailed to families, and then research workers may visit the homes to pick up the questionnaires and check them for completeness. In the opposite approach, questionnaires have been hand delivered by research workers with a request that the respondents mail the completed questionnaires to the research office. In general, when a research worker delivers the questionnaire, picks it up, or both, the completion rate seems higher than for straightforward mail surveys. Additional experimentation with this method is likely to point to other techniques for improving completion while reducing costs. Mail surveys are still the most common form of self-administered survey, however, and the remainder of this section is devoted to them.

Mail Distribution and Return

The basic method for collecting data through the mail is transmittal of a questionnaire accompanied by a letter of explanation and a self-addressed, stamped envelope for returning the questionnaire. You have probably received one or two in your lifetime. As a respondent, you are expected to complete the questionnaire, put it in the envelope, and mail it back. If, by any chance, you have received such a questionnaire and failed to return it, it is extremely valuable for you to recall your reasons for not returning it—and keep those in mind any time you plan to send questionnaires to others.

One big reason that people do not return questionnaires is that it seems like too much trouble. To overcome this problem, researchers have developed ways to make the return of questionnaires easier. One method involves a self-mailing questionnaire that requires no return envelope. The questionnaire is designed so that when it is folded in a particular fashion, the return address appears on the outside. That way, the respondent doesn't have to worry about losing the envelope.

Use this method with caution, however. U.S. Postal Service regulations specify permissible sizes and methods for sealing different types of mail. Although it is unlikely that a mail survey would be too small, self-mailing questionnaires can be larger than first-class regulations permit. And you would not be happy to learn that thousands of questionnaires you had distributed to respondents could not be returned legally.

Anything you can do to make the job of completing and returning the questionnaire easier will improve your study results. Imagine receiving a questionnaire that made no provisions for its return to the researcher. Suppose you had to (1) find an envelope, (2) write the address on it, (3) figure out how much postage it requires, and (4) put the stamps on it. How likely are you to return the questionnaire?

One factor to consider in the actual mailing of questionnaires is timing. In most cases, the holiday months of November, December, and January should be avoided. Overall mail volume is greatest during those periods, which can substantially slow down both the distribution and return of questionnaires. And because a greater volume of mail is flowing through post offices, people receive more mail of all types. If your questionnaire arrives in the company of glossy gift catalogs, holiday greetings, bills, and assorted junk mail, respondents will be more likely to discard the survey packet.

Warning Mailings, Cover Letters

The U.S. population, especially that proportion residing in urban areas, is becoming increasingly mobile. This mobility, together with the fact that sampling frames used to obtain addresses may be dated, has prompted researchers to use warning mailings for the purpose of verifying, or "cleaning," addresses. Certain types of warning mailings can also be effective in increasing response rates.

Warning mailings work like this. After researchers generate a sample, they send a postcard to the address of each selected respondent, with the notation "Address correction requested" printed on the postcard. If the addressee has moved and left a forwarding address, the actual questionnaire is sent to the new address. In cases where someone has moved and not left a forwarding address, or more than one year has elapsed and the post office no longer has information about a new address, the postcard is returned marked something like "Addressee unknown."

Selected persons who still reside at the original listed address are "warned" in suitable language to expect a questionnaire in the mail. In such cases, postcards should briefly describe the purpose of the survey for which the respondent has been selected.

Warning letters sent instead of postcards can be more effective in increasing response rates and still serve the purpose of cleaning addresses. Letters printed on letterhead stationery can present a longer description of the survey's purpose and a more reasoned explanation of why it is important for everyone to respond.

Cover letters accompanying the actual questionnaire offer a similar opportunity to increase response rates. Two features of cover letters warrant some attention. First, the content of the letter is obviously important. Your message should communicate your reasons for conducting a survey, how and why the respondent was selected, and why it is important for the respondent to complete your questionnaire. In line with our discussion of the protection of human subjects in Chapter 8, the cover letter should also assure respondents that their answers will be confidential.

The second aspect of cover letters is the institutional affiliation or sponsorship of the survey. The two alternatives are: (1) some institution that the respondent respects or can identify with and (2) a neutral but nonetheless impressive-sounding affiliation. For example, if you are conducting a mail survey of police chiefs, printing your cover letter on International Association of Chiefs of Police (IACP) stationery and having the letter signed by some official in the IACP may increase the response rate. Of course, you would not adopt such a procedure unless your survey actually was endorsed by the IACP.

By the same token, you should avoid controversial affiliations or those inappropriate for your target population. The National Organization for Reform of Marijuana Laws, for instance, is not suitable for most target populations. A university affiliation is appropriate in many cases, unless the university is on bad terms with the target population.

Monitoring Returns

As questionnaires are returned, you should not sit back idly but should begin to monitor the completed questionnaires. It's important to pay close attention to the response rate—what percentage of mailed questionnaires are completed and returned. Each questionnaire should be opened, scanned, and assigned an identification number. These numbers should be assigned serially as the questionnaires are returned, even if other identification numbers have already been assigned. An example illustrates the important advantage of this procedure.

Let's assume you are studying attitudes toward police in a large city. You mailed 800 questionnaires to a probability sample of residents in February 1991. About one week later, the amateur videotape of Rodney King's beating by four Los Angeles police officers dominates the news for several days. By knowing the date when TV stations began to show the tape and cover the story, you will be in a position to determine the effect of that incident on attitudes toward police. (Recall the discussion of history in connection with experiments.)

Follow-up Mailings

Follow-up mailings may be administered in a number of ways. In the simplest, nonrespondents are sent a letter of additional encouragement to participate. A better method, however, is to send a new copy of the survey questionnaire with the follow-up letter. If potential respondents have not returned their questionnaires after two or three weeks, the questionnaires probably have been lost or misplaced.

The methodological literature on follow-up mailings strongly suggests that they are an effective way to increase return rates in mail surveys. In general, the longer a potential respondent delays replying, the less likely he or she is to do so at all. Properly timed follow-up mailings provide additional stimuli to respond.

The effects of follow-up mailings may be seen by monitoring the number of questionnaires received over time. The initial mailings will be followed by a rise and subsequent subsiding of returns; the follow-up mailings will spur a resurgence of returns; and more follow-ups will do the same. In practice, three mailings (an original and two follow-ups) are the most effective.

The timing of follow-up mailings is also important. Here the methodological literature offers less precise guides, but two or three weeks is a reasonable space between mailings. (This period might be increased by a few days if the mailing time—out and in—is more than two or three days.)

If the individuals in the survey sample are not identified on the questionnaires, it may not be possible to remail to only nonrespondents. In such a case, you should send your follow-up mailing to all members of the sample, thanking those who may have already participated and encouraging those who have not to do so.

Acceptable Response Rates

A question frequently asked about mail surveys concerns the percentage return rate that should be achieved. It should be pointed out here that the body of inferential statistics used in connection with survey analysis assumes that *all* members of the initial sample complete and return their questionnaires. Since this almost never happens, response bias becomes a concern, with the researcher testing (and hoping for) the possibility that the respondents look essentially like a random sample of the initial sample and thus a somewhat smaller random sample of the total population.

Nevertheless, overall response rate is one guide to the representativeness of the sample respondents. If the response rate is high, then there is less chance of significant response bias than if the rate is low. But what is a high response rate?

A quick review of the survey literature uncovers a wide range of response rates. Each may be accompanied by a statement like "This is regarded as a relatively high response rate for a survey of this type." (A U.S. senator made this statement about a poll of constituents that achieved a 4 percent return rate!) Even so, it's possible to state some rules of thumb about return rates. A response rate of at least 50 percent is adequate for analysis and reporting. A response of at least 60 percent is good. And a response rate of 70 percent is very good. Bear in mind, however, that these are only rough guides; they have no statistical basis, and a demonstrated lack of response bias is far more important than a high response rate.

As you can imagine, one of the more persistent discussions among survey researchers concerns ways to increase response rates. Ingenious techniques have been developed to address this problem. Some researchers have experimented with novel formats. Others have tried paying respondents to participate. The problem with paying, of course, is that it's expensive to make meaningfully high payments to hundreds or thousands of respondents.

Don Dillman (1978) has undertaken an excellent review of the various techniques survey researchers have used to increase return rates on mail surveys, and he evaluates the impact of each. More important, Dillman stresses the necessity of paying attention to all aspects of the study—what he calls the *Total Design Method*—rather than one or two special gimmicks.

■ IN-PERSON INTERVIEW SURVEYS

The in-person interview is an alternative method of collecting survey data. Rather than asking respondents to read questionnaires and enter their own answers, researchers send interviewers to ask the questions orally and record respondents' answers. Most interview surveys require more than one interviewer, although you might undertake a small-scale interview survey yourself.

The Role of the Interviewer

In-person interview surveys typically attain higher response rates than mail surveys. Respondents seem more reluctant to turn down an interviewer who is standing on their doorstep than to throw away a mail questionnaire. A properly designed and executed interview survey ought to achieve a completion rate of at least 80 to 85 percent.

The presence of an interviewer generally decreases the number of "don't knows" and "no answers." If minimizing such responses is important to the study, the interviewer can be instructed to probe for answers ("If you had to pick one of the answers, which do you think would come closest to your feelings?").

Interviewers can also guard against confusing questionnaire items. If the respondent clearly misunderstands the intent of a question, the interviewer can clarify matters and thereby obtain a relevant response. Such clarifications must be strictly controlled, however, through formal specifications. (See the later section "Coordination and Control.")

Finally, the interviewer can observe as well as ask questions. For example, the interviewer can make observations about the quality of the dwelling, the presence of various possessions, the respondent's ability to speak English, the respondent's general reactions to the study, and so forth. Interviewers for the BCS and for a 1983 supplement to the NCVS made detailed observations of the physical conditions surrounding each respondent's home. Later analysis compared interviewer ratings of such things as litter and graffiti with respondent perceptions of the same problems (Maxfield, 1987b).

Survey research is of necessity based on an unrealistic stimulus–response theory of cognition and behavior. It must be assumed that a questionnaire item will mean the same thing to every respondent, and every given response must mean the same when given by different respondents. Although this is an impossible goal, survey questions are drafted to approximate the ideal as closely as possible. The interviewer must also fit into this ideal situation. The interviewer's presence should not affect a respondent's perception of a question or the answer given. The interviewer, then, should be a neutral medium through which questions and answers are transmitted.

If this goal is met, different interviewers will obtain exactly the same responses from a given respondent. (Recall earlier discussions of reliability.) This neutrality has a special importance in area samples. To save time and money, a given interviewer is typically assigned to complete all the interviews in a particular geographic area—a city block or a group of nearby blocks. If the interviewer does anything to affect the responses obtained, the bias thus interjected might be interpreted as a characteristic of that area.

General Rules for Interviewing

The way interviews ought to be conducted will vary somewhat by the survey population and survey content. Nevertheless, it is possible to provide some general guidelines that apply to most interviewing situations, including sample surveys and more specialized interviewing.

Appearance and Demeanor   As a general rule, the interviewer should dress in a fashion similar to that of the people he or she will be interviewing. An interviewer wearing business attire will probably have difficulty getting good cooperation and responses from poorer respondents. And a poorly dressed interviewer will have similar difficulties with richer respondents.

To the extent that the interviewer's dress and grooming differ from those of the respondents, it should be in the direction of cleanliness and neatness in modest apparel. Although middle-class neatness and cleanliness may not be accepted by all sectors of American society, they remain the primary norm and are likely to be acceptable to the largest number of respondents.

The importance of considering the target population cannot be overemphasized. Neat establishment clothes should be the norm when interviewing most criminal justice officials. On the other hand, the middle-class norm in clothing may foster suspicion among street people or incarcerated persons.

In demeanor, interviewers should be pleasant if nothing else. Because they will be prying into the respondent's personal life and thoughts, they must communicate a genuine interest in getting to know the respondent without appearing to spy. They must be relaxed and friendly without being too casual or clinging. Good interviewers also have the ability to quickly determine the kind of person the respondent will feel most comfortable with or would most enjoy talking to, and they adapt accordingly.

Familiarity with Questionnaire   The interviewer must be able to read the questionnaire items to respondents without stumbling over words and phrases. A good model for interviewers is the actor reading lines in a play or film. The interviewer must read naturally as though the questions were a natural conversation, but that conversation must precisely follow the language set down in the question.

By the same token, the interviewer must be familiar with the specifications prepared for administering the questionnaire. Inevitably some questions will not exactly fit a given respondent's situation, and the interviewer must determine how those questions should be interpreted in that situation. The specifications provided to the interviewer should give adequate guidance in such cases, but the interviewer must know the organization and contents of the specifications well enough to refer to them efficiently.

Probing for Responses   Probes are frequently required for eliciting responses to open-ended questions. For example, to a question about neighborhood crime problems, the respondent might simply reply "Pretty bad." The interviewer could obtain an elaboration on this response through a variety of probes. Sometimes the best probe is silence; if the interviewer sits quietly with pencil poised, the respondent will probably fill the pause with additional comments. Appropriate verbal probes are "How is that?" and "In what ways?" Perhaps the most generally useful probe is "Anything else?"

It is frequently necessary to probe for answers that will be sufficiently informative for analytic purposes. In every case, however, it is imperative that probes be completely neutral. The probe must not in any way affect the nature of the subsequent response. If you anticipate that a given question may require probing for appropriate responses, you should write one or more useful probes next to the question in the questionnaire. This practice has two important advantages. First, you will have more time to devise the best, most neutral probes. Second, all interviewers will use the same probes when they are needed. Thus, even if the probe is not perfectly neutral, the same stimulus is presented to all respondents. This is the same logical guideline discussed for question wording. Although a question should not be loaded or biased, it is essential that every respondent be presented with the same question, even a biased one.

Coordination and Control

Whenever more than one interviewer will administer a survey, it is essential that the efforts be carefully controlled. Two ways to ensure this control are by training interviewers and supervising them after they begin work.

Whether you will be administering a survey yourself or paying a professional firm to do it for you, you should be attentive to the importance of training interviewers. The interviewers should normally know what the study is all about. Even though the interviewers may be involved only in the data-collection phase of the project, they should understand what will be done with the interviews they conduct and what purpose will be served.

There may be some exceptions to this, however. For example, in her follow-up study of child abuse victims and controls, Widom did not inform the professional interviewers who gathered data that her interest was in the long-term effects of child abuse (Luntz and Widom, 1994).

This safeguard was used to avoid even the slightest chance that interviewers' knowledge of the study focus would affect how they conducted interviews.

Obviously, training should ensure that interviewers understand the questionnaire. Interviewers should also be clear on procedures to select respondents from among household members, and under what circumstances substitute sample elements may be used in place of addresses that no longer exist, families who have moved, or persons who simply refuse to be interviewed.

Training should include practice interviews, where interviewers administer the questionnaire to one another. The final stage of the training for interviewers should involve some "real" interviews conducted under conditions like those in the actual survey.

While interviews are being conducted, it is a good idea to review questionnaires as they are completed. This may reveal questions or groups of questions that respondents do not understand. Alternatively, reviewing completed questionnaires can signal that some individual interviewer is encountering difficulties.

■ *TELEPHONE SURVEYS*

For years, telephone surveys had a bad reputation among professional researchers. Telephone surveys are limited by definition to people who own telephones, so years ago, this method produced a substantial social-class bias by excluding poor people. Over time, however, the telephone has become a standard fixture in almost all American homes. The U.S. Census Bureau estimates that 94 percent of all households now have telephones, so the earlier class bias has been substantially reduced (U.S. Bureau of the Census, 1992: Table 884). The NCVS has increased its use of telephone interviews as part of the crime survey's redesign; by 1993, about one-third of all interviews were completed by telephone (U.S. Bureau of the Census, 1994).

On the other hand, phone surveys are much less suitable for individuals not living in households. Homeless people are obvious examples; those who live in institutions are also difficult to reach out and touch via telephone.

A related sampling problem involves unlisted numbers. If the survey sample is selected from the pages of a local telephone directory, it totally omits all those people who have requested that their numbers not be published. Also, as we mentioned in Chapter 9, recent movers and transient residents are not well represented in published telephone directories. This potential bias has been eliminated through random-digit dialing (RDD), a technique that has advanced telephone sampling substantially.

RDD samples use computer algorithms to generate lists of random telephone numbers—usually the last four digits. This procedure gets around the sampling problem of unlisted telephone numbers but may create an administrative problem instead. Randomly generating telephone numbers produces numbers that are not in operation or numbers that serve a business establishment or pay phone. In most cases, businesses and pay phones are not included in the target population; dialing these numbers and learning that they're "out of scope" will take time away from producing completed interviews with your target population.

Telephone surveys have many advantages that make them such a popular method. Probably the greatest advantages are money and time. In a face-to-face household interview, you may drive several miles to a respondent's home, find no one there, return to the research office, and drive back the next day—possibly finding no one there again. It's cheaper and quicker to let your fingers make the trips.

Interviewing by telephone, you can dress any way you please and it will have no effect on the answers respondents give. And sometimes respondents will be more honest in giving socially disapproved answers if they don't have to look you in the eye. Similarly, it may be possible to probe into more sensitive areas, although that is not necessarily the case. People are, to some extent, more suspicious when they can't see the person asking them questions—perhaps a consequence of telemarketing and salespeople conducting bogus surveys.

Telephone surveys can give you greater control over data collection if several interviewers are engaged in the project. If all the interviewers are calling from the research office, they can get clarification from the supervisor whenever problems occur, as they inevitably do. Alone in the field, an interviewer may have to wing it between weekly visits with the interviewing supervisor.

A related advantage is rooted in the growing diversity of U.S. cities. Because many major cities have growing immigrant populations, interviews may need to be conducted in different languages. Telephone interviews are usually conducted from a central site, so that one or more multilingual interviewers can be quickly summoned if an English-speaking interviewer makes contact with, for example, a Spanish-speaking respondent. In-person interview surveys present much more difficult logistical problems in handling multiple languages. And mail surveys would require printing and distributing questionnaires in different languages.

Another important factor in the growing use of telephone surveys is personal safety. Don Dillman (1978:4) describes perceptions of risk in in-person interviews:

■ Interviewers must be able to operate comfortably in a climate in which strangers are viewed with distrust and must successfully counter respondents' objections to being interviewed. Increasingly, interviewers must be willing to work at night to contact residents in many households. In some cases, this necessitates providing protection for interviewers working in areas of a city in which a definite threat to the safety of individuals exists.

Concerns for safety therefore work two ways to hamper face-to-face interviews. Potential respondents may refuse to be interviewed because they fear the stranger–inteviewer. And the interviewers themselves may be in danger. Telephone surveys avoid risks to interviewers and reduce the concerns of respondents who may be uneasy about opening their doors to strangers.

Telephone interviewing has its problems, however. As we mentioned, the method is hampered by the proliferation of bogus "surveys," which are actually sales campaigns disguised as research.

Also, changes in technology have raised two new challenges for telephone surveys. First, telemarketing is now easier and cheaper than ever. The volume of junk phone calls now rivals that of junk mail, and salespeople often begin their pitch by describing a "survey." Second, residential phone customers have much greater control over incoming calls through the proliferation of answering machines and other new phone services. Many people screen calls by listening to a caller's message. Caller identification enables subscribers to learn who is calling them before they answer a phone and to ignore incoming calls from unfamiliar sources.

The ease with which people can hang up is, of course, another shortcoming of telephone surveys. Once you are inside someone's home for an interview, he or she is unlikely to order you out of the house in mid-interview. It's much easier to terminate a telephone interview abruptly, saying something like, "Whoops! Someone's at the door. I gotta go" or simply hanging up.

Computer-Assisted Interviewing

Much of the growth in telemarketing has been fueled by advances in computer and telecommunications technology. Computers generate and dial phone numbers (in some cases computers even control recorded sales pitches); operators type customer and order information into forms displayed on computer screens. Beginning in the 1980s, much of the same technology came to be widely used in telephone surveys, referred to as *computer-assisted telephone interviewing* (CATI). Here's how it works.

Interviewers wearing telephone headsets sit at computer workstations. Computer programs dial sampled phone numbers, which can be either generated through random-digit dialing or extracted from a database of phone numbers compiled from some source. As soon as phone contact is made, the computer screen displays an introduction ("Hello, my name is . . . calling from the Survey Research Center at Ivory Tower University") and the first question to be asked, often a query about the number of residents who live in the household. As interviewers key in answers to each question, the computer program displays a new screen that presents the next question, until the end of the interview is reached.

CATI systems offer several advantages over older procedures in which an interviewer works through a printed interview schedule. Speed is one obvious plus. Forms on computer screens can be filled in more quickly than paper forms. Typing answers to open-ended questions is much faster than writing them by hand. And CATI software immediately formats responses into a data file as they are keyed in, which eliminates the later step of manually transferring answers from paper to computer.

Perhaps you've occasionally marveled at newspaper stories that report the results of a nationwide opinion poll the day after some major speech or event. The speed of CATI technology, coupled with random-digit dialing, makes these instant polls possible.

Accuracy is also enhanced by CATI systems in a couple of different ways. First, CATI programs can be designed to accept only valid responses to any given questionnaire item. If valid responses to respondent "gender" are *f* for female and *m* for male, the computer will accept only those two letters, emitting a disagreeable noise and refusing to proceed if something else is keyed in. Second, the software can be programmed to automate contingency questions and skip sequences, thus ensuring that the interviewer skips over inappropriate items and rapidly gets to the next appropriate question. This can be especially handy in a victim survey, where affirmative answers to screening questions automatically bring up detailed questions about each crime incident.

Computer technology is also coming into wider use for in-person interview surveys, as we saw in the example of computer-assisted personal interviewing in the 1994 BCS. Interviewers may now carry small notebook computers rather than an armful of questionnaires. Database software similar to that used by CATI systems automates face-to-face interviews, affording all the advantages of speed and accuracy.

COMPARISON OF THE THREE METHODS

We've now described the three ways you can collect survey data: self-administered questionnaires, in-person interviews, and telephone surveys. Although we've touched on some of the relative advantages and disadvantages of each, let's take a minute to compare them more directly. Self-administered questionnaires are generally cheaper to use than interview surveys. Moreover, if you use the self-administered mail format, it costs no more to conduct a national survey than a local one; the cost difference between a local and a national in-person interview survey is much greater. Telephone surveys are somewhere in between, and national surveys can inflate costs through long-distance telephone charges. Mail surveys typically require a small staff. One person can conduct a reasonable mail survey alone, although you should not underestimate the work involved.

Up to a point, cost and speed are inversely related. In-person interview surveys can be completed very quickly if a large pool of interviewers is readily available and funding is adequqate to pay them. On the other hand, if a small number of people are conducting a larger number of face-to-face interviews, costs are generally lower but the survey takes much longer to complete. Telephone surveys that use CATI technology are easily the fastest.

Self-administered surveys are usually more appropriate to use with especially sensitive issues if the surveys offer complete anonymity. Respondents are sometimes reluctant to report controversial or deviant attitudes or behaviors in interviews, but they may be willing to respond to an anonymous self-administered questionnaire. The successful use of computers for self-report items in the 1994 BCS suggests that interacting with a machine may promote more candid responses.

Interview surveys have many advantages, too. For example, they are more appropriate where respondent literacy may be a problem. Interview surveys also produce fewer incomplete questionnaires. Although respondents may skip questions in a self-administered questionnaire, interviewers

FIGURE 10-5
Card Sort

Q.17   I would like now to talk to you about how serious you personally think different crimes are.

[PLACE DOWN THE LOOSE CARDS HEADED 'Q.17' AND GIVE RESPONDENT THE 14 CRIME CARDS]

Written on these cards are descriptions of different crimes. Please will you sort them into different piles according to how serious you think they are. For example if you think a crime is very serious put it on this pile [POINT TO 'VERY SERIOUS' CARD]

Please have a look through all the crimes before you sort them into piles.

[WHEN RESPONDENTS HAVE SORTED ALL CRIME CARDS INTO THE FOUR PILES, ASK THEM TO READ OUT THE CRIMES IN EACH CATEGORY AND RECORD THE ANSWERS BELOW]

Crime Cards:

    Someone being mugged and robbed

        A car being stolen for a joy ride

           A home being broken into and something stolen

              A home being damaged by vandals

                  Someone smoking cannabis or marijuana

. . . .

Sort Piles:

very serious	fairly serious	not very serious	trivial

. . . .

Instructions to interviewers in capital letters, enclosed in brackets.

Source: Adapted from 1984 British Crime Survey, follow-up questionnaire.

---

are trained not to do so. The computer offers a further check on this in CATI and CAPI surveys.

Interview surveys, moreover, typically have higher completion rates than self-administered ones. In an analysis of response rates to 517 surveys, John Goyder (1985) concluded that the difference in response rates between interview and mail surveys has decreased in recent times and that the earlier differences were primarily a function of more extensive follow-up in interview surveys.

Although self-administered questionnaires may be more effective in dealing with sensitive issues, interview surveys are definitely more effective in dealing with complicated ones. Interviewers can explain complex questions to respondents and use visual aids that are not possible in mail or phone surveys. The 1984 BCS contained two examples of such techniques.

First, a series of questions to learn more about attitudes toward neighborhood watch programs

was planned for the BCS. Pretests of certain questionnaire items revealed that many people were unfamiliar with neighborhood watch. In conducting the actual survey, interviewers handed respondents a card that presented a brief description of neighborhood watch. Respondents were asked a battery of questions about their opinions of such programs after they had read the card.

In general, this may be called an "information-opinion" technique, in which each respondent is first exposed to a standard description of some object and is then asked to give an opinion about the object. This technique cannot be used effectively in self-administered questionnaires because respondents might skip over a lengthy written description and begin to answer questions right away.

The second type of unique in-person interview technique used in the 1984 BCS helps avoid response sets. Figure 10-5 shows a group of questions about crime seriousness that were presented to respondents as a *card sort.* Instructions to interviewers are in capital letters enclosed in brackets. We mentioned earlier how presenting a series of similar items can generate a response set. A card sort like the one in Figure 10-5 requires respondents to play a more active role in the interview and generally breaks the tedium that can set in after a long session (45 minutes or more at this point in the 1984 BCS). Obviously, card sorts and similar visual aids that are manipulated by interviewers can be used only in face-to-face interviews. Similarly, notebook computers and CAPI techniques can be used only in face-to-face interviews.

As mentioned earlier, interviewers who question respondents face to face are also able to make important observations aside from responses to questions asked in the interview. In a household interview, they may summarize characteristics of the neighborhood, the dwelling unit, and so forth. They may also note characteristics of the respondents or the quality of their interaction with the respondents—whether the respondent had difficulty communicating, was hostile, seemed to be lying, and so on. Finally, where safety to interviewers must be considered, a mail or phone survey has advantages.

Ultimately, you must balance all these advantages and disadvantages of the three methods in relation to your research needs and your resources.

■ STRENGTHS AND WEAKNESSES OF SURVEY RESEARCH

Like other modes of collecting data in criminal justice research, surveys have strengths and weaknesses. It is important to consider these as you decide whether the survey format is appropriate to your research goals.

Surveys are particularly useful in describing the characteristics of a large population. The NCVS has become an important tool for researchers and public officials because of its ability to describe levels of crime. A carefully selected probability sample in combination with a standardized questionnaire allows researchers to make refined descriptive statements about a neighborhood, a city, a nation, or some other large population.

Standardized questionnaires have an important strength in regard to measurement. Earlier chapters have discussed the ambiguous nature of concepts: They ultimately have no real meanings. One person's view about crime seriousness or punishment severity is quite different from another's. Although you must be able to define concepts in ways that are most relevant to your research goals, you may not find it easy to apply the same definitions uniformly to all subjects. The survey researcher is bound to this requirement by having to ask exactly the same questions of all subjects and having to impute the same intent to all respondents giving a particular response.

At the same time, survey research has its weaknesses. First, the requirement for standardization just mentioned might mean you are trying to fit round pegs into square holes. Standardized questionnaire items often represent the least common denominator in assessing people's attitudes, orientations, circumstances, and experiences. By designing questions that will be at least minimally appropriate to all respondents, you may miss what is most appropriate to many respondents. In this sense, surveys often appear superficial in their coverage of complex topics.

Similarly, survey research cannot readily deal with the context of social life. Although questionnaires can provide information in this area, the survey researcher can seldom develop a feel for the total life situation in which respondents are thinking and acting. That contrasts with the participant observer (see Chapter 11). Most researchers are dissatisfied with standard survey questions about important criminal justice concepts such as fear of crime, routine behavior, and crime prevention.

Although surveys are flexible in the sense mentioned earlier, they cannot be changed once interviewing has begun. Studies that involve direct observation can be modified as field conditions warrant, but surveys typically require that an initial study design remain unchanged throughout.

Using surveys to study crime and criminal justice policy presents special challenges. The target population frequently includes lower-income, transient persons who are difficult to contact through customary sampling methods. For example, homeless persons are excluded from any survey that samples households, but people who live on the street no doubt figure prominently as victims and offenders.

Crime surveys such as the NCVS and the BCS have been deficient in getting information about crimes of violence where the victim and offender have some prior relationship. This is particularly true for domestic violence.

Underreporting of domestic violence appears to be due, in part, to the very general nature of large-scale crime surveys. Catriona Mirrlees-Black (1995:8) of the British Home Office summarizes the trade-offs of using survey techniques to learn about domestic violence:

■ Measuring domestic violence is difficult territory. The advantage of the BCS is that it is based on a large nationally representative sample, has a relatively high response rate, and collects information on enough incidents to provide reliable details of their nature. One disadvantage is that domestic violence is measured in the context of a crime survey, and some women may not see what happened to them as "crime," or be reluctant to do so. Also, there is little time to approach the topic "gently." A specially designed questionnaire with carefully selected interviewers may well have the edge here.

In recent years, both the NCVS and the BCS have been changed to produce better measures of domestic and intimate violence. Chapter 6 described the NCVS redesign efforts in this regard. Estimates of domestic violence increased in the 1996 wave of the British Crime Survey, and BCS researchers think the increase reflects a greater willingness by respondents to discuss domestic violence with interviewers (Mirrlees-Black, Mayhew, and Percy, 1996).

We have mentioned that national crime surveys cannot be used to estimate the frequency of victimization in local areas like individual cities.

For this reason, the Census Bureau conducted a series of city victimization surveys in the 1970s. City crime surveys suffer problems of their own, however. Since sampling procedures are almost always based on some sample frame of city residents, city-specific surveys are not able to measure crimes that involve nonresident victims. For example, a random-digit dialing survey of Key West, Florida, residents could not possibly count the robbery of a visitor who came down from Cincinnati.

Survey research is generally weaker on validity and stronger on reliability. In comparison with field research, for instance, the artificiality of the survey format puts a strain on validity. As an illustration, most researchers agree that fear of crime is not well measured by the standard question, "How safe do you feel, or would you feel, out alone in your neighborhood at night?" Survey responses to that question are, at best, approximate indicators of what we have in mind when we conceptualize fear of crime.

Reliability is a different matter. Survey research, by presenting all subjects with a standardized stimulus, goes a long way toward eliminating unreliability in observations made by the researcher.

However, even this statement is subject to qualification. Critics of survey methods argue that questionnaires for standard crime surveys and many specialized studies embody a narrow legalistic conception of crime that cannot reflect the perceptions and experiences of minorities and women. Survey questions are based on male views and do not adequately tap victimization or fear of crime among women. For example, Hanmer and Saunders (1984) conducted intensive interviews with 129 women in Leeds, England. They found much higher levels of physical assault and harassment than were reported in BCS data. Concern that survey questions might mean different things to different respondents raises important questions about reliability and about the generalizability of survey results across subgroups of a population.

As with all methods of observation, a full awareness of the inherent or probable weaknesses of survey research may partially resolve them. Ultimately, though, you are on the safest ground when you can use a number of different research methods to study a given topic.

■ *OTHER WAYS OF ASKING QUESTIONS*

Sample surveys are perhaps the best known application of asking questions as a data-gathering strategy for criminal justice research. Often, however, more specialized interviewing techniques are appropriate. We will briefly discuss the scope of specialized interviewing applications in this section.

Specialized Interviewing

No precise definition of the term *survey* enables us to distinguish a survey from other types of interview situations. As a rule of thumb, a sample survey (even one that uses nonprobability sampling methods) is an interview-based technique for generalizing to a larger population. In contrast, specialized interviewing focuses on the views and opinions of only those individuals who are interviewed.

Let's say you are interested in how mental health professionals view different drug treatment programs for prison inmates. One approach is to conduct a sample survey of psychologists who work in state correctional facilities, where each sampled psychologist completes a structured questionnaire concerning drug treatment programs. This approach would enable you to generalize to the population of state prison psychologists.

Another approach is to study one or two correctional institutions (or some small number) intensively. You could interview a psychologist in each institution and present questions about various approaches to drug treatment therapy. In all likelihood, you would not use a highly structured questionnaire but rather a list of questions or topics you wished to discuss with each subject, and you would treat the interview as more of a directed conversation than a formal interview. Of course, you would not be able to generalize from

interviews with one or two prison psychologists to any larger population. However, you would gain an understanding (and probably a more detailed one) of how staff psychologists in specific institutions feel about different drug treatment programs.

Specialized interviewing asks questions of a small number of subjects, typically using an interview schedule that is much less structured than that used in sample surveys. Michael Quinn Patton (1990:280) distinguishes two variations of specialized interviews. The less structured alternative is to prepare a *general interview guide* that includes the issues, topics, or questions you wish to cover. Issues are not presented to respondents in any standardized order. The interview guide is more like a checklist than an interview schedule, ensuring that planned topics are addressed at some point in the interview. The *standardized open-ended interview* is more structured, using specific questions arranged in a particular order. In this situation, you would present each respondent with the same questions in the same sequence (subject to any contingency questions). The questions are open-ended, but their format and presentation are standardized. To underscore the flexibility of specialized interviewing, Patton describes how the two approaches can be used in combination (1990:287):

■ . . . it is also possible to combine an interview guide approach with a standardized open-ended approach. Thus a number of basic questions may be worded precisely in a predetermined fashion, while permitting the interviewer more flexibility in probing and . . . determining when it is appropriate to explore certain subjects in greater depth or even to undertake whole new areas of inquiry that were not originally included in the interview instrument.

Open-ended questions are ordinarily used because they capture rich detail better. The primary disadvantage of open-ended questions—having to categorize responses—is not a problem in specialized interviewing because of the small numbers of subjects and because researchers are more interested in describing than in generalizing.

Case studies, where a researcher studies a single subject or institution, often use specialized interviewing techniques. However, specialized interviewing can be incorporated into any research project as a supplementary source of information. If, for example, you are interested in the effects of determinant sentencing on prison population, you could analyze data from the *Census of State Adult Correctional Facilities,* conducted by the Bureau of Justice Statistics. You might also wish to interview a small number of corrections administrators, perhaps asking them to react to findings from your data analysis. Evaluation studies and other applied research projects (see Chapter 13) frequently use specialized interviewing techniques, alone or in combination with other sources of data.

Focus Groups

Like sample surveys, focus group techniques were refined by private sector market research firms in the years following World War II. As the name implies, *market research* explores questions about the potential for sales of consumer products. Since a firm may spend millions of dollars developing, advertising, and distributing some new item, market research is an important tool to test consumer reactions before large sums of money are invested in a product.

Surveys have two disadvantages in market research. First, a nationwide or large-scale probability survey can be expensive. Second, it may be difficult to present advertising messages or other product images in a survey format. **Focus groups** have proven more suitable for many market research applications. In recent years, focus groups are commonly used as substitutes for surveys in criminal justice and other social science research.

In a focus group, typically 12 to 15 people are brought together in a room to engage in a guided group discussion of some topic. Although focus groups cannot be used to make statistical estimates about a population, members are nevertheless selected to represent a target population. Krueger (1994) and Stewart and Shamdasani (1990) describe focus groups, their applications, and their advantages and disadvantages in detail.

For example, the location of community correctional facilities such as work-release centers and halfway houses often prompts a classic "Not in my back yard!" (NIMBY) response from people who live in neighborhoods where proposed facilities will be built. Recognizing this, a mayor who wants to find a suitable site without annoying neighborhood residents (voters) is well advised to convene a focus group that includes people who live in areas near possible facility locations. A focus group can test the "market acceptability" of a work-release center, which might include the best way to package and sell the product. Such an exercise might reveal that appealing to altruism ("We all have to make sacrifices in the fight against crime") is much less effective in gaining support than an alternative sales pitch that stresses potential economic benefits ("This new facility will provide jobs for neighborhood residents").

Generalizations from focus groups to target populations cannot be precise; however, a study by Ward, Bertrand, and Brown (1991) found that focus-group and survey results can be quite consistent under certain conditions. They conclude that focus groups are most useful in two cases: (1) when precise generalization to a larger population is not necessary, and (2) when focus-group participants and the larger population they are intended to represent are relatively homogeneous. So, for example, a focus group is not appropriate to predict how all city residents will react to a ban on handgun ownership. But a focus group of registered handgun owners could help evaluate a proposed city campaign to buy back handguns.

Focus groups may also be used in combination with survey research in one of two ways. First, a focus group can be extremely valuable in questionnaire development. When researchers are uncertain how to present items to respondents, a focus-group discussion about the topic can generate possible item formats. For instance, earlier we mentioned the 1984 BCS battery of items on neighborhood watch. These questions, together with the introductory explanation of neighborhood watch, were developed after three focus-group discussions with people living in inner-city London areas, a target group of greatest interest for the neighborhood watch items (NOP Market Research, 1985).

Second, after a survey has been completed and preliminary results tabulated, focus groups may be used to guide the interpretation of some results. After a citywide survey in which you found, for example, that recent immigrants from Southeast Asian countries were least supportive of community policing, you could conduct a focus group of Asian residents to delve more deeply into their concerns.

Focus groups are flexible and can be adapted to many uses in basic and applied research. Keep in mind, however, two key elements expressed in the name of this data-collection technique. *Focus* means that researchers present specific questions or issues for directed discussion. Having a free-for-all discussion about neighborhood watch, for example, would not have yielded much useful insight for developing a structured questionnaire for the 1984 BCS. *Group* calls your attention to thinking about who will participate in the focused discussions. Like market researchers, you should select participants from a specific target population that relates to your research questions. If you're interested in how residents of a specific neighborhood would feel about opening a work-release center, you would take care to select group participants who lived in the target neighborhood.

■ *SHOULD YOU DO IT YOURSELF?*

The final issue we address in this chapter is who should conduct surveys. Drawing a sample, constructing a questionnaire, and either conducting interviews or distributing self-administered instruments are not especially difficult. Equipped with the basic principles we have discussed so far in this book, you could complete an in-person or telephone survey of modest size yourself. Mail surveys of large numbers of subjects are entirely possible, especially with present-day microcomputer capabilities.

On the one hand, the different tasks involved in completing a survey require a lot of work and attention to detail. We have presented many tips for constructing questionnaires, but our guidelines barely scratch the surface. Many books describe survey techniques in more detail, and a growing number focus specifically on telephone or mail techniques (see the list of additional readings at the end of this chapter). In many respects, however, designing and executing a survey of modest size can be challenging.

Consider the start-up costs involved in in-person or telephone interview surveys of any size. Finding, training, and paying interviewers are time-consuming, not cheap, and require some degree of expertise. The price of computer equipment continues downward at this writing (1997), but a CATI setup still represents a substantial investment.

If interview surveys are beyond your means, you might fall back on a mail survey. Few capital costs are involved; most expenses are in consumables, such as envelopes, stamps, and stationery. One or two persons can orchestrate a mail survey reasonably well at minimal expense. But consider two issues.

First, the business of completing a survey involves a great deal of tedious work. In mail surveys, for example, questionnaires and cover letters must be printed, folded or stuffed into envelopes, stamped, and delivered (finally!) to the post office. None of this is much fun. The enjoyment starts when completed questionnaires begin to trickle in. It's rewarding to begin the actual experience part of empirical research, and your excitement may get you past the next stretch of tedium: going from paper questionnaires to actual data. So it's possible to do a mail survey yourself, but be prepared for lots of work; even then, it will be more work than you expect.

The second issue is more difficult to deal with and is often overlooked by researchers. We have described at some length the advantages and disadvantages of the three methods of questionnaire administration. Some methods are more or less appropriate than others for different kinds of research questions. If a telephone or an in-person interview survey is best for your research, conducting a mail survey would be a compromise, perhaps an unacceptable one. But your excitement to actually begin your research may lead you to overlook or minimize problems with doing a mail survey on the cheap, in much the same way that researchers are often not in a position to recognize ethical problems with their own work, as we saw in Chapter 8. Doing a mail survey because it's all you can afford does not make a mail survey worth doing.

The alternative to doing it yourself is to contract with a professional survey research firm or a company that routinely conducts surveys. Most research universities have a survey research center or institute, often affiliated with a sociology or political science department. Such institutes are usually available to conduct surveys for government organizations as well as university researchers, and they can often do so very economically. Market research firms are another possibility. Most have the capability to conduct all types of surveys as well as focus groups.

Using a professional survey firm or institute has several advantages. Chapter 9 described the basic principles of sampling, but actually drawing a probability sample can be complex. Professional firms regularly use sampling frames that can represent city, state, and national samples, or whatever combination is appropriate.

We have emphasized the importance of measurement throughout this book. Researchers should develop conceptual and operational definitions and be attentive to all phases of the measurement process. However, constructing an actual questionnaire requires attention to details that may not always be obvious to researchers. Survey firms are experienced in preparing standard demographic items, batteries of matrix questions, and complex contingency questions with appropriate skip sequences.

Although it is often best for researchers to discuss specific concepts and even to draft questions, professional firms offer the considerable benefit of experience in pulling it all together. This is not to say that a researcher should simply propose some ideas for questions and then leave the details to the pros. Working together with a survey

institute or market research firm to propose questionnaire items, review draft instruments, evaluate pretests, and make final modifications is usually the best approach.

Perhaps the chief benefit of contracting for a survey is that professional firms have a pool of trained interviewers or the equipment to conduct computer-assisted telephone interviews. Furthermore, such companies can more readily handle such administrative details as training interviewers, arranging travel for in-person surveys, coordinating mail surveys, and providing general supervision. This frees researchers from much of the tedium of survey research, while enabling them to focus on more substantive issues.

You must ultimately decide whether to conduct a survey yourself or contract with a professional firm. And the decision is best made after carefully considering the pros and cons of each approach. Too often, university faculty assume that students can get the job done while overlooking the important issues of quality control and whether doing a survey is a worthwhile investment of students' time. Similarly, criminal justice practitioners may believe that agency staff can handle a mail survey or conduct phone interviews from the office. Again, compromises in the quality of results, together with the opportunity costs of diverting staff from other tasks, must be considered. The do-it-yourself strategy may seem cheaper in the short run, but it often becomes a false economy when attention turns to data analysis and interpretation.

■ MAIN POINTS

- Survey research, a popular social research method, involves the administration of questionnaires to a sample of respondents selected from some population.

- Survey research is especially appropriate for descriptive studies of large populations, but surveys have many other uses in criminal justice research.

- Surveys are the method of choice for obtaining self-reported offending data. Continuing efforts to improve self-report surveys include using confidential computer-assisted personal interviews.

- Questions may be open-ended (respondents supply their own answers) or closed-ended (they select from a list of answers provided). Each technique for formulating questions has advantages and disadvantages.

- Short items in a questionnaire are usually better than long ones.

- Bias in questionnaire items encourages respondents to answer in a particular way or to support a particular point of view. Avoid it.

- Questionnaires may be administered in three basically different ways: Self-administered questionnaires may be completed by the respondents themselves; interviewers may administer questionnaires in face-to-face encounters, reading the items to respondents and recording the answers; or interviewers may conduct telephone surveys.

- It is generally advisable to plan follow-up mailings for self-administered questionnaires, sending new questionnaires to respondents who fail to respond to the initial appeal.

- The essential characteristic of interviewers is that they be neutral; their presence in the data-collection process must not have any effect on the responses given to questionnaire items.

- A probe is a neutral, nondirective question designed to get an interviewee to elaborate on an incomplete or ambiguous answer given in an interview in response to an open-ended question. Examples are: "Anything else?" "How is that?" "In what ways?"

- Surveys conducted over the telephone are fast and flexible. Random-digit dialing produces representative probability samples; computer-assisted telephone interviewing (CATI) techniques enhance the speed and reliability of telephone interviews.

- The advantages of a self-administered questionnaire over an interview survey are economy, lack of interviewer bias, and the possibility of respondent anonymity and privacy to encourage more candid responses on sensitive issues.

- The advantages of an interview survey over a self-administered questionnaire are fewer in-complete questionnaires and fewer misunderstood questions, generally higher return rates, and greater flexibility in terms of sampling, types of questions that may be asked, and special general observations.

- Telephone surveys have advantages over both interview surveys and self-administered questionnaires. Their chief advantage is speed. Telephone surveys are much less costly than in-person interviews, and not much more costly than self-administered questionnaires.

- Survey research has the weaknesses of being somewhat artificial and potentially superficial. It is difficult to gain a full sense of social processes in their natural settings through the use of surveys.

- Specialized interviews with a small number of people and focus groups are additional ways of collecting data by asking questions. Specialized interviews do not seek to generalize to a larger population. Focus groups engage small, homogeneous groups of people in directed discussion of open-ended questions.

- Although the particular tasks required to complete a survey are not especially difficult, researchers must carefully consider whether to conduct surveys themselves or contract with a professional organization.

■ REVIEW QUESTIONS AND EXERCISES

1. Find a questionnaire printed in a magazine or newspaper. Bring the questionnaire to class and critique it. Critique other aspects of the survey design.

2. For each of the open-ended questions listed, construct a closed-ended question that could be used in a questionnaire.

   a. What was your family's total income last year?

   b. How do you feel about shock incarceration, or "boot camp" programs?

   c. How do people in your neighborhood feel about the police?

   d. What do you feel is the biggest problem facing this community?

e. How do you protect your home from burglary?

3. A recent evaluation of a federal program to support community policing included sending questionnaires to a sample of about 1,200 police chiefs. Each questionnaire included a number of items asking about specific features of community policing and whether or not they were being used in the department. Almost all police chiefs had someone else complete the questionnaire. What's the unit of analysis in this survey? What problems might result from having an individual complete such a questionnaire?

■ *ADDITIONAL READINGS*

Babbie, Earl, *Survey Research Methods* (Belmont, CA: Wadsworth, 1990). A comprehensive overview of survey methods. This textbook covers many aspects of survey techniques that are omitted here.

Converse, Jean M., and Presser, Stanley, *Survey Questions: Handcrafting the Standardized Questionnaire* (Newbury Park, CA: Sage, 1986). This is a useful book for questionnaire design. It is readable and contains many helpful tips.

Dillman, Don A., *Mail and Telephone Surveys: The Total Design Method* (New York: Wiley, 1978).

An excellent review of the methodological literature on mail and telephone surveys. Dillman makes many good suggestions for improving response rates.

Fowler, Floyd J., Jr., *Improving Survey Questions: Design and Evaluation* (Thousand Oaks, CA: Sage, 1995). A comprehensive discussion of questionnaire construction, including a number of suggestions for pretesting questions.

General Accounting Office, *Using Structured Interviewing Techniques* (Washington, DC: General Accounting Office, 1991). This is another useful handbook in the GAO series on evaluation methods. In contrast to Patton (below), the GAO emphasizes getting comparable information from respondents through structured interviews. A very useful step-by-step guide.

Patton, Michael Quinn, *Qualitative Evaluation and Research Methods,* 2nd ed. (Thousand Oaks, CA: Sage, 1990). A thorough discussion of specialized interviewing. Patton's advice should also be useful in constructing questionnaires for surveys in general.

Stewart, D. W., and Shamdasani, P. N., *Focus Groups: Theory and Practice* (Newbury Park, CA: Sage, 1990). A practical and comprehensive introduction to focus groups. This book really lives up to its title, describing basic principles of focus groups together with numerous practical tips.

11 *Field Research*

What You'll Learn in This Chapter

You'll improve your ability to observe life in its natural habitat—going where the action is and watching. You'll learn how to prepare for the field, how to observe, how to make records of what you observe, and how to recognize the relative strengths and weaknesses of field research.

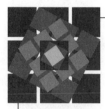

INTRODUCTION

TOPICS APPROPRIATE TO FIELD RESEARCH

THE VARIOUS ROLES OF THE OBSERVER

ASKING QUESTIONS

PREPARING FOR THE FIELD
Access to Formal Organizations
Access to Subcultures
Selecting Cases for Observation
Sampling in Field Research
Recording Observations
Field Notes
Structured Observations

LINKING FIELD OBSERVATIONS AND OTHER DATA

ILLUSTRATIONS OF FIELD RESEARCH
Shoplifting
How Many People Wear Seat Belts?
Bars and Violence

STRENGTHS AND WEAKNESSES OF FIELD RESEARCH
Validity
Reliability
Generalizability

MAIN POINTS

REVIEW QUESTIONS AND EXERCISES

ADDITIONAL READINGS

■ *INTRODUCTION*

We turn now to what may seem like the most obvious method of making observations: field research. If you want to know about something, why not just go where it's happening and watch it happen?

Field research encompasses two different methods of obtaining data, direct observation and asking questions. This chapter will concentrate primarily on observation, although we will briefly describe techniques for specialized interviewing in field studies.

Most of the observation methods discussed in this book are designed to produce data appropriate for quantitative (statistical) analysis. Surveys provide data from which to calculate the percentage of crime victims in a population, mean value of property lost in burglaries, and so forth. Field research may yield qualitative data—observations not easily reduced to numbers—in addition to quantitative data. For example, a field researcher who is studying burglars may note the number of times subjects have been arrested (quantitative) as well as whether individual burglars tend to select certain types of targets (qualitative).

Qualitative field research is often a theory- or hypothesis-generating activity as well. Yet in many types of field studies, researchers do not have precisely defined hypotheses to be tested. Field observation is often used to make sense out of an ongoing process that cannot be predicted in advance—making initial observations, developing tentative general conclusions that suggest further observations, making those observations and thereby revising your conclusions, and so forth.

For example, Homel, Tomsen, and Thommeny (1992) conducted a field study of violence in bars in Sydney, Australia, and found that certain situations tended to trigger violent incidents. A subsequent study tested a series of hypotheses about the links between certain situations and violence (Homel and Clark, 1994). Glaser and Straus (1967) refer to this process as *grounded theory.* Rather than following the hypothetico-deductive approach to theory building described in Chapter 2, grounded theory is based (or grounded) on

experience, usually through observations made in the field.

Field studies in criminal justice may also produce quantitative data that can be used to test hypotheses or evaluate some policy innovation. Typically, qualitative exploratory observations help define the nature of some crime problem and suggest possible policy responses. Following the policy response, further observations are made to assess the policy's impact. For example, we briefly described the situational crime prevention approach in Chapter 2. The first and last of the five stages in a situational crime prevention project illustrate the dual uses of observation for problem definition and hypothesis testing (Clarke, 1992b:5):

1. Collect data about the nature and dimensions of the specific crime problem.
5. Monitor results and disseminate experience.

By now, especially if you have experience as a criminal justice professional, you may be thinking that field research is not much different from what police officers and many other people do every day—make observations in the field and ask people questions. Police may also "collect data about the nature and dimensions of [a] specific crime problem," take action, and monitor results. So what's new here?

Compared to criminal justice professionals, researchers tend to be more concerned with making generalizations and then using systematic field research techniques to support those generalizations. For example, consider the different goals and approaches used by two people who might observe shoplifters: a retail store security guard and a criminal justice researcher. A security guard wishes to capture a thief and prevent the loss of shop merchandise. Toward those ends, a guard adapts surveillance techniques to the behavior of a particular suspected shoplifter. A researcher's interests are different, perhaps to estimate the frequency of shoplifting, describe characteristics of shoplifters, or evaluate some specific measure to prevent shoplifting. In all likelihood, researchers use more standardized methods of observation aimed toward a generalized understanding.

In a sense, we all do field research whenever we observe or participate in social behavior and try to understand it, whether at a corner tavern, in a doctor's waiting room, or on an airplane. Whenever we report our observations to others, we are reporting our field research efforts.

The purpose of this chapter is to discuss field research methods in some detail, providing a logical overview and suggesting some specific skills and techniques that make scientific field research more useful than the casual observation we all engage in. As we cover the various applications and techniques of field research, you may recall the distinction we made between ordinary human inquiry and social scientific research, way back in Chapter 1. Field methods illustrate how the common techniques of observation that we all use in ordinary inquiry can be deployed in systematic ways.

■ TOPICS APPROPRIATE TO FIELD RESEARCH

One of the key strengths of field research is the comprehensive perspective it gives the researcher. This aspect of field research enhances its *validity*. By going directly to the phenomenon under study and observing it as completely as possible, you can develop a deeper and fuller understanding of it. This mode of observation, then, is especially (though not exclusively) appropriate to research topics that appear to defy simple quantification. The field researcher may recognize nuances of attitude, behavior, and setting that might escape researchers using other methods.

For example, Shearing and Stenning (1992) describe how Disney World employs subtle but pervasive mechanisms of informal social control that are largely invisible to millions of theme park visitors. It is difficult to imagine any technique other than direct observation that could produce these insights:

■ Control strategies are embedded in both environmental features and structural relations. In both cases control structures and activities have other functions which are highlighted so that the control function is overshadowed. For example, virtually every pool, fountain, and flower garden serves both as an aesthetic object and to direct visitors away from, or towards, particular locations. Similarly, every Disney employee, while visibly and primarily engaged in other functions, is also engaged in the maintenance of order.

(1992:251)

Many of the different uses of field observation in criminal justice research are nicely summarized by George McCall. Comparing the three principal ways of collecting data—observing, asking questions, and consulting the written record—McCall (1978:8–9) states that observation is most appropriate for obtaining information about physical or social settings, behaviors, and events.

Observation is not the only way of getting data about settings, behaviors, and events, however. Information about the number of households on a block (setting) may be found in a city clerk's office; crime surveys routinely ask about victimization (events) and whether crimes were reported to police (behavior). In many circumstances, field observation is still the preferred method.

Field research is especially appropriate to the study of topics that can best be understood within their natural settings. Surveys may be able to measure behaviors and attitudes in somewhat artificial settings, but not all behavior is best measured this way. For example, field research is a superior method for studying how street-level drug dealers interpret behavioral and situational cues to distinguish potential customers, normal street traffic, and undercover police officers. It would be difficult to study these skills through a survey. Laud Humphreys's (1975) research on homosexual contacts in public rest rooms could have been conducted only through field observation.

Field research on actual crimes is an example of obtaining information about events. McCall (1978) points out that observational studies of vice—such as prostitution and drug use—are much more common than observational studies of other crimes, largely because these behaviors depend at least in part on being visible and attracting customers. One notable exception is research on shoplifting. A study by Baumer and Rosenbaum (1982) had two goals: (1) to estimate the incidence of shoplifting in a large department store, and (2) to assess the effectiveness of different store security measures. Each objective required some measure of shoplifting, which Baumer and Rosenbaum obtained through direct observation. Samples of persons were followed by research staff from the time they entered the store until they left. Observers, posing as fellow shoppers, watched for any theft by the person they had been assigned to follow. We will have more to say about this study later in the chapter.

Many aspects of physical settings are probably best studied through direct observation. The prevalence and patterns of gang graffiti in public places could not be reliably measured through surveys, unless the goal was to measure perceptions of graffiti. The work of Oscar Newman (1996, 1972), Ray Jeffery (1977), and Paul and Patricia Brantingham (1991a) on the relationship between crime and environmental design depends crucially on field observation of settings. If opportunities for crime vary by physical setting, then observation of the physical characteristics of a setting is required.

An evaluation of street lighting as a crime prevention tool in two areas of London illustrates how observation can be used to measure both physical settings and behavior. Kate Painter (1991) was interested in the relationships between street lighting, certain crime rates (measured by victim surveys), fear of crime, and nighttime mobility. Improvements in street lighting were made in selected streets; surveys of pedestrians and households in the affected areas were conducted before and after the lighting improvements. Survey questions included items about victimization, perceptions of crime problems and lighting quality, and reports about routine nighttime behavior in areas affected by the lighting.

Although the pretest and posttest survey items could be used to assess changes in attitudes and behavior associated with improved lighting, field observations provided better measures of behavior. Painter conducted systematic counts of pedestrians in areas both before and after street lighting was enhanced. Observations like this are better measures of such behavior than survey items because people often have difficulty recall-

ing something like how often they walk through some area after dark.

Painter's research also included provisions to observe physical settings. First, light levels (measured in lux units) were assessed in the experimental areas before and after changes in streetlighting equipment (1991:176). Second, interviewers who conducted household interviews made observations of physical settings in the areas around sampled households.

■ THE VARIOUS ROLES OF THE OBSERVER

The term *field research* is broader and more inclusive than the common term *participant observation*. Field researchers need not always participate in what they are studying, although they usually will study it directly at the scene of the action. Raymond Gold (1969:30–39) has discussed four different positions on a continuum of roles that field researchers may play in this regard: complete participant, participant-as-observer, observer-as-participant, and complete observer.

Gold (1969:33) describes the *complete participant* this way:

■ The true identity and purpose of the complete participant in field research are not known to those whom he observes. He interacts with them as naturally as possible in whatever areas of their living interest him and are acceptable to him in situations in which he can play or learn to play requisite day-to-day roles successfully.

The complete participant, in this sense, may be a genuine participant in what he or she is studying (for example, a participant in a demonstration against capital punishment) or may pretend to be a genuine participant. In any event, if you are acting as the complete participant, you let people see you only as a participant, not as a researcher.

Clearly, if you are not a genuine participant in what you are studying, you must learn to behave as though you were. If you are studying a group made up of uneducated and inarticulate people, it would not be appropriate for you to talk and act like a university professor or student.

Here we remind you of an *ethical* issue raised in Chapter 8. Is it ethical to deceive the people you are studying in the hope that they would confide in you as they would not confide in an identified researcher? Do the interests of science—the scientific values of the research—offset any ethical problems?

Related to this ethical consideration is a scientific one. No researcher deceives his or her subjects solely for the purpose of deception. Rather, it is done in the belief that the data will be more valid and reliable, that the subjects will be more natural and honest if they do not know the researcher is doing a research project. If the people being studied know they are being studied, they might modify their behavior. First, they might reject the researcher. Second, they might modify their speech and behavior to appear more respectable than would otherwise be the case. Third, the process being observed might radically change. These are among the justifications used by Humphreys (1975) in his participant observation study of homosexual contacts in public rest rooms.

On the other side of the coin, if you are a complete participant, you may affect what you are studying. To play the role of participant, you must *participate*, yet your participation may importantly affect the social process you are studying.

Additional problems may emerge in any participant observation study of active criminals. Legal and physical risks, also mentioned in Chapter 8, present obstacles to the complete participant in field research among criminals or delinquents.

Finally, complete participation in field studies of criminal justice institutions is seldom possible. Although it is common for police officers to become criminal justice researchers, practical constraints on the official duties of police present major obstacles to functioning effectively as a researcher. Similarly, the responsibilities of judges, prosecutors, probation officers, and corrections workers are not normally compatible with collecting data for research.

Because of these considerations—ethical, scientific, practical, and safety—the field researcher most often chooses a different role. In Gold's terminology, you might choose the role of *participant-as-observer*. You would participate with the group under study, but you would make it clear that you were also undertaking research. If you had been convicted of some offense and had been placed on probation, for example, you might be inspired to launch a study of probation officers.

McCall suggests that field researchers who study active offenders may comfortably occupy positions around the periphery of criminal activity. Certain types of leisure activities such as frequenting selected bars or dance clubs may be appropriate roles (McCall, 1978:30). Furthermore, McCall describes how making one's role as a researcher known to criminals and becoming known as a "right square" is more acceptable to research subjects than an unsuccessful attempt to masquerade as a colleague. There are dangers in this role also, however. The people being studied may shift much of their attention to the research project, and the process being observed may no longer be typical. Or, conversely, you yourself may come to identify too much with the interests and viewpoints of the participants. You may begin to "go native" and lose much of your scientific detachment.

The *observer-as-participant* is one who identifies himself or herself as a researcher and interacts with the participants in the course of their routine activities but makes no pretense of actually being a participant. Many observational studies of police patrol are examples of this approach. Researchers typically accompany police officers on patrol, observing routine activities and the interactions between police and citizens. Spending several hours in the company of a police officer also affords opportunities for unstructured interviewing.

Although a researcher's role in the eyes of police is exclusively observational, people with whom police come into contact may assume an observer is actually a plainclothes police officer. As a consequence, observation of citizens in their encounters with police tends to be less contaminated by the presence of a researcher than observation of police themselves.

McCall (1978:88) notes that "going native" is a common tendency among field workers, especially in observational studies of police. For example, observers may become more sympathetic toward officers' behavior and toward the views police express about the people they encounter. It is also possible that observers may actively assist officers on patrol. In either case, going native is often the product of the researcher's efforts to be accepted by police and the natural tendency of police to justify their actions to observers.

The *complete observer*, at the other extreme, observes some location or process without becoming a part of it in any way. The subjects of study might not even realize they are being studied because of the researcher's unobtrusiveness. A person making observations while sitting in a courtroom is an example. Although the complete observer is less likely to affect what is being studied and less likely to go native than the complete participant, he or she may be less able to develop a full appreciation of what is being studied. A courtroom observer, for example, witnesses only the public acts that take place in a courtroom, not private conferences between judges and attorneys.

McCall (1978:45) points out an interesting and often unnoticed trade-off between the role the observer adopts and the observer's ability to learn from what she or he sees. If your role as an observer is covert (complete participation) or detached (complete observation), you are less able to ask questions to clarify what you observe. As a complete participant, you take pains to conceal your observations and must exercise care in querying subjects. Similarly, complete observation means that it is generally not possible to interact with the persons or things being observed.

Think carefully about the trade-off. If it is most important that subjects not be affected by your role as observer, then complete participation or observation is preferred. If being able to ask questions about what you observe is important, then some role that combines participation and observation is better.

More generally, the appropriate role for you as an observer hinges on what you want to learn and the opportunities and constraints that affect your field inquiry. Different situations require different roles for the researcher. Unfortunately, there are no clear guidelines for making this choice, and you must rely on your understanding

of the situation and your own good judgment. In making your decision, however, you must be guided by both methodological and ethical considerations. Because these often conflict, your decision may be difficult, and sometimes you may find that your role limits your study.

■ ASKING QUESTIONS

Field research often involves going where the action is and simply watching and listening. You can learn a lot merely by being attentive to what's going on. Field research can also involve more active inquiry. Sometimes it's appropriate to ask people questions and record their answers. Wright and Bennett (1990) describe observing and interviewing as two complementary ways to study offenders.

We discussed interviewing in Chapter 10 on survey research. The interviewing you will do in connection with field observation falls into the category of specialized interviewing.

Field research interviews are usually much less structured than survey interviews. At one extreme, an unstructured interview is essentially a conversation in which the interviewer establishes a general direction for the conversation and pursues specific topics raised by the respondent. Ideally, the respondent does most of the talking. Michael Patton (1990) refers to this type as an *informal conversational interview*, which is especially well suited to in-depth probing.

Unstructured interviews are most appropriate when researchers have little knowledge about a topic, and in situations where it's reasonable for researchers to have a casual conversation with a subject. This is a good strategy for interviewing active criminals. Unstructured interviews are also appropriate when researchers and subjects are together for an extended time, such as a researcher accompanying police on patrol.

In other field research situations, your interviews will be somewhat more structured. The conversational approach may be difficult to use with officials in criminal justice or other agencies, who will respond best (at least initially) to a specific set of open-ended questions. This is because it is usually necessary to arrange appointments to conduct field research interviews with judges, prosecutors, bail commissioners, and other officials. Having arranged an appointment, it would be awkward to begin a casual conversation with a judge in hopes of eliciting the desired information.

On the other hand, one of the special strengths of field research is its flexibility in the field. Even during structured interviews with public officials, the answers evoked by your initial questions should shape your subsequent ones. It doesn't work merely to ask preestablished questions and record the answers. You need to ask a question, hear the answer, interpret its meaning for your general inquiry, and then frame another question either to dig into the earlier answer in more depth or to redirect the person's attention to an area more relevant to your inquiry. In short, you need to be able to listen, think, and talk almost at the same time.

The discussion of probes in Chapter 10 is a useful guide to getting answers in more depth without biasing later answers. Learn the skills of being a good listener; be more interested than interesting. Learn to say things like "How is that?" "In what ways?" "How do you mean that?" "What would be an example of that?" Learn to look and listen expectantly, and let the person you are interviewing break the silence.

At its best, a field research interview is much like normal conversation. Because of this, it is essential that you keep reminding yourself that you are not having a normal conversation. In normal conversations, each of us wants to come across as an interesting, worthwhile person. Often we don't really hear each other because we're too busy thinking of what we'll say next. As an interviewer, the desire to appear interesting is counterproductive to your job. You need to make the other person seem interesting by being interested yourself. By the way, if you do this, people will actually regard you as a great conversationalist.

Like other aspects of field research, interviewing improves with practice. Fortunately, it is something you can practice any time you want. Practice on your friends.

■ PREPARING FOR THE FIELD

Suppose that you have decided to undertake field research on a community corrections agency in a large city. Let's assume that you do not know a great deal about the agency and that you will identify yourself as a researcher to staff and other people you encounter. Your research interests are primarily descriptive. You want to observe the routine operation of the agency in the office and elsewhere. In addition, you would like to interview agency staff and persons who are serving community corrections sentences. This section will discuss some of the ways you might prepare before you conduct your interviews and direct observations.

As usual, you are well advised to begin with a search of the relevant literature, filling in your knowledge of the subject and learning what others have said about it. Because library research is discussed at length in Appendix A, we won't say anything more here.

Access to Formal Organizations

Any research on a criminal justice institution, or on persons who work either in or under the supervision of an institution, normally requires a formal request and approval. One of your first steps in preparing for the field, then, is to arrange access to the community corrections agency.

Obtaining initial approval can be confusing and frustrating. Many criminal justice agencies in large cities have a complex organization, combining a formal hierarchy with a bewildering variety of informal organizational cultures. For example, criminal courts are highly structured organizations, where a presiding judge may oversee court assignments and case scheduling for judges and many support personnel. On the other hand, courts are chaotic organizations in which three constellations of professionals—prosecutors, defense attorneys, and judges—episodically interact to process large numbers of cases.

To further complicate field research in criminal justice agencies, the obvious strategy of gaining approval from a single executive—such as a corrections commissioner or police chief—does not guarantee that operations staff at lower levels will cooperate. McCall points out that researchers may have to negotiate access at multiple levels.

In any event, your best strategy in gaining access to the community corrections agency, or to just about any other formal criminal justice organization, is to use a four-step procedure: sponsor, letter, phone call, and meeting. Our discussion of these steps assumes that you will begin your field research by interviewing the agency executive director and gaining that person's approval for subsequent interviews and observations.

Sponsor Your first step is to find a sponsor, a person who is personally known to and respected by the executive director. Ideally, a sponsor will be able to advise you on whom to contact, that person's formal position in the organization, and that person's informal status, including her or his relationships with other key officials. Such advice can be important in helping you initiate contact with the right person, while avoiding people who have bad reputations.

For example, you may initially think that a particular judge who is often mentioned in newspaper stories about community corrections would be a useful source of information. However, your sponsor may advise you that the judge is not held in high regard by prosecutors and community corrections staff. Your association with this judge would generate suspicion on the part of other officials whom you might eventually want to contact and may frustrate your attempts to get information.

Finding the right sponsor is often the most important step in gaining access. It may, in fact, require a couple of extra steps, since you might first need to ask a professor whether she or he knows someone. Then contact that person (with the sponsorship of your professor) and ask for further assistance.

For purposes of illustration, we will assume that your professor is knowledgeable, well connected, and happy to act as your sponsor. Your professor confirms your view that it is best to begin with the executive director of community corrections.

Letter Next, write a letter to the executive direc-

tor. Your letter should have three parts: introduction, brief statement of your research purpose, and action request. See Figure 11-1 for an example. The introduction begins by naming your sponsor, thus establishing your mutual acquaintance in the first sentence. This is a key part of the process; if you do not name a sponsor, or if you name the wrong sponsor, you might get no further.

Describe your research purpose succinctly. This is not the place to give a detailed description as you would do in a proposal. If possible, keep it to one or two paragraphs, as in Figure 11-1. If a longer description is necessary to explain what you will be doing, you should *still* include only a brief description in your introductory letter, and refer the reader to a separate attachment in which you summarize your research.

The action request describes what immediate role you are asking the contact person to play in your research. You may simply be requesting an interview, or you may want the person to help you gain access to other officials. Notice how the sample in Figure 11-1 mentions both an interview and "suggestions on further sources of information about community corrections." In any case, you will usually want to arrange to meet or at least talk with the contact person. That leads to the third step.

Phone Call You probably already know that it can be difficult to arrange meetings with public officials (and often professors) or even to reach people by telephone. You can simplify this task by concluding your letter with a proposal for this step: arranging a phone call. The example in Figure 11-1 specifies a date and approximate time when you will call. To be safe, specify a date about one week from the date of your letter. Notice also the request that the executive director call you if some other time would be convenient.

When you make the call, the executive director will have some idea who you are and what you want. She will also have the opportunity to contact your sponsor if she wants to verify any information in your introductory letter.

The actual phone call should go smoothly. Even if you are not able to talk with the executive director personally, you will probably be able

FIGURE 11-1
Sample Letter for Sponsor—Letter—Phone Call—Meeting

Jane Adams
Executive Director
Chaos County Community Corrections
Anxiety Falls, Colorado   1 May 1997

Dear Ms. Adams:

My colleague, Professor Steve Allen, suggested I contact you for assistance in my research on community corrections. I will be conducting a study of community corrections programs and wish to include the Chaos County agency in my research.

Briefly, I am interested in learning more about the different types of sentences that judges impose in jurisdictions with community corrections agencies. As you know, Colorado's community corrections statute grants considerable discretion to individual counties in arranging locally administered corrections programs. Because of this, it is generally believed that a wide variety of corrections programs and sentences have developed throughout the state. My research seeks to learn more about these programs as a first step toward developing recommendations that may guide the development of programs in other states. I also wish to learn more about the routine administration of a community corrections program such as yours.

I would like to meet with you to discuss what programs Chaos County has developed, including current programs and those that were considered but not implemented. In addition, any information about different types of community corrections sentences that Chaos County judges impose would be very useful. Finally, I would appreciate your suggestions on further sources of information about community corrections programs in Chaos County and other areas.

I will call your office at about 10:00 a.m. on Monday, May 8, to arrange a meeting. If that time will not be convenient, or if you have any questions about my research, please contact me at the number below.

Thanks in advance for your help.

Sincerely,

Alfred Nobel
Research Assistant
Institute for Advanced Studies
(518) 555-1212

to talk to an assistant and make an appointment for a meeting (the next step). Again, this will be possible because your letter described what you eventually want—a meeting with the executive director—and established your legitimacy by naming a sponsor.

Meeting The final step is meeting with or interviewing the contact person. Since you have used the letter—phone call—meeting procedure, the contact person may have already taken prelimi-

nary steps to help you. For example, because the letter in Figure 11-1 indicates that you wish to interview the executive director about different types of community corrections sentences, she may have assembled some procedures manuals or reports in preparation for your meeting.

This procedure generally works well in gaining initial access to public officials or other people who work in formal organizations. Approval to interview persons who are under correctional supervision can usually be arranged in much the same way.

Once initial access is gained, it is up to the researcher to use interviewing skills and other techniques to elicit the desired information. This is not as difficult as it might seem to novice (or apprentice) researchers for a couple of reasons. First, most people are at least a bit flattered that their work, ideas, and knowledge are of interest to a researcher. And researchers can take advantage of this with the right words of encouragement. Second, criminal justice professionals are often happy to talk about their work with a knowledgeable outsider. Police, probation officers, and corrections workers usually encounter only their colleagues and their clients on the job. Interactions with colleagues become routinized and suffused with office politics. Interactions with clients are common sources of stress for criminal justice professionals. Talking with an interested and knowledgeable researcher is often seen as a pleasant diversion.

By the same token, Wright and Decker (1994) report that most members of their sample of active burglars were both happy and flattered to discuss the craft of burglary. Because they were engaged in illegal activities, burglars had to be more circumspect about sharing their experiences, unlike the way many people talk about events at work. As a result, burglars enjoyed the chance to describe their work to interested researchers who both promised confidentiality and treated offenders ". . . as having expert knowledge normally unavailable to outsiders" (1994:26).

Access to Subcultures

Research by Wright and Decker illustrates how gaining access to subcultures in criminal justice—active criminals, deviants, juvenile gangs, inmates—requires tactics that are different in some respects from those used to meet with public officials. Letters, phone calls, and formal meetings are usually less appropriate for initiating field research among active criminals. However, the basic principle of using a sponsor to gain initial access operates in much the same way, although the word *informant* is normally used to re-

fer to someone who helps make contact with subcultures.

Informants may be people whose job involves working with criminals; police, juvenile caseworkers, probation officers, attorneys, and counselors at drug clinics are examples. Lawyers who specialize in criminal defense work can be especially useful sources of information about potential subjects.

McCall (1978:31) states that obtaining initial access to criminals is not usually difficult. Chains of referrals may be necessary:

■ If a researcher wants to make contact with, say, a bootlegger, he thinks of a person he knows who is closest to the social structure of bootlegging. Perhaps that person will be a police officer, a judge, a liquor store owner, a crime reporter, or a recently arrived Southern migrant. If he doesn't personally know a judge or a crime reporter, he surely knows someone (his own lawyer . . .) who does and who would be willing to introduce him. By means of a very short chain of such referrals, the researcher can obtain an introduction to virtually any type of criminal.

For example, in their study of New York heroin users, Johnson and others (1985:16, 195–197) initially recruited former addicts they contacted through methadone treatment centers. These persons, employed as research field workers, used their network of social contacts in two Harlem neighborhoods to identify active heroin users who would serve as research subjects. And the first group of research subjects identified additional heroin users and criminals, who themselves became subjects.

Wright and Decker (1994) were fortunate to encounter a former offender who was well connected with active criminals. Playing the role of sponsor, the ex-offender helped researchers in two related ways. First, he referred them to other people, who in turn found active burglars willing to participate in the study. Second, the ex-offender was well known and respected among burglars, and his sponsorship of researchers made it possible for them to study a group of naturally suspicious subjects.

A different approach for gaining access to sub-cultures is to hang around places where criminals hang around. Wright and Decker rejected that strategy as a time-consuming and uncertain way to find burglars, in part because they were not sure where burglars hung around. In contrast, Bruce Jacobs (1996) initiated contact with street-level drug dealers by hanging around and being noticed in locations known for crack availability. Consider how this tactic might make sense for finding drug dealers, whose illegal work requires customers. In contrast, the offense of burglary is more secretive, and it's more difficult to imagine how one would find an area known for the presence of burglars.

Whatever techniques are used to identify sub-jects among subcultures, your sample will not be a probability sample and cannot therefore be assumed to represent some larger population within specified confidence intervals. You should also think about potential selection biases in whatever procedures are used to recruit subjects. Notice that although we can't make probability statements about samples of active offenders, such samples may be representative of a subculture target population.

Selecting Cases for Observation

This brings up the more general question of how to select cases for observation in field research. The techniques used by Wright and Decker, as well as by many other researchers who have studied active criminals, combine the use of informants and what is called **snowball sampling.** As we mentioned in Chapter 9, snowball sampling means that initial research subjects (or informants) identify other persons who might also become subjects, who in turn suggest more potential subjects, and so on. In such a way, a group of subjects is accumulated through a series of referrals.

Wright and Decker's (1994) study provides a good example. The ex-offender contacted a few active burglars and a few "street-wise non-criminals" who in turn referred researchers to additional subjects, and so on. This process is illustrated in Figure 11-2, which shows the chain of referrals that accumulated a snowball sample of 105 individuals.

If you start at the top of Figure 11-2, the ex-offender put researchers in contact with two subjects directly (001 and 003), a small-time criminal, three street-wise non-criminals, a youth worker, a crack addict, and someone serving probation. Continuing downward, the small-time criminal was especially helpful, identifying 12 subjects who participated in the study (005, 006, 008, 009, 010, 021, 022, 023, 025, 026, 030, 032). Notice how the snowball effect continues, with subject 026 identifying subjects 028 and 029. Notice also that some subjects were themselves "nominated" by more than one source. In the middle of the bottom row in Figure 11-2, for example, subject 064 was mentioned by subjects 060 and 061.

There are, of course, other ways of selecting subjects for observation. Chapter 9 discussed the logic and the more conventional techniques involved in probability sampling. Although the general principles of representativeness should be remembered in field research, controlled sampling techniques are often not possible.

Consider the potential selection biases involved in a field study of deviants. Let's say you want to study a small number of drug dealers. You have a friend who works in the probation department of a large city who is willing to introduce you to people convicted of drug dealing and sentenced to probation. What selection problems might result from studying subjects identified in this way? How might your subjects not be representative of the general population of drug dealers? If you work your way backward from the chain of events that begins with a crime and ends with a criminal sentence, the answers should become clear.

First, drug dealers sentenced to probation may be first-time offenders or persons convicted of dealing small amounts of "softer" drugs. Repeat offenders and "kingpin" cocaine dealers would not be in this group. Second, it is possible that people initially charged with drug dealing were convicted of simple possession through a plea bargain; because of your focus on people convicted of dealing, your selection procedure would miss this group as well. Finally, by selecting dealers who had been arrested and convicted, you

FIGURE 11-2
"Snowball" Referral Chart

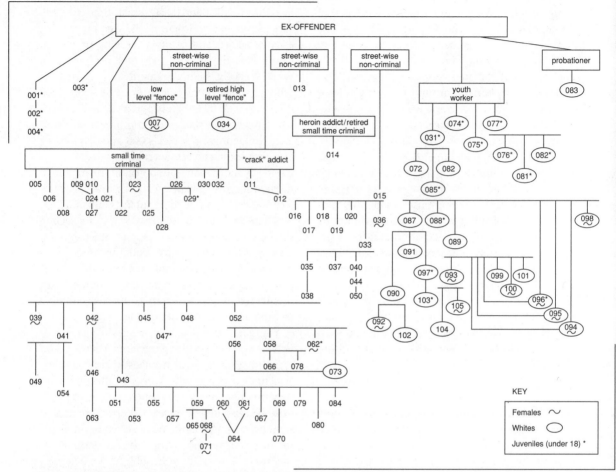

Source: Reprinted from Richard T. Wright and Scott H. Decker, *Burglars on the Job: Streetlife and Residential Break-ins* (Boston: Northeastern University Press, 1994), p. 19. Reprinted by permission of Sage Publications, Inc.

may be getting access to only those less skilled dealers who got caught. More skilled or experienced dealers may be less likely to get arrested in the first place; they could be different in important ways from the dealers you are studying.

To see why this raises an important issue in selecting cases for field research, let's return again to the sample of burglars studied by Wright and Decker. Notice that their snowball sample began with an ex-offender and sought out active burglars. An alternative approach would be to select a probability or other sample of convicted burglars, perhaps in prison or on probation. But Wright and Decker rejected this strategy for sam-

pling because of the possibility that they would overlook burglars who had not been caught. After accumulating their sample, the researchers were in a position to test this assumption by examining arrest records for their subjects. Only about one-fourth of the active burglars had ever been convicted of burglary; an additional one-third had been arrested for burglary but not convicted. More than 40 percent had no burglary arrests, and 8 percent had never been arrested for any offense (1994:12). Wright and Decker conclude that about three-fourths of their subjects would not have been eligible for inclusion if the researchers had based their sample on persons convicted of burglary. Thus, little overlap exists between the population of active burglars and the population of convicted burglars.

Sampling in Field Research

Sampling in field research tends to be more complicated than in other kinds of research. In many types of field studies, researchers attempt to observe everything within their field of study; thus, in a sense, they do not sample at all. In reality, of course, it is impossible to observe everything. To the extent that field researchers observe only a portion of what happens, then, what they do observe is a de facto sample of all the possible observations that might have been made. You can seldom select a controlled sample of such observations, but you should bear in mind the general principles of representativeness and interpret your observations accordingly.

The ability to systematically sample cases for observation depends on the degree of structure and predictability of the phenomenon being observed. This is more of a general guideline than a hard-and-fast rule. For example, the actions of youth gangs, burglars, and auto thieves are less structured and predictable than those of police officers. It is possible to select a probability sample of police officers for observation because the population of police officers in a given city is known. But since the population of active criminals is unknown, it is not possible to select a probability sample for observation.

This example should call to mind our discussion of sampling frames in Chapter 9. A roster of police officers and their assignments to patrol sectors and shifts could serve as a sampling frame for selecting subjects to observe. No such roster of gang members, burglars, and auto thieves is available. Criminal history records could serve as a sampling frame for selecting persons with previous arrests or convictions, subject to the problems of selectivity we have mentioned.

Now consider the case where a sampling frame is less important than the regularity of the process. The regular, predictable passage of people on city sidewalks makes it possible to systematically select a sample of cases for observation. There is no sampling frame of pedestrians, but

TABLE 11-1
Sampling Dimensions in Field Research

Sampling Dimension	Variation in
Population	Behavior and characteristics
Space	Behavior Physical characteristics of locations
Time, micro	Behavior by time of day, day of week Lighting by time of day Business, store, entertainment activities by time of day, day of week
Time, macro	Behavior by season, holiday Entertainment by season, holiday
Weather	Behavior by weather

studies such as Painter's research on the effects of street lighting can depend on the reliable flow of passersby who may be observed.

In an observational study such as Painter's, you might also make observations at a number of different locations on different streets. You could pick the sample of locations through standard probability methods or, more likely, you could use a rough quota system, observing wide streets and narrow ones, busy streets and quiet ones, or samples from different times of day. A study of pedestrian traffic might also observe people in different types of urban neighborhoods, comparing residential and commercial areas, for example.

Table 11-1 summarizes different sampling dimensions that might be considered in planning field research. The behavior of people, together with the characteristics of people and places, can vary by population group, location, time, and weather. We have had something to say about the first two already in this chapter, and now we will briefly discuss how sampling plans might consider time and weather dimensions.

People tend to engage in more out-of-door activity in fair weather than in wet or snowy conditions. In northern cities, people are outside more when the weather is warm. Any study of outdoor activity should therefore consider the potential effects of variation in the weather. For example, in Painter's study of pedestrian traffic before and after improvements in street lighting, it would be important to consider weather conditions during the times observations were made.

Behavior also varies by time, presented as micro and macro dimensions in Table 11-1. City streets in a central business district are busiest during working hours, while more people are in residential areas at other times. And, of course, people do different things on weekends than during the work week. Seasonal variation, the macro time dimension, may also be important in criminal justice research. Daylight is longer in summer months, which affects the amount of time people spend outdoors. Shopping peaks from Thanksgiving to Christmas, increasing the number of shoppers, who along with their automobiles may become targets for thieves. A study of assault in Dallas by Harries, Stadler, and Zdorkowski (1984) finds variation in assault rates by time of year and day of week; they tend to peak in summer months and on weekends. Felson and associates (1996) describe variations in the rhythms of activity at New York's Port Authority bus terminal. Time of day, day of week, season, and weather affect the facility's use by bus passengers, transients, and a wide variety of offenders.

In practice, controlled probability sampling is seldom used in field research. Different types of purposive samples are much more common. Michael Quinn Patton describes a broad range of approaches to purposive sampling, and offers a useful comparison of probability and purposive samples (1990:169):

■ The logic and power of probability sampling depends on selecting a truly random and statistically representative sample that will permit confident generalization. . . . The logic and power of purposeful sampling lies in selecting *information-rich cases* for study in depth. [emphasis in original]

Nonetheless, understanding the principles and logic of more formal sampling methods is likely to produce more effective purposeful sampling in field research.

In field research, bear in mind two stages of sampling. First, to what extent are the total situations available for observation representative of the more general class of phenomena you wish to describe and explain? Are the three juvenile gangs you are observing representative of all gangs? Second, are your actual observations within those total situations representative of all the possible observations? Have you observed a representative sample of the members of the three gangs? Have you observed a representative sample of the interactions that have taken place? Even when controlled probability sampling methods are impossible or inappropriate, the logical link between representativeness and generalizability still holds.

Recording Observations

Just as there is great variety in the types of field studies you might conduct, many options are available for making records of field observations. In conducting field interviews, for example, you will probably write notes of some kind, but you might also tape record your interviews. Videotaping may be useful in field interviews to capture visual images of dress and body language. Photographs or videotapes can be used to make records of visual images such as a block of apartment buildings before and after some physical design change, or as a pretest for an experimental neighborhood cleanup campaign.

Think of a continuum of methods for recording observations. At one extreme is traditional field observation and notetaking with pen and paper, such as you might use in field interviews. The opposite extreme includes various types of automated and remote measurement, such as videotaping, devices that count automobile traffic, or computer tabulations of mass transit users. In between is a host of methods that have many potential applications in criminal justice research.

Of course, the methods selected for recording observations are directly related to questions of measurement, especially how key concepts are operationalized. Thinking back to our discussion of measurement in Chapter 5, you should recognize why this is so. If you are interested in policies to increase nighttime pedestrian traffic in some city, you might want to know why people do or do not go out at night in addition to how many people stroll around different neighborhoods. Interviews—perhaps in connection with a survey—can determine people's reasons for going out or not, while video recordings of passersby can provide simple counts. By the same token, a traffic-counting device can produce information about the number of automobiles that pass a particular point on the road, but it cannot measure the blood alcohol content of drivers or whether riders are wearing seat belts.

Automated devices to record observations have many potential uses. We have mentioned research on electronic monitoring (ELMO) technology that records the physical location of individuals. In addition to the ELMO telephone technology—studied by Baumer, Maxfield, and Mendelsohn (1993)—other useful technological aids include devices for videotaping offenders in their home, devices that allow voice pattern recognition, and radio homing devices similar to those attached to animals whose movements are of interest to biologists.

Video cameras may be used in public places to record relatively simple phenomena, such as the passage of people or automobiles, or more complex social processes. For several years, London police have monitored traffic conditions at dozens of key intersections through video cameras permanently mounted on building rooftops in the city. Ronald Clarke (1996) studied speeding in Illinois, drawing on observations automatically recorded by cameras placed at several locations throughout the state.

In an effort to develop ways to control aggressive panhandlers in New York, George Kelling made videotapes of "squeegee people," who wipe the windshields of motorists stopped at intersections and then demand payment for their services. Kelling taped naturally occurring interactions between squeegee people and motorists, and he also staged contacts that involved plainclothes police in unmarked cars. The video recordings made it possible to study the specific tactics used by squeegee people to intimidate motorists, and the motorists' reaction to unwanted windshield service (Kelling and Cole, 1996:141–143).

Still photographs may be appropriate to record some types of observations, such as the presence of graffiti or litter. Photos have the added benefit of preserving visual images that can later be viewed and coded by more than one person, thus

facilitating interrater reliability checks, as described in Chapter 5. For example, if you were interested in studying pedestrian traffic on city streets, you might want to gather data about the types of people you saw in addition to how many there were. As the number and complexity of your observations increase, it becomes more difficult to reliably record how many males and females are seen, how many adults and juveniles, and so on. Taking photographs of sampled areas would enable you to be more confident in your measurements and would also make it possible for another person to check on your interpretation of the photographs.

In addition to their use in interviews, audiotape recorders are useful for dictating observations. For example, a researcher interested in patterns of activity on urban streets could dictate observations while riding through selected areas in an automobile. It is possible to dictate observations in an unstructured manner, describing each street scene as it unfolds. Or a tape recorder can be used more like an audio checklist, where observers dictate specified items seen in preselected areas.

Field Notes

In many field studies, observations are recorded as written notes, perhaps in a *field journal.* Even tape recorders and cameras cannot capture all the relevant aspects of social processes. Field notes should include both your empirical observations and your interpretations of them. You should record what you "know" you have observed and what you "think" you have observed. It is important, however, that these different kinds of notes be identified for what they are. For example, you might note that person X approached and handed something to person Y, a known drug dealer, that you think this was a drug transaction, and that you think person X was a new customer.

You can anticipate some of the most important observations before you begin the study; others will become apparent as your observations progress. Your notetaking can be made easier if you prepare standardized recording forms in advance. In a study of nighttime pedestrian traffic, for example, you might anticipate the characteristics of pedestrians that are the most likely to be useful for analysis—age, gender, ethnicity, and so forth—and prepare a form on which the actual observations can be recorded easily. Or you might develop a symbolic shorthand in advance to speed up recording. For studying participation at a meeting of a community crime prevention group, you might want to construct a numbered grid of the different sections of the meeting room; then you can record the locations of participants easily, quickly, and accurately.

None of this advance preparation should limit your recording of unanticipated events and aspects of the situation. Quite the contrary, the speedy handling of anticipated observations gives you more freedom to observe the unanticipated.

Every student is familiar with the process of taking notes. Good notetaking in field research requires more careful and deliberate attention and involves some specific skills. Three guidelines follow.

First, don't trust your memory any more than you have to; it's untrustworthy. Even if you pride yourself on having a photographic memory, it's a good idea to take notes, either during the observation or as soon afterward as possible. If you are taking notes during the observation, do it unobtrusively because people are likely to behave differently if they see you writing down everything they say or do.

Second, it's usually a good idea to take notes in stages. In the first stage, you may need to take sketchy notes (words and phrases) to keep abreast of what's happening. Then get off by yourself and rewrite your notes in more detail. If you do this soon after the events you've observed, the sketchy notes will help you recall most of the details. The longer you delay, the less likely it is that you'll recall things accurately and fully.

Third, you will inevitably wonder how much you should record. Is it really worth the effort to write out all the details you can recall right after the observation session? The general guideline here is yes. In field research, you can't be really sure of what's important and what's unimportant until you've had a chance to review and analyze a great volume of information, so you should record even things that don't seem important at the outset. They may turn out to be significant after all. In addition, the act of recording the details of something "unimportant" may jog your memory on something that is important.

Structured Observations

Field notes may be recorded on highly structured forms, where observers mark items in much the same way a survey interviewer marks a closed-ended questionnaire. For example, McCall (1978) presents a detailed coding form used in observational studies of police patrol. Steve Mastrofski and Roger Parks (1990) describe how police performance can be recorded on field observation questionnaires. Taylor, Shumaker, and Gottfredson (1985:265) developed forms to code a range of physical characteristics in a sample of Baltimore neighborhoods. Observers recorded information on closed-ended items about housing layout, street length and width, traffic volume, type of nonresidential land use, graffiti, persons hanging out, and so forth.

Since structured field observation forms often resemble survey questionnaires, the use of such forms has the benefit of producing numeric measures of conditions observed in the field. The Bureau of Justice Assistance (1993) has produced a handbook for conducting structured field observations, called **environmental surveys.** The name is significant because observers record information about the conditions of a specified environment:

■ [Environmental] surveys seek to assess, as systematically and objectively as possible, the overall physical environment of an area. That physical environment comprises the buildings, parks, streets, transportation facilities, and overall landscaping of an area as well as the functions and conditions of those entities.

(BUREAU OF JUSTICE ASSISTANCE, 1993:43)

Environmental surveys have come to be an important component of problem-oriented policing and situational crime prevention. For example, Figure 11-3 is adapted from an environmental survey form used by the Philadelphia Police Department in drug enforcement initiatives. Environmental surveys are conducted to

FIGURE 11-3

Example of Environmental Survey

Date:_____ Day of Week:_____ Time:_____

Observer:_____

Street name:_____

Cross streets:_____

1. Street width:

   Number of drivable lanes   _____

   Number of parking lanes   _____

   Median present? (yes = 1, no = 2)   _____

2. Volume of traffic flow: (check one)

   a. very light   _____

   b. light   _____

   c. moderate   _____

   d. heavy   _____

   e. very heavy   _____

3. Number of street lights   _____

4. Number of broken street lights _____

5. Number of abandoned automobiles _____

6. List all the people on the block and their activities:

Males	Hanging out	Playing	Working	Walking	Other
Young (up to age 12)	_____	_____	_____	_____	_____
Teens (13–19)	_____	_____	_____	_____	_____
Adult (20–60)	_____	_____	_____	_____	_____
Seniors (61+)	_____	_____	_____	_____	_____
Females					
Young (up to age 12)	_____	_____	_____	_____	_____
Teens (13–19)	_____	_____	_____	_____	_____
Adult (20–60)	_____	_____	_____	_____	_____
Seniors (61+)	_____	_____	_____	_____	_____

Source: Adapted from Bureau of Justice Assistance (1993: Appendix B).

plan police strategy in drug enforcement in small areas and to assess change in conditions following targeted enforcement. Notice that Figure 11-3 is used to record information about physical conditions (street width, traffic volume, street lights) as well as counts of people and their activities.

Like interview surveys, environmental surveys require that observers be carefully trained in what to observe and how to interpret it. For example, the instructions that accompany the environmental survey in Figure 11-3 include guidance on coding abandoned automobiles:

■ Count as abandoned if it appears nondrivable (i.e., has shattered windows, dismantled body parts, missing tires, missing license plates). Consider it abandoned if it appears that it has not been driven for some time and that it is not going to be for some time to come.

Other instructions provide details on how to count drivable lanes, what sorts of activities constitute "playing" and "working," how to estimate the age of people observed, and so on.

■ LINKING FIELD OBSERVATIONS AND OTHER DATA

Although criminal justice research may utilize field methods (or sample surveys) exclusively, a project will often collect data from several sources. This is consistent with our general advice to use appropriate measures and data-collection methods. Simply saying "I am going to conduct an observational study of youth gangs" restricts your focus at the outset to the kinds of information that can be gathered through observation. Although such a study may be useful and interesting, a researcher is better advised to consider what data-collection methods are necessary in any particular study.

For example, in their Baltimore study, Taylor and associates (1985) were interested in the effects of neighborhood physical characteristics on residents' perceptions of crime problems. Collecting data on physical characteristics required field observation, but sample surveys were necessary for gathering data on perceptions. So Taylor and colleagues conducted a survey of households in the neighborhoods where observations were made. Finally, they compared census data and crime reports from Baltimore police records with information from observations and household surveys.

These three sources of data provided different types of measures that, in combination, yielded a great deal of information about neighborhoods and neighborhood residents in the study sites. Surveys measured respondents' perceptions and beliefs about crime and other problems. Police records represented crimes reported to police by area residents. Field observations yielded data on physical characteristics and conditions of neighborhoods as rated by outside observers. And census data made it possible to control for the effects of socioeconomic status variables such as income, employment status, and housing tenure.

Research by Skogan and Maxfield (1981) on fear of crime similarly drew on data from surveys,

field observation, and police records. Their principal source of data was telephone surveys conducted in each of three cities, and in several neighborhoods within each city. Prior to conducting surveys, field observers were placed in each study neighborhood in each city, where they conducted informal and structured interviews with community leaders, public officials, and area residents. Observers produced more than 10,000 pages of field notes, together with a large number of tape-recorded interviews.

Skogan and Maxfield used information from field observations in two general ways. First, the field notes were helpful in developing telephone survey questionnaire items. Chapter 10 mentioned how focus groups can be useful in questionnaire development; extensive field research can provide similar benefits. Second, the field notes helped interpret survey results and "bring life to our quantitative data" (1981:18). For example, a large proportion of survey respondents from all neighborhoods indicated that they had special bars or locks on windows. Field notes from San Francisco's Mission neighborhood illustrated that such protective devices were especially evident in that area:

Person 2: Yeah, look at the bars on the windows. You never used to see that. Now they are everywhere.

Person 1: Yeah, bars on the windows. That tells you something about what is going on. It's just not safe anymore.

(SKOGAN AND MAXFIELD, 1981:209)

Field research could also be conducted after a survey. For example, a survey intended to measure fear of crime and related concepts might ask respondents to specify any area near their residence that they felt was particularly dangerous. Follow-up field visits to the named areas could then be conducted, where observers record information about physical characteristics, land use, numbers of people present, and so forth.

The box on p. 280 entitled "Conducting a Safety Audit" describes how structured field observations are combined with a focused group discussion to assess the scope for environmental design changes in Toronto, Canada.

The flexibility of field methods is one reason observation and field interviews can readily be incorporated into many research projects. And field observation often provides a much richer understanding of a phenomenon that is imperfectly revealed through a survey questionnaire. In Chapter 9, we mentioned how Baumer and Mendelsohn (1990) supplemented interviews with persons sentenced to electronic monitoring by actually wearing the devices themselves for several days. Their participant observation enabled them to experience the punitive features of home detention that would have been difficult to appreciate in any other way.

■ ILLUSTRATIONS OF FIELD RESEARCH

Before concluding this chapter on field research, let's examine some illustrations of the method in action. These descriptions will give you a clearer sense of how you might use field observations and interviews in your own criminal justice research.

Shoplifting

We have briefly mentioned the research on shoplifting by Baumer and Rosenbaum (1982). A fuller discussion of this unusual study illustrates much of the potential of field research, some problems that may be encountered, and the clever approaches to these problems adopted by Baumer and Rosenbaum.

This study was undertaken with two objectives: to estimate the prevalence of shoplifting and to assess the effectiveness of store security in identifying shoplifters. As we noted earlier, it is difficult to obtain reliable counts of offenses such as shoplifting and so-called victimless crimes. Shoplifting is usually counted only when an offense is seen by police or store security personnel. You might think that store inventory records could be used to estimate losses by customer theft, but Baumer and Rosenbaum describe why this is not possible because of employee theft and other sources of inventory loss. The approach they adopted was direct observation.

McCall (1978:20) describes three difficulties in observational studies of crime. First, most of-

fenses are relatively rare and unpredictable; an observer might spend weeks or months in the field without witnessing a single burglary, for example. Second, unless they are carefully concealed, the presence of field observers is likely to deter criminals anxious to keep their actions from public view. Finally, there is some danger to field workers who attentively observe crimes in progress while taking careful field notes.

Baumer and Rosenbaum recognized that shoplifting is largely immune from these problems. First, since shoplifting by definition takes place in only certain locations, observers can focus their attention on shops. Baumer and Rosenbaum selected a large department store in downtown Chicago as the site of their research. The second and third problems mentioned by McCall are also largely absent because shoplifters commit their offenses in the presence of other shoppers and the crime is one of stealth, not confrontation. Field workers could readily adopt the participant observation role of shoppers with no more fear for their own safety than that experienced by other shoppers.

Field observers could therefore be used in much the same way undercover retail security workers are deployed in many large stores: Pose as a shopper and watch for thefts by other shoppers. When a theft is witnessed, that's shoplifting.

What about selecting subjects for observation? And how can simple counts of observed thefts be used to estimate the prevalence of shoplifting? Shoplifting prevalence is defined as the number of shoppers who steal something during their visit to the store divided by the total number of shoppers. It is therefore necessary to obtain counts of shoppers as well as counts of shoplifters. Since shopping is a predictable activity (if it were not, there would be no shops!), it is possible to use systematic sampling methods to select people to observe.

Baumer and Rosenbaum chose a variety of days and times to conduct observations. During these times, observers and field supervisors were stationed at each entrance to the department store. Field supervisors counted everyone who entered the store and assigned observers to follow selected individuals from the time they entered until they left. Subjects were selected by systematic

Conducting a Safety Audit

Gisela Bichler-Robertson
Rutgers University

A SAFETY audit involves a careful inventory of specific environmental and situational factors that may contribute to feelings of discomfort, fear of victimization, or crime itself. The goal of a safety audit is to devise recommendations that will improve a specific area by reducing fear and crime.

Safety audits combine features of focus groups and structured field observations. To begin, the researcher assembles a small group of individuals (ten or fewer) considered to be vulnerable. Examples include: senior citizens, physically challenged individuals, young women who travel alone, students, youth, and parents with young children. Assembling diverse groups helps to identify a greater variety of environmental and situational factors for the particular area.

After explaining safety audit procedures, an audit leader then takes the group on a tour of the audit site. Since perceptions differ by time of day, at least two audits are conducted for each site—one during daylight and one after dark.

When touring audit sites, individuals do not speak to one another. The audit leader instructs group members to imagine that they are walking through the area alone. Each person is equipped with a structured form for documenting their observations and perceptions. Forms vary, depending on the group and site. In general, however, safety audit participants are instructed to document the following items:

I. Before walking through the area, briefly describe the type of space you are reviewing (e.g., a parking deck, park, shopping district). Record the number of entrances, general volume of users, design of structures, materials used in design, and type of lighting.

II. Complete the following while walking through the area.

General feelings of safety:

1. Identify the places in which you feel unsafe and uncomfortable.
2. What is it about each place that makes you feel this way?
3. Identify the places in which you feel safe.
4. What is it about each place that makes you feel this way?

General visibility:

1. Can you see very far in front of you?
2. Can you see behind you?
3. Are there any structures or vegetation that restrict your sightlines?
4. How dense are the trees/bushes?
5. Are there any hiding spots or entrapment zones?
6. Is the lighting adequate? Can you see the face of someone 15 meters in front of you?
7. Are the paths/hallways open or are they very narrow?
8. Are there any sharp corners (90° angles)?

sampling in which, say, every 20th person who entered during the observation period was followed by a field observer. Dividing the number of thefts witnessed by the number of shoppers observed yields an estimate of shoplifting prevalence. If observers were assigned to follow 500 people and witnessed thefts by 20 of them, the prevalence of shoplifting would be 4 percent.

Counts of observed thefts also provided one way to assess store security. Comparing the number of thefts witnessed by participant observers to the number detected by store security staff was one obvious way to evaluate store security. Baumer and Rosenbaum devised another method, however, one that solves a potential problem with their approach to counting shop-

Perceived control over the space:

1. Could you see danger approaching with enough time to choose an alternative route?
2. Are you visible to others on the street or in other buildings?
3. Can you see any evidence of a security system?

Presence of others:

1. Does the area seem to be deserted?
2. Are there many women around?
3. Are you alone in the presence of men?
4. What do the other people seem to be doing?
5. Are there any undesirables—vagrants (homeless or beggars), drunks, etc?
6. Do you see people who you know?
7. Are there any police or security officers present?

General safety:

1. Do you have access to a phone or other way of summoning help?
2. What is your general perception of criminal behavior?
3. Are there any places where you feel you could be attacked or confronted in an uncomfortable way?

Past experience in this space:

1. Have you been harassed in this space?
2. Have you heard of anyone who had a bad experience in this place (any legends or real experiences)?

3. Is it likely that you may be harassed here (e.g., drunk young men coming out of the pub)?
4. Have you noticed any social incivilities (minor deviant behavior—i.e., public drinking, vandalism, rough housing, or skate boarding)?
5. Is there much in the way of physical incivilities (broken windows, litter, broken bottles, vandalism)?

Following the site visit, the group finds a secure setting for a focused discussion of the various elements they identified. Harvesting observations about good and bad spaces helps to develop recommendations for physical improvement. Group members may also share perceptions and ideas about personal safety. This process should begin with a brain-storming discussion and finish with identifying the key issues of concern and most reasonable recommendations for addressing those issues.

This method of structured observation has proven to be invaluable. Much of the public space in Toronto including university campuses, public parks, transportation centers, and garages have been improved through such endeavors.

Source: Adapted from materials developed by the Metro Action Committee on Public Violence Against Women and Children (METRAC) (Toronto, Canada: METRAC, 1987).

lifting. The problem may have already occurred to you.

If you were an observer in this research, how confident would you be in your ability to detect shoplifting? Stated somewhat differently, how reliable would your observations be? Retail thieves are at least somewhat careful to conceal their crime. As a participant observer, you would have

to balance your diligence in watching people to whom you were assigned (observation) with care not to appear too interested in what your fellow shoppers were doing (participation).

Baumer and Rosenbaum used an ingenious adaptation of double-blind experimental methods, discussed in Chapter 7, to assess the reliability of field observers. Unknown to field observers, other research staff were employed as confederate shoplifters. Their job was to enter the store and steal something. Field supervisors, knowing when confederates would be entering the store, periodically instructed observers to follow one of these persons. Confederates committed known thefts and made it possible to determine whether observers were able to detect the incident.

In this way, the researchers could measure the reliability of field observations. If an observer detected 85 percent of the known thefts, that observer's count of shoplifting by real shoppers could be considered 85 percent accurate. Reliability figures were used to adjust estimates of shoplifting prevalence. For example, if the prevalence estimate for all observers was 4 percent and all observers were 85 percent reliable, then the adjusted prevalence rate would be 4.7 percent (.04/.85).

One of the lessons you should learn from this study is that simple observation is often not so simple. This is especially true when you are trying to observe people doing something they wish to conceal from observers. Our next example offers similar guidance in planning observations of people who are doing something required by law.

How Many People Wear Seat Belts?

Although nations in Europe and other parts of the world have required drivers to use seat belts for many years, laws mandating seat-belt use were rare in the United States until the 1980s. Problems in enforcing such laws, as well as general resistance to regulation, are among the reasons U.S. laws were late in coming. These concerns promoted interest in the degree of compliance with mandated seat-belt use. One study on this topic, conducted by Indiana University's Transportation Research Center (TRC), illustrates sampling issues in field observations and offers guidance on the importance of reliability. Our discussion is adapted from one of several research reports issued by TRC (Cornwell, Doherty, Mitter, and Drayer, 1989).

The first decision faced by TRC researchers was how to conduct the observations. They opted for stationary observers posted at roadsides rather than mobile observers who rode around in cars. The primary reason for this choice was the need to calculate the rates of seat-belt use, expressed as the number of people seen to be wearing belts divided by the number of cars observed. Keeping track of the number of vehicles observed is easier when they can be counted as they pass by some stationary point. Trying to count cars in view while riding in a car yourself is extremely difficult.

Where to place stationary observers was the next decision. Cornwell and associates describe how detecting seat-belt use in moving vehicles is difficult. For this reason, most observers were stationed at controlled intersections—those with a stop sign or traffic light. Since interstate highways do not have intersections, other observers were posted at entrance ramps where cars were traveling slowly.

Because it is impossible to know the number of autos in operation throughout Indiana at any given time, TRC researchers could not select a probability sample of vehicles to observe. Instead, they used systematic procedures to sample observations on three dimensions that might be associated with seat-belt use: time of day, roadway type, and observation site. In addition to considerations about site type, Cornwell and colleagues wished to stratify sites by density of auto ownership. Finding that this was highly correlated with population, they divided Indiana counties into three strata based on population and selected sites within each stratum. Small counties were oversampled to ensure that different geographic areas of the state were represented.

Roadway type included interstate highways, U.S. and state routes, and local streets. Observations were made for each day of the week and at different times of day to represent the various trip purposes. For example, weekday observations at 6:30–7:30 A.M. represented blue-collar home-to-work trips, later morning times were for white-collar commuters, midday hours represented lunch breaks, and so forth.

Standing by the roadside and trying to determine whether or not drivers and front-seat passengers are wearing safety belts is easier than observing shoplifters but still presented some difficulties. Cornwell and associates describe training procedures and steps they took to maximize the accuracy of observations. All observers completed a training period where they worked under the supervision of an experienced field worker. If you were a neophyte observer for the seat-belt study, here are some of the things you would be told about your role.

"First, you realize, of course, that we are complete observers, not participant observers. We don't try to conceal ourselves because we would not be able to see the cars very well if we hid behind signs or something. Sure, drivers can see us standing here with our clipboards, and they may wonder what we're doing. We've posted a sign that says 'Traffic Safety Research in Progress,' but there's no way they can know that we're checking seat-belt use. So try to relax and don't feel self-conscious about standing on the side of the road in your orange vest watching cars.

"Second, remember that you should check only passenger cars and station wagons. Trucks, buses, recreational vehicles, and taxicabs are not covered by the law. Also, this is Indiana, not California, so you won't see too many older cars that don't have shoulder belts. Even if you do, don't try to observe them because they aren't covered by the law either. And remember, we're interested only in front-seat occupants; ignore the back seat.

"On a related point, we are interested only in lap belt–shoulder belt combinations. Standing here on the roadside, it's not possible to tell whether or not someone is wearing a lap belt only. Because of this, observe the driver and, if present, the outboard front passenger only. There is no shoulder harness in the middle position of front seats, so ignore anybody sitting in the middle.

"Most important, record only safety belts that you can see. If you see a belt in use, great; mark a Y for yes on the coding form. If you see a belt that is NOT in use, mark N for no. But if you can't see that someone is wearing a belt and you can't ac-

tually see a safety belt that the person is not wearing, mark a U for uncertain. I know you're a good observer; we're all good observers. But sometimes cars go by so fast that you can't see whether a person is wearing a belt or not. It happens to all of us. Just be sure you mark U when you're uncertain.

"Now, I have been doing this for about six months and I've learned some things that they didn't tell me when I started. We have run into some problems that nobody thought about when they first designed this study. For example, you're lucky to be starting in May, when the weather is good and the sun is up. In wintertime, people are wearing heavy coats and it's much harder to tell whether or not they are wearing their safety belt. On cold mornings, the windows on many cars are all fogged up, making it hard to see inside. Also, when I started working the 6:30–7:30 A.M. shift in January, it was still dark and we couldn't see anything. We had to revise the time-of-day sampling plan because of that.

"From our site here we have four lanes of roadway to observe. Concentrate on the traffic lanes closest to us. You will be able to see the cars in those lanes better than you can see those in the far lanes. When traffic is stopped at the light it's not too bad, but when cars are moving you won't be able to observe everybody. Just remember, it's better to observe a smaller number of cars where you can confidently code Y or N than it is to try to see more cars but have to mark U because you can't be sure. There is no reason to expect that drivers in the far lanes will be any different than those in the near lanes. Code cars in all lanes when possible, but when in doubt, focus on those closest to you."

Bars and Violence

Researchers in the first two examples conducted systematic observations for specific purposes and produced quantitative estimates of shoplifting prevalence and seat-belt use. Field research is commonly used in more qualitative studies as well, where precise quantitative estimates are neither available nor needed. A fascinating study of violence in Australian bars by Ross Homel and associates (1992) provides an example.

Anyone with any sort of experience in or knowledge about crime will be at least casually familiar with the relationship between drinking and violence. Psychologists and medical researchers have found a physiological disinhibiting effect of alcohol that can lead to aggression and subsequent violence. In a large proportion of homicides, either the victim or offender (or both) had been drinking. Barroom brawls are known to most people by reputation if not by experience.

Homel and associates set out to learn how various situational factors of public drinking might promote or inhibit violence in Australian bars and nightclubs. Think for a moment about how you might approach their research question: "whether alcohol consumption itself contributes in some way to the likelihood of violence, or whether aspects of the drinkers or of the drinking settings are the critical factors" (1992:681). Examining police records could reveal that assault reports are more likely to come from bars than from, say, posh restaurants. Or a survey might find that self-reported bar patrons were more likely to have witnessed or participated in violence than respondents who did not frequent bars or nightclubs. But neither of these approaches could yield measures of the setting or situational factors that might provoke violence. Field research can produce direct observation of barroom settings and is well suited to addressing the question framed by Homel and associates.

Researchers began by selecting four "high-risk" and two "low-risk" sites based on Sydney police records and preliminary scouting visits. These six locations were visited five or more times, and an additional 16 sites were visited once in the course of scouting.

Visits to bars were conducted by pairs of observers who stayed two to six hours at each site. Their role is best described as complete participant because they were permitted one alcoholic drink per hour and otherwise played the role of bar patron. Observers made no notes while onsite. As soon as possible after leaving a bar, they wrote up separate narrative accounts. Later, at group meetings of all observers and research staff, the narrative accounts were discussed and any discrepancies were resolved. Narratives were later coded by the research staff to identify categories of situations, people, and activities that seemed to be associated with the likelihood of violence. These eventually included physical and social atmosphere, drinking patterns, characteristics of patrons, and characteristics of staff.

The researchers began their study by assuming that some thing or things distinguished bars where violence was common from bars where it was less common. But after beginning their field work, Homel and associates realized that circumstances and situations were the more important factors:

■ . . . during field research it soon became apparent that the violent premises are for most of the time not violent. Violent occasions in these places seemed to have characteristics that clearly marked them out from non-violent times. . . . This unexpectedly helped us refine our ideas about the relevant situational variables, and to some extent reduced the importance of comparisons with the premises selected as controls.

(1992:684)

In other words, the research question was partly restated. What began as a study to determine why some bars in Sydney were violent was revised to determine what *situations* seemed to contribute violence.

This illustrates one of the strengths of field research—the ability to make adjustments while in the field. You may recognize this as an example of inductive reasoning. Learning that even violent clubs were peaceful most of the time, Homel and associates were able to focus observers' attention on looking for more specific features of bar environment and staff and patron characteristics. Such adjustments "on the fly" would be difficult, if not impossible, if you were doing a survey.

Altogether, field observers made 55 visits to 23 sites, for a total of about 300 hours of field observation. During these visits, observers witnessed 32 incidents of physical violence. Examining detailed field notes, researchers traced violent incidents to a variety of interrelated factors.

With respect to patrons, violence was most likely to break out in bars frequented by young working-class males. However, these personal characteristics were deemed less important than the flow of people in and out of bars. Violent incidents were often triggered when groups of males entered a club and encountered other groups of males they did not know.

Physical features mattered little unless they contributed to crowding or other adverse characteristics of the social atmosphere. Chief among social features associated with violence were discomfort and boredom. A crowded, uncomfortable bar with no entertainment was trouble.

Drinking patterns made a difference; violent incidents were most common when bar patrons were very drunk. More important, certain management practices seemed to produce more drunk patrons. Fewer customers were drunk in bars that had either a restaurant or a snack table. Bars with high cover charges and cheap drinks produced a high density of drunk patrons and violence. The economics of this situation are clear: If you must pay to enter a bar that serves cheap drinks, you'll get more for your money by drinking a lot.

The final ingredient found to contribute to violence was aggressive bouncers. "Many bouncers seem poorly trained, obsessed with their own machismo (relating badly to groups of male strangers), and some of them appear to regard their employment as a license to assault people" (1992: 688). Rather than reducing violence by rejecting unruly patrons, bouncers sometimes escalated violence by starting fights.

You should recognize that field observation was necessary to identify what situations produce violence in bars. No other way of collecting data could have yielded the rich and detailed information that enabled Homel and associates to diagnose the complex relationships that produce violence in bars:

■ Violent incidents in public drinking locations do not occur simply because of the presence of young or rough patrons or because of rock bands, or any other single variable. Violent occasions are characterized by subtle interactions of several variables. Chief among

these are groups of male strangers, low comfort, high boredom, high drunkenness, as well as aggressive and unreasonable bouncers and floorstaff.

(1992:688)

■ STRENGTHS AND WEAKNESSES OF FIELD RESEARCH

We want to conclude the chapter by assessing the relative strengths and weaknesses of field research. This examination will be somewhat longer than those of earlier chapters because we want to spend some time comparing field research with surveys.

As we have indicated, field research is especially effective for studying the subtle nuances of behavior and for examining processes over time. For these reasons, the chief strength of this method is the depth of understanding it permits.

Field studies of behavior are often more appropriate than trying to measure behavior through surveys. Counts of seat-belt use or theft by shoppers obtained through observation are not subject to the effects of social desirability that we might expect in survey questions about those behaviors.

Flexibility is another advantage of field research. You can modify your research design at any time. Moreover, you are always prepared to engage in qualitative field research if the occasion arises, whereas launching a survey requires considerable advance work.

Field research can be relatively inexpensive. Other research methods may require costly equipment or an expensive research staff, but field research often can be undertaken by one researcher with a notebook and a pen. This is not to say that field research is never expensive. The shoplifting and seat-belt studies, for example, required many trained observers. Expensive recording equipment may be needed, or the researcher may wish to travel to Australia to replicate the study by Homel and associates.

Field research has its weaknesses, too. First, qualitative studies seldom yield precise descriptive statements about a large population. Observing casual discussions among corrections officers in a cafeteria, for example, does not yield trustworthy estimates about prison conditions. Nevertheless, it could provide important insights into some of the problems facing staff and inmates in a specific institution.

Second, field observation can produce systematic counts of behaviors and reasonable estimates for a large population of behaviors beyond those actually observed. However, since it is not usually possible to know the total population of phenomena—shoppers or drivers, for example—precise probability samples cannot normally be drawn. In designing a quantitative field study or assessing the representativeness of some other study, you must think carefully about the density and predictability of what will be observed. Then decide whether sampling procedures are likely to tap representative instances of cases you will observe.

More generally, the advantages and disadvantages of different types of field studies can be considered in terms of their validity, reliability, and generalizability. You'll recall that validity and reliability are both qualities of measurements. *Validity* concerns whether measurements actually measure what they are supposed to rather than something else. *Reliability,* on the other hand, is a matter of dependability: If you made the same measurement again and again, would you get the same result? Finally, *generalizability* refers to whether specific research findings apply to people, places, and things not actually observed. Let's see how field research stacks up in these respects.

Validity

Survey measurements are sometimes criticized as superficial and weak on validity. Observational studies have the potential to yield measures that are more valid. With respect to qualitative field research, "being there" is a powerful technique for gaining insights into the nature of human affairs.

Recall our discussion in Chapter 10 of some of the limits of using survey methods to study domestic violence. An alternative is a field study where the researcher interacts at length with victims of domestic violence. The relative strengths

of each approach are nicely illustrated in a pair of articles that examine domestic violence in England. Chapter 10 quoted from Catriona Mirrlees-Black's (1995) article on domestic violence as measured in the British Crime Survey. John Hood-Williams and Tracey Bush (1995) provide a different perspective through their study published in the same issue of the Home Office *Research Bulletin.*

Tracey Bush lived in a London public housing project (termed "housing estate" in England) for about five years. This enabled her to study domestic violence in a natural setting: "The views of men and women on the estate about relationships and domestic violence have been gathered through the researcher's network of friends, neighbours, acquaintances, and contacts" (Hood-Williams and Bush, 1995:11). Through long and patient field work, Bush learned that women sometimes "normalize" low levels of violence, seeing it as an unfortunate but unavoidable consequence of their relationship with a male partner. When violence escalates, victims may blame themselves. Victims may also remain in an abusive relationship in hopes that things will get better:

■ She reported that she wanted the companionship and respect that she had received at the beginning of the relationship. It was the earlier, non-violent man, whom she had met and fallen in love with, that she wanted back.

(1995:13)

Mirrlees-Black wrote that measuring domestic violence was "difficult territory" in part because women may not recognize assault by a partner as a crime. Field research such as that by Hood-Williams and Bush offers an example of this phenomenon and helps us understand why it exists.

Validity is a particular strength of field research. As we have pointed out, quantitative measurements based on surveys or on simple counts of some phenomenon give an incomplete picture of the fundamental concept we are interested in. Survey responses to questions about domestic violence victimization, however carefully phrased, are limited in their ability to count incidents that victims don't recognize as crimes. More important, survey methods cannot yield the rich understanding of domestic violence and its context that Tracey Bush discovered in her five years of field research.

In field research, validity often refers to whether you have accurately captured the intended meaning of things you observe or people you interview. In the case of interviews, Joseph Maxwell (1996) suggests getting feedback on your measures from the people you are studying. For example, Wright and Decker (1994) conducted lengthy semistructured interviews with their sample of burglars. The researchers recognized that their limited understanding of the social context of burglary may have produced some errors in interpreting what they learned from subjects. To guard against this, Wright and Decker had some of their subjects review what they thought they had learned:

■ . . . as the writing proceeded, we read various parts of the manuscript to selected members of our sample. This allowed us to check our interpretations against those of insiders and to enlist their help in reformulating passages they regarded as misleading or inaccurate. . . . The result of using this procedure, we believe, is a book that faithfully conveys the offender's perspective on the process of committing residential burglaries.

(1994:33–34)

You may recognize that this approach is possible only if subjects are aware of your role as a researcher. In that case, having informants review draft field notes or interview transcripts can be an excellent strategy for improving validity.

Reliability

Qualitative field research does have a potential problem with reliability. Suppose you were to characterize your best friend's political orientations based on everything you know about him or her. There's certainly no question about your assessment of that person's politics being superficial. The measurement you arrived at would appear to have considerable validity. We can't be sure, however, that someone else would charac-

terize your friend's politics the same way you did, even with the same amount of observation.

Field research measurements—though in-depth—are also often very personal. If, for example, you wished to conduct a field study of bars and honky-tonks near your campus, you might judge levels of disorder on a Friday night to be low or moderate. In contrast, older adults might view the same levels of noise and commotion and rate disorder as intolerably high. How we interpret the phenomena we observe depends very much on our own experiences and preferences.

The reliability of quantitative field studies can be enhanced by careful attention to the details of observation. We have seen examples of this in studies of shoplifting and seat-belt use. Environmental surveys can likewise promote reliable observations by including detailed instructions on how to classify what is observed. Reliability can be strengthened by reviewing the products of field observations. Homel and associates sought to increase the reliability of observers' narrative descriptions by having group discussions about discrepancies in reports from different observers.

In a more general sense, reliability will increase as the degree of interpretation required in making actual observations declines. Participant observation or unstructured interviews may require a considerable degree of interpretation on the part of the observer, and most of us draw on our own experiences and backgrounds in interpreting what we observe. At another extreme, electronic devices and machines can produce very reliable counts of persons who enter a store or of cars that pass some particular point. Somewhere in the middle are field workers who observe shoplifters, motorists, or pedestrians and tabulate some specific behavior.

Generalizability

One of the chief goals of social science is generalization. We study particular situations and events to learn about life in general. Usually nobody would be interested in the specific subjects observed by the researcher. Who cares, after all, about the 18 people who told National Crime

Victimization Survey interviewers about their stolen bicycles? We are interested only if their victimization experiences can be generalized to all U.S. households.

Generalizability can be a problem for qualitative field research. It crops up in two forms. First, the personal nature of the observations and measurements made by the researcher can produce results that would not necessarily be replicated by another independent researcher. If the observation depends in part on the particular observers, it is more valuable as a source of particular insight than as a general truth.

Second, because field researchers get a full and in-depth view of their subject matter, they can reach an unusually comprehensive understanding. By its very comprehensiveness, however, this understanding is less generalizable than results based on rigorous sampling and standardized measurements.

Let's say you set out to fully understand how the public defender's office in your city operates. You study each of the lawyers in great depth, learning about their ideological positions, why they decided to join the public defender's office, their career aspirations, who their friends and enemies are. You could learn about their family lives and see how personal feelings enter into their work representing indigent defendants. After such an in-depth study, you could probably understand the actions of the public defender's office really well. But would you be able to say much about public defenders in general? Surely, your study would have provided you with some general insights, but you wouldn't be able to carry over everything you learned from the specific to the general. Having learned all about the public defense bar in Atlanta, you might not be able to say much about Seattle's. You should, however, be in a position to organize a great study of public defenders in Seattle.

Even quantitative field studies may be weak on generalizability. Baumer and Rosenbaum's (1982) estimates of shoplifting prevalence were based on observations in a single large department store in downtown Chicago. The situation is likely to be different in smaller specialty shops, newer department stores in suburban malls, or other down-town stores in other cities. Similarly, conclusions about seat-belt use in Indiana may not apply in New York. Indiana's law calls for $25 fines for not wearing seat belts and may be invoked only if a driver is stopped for some other reason. Compliance may be different in states with stiffer penalties where police are permitted to stop drivers for not wearing seat belts.

On the other hand, some field studies are less rooted in the local context of the subject under study. Wright and Decker (1994) studied burglars in St. Louis, and it's certainly reasonable to wonder whether their findings apply to residential burglars in St. Petersburg, Florida. The actions and routines of burglars might be affected by local police strategies, differences in age or style of dwelling units, or even the type and amount of vegetation that might screen an intruder from the street. However, Wright and Decker draw general conclusions about how burglars search for targets, what features of dwellings signal vulnerability, how opportunistic knowledge can trigger an offense, and strategies for fencing stolen goods. It's likely that their findings about the technology and incentives that affect St. Louis burglars apply generally to residential burglars in other cities.

In reviewing reports of field research projects, you should determine where and to what extent the researcher is generalizing beyond her or his specific observations to other settings. Such generalizations may be in order, but you need to judge that. Nothing in this research method guarantees it.

As we've seen, field research is a potentially powerful tool for criminal justice research, one that provides a useful balance to the strengths and weaknesses of surveys.

■ *MAIN POINTS*

- Field research is a data-collection method that involves the direct observation of phenomena in their natural settings.
- Field observation is usually the preferred data-collection method for obtaining information about physical or social settings, behavior, and events.

- Field research in criminal justice may produce either qualitative or quantitative data. Grounded theory is typically built from qualitative field observations. Or observations that can be quantified may produce measures for hypothesis testing.
- Observations made through field research can often be integrated with data collected from other sources. In this way, field observations can help researchers interpret other data.
- Asking questions through a form of specialized interviewing is often integrated with field observation.
- You may or may not identify yourself as a researcher to the people you are observing. Identifying yourself as a researcher may have some effect on the nature of what you are observing, but concealing your identity may involve deceit.
- Preparing for the field involves negotiating or arranging access to subjects. Specific strategies depend on whether or not you identify yourself as a researcher, and whether you will be studying formal organizations, subcultures, or something in between.
- Controlled probability sampling techniques are not usually possible in field research. Different forms of quota sampling may be used in the attempt to achieve better representativeness in observations.
- Snowball sampling is a method by which you acquire an ever-increasing number of sample observations. You ask one participant in the event under study to recommend others for interviewing, and each of the subsequently interviewed participants is asked for more recommendations.
- If field observations will be made on a process that occurs with some degree of regularity, purposive sampling techniques can be used to select cases for observation.
- Alternatives for recording field observations range from video, audio, and other equipment to unstructured field notes. In between are observations recorded on structured forms; environmental surveys are examples.
- Field notes should be planned in advance to the greatest extent possible. However, note-taking should be flexible enough to make records of unexpected observations.
- Compared with surveys, field research measurements generally have more validity but less reliability, and field research results cannot be generalized as safely as those based on rigorous sampling and standardized questionnaires.

■ REVIEW QUESTIONS AND EXERCISES

1. Think of some group or activity you participate in or are very familiar with. In two or three paragraphs, describe how an outsider might effectively go about studying that group or activity. What should he or she read, what contacts should be made, and so on?
2. To show that you appreciate the differing strengths and weaknesses of surveys and field research, give brief descriptions of two studies especially appropriate to each method. Be sure each topic is most appropriately studied by the method you identify it with.
3. Review the box entitled "Conducting a Safety Audit" by Gisela Bichler-Robertson. Try conducting a safety audit on your campus or in an area near your campus.
4. Many police departments encourage citizen ride-alongs as a component of community policing. If this is the case for a police or sheriff's department near you, take advantage of this excellent opportunity to test your observation and unstructured interviewing skills.

■ ADDITIONAL READINGS

Bureau of Justice Assistance, *A Police Guide to Surveying Citizens and Their Environment* (Washington, DC: U.S. Department of Justice, Office of Justice Programs, Bureau of Justice Assistance, 1993). Intended for use in community policing initiatives, this publication is a useful source of ideas about conducting structured observations. Appendixes include detailed examples of environmental surveys. You can also download this publication in text form (no drawings) from the following web address: http://www.ncjrs.org/txtfiles/polc.txt

Johnson, Jeffrey C., *Selecting Ethnographic Informants* (Thousand Oaks, CA: Sage, 1990). The author discusses various strategies that apply to the task of sampling in field research.

King, Jean A., Morris, Lynn Lyons, and Fitz-Gibbon, Carol Taylor, *How to Assess Program Implementation* (Thousand Oaks, CA: Sage, 1987). Although it has an applied focus, this book offers detailed advice on how to plan, organize, and execute structured observations.

McCall, George J., *Observing the Law: Field Methods in the Study of Crime and the Criminal Justice System* (New York: Free Press, 1978). McCall does an excellent job of describing some of the field research issues that criminal justice researchers must confront. He offers suggestions and solutions to problems a field researcher might expect to encounter.

Patton, Michael Quinn, *Qualitative Evaluation Research Methods*, 2d ed. (Thousand Oaks, CA: Sage Publications, 1990). We mentioned this book in Chapter 10 as a good source of guidance on questionnaire construction. Likewise, Patton offers in-depth information on observation techniques, along with tips on conducting unstructured and semistructured field interviews. Finally, Patton describes a variety of purposive sampling techniques for qualitative interviewing and field research.

12 Agency Records, Content Analysis, and Secondary Data

CHAPTER

What You'll Learn in This Chapter

We'll examine three sources of existing data: agency records, content analysis, and data collected by other researchers. You'll learn about the many applications for these data in criminal justice research.

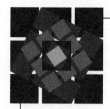

INTRODUCTION

**TOPICS APPROPRIATE
FOR AGENCY RECORDS**

TYPES OF AGENCY RECORDS
Published Statistics
Nonpublic Agency Records
New Data Collected by Agency Staff

UNITS OF ANALYSIS AND SAMPLING
Units of Analysis
Sampling

RELIABILITY AND VALIDITY
Sources of Reliability and Validity Problems

CONTENT ANALYSIS
Units of Analysis and Sampling
    in Content Analysis
Coding in Content Analysis
Illustrations of Content Analysis

SECONDARY ANALYSIS
Sources of Secondary Data
Advantages and Disadvantages
    of Secondary Data

MAIN POINTS

REVIEW QUESTIONS AND EXERCISES

ADDITIONAL READINGS

■ INTRODUCTION

Except for the complete observer in field research, the modes of observation discussed so far require the researcher to intrude to some degree into whatever he or she is studying. This is most obvious with survey research. Even the field researcher, as we've seen, can change things in the process of studying them.

In this chapter, we will discuss different ways of collecting data that do not involve intrusion by observers. We'll examine three different approaches to using information that has been collected by other persons, often as a routine practice.

First, a great deal of criminal justice research uses data collected by state and local agencies such as police, criminal courts, probation offices, juvenile authorities, and corrections departments. Federal organizations like the FBI, the Bureau of Justice Statistics, the Federal Bureau of Prisons, and the National Institute of Corrections compile information about crime problems and criminal justice institutions. In addition, nongovernment organizations such as the National Center for State Courts and the American Prosecutors' Research Institute collect data from members.

Government agencies gather a vast amount of crime and criminal justice data, probably rivaled only by efforts to produce economic and public health indicators. We will refer to such information as *data from agency records*. In this chapter, we will describe different types of such data that are available for criminal justice research, together with the promise and potential pitfalls of using information from agency records.

Second, in *content analysis*, researchers examine a class of social artifacts—typically written documents. Suppose, for example, you wanted to contrast the importance of criminal justice policy and health care policy for Americans in the 1980s and 1990s. One way would be to examine public opinion polls from these two periods. Another method would be to analyze newspaper articles from the two periods. The latter is an example of content analysis: the analysis of communications.

Finally, information collected by others is frequently used in criminal justice research, which in this case involves **secondary analysis** of existing data. Investigators who conduct research funded by federal agencies such as the National Institute of Justice are usually obliged to release their data for public use. Thus, for example, if you were interested in establishing a system for using bail guidelines to make pretrial release decisions, you might wish to analyze data collected by Goldkamp and Gottfredson (1983) in their research on judicial decision guidelines for bail. This chapter will discuss issues to consider in conducting secondary analysis. We will also briefly describe some sources of secondary data, which are covered more fully in Appendix D.

Before we begin to explore each of these sources of data in detail, recall our caution in Chapter 9 about obtrusive and unobtrusive measurement. When you go to the library to consult published statistics about persons under correctional supervision or to conduct secondary analysis of a prison inmate survey directed by the RAND Corporation, you are not interacting with research subjects. Do not, however, be too quick to describe such measurement as unobtrusive. Inmates interviewed by RAND researchers were certainly aware of their role in providing information for research, even if they had no idea that you would later examine the data. You may gather jail census figures from a published report, but those data were originally obtained from a survey questionnaire completed by one or more persons directly involved in the measurement process.

In a general sense, then, most data you obtain from agency records or research projects conducted by others are secondary data. Someone else gathered the original data, usually for purposes different from yours. This is less true for content analysis, as we will see later in the chapter. However, in most cases you will use data collected by other people for other reasons.

■ TOPICS APPROPRIATE FOR AGENCY RECORDS

Data from agency records or archives may have been originally gathered in any number of ways, from sample surveys to direct observation. Because of this, such data may, in principle, be appropriate for just about any criminal justice research topic.

Published statistics and agency records are most commonly used in descriptive or exploratory studies. This is consistent with the fact that many of the criminal justice data actually published by government agencies are intended to describe something. For instance, the Bureau of Justice Statistics (BJS) publishes annual figures on prison populations. If you were interested in describing differences in prison populations between states, or changes in prison populations from 1980 through 1995, a good place to begin would be the published data for each year. In a similar way, published figures on crimes reported to police, criminal victimization, felony court caseloads, drug use by high school seniors, and a host of other measures are available over time, for 20 years or longer in some cases.

Agency records may also be used in explanatory studies. Myers and Talarico (1986) examined more than 16,000 felony case records in Georgia to analyze different circumstances that affected the severity of sentences received by white and nonwhite defendants. They found that white defendants more often received prison sentences when they were found guilty in counties where a majority of the population was nonwhite.

Agency records are frequently used in applied studies as well. Evaluations of new policies that seek to reduce recidivism draw on arrest or conviction data for measures of recidivism. Studies of arrest as a presumptive response to domestic violence traced arrest records for experimental and control subjects (Sherman, 1992b). Baumer and Mendelsohn (1990) compared postrelease arrest records for subjects randomly assigned to simple home detention or to home detention with electronic monitoring. Sometimes records obtained from private firms can be used in applied studies; Bichler and Clarke (1996) examined records of international telephone calls in their evaluation of efforts to reduce telephone fraud in New York City.

In a different type of applied study, Blumstein, Cohen, and Miller (1980) combined data from prison sentences, arrest rates, and the U.S. census to develop a mathematical model that predicts future prison populations in Pennsylvania. This is an example of forecasting, in which past relationships among arrest rates and prison sentences for different age groups are compared to census estimates of future population by age group. Assuming that past associations between age, arrest, and prison sentences will remain constant in future years, demographic models of future population can be used to predict future admissions to prison.

Topics appropriate to research using content analysis center on the important links between communication, perceptions of crime problems, individual behavior, and criminal justice policy. The prevalence of violence on fictional television dramas has long been a concern of researchers and public officials (Gerbner and Gross, 1980). Skogan and Maxfield (1981) studied the link between mass media news stories about crime and people's perceptions. Numerous attempts have been made to explore relationships between exposure to pornography and sexual assault (e.g., Intons-Peterson and Roskos-Ewoldsen, 1989; U.S. Department of Justice, 1986; Donnerstein, Linz, and Penrod, 1987). Mass media also play an important role in affecting policy action by public officials. Many studies have examined the influence of media agenda setting for criminal justice policy (Fishman, 1980).

Research data collected by other investigators, through surveys or field observation, may be used for a broad variety of later studies. National Crime Victimization Survey (NCVS) data have been used by a large number of researchers in countless descriptive and explanatory studies since the 1970s. Robert Sampson and John Laub (1993) produced one of the most ambitious uses of secondary data in recent years. They recovered life history data on 500 delinquents and 500 nondelinquents originally collected by Sheldon and Eleanor Glueck in the 1940s. Taking advantage of theoretical and empirical advances in criminological research over the ensuing 40 years, Sampson and Laub produced a major contribution to knowledge of criminal career development in childhood.

Existing data may also be considered as a supplemental source of data. For example, if you were planning to survey corrections facility administrators about their views on the need for drug treatment programs, you would do well to examine existing data on the number of drug users sentenced to prison terms. Or, if you were evaluating an experimental morale-building program in a probation services department, statistics on absenteeism would be useful in connection with the data your own research would generate.

This is not to say that agency records and secondary data can always provide answers to research questions. If this were true, much of what you have read so far in this book would be unnecessary. The key to distinguishing appropriate and inappropriate uses of agency records, content analysis, and secondary data is understanding how these written records are produced. We cannot emphasize this point too strongly. Much of this chapter will underscore the importance of learning where data come from and how they are gathered. We begin by more closely examining different types of records produced by public agencies.

■ TYPES OF AGENCY RECORDS

Information collected by or for public agencies usually falls into one of three general categories: (1) published statistics, (2) nonpublic agency records routinely collected for internal use, and (3) new data collected by agency staff for specific research purposes. Each category varies in the extent to which data are readily available to the researcher and in the researcher's degree of control over the data-collection process.

Published Statistics

Many government organizations routinely collect and publish compilations of data. Examples are the Census Bureau, the FBI, the Administrative Office of U.S. Courts, the Federal Bureau of Prisons, and the BJS. Two of these organizations merit special mention. First, the Census Bureau conducts enumerations and sample surveys for several other federal organizations. Notable examples are the NCVS, Census of Children in Cus-

TABLE 12-1
Victimization Rates by Type of Crime, Form of Tenure, and Race of Head of Household (Rates per 1,000 Households)

	Home Owned or Being Bought		Rented	
	White	Black	White	Black
Household crimes				
Completed	112.5	171.3	176.0	174.0
Attempted	17.6	27.8	35.0	40.2
Burglary	39.7	61.1	71.7	84.9
Household larceny	74.5	102.2	112.6	91.6
Vehicle theft	15.9	35.8	26.6	37.7
Total number of households (1,000s)	55,795	4,938	27,157	6,345

Source: Adapted from Bureau of Justice Statistics (1992b: 48, Table 31).

tody, Survey of Inmates in Local Jails, Correctional Populations in the United States, and Survey of Justice Expenditure and Employment.

Second, the BJS compiles data from several sources and publishes annual and special reports on most data series. For example, *Criminal Victimization in the United States* reports summary data from the NCVS each year. Table 12-1 presents a sample breakdown of victimization rates by race and home ownership from the report for 1991. Annual reports entitled *Correctional Populations in the United States* present findings from sample surveys and enumerations of jail, prison, and juvenile facility populations. A sample tabulation of persons who are serving sentences in state and federal prisons is shown in Table 12-2. And *The Prosecution of Felony Arrests* reports detailed data on felony dispositions in selected cities.

The most comprehensive BJS publication on criminal justice data is the annual *Sourcebook of Criminal Justice Statistics*. Since 1972, this report has summarized hundreds of criminal justice data series, ranging from public perceptions about crime through characteristics of criminal justice agencies to, in the 1995 report, a table on how states execute capital sentences. Data from private sources, such as the Gallup Poll, are included with statistics collected by government agencies. Most important, each year's *Sourcebook* concludes

TABLE 12-2
Prisoners Under Jurisdiction of State and Federal Correctional Authorities

	Total 1990	Percent Change 1989–1990	Sentence 1 Year or More	
			1990	Percent Change 1989–1990
Northeast	123,392	8.3	119,063	8.8
Connecticut	10,500	12.9	7,771	23.2
Maine	1,523	4.7	1,480	3.4
Massachusetts	8,273	10.0	7,899	8.7
New Hampshire	1,342	15.1	1,342	15.1
New Jersey	21,128	8.7	21,128	8.7
New York	54,895	7.1	54,895	7.1
Pennsylvania	22,290	8.9	22,281	8.9
Rhode Island	2,392	−3.5	1,586	8.0
Vermont	1,049	15.9	681	8.8
Midwest	145,791	6.9	145,478	6.9
South	284,029	8.3	275,217	8.9
West	153,731	9.3	148,326	9.4

Source: Adapted from Bureau of Justice Statistics (1992a:86, Table 5.1).

with notes on data sources, appendixes summarizing data-collection procedures for major series, and addresses of organizations that either collect or archive original data.[1]

Published data on crime and criminal justice are readily available from many sources. Appendix D presents a more comprehensive list, together with some guidelines on how to get more information from the BJS and other major sources. At this point, however, we want to suggest some possible uses, and limits, of what Herbert Jacob (1984:9) refers to as being "like the apple in the Garden of Eden: tempting but full of danger . . . [for] the unwary researcher."

Referring to Tables 12-1 and 12-2, you may recognize that published data from series such as the NCVS or *Correctional Populations in the United States* are summary data, as we discussed in Chapter 6 with reference to Uniform Crime Reports (UCR). This means that data are presented in highly aggregated form and cannot be used to analyze the individuals from or about whom information was originally collected. For example, Table 12-2 shows that in 1990, 54,895 people

were serving sentences of one year or more in state and federal correctional institutions in New York. By comparing that figure to figures from other states, you could make some descriptive statements about prison populations in different states. You could also consult earlier editions of *Correctional Populations* to examine trends in prison populations over time, or to compare rates of growth from state to state.

Summary data could not, however, be used to reveal anything about individual correctional facilities, let alone facility inmates. Original data about institutions and individuals collected by the Census Bureau are available to the researcher, but not from published tabulations. We will provide information about sources of such original data later in this chapter.

This is not to say that published data are useless to criminal justice researchers. Highly aggregated summary data from published statistical series are frequently used in descriptive, explanatory, and applied studies. For example, Alfred Blumstein (1988) examined national and state-level prison population figures from the BJS, together with published FBI data on the age of persons arrested. His analysis of the summary data describes factors that contribute to prison crowding and assesses different policies for

[1]The *Sourcebook* is now (March 1997) available via the World Wide Web at this address: http://www.albany.edu/sourcebook

responding to the problem. In another study, Blumstein, Cohen, and Rosenfeld (1991) compare published UCR and NCVS data for burglary and robbery and conclude that the different measures of crime covaried relatively consistently from 1973 through 1985.

Ted Robert Gurr (1989) used published statistics on violent crime dating back to 13th-century England to examine how social and political events affected patterns of homicide through 1984. A long-term decline in homicide rates has been punctuated by spikes during periods of social dislocation, where:

■ significant segments of a population have been separated from the regulating institutions that instill and reinforce the basic Western injunctions against interpersonal violence. They may be migrants, demobilized veterans, a growing population of resentful young people for whom there is no social or economic niche, or badly educated young black men trapped in the decaying ghettos of an affluent society.

(1989:48–49)

Published data can therefore address questions about highly aggregated patterns or trends—crowding in state prisons, the covariation in two estimates of crime, or epochal change in fatal violence. Published data also have the distinct advantage of being readily available; a trip to the library or a letter to the BJS can quickly place several volumes of data series at your disposal. You can obtain copies of most publications by BJS and other Justice Department offices on the Internet; most documents published since about 1994 are available electronically (see Appendixes A, B, and D).

Published data series are available in several media. For example, you can obtain NCVS data through printed reports, microforms, computer tapes, diskettes, and compact disk formats. Subsets of NCVS data and many other criminal justice data series can also be downloaded from the Internet.

Electronic formats have many advantages. Data fields may be read directly into statistical or graphics computer programs for analysis. More important, complete data series are available in electronic formats. While printed reports of the NCVS limit you to summary tabulations such as those in Table 12-1, electronic and optical media include the original survey data from 100,000 or more respondents. We will have more to say about archived criminal justice data later in this chapter when our attention turns to secondary analysis.

Of course, before using either original data or tabulations from published sources, you must consider the issues of validity and reliability and the more general question of how well these data meet your specific research purpose. It would make little sense to use only FBI data on homicides in a descriptive study of domestic violence because murder records measure only incidents of fatal violence. Or data from an annual prison census would not be appropriate for research on changes in sentences to community corrections programs.

Nonpublic Agency Records

Despite the large volume of published statistics in criminal justice, those data represent only the tip of the proverbial iceberg. The FBI publishes the summary UCR, but each of the nation's several thousand law enforcement agencies produces an incredible volume of data not routinely released for public distribution. The BJS publication *Correctional Populations in the United States* presents statistics on prison inmates collected from annual surveys of correctional facilities, but any given correctional facility also maintains detailed case files on individual inmates. The volume *Court Caseload Statistics*, published by the National Center for State Courts, contains summary data on cases filed and disposed in state courts, but any courthouse in any large city houses paper or computer files on thousands of individual defendants. Finally, reports on the annual survey of expenditure and employment in criminal justice are sources of summary data on budgets and personnel, but every agency also maintains its own detailed records of expenditures and human resources.

Although we have labeled this data source "nonpublic agency records," most criminal justice organizations will make such data available to criminal justice researchers. But obtaining agency records is not as simple as strolling into a library and asking for a BJS publication, or clicking a download button on the Census Bureau's web page. Obtaining access to nonpublic records involves many of the same steps we outlined in Chapter 11 for gaining entry for field research.

At the outset, we want you to realize that the potential promise of agency records is not without cost. Jacob's caution about the hidden perils to unwary researchers who uncritically accept published data applies to nonpublic agency records as well. On the one hand, we could devote an entire book (or two) to describing the potential applications of agency records in criminal justice research, together with advice on how to use and interpret such data. On the other hand, we can summarize that unwritten book with one piece of advice: Understand how agency records are produced. Restated slightly, you can find the road to happiness in using agency records by following the paper trail.

By way of illustrating this humble maxim, we will now present two types of examples. First, we will describe two studies in which nonpublic agency records are used to reveal important findings about the etiology of crime and its spatial distribution. Second, we will briefly review two studies where the authors recognize validity and reliability problems, and we'll draw conclusions about the behavior of criminal justice organizations. At the end of this section, we will summarize the promise of agency records for research, together with cautions that must be exercised if such records are to be used effectively.

Child Abuse, Delinquency, and Adult Arrests In earlier chapters, we described Cathy Spatz Widom's research on child abuse as an example of a quasi-experimental design. For present purposes, this research illustrates the use of several different types of agency records.

Widom (1989b) identified cases of child abuse and neglect by consulting records from juvenile and adult criminal courts in a large midwestern city. Unlike adult courts, juvenile court proceedings are not open to the public, and juvenile records may not be released. However, after obtaining institutional review board approval, Widom was granted access to these files for research purposes by court authorities. From juvenile court records, Widom selected 774 cases of neglect, physical abuse, or sexual abuse. Cases of extreme abuse were processed in adult criminal court, where charges were filed against the offender. Criminal court records yielded an additional 134 cases.

As we described in Chapter 7, Widom constructed a comparison group of nonabused children through individual matching. Comparison subjects were found from two different sources of agency records. First, abused children who were aged 6 to 11 at the time of the abuse were matched to comparison subjects by consulting public school records. An abused child was matched with a comparison child of the same sex, race, and age (within 6 months) who attended the same school. Second, children who were younger than 6 at the time of abuse were matched on similar criteria by consulting birth records and selecting a comparison subject born in the same hospital.

These two types of public records and matching criteria—attending the same public school and birth in the same hospital—were used in an attempt to control for socioeconomic status. Although you may view such criteria with skepticism, Widom (1989a:360) points out that during this time period (1967–1971), school busing was not used and "elementary schools represented very homogeneous neighborhoods." Similarly, in the late 1960s, hospitals tended to serve local communities, unlike contemporary medical-industrial complexes that advertise their services far and wide. Widom assumed that children born in the same hospital were more likely to be from similar socioeconomic backgrounds than children born in different hospitals. Though far from perfect, school and birth records enabled Widom to construct approximate matches on socioeconomic status, which illustrates our advice in Chapter 9 to be creative while being careful.

Widom's research purpose was to examine the link between early child abuse and later delinquency or adult criminal behavior. These two dependent variables were measured by consulting additional agency records for information on arrests of abused subjects and comparison subjects for the years 1971 through 1986. Juvenile court files yielded information on delinquency. Adult arrests were measured from criminal history files maintained by local, state, and national law enforcement agencies. In an effort to locate as many subjects as possible, Widom searched state Bureau of Motor Vehicles files for current addresses and Social Security numbers. Finally, "marriage license bureau records were searched to find married names for the females" (1989a: 361).

Findings revealed modest but statistically significant differences between abused and comparison subjects. As a group, abused subjects were more likely to have records of delinquency or adult arrests (Widom, 1989b; Maxfield and Widom, 1996). However, Widom (1992) also found differences in these dependent variables by race and gender.

Now let's consider two potential validity and reliability issues that might be raised by Widom's use of nonpublic agency records. First, data from juvenile and adult criminal courts reveal only cases of abuse that come to the attention of public officials. Unreported and unsubstantiated cases of abuse or neglect are excluded, and this raises a question about the validity of Widom's measure of the independent variable. Second, dependent variable measures are similarly flawed because juvenile and adult arrests do not reflect all delinquent or criminal behavior.

Recognizing these problems, Widom is careful to point out that her measure of abuse probably reflects only the most severe cases, those that were brought to the attention of public officials. She also notes that cases in her study were processed before officials and the general public had become more aware of the problem of child abuse. Widom (1989a: 365–366) understood the limits of official records and qualified her conclusions accordingly: "These findings, then, are not generalizable to unreported cases of abuse or neglect. . . . Ours are also the cases in which agencies have intervened, and in which there is little doubt of abuse or neglect. Thus, these findings are confounded with the processing factor."

Crime "Hot Spots" Law enforcement officials and criminal justice researchers have long been interested in the spatial concentration of crime. Police patrol resources are allocated by beat according to crime volume. An influential article by Lawrence Cohen and Marcus Felson (1979) introduced a "routine activities" perspective on criminal victimization that linked the behavior of potential victims with characteristics of urban locations in a model of crime risk.

More recently, Sherman, Gartin, and Buerger (1989) examined the concentration of calls for police service in specific locations to draw conclusions about the criminogenic potential of crime "hot spots." Their analysis illustrates the potential uses of a long-neglected measure produced in great volume by police departments. Calls for service (CFS) represent the initial reports of crime and other problems to police departments. Most large police departments record basic information about CFS—location, time, nature of complaint—on audiotapes. Telephone operators respond to most CFS by dispatching a patrol car, a process that is automatically recorded on a computer. This produces a source of data on incidents brought to the attention of police.

Truly astonishing numbers of crime victims, witnesses, or people with some sort of noncrime problem telephone police departments each year. Sherman and associates (1989: 36) analyzed more than 300,000 such calls to the Minneapolis Police Department in 1986, proposing that "calls to the police provide the most extensive and faithful account of what the public tells the police about crime, with the specific errors and biases that that entails." As we pointed out earlier, UCR and similar data on recorded crime are subject to validity and reliability problems that reflect decisions by police and complainants. CFS are recorded (automatically) before most such decisions are made and are therefore less subject to screening by the police or the public. An additional advantage, and one crucial for Sherman's research on "the criminology of place," is that CFS data provide microlevel information on where incidents occur.

Since Sherman and colleagues (1989:37) were interested in the concentration of calls in certain locations, they required some measure of the number of distinct locations in Minneapolis. Consulting records from the city tax assessor's office, the Administrative Engineering Service, and the Traffic Engineering Office, researchers concluded that it was not possible to obtain a precise count of locations. A denominator of places for computing CFS rates was estimated at 115,000, which included 109,000 street addresses and 6,000 intersections.

In a slight digression, we point out that this approximation illustrates another point made by Jacob (1984:39). Given the many sources of potential error in published statistics and agency records, researchers who use such data should report rounded figures and thereby avoid the illusion of exaggerated accuracy that precise numbers imply. For example, there is no way of knowing whether Minneapolis has 107,037 or 111,252 street addresses because of varying definitions used by different agencies. It is therefore safer to state "about 109,000 street addresses" than to report either a specific estimate or a "precise" average of the two estimates (109,144.5), which implies a degree of accuracy that is unwarranted.

Addressing first the general question of concentration, Sherman and colleagues (1989:38) found that about 50 percent of calls for service occurred in just 3 percent of Minneapolis locations. Looking more closely at types of incidents shed light on the links between type of offense and type of place. For example, certain hot spots such as discount department stores and large parking lots produced large numbers of shoplifting reports and calls from motorists locked out of their cars. One hotel stood out with a large number of calls for burglary and violent crime but turned out to be more of a "cool spot" when standardized by the hotel's average daily population of more than 3,000 guests and employees. In contrast, the approximate robbery rate for a single bar that had an estimated daily population of about 300 was 83 per 1,000 persons at risk.

Even more interesting than simple data on the spatial concentration of CFS is the interpretation of these measures in the context of routine activity theory. Sherman and associates (1989:47–48) challenge the view that crime displacement is inevitable, arguing instead that the potential for displacement varies by type of incident. Predatory crimes such as robbery and burglary are at least partly dependent on an opportunity structure that can be modified. Citing measures for reducing convenience store robberies, the researchers propose that features of such places—physical design and staffing patterns—can deter motivated offenders. In contrast, incidents such as interpersonal violence and vice are less place-dependent. Domestic violence can occur any place two people live. Prostitution or drug sales depend on market attractions between seller and buyer. Parties to the transaction are mobile and can easily relocate to a place where surveillance or other inhibiting factors are absent. Thus, there is a greater potential for displacement of crimes linked to intimate or market relationships, while prevention may be possible for incidents that are more dependent on characteristics of place.

This example is different from Widom's study in many respects; however, each recognizes the potential promise and shortcomings of data from agency records—each is careful and creative. Despite the advantages of using CFS data, Sherman and associates describe three possible problems: the potential for duplicate records of the same incident; false reports, equivalent to false fire alarms; and misleading hot spots such as hospitals and police stations that produce secondary crime reports. After taking these problems into consideration, Sherman and colleagues concluded that the advantages of CFS data outweighed the disadvantages. Readers can form their own conclusions, aided by the careful description of the paper trail—how CFS data are produced—provided by Sherman, Gartin, and Buerger (1989).

Agency Records As Measures of Decision Making   Two studies we discussed in earlier chapters illustrate how flaws in agency recordkeeping practices can be used to infer something about agency behavior. In Chapters 5 and 7, we mentioned research by McCleary, Nienstedt, and Erven (1982) as an illustration of measurement problems and how those problems threaten certain quasi-experimental designs. Recall that McCleary and associates discovered that an apparent reduction in burglary rates was in fact due to changes in recordkeeping practices. Assigning officers from a special unit to investigate burglaries revealed that earlier investigative procedures sometimes resulted in double counts of a single incident; the special unit also reduced misclassification of larcenies as burglaries.

McCleary and colleagues became suspicious of police records when they detected an immediate decline in burglary rates following the introduction of the special unit, a pattern that was not reasonable given the technology of burglary. Following the paper trail, they were able to discover how changes in procedures affected these measures. In the same article, they describe similar examples—how replacement of a police chief and changes in patrol dispatch procedures produced apparent increases in crime and calls for service. But after carefully investigating how these records were produced, they were able to link changes in the indicators with changes in agency actions—rather than with changes in the frequency of crime.

Baumer, Maxfield, and Mendelsohn (1993) discovered a similar phenomenon when they detected inconsistencies between court records of juvenile probation violations and other indicators of probation client behavior. (See the box entitled "Home Detention" in Chapter 1.) After locating virtually no instances of probation violations in agency records, Baumer and associates found that arrest histories and data from electronic monitoring showed evidence of infractions. This led them to follow the paper trail through juvenile court, where they learned that juvenile probation staff were only minimally supervising their clients. Becoming more suspicious, the authors uncovered other inconsistencies in program implementation by juvenile court staff.

These two examples point to an important lesson in the use of agency records for criminal justice research: *Expect the expected.* If unexpected findings or patterns emerge, review data-collection procedures once again before accepting the unexpected. In these two examples, researchers suspected recordkeeping problems when data analysis produced results that were sharply discrepant with their expectations. Changing the way burglaries are investigated is unlikely to produce a pronounced, immediate decline in burglary. It is implausible that an experimental program for juvenile offenders will be 99 percent successful. Such clues prompted researchers to inquire further how such suspicious indicators were produced.

New Data Collected by Agency Staff

Thus far, we have concentrated on the research uses of information routinely collected by or for public agencies. As we have seen, such data are readily available, but researchers have little control over the actual collection process. Furthermore, agency procedures and definitions may not correspond with the needs of researchers.

It is sometimes possible to use a hybrid source of data in which criminal justice agency staff collect information for specific research purposes. We refer to this as a *hybrid* source because it combines the collection of new data—through observation or interviews—with day-to-day criminal justice agency activities. Virtually all criminal justice organizations routinely document their actions, from investigating crime reports to housing convicted felons. By slightly modifying forms normally used for recording information, you may be able to have agency staff collect original data for you.

For example, let's say you are interested in the general question of how many crimes reported to police involve nonresident victims. Reading about violent crime against European tourists in South Florida, you wonder how common such incidents are and decide to systematically investigate the problem. It doesn't take long to learn that no published data are available on the resident or nonresident status of Dade County crime victims. You next try the Miami and Dade County Police Departments, suspecting that such information might be recorded on crime report forms. No luck here either. Incident report forms include victim name and address, but you are told that police routinely record the local address for tourists, typically a hotel or guest house. Staff in the police crime records office inform you that sometimes officers will write down something like "tourist, resident of Montreal" in the comments section of the crime report form, but they are neither required nor asked to do this.

Assuming you can gain approval to conduct your study from police and other relevant parties, you may be able to supplement the standard police report form. Adding an entry such as the following would do the trick:

Is complainant a resident of Dade County?
_____ yes _____ no
If "no," record permanent address here

A seemingly simple modification of crime report forms may not happen quite so easily. Approval from the department is, of course, one of the first requirements. And recall our discussion in Chapter 11 on the need to gain approval for research from criminal justice agency staff at all levels. Individual officers who complete crime report forms must be made aware of the change and told why the new item was added. You might distribute a memorandum that explains the reasons for adopting a new crime report form. It would also be a good idea to have supervisors describe the new form at roll call before each shift of officers heads out on patrol. Finally, you should review samples of the new forms over the first few days they are used to determine the extent to which officers are completing the new item.

Incorporating new data collection into agency routine has two major advantages. The most obvious is that having agency staff collect data for you is much less costly than fielding a team of research assistants. It is difficult to imagine how original data on the resident status of Dade County victims could be collected in any other way.

Second, you have more control over the measurement process than you would by relying on agency definitions. Some Dade County officers might note information on victim residence, but most probably would not. Adding a specific question enhances the reliability of data collection. You might consider using an existing crime report item for "victim address," but the tendency of officers to record local addresses for tourists would undermine measurement validity. A specific "resident/nonresident" item is a more valid indicator.

This approach to data collection has many potential applications. Probation officers or other court staff in many jurisdictions complete some type of presentence investigation on convicted offenders. A researcher might be able to supplement standard interview forms with additional items appropriate for some specific research interest. In their experimental study of intensive probation, Petersilia and Turner (1991) obtained the cooperation of probation staff to complete three data-collection forms on each research subject. Intake forms yielded demographic and criminal history information. Review forms completed after 6 and 12 months documented the nature and types of services that probation staff delivered to experimental and control subjects (1991:621). Additional agency records provided data on probationer performance, but the supplementary data were needed to measure implementation of the intensive probation program.

The National Institute of Justice (1996a) has integrated new data collection into routine arrest procedures through its Drug Use Forecasting (DUF) system. As we described in Chapter 6, samples of persons arrested in each participating city are selected four times each year and asked to voluntarily submit a urine sample for anonymous testing. Results are tabulated to estimate the prevalence of drug use among people arrested for different types of offenses. Thus, research data are collected in connection with samples of arrested persons.

The latest wrinkle in this regard is the use of DUF as a "research platform," as illustrated in a study by Scott Decker, Susan Pennell, and Ami Caldwell (1997). You may recall from Chapter 6 that arrestees selected for DUF participation are interviewed in addition to contributing a urine sample. Since DUF began in 1987, these interviews have provided an ongoing source of information about the characteristics of arrestees who test positive for drug use. Decker and associates supplemented the interview questionnaire in 11 DUF sites to ask questions about firearm availability and use. The researchers found no association between drug use and firearm use, but they did discover that gun use was common among juvenile males and especially widespread among admitted gang members. By piggybacking on DUF in this way, Decker and associates were able to obtain information from more than 7,000 subjects at very low cost, which illustrates the principal strength of enlisting agency staff in your data-collection efforts.

On the other hand, having agencies collect original research data has some disadvantages. An obvious one is the need to obtain the cooperation of organizations and staff. The difficulty of this varies in direct proportion to the intrusiveness of data collection. Cooperation is less likely if some major additional effort is required of agency personnel, or if data-collection activities disrupt routine operations. The potential benefit to participating agencies is a related point. If a research project or an experimental program is likely to economize agency operations or improve staff performance, it will be easier to enlist their assistance on your behalf.

You will usually have less control over the data-collection process when you rely on agency staff. Petersilia (1989:442) points out that agency personnel have competing demands on their time and naturally place a lower priority on data collection than on their primary duties. If you were a probation officer serving a heavy caseload and were asked to complete detailed 6- and 12-month reports on services provided to individual clients, would you devote more attention to keeping up with your clients or filling out data-collection forms?

■ UNITS OF ANALYSIS AND SAMPLING

If you conclude that agency records will be suitable for some particular research purpose, then several decisions and tasks remain to be settled. We will mention two of them briefly because each is covered in more detail elsewhere in the book: units of analysis and sampling.

Units of Analysis

As we mentioned earlier in this chapter, archives and agency records may be based on units of analysis that are not suitable for particular research questions. If you are interested in studying individual probationers, for example, you require individual-level data about persons sentenced to probation. Summary data on the number of probationers served each week might not meet your research needs. Or if you wish to examine whether probationers convicted of drug offenses are supervised more closely than those convicted of assault, data on individuals sentenced to probation have to be aggregated into categories based on convicted offense.

A general rule we mentioned in Chapter 4 bears repeating here: It is possible to move from individual to aggregate units of analysis, but not the other way around. Thus, we could aggregate records on individual probationers into groups that reflected convicted offense, but we could not disaggregate weekly reports to produce information about individuals. In any case, if you will use agency records, you must be attentive to the match or mismatch between the units of analysis required to address your specific research questions and the level of aggregation represented in agency records.

Units of analysis can be especially troublesome in studies of criminal justice processes or studies of people moving through some institutional process. This is because criminal justice agencies use different units of count in keeping records of their activities. Figure 12-1, adapted from a report prepared by officials in a New York criminal justice agency (Poklemba, 1988), lists many of the counting units recorded at various stages of processing.

The units listed in Figure 12-1 can be grouped into two different categories: counts of events and counts of cases (Poklemba, 1988:III3). Counts of events—such as an arrest, indictment, or admission—are more straightforward because they are of short duration. Cases, however, may persist

FIGURE 12-1
Units of Count in Criminal Justice Data

Criminal Activity	Apprehension
Incidents	Arrests
Crimes violated	Offenders
Victims	Charges
Offenders	Counts
Court Activity	Corrections
Defendants	Offenders
Filings	Admissions
Charges and counts	Returns
Cases	Discharges
Appearances	
Dispositions	
Sentences	

Source: Adapted from Poklemba (1988:III1–III3).

over longer times that are bounded by initiating or terminating events. Cases are directly linked to individual persons, though in complex ways. For example, an indictment event begins a court case that does not terminate until a court disposition event. Or a prison admission begins an inmate case that ends at prison discharge. Further complicating matters is the multitude of possible relationships between units of count, where a court case can include multiple defendants, each facing multiple counts that can produce multiple dispositions.

The best solution for many research purposes is to define some equivalent to a person—a defendant, for example—as your unit of analysis. This is the approach used by Eisenstein and Jacob (1977:175–176) in their study of felony courts:

■ Indictments and cases are full of definitional ambiguities that vary from city to city. Some defendants are named in multiple indictments whereas others are not; many defendants are washed out of the process before being indicted but after receiving some punishment. Cases may involve a single defendant or many, and tend to be linked together if there are overlapping defendants or indictments. The concept of "defendants" suffers from none of these ambiguities. Using defendants as our unit of analysis permits us to discern the number of indictments each defendant faced, the

number of court cases in which each was involved, and the ultimate [disposition] each [defendant] faced.

Defining individual people as units can resolve the conceptual problems that emerge from complex relationships between different units of count. Practical difficulties may remain in linking individuals to other units of count, however, or in tracing the movement of individuals from one institution to another.

Sampling

It may sometimes be appropriate to select subsets of agency records for particular research purposes. Just as you would not need to interview every resident of New York to learn how residents of that city feel about subway crime, it may not be necessary to examine all court cases to understand patterns of case disposition or sentences.

You will be glad to hear that once units of analysis are defined, sampling agency records is relatively simple. In most cases, a target population and sample frame may be readily defined. If, for example, you want to study the disposition of felony arrests in New York, your target population might be all cases that reached final disposition in 1996. You could then get a list or computer file that contained identifying numbers for all 1996 felony cases and draw a sample using systematic or other sampling procedures we described in Chapter 9. You do have to be alert for potential biases in your sample frame, however, such as a recurring pattern in the listing of cases.

■ RELIABILITY AND VALIDITY

The key to evaluating the reliability and validity of agency records, as well as the general suitability of those data for a research project, is to understand as completely as possible how the data were originally collected. Doing so can help you identify potential new uses of data, as in Sherman, Gartin, and Buerger's (1989) study of hot spots. You will also be better able to anticipate and detect potential reliability or validity problems in agency records.

Any researcher who considers using agency records will benefit from a careful reading of Herbert Jacob's invaluable little guide, *Using Published Data: Errors and Remedies* (1984). In addition to warning readers to watch out for general problems with reliability and validity, such as those we discussed in Chapter 5, Jacob cautions users of these data to be aware of other potential errors that can be revealed by scrutinizing source notes. Clerical errors, for example, are unavoidable in such large-scale reporting systems as the UCR. These errors may be detected and reported in correction notices appended to later reports.

Users of data series collected over time must be especially attentive to changes in data-collection procedures or changes in the operational definitions of key indicators. As you might expect, such changes are more likely to occur in data series that extend over several years. James Garofalo (1990) describes changes in the NCVS between 1973 and 1986. In earlier chapters, we described the NCVS redesign that was completed in 1994. If you planned to conduct research on victimization over time, you should consider how changes in sample size and design, increased use of telephone interviews, and questionnaire revisions might affect your findings.

The longitudinal researcher must therefore diligently search for modifications of procedures or definitions over time in order to avoid attributing some substantive meaning to a change in a particular measure. Furthermore, as the time interval under investigation increases, so does the potential for change in measurement. Ted Robert Gurr (1989:24) cites a good example:

■ In the first two decades of the twentieth century many American police forces treated the fatalities of the auto age as homicides. The sharp increase in "homicide" rates that followed has led to some dubious conclusions. Careful study of the sources and their historical and institutional context is necessary to identify and screen out the potentially misleading effects of these factors on long-term trends.

This example suggests that cross-sectional researchers must be alert for a slightly different type of potential error. Roger Lane (1989:66–67) points out that the tendency to classify fatal accidents as homicides was greater in some cities than in others.

The general point, which we introduced in Chapters 5 and 6, is that researchers who analyze criminal justice data produced by different cities or states or other jurisdictions must be alert to variations in the definitions and measurement of key variables. Even in cases where definitions and measurement seem straightforward, you may run into problems. For example, Craig Perkins and Darrell Gilliard (1992:4)—statisticians at the Bureau of Justice Statistics—caution potential users of corrections data:

■ Care should be exercised when comparing groups of inmates on sentence length and time served. Differences may be the result of factors not described in the tables, including variations in the criminal histories of each group, variations in the offense composition of each group, and variations among participating jurisdictions in their sentencing and correctional practices.

Fortunately, most published reports on regular data series present basic information on definitions and collection procedures. Many BJS publications include copies of the questionnaires used in surveys and enumerations. You should, however, view summary descriptions in printed reports as no more than a starting point in your search for information on how data were collected. Before analyzing published data in earnest, you should contact the issuing organization to obtain details, perhaps in the form of technical reports.

All criminal justice researchers should read Jacob (1984). For more specific details on published data commonly used in criminal justice research, see the book, *Measuring Crime,* edited by MacKenzie, Baunach, and Roberg (1990).

Sources of Reliability and Validity Problems

Before shifting our attention to content analysis, we will conclude this section on agency records by briefly discussing some general characteristics of the recordkeeping process. You should think carefully about each of the features we mention, considering how they might apply to specific types of criminal justice research. It would also be extremely useful for you to think of some examples in addition to those we mention, perhaps discussing them with your instructor or others in your class.

Social Production of Data   Virtually all criminal justice recordkeeping is a social process. By this we mean that indicators of arrest, juvenile probation violations, court convictions, or rule infractions by prison inmates reflect decisions made by criminal justice officials in addition to the actual behavior of juvenile or adult offenders. As Baumer, Maxfield, and Mendelsohn state, "Researchers must realize that performance measures are *composites* of offenders' behavior, organizational capacity to detect behavior, and decisions about how to respond to offenders' misbehavior" (1993:139, emphasis added). A small number of classic articles illustrate the social production of crime records by police (Kitsuse and Cicourel, 1963; Black, 1970; Seidman and Couzens, 1974). Richard McCleary (1977) describes the social production of data by parole officers. They may fail to record minor infractions to avoid paperwork or, alternatively, they may keep careful records of such incidents in an effort to punish troublesome parolees by returning them to prison.

Discretionary actions by criminal justice officials and others affect the production of virtually all agency records. Police neither learn about all crimes nor arrest all offenders that come to their attention. Similarly, prosecutors, probation officers, and corrections staff are selectively attentive to charges filed or to rule violations by probationers and inmates. At a more general level, the degree of attention state legislatures and criminal justice officials devote to various crime problems varies over time. Tolerance of such behaviors as child abuse, drug use, acquaintance rape, and even alcohol consumption has changed over the years.

Agency Data Are Not Designed for Research   In many cases, criminal justice officials collect data because the law requires them to do so. Even more generally, agencies most commonly collect data for their own use, not for the use of researchers. Court disposition records are maintained in part because of legal mandates, and such records are designed for the use of judges, prosecutors, and other officials. Recordkeeping procedures reflect internal needs and directives from higher authorities. As a consequence, you might find it difficult to adapt agency records for your specific research purpose.

For example, Maxfield once wished to trace court dispositions for arrests made by individual police officers in Louisville, Kentucky. "No problem," he was assured by a deputy prosecutor, "we keep all disposition records on the computer." Following this electronic version of a paper trail to the county data-processing facility, Maxfield discovered that only the previous year's cases were maintained on computer tape. Such tapes were expensive (about $17), and nobody had authorized the data-processing staff to buy new tapes for each year's files. Instead, voluminous computer printouts from the previous year were microfilmed and saved, while the "costly" computer tape was erased for the new year. Maxfield abandoned the project after realizing that data collection would involve viewing hundreds of thousands of microfilmed case files, instead of a quick-and-easy computer search.

The general point is that your research needs may not be congruent with agency recordkeeping practices. Courts or police departments may use idiosyncratic definitions or methods of classifying information that make such records difficult to use. Also recognize that your conceptual and operational definitions of key concepts, however thoughtful and precise, will seldom be identical to actual measures maintained by criminal justice agencies.

Even when agencies have advanced recordkeeping and data management systems, researchers may still encounter problems. The Chicago Police Department, for example, has developed one of the most advanced systems for collecting and analyzing crime and calls for service data. Richard and Carolyn Block (1995) sought to take advantage of this in an analysis relating the density of taverns and liquor stores to police crime

How Many Parole Violators Were There Last Month?

By John J. Poklemba
New York State Division of Criminal Justice Services

QUESTION: How many parole violators were there last month?
Answer: It depends. More accurately, it depends on which agency is asked. Each of the three answers below is right in its own way:

New York State Commission of Correction	611
New York Department of Correctional Services	670
New York Division of Parole	356

The State Commssion of Correction (SCOC) maintains daily aggregate information on the local under-custody population. Data are gathered from local sheriffs, using a set of common definitions. SCOC defines a parole violator as follows: An alleged parole violator being held as a result of allegedly having violated a condition of parole—for example, a new arrest. This makes sense for local jails; a special category is devoted to counting alleged parole violators with new arrests. However, New York City does not distinguish between parole violators with and without new arrests, so the SCOC figure includes violators from upstate New York only.

The Department of Correctional Services (DOCS) is less interested in why people are in jail; their concern centers on the backlog of inmates whom they will soon need to accommodate. Furthermore, as far as DOCS is concerned, the only true parole violator is a technical parole violator. This makes sense for DOCS, since a parole violator convicted of a new crime will enter DOCS as a new admission, who—from an administrative standpoint—will be treated differently than a parolee returned to prison for a technical violation.

The Division of Parole classifies parole violators into one of four categories: (1) those who have violated a condition of parole; (2) those who have absconded; (3) those who have been

---

reports from taverns. The researchers wanted to learn whether areas with high concentrations of taverns and liquor stores generated a disproportionate number of crime reports where police had indicated "tavern or liquor store." Since the Chicago Police Department recorded addresses and type of location, and the city Department of Revenue recorded addresses for liquor license holders, the task seemed straightforward enough: Match the addresses from the two data sources and analyze the correspondence between crime and liquor establishments.

It wasn't so simple. The Blocks discovered inconsistent recording of addresses in crime reports. Sometimes police approximated a location by recording the nearest intersection—"Clark and Division." Some large establishments spanned several street addresses, and police recorded one address when the liquor license data had a different address. Other times police recorded the name of the tavern—"Red Rooster on Wilson Avenue." In sum, police recorded addresses to meet their needs—to locate a tavern or liquor store so that officers could find it—while the Department of Revenue recorded a precise address on a license application. Each address was accurate for each agency's purpose, but addresses did not match in about 40 percent of the cases analyzed by Richard and Carolyn Block.

For another example of how definitional differences can be traced to different agency needs, see the box entitled "How Many Parole Violators Were There Last Month?"

Tracking People, Not Patterns At the operational level, most officials in criminal justice organizations are more interested in keeping track of indi-

arrested for a new crime; and (4) those who have been convicted of a new crime. Once again, this makes sense, since the Division of Parole is responsible for monitoring parolee performance and wishes to distinguish different types of parole violations. The Division also classifies a parole violation as either alleged (yet to be confirmed by a Parole Board) or actual (the violation has been confirmed and entered into the parolee's file). Further differences in the fluid status of parolees and their violations, together with differences between New York City and other areas, add to the confusion.

Taking the varying persectives and roles of these three organizations into account, answers to the "How many" question can be made more specific:

SCOC: Last month, there were 611 alleged parole violators who are believed to have violated a condition of their parole by being arrested for a new offense, and are being held in upstate New York jails.

DOCS: Last month, there were 670 actual parole violators who have been judged to have violated a condition of their parole, and are counted among the backlog of persons ready for admission to state correctional facilities.

Parole Division: Last month, 356 parolees from the Division's aggregate population were actually removed from the Division's caseload and were en route to DOCS.

One of the major reasons that agency counts do not match is that agency information systems have been developed to meet internal operational needs. A systemwide perspective is lacking. Questions that depend on data from more than one agency are often impossible to answer with confidence. Recognize also that the availability and quality of state data depend on data from local agencies.

As stated above, the best answer to the question is: It depends.

Source: Adapted from Poklemba (1988:I1–I3).

---

vidual cases than in examining patterns. Police patrol officers and investigators deal with individual calls for service, arrests, or case files. Prosecutors and judges are most attentive to court dockets and clearing individual cases, while corrections officials maintain records on individual inmates. Although each organization produces summary reports on weekly, monthly, or annual activity, officials tend to be much more interested in individual cases. Michael Geerken (1994) makes this point clearly in his discussion of problems researchers are likely to encounter in analyzing police arrest records. Few rap sheet databases are regularly reviewed for accuracy; rather they simply accumulate arrest records submitted by individual officers.

With recent advances in computer and telecommunications technology, more justice agen-

cies are developing the capability to analyze data in addition to tracing individual cases. Crime analysis by police tracks spatial patterns of recent incidents; prosecutors are attentive to their scorecards; state corrections intake facilities consider prison capacity, security classification, and program availability in deciding where to send new admissions.

As problem-oriented and community approaches to policing become more widely adopted, many law enforcement agencies have improved their recordkeeping and crime analysis practices. For example, New York City's sharp reduction in reported crime for the years 1994–1996 is linked to the use of crime data by police managers to plan and evaluate specific anticrime tactics (Kelling and Coles, 1996). This illustrates an important general principle about the accuracy of agency-produced data: When agency managers routinely use data to make decisions, they will be more attentive to data quality.

However, recordkeeping systems used in most cities today are still designed more to track individual cases than to produce data for management or research purposes. This does not mean that computerized criminal history, court disposition, or prison intake records are of little use to researchers. However, you should be aware that even state-of-the-art systems may not be readily adaptable for research purposes. The Louisville system described above was fine for the needs of court staff who might have to check on some individual past case, but it was virtually unusable for Maxfield's research, which required data about patterns of dispositions.

Error Increases with Volume   There is a greater potential for clerical errors as the number of clerical entries increases. This seemingly obvious point is nonetheless important to keep in mind when analyzing criminal justice records. Sherman and Cohn (1989:34) describe the "mirror effect" of duplicate CFS records. Handling a large volume of CFS, phone operators in Minneapolis, or any large city for that matter, are not always able to distinguish duplicate reports of the same incident. An updated report about a CFS may be treated as a new incident. In either case, duplicate data result. McCleary, Nienstedt, and Erven (1982) describe a similar problem with burglary reports.

The relationship between volume of data entry and the potential for error can be especially troublesome for studies of relatively rare crimes or incidents. Although murder is uncommon compared to other crimes, information about individual homicides might be keyed into a computer by the same clerk who inputs data on parking violations. If a murder record is just one case among hundreds of parking tickets and petty thefts awaiting a clerk, there is no guarantee that the rare event will be treated any differently than the everyday ones.

While preparing a briefing for an Indianapolis commission on violence, Maxfield discovered that a single incident in which four people were murdered in a rural area appeared twice in computerized FBI homicide records. This was traced to the fact that officers from two agencies—sheriff's deputies and state police—investigated the crime, and each agency filed a report with the FBI. But the thousands of murders entered into FBI computer files for that year obscured the fact that duplicate records had been keyed in for one multiple murder in Indiana. See Loftin (1986) for a discussion of different types of error in murder records. For all their advantages, computers have the capacity to magnify clerical error with a vengeance.

In concluding our lengthy discussion of agency records, we do not mean to leave you with the impression that data produced by and for criminal justice organizations are fatally flawed. Thousands of studies making appropriate use of such data are produced each year. It is, however, essential that researchers understand potential sources of reliability and validity problems, together with how they can be overcome. Public agencies do not normally collect information for research purposes. The data they do collect often reflect discretionary decisions by numerous individuals. And, like any large-scale human activity, making observations on large numbers of people and processes inevitably produces some error.

■ CONTENT ANALYSIS

Content analysis methods may be applied to virtually any form of communication. Among the possible artifacts for study are books, magazines, newspapers, songs, speeches, letters, laws, and constitutions, as well as any components or collections of these. Suppose for a moment that you're interested in violence on television. Maybe you suspect that the manufacturers of men's products are more likely to sponsor violent TV shows than are other kinds of sponsors. Content analysis would be the best way of finding out if that's true.

Briefly, here's what you should do. First, you develop operational definitions of the two key variables in your inquiry: men's products and violence. Our later discussion of coding will explore some of the ways you can do that. Ultimately, you need a plan that allows you to watch television, classify sponsors, and rate the degree of violence on particular shows. Next, you have to decide what to watch: (1) what stations to watch, (2) for what days or period, and (3) at what hours. Then you stock up on some snacks and start watching, classifying, and recording. Once you have completed your observations, you can analyze the data you collected and determine whether men's product manufacturers sponsor more blood and gore than other sponsors.

Content analysis, then, is particularly well suited to the study of communications and to answering the classic question of communications research: Who says what, to whom, why, how, and with what effect? As a mode of observation, content analysis requires a considered handling of the *what*, and the analysis of data collected in this mode, as in others, addresses the *why* and *with what effect*.

Units of Analysis and Sampling in Content Analysis

In the study of communications, as in the study of people, it is usually impossible to directly observe all that interests you. In your study of television violence and sponsorship, you'd be well advised not to watch everything that's broadcast. It wouldn't be possible, and your brain would probably short-circuit before you got close to discovering that for yourself. Usually, then, it's appropriate to sample. Let's begin by looking again at units of analysis and then review some of the sampling techniques that might be applied to them in content analysis.

You'll recall from our earlier discussion in this chapter that determining appropriate units of analysis—the individual units about which or whom descriptive and explanatory statements are to be made—can be a complicated task. For example, we may wish to compare crime rates of different cities in terms of their sizes, geographic regions, racial composition, and other differences. Even though the characteristics of these cities are partly a function of the behaviors and characteristics of their individual residents, the cities would ultimately be the units of analysis.

The complexity of this issue is often more apparent in content analysis than in other research methods. That is especially the case when the units of observation differ from the units of analysis. A few examples should clarify this distinction.

Let's suppose we want to find out whether criminal law or civil law makes the most distinctions between juveniles and adults. In this instance, individual laws are both the units of observation and the units of analysis. We might select a sample of a state's criminal and civil laws and then categorize each law by whether it makes a distinction between juveniles and adults. In this fashion, we could determine whether criminal or civil law distinguishes more by age.

Now, let's look at a trickier example: the study of television violence and sponsors. What is the unit of analysis for the research question, "Are manufacturers of men's products more likely to sponsor violent shows than other sponsors?" Is it the TV show? The sponsor? The instance of violence? In the simplest study design, it would be none of these.

Although you might structure your inquiry in various ways, the most straightforward design would be based on the commercial as the unit of analysis. You would use two kinds of observational units: the commercial and the program that gets squeezed in between commercials. You'd want to observe both units. You would classify commercials by whether they advertised men's products and the programs by their violence. The program classifications would be transferred to the commercials that are near them. Figure 12-2 is an example of the kind of record you might keep.

Notice that in the research design illustrated in the figure, all the commercials that appear together are bracketed and get the same scores. Also, the number of violent instances recorded as following one commercial is the same as the number preceding the next commercial. This simple design allows us to classify each commercial by its sponsorship and the degree of violence associated with it. Thus, for example, the first Grunt Aftershave commercial is coded as being a men's product and as having 10 instances of violence associated with it. The Precious Perfume commercial is

FIGURE 12-2
Example of Recording Sheet for TV Violence

Sponsor	Men's Product?			Number of Instances of Violence	
	Yes	No	?	Before	After
Grunt aftershave	X			6	4
Reef-buster jet skis	X			6	4
Roperoot cigars	X			4	3
Grunt aftershave	X			3	0
Snowflake toothpaste		X		3	0
Godliness cleanser		X		3	0
Micro-zap computers			X	0	1
Snowflake toothpaste		X		1	0
Micro-zap computers			X	1	0
Precious perfume		X		0	0

coded as not being a men's product and as having no violent instances associated with it.

In Figure 12-2, we have four men's product commercials with an average of 7.5 violent instances each. The four commercials classified as definitely not men's products have an average of 1.75, and the two that might or might not be considered men's products have an average of 1 violent instance each. If this pattern of differences persisted across a much larger number of observations, we'd probably conclude that manufacturers of men's products are more likely to sponsor TV violence than other sponsors.

The point of this illustration is to demonstrate how units of analysis figure into data collection and analysis. You need to be clear about your unit of analysis before planning your sampling strategy, but in this case you can't sample commercials. Unless you have access to the stations' broadcasting logs, you won't know when the commercials are going to occur. Moreover, you need to observe the programming as well as the commercials. As a result, you must set up a sampling design that will include everything you need to observe.

In designing the sample, you would need to establish the universe to be sampled. In this case, what TV stations will you observe? What will be the period of the study, the number of days? And what hours of each day will you observe? Then, how many commercials do you want to observe and code for analysis? Watch television for a while and find out how many commercials occur each hour; then you can figure out how many hours of observation you'll need.

Now you're ready to design the sample selection. As a practical matter, you wouldn't have to sample among the different stations if you had assistants; each of you could watch a different channel during the same time period. But let's suppose you are working alone. Your final sampling frame, from which a sample will be selected and watched, might look something like this:

Jan. 7, Channel 2, 7–9 P.M.
Jan. 7, Channel 4, 7–9 P.M.
Jan. 7, Channel 9, 7–9 P.M.
Jan. 7, Channel 2, 9–11 P.M.
Jan. 7, Channel 4, 9–11 P.M.
Jan. 7, Channel 9, 9–11 P.M.
Jan. 8, Channel 2, 7–9 P.M.
Jan. 8, Channel 4, 7–9 P.M.
Jan. 8, Channel 9, 7–9 P.M.
Jan. 8, Channel 2, 9–11 P.M.
Jan. 8, Channel 4, 9–11 P.M.
Jan. 8, Channel 9, 9–11 P.M.
Jan. 9, Channel 2, 7–9 P.M.
Jan. 9, Channel 4, 7–9 P.M.

Notice that three decisions have been made for you in the illustration. First, it is assumed that Channels 2, 4, and 9 are the ones appropriate to your study. Second, it is assumed that the 7–11 P.M. prime time hours are the most relevant and that two-hour periods will do the job. January 7 was picked out of the hat for a starting date. In practice, of course, these decisions should be based on your careful consideration of what is appropriate to your particular study.

Once you have become clear about your units of analysis and the observations appropriate to those units and you have created a sampling frame like the one illustrated, sampling is simple and straightforward. The alternative procedures available to you are the same ones described in Chapter 9: random, systematic, stratified, and so on.

If you wished to analyze crime stories in major metropolitan newspapers, you might begin with a list of cities and then draw a systematic sample from that list. For cities with more than one newspaper, you would have to develop procedures for sampling papers within each city. Or let's say you were interested in studying how popular fiction depicted male and female detectives. Assuming you did not wish to read all published detective stories, you might consider stratifying by author's gender, and drawing samples of books by male and female authors. As another example, how would you sample movie videos for an analysis of violent acts by and against police officers? By thinking through these examples, you will gain a better understanding of sampling in general as well as of how sampling methods are used in content analysis.

Coding in Content Analysis

Content analysis is essentially a coding operation and, of course, coding represents the measurement process in content analysis. Communications—oral, written, or other—are coded or classified according to some conceptual framework. Thus, for example, newspaper editorials may be coded as liberal or conservative. Radio talk shows might be coded as propagandistic or not. Novels might be coded as detective fiction or not. Political speeches might be coded as containing bombastic rhetoric about crime or not. Recall that terms such as these are subject to many interpretations, and the researcher must specify definitions clearly.

Coding in content analysis involves the logic of conceptualization and operationalization as discussed in Chapter 5. In content analysis, as in other research methods, you must refine your conceptual framework and develop specific methods for observing in relation to that framework.

For all research methods, conceptualization and operationalization typically involve the interaction of theoretical concerns and empirical observations. If, for example, you believe some newspaper editorials support liberal and others support conservative crime policies, ask yourself why you think so. Read some editorials, asking which ones are liberal and which ones are conservative. Is the political orientation of a particular editorial most clearly indicated by its manifest content or by its overall tone? Is your decision based on the use of certain terms (for example, moral decay or need for rehabilitation) or on the support or opposition given to a particular issue, such as mandatory prison sentences versus job training for drug users?

As in other decisions relating to measurement, the researcher faces a fundamental choice between depth and specificity of understanding. Survey researchers must decide whether specific closed-ended questions or more general open-ended questions will better suit their needs. By the same token, the content analyst has a choice between searching for manifest or latent content. Coding the **manifest content**—the visible, surface content—of a communication more closely approximates the use of closed-ended items in a survey questionnaire. Alternatively, you may code the **latent content** of the communication: its underlying meaning. In the most general sense, manifest and latent content can be distinguished by the degree of interpretation required in measurement.

Throughout the process of conceptualizing manifest- and latent-content coding procedures, you should remember that the operational definition of any variable is composed of the attributes included in it. Such attributes, moreover, should be mutually exclusive and exhaustive. A newspaper editorial, for example, should not be described as both liberal and conservative, although you should probably allow for some to be middle-of-the-road. It may be sufficient for your purposes to code TV programs as being violent or not violent, but you may also want to consider that some could be antiviolence.

No coding scheme should be used in content analysis until it has been carefully pretested. You should decide what manifest or latent contents of communications will be regarded as indicators of

the different attributes that make up your research variables, write down these operational definitions, and use them in the actual coding of several units of observation. If you plan to use more than one coder in the final project, each of them should independently code the same set of observations so that you can determine the extent of agreement. In any event, you should take special note of any difficult cases: observations that were not easily classified using the operational definition. Finally, you should review the overall results of the pretest to ensure they will be appropriate to your analytic concerns. If, for example, all of the pretest newspaper editorials have been coded as liberal, you may want to reconsider your definition of that attribute.

Before beginning to code newspapers, crime dramas on TV, or detective fiction, you should make plans to assess the reliability of your coding. Fortunately, reliability in content analysis can readily be tested, if not guaranteed, in two related ways. First, interrater reliability can be determined by having two different people code the same message and then computing the proportion of items coded the same. For example, if 20 attributes of newspaper stories about crime are being coded and two coders score 18 attributes identically, their reliability is 90 percent. The second way to assess coding reliability is the test–retest method, in which one person codes the same message twice. Of course, some time should elapse between the two coding operations. Test–retest procedures can be used when only one person is doing the coding; reliability can be computed in the same way as if the interrater method were used.

Illustrations of Content Analysis

Let's look at some examples of content analysis in action. The first illustration uses content analysis to measure and characterize newspaper crime stories. The second describes content analysis of a different sort of message—body language.

Newspaper Stories about Crime In connection with a larger research project on reactions to crime, Gordon, Reis, and Tyler (1979) conducted a content analysis of crime stories in nine metropolitan newspapers serving three cities. They examined all stories in each newspaper issue from November 1977 through April 1978, coding information on more than 11,000 stories concerning violent crime during that period (pp. 4-1, 5-1). Gordon and associates coded extensive details about crime news coverage in each story. Some of their coding categories defined very specific types of information—what page the story appeared on; size of the article, measured in square inches; presence of photos; whether or not details are provided about victims, offenders, location, and so on. These are examples of manifest content, news story characteristics that required little or no interpretation and could be reliably coded.

Other features of crime news stories proved more difficult to code, largely because they referred to latent content and required more interpretation by coders. For example, each story was classified with respect to bias or slant, as applied to the overall tone of the story. Instructions to coders for this item read as follows: "The categories for this variable represent a continuum: objective—biasing word or two—somewhat sympathetic—biased, slanted. 'Toward victim' [is] construed to include 'against suspect,' and 'toward suspect' includes 'against victim'" (Gordon, Reis, and Tyler, 1979, Appendix E).

As you might expect, it was much more difficult for coders to interpret the bias or slant of a story than it was for them to determine, for example, whether the story was a news article, feature, or editorial. Evaluation of police action also proved difficult to code because a single story could be critical of an individual police officer, yet praise police administrators for handling the misbehavior of an individual officer.

Does Body Language Attract Assault?   Now consider another very different example of content analysis in which seemingly complex communication messages were readily reduced to coding categories. Betty Grayson and Morris Stein (1981:68) began a fascinating article by asking, "Are there specific movements or behaviors that identify a potential victim of an assault and which signal . . . this vulnerability to a criminal?" How would you go about answering that question? Notice the implicit reference to body language, not spoken communication. Grayson and Stein used a combination of data-collection methods—direct observation, field interviews, and content analysis—to produce behavioral profiles of more and less desirable mugging targets.

First, the researchers used videocameras to record, over a three-day period, people walking in a high-crime area in New York City. From tapes of a large number of individuals, 60 were grouped into four categories according to gender and approximate age. There were 15 tape segments each for older men, older women, younger men, and younger women (1981:69).

Second, two groups of prisoners who were serving sentences for assault against strangers viewed the tapes and rated each person on a ten-point scale ranging from 1 = "a very easy ripoff" to 10 = "would avoid it, too big a situation, too heavy" (1981:70). Based on these ratings, researchers classified taped persons with low scores as *victims* and those with higher scores as *nonvictims*.

Grayson and Stein then used a movement classification technique that had been developed for training dancers. Trained dance analysts, unaware of video subjects' victim/nonvictim classification, viewed each tape segment and coded 21 characteristics of body movement for each subject. These included such things as stride length, type of weight shift, foot height, and arm–leg coordination (1981:72).

Finally, researchers compared the ratings produced by dance analysts to the victim/nonvictim classifications by convicted muggers. This step revealed specific body language profiles that distinguished victims from nonvictims. Victims tended to have long or short strides, shifted their weight in two dimensions, lifted their feet when walking, and moved only one side of their body at a time. In contrast, nonvictims used medium stride length, shifted weight in three dimensions (sort of a rolling gait, rather than straight-ahead walking), swung their feet, and exhibited coordinated arm and leg movement in opposite directions (1981:73–74). In summary: "The prime difference between perceived victim and non-victim groups . . . seems to revolve around a 'wholeness' or consistency of movement. Non-victims have an organized quality about their body movements. . . . In contrast, the gestural movement of victims seems to communicate inconsistency and dissonance" (1981:74).

Through this form of content analysis, Grayson and Stein were able to classify the seemingly complex latent content of body language into quantifiable manifest-content categories. You may recognize some similarities between this study and what we had to say about observation in Chapter 11. Information was initially recorded through direct observation, and then those observations were analyzed as communications through content analysis. In much the same way, you might collect data on gang graffiti through field observation, and then use content analysis to categorize messages conveyed by the graffiti.

From these two very different examples, we expect that you can think of many additional applications of content analysis in criminal justice research. You might wish to consult Ray Surette's (1992) excellent book, *Media, Crime, and Justice: Images and Realities,* to get a better idea of the scope of topics for which content analysis can be used. The General Accounting Office (1996) has recently published an excellent guide to content analysis generally. See also the dated but still useful book by Ole Holsti (1969).

■ *SECONDARY ANALYSIS*

Our final topic encompasses all other sources of criminal justice data we have described in this and preceding chapters: content analysis, agency records, field observation, and surveys. We begin with an example of an unusually ambitious use of secondary data by a prolific criminal justice scholar.

For two decades, Wesley Skogan has examined the influence of crime on the lives of urban residents. In most cases, his research has relied on sample surveys to investigate questions about fear of crime (Skogan and Maxfield, 1981), community crime prevention (Skogan, 1988), and the

relationships between urban residents and police (Skogan, 1990b), among others. He has long recognized the importance of incivilities—symbols of social disorder—as indicators of neighborhood crime problems and as sources of fear for urban residents.

In 1990, Skogan published a comprehensive study of incivilities, drawing on his own earlier research as well as on studies by others (Skogan, 1990a). But instead of conducting new surveys to collect original data, Skogan's findings are based on secondary analysis of 40 surveys conducted in six cities from 1977 through 1983. He aggregated responses from about 13,000 individuals and examined questions about the sources of disorder, its impact, and the scope for action by individuals and police.

The secondary analysis of data collected by other researchers has become an increasingly important tool. Like Skogan, numerous criminal justice researchers have reanalyzed data collected by others. Several factors contribute to this, including the high cost of collecting original data through surveys or other means. More important, however, is that data for secondary analysis are readily available, largely due to efforts by the National Institute of Justice (NIJ), the BJS, and the Inter-university Consortium for Political and Social Research (ICPSR).

Are you interested in the relationship between delinquency, drug use, and school performance among adolescents? The National Youth Survey (NYS), which includes responses from 1,725 youths interviewed eight times from 1975 through 1989, would probably suit your needs nicely. NYS data were originally collected by Delbert Elliott and associates (for example, Elliott, Huizinga, and Ageton, 1985). However, like Lauritsen, Sampson, and Laub (1991)—who used the NYS to examine links between delinquency and victimization—you may be able to reanalyze the survey data to address your own research questions.

Or perhaps you wish to learn whether there are differences in the sentencing decisions of black and white judges. Cassia Spohn (1990) addressed this question using data originally collected by

Heumann and Loftin (1979), who were interested in how a new Michigan law affected plea bargaining. Spohn was able to conduct a secondary analysis of the same data to answer a different research question. Let's examine these examples more closely to see how they illustrate the uses and advantages of secondary analysis.

Original NYS data were collected by Elliott and associates (1985:91) for three related research purposes: (1) to estimate the prevalence and incidence of delinquency and drug use among U.S. adolescents, (2) to assess causal relationships between drug use and delinquency, and (3) to test a comprehensive theory of delinquency. The NYS was designed as a panel survey, in which a nationally representative sample of youths aged 11 to 17 in 1976 was interviewed once each year from 1976 through 1989. As we described in Chapter 4, this is an example of a longitudinal study, and it is especially well suited to disentangling the time ordering of such behaviors as drug use and delinquency.

Lauritsen, Sampson, and Laub (1991) were interested in the time order of somewhat different behaviors—delinquency and victimization—that were not directly addressed by the original researchers. A longitudinal design was equally important in this secondary analysis because Lauritsen and associates sought to determine whether youths experienced violent victimization after committing delinquent acts, or vice versa. Given this research interest, they faced two choices: collect original data by conducting a new panel survey, or reanalyze existing data from a panel survey that included questions on victimization and self-reported delinquency. Since the NYS included questions appropriate for their research purpose, Lauritsen and colleagues were spared the need and (considerable) expense of fielding a new panel study.

The second example mentioned earlier differs in two ways. First, the research questions addressed by Spohn and by Heumann and Loftin, who collected the original data, are quite different. Heumann and Loftin studied the impact of a new Michigan law that specified mandatory minimum prison sentences for defendants who used firearms in the course of committing a felony offense. Their primary interest was reductions in plea bargaining by prosecutors in Michigan's largest county following passage of the firearm statute. Spohn, however, used the same data to address the very different question of whether sentences imposed by black judges systematically differed from those imposed by white judges. Her research interest required data from a site with a sufficient number of black criminal court judges, a condition that was met by Detroit Recorder's Court in Wayne County (Michigan) where Heumann and Loftin had conducted their original research.

You may have already guessed the second difference between our two examples: Research by Spohn used data that had been collected from court records, while Lauritsen and associates conducted secondary analysis of survey data. Spohn could have gathered original information from court records, in Detroit or some other city, but was able to address her research question by conducting a new analysis of data that had already been collected from court records.

Sources of Secondary Data

As a college student, you probably would not be able to launch a five-wave panel study of a national sample of adolescents, or even gather records from some 2,600 felony cases in Wayne County. You do, however, have access to the same data used in those studies, together with data from thousands of other research projects, through the ICPSR at the University of Michigan. For more than 30 years, the ICPSR has served as a central repository of machine-readable data collected by social science researchers. Current holdings include data from thousands of studies conducted by researchers all over the world.

Of particular interest to criminal justice researchers is the National Archive of Criminal Justice Data (NACJD), established by the BJS in cooperation with ICPSR. Here you will find the NYS, Heumann and Loftin's sentencing data, along with each of the 40 surveys analyzed by Skogan for the book we mentioned earlier. There's more, including surveys on criminal justice topics by national polling firms, the NCVS from 1972 through the present, periodic censuses of juvenile detention and correctional facilities, a study of thefts from commercial trucks in New York City, and data from Marvin Wolfgang's classic study of a Philadelphia birth cohort. The possibilities are almost endless and grow each year as new data are added to the archives.

And you should realize that the Internet is a virtually unlimited source of secondary data. You can obtain documentation for most data archived by ICPSR and NACJD, as well as health statistics, census data, and other sources limited only by your imagination. See Appendix D for more information.

Advantages and Disadvantages of Secondary Data

The advantages of secondary analysis are obvious and enormous: It is cheaper and faster than collecting original data, and, depending on who did the original study, you may benefit from the work of topflight professionals.

There are disadvantages, however. The key problem involves the recurrent question of validity. When one researcher collects data for one particular purpose, you have no assurance that those data will be appropriate to your research interests. Typically, you'll find that the original researcher collected data that "come close" to measuring what you are interested in, but you may wish key variables had been operationalized just a little differently. Your question, then, is whether secondary data provide valid measures of the variable you want to analyze.

This closely resembles one of the key problems in the use of agency records. Perhaps a particular set of data do not provide a totally satisfactory measure of what interests you, but other sets of data are available. Even if no one set of data provides totally valid measures, you can build up a weight of evidence by analyzing all the possibilities. If each of the imperfect measures points to the same research conclusion, you will have developed considerable support for its accuracy. The use of replication lessens the problem.

In general, secondary data are least useful for evaluation studies. This is the case because evalua-tions are designed to answer specific questions about specific programs. It is always possible to reanalyze data from evaluations studies, but secondary data cannot be used to evaluate an entirely different program. Thus, for example, you could reanalyze data from Maxfield and Baumer's (1992) evaluation of pretrial home detention in Indianapolis, perhaps to verify their conclusion that home detention is more suitable for married than for unmarried persons, but you could not use those data to answer questions about a different home detention program in a different city.

In this book, the discussion of secondary analysis has a special purpose. As we conclude our examination of modes of observation in criminal justice research, you should have developed a full appreciation for the range of possibilities available to you in finding the answers to questions about crime and criminal justice policy. No single method of getting information unlocks all puzzles, yet there is no limit to the ways you can find out about things. And, more powerfully, you can zero in on an issue from several independent directions, gaining an even greater mastery of it.

■ MAIN POINTS

- Much criminal justice research uses data gathered from sources that have had no direct interaction with research subjects.
- Data and records produced by formal organizations may be the most common source of data in criminal justice research.
- Many public organizations produce statistics and data for the public record, and these data are often useful for criminal justice researchers.
- All organizations keep other nonpublic records for internal operational purposes or because such recordkeeping is mandated by law. These records are potentially valuable sources of data for criminal justice research.
- Public organizations can sometimes be enlisted to collect new data—through observation or interviews—for use by researchers.

- The units of analysis represented by agency data may not always be obvious. This is especially true in studies that examine processes, such as the movement of people through institutions. Agencies typically use different, and often unclear, units of count to record information about people and cases.
- Although agency records have many potential research uses, because they are produced for purposes other than research, they may be unsuitable for a specific study.
- Researchers must be especially attentive to possible reliability and validity problems when they use data from agency records. As a guard against such problems, it is essential that researchers understand how such records are produced.
- "Follow the paper trail" and "Expect the expected" are two general maxims for you to keep in mind when using agency records in your research.
- Content analysis is a research method appropriate for studying human communications. It may also be used to study other aspects of behavior.
- Units of communication, such as words, paragraphs, and books, are the usual units of analysis in content analysis.
- Manifest content refers to the directly visible, objectively identifiable characteristics of a communication, such as the specific words in a newspaper story. That is one focus for content analysis.
- Latent content refers to the meanings contained within communications. The determination of latent content requires judgments by the researcher.
- Coding is the process of transforming raw data—either manifest or latent content—into a standardized, quantitative form.
- Secondary analysis refers to the analysis of data collected earlier by another researcher for some purpose other than the topic of the current study.
- Archives of criminal justice and other social data are maintained by the ICPSR and NACJD for use by other researchers.

- The advantages and disadvantages of using secondary data are similar to those for agency records. Data previously collected by some researcher may not match your own needs.

■ REVIEW QUESTIONS AND EXERCISES

1. Consult an issue of a journal such as *Criminology, Journal of Research in Crime and Delinquency,* or *Justice Quarterly.* Scan each article and keep track of the source of data used: interviews, field observation, agency records, content analysis, or secondary data. For studies that use data from agency records, summarize how the agency produced its records. If the article does not present enough information for you to do this, describe what information you would need to assess reliability and validity.

2. Each year the BJS publishes the *Sourcebook of Criminal Justice Statistics,* a compendium of data from many different sources. From a recent edition of the *Sourcebook,* select a table of interest to you and describe how the data presented in that table were originally collected.

3. In New York City, police officers assigned to a specialized gang squad pay special attention to graffiti, or tagging. In doing so, they conduct a type of content analysis to study actions, threats, and other messages presented in this form of communication. Describe how you would plan a formal content analysis of graffiti. Be sure to distinguish manifest and latent content, units of analysis, and coding rules for your study.

■ ADDITIONAL READINGS

Bureau of Justice Statistics, *Sourcebook of Criminal Justice Statistics* (Washington, DC: U.S. Department of Justice, Bureau of Justice Statistics, annual). As its name implies, this annual compendium of crime and criminal justice data is a comprehensive source of information collected by government agencies and other organizations. Organized into six sections, each year's *Sourcebook* presents hundreds of tables, including extensive notes documenting original sources. You can find the *Sourcebook* on the Internet at: http://www.albany.edu/sourcebook

Geerken, Michael R., "Rap Sheets in Criminological Research: Considerations and Caveats," *Journal of Quantitative Criminology,* Vol. 10 (1994), pp. 3–21. You won't find a more thorough or interesting discussion of how police arrest records are produced and what that means for researchers. Anyone who uses arrest data should read this very carefully.

Holsti, Ole, *Content Analysis for the Social Sciences and Humanities* (Reading, MA: Addison-Wesley, 1969). A dated but still valuable overview of content analysis as a method. This excellent book examines the place of content analysis within the context of studying communication processes, discusses and illustrates specific techniques, and cites numerous reports using this method.

Jacob, Herbert, *Using Published Data: Errors and Remedies* (Newbury Park, CA: Sage, 1984). We have often referred to this small book. It is an extremely valuable source of insight into the promise and pitfalls of using agency records. All social scientists should read this book carefully.

Webb, Eugene T., Campbell, Donald T., Schwartz, Richard D., Sechrest, Lee, and Grove, Janet Belew, *Nonreactive Measures in the Social Sciences* (Boston: Houghton Mifflin, 1981). A compendium of unobtrusive measures. This book includes physical traces, a variety of archival sources, and observation and provides a good discussion of the ethics involved and the limitations of such measures.

PART 4

Pulling It All Together

IN this final section of the book, we draw on concepts and ideas from earlier chapters to bring you closer to the actual process of criminal justice research. Having examined the role of theory, cause and effect, measurement, experiments, and different ways of collecting data, we are now ready to see how these pieces come together.

As you have realized by now, criminal justice research can be conducted in many ways to answer many different types of questions. We have touched on different research purposes throughout the text, but the first chapter in this section examines a specific research purpose more closely. Since crime is an important and seemingly intractable social problem, applied research has attracted growing interest from researchers and public officials alike. Chapter 13 describes evaluation research, examining program evaluation and policy analysis. As we will see, carefully specifying concepts and being attentive to measures are as important for applied research as they are for other research purposes.

Chapter 14 takes up the question of analysis. After you have designed your research project, specified measures, and collected data, your attention will turn to a search for patterns and relationships for description, explanation, or evaluation, depending on your research purpose. In Chapter 14, we introduce you to descriptive and inferential statistics. Our goal is to familiarize you, as a research producer or consumer, with fundamental statistical analysis.

Chapter 15, you will be pleased to learn, presents no new material. Instead, it offers two examples of criminal justice research, describing each at some length and pointing out how each illustrates general principles of research discussed in earlier chapters. We think you'll find this chapter helpful as a review of earlier material as well as a valuable resource for future reference (of course, we expect you to keep the book). This way of pulling it all together should help you better understand how the individual pieces fit together.

CHAPTER 13 *Program Evaluation and Policy Analysis*

What You'll Learn in This Chapter

You'll come away from this chapter knowing more about applied criminal justice research. Evaluation studies are conducted to learn whether (and why) programs have succeeded or failed. Policy analysis helps officials anticipate the possible effects of new programs.

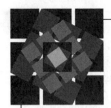

INTRODUCTION

TOPICS APPROPRIATE FOR EVALUATION RESEARCH AND POLICY ANALYSIS
The Policy Process
Linking the Process to Evaluation

GETTING STARTED
Evaluability Assessment
Problem Formulation
Measurement

DESIGNS FOR PROGRAM EVALUATION
Randomized Evaluation Designs
Home Detention: Two Randomized Studies
Quasi-experimental Designs

Nonexperimental Evaluation Studies
Other Types of Evaluation Studies

POLICY ANALYSIS
Modeling Prison Populations

POLITICAL CONTEXT OF APPLIED RESEARCH
Evaluation and Stakeholders
Politics and Objectivity

MAIN POINTS

REVIEW QUESTIONS AND EXERCISES

ADDITIONAL READINGS

■ INTRODUCTION

Evaluation research—sometimes called program evaluation—refers to a research purpose rather than a specific research method. Its special purpose is to evaluate the impact of interventions such as mandatory arrest for domestic violence, innovations in probation, new sentencing laws, and a wide variety of such programs. Other types of evaluation studies—policy analysis—are designed to help public officials choose from alternative future actions. Many methods, including surveys and experiments, can be used in evaluation research and policy analysis.

Evaluation research in criminal justice is probably as old as criminal justice research generally. Whenever people have instituted a new program for a specific purpose, they have paid attention to its actual consequences, even if they have not always done so in a conscious, deliberate, or sophisticated fashion. In recent years, however, the field of evaluation research has become an increasingly popular and active research specialty, which is reflected in the proliferation of textbooks, courses, and projects. As a consequence, you are likely to read increasing numbers of evaluation reports, and as a researcher you are likely to be asked to conduct evaluations.

In part, the growth of evaluation research no doubt reflects increasing desire on the part of criminal justice researchers to actually make a difference in the world. At the same time, we cannot discount the influence of two additional factors: (1) increased federal requirements for program evaluations to accompany the implementation of new programs and (2) the availability of research funds to meet that requirement. Many people know that the 1994 Crime Act authorized billions of federal dollars to support community policing, drug courts, and other criminal justice initiatives. Fewer people realize that the Crime Act also required that most of these new initiatives be evaluated. During the 1995–96 fiscal year, the National Institute of Justice alone spent more than $37 million on research and evaluation projects under the Crime Act. (National Institute of Justice, 1997:5)

By the same token, increased interest in program evaluation and policy analysis has followed heightened concern with the accountability of public officials and public policy. By this we mean that criminal justice agencies are increasingly being asked to justify the effectiveness and cost of their actions. If traditional approaches to probation supervision, for example, have questionable effects in deterring future lawbreaking, new approaches should be developed and their effectiveness should be assessed. Or, if using temporary detention facilities fabricated from recycled semi-truck trailers is less costly than constructing new jails, public officials should consider whether the lower-cost alternative will meet their needs for pretrial detention and short-term incarceration.

In this chapter, we're going to look at some of the key elements in this form of research. We'll start by considering the kinds of topics commonly subjected to evaluation and policy analysis, and then we'll move through some of the main operational aspects of it: measurement, study design, and execution. As we'll see, formulating questions is as important as answering them. Throughout the chapter, we present examples of applied studies, relating these to general research principles we have covered in earlier chapters.

In the final section of this chapter, we will consider some of the special problems raised by evaluation and policy analysis studies in criminal justice agencies. Particular logistical, ethical, and political issues are involved in evaluation research generally and in its specific technical procedures. As you review reports of applied studies, you should be especially sensitive to these problems.

■ TOPICS APPROPRIATE FOR EVALUATION RESEARCH AND POLICY ANALYSIS

Most fundamentally, evaluation research is appropriate whenever some policy intervention occurs or is planned. A policy intervention is an action taken for the purpose of producing some intended result. In its simplest sense, evaluation research is a process of determining whether the intended result was produced. Policy analysis focuses more on making choices about what intervention, if any, should be pursued. Given alternative courses of action, which is likely to be most costly, most effective, or most difficult to implement?

Our focus, of course, is on the analysis and evaluation of criminal justice policy and criminal justice agencies. However, it will be useful to first consider a simple general model of the policymaking process in order to understand various topics appropriate to evaluation and policy analysis.

The Policy Process

Figure 13-1 presents our model, adapted from Robert Lineberry's (1977:42–43) version of a policy system. A similar type of "input–output" model is described in a National Institute of Justice publication on evaluation guidelines (McDonald and Smith, 1989). Although we describe each step in turn, recognize that the policy process, like the research process generally (see Chapter 4), is fluid and does not always start at the beginning and conclude at the end.

The policy process begins with some demand that normally appears as support for some new course of action or opposition to existing policy. Such demands can emerge from within a public organization or from outside sources. For example, newspaper stories alleging racial discrimination in drug sentencing can generate demand for revised sentencing policies, or a prosecutor may independently decide to review all sentence recommendations made by deputies who prosecute drug cases. Before any action can be taken, demands must find a place on the policy agenda. A prosecutor might ignore accusations of discrimination published in an alternative newspaper held in low esteem, or she may decide not to take actions on suggestions for changes that emerge from within her office.

The next step actually encompasses several steps. Policymakers consider ultimate goals they wish to accomplish and different actions for achieving those goals. Does our prosecutor wish to achieve absolute equality in sentences recommended for all white and African American drug defendants, or should there be ranges of permissible variation based on criminal history and severity of charges? Resources must be allocated from available inputs, including personnel, equipment, supplies, and even time. Who will review sentence recommendations? How much time will that take, and will additional staff be required? Since the word *policy* implies some standard course of action about how to respond to some recurring problem or issue, routine practices and decision rules must be formulated. Will sentence recommendations for each case be reviewed as they are prepared, or is it sufficient to review all cases on a weekly basis?

Policy outputs refer to what is actually produced, in much the same manner that a manufacturer of office supplies produces paper clips and floppy disks. In our hypothetical example, the prosecutor's policy produces the routine review of sentence recommendations in drug cases. Or, to consider a different example, a selective traffic enforcement program intended to reduce auto accidents on a particular roadway may produce a visible police presence, together with traffic citations for speeding.

In the final stage, we consider the impact of policy outputs. Does the prosecutor's review process actually eliminate disparities in sentences? Are auto accidents reduced in the targeted enforcement area?

The distinction between policy outputs and their impacts is important for understanding applications of evaluation to different stages of the policy process. Impacts are fundamentally related to policy goals; they refer to the basic question of what a policy action is trying to achieve. Outputs embody the means to achieve desired policy goals. A prosecutor seeks to achieve equality in sentence recommendations; a review process is produced as a means to achieve that goal. Or a police executive allocates officers, patrol cars, and overtime pay to produce traffic citations in the expectation that this output will achieve the goal of reducing auto accidents.

Now consider the left side of Figure 13-1. Our policy model can be expressed as a simple cause-and-effect process. Some cause has produced the variation in sentences for African American and

FIGURE 13-1
The Policy Process

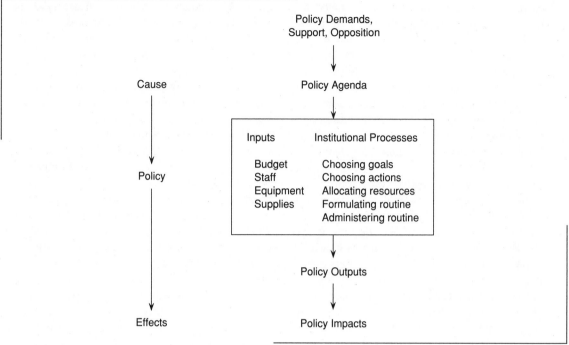

Source: Adapted from Lineberry (1977:42–43).

white defendants, or some cause has produced a concentration of auto accidents. Policies are formulated to produce some effect or impact. In this sense, a policy can be viewed as a hypothesis in which an independent variable is expected to produce change in some dependent variable. Sentence review procedures are expected to produce change in sentence disparities; targeted enforcement is expected to produce change in auto accidents. Goal-directed public policies may therefore be viewed as *if–then statements:* If some policy action is taken, then we expect some result to be produced.

Linking the Process to Evaluation

By comparing this simple model to a general definition of program evaluation in one of the most widely used texts on the subject, the topics appropriate to applied research will become clearer. Rossi and Freeman (1993:4) define program evaluation as "the systematic application of social science research procedures for assessing the conceptualization, design, implementation, and utility of social intervention programs." Throughout this book, we have been discussing systematic social science research procedures. Now let's substitute *criminal justice* for *social intervention* and see how this definition and Figure 13-1 suggest program evaluation applications.

Policy Analysis Activities listed under "Institutional Processes" in Figure 13-1 refer to conceptualization and design. For example, faced with a need to comply with a court order to maintain prison populations within established capacity, corrections officials would begin by conceiving and designing different ways to achieve this demand. Policy analysis is an example of a social science research procedure that would help corrections officials evaluate alternative actions, choose among them, and formulate routine practices for implementing a policy to comply with a court order.

One general approach might be to increase rated capacity through new construction or conversion of existing facilities. Another could be devising a program to immediately reduce the existing population. Still another might be to cut back on the admission of newly sentenced offenders. A more general goal that would certainly be considered is the need to protect public safety. Each specific goal implies different types of actions, together with different types and levels of resources, that would be considered within constraints implied by the need to protect public safety. If officials from other organizations—prosecutors, judges, or state legislators—were involved in conceptualization and design, then additional goals, constraints, and polices might be considered.

Increasing capacity would be the most costly approach in financial terms, but it might also be viewed as the most certain way to protect public safety. Early release of current inmates would be cheaper and much faster than building new facilities, but this goal implies other decisions, such as how persons would be selected and whether they would be released to parole or to halfway houses. And each of these alternatives requires some organizational capacity to choose inmates for release, place them in halfway houses, or supervise compliance with parole orders. Refusing new admissions would be least costly. Political support must be considered for each possible approach. Each alternative—spending money on new construction, accepting responsibility for early release, or tacitly passing the problem on to jails that must house inmates refused admission to state facilities—requires different types of political influence or courage.

Many other topics in criminal justice research are appropriate for policy analysis. Police departments use such techniques to help determine the boundaries of patrol beats. In most large cities, analysts examine the concentration of calls for service in space and time and consider how street layout and obstacles might facilitate or impede patrol car mobility. More recently, many law enforcement agencies have used computerized crime maps to detect emerging patterns in crime and develop appropriate responses. Similarly, problem-oriented policing uses policy analysis to identify patterns of crime problems, devise actions to eliminate the problems, and assess the results of those actions (Eck and Spelman, 1987).

Court administrators often make changes in how cases are scheduled for individual judges after estimating what effects such changes would have; estimates are usually based on analysis of past case volume and predicted future volume. Many states now conduct "prison-impact" studies to estimate shifts in prison populations that would result from legislative changes in sentence length. Later in this chapter, we will describe one prison population model.

Program Evaluation   Note that policy analysis, as we have described it, takes places in the policymaking stage. In contrast, program evaluation studies are conducted in later stages, seeking the answers to two types of questions: (1) Are policies being implemented as planned? (2) Are policies achieving their intended goals? Evaluation, therefore, seeks to link the intended actions and goals of criminal justice policy to empirical evidence that policies are being carried out as planned and that they are having the desired effects. These two types of questions correspond to two related types of program evaluations: **process evaluation** and **impact assessment.** Returning to our example of policies to reduce prison population as an illustration, we will consider first impact assessment and then process evaluation.

Let's assume that corrections department policy analysts select an early-release program to reduce the population of one large institution. Inmates who have less than 120 days remaining on their sentence, and who were committed for nonviolent offenses, will be considered for early release. Further assume that of those inmates selected for early release, some will be assigned to parole officers, and some will serve their remaining sentence in halfway houses—working at jobs during the week, but spending evenings and weekends in a community-based facility.

The program has two general goals: to reduce prison population to the court-imposed ceiling and to protect public safety. Although the first goal is pretty straightforward, the second is uncomfortably vague. What do we mean by "protecting public safety"? For now, let's say we will conclude that the program is successful in this regard if, after six months, persons in the two early-release conditions have aggregate rates of arrest for new offenses equal to or less than a comparison group of inmates released after completing their sentences.

Our impact assessment would examine data on prison population before and after the new program was implemented, together with arrest records for the two types of early releases and a comparison group. We might obtain something like the hypothetical results shown in Table 13-1.

Did the program meet its two goals? Your first reaction would probably be no, but Table 13-1 presents some interesting findings. The prison population certainly was reduced, but it did not reach the court-imposed cap of 1,350. Those released to halfway houses had lower arrest rates than others, but persons placed on early parole had higher arrest rates. Averaging arrest rates for all three groups shows that the total figure is about the same as that for persons released early. Notice also that almost twice as many people were released to early parole compared to those placed in halfway houses.

The impact assessment results in Table 13-1 would be more easy to interpret if we had conducted a *process evaluation*. A process evaluation focuses on program outputs, as represented in Figure 13-1, seeking answers to the question: Was the program implemented as intended? If we had conducted a process evaluation of this early-release program, we might have discovered that something was amiss in the selection process. Two pieces of evidence in Table 13-1 suggest that one of the selection biases we described in Chapter 7, "creaming," might be at work in this program. We defined creaming as the natural tendency of public officials to choose experimental subjects least likely to fail. In this case, selectivity is indicated by the failure of the early-release program to meet its target number, the relatively small number of persons placed in halfway houses, and the lower rearrest rates for these persons. A process evaluation would have monitored

TABLE 13-1
Early Prison Release Impact
Assessment (Hypothetical Results)

	Percent New Arrest After 6 Months	Number of Persons
Normal release	26%	142
Early release to halfway houses	17%	25
Early parole	33%	46
Subtotal early release	27%	71
Total	26%	213

Note: Preprogram population = 1,578; actual population after implementation = 1,402; court-imposed population cap = 1,350.

selection procedures and probably revealed evidence of excessive caution on the part of corrections officials in releasing offenders to halfway houses.

Ideally, impact assessments and process evaluations are conducted together. Our example illustrates the important general point that process evaluations make impact assessments more interpretable. In other cases, process evaluations may be conducted when an impact assessment is not possible. To better understand how process evaluations and impact assessments complement each other, let's now look more closely at how evaluations are conducted.

■ *GETTING STARTED*

Several steps are involved in planning any type of research project, as we discussed in Chapter 4. This is especially true in applied studies, where even more planning is often required. If you were thinking about evaluating a prison early-release program, you would need to think about design, measurement, sampling, data-collection procedures, analysis, and so on. You would also have to address such practical problems as obtaining access to people, information, and data needed in an evaluation.

In one sense, however, evaluation research differs slightly in the way research questions are developed and specified. Recall that we equated program evaluation with hypothesis testing; policies are equivalent to if–then statements postulating that some intervention will have some desired impact. Preliminary research questions, therefore, will already have been formulated for many types of evaluations. Policy analysis usually considers a limited range of alternative choices, process evaluations focus on whether programs are carried out according to plans, and impact assessments evaluate whether or not specified goals are attained.

This is not to say that evaluation research is a straightforward business of using social science methods to answer specific questions formulated by criminal justice officials. As we will see, it is often difficult to express policy goals in the form of if–then statements that are empirically testable. Another common problem is the presence of conflicting goals. Many issues in criminal justice are complex, involving different organizations and people. And different organizations and people may have different goals that make it difficult to define specific evaluation questions.

In most cases, researchers will have to help criminal justice officials formulate testable goals. Other obstacles may interfere with a researcher's access to important information. Because of these and similar problems, the evaluation researcher must first address the question of whether to evaluate at all.

Evaluability Assessment

An *evaluability assessment* is described by Rossi and Freeman (1993:145) as sort of a "preevaluation," where a researcher determines whether requisite conditions for conducting an evaluation are present. One obvious condition is support for the study from organizations delivering program components that will be evaluated. The word *evaluation* may be threatening to public officials, who fear that their own job performance is being rated. Cook and Campbell (1979) refer to this as *evaluation apprehension,* a problem we will say more about later in this chapter. Even if officials do not feel personally threatened by an impact assessment or other applied study, evaluation research can disrupt routine agency operations. Ensuring

agency cooperation and support is therefore an important part of evaluability assessment.

This and other steps in evaluability assessment may be accomplished by "scouting" a program and interviewing key personnel (Rossi and Freeman, 1993:147). Your focus in scouting and interviewing should be to obtain preliminary answers to questions that will eventually have to be answered in more detail if an evaluation is later conducted. What are general program goals and more specific objectives? How are these goals translated into program components? What kinds of records and data are readily available? Who will be the primary consumers of evaluation results? Do other persons or organizations have some sort of direct or indirect stakes in the program?

The answers to these and similar questions should be used to prepare a program description. Although "official" program descriptions may be available, evaluation researchers should always prepare their own description, one that reflects their own understanding of program goals, elements, and operations. Official documents may present incomplete descriptions, or descriptions intended for use by program staff, not evaluators. Even more important, official program documents often do not contain usable statements about program goals. As we will see, formulating goal statements that are empirically testable is one of the most important parts of conducting evaluation research.

McDonald and Smith (1989:1) describe slightly different types of questions to be addressed by criminal justice officials and evaluators in deciding whether or not to evaluate state-level drug control programs:

How central is the project to the state's strategy? How costly is it relative to others?
Are the project's objectives such that progress toward meeting them is difficult to estimate accurately with existing monitoring procedures?

Such questions are related to setting both program and evaluation priorities. If a project is not central to drug control strategies, or if existing information can help determine project effectiveness, then an evaluation should probably not be conducted. On the other hand, costly projects that are key elements in antidrug efforts should be evaluated so that resources can be devoted to new programs if existing approaches are found to be ineffective.

Although Rossi and Freeman describe it as a distinct type of research, an evaluability assessment does not need to be a major project in and of itself. Often a few questions posed to a few people, together with a careful reading of program documents, will yield sufficient information to decide whether to proceed further. If your scouting report indicates that a particular program would not be readily evaluable, it is far better to make that determination before beginning a full-blown study.

Problem Formulation

We mentioned that evaluation research questions may be defined for you. This is true in a general sense, but formulating applied research problems that can be empirically evaluated is an important and often difficult step. Evaluation research is a matter of finding out whether something is there or not there, whether something happened or didn't happen. To conduct evaluation research, we must be able to operationalize, observe, and recognize the presence or absence of what is under study.

This process normally begins by identifying and specifying program goals. The difficulty of this task, according to Rossi and Freeman (1993: 112), revolves around the fact that "goals are generally abstract, idealized statements of desired outcomes." Here are some examples of goal statements paraphrased from actual program descriptions:

Equip individuals with life skills to succeed (a state-level shock incarceration program; MacKenzie, Shaw, and Gowdy, 1993)

Enhance existing probation services (a community corrections program; Austin, Quigley, and Cuvelier, 1989)

Participants will accept the philosophy and principles of drug-free living (an urban drug court; Finn and Newlyn, 1993)

Hold serious, habitual offenders accountable for their actions (habitual juvenile offender pilot program in 13 cities; Speirs, 1988)

Each statement expresses a general but vague program objective that must be clarified before we can formulate research questions to be tested empirically. You probably have some idea what the first example means, but this goal statement should raise several questions in your mind. The objective is for individuals to succeed, but succeed at what? What is meant by "life skills"—literacy, job training, time management, self-discipline? You might also ask whether the program focuses on outputs (equipping people with skills) or on outcomes (success among people who are equipped with the skills). An evaluation of program outputs might assess individual learning of skills, without considering whether the skills enhance chances for success. On the other hand, an evaluation of program outcomes would obtain measures of success, such as stable employment or not being arrested within some specified time period.

In all fairness, these goal statements are taken somewhat out of context; source documents expand on program goals in more detail. They are, however, typical of stated goals, or initial responses you might get to the question: What are the goals of this program? Researchers, however, require more specific statements of program objectives.

Skogan (1985) cautions that official goal statements frequently "oversell" what a program might realistically be expected to accomplish. It's natural for public officials to be positive or optimistic in stating goals, and overselling may be evident in goal statements. Another reason officials and researchers embrace overly optimistic goals is that they fail to develop what Skogan (1985: 38) refers to as a *micro model* of a program production process. That is, officials do not adequately consider just how some specified intervention will work. Referring back to Figure 13-1, you can see that developing a micro model can be an important tool for laying out program goals and understanding how institutional processes are structured to achieve those goals. Skogan describes a micro model as:

■ ... part of what is meant by a "theory driven" evaluation. Researchers and program personnel should together consider just how each element of a program should affect its targets. If there is not a good reason why "X" *should* cause "Y" the evaluation is probably not going to find that it did! Micro-modeling is another good reason for monitoring the actual implementation of programs.

(1985:38, EMPHASIS IN ORIGINAL)

A micro model can also reveal another problem that sometimes emerges in applied studies: inconsistent goals.

For example, Maxfield and Baumer (1992) evaluated a pretrial home detention program in which persons awaiting trial for certain types of offenses were released from jail and placed on home detention with electronic monitoring. Five different criminal justice organizations played roles in implementation or had stakes in the program. The county sheriff's department (1) faced pressure to reduce its jail population. Under encouragement from the county prosecutor (2), the pretrial release program was established. Criminal court judges (3) had the ultimate authority to release defendants to home detention, following recommendations by bail commissioners in a county criminal justice services agency (4). Finally, a community corrections department (5) was responsible for actually monitoring persons released to home detention.

Maxfield and Baumer interviewed persons in each of these organizations, discovering that different agencies had different goals. Sheriff's police were anxious to release as many people as possible to free up jail space for convicted offenders and pretrial defendants who could not be released. Community corrections staff, charged with the task of monitoring pretrial clients, were more cautious and sought only persons who presented a lower risk of absconding or committing more offenses while on home detention. The county prosecutor viewed home detention as a way to exercise more control over some individuals who

would otherwise be released under less restrictive conditions. Some judges refused to release people on home detention, while others followed prosecutors' recommendations. Finally, bail commissioners viewed pretrial home detention as a form of jail resource management, adding to the menu of possible pretrial dispositions (jail, bail, or release on recognizance).

The different organizations involved in the pretrial release program comprised multiple **stakeholders**—persons and organizations that had some stake in the program. These different stakeholders had different goals and different views on how the program should actually operate—who should be considered for pretrial home detention, how they should be monitored, and what actions should be taken against persons who violated various program rules. After laying out these goals and considering different measures of program performance, Maxfield and Baumer (1992: 331) developed a micro model of home detention that indicated that electronic monitoring was suitable for only a small fraction of defendants awaiting trial.

Clearly specifying program goals, then, is a fundamental first step in conducting evaluation studies. If there is uncertainty about what a program is expected to achieve, it is not possible to determine whether goals are reached. Or, if multiple stakeholders embrace different goals, evaluators must specify different ways to assess those goals. Arguing that evaluators should take an activist role, Skogan (1985:49) shows that helping officials specify goals as clearly as possible is a crucial first step.

Measurement

After identifying program goals, your attention should turn to measurement, considering first how to measure a program's success in meeting goals. Rossi and Freeman (1993:112) state this in terms that should now be familiar: "For evaluation purposes, goal setting must lead to the operationalization of the desired outcome; that is, the condition to be dealt with must be specified in detail, together with one or more measurable criteria of success. Evaluation researchers often refer to these operationalized statements as *objectives*" (emphasis in original).

Obtaining evaluable statements of program goals is conceptually similar to the measurement process, where program objectives represent conceptual definitions of what a program is trying to accomplish. As we stated in the first sentence of Chapter 5, "This chapter deals with the process of moving from vague ideas about what you want to study to being able to recognize it and measure it in the real world."

Specifying Outcomes If a criminal justice program is intended to accomplish something, you must be able to measure that something. If you want to reduce fear of crime, you need to be able to measure fear of crime. If you want to increase consistency in sentences for drug offenses, you need to be able to measure that. Notice, however, that although outcome measures are derived from goals, they are not the same as goals. Program goals represent *desired outcomes*, while outcome measures are empirical indicators of whether or not those desired outcomes are achieved. Furthermore, if a program pursues multiple goals, then researchers may have to either devise multiple outcome measures or select a subset of possible measures to correspond with a subset of goals.

Keeping in mind our program-as-hypothesis simile, outcome measures correspond to *dependent variables*—the Y in a simple $X \rightarrow Y$ causal hypothesis. Since you already know what's involved in developing measures for dependent variables, you should also be able to describe how to formulate outcome measures. Pinning down program goals and objectives produces a conceptual definition. You specify an operational definition by describing empirical indicators of program outcomes.

In our earlier example, Maxfield and Baumer (1992) translated the disparate interests of organizations involved in pretrial home detention into three more specific objectives: (1) ensure appearance at trial, (2) protect public safety, and (3) relieve jail crowding. These objectives led to corresponding outcome measures: (1) failure-to-appear rates for persons released to pretrial home

TABLE 13-2
Pretrial Home Detention with Electronic Monitoring: Goals, Objectives, and Measures

Actor/organization	Goals
Sheriff	Release jail inmates
Prosecutor	More supervision of pretrial defendants
Judges	Protect public safety
Bail commission	Better jail resource management
Community corrections	Monitor defendant compliance Return violators to jail

Objectives	Measures
Ensure court appearance	Failure-to-appear courts
Protect public safety	Arrests while on program
Relieve jail crowding	N defendants $\times$ days served

Source: Adapted from Maxfield and Baumer (1992).

detention, (2) arrests while on home detention, and (3) estimates of the number of jail beds made available, computed by multiplying the number of persons on pretrial home detention by the number of days each person served on the program. Table 13-2 summarizes the goals, objectives, and measures defined by Maxfield and Baumer.

As another example, MacKenzie, Shaw, and Gowdy (1993) examined shock incarceration programs in Louisiana, referred to as "Intensive Motivational Program of Alternative Correctional Treatment" or IMPACT. According to program documents developed from state legislation, IMPACT had two broad goals:

Provide a satisfactory alternative to the long-term incarceration of primarily youthful first offenders, thereby helping to relieve crowded conditions that exist in prisons throughout Louisiana

Increase offenders' abilities to lead law-abiding, creative, fulfilling lives as contributing members of society (MacKenzie, Shaw, and Gowdy, 1993:1–2)

After observing different elements of the program and interviewing officials, MacKenzie and associates settled on three categories of indicators that would be examined: (1) inmate attitudes and behavior while in shock incarceration, (2) postrelease arrests or parole violations, and (3) estimated detention facility space freed through diversion to boot camp.

Interviews conducted with IMPACT participants and comparison groups of juvenile detention inmates yielded information on attitude measures of inmates' future outlook and on whether they believed they had learned useful skills. Agency records enabled the researchers to compare arrests, parole violations, and other postrelease measures among offenders in IMPACT and comparison programs. Finally, researchers used the number of IMPACT participants and how long they served in the program to estimate the number of juvenile detention facility beds that were made available.

Measuring Program Contexts Measuring the dependent variables directly involved in an impact assessment is only a beginning. As Riecken and Boruch (1974:120–121) point out, it is often appropriate and important to measure aspects of the context within which the program is conducted. These variables are external to the experiment itself, yet they affect it.

Consider, for example, an evaluation of a job-skills training program coupled with early prison release to a halfway house. The primary outcome measure might be participants' success at gaining employment after completing the program. You would, of course, observe and calculate the subjects' employment rates. You should also determine what has happened to the employment/ unemployment rates of the community and state where the program is located. A general slump in the job market should be taken into account in assessing what might otherwise seem a low employment rate for subjects. Or, if all the experimental subjects get jobs following the program, that might result more from a general increase in available jobs than from the value of the program itself.

There is no magic formula or set of guidelines for selecting measures of program context, any more than there is for choosing control variables

in some other type of research. Just as you read what other researchers have found with respect to some topic you are interested in for, say, explanatory research, you should also learn about the production process for some criminal justice program before conducting an evaluation.

Theory also plays an important role. If you study a program to provide job training so that participants can better compete for employment, you should understand how labor markets operate in general. This is part of a theory-driven evaluation: Understanding how a program should work in theory will better enable you to specify measures of program contexts that should be considered (Weiss, 1995).

Measuring Program Delivery Besides making measurements relevant to the outcomes of a program, it is also necessary to measure the program intervention—the experimental stimulus or independent variable. In some cases, this measurement will be handled by assigning subjects to experimental and control groups, if that's the research design. Assigning a person to the experimental group is the same as scoring that person "yes" on the intervention, and assignment to the control group represents a score of "no." In practice, however, it's seldom that simple.

Let's stick with the job-training example. Some inmates will participate in the program through early release; others will not. But imagine for a moment what job-training programs are probably like. Some subjects will participate fully; others might miss a lot of sessions or fool around when they are present. So we may need measures of the extent or quality of participation in the program. And if the program is effective, we should find that those who participated fully have higher employment rates than those who participated less.

Other factors may further confound the administration of the experimental stimulus. Suppose we were evaluating a new form of counseling designed to cure drug addiction. Several counselors administer it to subjects composing an experimental group. We'll compare the recovery rate of the experimental group with that of a control group (a group that received some other type of counseling or none at all). It might be useful to include the names of the counselors who treated specific subjects in the experimental group, since some may be more effective than others. If that turns out to be the case, we must find out why the treatment worked better for some counselors than for others. What we learn will further elaborate our understanding of the therapy itself.

Michael Dennis (1990) describes an excellent example of the importance of measuring interventions in this type of study. Intravenous drug users were randomly assigned to receive enhanced treatment (the experimental stimulus) or standard treatment from counselors. Recognizing that some counselors might be more skilled than others, Dennis also randomly assigned counselors to provide either enhanced or standard treatments. There was still some potential for variation in counseling within the enhanced and standard treatment groups, so Dennis tape-recorded sample sessions between patients and counselors. Research staff who were blind to the intended level of counseling then rated each recorded session according to whether they felt it represented enhanced or standard counseling.

Obtaining measures of the experimental intervention is very important for many types of evaluation designs. As we will see later in this chapter, variation in the levels of treatment delivered by a program can be a major threat to the validity of even randomized evaluation studies. Put another way, uncontrolled variation in treatment is equivalent to unreliable measurement of the independent variable.

Specifying Other Variables It is usually necessary to measure the population of subjects involved in the program being evaluated. In particular, it is important to define those for whom the program is appropriate. In evaluation studies, such persons are referred to as a program's *target population*. If we are evaluating a program that combines more intensive probation supervision with periodic urine testing for drug use, it's probably appropriate for convicted persons who are chronic users of illegal drugs, but how should we define and measure chronic drug use more specifically? The job-skills training program mentioned previously is probably appropriate for inmates who have poor employment histories, but a more specific definition is needed.

This process of definition and measurement has two aspects. First, the program target population must be specified. This is usually done in a manner similar to the process of defining program goals. Evaluators consult program officials to identify the intended targets or beneficiaries of a particular program. Since the hypothetical urine testing program is combined with probation, its target population would include persons who might receive suspended sentences with probation, but offenders convicted of crimes that carried nonsuspendible sentences would not be in the target population. Prosecutors and other participants may specify additional limits to the target population—employment or no previous record of probation violations, for example.

Most evaluation studies that use individual people as units of analysis also measure such background variables as age, gender, educational attainment, employment history, prior criminal record, and so forth. As you might expect, such measures are made to determine whether experimental programs work best for males, those over age 25, high school graduates, persons with fewer prior arrests, and so forth.

Second, in providing for the measurement of these different kinds of variables, there is a continuing choice: whether to create new measures or use ones that are already collected in the course of normal program operation. If your study addresses something that's not routinely measured, the choice is easy. More commonly, at least some of the measures you are interested in will be represented in agency records in some form or other. You then have to decide whether agency measures are adequate for your evaluation purposes, in the same way we discussed (in Chapter 12), deciding whether agency measures are appropriate for research purposes.

Since we are talking about measurement here, your decision to use your own measures or those produced by agencies should be based on an assessment of measurement reliability and validity. If you were evaluating the program that combined intensive probation with urinalysis, you would have more confidence in the reliability and validity of basic demographic information recorded by court personnel than you would in court records of drug use. In this case, you might want to obtain self-report measures of drug use and crime commission from subjects themselves, rather than relying on official records.

As you can see, measurement must be taken very seriously in evaluation research. You must carefully determine all the variables to be measured and get appropriate measures for each. However, you need to realize that such decisions are typically not purely scientific ones. Evaluation researchers often must work out their measurement strategy with the people responsible for the program being evaluated.

■ DESIGNS FOR PROGRAM EVALUATION

Chapter 7 gave a good introduction to a variety of experimental and other designs that researchers use in studying criminal justice. Recall that randomly assigning research subjects to experimental or control groups controls for many threats to internal validity. Here our attention turns specifically to the use of different designs in program evaluation. Along the way, we also consider appropriate applications for each design type and problems you may encounter.

Randomized Evaluation Designs

To illustrate the advantages of random assignment, consider this dialogue from Lawrence Sherman's book, *Policing Domestic Violence: Experiments and Dilemmas* (1992b:67):

■ When the Minneapolis domestic violence experiment was in its final planning stage, some police officers asked: "Why does it have to be a randomized experiment? Why can't you just follow up the people we arrest anyway, and compare their future violence risks to the people we don't arrest?"

Since this question reveals the heart of the logic of controlled experiments, I said, "I'm glad you asked. What kind of people do you arrest now?"

"Assholes," they replied. "People who commit aggravated POPO."

"What is aggravated POPO?" I asked.

"Pissing off a police officer," they answered. "Contempt of cop. But we also arrest people who look like they're going to be violent, or who have caused more serious injuries."

"What kind of people do you not arrest for misdemeanor domestic assault?" I continued.

"People who act calm and polite, who lost their temper but managed to get control of themselves," came the answer.

"And which kinds of people do you think would have higher risks of repeat violence in the future?" I returned.

"The ones we arrest," they said, the light dawning.

"But does that mean arrest caused them to become more violent?" I pressed.

"Of course not—we arrested them because they were more trouble in the first place," they agreed.

"So just following up the ones you arrest anyway wouldn't tell us anything about the effects of arrest, would it?" was my final question.

"Guess not," they agreed. And they went on to perform the experiment.

Sherman's dialogue portrays the obvious problems of selection bias in routine police procedures for handling domestic violence. In fact, one of the most important benefits of randomization is to avoid the selectivity that is such a fundamental part of criminal justice decision making. Police selectively arrest people, prosecutors selectively file charges, judges and juries selectively convict defendants, and offenders are selectively punished. In a more general sense, randomization is the great equalizer: Through probability theory we can assume that groups created by random assignment will be statistically equivalent.

On the other hand, randomized designs are not suitable for evaluating all experimental criminal justice programs. Certain requirements of randomized studies preclude their use in many situations.

Program and Agency Acceptance Random assignment of people to receive some especially desirable or punitive treatment may not be possible for legal, ethical, and practical reasons. We discussed ethics and legal issues in Chapter 8. Sometimes practical obstacles may also be traced to a misunderstanding of the meaning of random assignment. It is crucial that public officials understand why randomization is desirable and that they fully endorse the procedure. Petersilia (1989: 444) describes how RAND researchers obtained cooperation for an evaluation of intensive probation by appealing to the self-interest of program staff. Staff would be better served by learning what works and what doesn't, a determination that could best be made through a randomized experiment. Staff responsible for delivering an experimental program must understand, endorse, and agree to follow procedures for random assignment.

Minimize Exceptions to Random Assignment In any real-world delivery of alternative programs or treatments to victims, offenders, or criminal justice agency staff, exceptions to random assignment are all but inevitable. In a series of experiments in police policies for responding to domestic violence, officers responded to incidents in one of three ways, according to a random-assignment procedure (Sherman, 1992b). The experimental treatment was arrest, while control treatments included simply separating parties to the dispute or attempting to advise and mediate. Although patrol officers and police administrators accepted the random procedure, exceptions were made as warranted in individual cases, subject to an officer's discretionary judgment.

As the number of exceptions to random assignment increases, however, the statistical equivalence of experimental and control groups is threatened. You should recognize that when police (or others) make exceptions to random assignment, they are introducing bias into the selection of experimental and control groups. Randomized experiments are best suited for programs where such exceptions can be minimized.

Caseflow Adequate for Sample Size In Chapter 9, we explained the relationship between sample size

and accuracy in estimating population characteristics. As sample size increases (up to a point), estimates of population means and standard errors become more precise. By the same token, the number of subjects in groups created through random assignment is related to the researcher's ability to detect significant differences in outcome measures between groups. If each group has only a small number of subjects, statistical tests can detect only very large program effects or differences in outcome measures between the two groups. This is a problem with statistical conclusion validity and sample size, as we discussed in Chapters 7 and 9, and is best understood in the context of statistical inference, a topic we will cover in Chapter 14.

Caseflow represents the process through which subjects are accumulated in experimental and control groups. In Sherman's domestic violence evaluations, cases flowed into experimental and control groups as domestic violence incidents were reported to police. Evaluations of other types of programs will generate cases through other processes—offenders sentenced by a court or inmates released from a correctional facility.

If relatively few cases flow through some process and thereby become eligible for random assignment, it will take a longer time to obtain sufficient numbers of cases. The longer it takes to accumulate cases, the longer it will take to conduct an experiment and the longer experimental conditions must be maintained. Imagine filling the gas tank of your car with a small cup: It would take a long time, it would test your patience, and you would probably tarnish the paint with spilled gasoline as the ordeal dragged on. In a similar fashion, an inadequate flow of cases into experimental groups risks contaminating the experiment through other problems.

Getting information about caseflow in the planning stages of an evaluation is a good way to diagnose possible problems with numbers of subjects. For example, Sherman (1992b:293–295) conducted what he calls a "pipeline" study in Milwaukee to determine whether there would be enough suitable domestic violence cases for random assignment to three treatment conditions.

Maintaining Treatment Integrity Treatment integrity refers to whether an experimental intervention is delivered as intended. Sometimes called treatment consistency, treatment integrity is therefore roughly equivalent to measurement reliability. You'll recall that we described reliability as consistency in Chapter 5. Experimental designs in applied studies often suffer from problems related to treatment inconsistencies. If, for example, serving time in jail is the experimental treatment in a program designed to test different approaches to sentencing drunk drivers, treatment integrity would be threatened if some defendants were sentenced to one weekend in jail, while others served 30 days or longer.

Criminal justice programs can vary considerably in the amount of treatment applied to different subjects in experimental groups. For example, Petersilia (1989) describes how the concept of intensive probation supervision invites problems with treatment integrity. Intensive supervision, the experimental treatment, is defined as increased contact between probation officers and clients. Two types of problems can emerge. First, subjects in the experimental group might not receive enough increased contact with probation officers to constitute intensive supervision. Second, there may be some treatment spillover such that control-group subjects begin to have more contact with probation officers. In either case, subjects in experimental and control groups receive similar levels of treatment, which can reduce the differences between the two groups on outcome measures.

Midstream changes in experimental programs can also threaten treatment integrity. Rossi and Freeman (1993:290) point out that the possibility of midstream changes means that randomized designs are usually not appropriate for evaluating programs in early stages of development where such changes are more likely. For example, assume you were evaluating an intensive supervision probation program with randomized experimental and control groups. Midway through the experiment, program staff decide to require weekly urinalysis of everyone in the experimental group (those assigned to intensive supervision). If you detect differences in outcome measures between experimental and control groups (say, arrests one year after release), you would not know how much of the differences would be due to intensive supervision, and how much might be due to the midstream change of adding urine tests.

Randomized experiments therefore require that certain conditions be met. Staff responsible for program delivery must accept random assignment and further agree to minimize exceptions to randomization. Caseflow must be adequate to produce enough subjects in each group so that statistical tests will be able to detect significant differences in outcome measures. Finally, experimental interventions must be consistently applied to treatment groups and withheld from control groups.

These conditions, and the problems that can result if they are not met, can be summarized as two overriding concerns in field experiments: (1) equivalence between experimental and control groups before an intervention, and (2) ability to detect differences in outcome measures after an intervention is introduced. If there are too many exceptions to random assignment, experimental and control groups may not be equivalent. If there are too few cases, inconsistencies in administering a treatment, or treatment spillover to control subjects, outcome measures may be affected in such a way that you cannot detect the effects of an intervention.

Although these conditions are related to features of experimental design, more often they are practical issues when conducting experiments in natural settings. For this reason, you should carefully think through exactly how an experiment will be conducted *before* beginning. All procedures should be discussed with agency staff who will be involved in program delivery. Staff must both understand and accept the importance of maintaining the integrity of random assignment and experimental interventions.

Let's now look at an example that illustrates both the strengths of random experiments and

FIGURE 13-2
Home Detention for Convicted Adults: Caseflow and Random Assignment

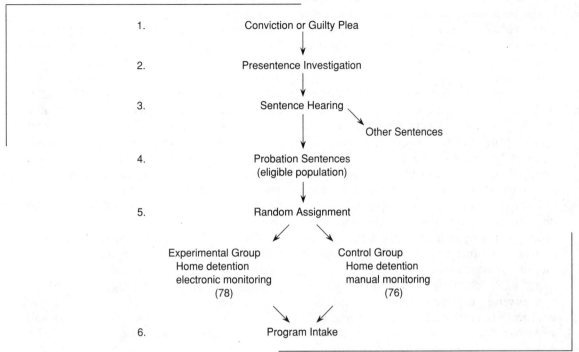

constraints on their use in criminal justice program evaluations.

Home Detention: Two Randomized Studies

Terry Baumer and Robert Mendelsohn conducted two random experiments to evaluate programs that combine home detention with electronic monitoring (ELMO). In earlier chapters, we mentioned how different features of these studies illustrated measurement principles; here our focus is on the mechanics of random assignment and program delivery.

In their first study, Baumer and Mendelsohn evaluated a program that targeted adult offenders convicted of nonviolent misdemeanor and minor felony offenses (Baumer and Mendelsohn, 1990; also summarized in Baumer, Maxfield, and Mendelsohn, 1993). The goal of the program was to provide supervision of offenders that was more enhanced than traditional probation but less restrictive and less costly than incarceration. Several measures of outcomes and program delivery were examined, as we have described in earlier chapters.

Baumer and Mendelsohn selected a randomized posttest-only design, where the target population was offenders sentenced to probation. Subjects were randomly assigned to an experimental group where the treatment was electronically monitored home detention, or a control group sentenced to home detention without electronic monitoring. Figure 13-2 summarizes caseflow into the evaluation experiment. After a guilty plea or trial conviction, probation office staff reviewed offenders' backgrounds and criminal records for the purpose of recommending an appropriate sentence. The next step was a hearing, where sentences are imposed by a criminal court judge.

Persons sentenced to probation were eligible for inclusion in the experiment. Their case files were forwarded to staff in the community corrections agency responsible for delivering the home detention programs. On receiving an eligible case file, community corrections staff telephoned the evaluation researchers, who, having prepared a random list of case numbers, assigned subjects to either the treatment or control group. Subject to two constraints, this process produced 78 treatment subjects and 76 control subjects.

If you recall our discussion of ethics in Chapter 8, you should be able to think of one constraint: informed consent. Researchers and program staff explained the evaluation project to subjects and obtained their consent to participate in the experiment. Those who declined to participate in the evaluation study could nevertheless be assigned to home detention as a condition of their probation. The second constraint was made necessary by the technology of electronic monitoring: Subjects could not be kept in the treatment group if they did not have a telephone that could be connected to the electronic monitoring equipment.

Notice that random assignment was made *after* sentencing. Baumer and Mendelsohn began their evaluation by randomizing subjects between stages 2 and 3 in Figure 13-2. This produced problems because judges occasionally overruled presentence investigation recommendations to probation, thus overriding random assignment. After detecting this problem, Baumer and Mendelsohn (1990:27–29) moved randomization "downstream," so that judicial decisions would not contaminate the selection process.

Baumer and Mendelsohn (1990:26) obtained agreement from community corrections staff, prosecutors, and judges to use random assignment by getting all parties to accept an assumption of "no difference":

■ That is, in the absence of convincing evidence to the contrary, they were willing to assume that there was no difference between the . . . methods of monitoring. This allowed the prosecutor to negotiate and judges to assign home detention as a condition of probation only, while permitting the community corrections agency to make the monitoring decision.

Convinced of the importance of random assignment, the community corrections agency "dele-gated" to researchers the responsibility for making the monitoring decision, a "decision" that was randomized.

In this example, the experimental condition, electronic monitoring, was readily distinguished from the control condition, home detention without electronic monitoring. There was no possibility of treatment spillover; control subjects could not unintentionally receive some level of electronic monitoring because they had neither the bracelet nor the home-base unit that embodied the treatment. Electronic monitoring could therefore be readily delivered to subjects in the experimental group and withheld from control subjects. This treatment was not necessarily consistent, however.

The second ELMO evaluation conducted by Baumer and Mendelsohn reveals how program delivery problems can undermine the strengths of random assignment (Baumer, Maxfield, and Mendelsohn, 1993). In their study of juvenile burglars, they used similar procedures for randomization, but eligible subjects were placed in one of four groups, as illustrated in the table:

Police Visits?	Electronic Monitoring?	
	No	Yes
No	C	E1
Yes	E2	E3

Juvenile burglars could be randomly assigned to three possible treatments: electronic monitoring only (E1), police visits to their home after school (E2), or electronic monitoring and police visits (E3). Subjects in the control group were sentenced to home detention only. As in the adult study, outcome measures included arrests after release.

Although there were no problems with random assignment, inconsistencies in the delivery of each of the two experimental treatments produced uninterpretable results:

■ Observations of day-to-day program operations revealed that, compared with the adult program, the juvenile court and cooperating agencies paid less attention to delivering program elements and using information from . . . the electronic monitoring equipment. Staff were less well-trained in operating the electronic monitoring equipment, and police visits were inconsistent.

(MAXFIELD AND BAUMER, 1991:5)

The box entitled "Home Detention" in Chapter 1 elaborates on differences in the operation of these two programs and a third ELMO program for pretrial defendants. However, the lesson from these studies bears repeating here: *Randomization does not control for variation in treatment integrity and program delivery.*

Randomized experiments can be powerful tools in criminal justice program evaluations. Realizing their potential, the National Institute of Justice has promoted the use of experimental designs to researchers and criminal justice agencies alike, urging each to be creative and flexible in designing evaluation projects (Lempert and Visher, 1988; McDonald and Smith, 1989).

At the same time, it is often impossible to maintain the desired level of control over experimental conditions. This is especially true for complex interventions that may change while an evaluation is under way. Experimental conditions are also difficult to maintain when different organizations work together in delivering some service—a community-based drug treatment provider coupled with intensive probation, for example.

Largely because of such problems, evaluation researchers are increasingly turning to other types of designs that are less "fragile"—less subject to problems if rigorous experimental conditions cannot be maintained.

Quasi-experimental Designs

Quasi-experiments are distinguished from "true" experiments by the lack of random assignment of subjects to an experimental and a control group. Random assignment of subjects is often impossible in criminal justice evaluations. Rather than forgo evaluation altogether in such instances, it is usually possible to create and execute research designs that will permit an evaluation of the program in question.

Quasi-experiments may also be "nested" into experimental designs as backups should one or more of the requisites for a true experiment break down. For example, Michael Dennis (1990) describes how a time-series design was nested into a series of random experiments to evaluate enhanced drug abuse counseling. In the event that caseflow was inadequate or random assignment to enhanced or standard counseling regimes broke down, the nested time-series design would salvage a quasi-experiment.

We discussed different classes of quasi-experimental designs—nonequivalent groups, cohorts, and time series—in Chapter 7, together with examples of each type. Each of these designs has been used extensively in criminal justice evaluation research. Here we will describe situations where quasi-experiments may be most appropriate, along with some cautions to keep in mind when planning a quasi-experimental study.

Ex Post Evaluations Often a researcher or public official may decide to conduct an evaluation sometime after an experimental program has gone into effect. Such situations are called *ex post evaluations* (Rossi and Freeman, 1993:300) and are not usually amenable to random assignment after the fact. For example, if a new job-skills training program is introduced in a state correctional facility, an ex post evaluation might compare rates of employment among released inmates with similar outcome measures for a matched comparison institution. Or an interrupted time-series design might examine records of alcohol-related accidents before and after a new law that allows administrative suspension of driver's licenses to take effect.

Full-Coverage Programs Interventions such as new national or statewide laws are examples of full-coverage programs where it is not possible to identify subjects who are not exposed to the intervention, let alone randomly assign persons to receive or not receive the treatment. Quasi-experimental designs may be the strongest possible approach for evaluating such programs. We mentioned different types of examples in Chapter 7: Miethe's (1987) cohort design to evaluate determinant sentencing in Minnesota, and the time-series study of gun control laws by Loftin, McDowall, Wiersma, and Cottey (1991).

Larger Treatment Units Similarly, some experimental interventions may be designed to affect all persons in some larger unit—a neighborhood crime prevention program, for example. It is not possible to randomly assign some neighborhoods to receive the intervention while withholding it from others. Nor is it possible to control which individuals in a neighborhood are exposed to the intervention. Different types of quasi-experimental designs can be used in such cases. For example, in their evaluation of fear reduction programs in two cities, Pate, Wycoff, Skogan, and Sherman (1986) set up storefront police stations in some neighborhoods. Surveys conducted before and after the stations were opened provided pretest and posttest measures of fear in the treatment neighborhoods and in comparison neighborhoods that were matched on socioeconomic variables and reported crime rates.

Nonequivalent-Groups Designs As we described in Chapter 7, quasi-experimental designs lack the built-in controls for selection bias and other threats to internal validity. Nonequivalent-groups designs, by definition, cannot be assumed to include treatment and comparison subjects who are statistically equivalent. For this reason, quasi-experimental program evaluations must be carefully designed and analyzed to rule out possible validity problems.

For evaluation designs that use nonequivalent groups, your attention should be devoted to constructing experimental and comparison groups that are as similar as possible on important variables that might account for differences in outcome measures. Rossi and Freeman (1993:304) caution that procedures for constructing such groups should be "based on prior knowledge and theoretical understanding of the social processes in question. Such knowledge instructs the evaluator in which specific ways a matched control group should resemble the experimental group."

In a study of recidivism by participants in shock incarceration programs, for example, you would certainly want to ensure that equal numbers of men and women were included in groups assigned to shock incarceration and groups that received some other sentence. Alternatively, you could restrict your analysis of program effects to only men or only women. Our discussion in Chapters 7 and 12 of Widom's (1989a) research on child abuse presents an example of theory-based matching criteria.

Time-Series Designs Interrupted time-series designs require attention to different issues because researchers cannot normally control how reliably the experimental treatment is actually implemented. Foremost among these issues are instrumentation, history, and construct validity. In many interrupted time-series designs, conclusions about whether an intervention produced change in some outcome measure rely on simple indicators that represent complex causal processes. The evaluation of the Washington, D.C., gun control law by Loftin and associates (1991) examined changes in public health records of death by homicide and suicide. These indicators represented complex processes, including motivation, situational factors, and the presence of other persons who might have prevented a murder or suicide, in addition to the primary concept of interest to the authors—weapon availability. The authors could not control for differences in the circumstances surrounding homicides and suicides, and their conclusions about the gun control law's impact assumed that declines in gun-related deaths were not produced by outside factors.

Understanding the causal process that produces measures used in time-series analysis is crucial for interpreting results. Such understanding can come in two related ways. First, you should have a sound conceptual grasp of the underlying causal forces at work in whatever process you are interested in. Second, you should understand how the indicators used in any time-series analysis are produced. The time-series experiments reported in McCleary, Nienstedt, and Erven (1982) present good examples of these two points. See Chapters 5, 7, and 12 to review our earlier remarks about this study.

As another example, Mayhew, Clarke, and Elliott (1989) concluded that laws requiring motorcycle riders to wear helmets produced a reduction in motorcycle theft. This might strike you as puzzling, until you consider the causal constructs involved in stealing motorcycles. Assuming that most motorcycle thefts are crimes of opportunity,

Mayhew and associates argue that few impulsive thieves stroll about carrying helmets. Even thieves are sufficiently rational to recognize that helmetless motorcycle riders would be unacceptably conspicuous—an insight that deters them from stealing motorcycles. Mayhew and colleagues considered displacement as an alternative explanation for the decline in motorcycle theft, but they found no evidence that declines in motorcycle theft were accompanied by increases in either stolen cars or bicycles. By systematically thinking through the causal process of motorcycle theft, Mayhew and associates were able to conclude that helmet laws were unintentionally effective in reducing theft.

Situational Crime Prevention We conclude our discussion of quasi-experimental evaluations by briefly describing certain crime prevention studies that have readily used such designs. In earlier chapters, we outlined the general rationale of situational crime prevention. Carefully considering the interaction between offender motivations and the situations that facilitate different types of crime can reveal approaches to reducing crime opportunities. The motorcycle theft study by Mayhew and colleagues is an example of situational crime prevention, albeit unintentional. Clarke's (1992a) evaluation of caller ID as a way to reduce obscene phone calls, described in Chapter 7, is another example. The periodical, *Crime Prevention Studies,* includes several examples of quasi-experimental evaluations based on the theoretical foundations of situational crime prevention.

One of these is a nonequivalent-groups quasi-experiment conducted by David Farrington and associates (1993) to evaluate different approaches to preventing shoplifting. The experiment was carried out in nine electronics stores operated in England by the same retailing chain. Stores were placed in one of four groups, matched on physical size, sales volume, and type of location. Three experimental interventions to prevent shoplifting were tested: physical redesign of store layout to reduce opportunities for shoplifting, electronic tagging of items so that they would trigger sensors at the exit to each shop, and uniformed guards posted at store entrances. In addition, one store in three of the four groups served as a com-

TABLE 13-3
Situational Crime Prevention of Shoplifting

	Percent of Items Stolen		
	Pretest	Posttest 1	Posttest 2
Group A			
Store 1 (R)	36.5	15.2	27.1
Store 2 (T)	30.8	7.3	4.4
Group B			
Store 3 (T)	17.3	1.4	5.5
Store 4 (G)	10.7	5.8	8.8
Store 5 (C)	15.3	10.4	NA
Group C			
Store 6 (C)	15.4	21.5	15.0
Store 7 (G)	6.9	8.1	18.6
Group D			
Store 8 (R)	24.4	5.0	NA
Store 9 (C)	13.6	29.6	22.0

Note: Experimental treatments: R = store redesign; T = electronic tagging; G = security guard; C = comparison.

Source: Adapted from Farrington and others (1993:108).

parison site, where no new measures to prevent shoplifting were introduced.

The outcome measure was based on a system where labels were placed on certain small items thought to be frequently stolen: audiotapes, videotapes, stereo headphones, and photographic film. Each item was fixed with a sticky label that sales clerks were to remove whenever an item was sold. The total number of labeled items before a store opened for the day was known. Comparing this total with the number of labels accumulated by clerks and the number of items remaining in the store at day's end yielded a count of missing items. Pretest measures were obtained for each store over a three-day period. Two posttest measures were made at most sites, one week and four weeks after introducing prevention measures. Table 13-3 summarizes the grouping of stores with experimental treatments and the results of the evaluation. The figures in this table represent the number of missing tags as a percent of all items that left the store (sold or stolen).

Notice first the different mixes of stores and experimental treatments. The four groupings of stores reflect within-group similarities and between-group differences in matching criteria. The experimental and control conditions across stores in different groups were mixed to compare prevention effectiveness to store characteristics.

Although we have omitted tests of statistical significance from Table 13-3, you can see some interesting patterns in the results. Electronic tagging (stores 2 and 3) reduced shoplifting in both the one- and four-week posttests. Store redesign was effective only in the first posttest (store 1); a second posttest showed an increase in shoplifting, which suggests that thieves learned to adapt to the new layout (only one posttest was conducted in the other redesign site, store 8). Uniformed guards (stores 4 and 7) had no consistent impact on shoplifting. Shoplifting in the three comparison sites (stores 5, 6, and 9) either increased or declined less than it did in matched experimental sites.

Several features of this evaluation warrant comment. First, randomization was not possible because the experimental treatment was delivered to a small number of large units—electronics stores. Second, Farrington and associates used matching criteria that could reasonably be expected to affect shoplifting rates. A related point is that all sites were franchise stores owned by the same large chain, which minimized differences in inventory mixes, management procedures, and the like. Third, the three experimental conditions were mixed and tested in different groups of matched stores. This produces a stronger test of the relative effectiveness of different prevention measures.

Finally, consider for a moment the degree of cooperation required between researchers and evaluation clients. Farrington and colleagues required some effort of store staff in collecting and counting tagged items, not to mention implementing different crime prevention measures. On the other hand, you should also see the potential benefits to retail stores from this quasi-experiment to determine what works in preventing shoplifting.

Nonexperimental Evaluation Studies

Random assignment, the ability to manipulate an experimental intervention, and other controls over experimental conditions are the general hallmarks of experimental designs. We have described quasi-experimental designs as those studies that are "sort of" experimental. By using matched comparison groups or time-series designs, we can incorporate many of the controls required to rule out alternative explanations for evaluation findings into nonrandomized designs. But what about situations where it is not possible to use comparison groups or to otherwise manipulate experimental conditions? Or what if a planned randomized study breaks down: inadequate caseflow, too many exceptions to random assignment, or too much variation in experimental interventions?

In many cases, useful evaluations may be performed even if requirements for experimental or quasi-experimental designs cannot be met. This is also true for evaluations initially designed with more rigorous experimental conditions that cannot be maintained. Nonexperimental evaluations, or case studies, may provide useful information to policymakers and other public officials. The study of pretrial ELMO conducted by Maxfield and Baumer (1992:316) is a good example:

■ An earlier attempt (not by the present authors) to evaluate pretrial home detention through a randomized experiment was terminated because of caseflow problems and treatment contamination. The current effort may be viewed as a salvage operation: a nonexperimental ex post evaluation . . . that was undertaken both to provide guidance to local officials, and to contribute to the small but growing body of literature on this increasingly popular alternative to incarceration [ELMO].[1]

The researchers examined program goals and objectives and developed measures of program success, as summarized earlier in Table 13-2. Maxfield and Baumer also compared results from their pretrial study to two randomized evaluations of ELMO, as reported in Baumer, Maxfield, and Mendelsohn (1993).

---

[1] Maxfield confesses to a certain fascination with Travis McGee, a salvage consultant operating out of Fort Lauderdale, whose fictional exploits were portrayed by the late John MacDonald. In the same spirit, one member of the project's advisory board described this as a "scrap metal" design.

In addition, they used what Rossi and Freeman (1993) referred to as *generic controls,* comparing failure-to-appear rates and new arrests with similar measures for persons assigned to other pretrial dispositions—release on recognizance and release on surety bond. In the absence of a matched comparison group, it is sometimes possible to compare subjects who receive some experimental treatment to a larger pool or class of similarly situated persons. You have probably seen generic controls used informally, as when newspaper reports compare crime rates in some city to nationwide average crime rates. Noncriminal justice examples are common: infant mortality rates, HIV-positive prevalence, or SAT scores. Generic controls are poor substitutes for matched comparison groups, but they may nonetheless afford some guidance to public officials anxious to compare program results to something. In other words, generic controls are usually better than no controls.

Whenever possible, randomized or quasi-experimental evaluations should be conducted. When this is not possible, a salvage evaluation or case study may be appropriate. Case studies can sometimes be designed to satisfy the definition of program evaluation we quoted at the beginning of this chapter, by systematically applying social science research procedures to examine some individual program or agency.

Our general advice in this regard is simple: Do the best you can. This requires two things: (1) understanding the strengths and limits of social science research procedures and (2) carefully diagnosing what is needed and what is possible in some particular application. Only by understanding possible methods and necessary program constraints can you properly judge whether any kind of evaluation study is worth undertaking with an experimental, quasi-experimental, or nonexperimental design, or whether an evaluation should not be undertaken at all.

Other Types of Evaluation Studies

Earlier in this chapter, we distinguished process evaluations from impact assessments. While the latter seek answers to questions about program effects, process evaluations monitor program implementation, asking whether programs are being delivered as intended.

Process evaluations can be invaluable aids in interpreting results from an impact assessment. We described how Baumer and Mendelsohn were better able to understand outcome measures in their evaluation of ELMO for juvenile burglars because they had monitored program delivery. Similarly, Petersilia (1989) notes the importance of process evaluation in monitoring levels of intensive supervision that were actually delivered to probationers. Without a process evaluation, information about program implementation cannot be linked to outcome measures.

Process evaluations can also be useful for criminal justice officials whose responsibility centers more on the performance of particular tasks than on the overall success of some program. For example, police patrol officers are collectively responsible for public safety in their beat, but their routine actions focus more on performing specific tasks such as responding to a call for service or, in community policing, diagnosing the concerns of neighborhood residents. Police supervisors are attentive to traffic tickets written, arrests made, and complaints against individual officers. Probation and parole officers are, of course, interested in the ultimate performance of their clients, but they are also task-oriented in their use of records to keep track of client contacts, attendance at substance abuse sessions, or job performance. Process evaluations center on measures of task performance—on the assumption that tasks are linked to program outcomes.

So process evaluations can be valuable in their own right, as well as important for diagnosing measures of program effects.

■ POLICY ANALYSIS

Program evaluation differs from policy analysis with respect to the time dimension and where each activity takes place in the policy process. Policy analysis is used to help design alternative courses of action and choose among them.

Because of this, policy analysis is a more future-oriented activity that frequently produces predictions, while most evaluation studies produce explanations.

In reality, the distinction between these two types of applied research is not quite so clear. Similar types of research methods are used to address policy analysis questions that explore, What would happen? as are brought to bear on program evaluation questions that explore, What did happen? Consider, for example, a definition of policy analysis from a prominent text: "Attempting to bring modern science and technology to bear on society's problems, policy analysis searches for feasible courses of action, generating information and marshalling evidence of the benefits and other consequences that would follow their adoption and implementation" (Quade, 1989:4). Except for the form of the verb—"*would follow*"—this is not too different from the way Rossi and Freeman define program evaluation. Results from program evaluations are frequently considered in deciding among future courses of action. Policy analysis depends as much on clearly specifying goals and objectives as does program evaluation. As a result, the achievement of goals and objectives worked out through policy analysis can be tested through program evaluation. Measurement is also a fundamental concern in both types of applied studies. Let's consider an example of policy analysis to illustrate its similarities to and differences from program evaluation.

Modeling Prison Populations

Growth in state and federal prison populations throughout the 1980s and 1990s caught many public officials only partly by surprise. For years, researchers like Alfred Blumstein (1988; Blumstein, Cohen, and Miller, 1980) used mathematical models to forecast future prison populations. More important, such models permit corrections officials and others to answer "what if" questions about future prison populations. For example, what would be the estimated impact on a state's prison population if the minimum sentence for possession of three grams of cocaine was increased from four to eight years? Or what would

happen if a larger proportion of arrested persons have prior felony convictions and therefore must be sentenced to prison under state law? Or will the natural aging of a state's population relieve pressure on prison crowding over the next ten years?

Although the mathematics of modeling prison populations can seem intimidating, the principles are relatively straightforward. Our discussion will draw heavily on prison population models developed in two states: the Pennsylvania model described by Blumstein, Cohen, and Miller (1980) and a model used by researchers in the New York State Division of Criminal Justice Services, Office of Policy Analysis, Research, and Statistical Services (Greenstein, van Alstyne, and Frederick, 1986).

In both cases, model projections are based on data that represent the demographic structure of a state's population, arrest rates broken down by demographic groups, and conviction and incarceration rates broken down by groupings of offenses. Models are first developed, or "initialized," using current population data and past information about criminal justice processing—arrest, conviction, and incarceration rates.

Figure 13-3 summarizes components of the model used in New York State; it shows the flow of persons from arrest through incarceration. The stages labeled "Arrest rates," "Probability of conviction," and "Probability of prison sentence" are based on past cases. The latter two are conditional probabilities computed from past data that represent the percentage of arrested defendants who are convicted and the percentage of convicted offenders who are sentenced to prison.

Two other general features of the box labeled "New prison commitments" are important. First, commitments are adjusted to include past information on sentence length, a factor that obviously affects prison population. Second, a further adjustment is required because of an especially vexing characteristic of criminal justice enforcement and prosecution. As we saw in the box in Chapter 12 ("How Many Parole Violators Were There Last Month?"), it's sometimes hard to figure out what to count. *People* are arrested and prosecuted, but individual people may be charged

FIGURE 13-3
Process Generating Prison Population

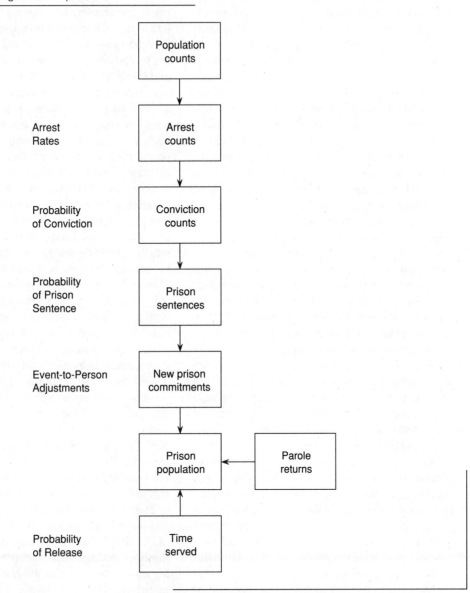

Source: Adapted from Greenstein, van Alstyne, and Frederick (1986:7).

with and convicted of more than one *offense* and more than one *count* for each offense, or more than one offender might be arrested in a single arrest event.

Consider, for example, an armed robbery in which two offenders rob three victims, one of whom is struck in the face with a handgun by offender 1; another is shot and seriously injured by offender 2. Both offenders are arrested the next day when they attempt to buy cocaine from an undercover police officer. This single arrest event could produce two defendants, each of whom faces three counts of robbery and one or more counts of weapon use while committing a felony; defendant 1 is charged with aggravated assault and defendant 2 with attempted murder; both also face drug charges; each has a prior felony conviction that precludes legal handgun ownership. The stage labeled "Event-to-Person Adjustments" in Figure 13-3 reflects the complicated relationships among arrest events, defendants, offenses, counts, and charges that must be taken into account in forecasting prison populations, which are, of course, based on numbers of people.

The next component of prison population models is an estimate of demographic change. As Blumstein, Cohen, and Miller (1980:8) point out, changes in demographic composition are based on three social processes: births, deaths, and migration. A state's population change depends on fertility, mortality, and people moving into and out of the state. Fortunately, these social processes are readily modeled, and demographic projections are relatively reliable. Since arrest rates vary by age, gender, and race, prison population forecasts almost always disaggregate demographic projections into groups based on these three characteristics. Blumstein and associates obtained demographic projections from the Pennsylvania Department of Education, while data from the National Planning Association were used to predict New York's population.

One final category of information is needed. Prison population is a function of intake, length of stay, and exits. We have discussed the complex process of estimating intake and sentence length; the last item is some estimate of exits. Since New York uses a parole system, that state's model incorporates past data on the proportion of inmates paroled to estimate exits.

We now have all of the pieces needed to project prison populations: (1) predictions of future state population, broken down by age, gender, and race; (2) past data on arrest rates for each demographic group, broken down by type of crime; (3) past data on conviction rates for persons arrested in each crime group; (4) past data on incarceration rates and imposed sentence length for persons convicted in each crime group; and

(5) past data on parole release rates. Having entered all of these data into a computer[2] and specified the relationships among all components, let's look at some actual projections.

Figure 13-4 presents forecasts from New York's model, adapted from Greenstein, van Alstyne, and Frederick (1986:65–66). Since we described such models as being most useful as tools for assessing "what if" questions, Figure 13-4 incorporates two scenarios about possible future change. Each scenario is projected with two estimates of parole release rates to produce four population estimates. Scenario A assumes no change in arrests or case processing; its projections reflect demographic change only. Scenario B adjusts for changes in types of arrests. A growing proportion of persons arrested have prior felony convictions, which affects the severity of charges that can be brought against them and therefore both the likelihood of being sentenced to prison and the probable sentence length. Each scenario is modeled with past parole release rates and higher release rates that the state Department of Corrections has targeted for future parole decision making.

According to Figure 13-4, under any of these assumptions New York's prison population would continue to grow through the early 1990s, thereafter leveling off (scenario B) or declining (scenario A). Assuming that more persons with prior felony conditions will be arrested in future years (scenario B) adds from 2,000 to 4,000 inmates. For each scenario, achieving the target higher parole release rates would make a difference.

Now put yourself in the role of a New York corrections official or state legislator. What are some of the things you might consider after studying these projections? You might think about building more prisons, given the likelihood of growth in any case. But this is the most costly solution, and what happens after 1999? Blumstein and colleagues show that the natural aging of Penn-

---

[2]This can be a challenging task, depending on the quality of data for all model components. Maxfield discovered this through his experience in developing such a model for the state of Indiana.

FIGURE 13-4
Prison Population Forecasts

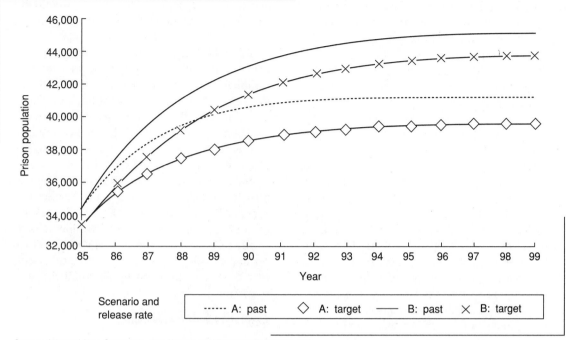

Source: Adapted from Greenstein, van Alstyne, and Frederick (1986:65–66).

sylvania's population will reduce the number of people at high risk of being sentenced to prison. If the same thing happens in New York, you might end up with empty prison cells after the turn of the century. On the other hand, Greenstein and associates (1986:71–72) cite evidence that differences in the future composition of New York's population will not produce any demographic relief. Achieving target figures for parole release rates would certainly help, and you may want to urge that corrections officials monitor this closely. Finally, since corrections policy analysts have noticed growing proportions of repeat offenders, you might want to consider legislative action to revise statutory sentences for habitual offenders. You could then go back to the analysts and ask them to run more projections after incorporating possible changes in sentence length into the model. This would give you an answer to the question: What if we reduced the length of mandatory sentences for repeat felons?

Prison population models are clearly useful tools for policymakers. You should recognize that the accuracy of forecasts diminishes with how far into the future they attempt to project, since intentional or unintentional policy changes may alter the flow of persons through courts to prison. In practice, the conditional probability estimates that form the core of projection models are regularly updated to reflect changes in arrest, conviction, and incarceration rates.

Blumstein and associates argue that error and interjurisdictional inconsistencies in data on criminal justice processing threaten the accuracy of estimates that depend too heavily on changes in caseflow. Demographic projections are less subject to such error and thus should be viewed as the driving force behind estimates of future prison population. On the other hand, the New York model shows that changes in parole decision making can, at least in principle, have a major effect on prison populations.

In any case, the difficulty of accurately modeling caseflow from arrest through new prison commitments is further evidence of the fundamental importance of measurement in applied and basic criminal justice research. Unreliable measures undermine mathematical models and other prediction tools, in the same way that they create problems in finding program impacts or making statements about cause and effect.

Our discussion has only scratched the surface of policy analysis applications in criminal justice. Other examples draw on methods of systems analysis, operations research, and economics for such purposes as cost-benefit studies, police patrol allocation, and making decisions about hiring probation officers. Although the mathematical tools that form the base of policy analysis are sophisticated, the underlying logic is often simple. For example, police departments have long used pin maps to represent the spatial and temporal concentration of reported crime. This example of "low-tech" policy analysis is conceptually similar to computer models of hot spots used in many departments to plan police deployment.

Over the last five years or so, rapid advances in computing and telecommunications have made their way to a growing number of justice agencies, especially police and sheriff's departments. Crime analysis used to be pretty much restricted to studying a pin map. Now, computerized mapping systems permit police to monitor changes in crime patterns on a daily or hourly basis and develop responses accordingly (Block, 1995). Reported crime and calls for service data fueled New York City's "Compstat" system, used in weekly meetings to develop district-level strategies for reducing crime (Bratton, 1995; Kelling and Coles, 1996).

■ POLITICAL CONTEXT OF APPLIED RESEARCH

Applied researchers bridge the gap between the body of research knowledge about crime and the practical needs of criminal justice professionals.

This role is accompanied by potential political, ideological, and ethical problems. In the final section of this chapter, we will turn our attention to applied research, describing some of the special problems that can emerge in such studies.

You will recognize similarities between this material and our discussion of ethics in Chapter 8. Although ethics and politics are often closely intertwined, the ethics of criminal justice research deal more with the methods used, whereas political issues are more concerned with the substance and use of research. Ethical and political aspects of applied research also differ in that there are no formal codes of accepted political conduct comparable to the codes of ethical conduct we discussed earlier. Although some ethical norms have political aspects—for example, not harming subjects clearly relates to our protection of civil liberties—no one has developed a set of political norms that could be agreed on by all criminal justice researchers.

Evaluation and Stakeholders

Any applied study usually involves multiple stakeholders—people who have some direct or indirect interest in the program or evaluation results (Rossi and Freeman, 1993:110). Some stakeholders may be enthusiastic supporters of an experimental program, others may oppose it, and still other stakeholders may be neutral. Different stakeholder interests in programs can produce conflicting perspectives on evaluations of those programs.

For example, in their study of pretrial home detention, Maxfield and Baumer (1992) found support for the program in the prosecutor's office and sheriff's department. Each was pleased by the prospect of freeing up jail space. Decision makers in the community corrections agency, responsible for delivering home detention, were less supportive, expressing concern over the increased workload and fear that too many persons released to pretrial home detention were bad risks. Some community corrections staff were more worried about the evaluation than the program, feeling that their job performance was under scrutiny. The National Institute of Justice funded the evaluation, hoping that results would document a successful program that could be adopted in other jurisdictions. Community corrections decision makers had a different perspective on the evaluation. They wanted to know what worked and what did not work.

Posavec and Carey (1992:36–40) describe such problems as dysfunctional attitudes toward program evaluation. Program supporters may have unrealistic expectations that evaluation results will document dramatic success or may worry that negative results will terminate a program. Agency staff may feel that day-to-day experience in delivering a program imparts a qualitative understanding of its success that could not be documented by a controlled experiment. Staff and other stakeholders may object that an evaluation consumes scarce resources that would be better spent on actually delivering a program.

We have two bits of advice in dealing with such problems: First, identify program stakeholders, their perspectives on the program, and their likely perspectives on the evaluation. In addition to agency decision makers and staff, stakeholders include program beneficiaries and competitors. For example, store owners in a downtown shopping district would benefit from an experimental program to deploy additional police on foot patrol, while people who live in a nearby residential area might argue that additional police should be assigned to their neighborhood.

Second, educate stakeholders about why an evaluation should be conducted. This is best done by explaining that applied research is conducted to determine what works and what does not. The National Institute of Justice, a strong supporter of randomized experiments and other types of evaluation studies, has issued brief documents that describe how evaluation can benefit criminal justice agencies by rationalizing their actions (Lempert and Visher, 1988; McDonald and Smith, 1989). Such publications, together with examples of completed evaluations, can be valuable tools for winning the support of stakeholders. It may be possible to point to other benefits of evalua-

tion. For example, Petersilia (1989:455) describes the generally high levels of support found in the 11 sites conducting experiments on intensive supervision programs: "The project seems to buy local practitioners visibility with the media and local funders, staff enthusiasm (at least initially), and because an outside agency is interested in studying them, added acceptance with their peers."

For an excellent description of the political and logistical problems involved in a complex evaluation that affects multiple stakeholders, see the appendix to Lawrence Sherman's (1992b) book on domestic violence experiments. He presents a detailed report on the process of planning one experiment in Milwaukee, from initial negotiations through project completion.

More generally, recognize that applied research is very much a cooperative venture. Accordingly, researchers and program staff are mutual stakeholders in designing and executing evaluations. In the words of Rossi and Freeman (1993:30):

■ Whereas scientific studies strive to meet a set of research standards set by the investigators' peers, evaluations need to be designed and implemented in ways that recognize the policy and program interests of the sponsors and stakeholders, and that will yield maximally useful information for decision makers given the circumstances.

Among other things, the existence of mutual stakeholders' perspectives implies that applied researchers have obligations to program sponsors, their collaborative partners in evaluation studies.

The flip side of our cautions about becoming caught in stakeholder conflict is the benefit of applied research in influencing public policy. Evaluation studies can provide support for continuing or expanding successful criminal justice programs, or evidence that ineffective programs should be modified or terminated. And policy analysis results can sometimes be used to influence actions by public officials. For an example, see the box entitled "When Politics Accommodate Facts," in which Tony Fabelo describes how

When Politics Accommodate Facts

Tony Fabelo
Executive Director, Texas Criminal Justice Policy Council

THE 1994 federal anticrime bill, and related politics emanating from this initiative, put pressure on the states to adopt certain sentencing policies as a condition for receiving federal funds. Among these policies is the adoption of a "three strikes and you're out" provision establishing a no parole sentence for repeat violent offenders. Facts have prevented a criminal justice operational gridlock in Texas by delineating to policymakers the operational and fiscal impact of broadly drafted policies in this area. Facts established through policy analysis by the Criminal Justice Policy Council (CJPC) have clearly stated that a broad application of the "three strikes and you're out" policy will have a tremendous fiscal impact.

Therefore, state policymakers have carefully drafted policies in this area. For example, during the last legislative session the adoption of life with no parole for repeat sex offenders was considered. State policymakers, after considering facts presented by the CJPC, adopted a policy that narrowly defined the group of offenders for whom the law is to apply. They also adopted a 35-year minimum sentence that must be served before parole eligibility, rather than a life sentence with no parole. The careful drafting of this policy limited its fiscal impact while still accomplishing the goal of severely punishing the selected group of sex offenders.

Unlike Texas, politics did not accommodate facts in California, where lawmakers adopted a fiscally unsustainable "three strikes and you're out" policy.

---

policy analysis dissuaded Texas legislators from costly lawmaking.

Politics and Objectivity

Politics and ideology can color research in ways even more subtle than those described by Fabelo. You may, for example, consider yourself an open-minded and unbiased person who aspires to be an objective criminal justice researcher. However, you may have strong views about different sentencing policies, believing that probation and restitution are to be preferred over long prison sentences. Since there is no conclusive evidence to favor one approach over the other, your beliefs would be perfectly reasonable.

Now, assume that one of the requirements for the course you are taking is to write a proposal for an evaluation project on corrections policy. In all likelihood, you would prepare a proposal to study a probation program rather than, say, a program on the use of portable jails to provide in-

creased detention capacity. That would be natural, and certainly legitimate, but your own policy preferences would have affected the topic you chose.

Or let's say that you deplore racism and racial discrimination in any form. Nonetheless, you know from other courses you have taken that African Americans are disproportionately arrested and imprisoned. You also know that there is some evidence of higher crime commission rates among African Americans than whites. You would probably reject an explanation that suggests genetic or other biological factors as the causes, believing that one race is not genetically superior to another. But how would you feel about a research project that searched for relationships between genetics and crime? Since genetic differences between races do exist, would you feel that such research was racist? Probably not, as we have described it here, but you may know that in 1992 and 1993, the U.S. National Institutes of Health

For my part, I need to maintain personal integrity and the integrity of the CJPC in defining the facts for policymakers. I have to be judged not only by "objectivity," which is an elusive concept, but by my judgment in synthesizing complex information for policy makers. To do this, I follow and ask my staff to follow these rules:

Consider as many perspectives as possible in synthesizing the meaning of information, including the perspectives of those stakeholders who will be affected.

State the limits of the facts and identify areas where drawing conclusions is clearly not possible.

Consult with your peers to verify methodological assumptions and meet accepted criteria to pass the scrutiny of the scientific community.

Provide potential alternative assumptions behind the facts.

Set clear expectations for reviewing reports and releasing information so that facts are not perceived as giving advantage to any particular interest group.

Judge the bottom-line meaning of the information for policy action based on a frame of reference broader than that of any particular party or constituency.

Finally, if the above is followed, never succumb to political pressure to change your judgment. Integrity cannot be compromised even once. In the modern crowded marketplace of information, your audience will judge you first for your motives and then for your technical expertise.

Source: Adapted from Fabelo (1996:2, 4).

---

canceled conferences to discuss research on the link between genetics and crime because of the racial implications of such research.

Ronald Clarke (1992b:28) describes political objections to applied studies of situational crime prevention: "Conservative politicians regard it as an irrelevant response to the breakdown in morality that has fueled the post-war rise in crime. Those on the left criticize it for neglecting issues of social justice and for being too accepting of the definitions of crime of those in power." By the same token, electronic monitoring is distrusted for being simultaneously too lenient by allowing offenders to do time at home, and too close to a technological nightmare that enables big government to spy on individuals. Evaluations of situational crime prevention or ELMO programs may be criticized for tacitly supporting either soft-on-crime or heavy-handed police-state ideologies.

So it is difficult to claim that criminal justice research, either applied or basic, is value-free. Our

own beliefs and preferences affect the topics we choose to investigate. Political preferences and ideology may also influence criminal justice research agendas by making funds available for some projects but not for others. For example, in 1995, the National Institute of Justice (1996b) awarded money for projects to study these topics: "An Evaluation of the Chicago Housing Authority's Anti-Drug Initiative" and "Evaluation of Two Models for Treating Sentenced Federal Drug Offenders." No awards were given, however, for such projects as "The Scope of Institutionalized Racism in the War on Drugs," or "Systematic Bias in Sentences for Crack Possession."

It is, of course, possible for researchers to become instruments for achieving political or policy objectives in applied research, consciously or unconsciously. For instance, the U.S. General Accounting Office (GAO) conducts evaluations of executive branch agencies in order to help Congress exercise its oversight function. Wallace Earl

Walker (1985) argues that GAO staff selectively plan evaluations, choosing agencies that they believe will show evidence of mismanagement. Or evaluators try to steer congressional staff to "request" evaluations that the GAO is eager to conduct.

It may sometimes seem difficult to maintain an acceptable level of objectivity or distance from evaluation results in criminal justice research. This can be further complicated if you have strong views one way or another about a particular program or policy. Most people deplore domestic violence, so researchers who evaluate an experimental program to prevent repeat offenders probably sincerely hope the program will work. However, substantially less consensus exists about other criminal justice problems and policies. How would you feel about a project to test the effects of restrictive handgun laws or mandatory jail sentences for abortion protesters?

We conclude this chapter with one final example that we expect will make you think about some of the political issues involved in applied research. In 1990, the elected prosecutor of Marion County, Indiana—in which Indianapolis is located—was sharply criticized by a series of newspaper stories that claimed to present evidence of racial disparity in drug sentences handed down in the county. Convicted minority offenders, it was asserted, received longer prison terms than white offenders. The prosecutor immediately responded, criticizing the data collected and methods used by the investigative reporter. He also contacted Maxfield and asked him to conduct an independent analysis of drug cases accepted for prosecution.

In the first place, the prosecutor claimed, he had had previous feuds with the author of the newspaper stories. Second, he categorically denied any discriminatory policies in making sentence requests in drug cases. Third, the prosecutor said he knew that the data and methods reported in the newspaper stories were deficient, even though the reporter would not reveal details about his information. Finally, if any pattern of racial disparity existed, it was certainly inadvertent and the prosecutor wanted to know about

it so that the problem could be fixed. Maxfield accepted the project and was paid to produce a report.

How do you feel about this example? Did Maxfield sell out? How would you feel if Maxfield turned up clear evidence of disparity in sentences? Or no evidence of disparity? What about political party affiliation—would it make a difference if the prosecutor and Maxfield identified with the same party? With different parties?

■ MAIN POINTS

- Evaluation research and policy analysis are examples of applied research in criminal justice.

- Different types of evaluation activities correspond to different stages in the policy process. Policy analysis may be used in program planning to help select alternative courses of action. Process evaluations examine whether a program is being implemented as intended. Impact assessments determine whether programs are achieving their intended goals.

- An evaluability assessment may be undertaken as a scouting operation or a preevaluation to determine whether it is possible to evaluate a particular program.

- A careful formulation of the problem, including relevant measurements and criteria of success or failure, is essential in evaluation research.

- For various reasons, organizations may not have clear statements or ideas about program goals. In such cases, researchers must work with agency staff to formulate mutually acceptable statements of goals before proceeding further.

- Evaluation research may use experimental, quasi-experimental, or nonexperimental designs. As in studies with other research purposes, designs that offer the greatest control over experimental conditions are preferred.

- Randomized field experiments are potentially the most powerful evaluation designs. Their use requires careful attention to random assignment, caseflow, and treatment integrity.

- Randomized designs cannot be used for evaluations that begin after a new program has been implemented and for full-coverage programs where it is not possible to withhold an experimental treatment from a control group. In such cases, nonequivalent groups or interrupted time-series designs may be appropriate.
- Process evaluations can be undertaken independently or in connection with an impact assessment. Process evaluations are all but essential for interpreting results from an impact assessment.
- Policy analysis is a more future-oriented applied research technique. However, policy analysis draws on the same social science research methods used in program evaluation.
- Evaluation research entails special logistical, ethical, and political problems because it is embedded in the day-to-day events of public policy and real life.

■ *REVIEW QUESTIONS AND EXERCISES*

1. From a newspaper or newsmagazine story about a criminal justice program, sketch out an evaluation design for that program. Be especially attentive to program goals. Are they clearly stated in the story, or would you require more information to specify evaluable goals?

2. Program evaluation studies are usually less concerned with external validity than basic research studies. Why is this the case? (You may want to review the discussion of external validity in Chapters 3 and 7.)

3. When programs do not achieve their expected results, it's due to one of two things: (a) the program was not a good idea to begin with or (b) it was a good idea but was not implemented properly. Discuss why it would be necessary to conduct both a process and an impact evaluation to learn why a program failed.

■ *ADDITIONAL READINGS*

Connell, James P., Kubisch, Anne C., Schorr, Lisbeth B., and Weiss, Carol H. (eds.), *New Approaches to Evaluating Community Initiatives: Concepts, Methods, and Contexts* (Washington, DC: Aspen Institute, 1995). Although this collection of essays is not specific to criminal justice, it offers much useful advice. Many of the chapters are best suited to readers who have a background in evaluation, but the chapter by Carol Weiss, "Nothing As Practical As Good Theory," is an excellent guide to the importance of thinking through the rationale underlying a program.

Kennedy, David M., and Moore, Mark H., "Underwriting the Risky Investment in Community Policing: What Social Science Should Be Doing to Evaluate Community Policing," *The Justice System Journal,* Vol. 17, no. 3 (1995), pp. 271–289. Kennedy and Moore describe how fundamental characteristics of community policing present problems in the use of traditional evaluation techniques. Although they do not propose specific solutions, their essay is an excellent discussion of the need for a flexible approach to evaluation.

Lempert, Richard O., and Visher, Christy A., *Randomized Field Experiments in Criminal Justice Agencies* (Washington, DC: U.S. Department of Justice, Office of Justice Programs, National Institute of Justice, 1988). Designed to be read by criminal justice professionals, this short report provides an excellent introduction to the value of experimental designs for program evaluations in criminal justice.

Pawson, Ray, and Tilley, Nick, "What Works in Evaluation Research?" *British Journal of Criminology,* Vol. 34 (1994), pp. 291–306. The authors criticize the inappropriate use of experimental and quasi-experimental designs in criminal justice evaluation. Although they overstate their case somewhat, this is a valuable discussion of the problems one encounters in doing applied research.

Petersilia, Joan, "Implementing Randomized Experiments: Lessons from BJA's Intensive Supervision Project," *Evaluation Review,* Vol. 13 (1989), pp. 435–458. This article describes the practical difficulties frequently encountered in randomized field experiments, together with how RAND Corporation researchers dealt with them.

Rossi, Peter H., and Freeman, Howard E., *Evaluation: A Systematic Approach,* 5th ed. (Newbury Park, CA: Sage, 1993). Of the many available "handbooks" on evaluation methods, this is the most widely read. Although the book is uneven in its coverage of recent developments, Rossi and Freeman provide a good general foundation in evaluation methods.

14 Interpreting Data

What You'll Learn in This Chapter

Here you'll learn about a few simple statistics frequently used in criminal justice research. You'll also become familiar with the fundamental logic of multivariate analysis. You'll come away from this chapter able to perform a number of simple, though powerful, analyses to describe data and reach research conclusions.

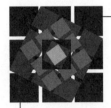

INTRODUCTION

DESCRIPTIVE STATISTICS
Univariate Analysis
Subgroup Comparisons
Bivariate Analysis
Multivariate Analysis
Measures of Association

INFERENTIAL STATISTICS
Univariate Inferences
Tests of Statistical Significance
The Logic of Statistical Significance
Chi Square
Cautions in Interpreting Statistical Significance

MAIN POINTS

REVIEW QUESTIONS AND EXERCISES

ADDITIONAL READINGS

■ INTRODUCTION

Many people are intimidated by empirical research because they feel uncomfortable with mathematics and statistics. And indeed, many research reports are filled with unspecified computations. The role of statistics in criminal justice research is very important, but it is equally important for that role to be seen in its proper perspective.

Empirical research is first and foremost a logical rather than a mathematical operation. Mathematics is merely a convenient and efficient language for accomplishing the logical operations inherent in good data analysis. Statistics is the applied branch of mathematics especially appropriate to a variety of research analyses.

We'll be looking at two types of statistics: descriptive and inferential. **Descriptive statistics** is a medium for describing data in manageable forms. **Inferential statistics,** on the other hand, helps you form conclusions from your observations; typically, that involves forming conclusions about a population from the study of a sample drawn from it.

Before exposing you to any numbers, we want to assure you that the level of statistics used in the rest of this chapter has been proven safe for humans. Our introduction to this important phase of criminal justice research is just that—an introduction. Our intent is to familiarize future producers and consumers of empirical criminal justice research with fundamental concepts of quantitative analysis. Many published criminal justice studies use sophisticated statistical techniques that are best learned in specialized courses. But the logic and fundamental techniques of statistics are not at all complicated.

We assume that you are taking a course in research methods for criminology and criminal justice because you are interested in the subjects of crime and criminal justice policy. We suggest you approach this chapter by thinking about statistics as tools for describing and explaining crime and criminal justice policy. Learning how to use these tools will help you better understand this fascinating subject. And learning how to summarize and interpret data about a subject you find inherently interesting is the least painful and most rewarding way to becoming acquainted with statistics.

■ DESCRIPTIVE STATISTICS

Descriptive statistics is a method for presenting quantitative descriptions in a manageable form. Sometimes we want to describe single variables; this procedure is known as *univariate analysis.* At other times we want to describe the associations that connect one variable with another. *Bivariate analysis* refers to descriptions of two variables, and *multivariate analysis* examines relationships among three or more variables.

Let's look at some of the ways statistics are used to describe variables and the relationships among them.

Univariate Analysis

Univariate analysis examines the distribution of cases on only one variable at a time. We'll begin with the logic and formats for the analysis of univariate data.

Distributions The most basic way to present univariate data is to report all individual cases—that is, to list the attribute for each case under study in terms of the variable in question. Suppose you are interested in the ages of criminal court judges; your data might have come from a directory of judges prepared by your state bar association. The most direct manner of reporting the ages of judges would be to list them: 63, 57, 49, 62, 80, 72, 55, and so forth. Such a report would provide your reader with complete details of the data, but it would be too cumbersome for most purposes. You could arrange your data in a somewhat more manageable form without losing any of the detail by reporting that 5 judges were 38 years old, 7 were 39, 18 were 40, and so forth. Such a format would avoid duplicating data on this variable.

For an even more manageable format—with a certain loss of detail—you could report judges' ages as *marginals,* which are **frequency distributions** of *grouped data:* 246 judges under 45 years of age, 517 between 45 and 50 years of age, and so forth. Your reader would have less data to examine and interpret, but he or she would not be able to reproduce fully the original ages of all the judges. Thus, for example, the reader would have no way of knowing how many judges were 41 years old.

The preceding example presented marginals in the form of raw numbers. An alternative form is the use of *percentages*. Thus, for example, you could report that *x* percent of the judges were younger than 45, *y* percent were between 45 and 50, and so forth. The accompanying table shows an example.

Ages of Criminal Court Judges (Hypothetical)

Age	Percent
Under 35	9%
36–45	21
46–55	45
56–65	19
65 and older	6
Total	100% = 433
No data	18

In computing percentages, you must frequently determine the base from which to compute: the number that represents 100 percent. In the most straightforward examples, the base is the total number of cases under study. A problem arises, however, whenever some cases have missing data. Let's assume, for example, that you have conducted a survey in which respondents were asked to report their ages. If some respondents failed to answer that question, you have two alternatives. First, you might still base your percentages on the total number of respondents, reporting those who failed to give their ages as a percentage of the total. Second, you could use the number of persons who gave an answer as the base from which to compute the percentages; the approach is illustrated in the accompanying table. You should still report the number who did not answer, but they would not figure in the percentages.

The choice of a base depends wholly on the purposes of the analysis. If you wish to compare the age distribution of your survey sample with comparable data on the population from which the sample was drawn, you will probably want to omit the "no answers" from the computation. Your best estimate of the age distribution of all respondents is the distribution for those who answered the question. Because "no answer" is not a meaningful age category, its presence among the base categories would confuse the comparison of sample and population figures.

Central Tendency Beyond simply reporting marginals, you may choose to present your data in the form of summary **averages,** or measures of *central tendency.* Your options in this regard are the **mode** (the most frequent attribute, either grouped or ungrouped), the arithmetic **mean,** and the **median** (the middle attribute in the ranked distribution of observed attributes). Here's how the three averages are calculated from a set of data.

Suppose you are conducting an experiment that involves teenagers as subjects. They range in age from 13 to 19, as indicated in this frequency distribution:

Age	Number
13	3
14	4
15	6
16	8
17	4
18	3
19	3

Now that you know the actual ages of the 31 subjects, how old would you say they are in general, or on the average? Let's look at three different ways you might answer that question.

The easiest average to calculate is the *mode,* the most frequent value. As you can see, there are more 16-year-olds (eight of them) than any other age, so the modal age is 16, as indicated in Figure 14-1.

Figure 14-1 also demonstrates the calculation of the *mean.* There are three steps: (1) multiply each age by the number of subjects who are that age, (2) total the results of all those multiplications, and (3) divide that total by the number of subjects. As indicated in Figure 14-1, the mean age in this illustration is 15.87.

FIGURE 14-1
Three "Averages"

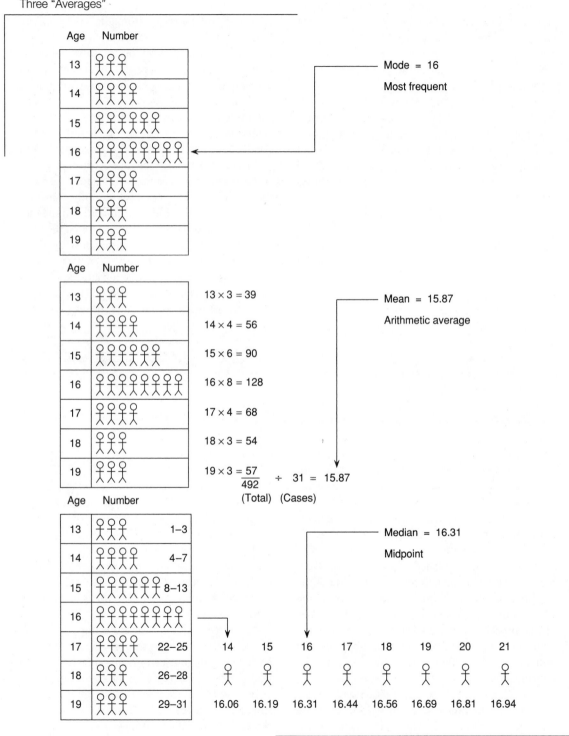

The *median* represents the "middle" value; half are above it and half below. If we had the precise age of each subject (for instance, 17 years and 124 days), we'd be able to arrange all 31 subjects in order by age, and the median for the whole group would be the age of the middle subject.

As you can see, however, we do not know precise ages; our data constitute "grouped data" in this regard: Three people who are not precisely the same age have been grouped in the category "13 years old," for example.

Figure 14-1 illustrates the logic of calculating a median for grouped data. Since there are 31 subjects altogether, the "middle" subject is number 16 when they are arranged by age—15 are younger and 17 are older. Look at the bottom portion of Figure 14-1 and you'll see that the middle person is one of the eight 16-year-olds. In the enlarged view of that group, we see that number 16 is the third from the left.

Dispersion In the research literature, you will find both means and medians presented. Whenever means are presented, you should be aware that they are susceptible to extreme values: A few very large or very small numbers can change the mean dramatically. Because of this, it is usually important to examine measures of **dispersion** about the mean.

The simplest measure of dispersion is the **range:** the distance separating the highest from the lowest value. Thus, besides reporting that our subjects have a mean age of 15.87, we might also indicate that their ages range from 13 to 19. A somewhat more sophisticated measure of dispersion is the **standard deviation,** which can be described as the average amount of variation about the mean. If the mean is the average value of all observations in a group, then the standard deviation represents the average amount each individual observation varies from the mean. Table 14-1 presents some hypothetical data on the ages of persons in juvenile and adult court that will help illustrate the concepts of deviation and average deviation. Let's first consider the top of Table 14-1.

The first column shows the age for each of ten juvenile court defendants. The mean age for these ten juveniles is 14. The second column shows how much each individual's age deviates from the mean. Thus, the first juvenile is two years younger than the mean, the second is one year older, and the third is the same age as the mean.

You might first think that the average deviation would be calculated in the same way as the mean—add up all individual deviations for each case and divide by the number of cases. We have done that in Table 14-1, but you can see that the total deviation is zero; therefore, the average deviation would be zero. You should recognize that the sum of deviations from the mean will always be zero. Some individual deviations will be negative, some will be positive, and the positive and negative values will always cancel each other out.

For this reason (and other reasons too complex to describe here), the standard deviation measure of dispersion is based on the squared deviations from the mean. Squaring any number always produces a positive value, so when we add all the squared deviations together, we will not get zero for the total. Summing these squared deviations in the top half of Table 14-1 produces a total of 20, and dividing by the number of observations produces an "average" deviation of 2. This quantity—the sum of squared deviations from the mean divided by the number of cases—is known as the *variance*. Taking the square root of the variance produces the standard deviation, which equals 1.41 for juveniles in Table 14-1.

You might wonder how to interpret a standard deviation of 1.41, or any other value for that matter. Any particular value for the standard deviation has no real intuitive meaning. This measure of dispersion is most useful in a comparative sense. Comparing the relative values for the standard deviation and the mean indicates how much variation there is in a group of cases, relative to the average. Similarly, comparing standard deviations for different groups of cases indicates relative amounts of dispersion within each group.

In our example of juvenile court cases, the standard deviation of 1.41 is rather low relative to the mean of 14. Now compare the data for juvenile court to the bottom half of Table 14-1, which presents ages for a hypothetical group of adult

TABLE 14-1
Standard Deviation for Two Hypothetical Distributions

	Juvenile Court		
	Age	Deviation from Mean	Squared Deviation from Mean
	12	−2	4
	15	1	1
	14	0	0
	13	−1	1
	15	1	1
	14	0	0
	16	2	4
	16	2	4
	12	−2	4
	13	−1	1
Sum	140	0	20
Average	14	(0)	(2)
Standard deviation			1.41

	Adult Court		
	Age	Deviation from Mean	Squared Deviation from Mean
	18	−10	100
	37	9	81
	23	−5	25
	22	−6	36
	25	−3	9
	43	15	225
	19	−9	81
	50	22	484
	21	−7	49
	22	−6	36
Sum	280	0	1,126
Average	28	(0)	(112.6)
Standard deviation			10.61

court defendants. The mean is higher, of course, since adults are older than juveniles. More important (for illustrating the standard deviation), there is greater variation in the distribution of adult court defendants, as illustrated by the standard deviation and the columns that show raw deviations and squared deviations from the mean of 28. The standard deviation for adult cases (10.61) is much higher relative to the mean of 28 than the relative values of the standard deviation and mean for juvenile cases. In this hypothetical example, the substantive reason for this is obvious: There is much greater age variation in adult court than in juvenile court because there is much greater age variation in adults (18 to whatever) than there is in juveniles (1 to 17). As a result, the standard deviation for adult defendants indicates greater variation than the same measure for juvenile defendants.

In addition to providing a summary measure of dispersion, the standard deviation plays a role in the calculation of other descriptive statistics, some of which we will mention later in this chapter. Furthermore, the standard deviation is a central component of many inferential statistics used to make generalizations from a sample of observations to the population from which the sample was drawn.

TABLE 14-2
A Distribution of Prior Arrests (Hypothetical Data)

Number of Prior Arrests	Number of Cases	Percent of Cases	Percentile/ Quartile
0	1	0.56	
1	16	8.89	
2	31	17.22	25th/1st
3	23	12.78	
4	20	11.11	50th/2nd
5	16	8.89	
6	19	10.56	
7	18	10.00	75th/3rd
8	11	6.11	
9	14	7.78	
10	5	2.78	
30	3	1.67	
40	2	1.11	
55	1	0.56	
Total	180	100%	
Mode	2		
Median	4		
Mean	5.76		
Range	0–55		
Standard deviation	6.64		

Comparing Measures of Dispersion and Central Tendency
Many other measures of dispersion can help you interpret measures of central tendency. One useful indicator that expresses both dispersion and grouping of cases is the *percentile,* which indicates what percentage of cases fall at or below some value. For example, scores on achievement tests, such as the SAT, are usually reported in percentiles as well as raw scores. Thus, a raw score of 630 might fall in the 80th percentile, indicating that 80 percent of persons who take the SAT achieve scores of 630 or less; alternatively, the 80th percentile means that 20 percent of scores were higher than 630. Percentiles may also be grouped into quartiles, which give the cases that fall in the first (lowest), second, third, and fourth (highest) quarters of a distribution.

Table 14-2 presents a distribution of prior arrests for some hypothetical population of, say, probationers to illustrate the different measures of central tendency and dispersion we have discussed. Notice that while the number of prior arrests ranges from 0 to 55, cases cluster in the lower end of this distribution. Half the cases have 4 or fewer prior arrests, as indicated by three descriptive statistics in Table 14-2: median, 50th percentile, and 2nd quartile. Only one-fourth of the cases have 8 or more prior arrests.

Notice also the different values for our three measures of central tendency. The mode for prior arrests is 2, and the mean or average number is 5.76, which indicates that the mean is distorted by a small number of persons with many prior arrests. The standard deviation of 6.64 further documents that our small population has quite a bit of variability. Figure 14-2 presents a graphic representation of the dispersion of cases and the different values for the three measures of central tendency.

Distributions such as that shown in Table 14-2 and Figure 14-2 are known as *skewed distributions.* Although most cases cluster near the low end, a few are spread out over very high values for prior arrests. Many variables of interest to

FIGURE 14-2
Graphic Representation of a Distribution of Prior Arrests (Hypothetical Data)

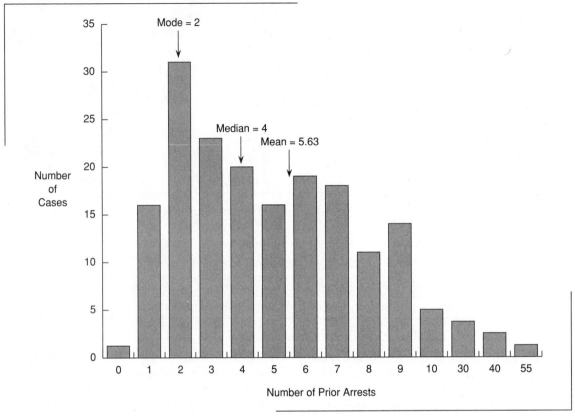

criminal justice researchers are skewed in similar ways, especially when examined for some general population. Most people have no prior arrests, but a small number of persons will have many. Similarly, most people suffer no victimization from serious crime in any given year, but a small number of persons are repeatedly victimized.

Continuous and Discrete Variables The preceding calculations are not appropriate for all variables. To understand this, we must examine two types of variables: *continuous* and *discrete*. Age and number of prior arrests are continuous ratio variables; they increase steadily in tiny fractions instead of jumping from category to category as does a discrete variable such as gender or marital status. If discrete variables are being analyzed—a nominal

or ordinal variable, for example—then some of the techniques discussed previously are not applicable. Strictly speaking, medians and means should be calculated for only interval and ratio data, respectively. If the variable in question is gender, for instance, raw number or percentage marginals are appropriate and useful measures. Calculating the mode is a legitimate, though not very revealing, analysis, but reports of mean, median, or dispersion summaries would be inappropriate. Although researchers can sometimes learn something of value by violating rules like these, you should do so only with caution.

Computing Rates Rates of things are fundamental descriptive statistics in criminal justice research. In most cases, rates are used to standardize some measure for comparative purposes. For example, see the accompanying table, which gives figures on total murders for 1995 in four states.[1]

	Total Murders, 1995	1995 Population
California	3,531	31,589,000
Florida	1,037	14,166,000
Louisiana	740	4,342,000
Pennsylvania	755	12,072,000

Obviously, California had far more murders than the other three states, but these figures are difficult to interpret because of large differences in the states' total populations. Computing rates enables us to standardize by population size and make more meaningful comparisons, as the next table shows.

Murder Rates Per 100,000 Population, 1995

California	11.2
Florida	7.3
Louisiana	17.0
Pennsylvania	6.3

Here we see that Louisiana, with the smallest number of murders in 1995 (among the states reported here), actually had the highest murder rate. Notice also that the murder rate is expressed as the number of murders per 100,000 population. This is a common convention in reporting rates of crime and other rare events. To get the actual rate of murder per person, move the decimal point five places to the left in each of the figures in the second table.

The arithmetic of calculating rates could not be much easier. What is not so simple, and in any event requires careful consideration, is deciding on the basic two components of rates: numerator and denominator. The numerator represents the central concept you are interested in measuring, so selecting the numerator involves all the considerations of measurement we have discussed else-

where. Murder rates, arrest rates, conviction rates, and incarceration rates are common examples where the numerator is relatively straightforward.

Choosing the right denominator sometimes presents problems. In most cases, you compute rates to standardize by some population eligible to be included in the numerator. Sometimes the choice is fairly obvious, as in our use of each state's total population to compute murder rates. To compute rates of rape or sexual assault, you would probably want to use a population of adult women in the denominator, although you might consider how to handle the possibility of homosexual rape. Since households are at risk of residential burglary, burglary rates should be computed using some count of households. In computing auto theft rates, use some indicator of registered autos.

More difficult problems can arise in computing rates to express some characteristic of a mobile population. For example, residents of Miami are at risk of criminal victimization in that city, but so are tourists and other visitors to Miami. Because many nonresidents visit or pass through the city in any given year, a measure of Miami's crime rate that was based only on the city's resident population (such as the U.S. Census) would tend to overestimate the number of crimes standardized by the population at risk; many people at risk would not be counted in the denominator. Or what about estimating the crime rate on a subway system? The population at risk here is users, who may amount to hundreds of thousands of persons per day.

Rates are very useful descriptive statistics that may be easily computed. You should, however, be careful in selecting numerators and denominators. And you should recognize that this caution refers as much to questions of *measurement* as it does to questions of computing descriptive statistics. The box entitled "Murder on the Job" is presented later in this chapter as an example of confusion about the meaning of rates.

Detail Versus Manageability   In presenting univariate—and other—data, you will be constrained by two often conflicting goals. On the one hand, you

---

[1] Murder and population data are from *Crime in the United States 1995* (Federal Bureau of Investigation, 1996:62–66).

TABLE 14-3

Illustration of Subgroup Comparisons: Length of Prison Sentence by Felony Criminal History (Hypothetical Data)

Felony Criminal History	Median Sentence Length
No arrests or convictions	6 months
Prior arrests only	11 months
Prior convictions	23 months

TABLE 14-4

Gun Ownership Among Men and Women in 1994

Gun Ownership	Men	Women
Yes	51%	33%
No	49	67
100% = 12 months?	(861)	(1,108)

Source: 1994 General Social Survey, accessed from: http://bravo. berkeley.edu/cgi-bin/hcsa3

should attempt to provide your reader with the fullest degree of detail regarding those data. On the other hand, the data should be presented in a manageable form. Since these two goals often go directly counter to each other, you must seek the best compromise between them. One useful solution is to report a given set of data in more than one form. In the case of age, for example, you might report the marginals on ungrouped ages plus the mean age and standard deviation.

As you can see from this introductory discussion of univariate analysis, this seemingly simple matter can be rather complex. The lessons of this section will be important as we move now to a consideration of subgroup comparisons and bivariate analyses.

Subgroup Comparisons

Univariate analyses describe the units of analysis of a study and, if they are a sample drawn from some larger population, allow us to make descriptive inferences about the larger population. Bivariate and multivariate analyses are aimed primarily at explanation. Before turning to explanation, however, we will consider the case of subgroup description.

Often it's appropriate to describe subsets of cases, subjects, or respondents. Table 14-3, for example, presents hypothetical data on sentence length for offenders grouped by prior felony record. In some situations, the researcher presents subgroup comparisons purely for descriptive purposes. More often, the purpose of subgroup descriptions is comparative. In this case, comparing sentences for subgroups of convicted

offenders implies some causal connection between prior felony record and sentence length. Similarly, if we compared sentence lengths for men and women, it would imply that something about gender has a causal effect on sentence length.

Bivariate Analysis

In contrast to univariate analysis, subgroup comparisons constitute a kind of **bivariate analysis** in that two variables are involved. As we noted earlier, the purpose of univariate analysis is purely descriptive. The purpose of subgroup comparisons is also largely descriptive—independently describing the subgroups—but the element of comparison is added. Most bivariate analysis in criminal justice research adds another element: relationships among the variables themselves. Thus, univariate analysis and subgroup comparisons focus on describing the *people* (or other units of analysis) under study, and bivariate analysis focuses on the *variables*.

Notice, then, that Table 14-4 could be regarded as a subgroup comparison: It independently describes gun ownership among men and women, as reported in the 1994 General Social Survey. It shows—comparatively and descriptively—that fewer women than men report owning a gun.

The same table seen as an explanatory bivariate analysis tells a somewhat different story. It suggests that the variable gender has an effect on the variable gun ownership. The behavior is seen as a dependent variable that is partially determined by the independent variable, gender. Explanatory bivariate analyses, then, involve the "variable language" we introduced in Chapter 1. In a subtle shift of focus, we are no longer talking about men and women as different subgroups but about gender as a variable—a variable that has an influence on other variables.

Adding the logic of causal relationships among variables has an important implication for the construction and reading of percentage tables. One of the chief bugaboos for new data analysts is deciding on the appropriate "direction of percentaging" for any given table. In Table 14-4, for example, we have divided the group of subjects into two subgroups—men and women—and then described the behavior of each subgroup. That is the correct way to construct this table.

Notice, however, that it would have been possible, though inappropriate, to construct the table differently. We could have first divided the subjects into different categories of gun ownership, and then we could have described each of those subgroups by the percentage of men and women in each. This method would make no sense in terms of explanation, however; owning a gun cannot make you a woman or a man.

Table 14-4 suggests that gender affects gun ownership. Had we used the other method of construction, the table would suggest that gun ownership affects whether you are a man or a woman—which makes no sense.

Another related problem complicates the lives of new data analysts. How do you read a percentage table? There is a temptation to read Table 14-4 as follows: "Of the women, only 33 percent owned a gun, and 67 percent did not; therefore, being a woman makes you less likely to own a gun." That is *not* the correct way to read the table, however. The conclusion that gender—as a variable—has an effect on gun ownership must hinge on a comparison between men and women. Specifically, we compare the 33 percent with the 51 percent and note that women are less likely than men to own a gun. The comparison of subgroups, then, is essential in reading an explanatory bivariate table.

In constructing and presenting Table 14-4, we have used a convention called *percentage down*. This term means that you can add the percentages down each column to total 100 percent. You read this form of table across a row. For the row

labeled Yes, what percentage of the men own a gun? What percentage of the women own a gun?

The direction of percentaging in tables is arbitrary, and some researchers prefer to percentage across. They would organize Table 14-4 so that "Men" and "Women" were shown on the left side of the table, identifying the two rows, and "Yes" and "No" appeared at the top to identify the columns. The actual numbers in the table would be moved around accordingly, and each row of percentages would total 100 percent. In that case, you would read the table down a column, still asking what percentage of men and women owned guns. The logic and the conclusion would be the same in either case; only the form would be different.

In reading a table that someone else has constructed, therefore, you need to find out in which direction it has been percentaged. Usually that will be apparent in the labeling of the table or in the logic of the variables being analyzed. As a last resort, however, you should add the percentages in each column and each row. If each of the columns totals 100 percent, the table has been percentaged down. If the rows total 100 percent each, it has been percentaged across. Follow these rules of thumb:

If the table is percentaged down, read across.
If the table is percentaged across, read down.

By the way, we constructed Table 14-4 from General Social Survey (GSS) data available on the Internet, as you may have guessed from the Internet address shown at the bottom of the table. Annual GSS data from 1976 onward can be accessed directly through a service provided by the University of California at Berkeley. You can access all GSS variables at the Berkeley site and use a simple program, "Conversational Data Analysis," to construct your own percentage tables. This will give you invaluable practice in constructing bivariate percentage tables.

Percentaging a Table Here's another example. Suppose we are interested in investigating newspaper editorial policies regarding the legalization of marijuana. We undertake a content analysis of editorials on this subject that have appeared during a given year in a sample of daily newspapers across the nation. Each editorial has been classified as favorable, neutral, or unfavorable with regard to the legalization of marijuana. Perhaps we wish to examine the relationship between editorial policies and the types of communities in which the newspapers are published, thinking that rural newspapers might be more conservative than urban ones. Thus, each newspaper (hence, each editorial) is classified in terms of the population of the community in which it is published.

Table 14-5 presents some hypothetical data describing the editorial policies of rural and urban newspapers. Note that the unit of analysis in this example is the individual editorial. Table 14-5 tells us that there were 127 editorials about marijuana in our sample of newspapers published in communities with populations under 100,000. (*Note:* This choice of 100,000 is for simplicity of illustration and does not mean that rural refers to a community of less than 100,000 in any absolute sense.) Of these, 11 percent (14 editorials) were favorable toward the legalization of marijuana, 29 percent were neutral, and 60 percent were unfavorable. Of the 438 editorials that appeared in our sample of newspapers published in communities with more than 100,000 residents, 32 percent (140 editorials) were favorable toward legalizing marijuana, 40 percent were neutral, and 28 percent were unfavorable.

When we compare the editorial policies of rural and urban newspapers in our imaginary study, we find—as expected—that rural newspapers are less favorable toward the legalization of marijuana than urban newspapers. That is determined by noting that a larger percentage (32 percent) of the urban editorials were favorable than the rural ones (11 percent). We might note, as well, that more rural than urban editorials were unfavorable (60 percent compared to 28 percent). Note that this table assumes that the size of a community might affect its newspapers' editorial policies on this issue, rather than that editorial policy might affect the size of communities.

Constructing and Reading Tables Before introducing multivariate analysis, let's review the steps in-

TABLE 14-5

Hypothetical Data Regarding Newspaper Editorials on the Legalization of Marijuana

Editorial Policy Toward Legalizing Marijuana	Community Size	
	Under 100,000	Over 100,000
Favorable	11%	32%
Neutral	29	40
Unfavorable	60	28
100% =	(127)	(438)

volved in the construction of explanatory bivariate tables:

1. The cases are divided into groups according to attributes of the independent variable.
2. Each of these subgroups is then described in terms of attributes of the dependent variable.
3. Finally, the table is read by comparing the independent variable subgroups with one another in terms of a given attribute of the dependent variable.

In the example of editorial policies regarding the legalization of marijuana, size of community is the independent variable, and a newspaper's editorial policy is the dependent variable. The table is constructed as follows:

1. Divide the editorials into subgroups according to the sizes of the communities in which the newspapers are published.
2. Describe each subgroup of editorials in terms of the percentages favorable, neutral, or unfavorable toward the legalization of marijuana.
3. Compare the two subgroups in terms of the percentages favorable toward the legalization of marijuana.

Bivariate analyses typically have an explanatory causal purpose. This hypothetical example has hinted at the nature of causation as it is used by social scientists. We hope the rather simplified approach to causation in these examples will have commonsense acceptability for you at this point.

Bivariate Table Formats Tables such as those we've been examining are commonly called **contin-**

gency tables: Values of the dependent variable are contingent on values of the independent variable. Although contingency tables are commonly used in criminal justice research, their format has never been standardized. As a result, a variety of formats will be found in research literature. As long as a table is easy to read and interpret, there is probably no reason to strive for standardization; however, these guidelines should be followed in the presentation of most tabular data.

1. A table should have a heading or a title that succinctly describes what is contained in the table.
2. The original content of the variables should be presented clearly—in the table itself if at all possible or in the text with a paraphrase in the table. This information is especially critical when a variable is derived from responses to an attitudinal question because the meaning of the responses will depend largely on the wording of the question.
3. The attributes of each variable should be clearly indicated. Complex categories will have to be abbreviated, but the meaning should be clear in the table and, of course, the full description should be reported in the text.
4. When percentages are reported in the table, the base on which they are computed should be indicated. It is redundant to present all the raw numbers for each category because these could be reconstructed from the percentages and the bases. Moreover, the presentation of both numbers and percentages often confuses a table and makes it more difficult to read.
5. If any cases are omitted from the table because of missing data ("no answer," for example), their numbers should be indicated in the table.

By following these guidelines and by thinking carefully about the kinds of causal and descriptive relationships you want to examine, you will find that contingency tables can address many policy and research questions in criminal justice. We want to emphasize, however, the importance of thinking through the logic of contingency tables. Any descriptive statistics—contin-

gency tables, measures of central tendency, or rates—are sometimes misrepresented or misinterpreted. See the box entitled "Murder on the Job" for an example of this.

Multivariate Analysis

A great deal of criminal justice research uses multivariate techniques to examine relationships among several variables. Like much statistical analysis, the logic of **multivariate analysis** is straightforward, but the actual use of many multivariate statistical techniques can be complex. A full understanding requires a good background in statistics and is beyond the scope of this book. In this section, we will briefly discuss the construction of multivariate tables—those constructed from three or more variables—and the comparison of multiple subgroups.

Multivariate tables may be constructed on the basis of a more complicated subgroup description by following essentially the same steps outlined previously for bivariate tables. Instead of one independent variable and one dependent variable, however, we will have more than one independent variable. Instead of explaining the dependent variable on the basis of a single independent variable, we'll seek an explanation through the use of more than one independent variable. Let's consider an example from research on victimization.

Multivariate Tables: Lifestyle and Street Crime If you consult any source of published statistics on victimization (we discussed these in Chapter 12), you will find several tables that document a relationship between age and personal crime victimization—younger people are more often victims of assault and robbery, for example. An influential book by Michael Hindelang, Michael Gottfredson, and James Garofalo (1978) suggests a "lifestyle" explanation for this relationship. The lifestyle of many younger people—visiting bars and clubs for evening entertainment, for example—exposes them to street crime and potential predators more than does the less hectic lifestyle of older people. This is certainly a sensible hypothesis, and Hindelang and associates found general support for the lifestyle explanation in

Murder on the Job

"HIGH Murder Rate for Women on the Job," read the headline for a brief story in *The New York Times*, reporting on a study released by the U.S. Department of Labor. The subhead was equally alarming, and misleading, to casual readers: "40% of women killed at work are murdered, but figure for men is only 15%." Think about this statement, in light of our discussion of how to percentage a table. You should be able to imagine something like the following:

Cause of Death at Work

	Women	Men
Murder	40%	15%
Other	60	85
Total	100%	100%

This table indicates that of those women who die while on the job at work, 40% are murdered, and is consistent with the opening paragraphs of the story. Notice that so far nothing has been said about *how many* women and men are murdered, or *how many* women and men die on the job from all causes. Later on, the story provides more details.

■ "Vehicle accidents caused the most job-related deaths, 18 percent or 1,121 of the 6,083 work-related deaths in 1992. . . .

"Homicides, including shootings and stabbings, were a close second with 17 percent, or 1,004 deaths, said the study by the department's Bureau of Labor Statistics."

This information enables us to supplement the table by adding row totals: 6,083 people died on the job in 1992, 1,004 of them were murdered, and 5,079 (6,083 − 1,004) died from other causes.

One more piece of information is needed to construct a contingency table: the total number of men and women killed on the job. The story does not tell us that directly, but provides enough information to approximate the answer: "Although men are 55 percent of the work force, they comprise 93 percent of all job-related deaths." Men must therefore be 93 percent of the 6,083 total workplace deaths, or approximately 5,657; this leaves approximately 426 deaths of women on the job. "Approximate" is an important qualifier here, since computing numbers of cases from percentages creates some inconsistencies due to rounding off percents reported in the newspaper story. Let's now construct a contingency table to look at the numbers of workplace deaths. The accompanying table shows computed numbers in parentheses.

their analysis of data from early versions of the National Crime Victimization Survey. But the U.S. crime survey data did not include direct measures of lifestyle concepts.

Questionnaire items in the British Crime Survey (BCS) provided better measures of individual behaviors. Using these data, Clarke, Ekblom, Hough, and Mayhew (1985) examined the link between exposure to risk and victimization, while holding age and gender constant. Specifically, Clarke and colleagues hypothesized that older persons were less often victims of street crime because they spent less time on the streets. The

1982 BCS asked respondents whether they had left their homes in the previous week (that is, the week just before they were interviewed) for any evening leisure or social activities. Those who responded yes were asked which specific nights they had gone out and what they had done.

Hypothesizing that some types of evening activities are more risky than others, Clarke and associates restricted their analysis to leisure pursuits away from the respondent's home, such as visiting a pub, nightclub, or theater. Their dependent variable, street crime victimization, was also carefully defined to include only crimes against per-

Cause of Death at Work

	Women	Men	Total	
Murder	(170)	(849)	1,004	(1,019)
Other	(256)	(4,808)	5,079	(5,064)
Total	(426)	(5,657)	6,083	

The results are interesting. Although a greater percent of women than men are murdered, a much larger *number* of men than women are murdered.

Now, recall the story's headline, "High Murder *Rate*." This implies that the number of women murdered on the job, divided by the total number of women at risk of murder on the job, is higher than the same computed rate for men. We need more information than the story provides to verify this claim, but there is a clue. Women are about 45 percent of the workforce, so there are about 1.2 men in the workforce for every woman (55% ÷ 45%). But about five times as many men as women are murdered on the job (849 ÷ 170).

This should tip you off that the headline is misleading. If the ratio of male to female murders is 5 to 1, but the ratio of male to female workers is 1.2 to 1, how could the murder rate for women be higher? You could compute actual rates of murder on the job by finding a suitable

denominator; in this case, the number of men and women in the workforce would be appropriate. Consulting the Census Bureau publication *Statistical Abstract of the United States* would provide this information and enable you to compute rates as in our final table:

	Women	Men
Civilian work force (1,000s)	53,284	63,593
Murdered at work	170	849
On-the-job murder rate per 100,000 workers	.319	1.335

So *The New York Times* got it wrong; there is a higher murder rate for men on the job. Women are less often killed on the job by any cause, including murder. But women who die on the job (in much smaller numbers than men) are more likely to die from murder than are men who die on the job. A murder rate expresses the number of people murdered divided by the population at risk.

Rates are often computed with inappropriate denominators. But it is less common to find the term *rate* used so inaccurately.

Sources: "High Murder Rate for Women on the Job," 1993; U.S. Bureau of the Census, 1992.

sons (actual and attempted assault, robbery, rape, and thefts from the person) that occurred away from victims' homes, workplaces, or the homes of friends. Furthermore, since the leisure behavior questions asked about evening activities, only street crime victimizations that took place between 6:00 P.M. and midnight were included.

Clarke and associates therefore propose a very specific hypothesis that involves three carefully defined concepts and variables: Older persons are less often victims of street crime because they less often engage in behavior that exposes them to risk of street crime. Parts A through C of Table 14-6

present cross-tabulations for the three possible bivariate relationships among these variables: evening street crime victimization by age and evening leisure pursuits, and evening leisure pursuits by age.[2]

The relationships illustrated in these tables are consistent with the lifestyle hypothesis of personal

[2]These tables are simplified from those included in the analysis by Clarke and associates and required some recalculation of percents. Also, the original article includes additional tables to assess differences in victimization by gender and by mode of transportation.

TABLE 14-6A
Evening Street Crime Victimization by Age

Street Crime Victim	16–30	31–60	61+
Yes	4.8%	1.0%	0.3%
No	95.2	99.0	99.7
100% =	(2,738)	(4,460)	(1,952)

TABLE 14-6B
Evening Street Crime Victimization
by Evenings Out During Previous Week

Street Crime Victim	None	1 or 2	3+
Yes	1.2%	1.6%	3.8%
No	98.9	98.4	96.2
100% =	(3,252)	(3,695)	(2,203)

TABLE 14-6C
Evening Out During Previous Week by Age

Evenings Out	16–30	31–60	61+
None	20.6%	35.2%	57.2%
1 or 2	38.6	44.9	32.5
3+	40.9	19.8	10.2
100% =	(2,738)	(4,460)	(1,952)

TABLE 14-6D
Evening Street Crime Victimization
by Age and Evenings Out

	Percent Victims		
Evenings Out	16–30	31–60	61+
None	3.9	1.0	0.2
	(563)	(1,572)	(1,117)
1 or 2	3.8	0.9	0.2
	(1,056)	(2,004)	(635)
3+	6.2	1.4	1.1
	(1,119)	(884)	(200)
Total N =	(2,738)	(4,460)	(1,952)

Source: Adapted from Clarke, Ekblom, Hough, and Mayhew (1985, Tables 1, 2, and 3). Percentages and numbers of cases computed from published tabulations.

crime victimization. First, victimization is more common for younger people (ages 16–30) and for those who pursued leisure activities outside their home three or more evenings in the previous week (parts A and B of Table 14-6). Second, as shown in part C, the attributes of young age and frequent exposure to risk are positively re-

lated: About 41 percent of the youngest group had gone out three or more nights, compared to 20 percent of those aged 31–60 and only 10 percent of those over age 60.

However, since we are interested in the effects of two independent variables—lifestyle and age—on victimization, we must construct a table that includes all three variables.

Several of the tables presented in this chapter are somewhat inefficient. When the dependent variable—street crime victimization—is dichotomous (two attributes), knowing one attribute permits the reader to easily reconstruct the other. Thus, if we know from Table 14-6A that 1 percent of respondents aged 31–60 were victims of street crime, then we know automatically that 99 percent were not victims. So reporting the percentages for both values of a dichotomy is unnecessary. On the basis of this recognition, Table 14-6D presents the relationship between victimization and two independent variables in a more efficient format.

In Table 14-6D, the percentages of respondents who reported a street crime victimization are shown in the cells at the intersections of the two independent variables. The numbers presented in parentheses below each percentage are the numbers of cases on which the percentages are based. Thus, for example, the reader knows that 563 people aged 16–30 did not go out for evening leisure in the week before their interview, and that 3.9 percent of them were victims of street crime in the previous year. We can calculate from this that 22 of those 563 people were victims and the other 541 people were not victims.

Let's now interpret the conclusions implied by this table.

1. Within each age group, persons who pursued outside evening leisure activities three or more times per week were more often victimized. There is not much difference between those who went out once or twice per week and those who stayed home.

2. Within each category for evening leisure activities, street crime victimization declines as age increases.

3. Exposure to risk through evenings out is less strongly related to street crime victimization than is age.

4. Age and exposure to risk have independent effects on street crime victimization. Within a given attribute of one independent variable, different attributes of the second are still related to victimization.

5. Similarly, the two independent variables have a cumulative effect on victimization. Younger people who went out three or more times per week were most often victimized.

Returning to the lifestyle hypothesis, what can we conclude from Table 14-6D? First, this measure of exposure to risk is in fact related to street crime victimization. People who go out more frequently are more often exposed to risk and are in fact more often victims of street crime. As Clarke and associates point out, however, differences in exposure to risk do not account for lower rates of victimization among older persons: Within categories of exposure to risk, victimization still declines with age. So lifestyle is related to victimization, but this measure of behavior—exposure to risk of street crime—does not account for all age-related differences in victimization. Furthermore, what we might call lifestyle "intensity" plays a role here. Going out once or twice does not have as much impact on victimization as going out more often. So the most intensely active night people aged 30 or younger are most often victims of street crime.

Multivariate contingency tables are powerful tools for examining relationships between a dependent variable and multiple independent variables measured at the nominal or categorical level. Contingency tables can, however, become cumbersome and difficult to interpret if independent variables have several categories, or if more than two independent variables are included in a table. In practice, criminal justice researchers often employ more sophisticated techniques for multivariate analysis of discrete or nominal variables. The "Additional Readings" section at the end of this chapter includes some references for advanced multivariate analysis of nominal data. Although the logic of such analysis is not especially difficult, most people learn these techniques through advanced courses in statistics.

TABLE 14-7
Assault Rates, Poverty, and Mobility in 60 Boston Neighborhoods

Poverty	Mobility		
	Low	High	Total
Low	12.2 (22)	19.5 (21)	15.8 (43)
High	43.8 (4)	25.0 (13)	29.4 (17)
Total	17.1 (26)	21.6 (34)	19.6 (60)

Source: Adapted from Warner and Pierce (1993, Table 2). Row and column total assault rates computed from published tabulations.

Multiple-Subgroup Comparisons: Social Disorganization and Boston Neighborhoods Just as subgroup comparisons can constitute a type of bivariate analysis, comparing values on some dependent variable across multiple subgroups is a type of multivariate analysis. In a sense, Table 14-6D compared victimization for multiple subgroups defined by age and evening leisure activities.

Multiple-subgroup comparisons are most frequently used to compare values for dependent variables measured at the interval or ratio level. For example, you may wish to compare crime rates among urban areas that have been classified according to different attributes. Table 14-7 is adapted from research by Barbara Warner and Glenn Pierce (1993) that examines the relationship between measures of social disorganization and crime problems.

Drawing on earlier studies by Shaw and McKay (1969) and by William Julius Wilson (1987), Warner and Pierce compared calls for police service from 60 Boston neighborhoods to two measures of social disorganization—poverty and population mobility—each computed from census data for Boston neighborhoods. Their poverty measure expresses the percentage of neighborhood residents with incomes below the poverty line in 1980; mobility measures the percentage of residents who have lived in the same dwelling for less than five years. Classifying each neighborhood as high or low on each of these two measures produces the two subgroups shown in Table 14-7. Each cell indicates the mean rate of police calls to report assaults for neighborhoods in each subgroup.

The table shows that assaults are more common in high-poverty neighborhoods, regardless of residential mobility. No surprises here; this finding is consistent with virtually all research on social disorganization, from Shaw and McKay onward. However, the relationship between mobility and assaults varies, depending on neighborhood poverty levels. In low-poverty areas (the first row of Table 14-7), the mean assault rate is greater for high-mobility neighborhoods, but the opposite is true for high-poverty neighborhoods (the second row). Warner and Pierce refer to Wilson's influential book, *The Truly Disadvantaged: The Inner City, the Underclass, and Public Policy* (1987), to interpret this finding: Assaults are more common in poor stable neighborhoods—those where poverty is persistent and mobility is limited. As Warner and Pierce (1993:507) state, these are "neighborhoods where people remain because they have no choice. This type of stability appears to have an impact on crime in a very different way. Rather than building cohesiveness, it may build resentment, frustration, and isolation."

Notice how it is necessary to compare the combined categories of poverty and mobility to reveal this finding. If we examined the mean number of assaults for each variable separately, shown in the row and column totals for Table 14-7, we would conclude that assaults are more common in high-poverty neighborhoods and in high-mobility neighborhoods. Comparing multiple subgroups defined by the intersection of poverty and mobility is a form of multivariate analysis that enabled Warner and Pierce to sort out the subtle relationships between these two independent variables and neighborhood assault rates. Later in this chapter, we will return to this study to illustrate the use of a more powerful multivariate technique. But multiple-subgroup comparison can provide useful information about the relationship between more than one independent variable and dependent variables measured at the interval or ratio level.

Measures of Association

As we've suggested, descriptive statistics is a method for presenting quantitative descriptions in a manageable form. Sometimes we want to describe single variables, and sometimes we want to describe the associations that connect one variable with another. Let's look more closely at some of the ways that is done.

Bivariate contingency tables are one way to examine the association between two variables. But sometimes contingency tables can be quite complex, presenting several different response categories for row and column variables. Nevertheless, a contingency table represents the association between two variables as a data matrix. Table 14-8 presents such a matrix, showing hypothetical data for the joint frequency distribution of education and support for gun control laws. It provides all the information needed to determine the nature and extent of the relationship between education and support for gun control. Notice, for example, that 23 people (1) have no education and (2) scored low on support for gun control; 77 people (1) have graduate degrees and (2) scored high on support for gun control.

However, this matrix gives you more information than you can easily comprehend. If you study the table carefully, you will note that as education increases from "None" to "Graduate degree," there is a general tendency for gun control support to increase, although no more than a general impression is possible. A variety of descriptive statistics can summarize this data matrix. Selecting the appropriate measure depends initially on the nature of the two variables.

We'll turn now to some of the options available for summarizing the association between two variables. This discussion and those to follow are taken largely from an excellent statistics textbook by Linton C. Freeman (1968). Each measure of association we'll discuss is based on the same model—*proportionate reduction of error* (PRE). To see how this model works, let's assume that we asked you to guess respondents' attributes on a given variable: for example, whether they answered yes or no to a given questionnaire item.

TABLE 14-8

Hypothetical Raw Data on Education and Support for Gun Control Laws

Support for Gun Control	Educational Level				
	None	Grade School	High School	College	Graduate Degree
Low	23	34	156	67	16
Medium	11	21	123	102	23
High	6	12	95	164	77

To assist you, let's first assume you know the overall distribution of responses in the total sample—say, 60 percent said yes and 40 percent said no. You would make the fewest errors in this process if you always guessed the modal (most frequent) response: yes.

Second, let's assume you also know the empirical relationship between the first variable and some other variable—say, gender. Now, each time we ask you to guess whether a respondent said yes or no, we'll tell you whether the respondent is a man or a woman. If the two variables are related, you should make fewer errors the second time. It is possible, therefore, to compute the PRE by knowing the relationship between the two variables: The stronger the relationship, the greater the reduction of error.

This basic PRE model is modified slightly to take account of different levels of measurement—nominal, ordinal, or interval. The following sections will consider each level of measurement and present one measure of association appropriate to each. You should realize that the three measures discussed are only an arbitrary selection from among many appropriate measures.

Nominal Variables If the two variables consist of nominal data (for example, gender, marital status, race), lambda (λ) is one appropriate measure. Lambda is based on your ability to guess values on one of the variables: the PRE achieved through knowledge of values on the other variable. A simple hypothetical example will illustrate the logic and method of lambda. Table 14-9 presents hypothetical data relating gender to a common measure of fear of crime, based on the question: "How safe do you feel, or would you feel, walking alone on your neighborhood streets at night?"

Overall, we note that 1,100 people answered "safe" on the fear question, and 900 answered "unsafe." If you were to predict how people responded to the fear-of-crime question, knowing only the overall distribution on that variable, you would always predict "safe" because that would result in fewer errors than always predicting "unsafe." Nevertheless, this strategy would result in 900 errors out of 2,000 predictions.

Let's suppose that you had access to the data in Table 14-9 and you were told each person's gender before making your prediction about fear of crime. Your strategy would change in that case. For every man, you would predict "safe," and for every woman, you would predict "unsafe." In this instance, you would make 300 errors—the 100 men who responded "unsafe" and the 200 women who responded "safe"—600 fewer errors than you would make without knowing the person's gender.

Lambda, then, represents the reduction in errors as a proportion of the errors that would have been made on the basis of the overall distribution. In this hypothetical example, lambda would equal .67—that is, 600 fewer errors divided by the 900 total errors based on fear of crime alone. In this fashion, lambda measures the statistical association between gender and fear of crime.

TABLE 14-9

Hypothetical Data Relating Gender to Fear of Crime

Fear[a]	Men	Women	Total
Safe	900	200	1,100
Unsafe	100	800	900
Total	1,000	1,000	2,000

[a] Text of fear question: "How safe do you feel, or would you feel, walking alone on your neighborhood streets at night?"

If gender and fear were statistically independent, we would find the same distribution of fear of crime for men and women. In this case, knowing gender would not affect the number of errors made in predicting fear, and the resulting lambda would be zero. If, on the other hand, all men had responded "safe" and all women had responded "unsafe," then by knowing gender you would avoid all errors in predicting fear of crime. You would make 900 fewer errors (out of 900), so lambda would be 1.0—representing a perfect statistical association.

Lambda is only one of several measures of association appropriate to the analysis of two nominal variables. You might want to look at Freeman (1968) for a discussion of other appropriate measures.

Ordinal Variables If the variables being related are ordinal (for example, occupational status or education), gamma (γ) is one appropriate measure of association. Like lambda, gamma is based on your ability to guess values on one variable by knowing values on another. Instead of exact values, however, gamma is based on the ordinal arrangement of values. For any given pair of cases, you guess that their ordinal ranking on one variable will correspond (positively or negatively) to their ordinal ranking on the other. For example, if you suspect that political conservatism is negatively related to support for gun control, and if person A is more conservative than person B, then you guess that A is less supportive of gun control than B. Gamma is the proportion of paired comparisons that fits this pattern.

Table 14-10 presents hypothetical data relating political ideology to support for gun control. The general nature of the relationship between these two variables is that as conservatism increases, support for gun control decreases. There is a negative association between conservatism and support for gun control.

Gamma is computed from two quantities: (1) the number of pairs that have the same ranking on the two variables and (2) the number of pairs that have the opposite ranking on the two variables. The pairs that have the same ranking are computed as follows: The frequency of each

TABLE 14-10
Hypothetical Data Relating Political
Ideology and Support for Gun Control

Support for Gun Control	Liberal	Moderate	Conservative
Low	200	400	700
Medium	500	900	400
High	800	300	100

cell in the table is multiplied by the sum of all cells appearing below and to the right of it—with all these products being summed. In Table 14-10, the number of pairs with the same ranking is $200(900 + 300 + 400 + 100) + 500(300 + 100) + 400(400 + 100) + 900(100)$, or $340,000 + 200,000 + 200,000 + 90,000 = 830,000$.

The pairs that have the opposite rankings on the two variables are computed as follows: The frequency of each cell in the table is multiplied by the sum of all cells appearing below and to the left of it—with all these products being summed. In Table 14-10, the number of pairs with opposite rankings is $700(500 + 800 + 900 + 300) + 400(800 + 300) + 400(500 + 800) + 900(800)$, or $1,750,000 + 440,000 + 520,000 + 720,000 = 3,430,000$. Gamma is computed from the numbers of same-ranked pairs and opposite-ranked pairs as follows:

$$\text{Gamma} = \frac{\text{same} - \text{opposite}}{\text{same} + \text{opposite}}$$

In our example, gamma equals ($830,000 - 3,430,000$) divided by ($830,000 + 3,430,000$), or $-.61$. The negative sign in this answer indicates the negative association suggested by the initial inspection of the table. Conservatism and support for gun control, in this hypothetical example, are negatively associated. The numerical figure for gamma indicates that 61 percent more of the pairs examined had opposite rankings than the same ranking.

Note that whereas values of lambda vary from 0 to 1, values of gamma vary from -1 to $+1$ and represent the direction as well as the magnitude of the association. Because nominal variables have no ordinal structure, it makes no sense to speak of the direction of the relationship. (A negative lambda would indicate that you made more errors in predicting values on one variable while knowing values on the second than you made in ignorance of the second, and that's not logically possible.)

Interval or Ratio Variables If interval or ratio variables (for example, age, income, number of arrests) are being associated, one appropriate measure of association is *Pearson's product-moment correlation* (r). The derivation and computation of this measure of association are complex enough to lie outside the scope of this book, so we will make only a few general comments.

Like both gamma and lambda, r is based on guessing the value of one variable by knowing the other. For continuous interval or ratio variables, however, it is unlikely that you can predict the precise value of the variable. But on the other hand, predicting only the ordinal arrangement of values on the two variables does not take advantage of the greater amount of information conveyed by an interval or ratio variable. In a sense, r reflects how closely you can guess the value of one variable through your knowledge of the value of the other.

To understand the logic of r, consider how you might hypothetically guess values that particular cases have on a given variable. With nominal variables, we have seen that you might always guess the modal value. But for interval or ratio data, you would minimize your errors by always guessing the mean value of the variable. Although this practice produces few, if any, perfect guesses, you will minimize the extent of your errors.

In the computation of lambda, we noted the number of errors produced by always guessing the modal value. In the case of r, errors are measured in terms of the sum of the squared differences between the actual value and the mean. This sum is called the *total variation* and is used to calculate the standard deviation, as we discussed earlier in this chapter.

To understand that concept, we must expand the scope of our examination. Let's look at the logic of regression analysis, and we'll return to correlation within that context.

FIGURE 14-3
Simple Scattergram of Values of X and Y

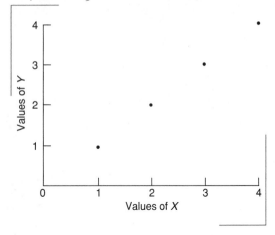

Regression Analysis The general formula for describing the association between two variables is: $Y = f(X)$. This formula is read "Y is a function of X," which means that values of Y can be explained in terms of variations in the values of X. Stated more strongly, we might say that X causes Y, so the value of X determines the value of Y. **Regression analysis** is a method of determining the specific function relating Y to X. There are several forms of regression analysis, depending on the complexity of the relationships being studied. Let's begin with the simplest.

The regression model can be seen most clearly in the case of a perfect linear association between two variables. Figure 14-3 is a scattergram presenting in graphic form the values of X and Y produced by a hypothetical study. It shows that for the four cases in our study, the values of X and Y are identical in each instance. The case with a value of 1 on X also has a value of 1 on Y, and so forth. The relationship between the two variables in this instance is described by the equation $Y = X$; this is called the *regression equation*. Because all four points lie on a straight line, we could superimpose that line over the points; this is the *regression line*.

The linear regression model has important descriptive uses. The regression line offers a graphic picture of the association between X and Y, and

FIGURE 14-4

A Scattergram of the Values of Two Variables with Regression Line Added (Hypothetical)

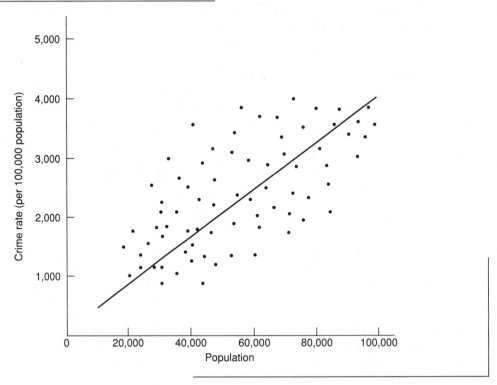

the regression equation is an efficient form for summarizing that association. The regression model has inferential value as well. To the extent that the regression equation correctly describes the general association between the two variables, it may be used to predict other sets of values. If, for example, we know that a new case has a value of 3.5 on X, then we can predict the value of 3.5 on Y as well.

In practice, of course, studies are seldom limited to four cases, and the associations between variables are seldom as clear as the one presented in Figure 14-3.

Figure 14-4 is a somewhat more realistic example that represents a hypothetical relationship between population and crime rate in small to medium-sized cities. Each dot in the scattergram is a city, and its placement reflects that city's population and its crime rate. As in our previous example, the values of Y (crime rates) generally cor-

respond to those of X (populations), and as values of X increase, so do values of Y. However, the association is not nearly as clear as it was in Figure 14-3.

It is not possible in Figure 14-4 to superimpose a straight line that will pass through all the points in the scattergram. But we can draw an approximate line showing the best possible linear representation of the several points.

If you've ever studied geometry, you know that any straight line on a graph can be represented by an equation of the form $Y = a + bX$, where X and Y are values of the two variables. In this equation, a equals the value of Y when X is 0, and b represents the slope of the line. If we know the values of a and b, we can estimate Y for every value of X.

Regression analysis is a technique for establishing the regression equation representing the geometric line that comes closest to the distribution of points. This equation is valuable both descriptively and inferentially. First, the regression equation provides a mathematical description of the relationship between the variables. Second, the regression equation allows us to infer values of Y when we have values of X. Recalling Figure 14-4, we could estimate crime rates of cities if we knew their populations.

To improve your guessing, you construct a regression line, stated in the form of a regression equation that permits the estimation of values on one variable from values on the other. The general format for this equation is $Y' = a + b(X)$, where a and b are computed values, X is a given value on one variable, and Y' is the estimated value on the other. The values of a and b are computed to minimize the differences between the actual values of Y and the corresponding estimates (Y') based on the known value of X. The sum of squared differences between actual and estimated values of Y is called the *unexplained variation* because it represents errors that exist even when estimates are based on known values of X.

The *explained variation* is the difference between the total variation and the unexplained variation. Dividing the explained variation by the total variation produces a measure of the proportionate reduction of error corresponding to the similar quantity in the computation of lambda. In the present case, this quantity is the correlation squared: r^2. Thus, if $r = .7$, then $r^2 = .49$, which means that about half the variation has been explained. In practice, we compute r rather than r^2 because the product-moment correlation can take either a positive or a negative sign, depending on the direction of the relationship between the two variables. (Computing r^2 and taking a square root would always produce a positive quantity.) See Freeman (1968) or any other standard statistics textbook for the method of computing r, although most readers who use this measure will have access to computer programs designed for this function.

Multiple Regression Analysis Often criminal justice researchers find that a given dependent variable is affected by several independent variables simultaneously. *Multiple regression analysis* provides

a means for analyzing such situations. That was the case when Warner and Pierce (1993) set about studying social disorganization and calls for police services in Boston neighborhoods. Their expectations may be stated in the form of a multiple regression equation:

$$AR = b_0 + b_1X_1 + b_2X_2 + b_3X_3 + e$$

where

AR = assault rate
X_1 = poverty
X_2 = residential mobility
X_3 = racial heterogeneity
b = regression weight
e = residual

Notice that in place of the single X variable in a linear regression, there are several X's, and there are also several b's instead of just one. Also, the equation ends with a residual factor (e), which represents the variance in Y that is not accounted for by the X variables analyzed.

Warner and Pierce then calculated the values of the several b's to show the relative contributions of the several independent variables in neighborhood assault rates. They also calculated the multiple-correlation coefficient as an indicator of the extent to which the three independent variables predict the dependent variable. This follows the same logic as the simple bivariate correlation discussed earlier, and it is traditionally reported as a capital R. In this case, $R = .77$, which means that about 58 percent of the variance in neighborhood assault rates is explained by the three variables acting in concert.

Cautions in Regression Analysis The use of regression analysis for statistical inferences is based on the same assumptions made for correlational analysis: simple random sampling, the absence of nonsampling errors, and continuous interval data. Because criminal justice research seldom completely satisfies these assumptions, you should use caution in assessing the results of regression analyses.

Also, regression lines can be useful for interpolation (estimating cases that lie between those observed), but they are less trustworthy when used for extrapolation (estimating cases that lie beyond the range of observations). This limitation on extrapolations is important in two ways. First, you are likely to come across regression equations that seem to make illogical predictions. An equation that links population and crimes, for example, might seem to suggest that small towns with, say, a population of 1,000 should produce −123 crimes a year. This failure in predictive ability does not disqualify the equation but dramatizes that its applicability is limited to a particular range of population sizes. Second, researchers sometimes overstep this limitation, drawing inferences that lie outside their range of observation, and you are right in criticizing them for that.

■ INFERENTIAL STATISTICS

Many criminal justice research projects examine data collected from a sample drawn from a larger population. A sample of people may be interviewed in a survey; a sample of court records may be coded and analyzed; a sample of newspapers may be examined through content analysis. Researchers seldom, if ever, study samples just to describe the samples per se; in most instances, their ultimate purpose is to make assertions about the larger population from which the sample has been selected. Frequently, then, you will wish to interpret your univariate and multivariate sample findings as the basis for inferences about some population.

This section will examine the statistical measures used for making such inferences and their logical bases. We'll begin with univariate data and then move to bivariate.

Univariate Inferences

The opening sections of this chapter dealt with methods of presenting univariate data. Each summary measure was intended to describe the sample studied. Now we will use those measures to make broader assertions about the population. This section will address two univariate measures: percentages and means.

If 50 percent of a sample of people say they received traffic tickets during the past year, then 50 percent is also our best estimate of the proportion of people who received traffic tickets in the total population from which the sample was drawn. (This estimate assumes a simple random sample, of course.) It is rather unlikely, however, that precisely 50 percent of the population have gotten tickets during the year. If a rigorous sampling design for random selection has been followed, we will be able to estimate the expected range of error when the sample finding is applied to the population.

The section in Chapter 9 on sampling theory covered the procedures for making such estimates, so they will only be reviewed here. The quantity

$$s = \sqrt{\frac{p \times q}{n}}$$

where p is a percentage, q equals $1 - p$, and n is the sample size, is called the *standard error*. As noted in Chapter 9, this quantity is very important in the estimation of sampling error. We may be 68 percent confident that the population figure falls within plus or minus one standard error of the sample figure, we may be 95 percent confident that it falls within plus or minus two standard errors, and we may be 99.9 percent confident that it falls within plus or minus three standard errors.

Any statement of sampling error, then, must contain two essential components: the *confidence level* (for example, 95 percent) and the *confidence interval* (for example, 2.5 percent). If 50 percent of a sample of 1,600 people say they have received traffic tickets during the year, we might say we are 95 percent confident that the population figure is between 47.5 percent and 52.5 percent.

Recognize in this example that we have moved beyond simply describing the sample into the realm of making estimates (inferences) about the larger population. In doing that, we must be wary of three assumptions.

First, the sample must be drawn from the population about which inferences are being made.

A sample taken from a telephone directory, for example, cannot legitimately be the basis for statistical inferences about the population of a city.

Second, the inferential statistics assume simple random sampling, which is virtually never the case in sample surveys. The statistics assume sampling with replacement, which is almost never done, but that is probably not a serious problem. Although systematic sampling is used more frequently than random sampling, that, too, probably presents no serious problem if done correctly. Stratified sampling, since it improves representativeness, clearly presents no problem. Cluster sampling does present a problem, however, because the estimates of sampling error may be too small. Clearly, street-corner sampling does not warrant the use of inferential statistics. This standard error sampling technique also assumes a 100 percent completion rate. This problem increases in seriousness as the completion rate decreases.

Third, inferential statistics are addressed to sampling error only; they do not take account of **nonsampling errors.** Thus, although it might be correct to state that between 47.5 and 52.5 percent of the population (95 percent confidence) would report getting a traffic ticket during the previous year, we could not so confidently guess the percentage who had actually received them. Because nonsampling errors are probably larger than sampling errors in a respectable sample design, we need to be especially cautious in generalizing from our sample findings to the population.

Tests of Statistical Significance

There is no scientific answer to the question of whether a given association between two variables is significant, strong, important, interesting, or worth reporting. Perhaps the ultimate test of significance rests with your ability to persuade your audience (present and future) of the association's significance. At the same time, a body of inferential statistics—called parametric tests of significance—can assist you in this regard. As the name suggests, parametric statistics make certain assumptions about the parameters that describe the population from which the sample is selected.

Although **tests of statistical significance** are widely reported in criminal justice literature, the logic underlying them is subtle and often misunderstood. Tests of significance are based on the same sampling logic that has been discussed elsewhere in this book. To understand that logic, let's return for a moment to the concept of sampling error in regard to univariate data.

Recall that a sample statistic normally provides the best single estimate of the corresponding population parameter, but the statistic and the parameter are seldom identical. Thus, we report the probability that the parameter falls within a certain range (confidence interval). The degree of uncertainty within that range is due to normal sampling error. The corollary of such a statement is, of course, that it is improbable that the parameter would fall outside the specified range only as a result of sampling error. Thus, if we estimate that a parameter (99.9 percent confidence) lies between 45 percent and 55 percent, we say by implication that it is extremely improbable that the parameter is actually, say, 90 percent if our only error of estimation is due to normal sampling. That is the basic logic behind tests of significance.

The Logic of Statistical Significance

The logic of statistical significance can be illustrated in a series of diagrams representing the selection of samples from a population. The elements in the logic we will illustrate are:

1. Assumptions regarding the *independence* of two variables in the population study
2. Assumptions regarding the *representativeness* of samples selected through conventional probability sampling procedures
3. The observed *joint distribution* of sample elements in terms of the two variables

Figure 14-5 represents a hypothetical population of 256 people, half women and half men. The diagram indicates how each person feels about laws restricting gun ownership. In the diagram, those who favor gun control laws have open circles; those who oppose it have their circles shaded in.

FIGURE 14-5

A Hypothetical Population of Men and Women Who Either Favor or Oppose Gun Control Laws

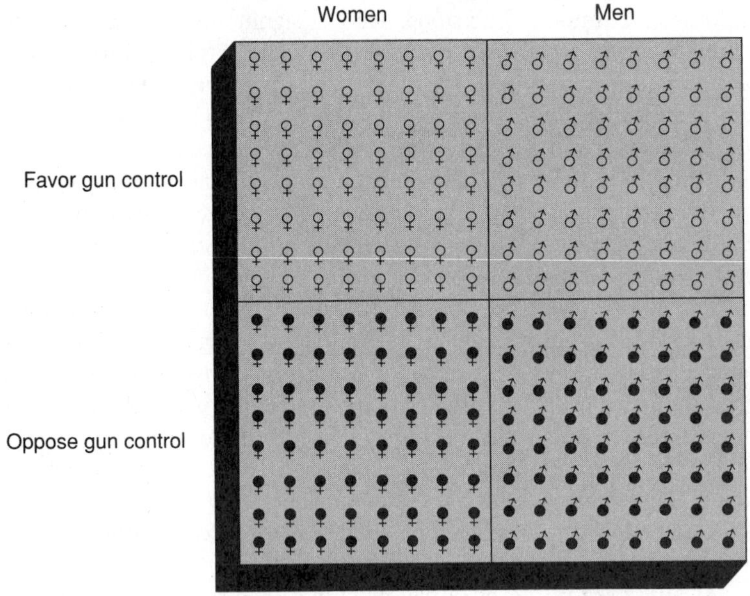

	Women	Men
Favor gun control	50%	50%
Oppose gun control	50%	50%
	100%	100%

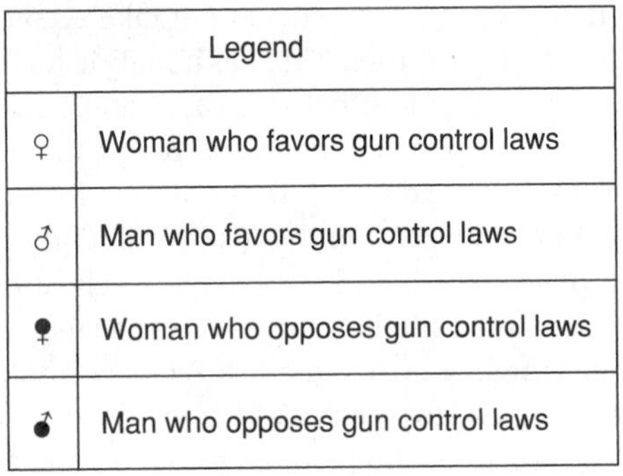

The question we'll be investigating is whether there is any relationship between gender and opinions about gun control laws. More specifically, we'll see whether women are more likely to favor gun control than men. Take a moment to look at Figure 14-5 and see what the answer to that question is.

The figure indicates that there is no relationship between gender and attitudes about gun control. Exactly half of each group favors gun control and half opposes it. Recall the earlier discussion of proportionate reduction of error. In this instance, knowing a person's gender would not reduce the "errors" we'd make in guessing his or her attitude toward gun control laws. The table at the bottom of Figure 14-5 provides a tabular view of what you can observe in the graphic diagram.

Figure 14-6 represents the selection of a one-fourth sample from the hypothetical population. In terms of the graphic illustration, a "square" selection from the center of the population provides

FIGURE 14-6
A Representative Sample

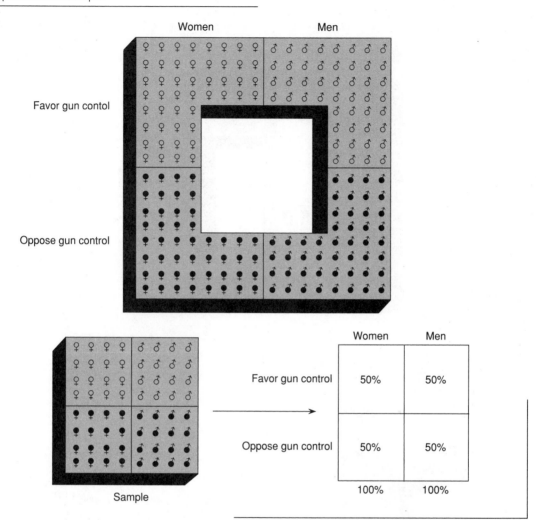

a representative sample. Notice that our sample contains 16 of each type of person: Half are men and half are women; half of each gender group favors gun control, and the other half opposes it.

The sample selected in Figure 14-6 would allow us to draw accurate conclusions about the relationship between gender and attitudes toward gun control in the larger population. Following the sampling logic you learned in Chapter 9, we would note there was no relationship between gender and gun control attitudes in the sample.

Thus, we'd conclude that there was similarly no relationship in the larger population—since we've presumably selected a sample according to the conventional rules of sampling.

Of course, real-life samples are seldom such perfect reflections of the populations from which they are drawn. It would not be unusual for us to have selected, say, one of two extra men who opposed gun control and a couple of extra women who favored it—even if there was no relationship between the two variables in the population.

FIGURE 14-7
An Unrepresentative Sample

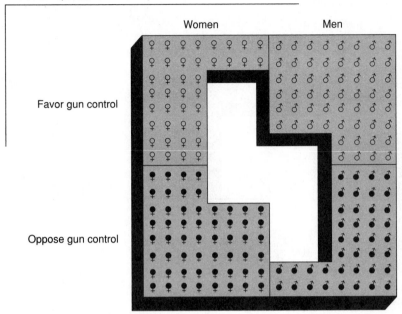

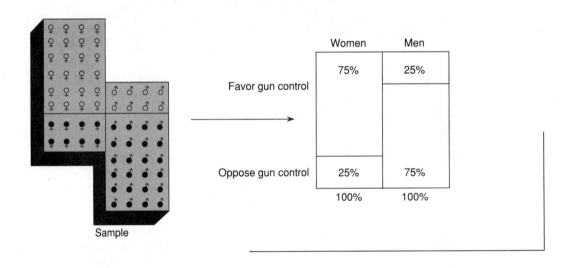

Sample

Such minor variations are part and parcel of probability sampling, as you learned in Chapter 9.

Figure 14-7, however, represents a sample that falls far short of the mark in reflecting the larger population. Notice that it has selected far too many supportive women and too many opposing men. As the table shows, three-fourths of the women in the sample support gun control, but only one-fourth of the men do so. If we had selected this sample from a population in which the two variables were unrelated, we'd be sorely misled by the analysis of our sample.

As you'll recall, it's unlikely that a properly drawn probability sample would ever be as inaccurate as the one shown in Figure 14-7. In fact, if we actually selected a sample that gave us those

FIGURE 14-8

A Representative Sample from a Population in Which the Variables Are Related

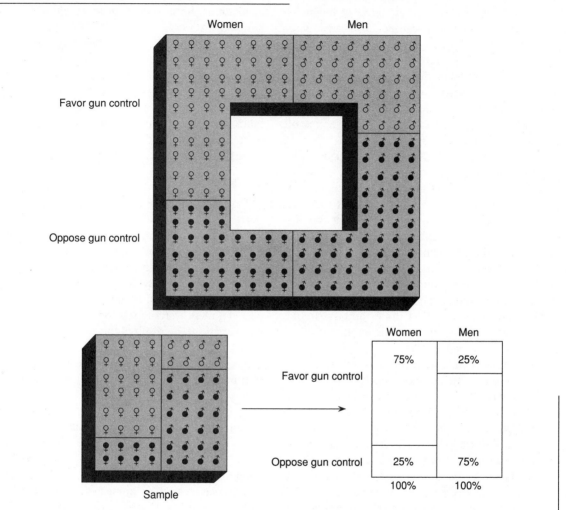

results, we'd look for a different explanation. Figure 14-8 illustrates that other explanation.

Notice that the sample selected in Figure 14-8 also shows a strong relationship between gender and opinion about gun control. The reason is quite different this time. We've selected a perfectly representative sample, but we see that there is actually a strong relationship between the two variables in the population at large. In this figure, women are more likely to support gun control than men: That's the case in the population, and the sample reflects it.

In practice, of course, we never know what's so for the total population; that's why we select samples. So if we selected a sample and found the strong relationship presented in Figures 14-7 and 14-8, we would need to decide whether that finding accurately reflected the population or was simply a product of sampling error.

The fundamental logic of tests of statistical significance, then, is this: Faced with *any* discrepancy between the assumed independence of variables in a population and the observed distribution of sample elements, we may explain that discrepancy in either of two ways: (1) We may attribute it to an unrepresentative sample, or (2) we may reject the assumption of independence. The logic and statistics associated with probability sampling methods offer guidance about the varying probabilities of different degrees of unrepresentativeness (expressed as sampling error). Most simply put, there is a high probability of a small degree of unrepresentativeness and a low probability of a large degree of unrepresentativeness.

The **statistical significance** of a relationship observed in a set of sample data, then, is always expressed in terms of probabilities. Significant at the .05 level ($p \leq .05$) simply means that the probability of a relationship as strong as the observed one being attributable to sampling error alone is no more than 5 in 100. Put somewhat differently, if two variables are independent of each other in the population and if 100 probability samples were selected from that population, then no more than 5 of those samples should provide a relationship as strong as the one that has been observed.

There is, then, a corollary to confidence intervals in tests of significance, which represent the probability of the measured associations being due to only sampling error. This is called the **level of significance.** Like confidence intervals, levels of significance are derived from a logical model in which several samples are drawn from a given population. In the present case, we assume that no association exists between the variables in the population, and then we ask what proportion of the samples drawn from that population would produce associations at least as great as those measured in the empirical data. Three levels of significance are frequently used in research reports: .05, .01, and .001. These mean, respectively, that the chances of obtaining the measured association as a result of sampling error are no more that 5/100, 1/100, and 1/1,000.

Researchers who use tests of significance normally follow one of two patterns. Some specify in advance the level of significance they will regard as sufficient. If any measured association is statistically significant at that level, they will regard it as representing a genuine association between the two variables. In other words, they are willing to discount the possibility of its resulting from sampling error only.

Other researchers prefer to report the specific level of significance for each association, disregarding the conventions of .05, .01, and .001. Rather than reporting that a given association is significant at the .05 level, they might report significance at the .023 level, indicating the chances of its having resulted from sampling error as no more than 23 out of 1,000.

Chi Square

Chi square (χ^2) is a frequently used test of significance in criminal justice research. It is based on the **null hypothesis:** the assumption that there is no relationship between the two variables in the total population. Given the observed distribution of values on the two separate variables, we compute the conjoint distribution that would be expected if there were no relationship between the two variables. The result of this operation is a set of expected frequencies for all the cells in the contingency table. We then compare this expected distribution with the distribution of cases actually found in the sample data, and we determine the probability that the discovered discrepancy could have resulted from sampling error alone. An example will illustrate this procedure.

Let's assume we are interested in the possible relationship between gender and whether people avoid areas near their home because of crime, which we will refer to as *avoidance behavior.* To test this relationship, we select a sample of 100 people at random. Our sample is made up of 40 men and 60 women; 70 percent of our sample report avoidance behavior, whereas the remaining 30 percent do not.

If there is no relationship between gender and avoidance behavior, then 70 percent of the men in the sample should report avoiding areas near their home, and 30 percent should report no avoidance behavior. Moreover, women should describe avoidance behavior in the same proportion. Table 14-11 (Part I) shows that, based on this model, 28 men and 42 women would say

TABLE 14-11
A Hypothetical Illustration of Chi Square

I. Expected Cell Frequencies

	Men	Women	Total
Avoid areas[a]	28	42	70
Do not avoid areas	12	18	30
Total	40	60	100

II. Observed Cell Frequencies

	Men	Women	Total
Avoid areas	20	50	70
Do not avoid areas	20	10	30
Total	40	60	100

III. (Observed − Expected)^2 ÷ Expected

	Men	Women	
Avoid areas	2.29	1.52	Chi sq. = 12.70
Do not avoid areas	5.33	3.56	$p < .001$

[a]"Is there any area around here—that is, within a city block—that you avoid at night because of crime?"

they avoided areas at night, with 12 men and 18 women reporting no avoidance.

Part II of Table 14-11 presents the observed avoidance behavior for the hypothetical sample of 100 people. Note that 20 of the men say they avoid areas at night, and the remaining 20 say they do not. Among the women in the sample, 50 avoid areas and 10 do not. Comparing the expected and observed frequencies (Parts I and II), we note that somewhat fewer men reported avoidance behavior than expected, whereas somewhat more women than expected avoid areas near their home at night.

Chi square is computed as follows. For each cell in the tables, the researcher (1) subtracts the expected frequency for that cell from the observed frequency, (2) squares this quantity, and (3) divides the squared difference by the expected frequency. This procedure is carried out for each cell in the tables, and the results are added. (Part III of Table 14-11 presents the cell-by-cell computations.) The final sum is the value of chi square: 12.70 in the example.

This value is the overall discrepancy between the observed conjoint distribution in the sample and the distribution we would expect if the two variables were unrelated. Of course, the mere discovery of a discrepancy does not prove that the two variables are related, since normal sampling error might produce discrepancies even when there was no relationship in the total population. The magnitude of the value of chi square, however, permits us to estimate the probability of that having happened.

To determine the statistical significance of the observed relationship, we must use a standard set of chi-square values. That will require the computation of the *degrees of freedom*. For chi square, the degrees of freedom are computed as follows: The number of rows in the table of observed frequencies, minus one, is multiplied by the number of columns, minus one. This may be written as $(r - 1)(c - 1)$. In the present example, we have two rows and two columns (discounting the totals), so there is one degree of freedom.

Turning to a table of chi-square values (see Appendix E), we find that for one degree of freedom and random sampling from a population in which there is no relationship between two variables, 10 percent of the time we should expect a chi square of at least 2.7. Thus, if we selected 100 samples from such a population, we should expect about 10 of those samples to produce chi squares equal to or greater than 2.7. Moreover, we should expect chi-square values of at least 6.6 in only 1 percent of the samples and chi-square values of 10.8 in only .1 percent of the samples. The higher the chi-square value, the less probable it is that the value could be attributed to sampling error alone.

In our example, the computed value of chi square is 12.70. If there were no relationship between gender and avoidance behavior and a large number of samples had been selected and studied, we would expect a chi square of this magnitude in fewer than .1 percent of those samples. Thus, the probability of obtaining a chi square of this magnitude is less than .001 if random sampling has been used and there is no relationship in the population. We report this finding by saying the relationship is statistically significant at the .001 level. Because it is so improbable that the observed relationship could have resulted from sampling error alone, we are likely to reject the null hypothesis and assume that a relationship does exist between the two variables.

Many measures of association can be tested for statistical significance in a similar manner. Standard tables of values permit us to determine whether a given association is statistically significant and at what level. Any standard statistics textbook provides instructions on the use of such tables, so we will not pursue the matter further here.

Cautions in Interpreting Statistical Significance

Tests of significance provide an objective yardstick against which to estimate the significance of associations between variables. They assist us in ruling out associations that may not represent genuine relationships in the population under study. The researcher who uses or reads reports of significance tests should remain wary of certain dangers in their interpretation, however.

First, we have been discussing tests of *statistical* significance; there are no objective tests of substantive significance. Thus, we may be legitimately convinced that a given association is not due to sampling error, but we may still assert without fear of contradiction that two variables are only slightly related to each other. Recall that sampling error is an inverse function of sample size; the larger the sample, the smaller the expected error. Thus, a correlation of, say, .1 might well be significant (at a given level) if discovered in a large sample, whereas the same correlation between the same two variables would not be significant if found in a smaller sample. Of course, that makes perfectly good sense if one understands the basic logic of tests of significance: In the larger sample, there is less chance that the correlation could be simply the product of sampling error.

Consider, for example, Table 14-12, in which 20 cases are distributed in the same proportions across row and column categories as in Table 14-11. In each table, 83 percent of women report avoidance behavior (10/12 in Table 14-12, and 50/60 in Table 14-11). But with one-fifth the number of cases in Table 14-12, the computed value of chi square is only one-fifth that obtained in Table 14-11. Consulting the distribution of chi-square values in Appendix E, we see that the probability of obtaining a chi square of 2.54 with one degree of freedom lies between .10 and .20. Thus, if there were no relationship between these two variables, we would expect to obtain a chi square of this size in 10 to 20 percent of samples drawn. Most researchers would not reject the null hypothesis of no relationship in this case.

We mentioned the point illustrated by this example in Chapter 13 because it has special meaning for applied studies, particularly those using experimental designs. With small sample sizes, even moderately large differences might result from sampling error. Because randomized experiments are costly and time-consuming, they are often conducted with relatively small numbers of subjects in experimental and control groups. With small numbers of subjects, only large differences in outcome variables will be statistically significant.

The distinction between statistical and substantive significance is perhaps best illustrated by those cases where there is absolute certainty that observed differences cannot be a result of sampling error. That would be the case when we observe an entire population. Suppose we were able to learn the age and gender of every murder victim in the United States for 1996. For argument's

TABLE 14-12
Chi Square Sensitivity to Sample Size: A Hypothetical Illustration

I. Expected Cell Frequencies

	Men	Women	Total
Avoid areas[a]	5.6	8.4	14
Do not avoid areas	2.4	3.6	6
Total	8	12	20

II. Observed Cell Frequencies

	Men	Women	Total
Avoid areas	4	10	14
Do not avoid areas	4	2	6
Total	8	12	20

III. (Observed − Expected)^2 ÷ Expected

	Men	Women	
Avoid areas	0.46	0.30	Chi sq. = 2.54
Do not avoid areas	1.07	0.71	$10 < p < 20$

[a]"Is there any area around here—that is, within a city block—that you avoid at night because of crime?"

sake, let's assume that the average age of male murder victims was 25, as compared to, say, 26 for female victims. Because we would have the ages of all murder victims, there would be no question of sampling error. We know with certainty that the female victims are older than their male counterparts. At the same time, we would say that the difference was of no substantive significance. We'd conclude, in fact, that they were essentially the same age.

Second, lest you be misled by this hypothetical example, you should not calculate statistical significance on relationships observed in data collected from whole populations. Remember, tests of statistical significance measure the likelihood of relationships between variables being only a product of sampling error, which of course assumes that data come from a sample. If there's no sampling, there's no sampling error.

Third, tests of significance are based on the same sampling assumptions we used to compute confidence intervals. To the extent that these assumptions are not met by the actual sampling design, the tests of significance are not strictly legitimate.

In practice, tests of statistical significance are frequently used inappropriately. If you were to review any given issue of an academic journal in criminal justice, we'd be willing to bet you would find one or more of these technically improper uses:

1. Tests of significance computed for data representing entire populations
2. Tests based on samples that do not meet the required assumptions of probability sampling
3. Tests applied to measures of association that have been computed in violation of the assumptions made by those measures (for example, product-moment correlations computed from ordinal data)
4. Interpretation of statistical significance as a measure of association (a "relationship" of $p = .001$ is "stronger" than one of $p = .05$)

We do not mean to a suggest a "purist" approach by these comments. We encourage you to use any statistical technique—any measure of association or any test of significance—on any set of data if it will help you understand your data. In doing so, however, you should recognize what measures of association and statistical significance can and cannot tell you, as well as the assumptions required for various measures. Any individual statistic or measure tells only part of the story, and you should try to learn as much of the story as you possibly can.

■ *MAIN POINTS*

- Descriptive statistics are used to summarize data under study. Some descriptive statistics summarize the distribution of attributes on a single variable; others summarize the associations between variables.

- Descriptive statistics that summarize the relationships between variables are called measures of association.

- Univariate analysis is the analysis of a single variable.

- A frequency distribution shows the number of cases that have each of the attributes of a given variable.

- Measures of central tendency (the mean, median, and mode) reduce data to an easily manageable form, but they do not convey the detail of the original data.

- Measures of dispersion give a summary indication of the distribution of cases around an average value.

- Rates are descriptive statistics that standardize some measure for comparative purposes. The measure of interest—number of persons under correctional supervision in a state, for example—is divided by the population eligible for inclusion in the measure. Rates can be misleading if calculated with an inappropriate denominator.

- To undertake a subgroup comparison: (1) divide cases into the appropriate subgroups, (2) describe each subgroup in terms of a given variable, and (3) compare those descriptions across the subgroups.

- Bivariate analysis is nothing more than a different interpretation of subgroup comparisons: (1) divide cases into subgroups in terms of their attributes on some independent variable, (2) describe each subgroup in terms of some dependent variable, (3) compare the dependent variable descriptions of the subgroups, and (4) interpret any observed differences as a statistical association between the independent and dependent variables.

- The rules of thumb in interpreting bivariate percentage tables are: (1) "percentage down" and "read across" in making the subgroup comparisons, or (2) "percentage across" and "read down" in making subgroup comparisons.

- Multivariate analysis is a method of analyzing the simultaneous relationships among several variables and may be used to more fully understand the relationship between two variables.

- Many measures of association are based on a proportionate reduction of error (PRE) model. This model is based on a comparison of (1) the number of errors we would make in attempting to guess the attributes of a given variable for each of the cases under study—if we knew nothing but the distribution of attributes on that variable—and (2) the number of errors we would make if we knew the joint distribution overall and were told for each case the attribute of one variable each time we were asked to guess the attribute of the other.

- Lambda (λ) is an appropriate measure of association to be used in the analysis of two nominal variables. It also provides a clear illustration of the PRE model.

- Gamma (γ) is an appropriate measure of association to be used in the analysis of two ordinal variables.

- Pearson's product-moment correlation (r) is an appropriate measure of association to be used in the analysis of two interval or ratio variables.

- Regression analysis represents the relationships between variables in the form of equations, which can be used to predict the values of a dependent variable on the basis of values of one or more independent variables.

- The basic regression equation—for a simple linear regression—is of the form $Y = a + bX$. In this case, Y is the value (estimated) of the dependent variable; a is some constant value; and b is another numerical value, which is multiplied by X, the value of the independent variable.

- Regression equations are computed on the basis of a regression line: that geometric line that represents, with the least amount of discrepancy, the actual location of points in a scattergram.

- A multiple regression analysis results in a regression equation, which estimates the values of a dependent variable from the values of several independent variables.

- Inferential statistics are used to estimate the generalizability of findings arrived at in the analysis of a sample to the larger population from which the sample has been selected. Some inferential statistics estimate the single-variable characteristics of the population; others—tests of statistical significance—estimate the relationships between variables in the population.

- Inferences about some characteristic of a population—such as the percentage who favor gun control laws—must contain an indication of a confidence interval (the range within which the value is expected to be: for example, between 45 and 55 percent favor gun control) and an indication of the confidence level (the likelihood the value does fall within that range: for example, 95 percent confidence). Computations of confidence levels and intervals are based on probability theory and assume that conventional probability sampling techniques have been employed in the study.

- Inferences about the generalizability to a population of the associations discovered between variables in a sample involve tests of statistical significance. Most simply put, these tests estimate the likelihood that an association as large as the observed one could result from normal sampling error if no such association exists between the variables in the larger population. Tests of statistical significance, then, are also based on probability theory and assume that conventional probability sampling techniques have been employed in the study.

- Statistical significance must not be confused with substantive significance, which means that an observed association is strong, important, or meaningful.

- The level of significance of an observed association is reported as the probability that that association could have been produced merely by sampling error. To say that an association is significant at the .05 level is to say that an association as large as the observed one could not be expected to result from sampling error more than 5 times out of 100.

- Tests of statistical significance, strictly speaking, make assumptions about data and methods that are almost never satisfied completely by real social research. Despite this, the tests can serve a useful function in the analysis and interpretation of data. You should be wary of interpreting the "significance" of the test results too precisely, however.

■ REVIEW QUESTIONS AND EXERCISES

1. Using the data in the accompanying table, construct and interpret tables showing:
   a. The bivariate relationship between age and attitude toward capital punishment
   b. The bivariate relationship between political orientation and attitude toward capital punishment
   c. The multivariate relationship linking age, political orientation, and attitude toward capital punishment

Age	Political Orientation	Attitude Toward Capital Punishment	Frequency
Young	Conservative	Favor	90
Young	Conservative	Oppose	10
Young	Liberal	Favor	60
Young	Liberal	Oppose	40
Old	Conservative	Favor	60
Old	Conservative	Oppose	10
Old	Liberal	Favor	5
Old	Liberal	Oppose	15

2. In your own words, explain the logic of proportionate reduction of error (PRE) measures of associations.

3. Distinguish between measures of association and tests of statistical significance.

4. This exercise requires that you have access to the World Wide Web and a browser with

graphics capability. Go to the General Social Survey site identified at the bottom of
Table 14-4.

   a. Prepare bivariate contingency tables for
      analyzing the relationship between gun
      ownership and these variables: political
      party affiliation, education, and
      rural/urban/suburban residence.

   b. Prepare a three-way contingency table for
      analyzing gun ownership, gender, and each
      of the variables from the first part of this
      exercise.

■ ADDITIONAL READINGS

Babbie, Earl, and Halley, Fred, *Adventures in Social Research* (Newbury Park, CA: Pine Forge
Press, 1995). This book introduces you to data
analysis through SPSS, a widely used computer program for statistical analysis. Several
of the basic techniques described in this chapter are illustrated and discussed further.

Blalock, Hubert M., Jr. *Social Statistics,* 3rd ed.
(New York: McGraw-Hill, 1979). Blalock's
text has been a standard for social science
students and faculty for decades.

Fienberg, Stephen E., *The Analysis of Cross-Classified
Data* (Cambridge, MA: MIT Press, 1977). This
book presents a conceptual treatment of the
principles of multivariate analysis of nominal
variables. Many important criminal justice
variables are measured at the nominal level,
and criminal justice researchers have increasingly adopted multivariate techniques for
such variables. Several different approaches
are currently used, but Fienberg's excellent
little book clearly presents the underlying
logic common to all approaches.

Finkelstein, Michael O., and Levin, Bruce, *Statistics for Lawyers* (New York: Springer-Verlag,
1990). Law school trains people to be analytic, but few lawyers know much about statistics. This book provides a straightforward
explanation of many basic statistical concepts.
Examples are drawn from actual cases to illustrate how to calculate and interpret statistics. Additionally, you'll gain insight into how
to reason with statistics.

Mohr, Lawrence B., *Understanding Significance Testing* (Newbury Park, CA: Sage, 1990). An excellent and comprehensive examination of the
topic, covering both the technical details and
the substantive meaning of significance tests.

Schroeder, Larry D., Sjoquist, David L., and
Stephan, Paula E., *Understanding Regression
Analysis: An Introductory Guide* (Newbury Park,
CA: Sage, 1986). If you wish to learn more
about regression as an analytic technique, this
book would be an excellent next step. The
authors offer an understandable introduction
to a complex topic.

CHAPTER

15 *Pulling It All Together: Annotated Examples*

What You'll Learn in This Chapter

In this final chapter, we will describe examples of criminal justice research at some length to illustrate what you have learned in earlier chapters. You'll find that this chapter helps you pull it all together.

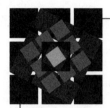

INTRODUCTION

NATIONAL INSTITUTE OF JUSTICE RESEARCH PLAN 1995–96
Writing Your Grant Proposal

JUVENILE VICTIMIZATION AND OFFENDING
Research Program Statement
Proposal: Longitudinal Design
    Using Available Data
The Research Report

CRIME COMMISSION RATES
Research Program Statement
Proposal: Inmate Self-report Survey
The Research Report

CONCLUSION

■ INTRODUCTION

As you'll gather, we are getting close to the conclusion of your venture into criminal justice research. We imagine some parts have been pretty simple for you, and others have been a bit more challenging—and some may have seemed more challenging than absolutely necessary. Whatever the balance of these materials for you, we are pleased to report there's no new technical material in this chapter; you've already covered everything you need to know in your introduction to criminal justice research. The purpose of this chapter is to bring things together and help you retain and use what you've already learned.

Our plan in this regard is to lead you through more examples of research. We have, of course, mentioned many examples along the way to illustrate various principles of the research process as they were covered in individual chapters. Here we adopt a slightly different approach.

We will describe two actual research projects at some length, pointing out how these examples represent different elements of research, from design through measurement, data collection, and analysis. Previous chapters are organized around specific topics, incorporating various examples to illustrate those topics. Our final chapter is organized around examples, incorporating commentary to guide you back to topics from earlier chapters.

You may find yourself leafing back through the book as you read this chapter. In fact, that's an activity we want to encourage. We presented a great deal of material in the first 14 chapters, and there is no way you can expect to absorb it all after a single reading. So as we work through these two examples, we will frequently pause along the way to direct your attention to general principles and issues in conducting criminal justice research.

We'll begin by describing one source of interests and ideas about criminal justice research projects. For more than 25 years, the National Institute of Justice (NIJ) has promoted basic and applied research. Its annual *Research Plan* presents priority research topics that the institute seeks to promote.

Our purpose in organizing much of this chapter around NIJ's research program and examples of NIJ-sponsored research is neither to praise the institute nor to imply that it is the sole source of ideas about criminal justice research topics. Some researchers feel that NIJ focuses too narrowly on questions of crime control, to the exclusion of other worthy topics. Others may believe that concentrating research on applied policy or management issues diverts attention from basic research questions about the causes of crime. In any event, no prospective researcher should feel bound to restrict his or her inquiry to questions of interest to a single government organization.

We chose to organize the first part of this chapter around the NIJ *Research Plan* for three reasons. First, the *Research Plan* does in fact stimulate research that might not otherwise be conducted by providing funding for projects in specific areas. In this way, NIJ influences the agenda for criminal justice research. As a related point, NIJ encourages research by professionals in criminal justice organizations in addition to studies by university professors. In 1996, the institute began funding "partnership" studies that involved research collaboration between justice professionals and professional researchers.

Second, each year's plan lays out specific requirements for research proposals, in much the same way that we described the general elements of a research proposal in Chapter 4. In doing this, the *Research Plan* thus serves as our first example of a topic from earlier chapters.

Third, NIJ's statement of research priorities serves as the starting point in our efforts to illustrate how researchers move from general ideas and interests (whatever their source) to creating a research proposal, to producing reports of research results. After describing the Institute's *Research Plan*, we will turn to two specific research projects that were funded by NIJ. Each example begins with a brief description of the research purpose. We will next describe the actual proposal submitted to NIJ, pointing to elements of the research process exhibited by each proposal. Finally, we will briefly examine some of the findings that resulted from each project.

We think this approach will give you a better understanding of the overall research process and the specific elements of that process.

■ NATIONAL INSTITUTE OF JUSTICE RESEARCH PLAN 1995–96

Let's begin with an excerpt from the introduction to an earlier NIJ Program Plan:

■ Research takes many forms and involves a number of steps if it is to be useful. Accordingly, NIJ:

- Develops research studies to expand understanding of why and how specific violence and crime problems arise.
- Evaluates programs to learn what is working to prevent and reduce violent crime.
- Demonstrates how new knowledge can be put into practice.
- Communicates new ideas for action that can benefit communities seeking better approaches. (National Institute of Justice, 1994:iii)

This brief statement of NIJ's mission should prompt you to recall different research purposes described in Chapter 4. "Expand understanding of why and how" implies descriptive, exploratory, and explanatory research purposes. Evaluating programs and putting new knowledge into practice are clearly examples of application. And, of course, research findings, applied and otherwise, should be communicated to others.

Beginning with the 1993 plan, NIJ organized its research interests around long-range goals that establish topics for research within the general purposes of description, exploration, explanation, and application. The 1995–96 *Research Plan* lays out these goals and describes more specific priority areas within each:

■ I. Reduce violent crimes.

   II. Reduce drug- and alcohol-related crime.

   III. Reduce the consequences of crime.

   IV. Improve the effectiveness of crime prevention programs.

   V. Improve law enforcement and the criminal justice system.

   VI. Develop new technology for law enforcement and the criminal justice system. (p. 2)

Incidentally, NIJ developed these long-range goals and other aspects of its research activities by using focus groups (see Chapter 10). Group participants were selected to represent criminal justice professionals and researchers.

Priority areas within each goal describe both basic and applied research interests, many of which were reflected in widely publicized incidents and issues from the early 1990s. For example, gangs, firearms, and youth violence are specifically mentioned as topics of interest under the first goal. The second goal broadens a long-term interest in the relationships between drugs and crime to cite several specific questions about alcohol and crime.

The second goal also touches on an issue we raised in Chapter 12—supplementing existing data-collection activities to obtain creative but economical measures:

■ Researchers are encouraged to develop proposals that present innovative ways of utilizing the Drug Use Forecasting (DUF) program as a research "platform" for pursuing a wide range of hypotheses related to drug use and criminal activity. For instance, in collaboration with existing DUF sites, the basic data collection protocol could be supplemented with additional interview assessments or bio-assays. NIJ is also interested in proposals that examine specific research questions by applying the DUF protocol to targeted samples of arrestees such as those in suburban or rural jails, or those arrested for specific offenses.

As we mentioned in Chapter 12, Scott Decker and associates (1997) used DUF as a platform to investigate access to firearms.

In addition to the rather broad request for research proposals outlined under the six goals, NIJ issues solicitations that call for more specific research or evaluation projects. Since the passage of the 1994 "Crime Act," the institute has supported a number of projects in connection with various provisions of the legislation.

Finally, NIJ offers support for a variety of purposes that might not fit neatly into other categories. Some of these will be of particular interest to students in criminal justice:

- Research projects by graduate students or law students
- Internships for undergraduate or graduate students to work at NIJ
- Small grants ($1,000–$50,000) for basic or applied research in areas not specifically covered within other goals
- Intensive educational programs for criminal justice executives
- Data resources grants enabling researchers to complete short-term projects that analyze previously collected data
- Graduate research fellowships for students at historically black colleges and universities
- Fellowships to support senior researchers and criminal justice practitioners who work at the institute. (National Institute of Justice, 1997:10)

Some of these activities target small projects by criminal justice professionals or other researchers, some support traditional education, and still others afford students some practical experience through internships or visiting fellowships.

As you've worked your way through the first 14 chapters of this book, you may have occasionally had ideas about research projects you would like to conduct yourself. Perhaps you thought about a possible project for a senior or master's thesis. Or maybe the idea of spending a semester in Washington as an intern working with staff researchers at NIJ is appealing to you. In either case, opportunities exist for students to apply many of the research principles and tools we have covered.

Writing Your Grant Proposal

Let's say you've decided to apply for a student fellowship to conduct research on school-based crime prevention. You want to study a violence prevention program in a local high school, planning an applied study to evaluate the program's effectiveness. You have a good grasp of basic research principles, have worked out a quasi-experimental design, and plan to collect data from school records and from interviews with students and teachers.

Reviewing Chapter 4, you also understand how to organize your research proposal. Since your proposal will request funding from a specific agency, however, you naturally seek further guidance from the funding source on what kinds of things should be included and how the proposal should be organized. Turning to NIJ's 1995–96 *Research Plan*, you find just what you're looking for—questions and answers about the contents and format of grant proposals. Excerpts are presented in Figure 15-1.

These guidelines are slightly different from those we presented in Chapter 4. For one thing, NIJ is especially interested in applied research. You should, however, recognize many similarities as well.

Question 10 describes exactly what should be included in your application for grant funds, and questions 18 and 19 describe how a decision will be made about whether or not to accept your proposal. "Impact of the proposed project" means that proposals will be judged in part on how a project is likely to contribute to criminal justice research and policy. Another criterion is whether the peer review panel believes a project is feasible—in other words, whether it can actually be carried out as described. Reviewers also consider the qualifications of research staff (that's why you include your curriculum vitae, or resume) and the costs of the project.

Finally, you will, of course, be interested in whether you are eligible to apply for research funds from NIJ. As an individual, a student, and perhaps an employee of a public agency or other organization, you are certainly eligible. And, since you've gotten this far in a book that describes how to do criminal justice research, we're pretty confident about your capability.

Let's now turn to the first of our examples—a study based on the secondary analysis of existing data, a topic we described in Chapter 12. Because

FIGURE 15-1

National Institute of Justice Recommendations to Grantwriters

1. **What is the subject or problem you wish to address?** Describe the subject or problem and how it affects the criminal justice system and the public. . . .

2. **What do you want to do?** Explain the goal(s) of the project in simple, straightforward terms. . . .

3. **How will you do it?** Describe the methodology carefully so that what you propose to do and how you would do it are clear. All proposed tasks should be set forth so that a reviewer can see a logical progression of tasks and relate those tasks directly to the accomplishment of the project's goal(s). . . .

4. **What should you include in a grant application for a program evaluation?** An evaluation should determine whether the proposed program, training, procedure, service, or technology accomplished the objectives it was designed to meet. Applicants seeking support for a proposed evaluation should describe the criteria that will be used to evaluate the project's effectiveness and identify program elements that will require further modification. . . .

5. **How will others learn about your findings?** Include a plan to disseminate the results of the research, evaluation, technology, or demonstration beyond the jurisdictions and individuals directly affected by the project. . . .

6. **What are the specific costs involved?** The budget application should be presented clearly. Major budget categories such as personnel, benefits, travel, supplies, equipment, and indirect costs should be identified separately. . . .

. . .

10. **What technical materials should be included in the application?**
   - A one-page abstract of the full proposal, highlighting the project's purpose, methods, activities, and when known, the location(s) of field research.
   - A program narrative, which is the technical portion of the proposal. It should include a clear, concise statement of the problem, goals, and objectives of the project, and related questions to be explored. A discussion of the relationship of the proposed work to the existing literature is expected.
   - A statement of the project's anticipated contribution to criminal justice policy and practice. . . .
   - A detailed statement of the proposed research or study design and analytical methodologies. The proposed data sources, data collection strategies, variables and issues to be examined, and procedures of analysis to be employed should be delineated carefully and completely. When appropriate, experimental designs are encouraged because of their potential relevance to policymaking and the strength of the evidence they can produce.
   - The organization and management plan to conduct the study. A list of major milestones of events, activities, and products and a timetable for completion that indicates the time commitments to individual project tasks should be included. . . .
   - The applicant's curriculum vitae should summarize education, research experience, and bibliographic information related to the proposed work. . . .

. . .

18. **What does the review process entail?** After all applications for a competition are received, NIJ will convene a series of peer review panels of criminal justice professionals and researchers. NIJ will assign proposals to peer panels that it deems most appropriate. Panel members read each proposal and meet to assess the technical merits and policy relevance of the proposed research. Panel assessments of the proposals, together with assessments by NIJ staff, are submitted to the Director, who has sole and final authority over approval and awards. . . .

19. **What are the criteria for an award?** The essential question asked of each applicant is, "If this study were successful, how would criminal justice policies or operations be improved?" Four criteria are applied in the evaluation process:
   - Impact of the proposed project.
   - Feasibility of the approach to the issue, including technical merit and practical considerations.
   - Originality of the approach, including creativity of the proposal and capability of the research staff.
   - Economy of the approach.

. . .

21. **Who is eligible to apply?** NIJ awards grants to educational institutions, nonprofit organizations, public agencies, individuals, and profitmaking organizations that are willing to waive their fees.

Source: National Institute of Justice (1995:23–27).

we want to describe the research process from getting started to producing written reports, our examples are drawn from earlier NIJ Program Plans. It takes some time to move from the proposal stage to actually publishing results, so we will begin by examining the research agenda for victims of crime set by NIJ's 1989 Program Plan.

■ JUVENILE VICTIMIZATION AND OFFENDING

NIJ has sponsored research on victimization for several years; this topic is a regular feature of each year's Program Plan. As we have occasionally pointed out in earlier chapters that cite victimization examples, younger people are more likely to be victims of crimes. Younger people are also more likely to be offenders in many types of crime. The overlap between victimization and offending is the focus of our first example.

Research Program Statement

The 1989 Program Plan for victims of crime begins by laying out the rationale for research on victims. This is done, in part, by citing some statistics on the scope of crime victimization: "Over an entire lifetime, at current crime rates, five-sixths of us will be victims of personal theft at least three times, and victims of violent crime at least once. Half of all urban households will be victims of two or more burglaries in a 20-year period. These are national rates. For some subpopulations, rates are considerably higher" (National Institute of Justice, 1988:31). The introductory rationale continues by noting that although national rates of victimization continue their steady decline, public concern about crime remains high, and those who do become victims can take small comfort in such general trends.

By way of background, the 1970s and 1980s produced a large number of studies of crime victims. In part, this new research focus was fueled by the introduction, in 1972, of what was to become the National Crime Victimization Survey (NCVS). As we described earlier, the NCVS is a nationally representative annual survey of households. Hav-

ing a rigorous, standardized source of annual data enabled hundreds of researchers to produce exploratory, descriptive, and explanatory research on victimization.

Reviewing recent research on victimization, the Program Plan described how past studies point to continued needs for further research in several general areas. Two of these were highlighted as priority topics for NIJ:

1. Studies of the etiology or process of victimization that include consideration of routine daily activities and environmental characteristics as factors in the victimization of persons and property. Studies of how these factors may change over time. Implications for individual or collective actions and behavior, as well as for policy at a broader level.
2. Studies of the financial, psychological, and behavioral costs and consequences of criminal victimization . . . of satisfaction/dissatisfaction with the criminal justice system. How these aftermaths may vary with types of crime, or victim, or of societal response. (National Institute of Justice, 1988:33)

We do not expect that these statements will be immediately clear to you, although the second priority area is fairly straightforward. In the next section, we will expand on the first priority area.

At this point, you should simply understand that these statements of priority research areas represent a first step in the research process we described in Chapter 4. The Program Plan for victims of crime implies specific interests, ideas, theories, or new programs that mark the beginning for a research project. An agenda has been set for researchers or public officials interested in the process of victimization or its consequences. Furthermore, this agenda is supported by a review of past research on victimization, since the Program Plan description cites recent advances in knowledge. As we pointed out in Chapter 4, finding out what research has been done in the past is a crucial first step in formulating new research questions.

Let's now examine how one research proposal responded to this program announcement. We will also draw on the proposal to explain a bit more about what is involved in studying the etiology of victimization.

Proposal: Longitudinal Design Using Available Data

We pointed out in Chapter 4 that a research proposal normally begins by stating a problem or research objective. NIJ's Program Plan has already done this to some extent by specifying priority areas. A good proposal in response to this statement will present more specific research objectives that are consistent with NIJ's stated priorities.

Robert Sampson's proposal (1989) did just that. Beginning with a review of recent research, Sampson stated his objective like this:

■ Limitations of past research have produced a gap in our understanding of juvenile and young adult victimization, especially with regard to prevention. As a result, important theoretical and policy questions remain unanswered. . . . What are the causes of victimization among teenagers? . . . What specific lifestyle and opportunity factors are relevant to young persons? Are juvenile victims also juvenile *offenders?* Do the assumptions of current victim policies, often built on findings from older adults, hold for those most at risk—teenagers and young adults? . . . It is the purpose of this project to address these and other questions by providing both a descriptive and causal analysis of juvenile and young adult victimization. (Sampson, 1989:5–6, emphasis in original)

A successful research proposal states the objectives clearly. Proposals that seek outside funding are most successful if they respond, as Sampson has done, directly to stated objectives.

Research Guided by Theory Beyond matching the proposed study directly to NIJ's Program Plan, Sampson casts his research within a loosely integrated body of theory that explains victimization as a product of lifestyle, routine activities, or opportunity. We mentioned lifestyle theory in Chapter 14, citing research by Ronald Clarke and associates (1985) that examined the relationship between nighttime leisure activities and personal crime victimization. Others have described the similarities between the lifestyle theory developed by Hindelang, Gottfredson, and Garofalo (1978) and the routine activity theory described by Cohen and Felson (1979).

Each theory proposes a straightforward but appealing explanation for why some individuals become victims while others do not: "What people do, how they behave, places them at more or less risk of criminal victimization" (Maxfield, 1987c: 275). Those who spend time in public places are at greater risk of street crime. Since most burglaries occur while a residence is vacant, those whose homes are unoccupied regularly or for long times are at greater risk of burglary. Routine behavior or lifestyle thus affects the opportunity structure for crime.

Sampson draws on these theoretical perspectives in his proposal to examine the etiology of victimization. In doing this, he is following the deductive model we described in Chapter 2 and is again being directly responsive to the first-priority topic in the NIJ Program Plan. Consider, for example, these excerpts from the "Conceptual Framework" section of Sampson's proposal:

■ Young persons go out at night and spend time in public places more than older persons, thus increasing their risk of victimization. . . . (p. 7)

■ Younger persons are more likely to be victims of violent crime than older persons because the former are more likely to associate with other youth who are themselves disproportionately involved in violence. . . . (p. 7)

■ Membership in a gang, for example, involves close proximity to fellow offenders and criminal events. (p. 7)

■ According to lifestyle theory, persons who drink extensively, especially at night, are at higher risk for assault because such behavior often occurs at parties and other social gatherings where victimization risk is increased. Drinking to excess also lowers guardianship potential and thus may increase victimization risk . . . for other personal crimes such as robbery. (pp. 8–9)

Lifestyle and routine activity theories lead Sampson to three objectives that incorporate descriptive and explanatory research purposes: (1) assess how this body of theory accounts for victimization of juveniles and young adults, (2) examine the role of drug and alcohol use in victimization, and (3) examine the link between victimization and offending. The third objective tests the theoretical proposition that juveniles who commit delinquent or criminal acts are more likely to be crime victims themselves. That is, juvenile offending and victimization are both associated with similar patterns of lifestyle and routine activities.

Conceptualization and Measurement One of the major shortcomings of explanatory research on victimization has been inadequate measurement, especially for concepts that are operationalized as independent variables. We mentioned this in Chapter 14, in discussing research by Clarke and associates. Sampson proposes specific measures of behaviors that represent lifestyle concepts: amount of time spent with family and friends; time spent in such conventional activities as school, sports, studying, watching TV, shopping, going to parties, and so on; use of marijuana and alcohol; and involvement in assault, theft, or vandalism.

The focus on juveniles and young adults is also an important feature of Sampson's conceptualization. Among the U.S. population as a whole, victimization is a rare event. As we noted in Chapters 6 and 9, this is the principal reason victim surveys require large sample sizes. However, since young people are most often victims of most types of crime, Sampson proposes that juveniles and young adults are the most appropriate research subjects for studying the etiology of victimization. He also points out that most lifestyle and routine behavior concepts linked to victimization risk are more common among the young. This is also true for delinquency and many types of criminal offenses.

Source of Data A sample survey is the best source of data to address the questions posed by Sampson. We saw in Chapter 6 that victim surveys are best suited for measuring crimes not reported to police; many incidents involving young victims produce minor losses or injury and are less com-

monly reported (Garofalo, Siegel, and Laub, 1987). Chapter 6 also pointed out that self-report surveys are best suited for measuring delinquency. As we noted in Chapter 10, self-report measures of delinquency and offending are subject to reliability problems, and victimization surveys are flawed in various ways. But the advantages of survey methods outweigh their disadvantages in this case.

Rather than launch a new sample survey of juveniles and young adults, Sampson proposed to use two sources of available data. Both the National Youth Survey (NYS) and the Monitoring the Future (MTF) survey of high school seniors include appropriate questionnaire items to measure the dependent variable (victimization) and independent variables (lifestyle concepts and self-reports). According to Sampson (1989:12), "While each data set has different strengths and limitations, both share a common core of items and method that allow us to propose a . . . complementary approach to the problem of juvenile and young adult victimization."

We described the secondary analysis of existing data in Chapter 12; its principal advantage is low cost. Rather than complete all the steps necessary to design and execute complex nationwide surveys of young adults and juveniles, Sampson obtained complete NYS and MTF data from the University of Michigan's Inter-university Consortium for Political and Social Research (see Appendix D).

What about the weaknesses of secondary analysis? You'll recall from Chapter 12 that the biggest drawback relates to validity: The design and measures used in a study by some other researcher may not meet your own needs. Much of Sampson's proposal weighs the strengths and weaknesses of the NYS and MTF studies and concludes that these two surveys closely match his research purposes.

Sampson (1989:31–32) describes an additional reason for using data from two independent surveys: "These data present a unique opportunity for replication of our major hypotheses." In Chapters 1 and 4, we discussed the role of replication in scientific research. Lifestyle and routine activity theories would be more strongly supported if consistent findings are obtained through survey data collected from different populations.

Causal Inference and Longitudinal Designs Recall from Chapters 4 and 10 that cross-sectional surveys measure concepts at one point in time. As a result, they are often deficient in explanatory research because the time ordering of cause and effect is one immutable requirement for causal inference. Think about the importance of this for addressing Sampson's research questions about the links between delinquency, lifestyle measures, and victimization. Respondents may inaccurately recall the time order of different events if they are interviewed only once.

The NYS and MTF data were produced by different types of longitudinal designs and are therefore more appropriate for sorting out the time order of independent and dependent variables: "The longitudinal nature of the data allow[s] us to specify and explore the causal ordering of variables. In particular, the design permits specification of lifestyle and delinquent activities . . . as temporally prior to victimization" (Sampson, 1989:15). The NYS is a panel study in which a sample of youths aged 11 to 17 were interviewed annually from 1977 through 1981, and at irregular intervals since then, producing multiple interviews over time with the same respondents. The NYS used multistage cluster sampling techniques to produce a representative sample of U.S. households. Respondents were then selected from sampled households and interviewed in person. In the first (1977) wave of the panel, 1,725 youths were interviewed to produce a response rate of about 73 percent (Sampson, 1989:13).

What about the weaknesses of panel studies? We mentioned mortality in Chapters 4 and 7; some respondents interviewed in the first wave may drop out of the study and not be reinterviewed in subsequent waves. The danger is that those who drop out may be different from other respondents in some important way. In a five-year study of youth, some of whom will have aged from 17 to 22, it is likely that some proportion of respondents will not be located for later waves. Recognizing this potential problem,

Sampson (1989:13) describes mortality for the first three waves of the NYS:

■ Respondent loss between waves was found to be small, with a cumulative loss of approximately 6 percent. There was, however, a small loss by ethnicity, social class, and place of residence in the third wave, with lower class and black youths more likely to have been lost in this reinterview. Elliott et al. (1983)[1] also found that there was no significant selective loss by self-reported levels of delinquency.

Sampson devotes considerable attention to the issue of mortality. His proposal presents a preliminary analysis of victimization for each of three panel waves. He found no statistically significant differences in victimization between respondents who were interviewed in each wave and those who dropped out of later waves (1989:29).

Replication As we described in Chapter 6, the MTF survey is a different type of longitudinal design. Independent samples of high school seniors are interviewed each year. The MTF also incorporates an interesting application of the general cluster sampling techniques we covered in Chapter 9.

The multistage cluster design involves three stages of sampling. First, 74 primary sampling units (PSUs) are selected to represent the 12 largest metropolitan areas in the country as well as 62 other areas across different regions proportionate to regional populations. In the next two stages, high schools are selected within each PSU, and samples of 400 seniors are selected within each high school. Of course, some schools had fewer than 400 seniors; in most of these cases, all seniors participated. Sampled seniors completed self-administered questionnaires, usually in a classroom (Johnston, O'Malley, and Bachman, 1996). Sampson proposed to use data collected in 1976, 1980, and 1986, years in which about 3,000 seniors completed questionnaire items central to research questions.

Since the same persons are not interviewed from year to year in the MTF survey, it cannot

---

[1]This reference is to Delbert Elliot and associates, who designed and executed the original NYS.

ensure the precise causal ordering possible with the NYS. The principal reason for examining MTF data is to replicate NYS findings. Similar results across four independently selected samples (the NYS panel and three MTF samples) would enhance external validity.

In addition, the longer time period covered by MTF data makes it possible to assess changes over time in the frequency of victimization and offending among high school seniors. Comparing the NYS and MTF data provides a good example of the metaphor for longitudinal studies we mentioned in Chapter 4. The MTF is what Devine and Wright (1993:19) call a *slide show:* It presents a series of pictures of high school seniors from year to year, thus illustrating trends. The NYS is a *motion picture:* It displays moving images of the same sample of youths as they age and otherwise change over time.

As we mentioned in Chapter 6, because the MTF survey is based on a sample of high school seniors, it cannot represent people who drop out of high school before their senior year. Sampson reports that this excludes about 15 percent of persons near age 18. "Furthermore," he says, "since no provision is made to contact students absent from school the day of [questionnaire] administration, we might also expect that the sample is biased" (1989:36). You might reasonably expect that high school dropouts and students who are chronically absent would be disproportionately involved in delinquent or criminal acts.

Despite these potential problems, Sampson (1989:37) concludes that "our primary hypotheses can thus be tested with the [MTF] and the findings replicated across time with independent samples." The proposal does a thorough and thoughtful job in describing data sources and measures, so that readers can decide for themselves whether or not they agree with Sampson.

Analysis   The proposal is less detailed in describing what types of data analysis will be conducted. Sampson mentions descriptive and causal analyses and implies that different multivariate techniques will be used.

In one sense, this might be a serious deficiency in a research proposal. It is less important in this particular case for two reasons. First, Sampson's conceptual discussion of how questionnaire items from the two surveys will be used to test specific hypotheses is so thorough that knowledgeable readers can easily visualize the analyses that will be conducted. As a general principle, careful conceptualization will readily point to appropriate analysis techniques.

Second, Sampson and other members of the research team (Janet Lauritsen and John Laub) have considerable experience in victimization research, as documented in a later section of the proposal: "Between them, Dr. Sampson and Dr. Laub have published over 20 articles and monographs in the area of victimization" (Sampson, 1989:46).

Significance, Management Plan, Products   The final sections of the proposal return to linking planned research activities to NIJ priorities, a description of the project time schedule, and a budget. Sampson does not directly discuss the policy implications of his proposed research, but he does point out that the project will provide new descriptive and explanatory information on victimization that may contribute to developing crime prevention policy.

Since no new data will be collected, the project's management plan is simple. Sampson describes computing facilities at the University of Illinois, where the project will be conducted. This section of the proposal also presents the qualifications of researchers, lays out a time frame for the project (it will last 15 months), and describes anticipated products (a final report to NIJ and papers to be presented at professional conferences and published in scientific journals).

Let's now look at two of the published products that resulted from this project.

The Research Report

Professors Janet Lauritsen and John Laub collaborated with Robert Sampson to coauthor two published reports from this project on juvenile and young adult victimization. One focused on the link between victimization and offending, examining whether young persons who commit juvenile or adult offenses are more often victims of crime (Lauritsen, Sampson, and Laub, 1991). The other report assessed the relationships between lifestyle measures and victimization and discussed the policy implications of the study's findings (Lauritsen, Laub, and Sampson, 1992).

Appendix C of this book presents some general guidelines on planning and writing research reports. As we point out, reports can take many forms, depending on your audience and research purposes. Most, however, will have some basic elements in common. One published report from Sampson's study nicely illustrates this general format. The article "Conventional and Delinquent Activities: Implications for the Prevention of Violent Victimization Among Adolescents" (Lauritsen, Laub, and Sampson, 1992) is organized into these sections:

1. Introduction
2. Prior Research
3. Theoretical Issues
4. Data and Measures
5. Findings
6. Discussion
7. References
8. Appendixes

The first section has two paragraphs that briefly summarize the purpose of the study: "Using two well-known national data sources . . . and an analytical framework derived from lifestyle/routine activity theories, we examine the relationship between conventional and delinquent activities and violent victimization among adolescents in the United States" (Lauritsen, Laub, and Sampson, 1992:91–92). The authors' review of prior research is also brief and flows directly into the "Theoretical Issues" section. Lifestyle and routine activity theories are summarized, linked to past research, and presented as a rationale for conducting the current study: "Drawing on lifestyle/ routine activity theories, we expect that involvement in conventional activities will reduce the risk of victimization for adolescents" (1992:94). Their discussion of theory leads to specific hypotheses, proposing that adolescents whose lifestyle includes conventional activities—sports or social pursuits connected with schools, family, or community organizations—will be less often victims of crime than adolescents whose lifestyle includes delinquent or deviant activities.

As its title implies, the fourth section describes NYS and MTF design and indicates how questionnaire items will be used to operationalize independent and dependent concepts.

The first four sections of this article are shorter versions of introductory sections from the original NIJ proposal. This illustrates that good planning pays off. The authors' research proposal reviewed the literature, derived hypotheses from theory, and examined available data for testing hypotheses. Careful planning at the proposal stage also helped the research team to obtain funding for their work.

Findings A good general rule in presenting results is to begin simply. Lauritsen and associates do just that, first presenting bivariate analysis of the relationships between violent crime victimization (the dependent variable) and self-reported delinquency.

Analyzing five waves of the NYS and three samples of high school seniors from MTF data, they find that in each case, respondents who report committing some delinquent act are more commonly victims of assault. Delinquency was also positively related to robbery victimization among NYS respondents (there were no questions about robbery in the MTF). For these eight comparisons (five NYS and three MTF), delinquents were on the average about 3.5 times more likely to be assault victims.[2]

Turning next to the question of whether engaging in conventional activities reduced victimization, Lauritsen and colleagues examine Pearson product-moment correlations between independent and dependent variables. For NYS respondents, they found that assault victimization was negatively related to: time spent studying, grade-point average, feelings of attachment to school and family, and involvement in family-centered activities. Victimization was positively related to

---

[2] Computed from data presented in Lauritsen, Laub, and Sampson (1992:97, Table 1).

alcohol and marijuana use, participation in community activities, and having friends who were involved in delinquent acts (1992:98, Table 2). MTF data revealed no relationships between conventional activities and victimization, but MTF respondents who used alcohol or marijuana and those who spent more time with friends were more often victims of assault (1992:99, Table 3).

Finding limited support for lifestyle theories in bivariate analysis, Lauritsen and associates next conducted a type of multivariate analysis to examine the effects of lifestyle variables on victimization, while statistically controlling for respondent characteristics and involvement in delinquency. Correlations between lifestyle and victimization disappeared when they took delinquency and demographics into account. The authors conclude that engaging in conventional activities reduces victimization only among adolescents who do not themselves commit delinquent acts. Similarly, measures of lifestyle and routine activity do not account for differences in victimization by gender, age, and race (1992:100–101).

Although they used different multivariate statistical procedures than those we discussed in Chapter 14, Lauritsen and colleagues followed the same logical steps in their analysis. They first examined bivariate relationships between the dependent variable (victimization) and two categories of independent variables (lifestyle and delinquency). Each set of bivariate relationships was in the expected direction; victimization was positively related to delinquency and negatively related to some measures of conventional activities. However, multivariate analysis revealed that participating in conventional activities did not reduce victimization for those who committed delinquent acts.

Policy Implications   As you might expect from our brief discussion of results, Lauritsen and associates conclude that lifestyle theories offer only limited explanations for why some youths become crime victims while others do not. The authors further suggest that lifestyle theories of victimization should be linked with lifestyle theories of offending. Certain types of activities reduce violent victimization, but only among youths who do not commit delinquent acts.

In addition to considering the theoretical meaning of their findings, Lauritsen and associates (1992:101) suggest some new directions for policy:

■ A key component in the prevention of adolescent violence is delinquency prevention. Not only would delinquency prevention reduce the risk of violence among delinquency-prone subgroups, but the risk of violence for other groups in proximity to delinquents should be reduced as well. This is likely to occur because efforts to reduce delinquent involvement among youth will influence the very same factors which affect victimization risk.

It is useful for you to think through the logic of this conclusion. First, engaging in conventional activities reduces victimization for nondelinquents, but such activities have no impact on victimization among delinquents. Second, participating in delinquency increases victimization regardless of participation in more conventional activities. Therefore, actions to reduce victimization by promoting adolescent participation in conventional activities can be effective only for nondelinquents. It is more likely that victimization can be reduced by policies that target delinquency.

Lauritsen and colleagues do a nice job of linking this policy implication to further efforts to develop lifestyle theory. Lifestyle, victimization, and offending are interrelated. Theories that attempt to predict or explain victimization as a product of lifestyle must also address the association between lifestyle and offending.

■ CRIME COMMISSION RATES

When Julie Horney and Ineke Haen Marshall set out to study offending rates among incarcerated felons, they submitted a proposal to NIJ's research program on Criminal Careers and the Control of Crime. Unlike the authors in our first example, Horney and Marshall did not propose a project within one of the institute's priority topics. Instead, they wished to conduct research on the more general issue of criminal careers, with a specific focus on measuring rates of offending.

Research Program Statement

We briefly described research on criminal careers in Chapters 2 and 3. Drawing on developmental theories of crime, criminal career studies focus on two central concepts: crime participation rates and individual offending rates (Blumstein, Cohen, and Farrington, 1988). Participation rates refer to the proportion of individuals in some population who have committed some crime within some time period. For example: What proportion of male high school seniors have committed assaults within the past six months? Individual offending rates express how many crimes are committed by an individual offender during some specified period of time. Given that some person admits having committed an assault, an offending rate would measure the actual number of assaults that person committed in, say, the previous six months.

The 1988 NIJ program plan expressed a general interest in criminal career research, including efforts to develop better measures of participation rates and offending rates. This is linked to NIJ's role in policy development because, as we mentioned in Chapter 2, information on individual participation and offending rates is central to developing selective incapacitation policies.

Proposal: Inmate Self-report Survey

Horney and Marshall (1988) proposed to test different measures of offending rates by interviewing men admitted to Nebraska correctional facilities. Although they did not respond to research priority areas specifically identified by NIJ, their proposal was well within the scope of the institute's interest in criminal careers. Their proposal presents examples of issues in conceptualization and measurement, questionnaire design, subject selection, the use of randomization, and human subjects protection.

Conceptualization The research proposal begins by reviewing the genesis of criminal career research, starting with Marvin Wolfgang's influential research on a Philadelphia birth cohort (Wolfgang, Figlio, and Sellin, 1972) through studies by Alfred Blumstein and associates (Blumstein, Cohen, Roth, and Visher, 1986) and by researchers at the RAND Corporation (Peterson and Braiker,

1980; Chaiken and Chaiken, 1982). Following the lead established by these earlier studies, Horney and Marshall (1988:1) describe some of the central issues in measuring criminal careers:

■ In order to understand differences in offending patterns, the focus of criminal careers research is on gathering individual level data on the onset and termination of criminal careers, the rate of offending over time, and the seriousness and variety of offenses. . . . Because actual rates of committing crimes are poorly represented by official [crime records], one major approach to studying criminal careers has been through self-report.

We discussed units of analysis at some length in Chapter 4. Horney and Marshall point out that the concept of a criminal career implies the need for individual-level data to measure individual participation and offending rates. Although it is possible to conceptualize an aggregate-level participation rate—the proportion of males in Omaha, Nebraska, who were arrested for burglary in the past year, for example—an aggregate offending rate would not be very meaningful. Try to think for a moment how you might measure an aggregate-level offending rate.

So individuals are the units of analysis. And since Horney and Marshall are interested in offending rates rather than participation rates, they propose to study a group of known offenders—men under correctional supervision in Nebraska. As we pointed out in our examination of self-report surveys in Chapter 10, the concept of offending rates is more central to a population of actual offenders. Information on participation rates is more meaningful when applied to a general population.

You should recognize from Chapter 6 on measuring crime and Chapter 10 on survey methods why offending rates are best measured through self-report methods. If we are interested in how many crimes are committed by individual offenders, official police data provide incomplete information. Police records cannot link particular offenses to individual people unless someone is arrested. And only a fraction of most types of offenses result in arrest.

Measurement Horney and Marshall introduce their own proposed study design by reviewing previous criminal career research on known offenders. Most notably, this includes RAND Corporation surveys of prison inmates in California, Texas, and Michigan (Peterson and Braiker, 1980; Chaiken and Chaiken, 1982). Replications in Colorado (Mande and English, 1987) and in two urban counties (Chaiken and Chaiken, 1987) incrementally modified research procedures used in the RAND studies.

The RAND studies and other surveys of inmates contributed substantially to knowledge about offending patterns. However, Horney and Marshall point out that inconsistent estimates of offending rates raised questions of measurement validity and reliability. Their own objective is "the development of improved self-report methodology designed to obtain more valid and reliable measures of criminality" (1988:2). They propose to do this through changes in questionnaire design, with a goal of producing more precise estimates of the number of crimes committed within time periods.

Self-report questionnaire items are examples of questions that ask about past behavior, a challenging measurement problem. This is especially true for behavior in the distant past and for routine behavior. As an example, imagine designing a questionnaire to measure how often people violated some traffic law in the past three years. Even if we limited our questions to exceeding the speed limit on interstate highways, it would be difficult for respondents to accurately recall the number of times they committed this infraction and how often they did so each month. Asking a sample of incarcerated felons how often they committed different crimes over a three-year period presents similar difficulties, especially for high-rate offenders.

Horney and Marshall proposed to modify "crime calendar" procedures used by RAND researchers. The general crime calendar approach presents a printed calendar of months to respondents; each month lists different offenses. Respondents are asked to indicate how often they committed each offense in each month.

Of course, recall error is a potential danger in such methods, so Horney and Marshall proposed to adapt RAND procedures to reduce this problem. Respondents would first be shown a general activity calendar, in which they would indicate their city of residence in specific months and whether they engaged in a variety of activities: working, having a spouse or girlfriend, being on parole or probation, being in school, using drugs or alcohol, and so on. This was intended to prompt respondents' recall of their general activities each month over a three-year period and establish the context for later questions about offending. To relate this to our example, we might preface questions about speeding on interstate highways in July 1997 by first asking respondents whether they owned or had access to a car in July 1997; we could follow that up by asking whether they drove to work on interstate highways or had taken a trip by car in July 1997.

After indicating their residence and general activities, respondents would work through a second calendar that showed the same months, indicating which crimes they had committed and how often they committed them. Horney and Marshall (1988:6) describe the advantages of this approach to measuring offending rates:

■ We believe that getting this detailed information from the respondent provides a good frame of reference for asking the . . . more specific questions on frequency of criminal behaviors. Some of our respondents have reported,[3] for example, "Oh, yes, it was when I moved to Atlanta that I started doing a couple of burglaries a month," or "Well, it was during those four months when I was drinking heavily that I was doing the burglaries at a high rate."

From their examination of earlier inmate surveys, Horney and Marshall expected that offending rates would vary over time. The preceding quote, for example, suggests that before moving to Atlanta, the respondent committed burglar-

---

[3]Here the authors refer to a pilot study in which they tested the two-calendar questionnaire procedure.

FIGURE 15-2
Questionnaire Items for Estimating Burglary Offending Rate

Now, I want you to think about how many burglaries you were doing at different times. Let's think of months when you were doing burglaries at low, medium, or high rates. These can be defined in terms of any numbers you want.

1A. During which months did you do burglaries at a low rate?

(Write a "1" in the months during which
burglaries were committed at a low rate)

1B. In these low-rate months, when you did burglaries, how often did you usually do them?

(Check one box in column A, write
numbers in columns B and C)

	A			B		C
Every day or almost every day	☐	How many per day?	☐	How many days a week usually?	☐	
Several times a week	☐	How many per week?	☐			
Every week or almost every week	☐	How many per month?	☐			
Less than every week	☐	How many per month?	☐			

Source: Adapted from Horney and Marshall (1988: Appendix A, p. 12).

ies less often than a couple of times per month. Procedures for questioning respondents about monthly offending must therefore strive to stimulate recall about offending frequency.

The questionnaire designed by Horney and Marshall did this by devoting careful attention to ordering questions in a questionnaire. For example, if a respondent said he had committed burglary during any months shown on the crime calendar, he was presented with the sequence of questions shown in Figure 15-2. In answering question 1A, a respondent would refer to the crime calendar and point to those months when he committed burglaries at the self-defined low rate. Next the respondent would be asked question 1B, in which he would operationalize what he meant by "low rate."

With month-by-month information, Horney and Marshall expected to produce more accurate estimates of offending rates than those reported in earlier surveys.

Approximating a Longitudinal Design In addition to producing enhanced measures of offending rates, Horney and Marshall included several types of

questions to measure independent variables that might affect offending rates. Many of the items included in the general activity calendar could plausibly be related to offending rates—drug use or being unemployed, for example.

Unlike our first example in this chapter, Horney and Marshall proposed to conduct a single interview with offenders—a cross-sectional design or snapshot. They could not, therefore, take advantage of the special features of a longitudinal design to establish the causal order of independent and dependent variables.

You should recognize, however, that Horney and Marshall have approximated a longitudinal design in one of the ways we mentioned in Chapter 4. Using a retrospective design, respondents are asked to reconstruct their activities over time on a month-by-month basis, thus establishing an estimate of time ordering. So, for example, it would be possible to establish that a respondent first moved to Atlanta and then began committing more burglaries.

Chapter 4 pointed out that faulty recall by respondents is the principal danger in retrospective studies. We have described the several ways Horney and Marshall sought to jog the memories of their respondents and help them to reconstruct various activities and events.

Subject Selection   Rather than select a sample of current inmates, Horney and Marshall designed their study to represent an intake cohort. We mentioned this in Chapter 9 in our discussion of different techniques for nonprobability sampling. There were two reasons for this approach. First, subjects were to be asked about crime commission and other activities during a "window period." This referred to street time, periods when subjects were not incarcerated and were therefore able to commit offenses. Horney and Marshall argue that subjects' recall would be more accurate if they were interviewed as they began a period of incarceration, rather than after they had been in prison for several months or more.

Second, it was felt that response rates for an intake cohort would be higher than for a sample of institutionalized offenders. People entering an institution are not yet assigned to work details or educational programs, thus reducing the possibility of scheduling conflicts. Horney and Marshall also point out that an intake cohort is less subject to peer influence that could produce disincentives to participate. Since they would not have had an opportunity to be absorbed into the institutional culture, members of an intake cohort would be more likely to cooperate with researchers and thus produce a higher response rate (1988:15).

An intake cohort is an example of a natural institutional process, as we described in Chapters 7 and 9. If you have no reason to expect that a process is biased in some way that would affect your research questions, you can use something like an intake cohort to select subjects.

In-Person Interviews   With a complex questionnaire, Horney and Marshall proposed to conduct in-person interviews rather than use a self-administered questionnaire. They contrast this approach to procedures used in other surveys where groups of inmates filled out questionnaires. Horney and Marshall cite other studies that found substantial error and inconsistencies for many items in the RAND surveys.

Although in-person interviews are more costly and time-consuming, they are more likely to produce reliable data. We discussed this point in Chapter 10, noting the various ways interviewers can help a respondent work through complex questionnaire items.

In Chapter 10, we also considered the relative advantages and disadvantages of conducting a survey yourself versus hiring a professional firm. Horney and Marshall chose to do it themselves by training graduate students to conduct the actual interviews. Notice that they faced no particular problems in subject selection that would require expert assistance in drawing a complex sample. Interviews were conducted at a central site, the intake facility for Nebraska's Department of Corrections. Having graduate students conduct in-person interviews, after being trained by Horney and Marshall, was feasible and contributed to the professional training of student interviewers. Considered against the general rules of thumb we offered in Chapter 10, you should understand why Horney and Marshall decided to do it themselves.

Randomization   One of the research purposes for Horney and Marshall was to compare their procedures for measuring offending rates to those used in other inmate surveys. They felt that more precise month-by-month measurement would produce lower estimates of offending; they cited high-rate saliency as a problem with other studies that asked respondents to estimate the number of crimes committed in a typical week or month. High-rate saliency means that offenders might most clearly recall time periods when they were committing a large number of offenses and incorrectly report them as typical.

However, simply comparing their estimates of offending rates to those produced by, for example, RAND researchers was not possible. RAND studies were conducted in California, Texas, and Michigan, while Horney and Marshall proposed to conduct their research in Nebraska. It is plausible to expect that prison inmates in different states might systematically differ on offending rates. For example, with a smaller population than California, Texas, and Michigan, Nebraska officials may face fewer pressures from overcrowded prisons and sentence a larger proportion of offenders to longer periods of incarceration. This would have the effect of producing lower estimates of offending rates among a Nebraska cohort, as compared to offending rates for samples of inmates in other states.

Horney and Marshall (1988:17) dealt with this problem by proposing a randomized design:

■ Subjects in our intake cohort will be randomly assigned to two groups. Those in the experimental [group] will be interviewed using our modifications on rate questions . . . and more detailed calendars. Those in the control [group] will be interviewed with the same survey instrument with the exception that the rate questions and calendar methods will be those used in the RAND and Colorado studies.

Recall from Chapters 7 and 13 that randomization is the great equalizer. Subjects randomly assigned to an experimental or control group can be assumed to be statistically equivalent, thereby ruling out most threats to internal validity. In this example, the experimental stimulus is a revised questionnaire. Rather than test an experimental intervention, this proposal uses randomization to test an experimental measurement instrument. If the instrument used by Horney and Marshall does in fact produce lower estimates of offending rates, then rates for inmates who receive the experimental stimulus should be lower than those for inmates in the control group.

On a related point, notice how Horney and Marshall have creatively used the building blocks of experimental design we mentioned in Chapter 7. Unable to directly compare their results with those from earlier inmate self-report studies, the researchers adapted random-assignment techniques in a way that suited their purpose nicely.

Protecting Human Subjects We're sure you can recognize several potential ethical questions raised by this study. In Chapter 8, we pointed out that researchers have particular obligations in conducting research on special populations such as prisoners. Participation must be voluntary; undue influence or coercion cannot be used to induce subjects to participate. We also mentioned that asking about illegal behavior obliges researchers to ensure that respondents' answers will not cause them embarrassment or legal harm.

Horney and Marshall followed two standard procedures for complying with these and other ethical principles we discussed in Chapter 8. First, their proposal was reviewed by an institutional review board (IRB) at the University of Nebraska at Omaha. IRB approval is required for research conducted at an institution that receives federal funds. Horney and Marshall were required to document how their proposed research would minimize the potential harm to participants, and how they would guard the confidentiality of their interview data.

The second protection, informed consent, is required before an IRB will approve research of this type—research using prisoners as subjects, or research that asks about illegal actions. Informed consent also satisfies the more general ethical principle of voluntary participation. Figure 15-3 presents the informed consent statement used by Horney and Marshall. This detailed, thorough statement clearly explains research procedures, subject rights, confidentiality, and potential risks and benefits.

Analysis The primary purpose of this proposal is to describe offending rates. Therefore, most of the analysis section describes how the authors plan to compute these rates. Following other researchers, Horney and Marshall propose to compute annualized offending rates. This means that they will calculate a rate that expresses the approximate number of crimes committed by each offender over the course of a year.

The basic formula is straightforward, as this example for burglary illustrates:

$$\text{Annualized burglary offending rate} = \frac{\text{total burglaries committed}}{\text{window period}/12 \text{ months}}$$

As we described in Chapter 14, rates are fundamental descriptive measures in criminal justice research, but they must be computed with care. Let's look at this example as an illustration.

FIGURE 15-3

Informed Consent Crime Commission Rates Among Incarcerated
Felons in Nebraska
by Julie Horney and Ineke Marshall

Invitation to Participate
You are invited to participate in research conducted by researchers from the University of Nebraska at Omaha.

Basis for Subject Selection
You are asked to participate in this research because of your recent admission to the Diagnostic and Evaluation Unit. All men admitted over a period of about one year will be invited to participate.

Purpose of the Study
The purpose of the study is to collect information from men who have been recently convicted and sentenced to the Nebraska Department of Corrections to find out your opinions and experiences with the criminal justice system, and what are your opinions, past activities, and experiences in doing crime. We are trying to see if differences in the way questions are asked can help you be more accurate in some of your answers.

Explanations of Procedures
If you agree to participate in the survey you will be asked a series of questions that will probably take you about 45 minutes to one hour to answer. In this study, we use two slightly different sets of questions. Which of the two sets of questions you are asked will be determined purely by chance. We will also collect information about your arrests and treatment by the criminal justice system from records kept by the Department of Corrections.

Potential Risks and Discomforts
You will be asked questions about your past criminal activities, and you may be concerned that your answers would become known to people who may make decisions about your future. Any such risk is extremely unlikely because we will take a number of steps to insure the confidentiality of your answers.

Potential Benefits
There are no potential benefits to you. The potential benefits to society would be in improving our understanding of the causes and nature of criminal behavior.

Financial Compensation for Participation
If you participate in the survey you will receive a payment of $5.00 credited to your account. Your payment will only be received if you complete the survey.

Assurance of Confidentiality
The interviewer will have a booklet of questions to ask you. The booklet has a number on it but your name will not be on this booklet. I will print your name on a separate sheet that has the same number as the booklet. This sheet with your name will always be kept in a separate place from your answers.

UNO researchers will use the number sheet to combine your answers with information from the Department of Corrections records. All information obtained will be kept under locked conditions, and after records data have been

The concept of "annualized burglary offending rate" refers to the average number of burglaries committed in a one-year period. Although rates could be computed on other units of time, annualized rates have become a standard in criminal careers research. Looking at the preceding formula, you might initially wonder why we don't express it as the total number of burglaries divided by the total number of years. Conceptually, that is exactly what the formula does express. However, criminal careers are commonly interrupted by arrests, during which time an offender is incapacitated or not able to commit offenses. So, as we mentioned above, Horney and Marshall calculate a window period that expresses street time—the amount of time someone is not institutionalized and therefore is able to commit burglaries.

As an example, let's assume a subject reports committing 18 burglaries over a three-year period (36 months). Our subject was in jail for 14 of those months, which leaves a 22-month window period, or street time. We standardize the window period by dividing it by 12, the number of months in a year, to yield 1.83 years during which the subject was able to commit burglary ($22/12 = 1.83$). We then divide the number of burglaries (18) by the number of years (1.83), producing an annualized burglary rate of 9.84.

FIGURE 15-3 *(continued)*

collected, the sheet with your name on it will be destroyed. There would then be no way of associating your name with any of the information.

The UNO researchers will use your answers to questions in the survey booklet and the information they collect from the records *only for the purpose of research.* Your answers and all of the other information collected by the researchers will be kept strictly confidential. The researchers are in no way associated with the Department of Corrections.

Withdrawal from the Study

Participation is voluntary. Your decision whether or not to participate will not affect your present or future treatment by the Department of Corrections or the Nebraska Board of Parole. If you decide to participate, you are free to withdraw from this study at any time.

Offer to Answer Questions

If you have any questions, please do not hesitate to ask. If you think of questions later, please feel free to contact the investigators listed below. If you have any questions concerning your rights as a research subject, you may contact the University of Nebraska Institutional Review Board (IRB), telephone [phone].

Concluding Consent Statement

YOU ARE VOLUNTARILY MAKING A DECISION WHETHER OR NOT TO PARTICIPATE IN THIS RESEARCH STUDY. YOUR SIGNATURE CERTIFIES THAT YOU HAVE DECIDED TO PARTICIPATE HAVING READ AND UNDERSTOOD THE INFORMATION PRESENTED. YOUR SIGNATURE ALSO CERTIFIES THAT YOU HAVE HAD AN ADEQUATE OPPORTUNITY TO DISCUSS THIS STUDY WITH THE INVESTIGATOR AND YOU HAVE HAD ALL YOUR QUESTIONS ANSWERED TO YOUR SATISFACTION. YOU WILL BE GIVEN A COPY OF THIS CONSENT FORM TO KEEP.

_____   _____
SIGNATURE OF SUBJECT   DATE

IN OUR JUDGMENT THE SUBJECT IS VOLUNTARILY AND KNOWINGLY GIVING INFORMED CONSENT AND POSSESSES THE LEGAL CAPACITY TO GIVE INFORMED CONSENT TO PARTICIPATE IN THIS RESEARCH STUDY.

_____   _____
SIGNATURE OF INVESTIGATORS   DATE

Identification of Investigators

I. Marshall, Ph.D.   J. Horney, Ph.D.   [phone]

Source: Horney and Marshall (1988).

The actual calculations described by Horney and Marshall vary somewhat depending on which questionnaire (experimental or control) a respondent completes. Using the month-by-month estimates of offending frequency (from the experimental questionnaire) requires that actual rate calculations take monthly variations into account.

Significance, Management Plan   The proposal is careful to link its descriptive research purpose to criminal career research and to the policy implications of better understanding patterns of offending:

■ If it is indeed possible to clearly differentiate between high-rate and low-rate offenders, prison overcrowding may be alleviated by the greater use of alternative, non-prison sentences [for] low-rate offenders. If such differentiation is possible, it is not only prison resources that may be used more efficiently, but also police and prosecutorial resources.

(HORNEY AND MARSHALL, 1988:12)

The authors do not claim that their research will solve problems of prison crowding, but they do succinctly link their interests in more precise measurement to the policy needs of criminal justice officials.

Since Horney and Marshall propose to collect original data, they face additional requirements concerning project management that Sampson did not have to contend with. We have already discussed the need for human subjects review. Additionally, the proposal must clear two other hurdles: (1) show evidence of host agency cooperation, and (2) demonstrate that the investigators will be able to execute and manage their project.

What if you designed a research project in which you proposed to interview 700 incarcerated felons, but when you showed up at the institution with an armful of questionnaires, you were refused permission to interview anybody? This may strike you as a silly question, but it does point out an essential element of planning—obtaining advance approval from a host agency to conduct research. NIJ requires that proposals provide evidence that researchers have obtained permission to conduct research in host organizations. Horney and Marshall included in their proposal a letter of support from the Nebraska Department of Corrections, indicating that the department approved of the project and would assist researchers in their efforts to conduct interviews.

Horney and Marshall demonstrated their ability to execute and manage such a project in two ways. First, they describe their research experience and present a brief timetable for proposed project activities. Second, they describe the results of a pilot study they had already conducted to test their interview procedures on a sample of Nebraska inmates.

With evidence that the authors had already successfully tested many of their research procedures, members of the NIJ peer review panel could be confident that the proposed project would be executed successfully.

The Research Report

Two published articles from this project reported results from the revised procedures for measuring offending rates (Horney and Marshall, 1991, 1992a). A third article compared offending rates to respondents' perceived risk of arrest while committing an offense (1992b). Here we will focus on the article that described the experimental comparison of crime calendar methods (Horney and Marshall, 1992a).

As with Sampson's research, the careful planning Horney and Marshall devoted to their proposal is reflected in published results. Introductory sections describing past research and the design and methods used are simply adapted from the proposal. The hours spent planning a project have many benefits. Data collection will proceed more smoothly, the types of data analysis needed to test your hypotheses will be clear in your mind, and when it comes time to write up the results, much of your introductory material will all but write itself.

Response Rate   One reason for interviewing an intake cohort, rather than a sample of facility inmates, was the expectation that response rates would be higher among people just entering prison. This proved to be true.

Seeking to interview 700 convicted male offenders, Horney and Marshall (1992a:107) reached that target after inviting 746 persons to participate, for a response rate of 94 percent. Such a high response rate inspires confidence that subjects accurately represent the target population.

Findings   Because they were conducting their research on a different population than those used in earlier studies, Horney and Marshall could not directly assess whether their revised questionnaire produced different estimates of offending rates. Their analysis, therefore, centers on comparing rates between respondents who completed the experimental and control questionnaires.

Of 700 respondents, exactly half were randomly assigned to be interviewed with the experimental and control questionnaires. Since subjects were randomly assigned, tests of statistical significance can be used to compare differences in offending rates. Note that this is somewhat different from our discussion in Chapter 14 of the assumptions necessary to test statistical significance. Even though respondents were not selected through random sampling, their random assignment to groups produces a similar type of null hypothesis: that measures of offending rates will not differ by group, corresponding to questionnaire type. Random assignment is the key here and enables Horney and Marshall to assume that experimental and control groups are equivalent. Because of this, any differences in offending

TABLE 15-1
Estimates of Annualized Offending Rates

	Median	Mean	90th Percentile	Percent Active Offenders
Burglary				
Experimental	1.7	29.9	49.4	22
Control	2.2	67.3	154.8	23
All nondrug crime				
Experimental	4.0	175.1	285.6	60
Control	4.4	180.8	341.6	56

Source: Adapted from Horney and Marshall (1992a:114, Table 1).

rates can be reasonably attributed to measurement techniques.

Table 15-1 shows offending rates for burglary and for all crimes except drug sales. This table presents three of the descriptive statistics we discussed in Chapter 14. The median and mean measure central tendency for annualized offending rates. Percentiles express clustering, sort of a combination of central tendency and dispersion. The 90th percentile means that 90 percent of annualized offending rates are equal to or below the figures shown in Table 15-1. For example, 90 percent of respondents in the experimental group report annualized offending rates of 49.4 or less.

The last column of Table 15-1 shows the crime participation rate, or percentage of respondents who reported having committed at least one burglary or one nondrug crime. Calculations for the other statistics in Table 15-1 are based on numbers of cases represented by the participation rate. Thus, with 350 respondents in each group, 77 in the experimental group had committed at least one burglary (350 × .22) compared to 81 in the control group (350 × .23).

Table 15-1 illustrates a point we made in Chapter 14 about measures of central tendency. Recall that the mean expresses an average value, computed by summing all burglaries committed by all subjects and dividing by the number of subjects. The median expresses the midpoint of a distribution, so that equal numbers of cases are above and below the median.

Examining Table 15-1, you should recognize an example of how the average or mean value of a distribution is distorted by cases with extreme values. The median for the experimental group

indicates that only half the 77 cases committed burglaries at a rate higher than 1.7 per year, but the "average" burglary offending rate is almost 30 per year. Obviously, a small number of subjects committed an extremely large number of burglaries and thus distorted the mean. The 90th percentile verifies this. Recalling that the median represents the 50th percentile, you can see that 40 percent of active burglars in the experimental group committed between 1.7 and 49.4 burglaries per year. There is even greater variation in burglary offending among subjects in the control group.

Because of this, Horney and Marshall (1992a: 115) report several measures of central tendency and dispersion to provide a more thorough quantitative description of their data:

■ The mean is not an adequate measure because it is so sensitive to the extreme values of the highest rate offenders. The median is also not completely satisfactory because it conveys so little information about those high-rate individuals. . . . We thus present the mean, median, and 90th percentile, as well as the percent active in each category.

By comparing these different measures, you can better understand both extreme values and the more typical values for annualized offending rates.

Another consequence of the distribution of extreme values is that common tests of statistical significance cannot be used to compare offending rates by questionnaire type. A full understanding of this point requires much greater familiarity with inferential statistics than we can provide in this book.

You may recall from our discussion of sampling in Chapter 9 something about the importance of a normal distribution. We presented an example of a normal distribution in Figure 9-9. Most tests of statistical significance assume that cases are normally distributed, as shown in Figure 9-9. If you turn back to that figure, you will see that most values are clustered about the average value, with only a few cases at the extremes of a distribution. And in a normal distribution, the mean, median, and mode are identical. This contrasts sharply with the distribution of offending rates found by Horney and Marshall, as illustrated by very different values for the mean and median in Table 15-1.

Horney and Marshall were able to compute two different tests of statistical significance on their data. One of these, the Mann–Whitney U test, does not require the assumption that cases are normally distributed (Blalock, 1972:243). Although this test is not as common as many others used in social science research, it is acceptable for distributions with extreme values.

The other test was chi square, used to test for differences in participation rates between experimental and control groups. From our discussion in Chapter 14 and the information in Table 15-1, you should be able to compute chi square for burglary and all nondrug offenses. Begin by reviewing Tables 14-11 and 14-12. Then construct contingency tables using data computed from Table 15-1. Are there significant differences in participation rates?

Computing the Mann–Whitney U test for offending rates, Horney and Marshall found no significant differences between experimental and control groups for nine different offenses. When they restricted their analysis to respondents who reported committing at least ten offenses in each category, they found offending rates to be lower among experimental subjects for burglary, but not for other crimes.

A Successful Replication   Most of us hope that our hypotheses will be supported by data analysis. We suspect that was the case for Horney and Marshall as well. However, don't lose sight of a point we raised in Chapter 8—the unfortunate myth that negative findings aren't worth reporting. Let's also consider how the study by Horney and Marshall contributed to scientific knowledge about criminal careers.

First, by comparing different methods for obtaining self-report data and finding no significant differences, the authors add support to the accuracy and validity of other self-report studies. In this sense, Horney and Marshall have replicated results obtained in California, Colorado, Michigan, and Texas with their study of incarcerated felons in Nebraska. They have also inadvertently responded to critics of self-report studies by showing that different measurement techniques produce similar measures of offending rates. Their results lend support to the internal and external validity of self-report procedures for measuring criminal careers.

A second point relates to some of the specific changes Horney and Marshall introduced into their experimental questionnaire. Hypothesizing that high-rate saliency would inflate estimates of offending rates, the authors found no differences. They interpret this as possible evidence that "when respondents are asked about their 'typical' rates of [offending] they do a fairly good job of averaging over their different rates" (1992a: 119). This adds confidence to researchers whose measurement techniques rely on recall of past behavior.

Researchers devote a great deal of attention to trying to develop better measures of central criminal justice concepts. In part, this is because measurement is often difficult and usually imprecise. Studies such as that by Horney and Marshall represent progress by showing that different measurement procedures can produce similar estimates of offending rates.

■ CONCLUSION

Equipped with the knowledge and skills we have presented in this book, you could design and execute a criminal justice research project such as those we have just described. Of course, we have not covered everything you need to know. Chapter 2, for example, described the importance of theory in systematic inquiry, but you need to know more about the substance of theories and paradigms in criminal justice before you can use them to guide your own research. Each of the two examples presented in this chapter was guided by a thorough understanding of theory and previous research.

Our overview of statistical analysis techniques in Chapter 14 provides a good foundation in the logic of quantitative analysis. Using many statistical tools, however, requires a more detailed understanding than we can present in a general research methods book. This is especially true for advanced multivariate techniques that you may have encountered in reading research reports in academic and professional journals.

The chances are not good ($p < .001$) that you'll ever be responsible for designing and running a multistage probability survey of the nation's households for the purpose of determining whether there's a statistically significant relationship between gun ownership and victimization. But notice that you know basically what that means and you could say something about the steps involved in such a study: questionnaire design, sampling, data collection, calculating rates of gun ownership and victimization, and so on. Even if you needed to refer to this and other books to refresh your memory on some details, that's what professionals do all the time.

As a rough estimate, you now know more about criminal justice research than 99.98 percent of the world's population. (If that concerns you, tell all your friends to take this course.) Even if you aren't fully prepared to undertake major research projects on your own, you have become an "informed consumer." Even if you never con-

duct a major project of your own, you are able to evaluate criminal justice research conducted by others.

This is not an insignificant ability. Since the first edition of this book was published, the 1994 Crime Act became law. We have mentioned the sharp growth of applied research funded under the Crime Act. You may also know something of its other provisions: expanding the death penalty, requiring mandatory life sentences for repeat offenders, adding 100,000 officers to local law enforcement agencies, restricting gun ownership, and providing special initiatives that target violence against women. These and other parts of the Crime Act have attracted comments from reporters, ideologues, and lots of other people with more or less informed views on what to do about crime.

Your new skills in research can make you an active and critical consumer in the face of rapid change in criminal justice policy. You should be spared the frustration of contradictions in what the "experts" say. You'll be able to make some sense of professional disagreements and even judge which results are most appropriate to which situations and purposes in your life. And when experts weigh in with competing views on what causes crime to go down or up, your knowledge of how to be careful but creative in doing research will enable you to make up your own mind.

Whether you actively pursue a career in criminal justice research or simply focus your skills on being an empowered consumer, we hope this venture into the scientific study of crime and criminal justice policy has conveyed some of the excitement this field has to offer.

Appendixes

A   USING THE LIBRARY: TRADITIONAL AND COMPUTER-BASED INFORMATION SOURCES

B   NATIONAL CRIMINAL JUSTICE REFERENCE SERVICE

C   THE RESEARCH REPORT

D   SOURCES OF SECONDARY DATA

E   DISTRIBUTION OF CHI SQUARE

APPENDIX A
Using the Library: Traditional and Computer-Based Information Sources

■ INTRODUCTION

Throughout this book, we have assumed that you will be reading reports of criminal justice research. In this appendix, we want to talk a little about how you'll find reports to read.

You live in a world where daily reports of criminal justice research are the norm. Most newspapers, magazines, and television and radio news programs and features include news items, factoids, or summaries of crime problems and possible solutions. A variety of technical journals treat the same subjects from a more professional or academic standpoint.

This appendix is organized into two general sections. First we discuss using the library in the library. Going to your college or university library, or to a public or other library, is still an important starting point for most people. The second section describes examples of remote computer access to library and other information resources, including the Internet and World Wide Web. The section is much less complete for two related reasons. First, computer-assisted information resources are changing daily. No published guide could hope to keep pace, so you should view our suggestions as starting points.

Second, because of the phenomenal pace of development, the "virtual" library is a much less orderly place than the building where they keep the books. Internet tools and guides are continually being developed, but information technology changes much more quickly than guides to

that technology. This fact may seem disconcerting, but relax. We will guide you to particular sources of information that are likely to remain relatively stable.

■ USING THE LIBRARY IN THE LIBRARY

Usually you'll begin to pursue your interest in a particular topic through your college or university library. We'll give you just a brief overview here. Check your college or university library for customized guides to library and other resources.

Getting Help

When you want to find something in the library, your best friend is the reference librarian, who is specially trained to find things in the library. Sometimes it's hard to ask people for help, but you'll do yourself a real service to make an exception in this case.

Some libraries have specialized reference librarians—for the social sciences, humanities, government documents, and so forth. Find the one you need and describe what you're interested in. The reference librarian will probably put you in touch with some of the many available reference sources.

You may find that your library does not own a copy of some specific book or other item that interests you. In that case, your librarian may be able to obtain a copy through interlibrary loan. Most college and university libraries share their resources. Again, ask your librarians to help you; that's their job.

Reference Sources

You have probably heard about the information explosion. Your library is one of the main battlefields. Fortunately, a large number of reference volumes offer a guide to the information that's available.

Here are two lists of reference sources that you should find especially useful. The first presents reference materials designed for criminal justice or criminology research. Following that is a longer list for other social sciences. Neither of these lists is complete, but each presents some good starting points.

Criminal Justice Reference Sources

- *Criminal Justice Abstracts*
- *Criminal Justice Periodical Index*
- *Criminology, Penology, and Police Science Abstracts*
- *Abstracts on Juvenile Justice and Delinquency*
- *Abstracts on Police*
- *Police Science Abstracts*

General Social Science and Information Reference Sources

- *Social Science Index*
- *Social Science Citation Index*
- *Sociological Abstracts*
- *Psychological Abstracts*
- *Public Affairs Information Service Bulletin*
- *ABC Political Science*
- *Social Work Research and Abstracts*
- *New York Times Index*
- *Facts on File*
- *Business Periodicals Index*
- *Education Index*

Using the Stacks

For serious research, you should learn to use the stacks, where most of the library's books are stored. In this section, we'll give you some information about finding books in the stacks.

The Card Catalog Your library's card catalog is the main reference system for finding out where books are stored. Traditionally, each book is described on three separate 3 × 5 cards. The cards are then filed in three alphabetic sets. One set is arranged by author, another by title, and the third by subject matter.

If you want to find a particular book, you can look it up in either the author file or the title file. If you only have a general subject area of interest, you should thumb through the subject catalog.

On-Line Card Catalogs In recent years, card catalogs in many libraries have been shifted to computerized systems. Some libraries may have all their holdings in a computerized "card catalog," while others retain card catalogs for older library materials but enter all new acquisitions into on-line catalogs. In this section we refer to computerized systems as "on-line catalogs," as distinguished from the traditional "card catalog."

Several different software systems are used for on-line catalogs in different college and university libraries, but all are accessed in some way through computer terminals. The existence of different software systems slightly complicates the task of briefly summarizing on-line card catalogs. Fortunately, most software systems are designed for ease of use by library patrons, and most are based on the familiar logic of traditional card catalogs. This means that most on-line catalogs can be searched by author, title, or subject, just like card catalogs.

In addition, several popular systems can be searched by keyword, in which case you can specify any word that appears in a computer record as a keyword.

Let's consider an example, searching Indiana University's on-line catalog with the NOTIS software system. Searching first by author, let's see what the library has under Earl Babbie:

```
a=babbie earl
```

This produces a list of 51 entries! Now, Babbie has not written 51 books; the large number of entries includes duplicate holdings in different libraries of the Indiana University system.

If you are interested in one of Babbie's books— *Survey Research Methods*, for example—you may search by title, typing in the command:

```
t=survey research methods
```

You find this:

Author: Babbie, Earl R.
Title: Survey research methods / Earl R. Babbie.
Edition: 2nd edition
Published: Belmont, Calif. : Wadsworth Pub. Co., c1990.
Description: xx, 395 p. ; 24 cm.

LOCATION:	CALL NUMBER
Blgtn BUSINESS/SPEA	H62 .B23 1990

STATUS:
Charged, Due: 04/09/97
Ask about recall.

You find detailed information on the book, including the call number, just like you would in a card catalog. In this case, you also find some useful information that saves you a trip to the stacks: The book is currently charged to a library patron (Babbie's books are popular), but you can check with a librarian about recalling the book for your use.

Searching by subject and keyword is a bit trickier. For example, a search of the Indiana University on-line catalog for the subject "criminal justice" (s=criminal justice) produces 5,000 entries. It's best to state subject and keyword searches as specifically as possible.

The NOTIS system is used in many other college and university libraries—the University of Michigan and Northwestern University, for example. Other systems use similar commands. For example, at Rutgers University commands are specified as follows:

author	aut=
title	til=
subject	sub=
keyword	key=

We mention different on-line software systems for two reasons. First, we want you to have an idea of what you might encounter at your own library. Second, as you will see later, becoming familiar with basic search commands in different software systems will enable you to search the on-line catalogs of libraries around the world.

With a little practice, you will soon find yourself zipping through on-line catalogs with speed and efficiency. The efficiency part is important. You certainly want to avoid having to sift through the 5,000 entries you find at Indiana University by simply typing s=criminal justice. Efficiency also comes with practice, but a few minutes of instruction from a librarian will more than pay off.

Bibliographic Databases

In addition to having on-line catalogs, college and university libraries now have access to other computerized reference tools. For example, the Educational Resources Information Center (ERIC) system allows you to search through hundreds of major educational journals to find articles published in your area of interest (within the field of education). Once you identify the articles you are interested in, the computer will print out abstracts of those articles. The publications *Sociological Abstracts and Psychological Abstracts* present summaries of books and articles—often prepared by the original authors—so that you can locate a great many relevant references easily and effectively. As you find relevant references, you can track down the original works and see the full details. The summaries are available in both written and computerized forms.

One specialized bibliographic database is of special interest to criminal justice researchers and students. *Criminal Justice Abstracts* is the best single reference tool for criminal justice journals and published books; this is also an excellent source of information on government documents. Each year the *Abstracts* adds thousands of new records that can be searched on more than a dozen fields.

Here are some other bibliographic databases found increasingly in college libraries. Some of these include abstracts of articles, while others simply present citations for books, scholarly journals, or periodical articles.

- *Newsbank.* Selected articles from more than 450 local and regional U.S. newspapers. 1982–current.

- *National Newspaper Index.* Articles from five nationally significant newspapers: *New York Times, The Wall Street Journal, Washington Post, Los Angeles Times,* and *Christian Science Monitor.* Most recent four years.
- *Dissertation Abstracts Ondisc.* Abstracts for doctoral dissertations completed at hundreds of North American universities. 1980–current.
- *Public Affairs Information Service CD-ROM.* Indexes of books, periodicals, and government publications on public policy, government, and legal issues. 1991–current.
- *Social Sciences Index.* English-language periodicals on current events in politics, economics, sociology, criminology, and other social sciences. 1983–current.
- *Social Sciences Citation Index.* Index of leading social science journals by author, article or journal title, cited author, and cited title. 1981–current.
- *County and City Databook.* Computerized version of the Census Bureau publication, including social, demographic, and economic data on counties and cities with populations greater than 25,000. Revised every five years.
- *LegalTrac.* Scholarly journals and some specialized newsletters covering law and legal issues. 1980–current.

These are just a sample of computerized library research tools available on compact disc (CD-ROM). Ask your librarian for help in getting started.

Government Documents

Many especially useful sources of data and information about crime and criminal justice are government publications. Larger universities have special departments for government publications; smaller institutions may house government documents in general collections.

Unfortunately, material published by federal, state, local, or foreign governments is often not included in card catalogs. Instead, various published indexes, bibliographies, or computer databases must be consulted to search for government documents. These bibliographic resources are often difficult to use. Because of this, finding government publications in library stacks often requires help from a specialized librarian.

This situation is changing rapidly, however. Most federal agencies, and a growing number of state and local governments, make electronic copies of publications available on the Internet. For example, Maxfield obtained crime data for Idaho (reported in Chapter 6) by connecting to the Idaho Department of Law Enforcement on the Internet.

National Criminal Justice Reference Service Criminal justice researchers are fortunate in having access to an exceptionally useful source of government documents and other unpublished materials through the National Criminal Justice Reference Service (NCJRS). Appendix B describes NCJRS and its services in detail.

■ REMOTE ACCESS TO LIBRARIES

Students and researchers traditionally have gone to libraries to use the computerized tools we have mentioned so far. However, rapid changes in computer and telecommunications technology bring many library research tools to your desktop. With a personal computer, modem, and communications software, you might be able to use many university library resources from home. Again, because of the wide variety of systems and astonishing development of new technologies, we can only present examples. But many of you will find these tools available right now.

Calling Your Library from Home

If your college or university library has a computerized on-line catalog, you may be able to connect to it through remote access. For example, Maxfield can call up the Indiana University Library on-line catalog by connecting to the university computing system. This does not require state-of-the-art technology, by the way; on-line library catalogs can be accessed with very simple software and computers dating to the early 1980s.

At present, several Indiana University resources are available to anyone who has a personal computer and a modem. The on-line card catalog can be searched by author, title, subject, or keyword at home or in the library. Selected computerized indexes are also available, including the *National Newspaper Index* mentioned earlier, together with indexes of scholarly journals and popular periodicals. Most other large universities allow Internet users to access their card catalogs and certain other library resources.

The Internet and World Wide Web

Remote access to your library's on-line catalog is just the beginning. By connecting to the Internet or the World Wide Web, you can access library and other information resources at colleges and universities throughout the world.

The basic technology underlying the Internet—remotely connecting to a central computer facility—has been possible for many years. But since the early 1990s, countless computers have become linked through sophisticated software that carries photographs, sound, and even video images. All of this has made it possible for you to access a vast, almost unimaginable body of information from around the world.

The best way to learn what you can do on the net and the web is to experiment: Find a computer that's connected to the web and explore. Few reliable guides to the Internet currently exist. Change is occurring so fast that anything written about the Internet is obsolete before it can be published. In the future, things will become better documented. Perhaps your college or university computing center has useful guides or other publications. For now, however, our best advice to you is to see what you can find. If you're uncomfortable with that, think of exploring the Internet as the electronic equivalent of wandering around your library's stacks and looking for interesting things.

Browsing Software Rather sophisticated web browsers have become all but essential tools for exploring the Internet. Graphical browsers enable you to view pictures, graphs, and tables, as well as publication-quality text. Such software has become pretty much the norm, but much simpler text-based browsers remain useful.

As its name implies, a text-based browser does not make it possible to receive graphics images. This limit may be unacceptable for many people, but this disadvantage is offset by the speed of text-based browsers. Most colleges and universities have both text-based and graphical browsers, so you can determine which best meets your needs. See computing center staff for more information.

Plan Your Internet Research Once you're on the web, using graphical or text browsers, you have access to limitless sources of information. As we said earlier, wandering around is the best way to become comfortable with finding things on the web. But when it comes time to do background reading for a research project or a class paper, you should have a more conscious plan about what you're looking for and where to look. Librarians can be helpful here because they are trained to catalog and find information. As more and more information is placed on and retrieved from the web, librarians make it their business to learn efficient strategies for electronic searches.

Keep two things in mind before beginning your search of Internet resources. First, Internet sites and web pages come and go. What we have identified here is current as of April 1997; individual sites may have been moved or discontinued without notice. So be prepared to hit some deadends. Second, the Internet can be a marvelous research tool, but it can also be a trap. It's easy to get distracted by photos from the O. J. Simpson trial, for example, when you're looking for information on the outcomes of murder trials. Just as going to a university library can be an intellectual or social experience, using the Internet to search for information can save time or waste time.

Different Ways to Find Information Librarians at the State University of New York at Albany have produced an excellent guide to conducting research on the Internet.[1] The guide describes five basic ways to find information, three of which we'll summarize here.

---

[1] University at Albany Libraries, "Conducting Research on the Internet," University at Albany, State University of New York, April 1996.

- *Go directly to a specific Internet address.*   If you know or suspect that some particular site will be useful, specify the site's *Uniform Resource Locator* (URL) address. At the end of this appendix, we list the URLs for several sites that will be useful to criminal justice researchers.
- *Browse.*   Undirected wandering is rarely an efficient way to do research, but using a particular site as a starting point for your browsing can sometimes pay off. For example, the Library of Congress "Research Tools" site or the Bureau of Justice Statistics home page can be a useful point of departure for directed browsing.
- *Use a search tool.*   To use search tools, sometimes called "search engines," type in a few terms or key words that relate to your topic of interest. In this way, Internet search engines work much the same as on-line card catalogs. A number of commercial search engines are available on the Internet. Many specific sites have their own search tools that often allow for more efficient searching.

Basic Criminal Justice Sources

In this section we list some web and Internet sites that should serve as starting points in your search. We specify URL addresses for each site. Type each address exactly as it appears, beginning with the characters: http://

http://www.ojp.usdoj.gov/bjs

This home page for the Bureau of Justice Statistics (BJS) includes BJS publications, news releases, and many useful links.

http://www.ncjrs.org/homepage.htm

Start here to search for documents and publications produced by the National Institute of Justice and other national government agencies. You'll find some references to state and local documents as well. See Appendix B for more on the NCJRS.

http://www.fsu.edu/~crimdo/cj.html

Florida State University professor Cecil Greek has assembled a wide variety of criminal justice resources and links. You might want to start here, but be aware of two potential ob-

stacles. First, this site has become popular and is therefore sometimes hard to access. Second, the site includes many "bells and whistles" that look quite nice but tend to slow things down. All in all, this is an excellent resource.

http://www.open.gov.uk/home_off/rsd/rsdhome.htm

This site is maintained by the British Home Office Research and Statistics Directorate. Here you will find information about the excellent series of publications produced by this organization.

http://www.nida.nih.gov/NIDACapsules/NCIndex.html

Maintained by the National Institute on Drug Abuse (NIDA), this site gives access to the latest reports on drug abuse issues.

http://www.cdc.gov/ncipc/ncipchm.htm

Another nonjustice organization, the Centers for Disease Control have expanded research on violence. You will find useful information and links on this page.

http://bravo.berkeley.edu/cgi-bin/hcsa?harc3

Go to the University of California at Berkeley to access the General Social Survey (GSS) data online. You can find out about the GSS at other sites, but here you can actually do analysis of GSS data over the web.

http://www.icpsr.umich.edu/NACJD/index.html
http://www.icpsr.umich.edu/INTRA/index.html
http://dawww.essex.ac.uk/

The first two sites will lead you to detailed information about criminal justice and other social science data held at the University of Michigan. You can also download data directly via links on these sites. See Appendix D for more information. The third address specifies the University of Essex Data Archive, the most complete source of social science data in the United Kingdom. The Essex page also lists additional data archives in other nations.

Other Useful Sources

http://www.loc.gov

The Library of Congress card catalog is accessible from this location. You will also find the Library of Congress to be a good starting point for finding many valuable Internet resources. See especially the "Research Tools" link.

http://www.indiana.edu/~librcsd/

This is the home page for the Research Collections and Services Department of Indiana University's library. Like many Internet sites maintained by large libraries, this page will point you to a variety of other sources of reference information.

http://www.apa.org/science/research.html
http://www.asanet.org/default.htm

These sites are maintained by the American Psychological Association and the American Sociological Association, respectively. Point your browser here for information on research ethics.

http://www.nytimes.com
http://www.washingtonpost.com
http://www.latimes.com

Here are home pages for three major newspapers. Access to each is free of charge at this writing (April 1997), although the *New York Times* requires that you register. Hundreds of other newspapers can be found on the web.

■ ADDITIONAL READINGS

Benamati, Dennis C., Schultze, Phyllis A., Bouloukos, Adam C., and Newman, Graeme R. *Criminal Justice Information: How to Find It, How to Use It* (Phoenix: Oryx Press, 1997). This new guide to criminal justice information is prepared by respected scholars and reference librarians. It should become an invaluable resource for criminal justice researchers.

Booth, Wayne C., Colomb, Gregory G., and Williams, Joseph M., *The Craft of Research* (Chicago: University of Chicago Press, 1995). Here is an excellent guide to how to find and read scholarly literature. The authors also provide great advice on how to make your notetaking more efficient and useful. Read

this book before you go to the library or log onto the Internet.

Lutzker, Marilyn, and Ferrall, Eleanor, *Criminal Justice Research in Libraries* (New York: Greenwood Press, 1986). This book presents detailed advice on how to get the most out of the time you spend in a library. The authors provide tips on notetaking and keeping track of the information you find. Specialized criminal justice reference sources are described, in addition to social science materials of interest to criminal justice researchers. There is even an appendix on Library of Congress subject headings that can make your searches of card or on-line library catalogs much more efficient.

O'Block, Robert L., *Criminal Justice Research Sources*, 3rd ed. (Cincinnati, OH: Anderson, 1992). This invaluable book offers advice on getting started with your research topic, as well as comprehensive guides to a large variety of information sources. Each of the book's 17 chapters begins with general advice on locating different sources of information and then presents descriptive lists of resources ranging from books to statistical data.

New published guides to using the Internet appear frequently. Here are some recent and classic samples worth consulting:

Kardas, Edward P., and Milford, Tommy M., *Using the Internet for Social Science Research and Practice* (Belmont, CA: Wadsworth, 1996). As the title indicates, this introduction to the net focuses on the resources specifically relevant to social science research. It is loaded with web sites and more, and an enclosed diskette makes it easier for you to use them.

Kehoe, Brendan P., *Zen and the Art of the Internet: A Beginner's Guide*, 3rd ed. (Englewood Cliffs, NJ: Prentice-Hall, 1994).

Laquey, Tracy, *The Internet Companion: A Beginner's Guide to Global Networking*, 2nd ed. (Reading, MA: Addison-Wesley, 1994).

B National Criminal Justice Reference Service

■ INTRODUCTION

The National Criminal Justice Reference Service (NCJRS), established by the National Institute of Justice (NIJ) in 1972, is an important specialized bibliographic resource. NCJRS serves hundreds of thousands of criminal justice researchers and professionals from many different nations.

Although NCJRS was established with the primary purpose of disseminating information on research and policy development to criminal justice professionals, its services are an important resource for researchers, students, and the general public. Many people, especially those who lack ready access to a library with an extensive government documents collection, find NCJRS invaluable for keeping up on new developments in applied criminal justice research.

In this appendix, we will describe some of the information available to you through the NCJRS World Wide Web site. We'll also summarize some of the major reports and bulletins produced by two bureaus in the Office of Justice Programs, an organization within the U.S. Department of Justice.

■ DOCUMENT COLLECTIONS

First and foremost, NCJRS is the central repository and distribution center for a wide variety of publications. Books, articles, government reports, and other criminal justice documents are included in general and specialized collections.

The NCJRS traditionally distributed copies of publications in response to special requests by telephone or mail. Since 1995, a rapidly growing number of documents have become available via the Internet. The bulk of NCJRS holdings from earlier years are maintained as printed or microformed documents that have been indexed in a bibliographic database. The database entry for each document includes a full bibliographic citation, together with a 100- to 200-word summary of contents.

You can probably access the NCJRS database through your college librarian. Many libraries have access to a networked information retrieval service, DIALOG. Through DIALOG, you and your librarian can search the NCJRS bibliographic database and obtain brief summaries of documents that meet your research needs.

Justice Information Center

Most people who have access to a graphical or text-based Internet browser will want to visit the NCJRS web page, the Justice Information Center, at this address:

http://www.ncjrs.org/homepage.htm

The Justice Information Center is the starting point for identifying two general types of information: on-line copies of documents and links to other web sites. Let's look at an example.

The Justice Information Center home page starts by displaying ten topical subareas:

corrections	international
courts	juvenile justice
crime prevention	law enforcement
criminal justice statistics	research and evaluation
drugs and crime	victims

Clicking on "crime prevention" produces two choices: World Wide Web sites and documents. Each of these choices leads to more information about crime prevention. Here are some examples of web sites you would find under "crime prevention":

- Canadian Crime Prevention Centre
    http://www.telusplanet.net/public/ccpc/
- Florida Citizen Safety Center
    http://www.legal.firn.edu/safe_cen.html
- National Crime Prevention Council—United States
    http://www.weprevent.org/
- Partnerships Against Violence
    http://www.pavnet.org

Clicking instead on "documents" produces a list of dozens of on-line publications about crime prevention. One example is *A Police Guide to Surveying Citizens and Their Environment.* We mentioned this document in Chapter 11 as an example of how to do structured observations in the form of an environmental survey. Figure 11-3 was adapted from that document, and you could obtain a complete copy of the publication from the NCJRS web site.

The Justice Information Center also includes a search tool. As we described in Appendix A, such tools can be very helpful in searching for specific types of documents in a large database. At present (April 1997), NCJRS searches are not as useful as they might be because the complete text of on-line documents is searched. This means that if you search for "crime prevention," your results will include documents where the words "crime" and "prevention" appear anywhere in the text.

We emphasize here that the Justice Information Center is a *starting point.* Beginning here you will find a large number of links to additional resources that will take you, virtually, around the world. For example, Figure B-1 shows what you find by clicking "international" on the Justice Information Center home page. And clicking on the map shown in Figure B-1 can take you from Canada (numbers 4 and 5) to Uganda (number 11) to Australia (number 1).

Specialized Publications

NCJRS and its web site are gateways to publications issued by different organizations within the Department of Justice. Additionally, bureaus within the Office of Justice Programs maintain their own specialized information centers. Each of these bureaus has a web page that can be reached through the Justice Information Center.

Two bureaus issue specialized publications of particular interest. Each presents recent research findings, statistical reports, or guidelines on policy development that are valuable for researchers, students, and criminal justice professionals. Most documents issued since 1995, and some documents published earlier, are available on-line from the Justice Information Center. Here we list brief descriptions of only a sample of documents produced by NIJ and BJS.

National Institute of Justice

- *Research in Brief.* This series presents findings from research projects sponsored by NIJ or research conducted by institute staff. Known colloquially as "RIBs," each report presents a 6- to 12-page summary of research results from projects of current interest. Many RIBs are succinct reports adapted from more detailed books or articles.
- *Research Preview.* Preliminary results from ongoing NIJ-sponsored projects are sometimes described in this series.
- *Research in Action.* While RIBs may report on basic or applied research findings, the Research in Action series focuses on new policy or program developments of particular interest to criminal justice professionals. For example, recent titles describe alternative strategies for prosecuting high-rate offenders and experimental interventions in cases of child abuse.
- *Perspectives on Policing.* NIJ and Harvard University jointly convened a series of conferences where leading researchers and police executives discussed management and policy issues in policing. Reports from these conferences are valuable resources for research and policy development in such law enforcement

FIGURE B-1
National Institute of Justice UNOJUST

Welcome to UNOJUST   http://www.ncjrs.org/unojust/

National Institute of Justice
UNOJUST

About Us • What's New • Publications • Calendar of Events • Guestbook

The <u>National Institute of Justice (NIJ)</u>, the research arm of the <u>U.S. Department of Justice</u>, developed the United Nations Online Crime and Justice Clearinghouse (UNOJUST) to assist member criminological institutes around the world in developing their capacity to exchange information electronically. Use this site to explore NIJ's international activities, NIJ-sponsored research, and a calendar of international events, and to link to other UNOJUST member organizations.

☐ <u>Other WWW Links</u>
☐ <u>Contacts</u>

United Nations Online Crime and Justice Clearinghouse

Member of:

UNOJUST
network

1. <u>AIC Canberra</u>	2. <u>ASSTC, Riyadh</u>
3. <u>HEUNI, Helsinki</u>	4.<u>ICCLRCJP, Vancouver</u>
5. <u>ICPC, Montreal</u>	6. <u>ILANUD, San Jose</u>
7. <u>ISISC, Siracusa</u>	8. <u>ISPAC, Milan</u>
9. <u>NIJ, Washington</u>	10. <u>UNAFEI, Fuchu</u>
11. <u>UNAFRI, Kampala</u>	12. <u>UNCPCJ, Vienna</u>
13. <u>UNICRI, Rome</u>	14. <u>Raoul Wallenberg Institute</u>

Source: Printed from the National Institute of Justice UNOJUST web page at url: http://www.ncjrs.org/unojust/
Accessed March 29, 1997.

areas as community policing and drug control strategies.

Bureau of Justice Statistics BJS publishes several series of documents that reflect the bureau's responsibility for collecting, analyzing, and disseminating statistical information about crime and the operation of criminal justice agencies. Most reports present summary statistics from various data series; others report data analysis by BJS staff. Although many BJS reports are available through the Justice Information Center, you should also check the BJS web page at: http://www.ojp.usdoj. gov/bjs/

• *Corrections Reports.* Results of sample surveys and censuses of jails, prisons, parole, probation, and other corrections data.

- *Federal Statistics.* Federal case processing: investigation through prosecution, adjudication, sentencing, incarceration.
- *Drugs and Crime.* Sentencing and time served by drug offenders, drug use at time of crime by jail inmates and state prisoners, and other quality data on drugs, crime, and law enforcement.
- *Justice Expenditure and Employment.* National data on state and local police and sheriffs' departments; operations, equipment, personnel salaries, spending, policies, and programs.
- *BJS Bulletins and Special Reports.* Timely reports of the most current justice data.
- *National Crime Victimization Survey Reports.* The only ongoing national survey of crime victims. Reports are issued in two series each year, brief summary reports and detailed tabulations.
- *Sourcebook of Criminal Justice Statistics* (annual). Broad-based data from more than 150 sources (400+ tables, 100+ figures, subject index, annotated bibliography, addresses of sources). Beginning with the 1995 edition, the *Sourcebook* is available on-line at this address: http://www.albany.edu/sourcebook

Further Information

The best source of additional information on research resources available from NCJRS is the Justice Information Center web page. You can also subscribe to an electronic mailing list and receive a free copy of a bimonthly newsletter from NCJRS. The newsletter will be sent to your e-mail address. To subscribe, log onto your e-mail account and send a message like the following (substituting your name for Maxfield's):

```
subscribe    justinfo    michael
maxfield
```

Send the message to:

```
listproc@ncjrs.org
```

Don't include anything else in your message; just send it as shown here. If you have any question about NCJRS services, send an e-mail message describing your question to:

```
askncjrs@ncjrs.org
```

C The Research Report

■ INTRODUCTION

This book has considered the variety of activities involved in doing criminal justice research. In this appendix, we'll turn to an often neglected subject: reporting the research to others. Unless the research is properly communicated, all the efforts devoted to procedures will go for naught.

Before proceeding further on this topic, we should suggest one absolutely basic guideline. Good research reporting requires good English (unless you are writing in a foreign language). We need to communicate our results clearly and precisely; nothing should be left to the reader's imagination. Whenever we use unduly complex terminology or sentence structure, communication is reduced. Every researcher should read and reread (at approximately three-month intervals) an excellent small book by William Strunk, Jr., and E. B. White: *The Elements of Style*. If you do this faithfully, and if even 10 percent of the contents rub off, you stand a good chance of making yourself understood and your findings perhaps appreciated.

Research reporting has three functions, and it is a good idea to keep these in mind. First, the report communicates to an audience a body of specific data and ideas. The report should provide those specifics clearly and with sufficient detail to permit an informed evaluation. Second, the research report should be viewed as a contribution to the general body of scientific knowledge. While remaining appropriately humble, you should always regard your research report as an addition to what we know about behavior. Finally, the report should stimulate and direct further inquiry.

■ SOME BASIC CONSIDERATIONS

Despite these general guidelines, different reports serve different purposes. A report appropriate for one purpose might be wholly inappropriate for another. This section deals with some basic considerations in this regard.

Audience

Before drafting your report, you must ask yourself who you hope will read it. Normally, you should make a distinction between fellow researchers and general readers. If you are writing for the former, you may make certain assumptions about their existing knowledge and perhaps summarize certain points rather than explaining them in detail. Similarly, you may use more technical language than would be appropriate for a general audience.

At the same time, you should remain aware that criminal justice, just like any other social science, is composed of factions or cults. Terms and assumptions acceptable to your immediate colleagues may only confuse other scientists. That applies with regard to substance as well as techniques. A researcher describing an evaluation of community policing to a general audience, for example, should explain previous findings in more detail than would be necessary if he or she were addressing an audience of others who specialize in research on policing.

Form and Length of the Report

It is useful to think about the variety of reports that might result from a research project. To begin, you may wish to prepare a short research note for publication in an academic or technical journal. Such reports should be approximately one to five pages in length (typed, double-spaced) and should be concise and direct. In a short space, you will not be able to present the state of the field in any detail, and your methodological notes must be somewhat abbreviated as well. Basically, you should tell the reader why you feel a brief note is justified by your findings, then tell what those findings are.

Often researchers must prepare reports for the sponsors of their research. These may vary greatly in length, of course. In preparing such a report, however, you should bear in mind the audience for the report—scientific or lay—and their reasons for sponsoring the project in the first place. It is both bad politics and bad manners to bore the sponsors with research findings that have no interest or value to them. At the same time, it may be useful to summarize the ways the research has advanced basic scientific knowledge (if it has).

Working papers or monographs are another form of research reporting. Especially in a large and complex project, it is useful to obtain comments on your analysis and the interpretation of your data. A working paper is a tentative presentation with an implicit request for comments. Working papers can also vary in length; they may present all the research findings of the project or only a portion of them. Because your professional reputation is not at stake in a working paper, you should feel free to present tentative interpretations that you cannot altogether justify—identifying them as such and asking for evaluations.

Many research projects result in papers delivered at professional meetings. Often these serve the same purpose as working papers. You are able to present findings and ideas of possible interest to your colleagues and ask for their comments. The length of professional papers may vary depending on the requirements of the particular meetings; however, it's usually better to say too little rather than too much. Although a working paper may ramble somewhat through a variety of tentative conclusions, conference participants should not be forced to sit through an oral unveiling of the same. Interested listeners can al-

ways ask for more details later, and uninterested ones can gratefully escape.

Probably the most popular research report is the article published in an academic journal. Again, lengths vary; examine the lengths of articles previously published by a particular journal. As a rough guide, however, 25 typed pages is as good as any. A subsequent section on the organization of the report is primarily based on the structure of a journal article, so we will say no more at this point, except to indicate that student term papers should be written on this model. As a general rule, a term paper that would make a good journal article also makes a good term paper.

A book is the most prestigious form of research report. It has the advantages of the working paper, but it should be a more polished document. Because the publication of research findings as a book gives those findings an appearance of greater substance and worth, you have a special obligation to your audience. Although you will still hope to receive comments from colleagues, possibly leading you to revise your ideas, you must realize that other readers may be led to accept your findings uncritically.

Aim of the Report

Earlier in this book, we considered the different purposes of criminal justice research projects. In preparing your report, you should keep these different purposes in mind.

Some reports focus primarily on the exploration of a topic of interest. Inherent in this aim is the tentativeness and incompleteness of the conclusions. You should clearly indicate to your audience the exploratory aim of the study and point to the shortcomings of the particular project. An important aspect of an exploratory report is to point the way to more refined research on the topic.

Many studies have a descriptive purpose, and the research reports from these studies have a descriptive element. You should carefully distinguish for the reader those descriptions that apply to only the sample and those that are inferred to the population. Whenever inferential descriptions are to be made, you should give your audience some indication of the probable range of error in those descriptions.

Other reports have an explanatory aim; you wish to point to causal relationships among variables. Depending on the probable audience for your report, you should carefully delineate the rules of explanation that lie behind your computations and conclusions and, as in the case of description, you must give your readers some guide to the relative certainty of your conclusions.

Finally, some research reports have the aim of proposing action. For example, an evaluation of a program that set alternative punishments for drunk driving may wish to suggest ways drunk driving may be reduced, on the basis of the research findings. This aim often presents knotty problems, however, because your own values and orientations may interfere with your proposals. Although it is perfectly legitimate for your proposals to be motivated by personal values, you must ensure that the specific actions you propose are warranted by your data. Thus, you should be especially careful to spell out the logic by which you move from empirical data to proposed action.

■ ORGANIZATION OF THE REPORT

Although the organization of reports differs somewhat on the basis of form and purpose, it is possible to suggest a general format for presenting research data. The following comments apply most directly to a journal article, but with some modification, they apply to most forms of research reports.

Purpose and Overview

It is always helpful to the reader if you begin with a brief statement of the purpose of the study and the main findings of the analysis. In a journal article, this overview may sometimes be given in the form of an abstract or synopsis.

Some researchers find this difficult to do. For example, your analysis may have involved considerable detective work, with important findings revealing themselves only as a result of imaginative deduction and data manipulation. You may

wish, therefore, to lead the reader through the same exciting process, chronicling the discovery process with suspense and surprise. To the extent that this form of reporting gives an accurate picture of the research process, it has considerable instructional value. Nevertheless, many readers may not be interested in following your entire research account, and not knowing the purpose and general conclusions in advance may make it difficult for them to understand the significance of the study.

An old forensic dictum says: "Tell them what you're going to tell them; tell them; and tell them what you told them." You would do well to follow this dictum in the preparation of research reports.

Review of the Literature

Because every research report should be placed in the context of the general body of scientific knowledge, it is important to indicate where your report fits in that picture. Having presented the general purpose of your study, you should then bring the reader up to date on the previous research in the area, pointing to general agreements and disagreements among previous researchers.

In some cases, you may wish to challenge previously accepted ideas. You should carefully review the studies that led to the acceptance of those ideas and then indicate the factors that were not previously considered or the logical fallacies present in the previous research.

When you are concerned with resolving a disagreement among previous researchers, you should organize your review of the literature around the opposing points of view. You should summarize the research supporting one view, then summarize the research supporting the other, and finally suggest the reasons for the disagreement.

To an extent, your review of the literature serves a bibliographic function for readers by indexing the previous research on a given topic. This can be overdone, however, and you should avoid an opening paragraph that is three pages long and mentions every previous study in the field. The comprehensive bibliographic function can best be served by a bibliography at the end of the report, and the review of the literature should focus on only those studies that have direct relevance to the present study.

Avoiding Plagiarism

Whenever you are reporting on the work of others, it is important that you be clear about who said what. It is essential that you avoid plagiarism: the theft of another's words and/or ideas—whether intentional or accidental—and the presentation of those words and ideas as your own. Because this is a common and sometimes unclear problem for college students, let's take a minute to examine it in some detail. Here are the main ground rules regarding plagiarism:

- You cannot use another writer's exact words without using quotation marks and giving a complete citation, which indicates the source of the quotation such that your reader could locate that quotation in its original context. As a rule of thumb, taking a passage of eight or more words without citation is a violation of federal copyright laws.
- It is not acceptable to edit or paraphrase another's words and present the revised version as your own work.
- Finally, it is not even acceptable to present another's ideas as your own—even if you use totally different words to express those ideas.

The following examples should clarify what is and is not acceptable in the use of another's work.

The Original Work

■ *Laws of Growth*

   Systems are like babies: once you get one, you have it. They don't go away. On the contrary, they display the most remarkable persistence. They not only persist; they grow. And as they grow, they encroach. The growth potential of systems was explored in a tentative, preliminary way by Parkinson, who concluded that administrative systems maintain an average growth of 5 to 6 percent per annum regardless of the work to be done. Parkinson was right so far as he goes, and we must give him full honors for

initiating the serious study of this important topic. But what Parkinson failed to perceive, we now enunciate—the general systems analogue of Parkinson's Law.[1]

Acceptable and Unacceptable Uses   First let's look at some of the acceptable ways you might make use of Gall's work in a term paper.

- **Acceptable:**   John Gall, in his work on Systemantics, draws a humorous parallel between systems and infants: "Systems are like babies: once you get one, you have it. They don't go away. On the contrary, they display the most remarkable persistence. They not only persist; they grow."[2]
- **Acceptable:**   John Gall warns that systems are like babies. Create a system and it sticks around. Worse yet, Gall notes, systems keep growing larger and larger.[3]
- **Acceptable:**   It has also been suggested that systems have a natural tendency to persist, even grow and encroach (Gall, 1975:12). [*Note:*   This format requires that you give a complete citation in your bibliography.]

Here are some unacceptable uses of the same material, reflecting some common errors.

- **Unacceptable:**   In this paper, I want to look at some of the characteristics of the social systems we create in our organizations. First, systems are like babies: once you get one, you have it. They don't go away. On the contrary, they display the most remarkable persistence. They not only persist; they grow. [It is unacceptable to quote someone else's material directly without using quotation marks and giving a full citation.]

---

[1] John Gall, *Systemantics: How Systems Work and Especially How They Fail* (New York: Quadrangle, 1975), pp. 12–14. *Note:* Gall previously gave a full citation for Parkinson.

[2] John Gall, *Systemantics: How Systems Work and Especially How They Fail* (New York: Quadrangle, 1975), p. 12.

[3] John Gall, *Systemantics: How Systems Work and Especially How They Fail* (New York: Quadrangle, 1975), p. 12.

- **Unacceptable:** In this paper, I want to look at some of the characteristics of the social systems we create in our organizations. First, systems are a lot like children: once you get one, it's yours. They don't go away; they persist. They not only persist, in fact: they grow. [It is unacceptable to edit another's work and present it as your own.]

- **Unacceptable:** In this paper, I want to look at some of the characteristics of the social systems we create in our organizations. One thing I've noticed is that once you create a system, it never seems to go away. Just the opposite, in fact: They have a tendency to grow. You might say systems are a lot like children in that respect. [It is unacceptable to paraphrase someone else's ideas and present them as your own.]

These unacceptable examples are plagiarism—a serious offense. Admittedly, there are some "gray areas." Some ideas are more or less in the public domain, not "belonging" to any one person. Or you may reach an idea on your own that someone else has already put in writing. If you have a question about a specific situation, discuss it with your instructor in advance.

We have discussed this topic in some detail because it is important that you place your research in the context of what others have done and said, and yet the improper use of their materials is a serious offense. Mastering this matter, however, is a part of your "coming of age" as a scholar.

Study Design and Execution

A research report that contains interesting findings and conclusions can be frustrating to the reader who is unable to determine the methodological design and execution of the study. The worth of all findings depends heavily on the manner in which the data were collected and analyzed.

In reporting the design and execution of a survey, for example, you should always include the following: the population, the sampling frame, the sampling method, the sample size, the data-collection method, the completion rate, and the

methods of data processing and analysis. Comparable details should be given if other methods are used. The experienced researcher is able to report these details in a rather short space without omitting anything required for the reader's evaluation of the study.

Analysis and Interpretation

Having set the study in the perspective of previous research and having described the design and execution of it, you should then present your data. The next major section will provide further guidelines in this regard. For now, a few general comments are in order.

The presentation of data, the manipulations of those data, and your interpretations should be integrated into a logical whole. It is frustrating to the reader to discover a collection of seemingly unrelated analyses and findings with a promise that all the loose ends will be tied together later in the report. Every step in the analysis should make sense—at the time it is taken. You should present your rationale for a particular analysis, present the data relevant to it, interpret the results, then indicate where that result leads next.

Summary and Conclusions

Following the forensic dictum mentioned earlier, you must summarize the research report. You should avoid reviewing every specific finding, but you should review all of the significant ones, pointing once more to their general significance.

The report should conclude with a statement of what you have discovered about your subject matter and where future research might be directed. A quick review of recent journal articles will probably indicate a very high frequency of the concluding statement "It is clear that much more research is needed." This is probably always a true conclusion, but it is of little value unless you can offer pertinent suggestions about the nature of that future research. You should review the particular shortcomings of your own study and suggest ways those shortcomings might be avoided by future researchers.

■ GUIDELINES FOR REPORTING ANALYSES

The presentation of data analyses should provide a maximum of detail without being cluttered. You can accomplish that best by continually examining your report to see whether it achieves the following aims.

Quantitative data should be presented in a way that permits recomputations by the reader. In the case of percentage tables, for example, the reader should be able to collapse categories and recompute the percentages. Readers should be given sufficient information to compute percentages in the table in the opposite direction from your own presentation.

All aspects of the analysis should be described in sufficient detail to permit a secondary analyst to replicate the analysis from the same body of data. This means that he or she should be able to create the same measures, produce the same tables, and so forth. That is seldom done, of course, but if the report is presented in a manner that makes it possible, the reader will be far better equipped to evaluate the report.

If you are doing a qualitative analysis, it is important to provide sufficient details from your observations so that your reader has a sense of having been there with you. Presenting only those data that support your interpretations is not acceptable. You must also share with your reader those data that conflict with the way you have made sense of things. Ultimately, you should provide your readers with enough varied information that they might reach a different conclusion than you did—though one hopes your interpretation will be the one that makes the most sense.

Be explicit in drawing conclusions. Although research is typically conducted for the purpose of drawing general conclusions, you should carefully note the specific basis for such conclusions. Otherwise, you may lead your reader into accepting unwarranted conclusions.

Point to any qualifications or conditions warranted in the evaluation of conclusions. Typically, you are in the best position to know the shortcomings and tentativeness of your conclusions, and you should give the reader the advantage of that knowledge. Failure to do so can misdirect future research and result in a waste of research funds.

A final guide to the reporting of methodological details is that the reader should be in a position to completely replicate the entire study independently. It should be recalled from an earlier discussion that replicability is an essential norm of science generally. A single study does not prove a point; only a series of studies can begin to do so. Unless studies can be replicated, there can be no meaningful series of studies.

We will conclude with a point made at the outset of this appendix, since it is extremely important. Research reports should be written in the best possible literary style. Writing lucidly is easier for some people than for others, and it is always harder than writing poorly. You are again referred to the Strunk and White book. Every researcher would do well to follow this procedure: Write. Read Strunk and White. Revise. Reread Strunk and White. Revise again. That will be a difficult and time-consuming endeavor, but so is science.

A perfectly designed, carefully executed, and brilliantly analyzed study will be worthless unless you are able to communicate your findings to others. This appendix has attempted to provide some general and specific guidelines toward that end. The best guides are logic, clarity, and honesty. Ultimately, there is probably no substitute for practice.

■ ADDITIONAL READINGS

Becker, Howard S., *Writing for Social Scientists: How to Start and Finish Your Thesis, Book, or Article* (Chicago: University of Chicago Press, 1986). You will not find a more informative (or more entertaining) discussion of how to write and how to write well. Strunk and White (below) present a classic and important description of writing principles. Read Becker for advice on how to transform principles into practice.

Booth, Wayne C., Colomb, Gregory G., and Williams, Joseph M., *The Craft of Research* (Chicago: University of Chicago Press, 1995). This is an excellent and highly readable source of tips and information on thinking, researching, and writing. In addition, the authors offer valuable advice on how to present data, including the relative strengths of tables and different styles of graphs. Finally, you will find more guidance on how to avoid even inadvertent plagiarism.

Strunk, William, Jr., and White, E. B., *The Elements of Style* (New York: Macmillan, 1979). As we stated earlier, everyone who writes should read and reread this book.

D Sources of Secondary Data

■ INTRODUCTION

Much of Chapter 12 described how data and information collected by other researchers or routinely gathered by government or other organizations can be used in criminal justice research. Using data collected by other researchers was called *secondary analysis*. Data gathered by government organizations were included under the general label of *agency records*.

Criminal justice researchers are fortunate in having access to a vast array of data produced by other researchers, government agencies, and various organizations. Available data represent every method for collecting information we have described in this book and just about every conceivable type of design.

Our discussion of how to obtain secondary data focuses on central repositories—most notably the National Archive of Criminal Justice Data (NACJD) and the Inter-university Consortium for Political and Social Research (ICPSR), both maintained at the University of Michigan. As you will see, NACJD and ICPSR holdings are rich and varied; we estimate that data from at least two-thirds of the studies we have mentioned in this book are available from these sources.

However, as you learn more about what data are out there, you should not lose sight of two limitations. First, central repositories are incomplete; data may also be available from the original source. Second, recall our discussion of reliability and validity as it applies to secondary data. You have no control over the measurement and data-collection process, which can mean that measures and variables used in available data don't match your own needs well. You also have no control over measurement reliability and other quality-control issues in data collection. We do not mean to scare you away from secondary analysis. But you should always be careful and not assume that because data have been collected by a respected researcher or by a government agency, there are no problems.

■ INTER-UNIVERSITY CONSORTIUM FOR POLITICAL AND SOCIAL RESEARCH

We begin by describing the ICPSR, since it is the "parent" organization that includes NACJD as a subset. Founded at the University of Michigan in 1962, the ICPSR has evolved into the world's largest central repository for machine-readable social science data. Its holdings include thousands of data resources collected by researchers and by government agencies. Many of the latter are ongoing data series such as the decennial census, national election studies, Uniform Crime Reports (UCR), and National Crime Victimization Survey (NCVS).

The word *consortium* is significant, denoting an association or partnership of hundreds of colleges and universities throughout the world. These member institutions provide financial support to the consortium in return for unlimited access to its data archives. In many cases, official representatives are linked to political science departments, reflecting ICPSR roots in that social science discipline.

It's difficult to succinctly classify ICPSR's social science holdings. Among the categories of interest to a variety of social science researchers are the following:

- *General Social Survey (GSS)*. Conducted by the National Opinion Research Center since 1972, the GSS includes questions on attitudes, opinions, and demographics. This survey has become an important source of data for social scientists in many disciplines. As we demonstrated in Chapter 14, GSS data may also be analyzed directly by connecting to the University of California at Berkeley at the following URL: http://bravo.berkeley.edu/cgi-bin/hcsa3
- *National Election Studies*. The ICPSR was established in large part to make survey data from national election studies available to political scientists and others. These surveys have been conducted since 1944, usually in all even-numbered years; all presidential election years are represented.
- *Decennial Census of Population and Housing*. Census data in a variety of formats and levels of aggregation are among the ICPSR resources of most general use to social scientists.
- *Mortality Detail Files*. These data are collected by the National Center for Health Statistics to provide detailed information on deaths as reported on individual death certificates filed in the United States. These files, dating to 1968, are of special interest to homicide researchers.

For a complete listing of data files, see the *ICPSR Guide to Resources and Services,* a publication you will find at the office of your official ICPSR representative. Alternatively, you can search ICPSR data holdings on-line by contacting this URL: http://www.icpsr.umich.edu/contents.html

ICPSR also provides three types of training services of interest to criminal justice researchers: (1) quantitative analysis techniques, most notably sophisticated multivariate procedures; (2) general computer use; and (3) instruction in using specific large, complex data files such as the decennial census and the NCVS.

■ NATIONAL ARCHIVE OF CRIMINAL JUSTICE DATA

The Bureau of Justice Satistics (BJS), in cooperation with ICPSR, established the National Archive of Criminal Justice Data in 1978. In general, this archive is a subset of ICPSR holdings of special interest to criminal justice researchers and professionals. Criminal justice data are routinely deposited in the archive from a variety of sources, including four Department of Justice organizations: BJS, National Institute of Justice (NIJ), Federal Bureau of Investigation, and Office of Juvenile Justice and Delinquency Prevention.

Here's a summary of what the NACJD does, reproduced from the organization's web page:[1]

■ The central mission of the NACJD is to facilitate and encourage research in the field of criminal justice through the preservation and sharing of data resources, and the provision of specialized training in quantitative analysis of crime and justice data. Specific activitiess of the NACJD include:

- Archiving and dissemination of computerized data, documentation, and software for the quantitative study of crime and the criminal justice system.
- Development of specialized collections of data sets on themes of interest in criminal justice.
- Training in quantitative methods of social science research to facilitate secondary analysis of criminal justice data.
- Technical assistance for selecting data collections and the computer hardware and software to analyze data efficiently and effectively.
- Customized reproduction of data sets on alternative media, including CD-ROM and diskette.

What this means to criminal justice researchers is that a wide variety of criminal justice data is available for an equally wide variety of purposes. The best way to learn about what's available is to visit the NACJD web site and browse through the

---

[1] http://www.icpsr.umich.edu/NACJD/mission.html Accessed March 25, 1997.

holdings. To give you an idea about what you can find there, we demonstrate by working through the index of NACJD holdings to obtain descriptions of data from two studies we frequently mentioned in earlier chapters.

If you point your web browser at the NACJD Archive index, you will get a screen something like the one in Figure D-1.[2] This figure shows the major subject areas under which NACJD data are organized, from "I. Attitude surveys" to "XI. Drugs, alcohol, and crime." From this screen you can search for a particular study by specifying either a researcher's name or keywords that identify the study. For example, searching for "victimization" would produce descriptions of the National Crime Victimization Survey, the British Crime Survey, and several others. The columns labeled "Title" and "P.I." refer to the title of the research project and the project's principal investigator, respectively. Clicking on "M" under "P.I." would then produce a list of all principal investigators whose last names began with M. Or you can click on one of the subject headings for a list of studies and data under that heading. That's the approach we'll take in continuing our example.

Clicking on "VII. Crime and delinquency" would yield a screen like that shown in Figure D-2, the first of several screens listing studies under this heading. The columns labeled "Study Title" and "Principal Investogator" are self-explanatory; the final column simply lists the study's index number in the NACJD database. The first two columns, labeled "Abstracts & Datasets," are routes to obtain summary descriptions of the study ("AB" in Figure D-2) and the actual data ("DA" in Figure D-2). Clicking on "DA" would lead you through a series of screens to a point where you could eventually download many

data files directly to your own computer. Be aware that some files are extremely large and would require quite a long time to access via a telephone connection.

Scanning the study titles shown in Figure D-2, you should see some titles that are familiar. Notice that the classic "Delinquency in a Birth Cohort" studies are listed. You should also recognize Cathy Spatz Widom's study on child abuse, and the study of residential burglars by Richard Wright and Scott Decker. Clicking on "AB" would lead you to screens like those shown in Figures D-3 and D-4.

If you've read our discussion in earlier chapters, the material under "SUMMARY" should be familiar to you. Notice also the information under "DATA SOURCE"—arrest records for Widom and personal interviews for Wright and Decker. The summary discussion of sampling for the burglary study should remind you of what we said about snowball sampling in Chapters 9 and 11. The comment "COLLECT NOTE" for Wright and Decker indicates that the data are transcripts from interviews, so you could review burglars' "verbatim answers to interviewers' questions," excluding identifying information and profanity. Subsequent screens for each study present more detailed information on how data are organized.

These examples should give you some idea of what kind of information is included about each study in the NACJD holdings. By browsing through the major catagories listed in Figure D-1, you can learn more about the scope of topics covered. That scope is extensive, and we invite you to learn more by visiting the NACJD.

■ *NATIONAL INSTITUTE OF JUSTICE DATA RESOURCES PROGRAM*

The initial collaboration between BJS and ICPSR to establish the criminal justice data archive reflected the organizational mission of BJS: to collect, analyze, and disseminate statistical information about crime and criminal justice agencies. Following this example, in 1984 NIJ established its

[2]This and other figures in this appendix were printed directly from screens displayed by a version of Netscape, a commercially produced web browser widely available without charge. Different versions of Netscape or other web browsers would produce slightly different images than those shown in Figures D-1 through D-4. But you should be able to see or print the essential content shown in each figure.

FIGURE D-1
NACJD Archive Index

NACJD   http://www.icpsr.umich.edu/NACJD/archive.html

non-tables version of this page
Criminal Justice Data - ICPSR Home - B J S
archive - contacts - forums - sites

N A C J D Archive

Note: All of the search and browse utilities on this page now access the most up-to-date information available. Please report studies which appear to be mistakenly omitted to webmaster.

Search Holdings	Browse Holdings by Subject, Title, PI or Study #				
	Subject	**Title**	**P.I.**	**Study #**	
	I. Attitude surveys	A	A		
		B	B		
	II. Community studies	C	C		
		D	D	3000s	7800s
Search Notes:	III. Corrections	E	E	5000s	7900s
		F	F	6000s	8000s
Searching is **not**	IV. Court case processing	G	G	6100s	8100s
case sensitive.		H	H	6200s	8200s
Multiple, space-	V. Courts	I	I	6300s	8300s
delimited terms		J	J	6400s	8400s
are interpreted	VI. Criminal justice system	K	K	6500s	8500s
as AND queries.		L	L	6600s	8600s
Quoted queries	VII. Crime and delinquency	M	M	6700s	8700s
are interpreted		N	N	6800s	8800s
as a single	VIII. Official statistics	O	O	6900s	8900s
search term.		P	P	7000s	9000s
	IX. Police	Q	Q	7100s	9100s
		R	R	7200s	9200s
	X. Victimization	S	S	7300s	9300s
		T	T	7400s	9400s
	XI. Drugs, alcohol, and crime	U	U	7500s	9500s
		V	V	7600s	9600s
		W	W	7700s	9700s
		X	X		9800s
		Y	Y		9900s
		Z	Z		

criminal justice issues || website technical issues
NACJD : http://www.icpsr.umich.edu/nacjd

Source: Printed from the National Archive of Criminal Justice Data web page at url: http://www.icpsr.umich.edu/NACJD/archive.html. Accessed March 25, 1997.

own data resources program through the ICPSR.

Researchers like Widom, Wright, and Decker, whose projects are funded by NIJ, are required to submit copies of machine-readable data when their project is completed. These data are then sent to ICPSR for inclusion in the criminal justice data archive. In contrast to most BJS data series, the NIJ program archives data from specific research and evaluation projects. This means that data from virtually any NIJ-funded study completed in the last 14 years are available from ICPSR for secondary analysis by researchers.

FIGURE D-2

Partial Listing NACJD Archive Crime and Delinquency Data

ICPSR - Subject Search   http://www.icpsr.umich.edu/cgi/subject.prl?path=NACJD&format=tb&query=VII

		Criminal Justice Data - ICPSR Home - B J S archive - contacts - forums - sites		
		Crime and delinquency		
Abstracts & Datasets		Study Title	Principal Investigator	Study Number
AB	DA	Adult Criminal Careers in New York, 1972-1983	Blumstein, Alfred and Jacqueline Cohen.	9353
AB	DA	Adult Criminal Careers, Michigan: 1974-1977	Blumenstein, Alfred. Jacqueline Cohen.	8279
AB	DA	Anticipating and Combating Community Decay and Crime in Washington, D.C., and Cleveland, Ohio, 1980-1990	Harrell, Adele and Caterina Gouvis.	6486
AB	DA	Autobiographical Accounts of Property Offenses by Youths at UCLA, 1983-1984	Katz, Jack.	8950
AB	DA	Cambridge Study in Delinquent Development [Great Britain], 1961-1981	Farrington, David P.	8488
AB	DA	Child Abuse, Neglect, and Violent Criminal Behavior in a Midwest Metropolitan Area of the United States, 1967-1988	Widom, Cathy Spatz	9480
AB	DA	Criminal Careers of Juveniles in New York City, 1977-1983	Winterfield, Laura A.	9986
AB	DA	Deinstitutionalization of Status Offenders: A Study of Intervention Practices for Youth in Seven Cities in the United States, 1987-1991	Klein, Malcolm, and Cheryl Maxson.	6039
AB	DA	Delinquency in a Birth Cohort II: Philadelphia, 1958-1986	Figlio, Robert M., Paul E. Tracy, and Marvin E. Wolfgang.	9293
AB	DA	Delinquency in a Birth Cohort in Philadelphia, Pennsylvania, 1945-1963	Wolfgang, Marvin E., Robert Figlio, and Thorsten Sellin	7729
AB	DA	Deterrent Effects of Antitrust Enforcement [United States]: The Ready-Mix Concrete Industry, 1970-1980	Block, Michael K. and Fredrick C. Nold.	9040
AB	DA	Deterrent Effects of the New York Juvenile Offender Law, 1974-1984	Singer, Simon I.	9324
AB	DA	Disturbed Violent Offenders in New York, 1985	Toch, Hans and Kenneth Adams.	9325
AB	DA	Domestic Terrorism: Assessment of State and Local Preparedness in the United States, 1992	Riley, Kevin Jack and Bruce Hoffman.	6566
AB	DA	Early Identification of the Chronic Offender, [1978-1980: California]	Haapenan, Rudy and Carl F. Jesness.	8226
AB	DA	Exploring the House Burglar's Perspective: Observing and Interviewing Offenders in St. Louis, 1989-1990	Wright, Richard and Scott H. Decker.	6148

Source: Printed from the National Archive of Criminal Justice Data web page at url: http://www.icpsr.umich.edu/cgi/subject.prl?path= NACJD&format=tb&query=VII. Page 1 of 5, accessed March 25, 1997.

FIGURE D-3
Partial Listing NACJD Archive Abstract: Child Abuse, Neglect, and Violent Criminal Behavior

ICPSR Abstract   http://www.icpsr.umich.edu/cgi/ab.prl?file=9480

STUDYNO = 09480;

DATE-ADDED = March 5, 1991;

DATE-UPDATED = March 31, 1995;

INVESTIGATOR = Widom, Cathy Spatz.;

TITLE = CHILD ABUSE, NEGLECT, AND VIOLENT CRIMINAL BEHAVIOR IN A MIDWEST METROPOLITAN AREA OF THE UNITED STATES, 1967–1988;

SUMMARY = These data examine the relationships between childhood abuse and/or neglect and later criminal and violent criminal behavior. In particular, the data focus on whether being a victim of violence and/or neglect in early childhood leads to being a criminal offender in adolescence or early adulthood and whether a relationship exists between childhood abuse or neglect and arrests as a juvenile, arrests as an adult, and arrests for violent offenses. For this data collection, adult and juvenile criminal histories of sampled cases with backgrounds of abuse or neglect were compared to those of a matched control group with no official record of abuse or neglect. Variables contained in Part 1 include demographic information (age, race, sex, and date of birth). In Part 2, information is presented on the abuse/neglect incident (type of abuse/neglect, duration of the incident, whether the child was removed from the home and, if so, for how long, results of the placement, and whether the individual was still alive). Part 3 contains family information (with whom the child was living at the time of the incident, family disruptions, and who reported the abuse or neglect) and data on the perpetrator of the incident (relation to the victim, age, race, sex, and whether living in the home of the victim). Part 4 contains information on the charges filed within adult arrest incidents (occasion for arrest, multiple counts of the same type of charge, year and location of arrest, and type of offense or charge), and Part 5 includes information on the charges filed within juvenile arrest incidents (year of juvenile charge, number of arrests, and type of offense or charge). The unit of analysis for Parts 1 through 3 is the individual at age 11 or younger, for Part 4 the charge within the adult arrest incident, and for Part 5 the charge within the juvenile arrest incident.;

EXTENT.COLLECT = 5 data files + machine-readable documentation (text) + SAS data definition statements + SPSS data definition statements;

EXTENT.PROCESS = DDEF.ICPSR/ MDATA.PR/ RECODE/ REFORM.DATA/ SCAN/ UNDOCCHK.ICPSR;

DATA.TYPE = event/transaction data;

TIME.PERIOD = 1967–1988;

DATE.OF.COLLECT = August 1, 1986–December 31, 1989;

FUNDING.AGENCY = United States Department of Justice. National Institute of Justice.;

GRANT.NUMBER = 86–IJ-CX-0033;

DATA.SOURCE = adult arrest records at the local, state, and federal levels, county juvenile court and juvenile probation department records, birth records (control group), Bureau of Motor Vehicle records, and marriage license bureau records;

DATA.FORMAT = LRECL with SAS and SPSS data definition statements;

Source: Printed from the National Archive of Criminal Justice Data web page at url: http://www.icpsr.umich.edu/cgi/ab.prl?file=9480. Page 1 of 3, accessed March 25, 1997.

FIGURE D-4
Partial Listing NACJD Archive Abstract: Exploring the House Burglar's Perspective

ICPSR Abstract   http://www.icpsr.umich.edu/cgi/ab.prl?file=6148

STUDYNO = 06148;

DATE-ADDED = March 10, 1994;

DATE-UPDATED = March 10, 1994;

INVESTIGATOR = Wright, Richard, and Scott H. Decker.;

TITLE = EXPLORING THE HOUSE BURGLAR'S PERSPECTIVE: OBSERVING AND INTERVIEWING OFFENDERS IN ST. LOUIS, 1989-1990;

SUMMARY = These data investigate the behaviors and attitudes of active residential burglars, not presently incarcerated, operating in St. Louis, Missouri. Through personal interviews, information was gathered on the burglars' motivation and feelings about committing crimes, peer pressure, burglary methods, and stolen goods disposal. Respondents were asked to describe their first residential burglary, to recreate verbally the most recent residential burglary they had committed, to discuss their perceptions of the risk values involved with burglary, and to describe the process through which they selected potential targets for burglaries. In-depth, semistructured interviews lasting from 1.5 to 3 hours were conducted in which participants were allowed to speak freely and informally to the investigator. These interviews were tape-recorded and transcribed verbatim, and some were later annotated with content-related markers or ''tags'' to facilitate analysis. Information was also elicited on age, race, sex, marital status, employment status, drug history, and criminal offense history.;

EXTENT.COLLECT = 1 data file + data collection instrument;

EXTENT.PROCESS = BLANKS/ NONNUM;

DATA.TYPE = machine-readable text;

TIME.PERIOD = 1989-1990;

DATE.OF.COLLECT = 1989-1990;

FUNDING.AGENCY = United States Bureau of Justice. National Institute of Justice.;

GRANT.NUMBER = 89-IJ-CX-0046;

DATA.SOURCE = personal interviews;

DATA.FORMAT = LRECL;

COLLECT.NOTE = This dataset is a machine-readable text file containing verbatim answers to interviewers' questions. For reasons of confidentiality, names have been removed. Profanity has been deleted as well.;

SAMPLING = The study employed a ''snowball'' sampling technique, whereby offenders known to the investigators were asked to refer other active offenders who, in turn, were asked to refer still more active offenders until a suitable sample size was attained. To keep the sample from containing a disproportionately high number of offenders who had been previously apprehended, no referrals from law enforcement or other criminal justice personnel were used. All 105 individuals who agreed to an interview were included in the sample. Of the sample, 87 were male and 18 were female, 72 were Black and 33 were white, and 27 were juveniles. At the time of interview, 21 of the subjects were on probation, parole, or serving suspended sentences.;

Source: Printed from the National Archive of Criminal Justice Data web page at url: http://www.icpsr.umich.edu/cgi/ab.prl?file=6148. Page 1 of 2, accessed March 25, 1997.

■ *HOW TO GET ICPSR AND CRIMINAL JUSTICE ARCHIVE DATA*

You may be able to get copies of ICPSR and NACJD data on-line. Depending on your computer setup and the size of the data file, you will probably use a special computer program called File Transfer Protocol (FTP). Although the procedures for using FTP or other methods to get copies of data files are simple enough, we suggest you check with staff at your computing center if you have not downloaded data files before.

BJS and NIJ have begun to distribute selected data files reproduced on CD-ROM disks. For example, in 1995 NIJ released a CD-ROM that contained data from more than 40 studies on vio-lence. Check the NACJD web site for information on how to obtain criminal justice data on CD-ROM.

While we're on the subject of computers and computing centers, you should be aware that some criminal justice data files can be very large or very complex, or both. Using the NCVS, for example, presents formidable challenges that will test the computer skills of any researcher and tax the resources of any computer installation.

We suggest that before ordering any data file from ICPSR or NACJD, you get further information about the size and format of specific files that interest you. Check with staff at your computing center, or send a message via e-mail to ICPSR staff.

E Distribution of Chi Square

	Probability						
df	.99	.98	.95	.90	.80	.70	.50
1	$.0^3157$	$.0^3628$	.00393	.0158	.0642	.148	.455
2	.0201	.0404	.103	.211	.446	.713	1.386
3	.115	.185	.352	.584	1.005	1.424	2.366
4	.297	.429	.711	1.064	1.649	2.195	3.357
5	.554	.752	1.145	1.610	2.343	3.000	4.351
6	.872	1.134	1.635	2.204	3.070	3.828	5.348
7	1.239	1.564	2.167	2.833	3.822	4.671	6.346
8	1.646	2.032	2.733	3.490	4.594	5.528	7.344
9	2.088	2.532	3.325	4.168	5.380	6.393	8.343
10	2.558	3.059	3.940	4.865	6.179	7.267	9.342
11	3.053	3.609	4.575	5.578	6.989	8.148	10.341
12	3.571	4.178	5.226	6.304	7.807	9.034	11.340
13	4.107	4.765	5.892	7.042	8.634	9.926	12.340
14	4.660	5.368	6.571	7.790	9.467	10.821	13.339
15	5.229	5.985	7.261	8.547	10.307	11.721	14.339
16	5.812	6.614	7.962	9.312	11.152	12.624	15.338
17	6.408	7.255	8.672	10.085	12.002	13.531	16.338
18	7.015	7.906	9.390	10.865	12.857	14.440	17.338
19	7.633	8.567	10.117	11.651	13.716	15.352	18.338
20	8.260	9.237	10.851	12.443	14.578	16.266	19.337
21	8.897	9.915	11.591	13.240	15.445	17.182	20.337
22	9.542	10.600	12.338	14.041	16.314	18.101	21.337
23	10.196	11.293	13.091	14.848	17.187	19.021	22.337
24	10.856	11.992	13.848	15.659	18.062	19.943	23.337
25	11.524	12.697	14.611	16.473	18.940	20.867	24.337
26	12.198	13.409	15.379	17.292	19.820	21.792	25.336
27	12.879	14.125	16.151	18.114	20.703	22.719	26.336
28	13.565	14.847	16.928	18.939	21.588	23.647	27.336
29	14.256	15.574	17.708	19.768	22.475	24.577	28.336
30	14.953	16.306	18.493	20.599	23.364	25.508	29.336

continued

For larger values of df, the expression $\sqrt{2\chi^2} - \sqrt{2df - 1}$ may be used as a normal deviate with unit variance, remembering that the probability of χ^2 corresponds with that of a single tail of the normal curve.

Source: We are grateful to the Literary Executor of the late Sir Ronald A. Fisher, F.R. S., to Dr. Frank Yates, F.R. S., and to Longman Group Ltd., London, for permission to reprint Table IV from their book *Statistical Tables for Biological, Agricultural, and Medical Research* (6th Edition, 1974).

Probability

df	.30	.20	.10	.05	.02	.01	.001
1	1.074	1.642	2.706	3.841	5.412	6.635	10.827
2	2.408	3.219	4.605	5.991	7.824	9.210	13.815
3	3.665	4.642	6.251	7.815	9.837	11.341	16.268
4	4.878	5.989	7.779	9.488	11.668	13.277	18.465
5	6.064	7.289	9.236	11.070	13.388	15.086	20.517
6	7.231	8.558	10.645	12.592	15.033	16.812	22.457
7	8.383	9.803	12.017	14.067	16.622	18.475	24.322
8	9.524	11.030	13.362	15.507	18.168	20.090	29.125
9	10.656	12.242	14.684	16.919	19.679	21.666	27.877
10	11.781	13.442	15.987	18.307	21.161	23.209	29.588
11	12.899	14.631	17.275	19.675	22.618	24.725	31.264
12	14.011	15.812	18.549	21.026	24.054	26.217	32.909
13	15.119	16.985	19.812	22.362	25.472	27.688	34.528
14	16.222	18.151	21.064	23.685	26.873	29.141	36.123
15	17.322	19.311	22.307	24.996	28.259	30.578	37.697
16	18.841	20.465	23.542	26.296	29.633	32.000	39.252
17	15.511	21.615	24.769	27.587	30.995	33.409	40.790
18	20.601	22.760	25.989	28.869	32.346	34.805	42.312
19	21.689	23.900	27.204	30.144	33.687	36.191	43.820
20	22.775	25.038	28.412	31.410	35.020	37.566	45.315
21	23.858	26.171	29.615	32.671	36.343	38.932	46.797
22	24.939	27.301	30.813	33.924	37.659	40.289	48.268
23	26.018	28.429	32.007	35.172	38.968	41.638	49.728
24	27.096	29.553	33.196	36.415	40.270	42.980	51.179
25	28.172	30.675	34.382	37.652	41.566	44.314	52.620
26	29.246	31.795	35.563	38.885	42.856	45.642	54.052
27	30.319	32.912	36.741	40.113	44.140	46.963	55.476
28	31.391	34.027	37.916	41.337	45.419	48.278	56.893
29	32.461	35.139	39.087	42.557	46.693	49.588	58.302
30	35.530	36.250	40.256	43.773	47.962	50.892	59.703

Bibliography

American Psychological Association. 1995. "Ethical Principles of Psychologists and Code of Conduct." Washington, DC: American Psychological Association. http://www.apa.org/ethics/code.html Accessed January 25, 1997.

American Sociological Association. 1996. "Code of Ethics." Washington, DC: American Sociological Association. http://www.asanet.org/ecoderev.htm Accessed January 25, 1997.

Austin, James, Peter Quigley, and Steve Cuvelier. 1989. *Evaluating the Impact of Ohio's Community Corrections Programs on Public Safety and Costs.* San Francisco: National Council on Crime and Delinquency.

Babbie, Earl. 1995. *The Practice of Social Research,* 7th ed. Belmont, CA: Wadsworth.

Bachman, Ronet, and Linda E. Saltzman. 1995. *Violence Against Women: Estimates from the Redesigned Survey.* Washington, DC: U.S. Department of Justice, Office of Justice Programs, Bureau of Justice Statistics.

Bachman, Ronet, and Bruce M. Taylor. 1994. "The Measurement of Family Violence and Rape by the Redesigned National Crime Victimization Survey." *Justice Quarterly* 11:499–512.

Baldus, David C., Charles Pulaski, and George Woodworth. 1983. "Comparative Review of Death Sentences: An Empirical Study of the Georgia Experience." *Journal of Criminal Law and Criminology* 74:661–753.

Ball, John C., Lawrence Rosen, John A. Flueck, and David N. Nurco. 1982. "Lifetime Criminality of Heroin Addicts in the United States." *Journal of Drug Issues* 3:225–39.

Baumer, Terry L., and Robert I. Mendelsohn. 1990. *The Electronic Monitoring of Non-violent Convicted Felons: An Experiment in Home Detention.* Final report to the National Institute of Justice. Indianapolis: Indiana University, School of Public and Environmental Affairs.

Baumer, Terry L., and Dennis Rosenbaum. 1982. *Combatting Retail Theft: Programs and Strategies.* Boston: Butterworth.

Baumer, Terry L., Michael G. Maxfield, and Robert I. Mendelsohn. 1993. "A Comparative Analysis of Three Electronically Monitored Home Detention Programs." *Justice Quarterly* 10:121–42.

Berecochea, John E., and Joel B. Gibbs. 1991. "Inmate Classification: A Correctional Program That Works." *Evaluation Review* 15:333–63.

Beveridge, William I. B. 1950. *The Art of Scientific Investigation.* New York: Vintage Books.

Bichler, Gisela, and Ronald V. Clarke. 1996. "Eliminating Pay Phone Toll Fraud at the Port Authority Bus Terminal in Manhattan." In *Preventing Mass Transit Crime,* ed. Ronald V. Clarke, 93–115. Crime Prevention Studies, vol. 6. Monsey, NY: Criminal Justice Press.

Black, Donald. 1970. "The Production of Crime Rates." *American Sociological Review* 35:733–48.

Blalock, Hubert M., Jr. 1972. *Social Statistics,* 2d ed. New York: McGraw-Hill.

Block, Carolyn Rebecca. 1995. "STAC Hot Spot Areas: A Statistical Tool for Law Enforcement Agencies." In *Crime Analysis Through Computer Mapping,* ed. Carolyn Rebecca Block, Margaret Dabdoub, and Suzanne Fregly, 15–32. Washington, DC: Police Executive Research Forum.

Block, Richard L. 1995. "Spatial Analysis in the Evaluation of the CAPS Community Policing Program in Chicago." In *Crime Analysis Through Computer Mapping,* ed. Carolyn Rebecca Block, Margaret Dabdoub, and Suzanne Fregly, 251–58. Washington, DC: Police Executive Research Forum.

Block, Richard L., and Carolyn Rebecca Block. 1980. "Decisions and Data: The Transformation of Robbery Incidents Into Official Robbery Statistics." *Journal of Criminal Law and Criminology* 71:622–36.

———. 1995. "Space, Place, and Crime: Hot Spot Areas and Hot Spot Places of Liquor-related Crime." In *Crime and Place,* ed. John E. Eck and David Weisburd, 145–83. Crime Prevention Studies, vol. 4. Monsey, NY: Criminal Justice Press.

Blumstein, Alfred. 1988. "Prison Populations: A System Out of Control?" In *Crime and Justice: An Annual Review of Research,* ed. Michael Tonry and Norval Morris, 231–66. Chicago: University of Chicago Press.

Blumstein, Alfred, Jacqueline Cohen, and David P. Farrington. 1988. "Criminal Career Research: Its Value for Criminology." *Criminology* 26(1):1–35.

Blumstein, Alfred, Jacqueline Cohen, and Harold D. Miller. 1980. "Demographically Disaggregated Projections of Prison Populations." *Journal of Criminal Justice* 8:1–26.

Blumstein, Alfred, Jacqueline Cohen, and Richard Rosenfeld. 1991. "Trend and Deviation in Crime Rates: A Comparison of UCR and NCS Data for Burglary and Robbery." *Criminology* 29:237–63.

Blumstein, Alfred, Jacqueline Cohen, Jeffrey A. Roth, and Christy A. Visher, eds. 1986. *Criminal Careers and "Career Criminals."* Washington, DC: National Academy Press.

Boland, Barbara. 1996. "What Is Community Prosecution?" *National Institute of Justice Journal* (231) (August):35–40.

Bonta, James, and Laurence L. Motiuk. 1990. "Classification to Halfway Houses: A Quasi-experimental Evaluation." *Criminology* 28:497–506.

Brantingham, Patricia L., and Paul J. Brantingham. 1991. "Notes on the Geometry of Crime." In *Environmental Criminology,* ed. Paul J. Brantingham and Patricia L. Brantingham, 2d ed., 27–54. Prospect Heights, IL: Waveland.

Brantingham, Paul J., and Patricia L. Brantingham, eds. 1991a. *Environmental Criminology,* 2d ed. Prospect Heights, IL: Waveland.

———. 1991b. "Introduction: The Dimensions of Crime." In *Environmental Criminology,* ed. Paul J. Brantingham and Patricia L. Brantingham, 2d ed., 7–26. Prospect Heights, IL: Waveland.

Brantingham, Paul J., and C. Ray Jeffery. 1991. "Afterword: Crime, Space, and Criminological Theory." In *Environmental Criminology,* ed. Paul J. Brantingham and Patricia L. Brantingham, 2d ed., 227–37. Prospect Heights, IL: Waveland.

Bratton, William J. 1995. "Great Expectations: How Higher Expectations for Police Departments Can Lead to a Decrease in Crime." Paper prepared for presentation at the National Institute of Justice Policing Research Institutes Meeting, Measuring What Matters, Washington, DC.

Brownstein, Henry H. 1996. *The Rise and Fall of a Violent Crime Wave: Crack Cocaine and the Social Construction of a Crime Problem.* Guilderland, NY: Harrow and Heston.

Bureau of Justice Assistance. 1993. *A Police Guide to Surveying Citizens and Their Environment.* Washington, DC: U.S. Department of Justice, Office of Justice Programs, Bureau of Justice Assistance.

Bureau of Justice Statistics. 1992a. *Correctional Populations in the United States, 1990.* Washington, DC: U.S. Department of Justice, Office of Justice Programs, Bureau of Justice Statistics.

———. 1992b. *Criminal Victimization in the United States, 1991.* Washington, DC: U.S. Department of Justice, Office of Justice Programs, Bureau of Justice Statistics.

———. 1994. *Criminal Victimization in the United States, 1992.* Washington, DC: U.S. Department of Justice, Office of Justice Programs, Bureau of Justice Statistics.

———. 1996a. *Criminal Victimization 1994.* Washington, DC: U.S. Department of Justice, Office of Justice Programs, Bureau of Justice Statistics.

———. 1996b. *Criminal Victimization in the United States, 1993.* Washington, DC: U.S. Department of Justice, Office of Justice Programs, Bureau of Justice Statistics.

Burgess, Ernest W. 1925. "The Growth of the City." In *The City: Chicago,* ed. Robert E. Park, Ernest W. Burgess, and Roderic D. McKenzie. Chicago: University of Chicago Press.

Campbell, Donald T., and Julian Stanley. 1966. *Experimental and Quasi-experimental Designs for Research.* Chicago: Rand McNally.

Caspi, Avshalom, Terrie E. Moffitt, Phil A. Silva, Magda Stouthamer-Loeber, Robert F. Krueger, and Pamela S. Schmutte. 1994. "Are Some People Crime Prone? Replications of the Personality–Crime Relationship Across Countries, Genders, Races, and Methods." *Criminology* 32:163–95.

Chaiken, Jan M., and Marcia R. Chaiken. 1982. *Varieties of Criminal Behavior.* Santa Monica, CA: Rand.

———. 1987. *Selecting "Career Criminals" for Priority Prosecution.* Washington, DC: U.S. Department of Justice, National Institute of Justice.

———. 1990. "Drugs and Predatory Crime." In *Crime and Justice: A Review of Research: Vol. 13. Drugs and Crime,* ed. Michael Tonry and James Q. Wilson. Chicago: University of Chicago Press.

Chicago Community Policing Evaluation Consortium. 1996. *Community Policing in Chicago, Year Three.* Chicago: Illinois Criminal Justice Information Authority.

Clarke, Ronald V. 1992a. "Deterring Obscene Phone Callers: The New Jersey Experience." In *Situational Crime Prevention: Successful Case Studies,* ed. Ronald V. Clarke, 124–32. New York: Harrow and Heston.

———. 1992b. "Introduction." In *Situational Crime Prevention: Successful Case Studies,* ed. Ronald V. Clarke, 3–36. New York: Harrow and Heston.

———. 1995. "Situational Crime Prevention." In *Crime and Justice: An Annual Review of Research,* ed. Michael Tonry and David Farrington, 91–150. Chicago: University of Chicago Press.

———. 1996. "The Distribution of Deviance and Exceeding the Speed Limit." *British Journal of Criminology* 36:169–81.

Clarke, Ronald V., and Patricia Mayhew. 1980. *Designing Out Crime*. London: Her Majesty's Stationery Office.

Clarke, Ronald, Paul Ekblom, Mike Hough, and Pat Mayhew. 1985. "Elderly Victims of Crime and Exposure to Risk." *The Howard Journal* 24:1–9.

Cohen, Lawrence E., and Marcus Felson. 1979. "Social Change and Crime Rate Trends: A Routine Activity Approach." *American Sociological Review* 44:588–608.

Cook, Thomas D., and Donald T. Campbell. 1979. *Quasi-experimentation: Design and Analysis Issues for Field Settings*. Boston: Houghton Mifflin.

Cornish, D. B., and Ronald V. Clarke, eds. 1986. *The Reasoning Criminal: Rational Choice Perspectives on Offending*. New York: Springer-Verlag.

Cornwell, J. Phillip, Michael J. Doherty, Eric L. Mitter, and Scarlet L. Drayer. 1989. *Roadside Observation Survey of Safety Belt Use in Indiana*. Bloomington, IN: Indiana University, Transportation Research Center.

Daly, Martin, and Margo Wilson. 1988. *Homicide*. Hawthorne, NY: Aldine de Gruyter.

Decker, Scott H. 1996. "Collective and Normative Features of Gang Violence." *Justice Quarterly* 13:243–64.

Decker, Scott H., Susan Pennell, and Ami Caldwell. 1997. *Illegal Firearms: Access and Use by Arrestees*. Research in Brief. Washington, DC: U.S. Department of Justice, Office of Justice Programs, National Institute of Justice.

Decker, Scott H., and Barrik Van Winkle. 1996. *Life in the Gang: Family, Friends, and Violence*. New York: Cambridge University Press.

Dennis, Michael L. 1990. "Assessing the Validity of Randomized Field Experiments: An Example from Drug Abuse Treatment Research." *Evaluation Review* 14:347–73.

Devine, Joel A., and James D. Wright. 1993. *The Greatest of Evils: Urban Poverty and the American Underclass*. Hawthorne, NY: Aldine de Gruyter.

Dillman, Don A. 1978. *Mail and Telephone Surveys: The Total Design Method*. New York: Wiley.

Donnerstein, Edward, Daniel Linz, and Stephen Penrod. 1987. *The Question of Pornography: Research Findings and Policy Implications*. New York: Free Press.

Eck, John E., and Nancy G. LaVigne. 1994. *Using Research: A Primer for Law Enforcement Managers*, 2d ed. Washington, DC: Police Executive Research Forum.

Eck, John E., and William Spelman. 1987. *Problem-solving: Problem-oriented Policing in Newport News*. Washington, DC: Police Executive Research Forum.

Eisenstein, James, and Herbert Jacob. 1977. *Felony Justice: An Organizational Analysis of Criminal Courts*. Boston: Little, Brown.

Elliott, Delbert S., and David Huizinga. 1984. "The Relationship Between Delinquent Behavior and ADM Problems." Unpublished paper prepared for the Alcohol, Drug Abuse, and Mental Health Administration/Office of Juvenile Justice and Delinquency Prevention State-of-the-Art Conference on Juvenile Offenders with Serious Drug, Alcohol, and Mental Health Problems.

Elliott, Delbert S., David Huizinga, and Suzanne S. Ageton. 1985. *Explaining Delinquency and Drug Use*. Thousand Oaks, CA: Sage.

Elliott, Delbert S., David Huizinga, and Scott Menard. 1989. *Multiple Problem Youth: Delinquency, Substance Use, and Mental Health Problems*. New York: Springer-Verlag.

Elliston, Frederick, and Norman Bowie. 1982. *Ethics, Public Policy, and Criminal Justice*. Cambridge, MA: Oelgeschlager, Gunn and Hain.

Erez, Edna. 1985. "Random Assignment, the Least Fair of Them All: Prisoners' Attitudes Toward Various Criteria of Selection." *Criminology* 23:365–79.

Ericson, Richard V., Patricia M. Baranek, and Janet B. L. Chan. 1991. *Representing Order: Crime, Law, and Justice in the News Media*. Toronto: University of Toronto Press.

Esbensen, Finn-Aage, and Delbert S. Elliott. 1994. "Continuity and Discontinuity in Illicit Drug Use: Patterns and Antecedents." *Journal of Drug Issues* 24(1):75–97.

Fabelo, Tony. 1995. "What is Recidivism? How Do You Measure It? What Can It Tell Policy Makers?" Bulletin from the Executive Director, Number 19. Austin, TX: Criminal Justice Policy Council.

———. 1996. "When Politics Accommodate Facts to Make Better Criminal Justice Policies." Bulletin from the Executive Director, Number 21. Austin, TX: Criminal Justice Policy Council.

Farrell, Ronald A., and Victoria Lynn Swigert. 1978. "Prior Offense Record As a Self-fulfilling Prophecy." *Law and Society* 12:437–53.

Farrington, David P., Sean Bowen, Abigail Buckle, Tony Burns-Howell, John Burrows, and Martin Speed. 1993. "An Experiment in the Prevention of Shoplifting." In *Crime Prevention Studies*, Vol. 1, ed. Ronald V. Clarke, 93–119. Monsey, NY: Criminal Justice Press.

Farrington, David P., Rolf Loeber, Magda Stouthamer-Loeber, Welmoet B. Van Kammen, and Laura Schmidt. 1996. "Self-reported Delinquency and a Combined Delinquency Seriousness Scale Based on Boys, Mothers, and Teachers: Concurrent and Predictive Validity for African-Americans and Caucasians." *Criminology* 34:493–517.

Farrington, David P., Lloyd E. Ohlin, and James Q. Wilson. 1986. *Understanding and Controlling Crime:*

Toward a New Research Strategy. New York: Springer-Verlag.

Federal Bureau of Investigation. 1988. *National Incident-based Reporting System: Data Collection Guidelines.* Washington, DC: U.S. Department of Justice, Federal Bureau of Investigation.

———. 1996. *Crime in the United States 1995.* Washington, DC: U.S. Department of Justice, Federal Bureau of Investigation.

Felson, Marcus, Mathieu E. Belanger, Gisela M. Bichler, Chris D. Bruzinski, Glenna S. Campbell, Cheryl L. Fried, Kathleen C. Grofik, Irene S. Mazur, Amy B. O'Regan, Patricia J. Sweeney, Andrew L. Ulman, and LaQuanda M. Williams. 1996. "Redesigning Hell: Preventing Crime and Disorder at the Port Authority Bus Terminal." In *Preventing Mass Transit Crime,* ed. Ronald V. Clarke, 5–92. Crime Prevention Studies, vol. 6. Monsey, NY: Criminal Justice Press.

Finn, Peter, and Andrea K. Newlyn. 1993. *Miami's Drug Court: A Different Approach.* Program Focus. Washington, DC: U.S. Department of Justice, Office of Justice Programs, National Institute of Justice.

Fishman, Mark. 1980. *Manufacturing the News.* Austin, TX: University of Texas Press.

Freeman, Linton. 1968. *Elementary Applied Statistics.* New York: Wiley.

Garofalo, James. 1990. "The National Crime Survey, 1973–1986: Strengths and Limitations of a Very Large Data Set." In *Measuring Crime: Large-scale, Long-range Efforts,* ed. Doris L. MacKenzie, Phyllis J. Baunach, and Roy R. Roberg. Albany, NY: State University of New York Press.

Garofalo, James, Leslie Siegel, and John H. Laub. 1987. "School-related Victimizations Among Adolescents: An Analysis of National Crime Survey Narratives." *Journal of Quantitative Criminology* 3:321–38.

Geerken, Michael R. 1994. "Rap Sheets in Criminological Research: Considerations and Caveats." *Journal of Quantitative Criminology* 10:3–21.

General Accounting Office. 1996. *Content Analysis: A Methodology for Structuring and Analyzing Written Material.* Transfer paper 10.3.1. Washington, DC: U.S. General Accounting Office.

Gerbner, G., and L. Gross. 1980. "The Violent Face of Television and Its Lessons." In *Children and the Faces of Television,* ed. E. Palmer and A. Dorr, 149–62. New York: Academic Press.

Gfroerer, Joseph. 1993. "An Overview of the National Household Survey on Drug Abuse and Related Methodological Research." In *Proceedings of the Survey Research Section of the American Statistical Association, August 1992.* Boston: American Statistical Association.

———. 1996. *Preliminary Estimates from the 1995 National Household Survey on Drug Abuse.* Advance Report Number 18. Rockville, MD: U.S. Department of Health and Human Services, Substance Abuse and Mental Health Services Administration. http://www.health.org/pubs/95hhs/ar18txt.htm Accessed December 18, 1996.

Glaser, Barney G., and Anselm Straus. 1967. *The Discovery of Grounded Theory.* Chicago: University of Chicago Press.

Glueck, Sheldon, and Eleanor T. Glueck. 1950. *Unraveling Juvenile Delinquency.* Cambridge, MA: Harvard University Press.

Gold, Raymond L. 1969. "Roles in Sociological Field Observation." In *Issues in Participant Observation,* ed. George J. McCall and J. L. Simmons. Reading, MA: Addison-Wesley.

Goldkamp, John S., and Michael R. Gottfredson. 1983. *Judicial Decision Guidelines for Bail: The Philadelphia Experiment.* Washington, DC: U.S. Department of Justice, Office of Justice Programs, National Institute of Justice.

Gordon, Margaret T., Janet Reis, and Thomas Tyler. 1979. *Crime in the Newspapers: Some Unintended Consequences.* Evanston, IL: Northwestern University, Center for Urban Affairs and Policy Research.

Gottfredson, Michael R., and Travis Hirschi. 1990. *A General Theory of Crime.* Stanford, CA: Stanford University Press.

Gottfredson, Stephen D., and Don M. Gottfredson. 1994. "Behavioral Prediction and the Problem of Incapacitation." *Criminology* 32:441–74.

Goyder, John. 1985. "Face-to-face Interviews and Mailed Questionnaires: The Net Difference in Response Rate." *Public Opinion Quarterly* 49:234–52.

Grayson, Betty, and Morris I. Stein. 1981. "Attracting Assault: Victims' Nonverbal Cues." *Journal of Communication* 31:68–75.

Greenstein, Steven C., David J. van Alstyne, and Bruce C. Frederick. 1986. *A Model for Forecasting Long-term Trends in the New York State Prison Population.* Albany, NY: New York State Division of Criminal Justice Services, Office of Policy Analysis, Research, and Statistical Services.

Greenwood, Peter. 1975. *The Criminal Investigation Process.* Santa Monica, CA: RAND Corporation.

Gurr, Ted Robert. 1976. *Rogues, Rebels, and Reformers.* Thousand Oaks, CA: Sage.

———. 1989. "Historical Trends in Violent Crime: Europe and the United States." In *Violence in America: The History of Crime,* ed. Ted Robert Gurr. Thousand Oaks, CA: Sage.

Haney, Craig, Curtis Banks, and Philip Zimbardo. 1973. "Interpersonal Dynamics in a Simulated Prison." *International Journal of Criminology and Penology* 1:69–97.

Hanmer, Jalna, and S. Saunders. 1984. *Well-founded Fear: A Community Study of Violence to Women.* London: Hutchinson.

Hansen, Hugh J., Samuel P. Caudill, and Joe Boone. 1985. "Crisis in Drug Testing: Results of a CDC Blind Study." *Journal of the American Medical Association* 253:2382–87.

Harries, Keith D., Stephen J. Stadler, and R. T. Zdorkowski. 1984. "Seasonality and Assault: Explorations in Inter-neighborhood Variation, Dallas 1980." *Annals of the Association of American Geographers* 74:590–604.

Heeren, T., R. A. Smith, S. Morelock, and S. Hingson. 1985. "Surrogate Measures of Alcohol Involvement in Fatal Crashes: Are Conventional Indicators Adequate?" *Journal of Safety Research* 16:127–34.

Hempel, Carl G. 1952. "Fundamentals of Concept Formation in Empirical Science." In *International Encyclopedia of Unified Science: Foundations of the Unity of Science,* 2. Chicago: University of Chicago Press.

Hesseling, Rene B. P. 1994. "Displacement: A Review of the Empirical Literature." In *Crime Prevention Studies,* Vol. 3, ed. Ronald V. Clarke, 197–230. Monsey, NY: Criminal Justice Press.

Heumann, Milton, and Colin Loftin. 1979. "Mandatory Sentencing and the Abolition of Plea Bargaining: The Michigan Felony Firearm Statute." *Law and Society Review* 13:393–430.

Hindelang, Michael J., Michael R. Gottfredson, and James Garofalo. 1978. *Victims of Personal Crime: An Empirical Foundation for a Theory of Personal Victimization.* Cambridge, MA: Ballinger.

Holsti, Ole R. 1969. *Content Analysis for the Social Sciences and Humanities.* Reading, MA: Addison-Wesley.

Homan, Roger. 1991. *The Ethics of Social Research.* New York: Longman.

Homel, Ross, and Jeff Clark. 1994. "The Prediction and Prevention of Violence in Pubs and Clubs." In *Crime Prevention Studies,* Vol 3, ed. Ronald V. Clarke, 1–46. Monsey, NY: Criminal Justice Press.

Homel, Ross, Steve Tomsen, and Jennifer Thommeny. 1992. "Public Drinking and Violence: Not Just an Alcohol Problem." *Journal of Drug Issues* 22:679–97.

Hood-Williams, John, and Tracey Bush. 1995. "Domestic Violence on a London Housing Estate." *Research Bulletin* (37): 11–18.

Hoover, Kenneth R. 1992. *The Elements of Social Scientific Thinking,* 5th ed. New York: St. Martin's Press.

Horney, Julie, and Ineke Haen Marshall. 1988. *Crime Commission Rates Among Incarcerated Felons in Nebraska.* Proposal submitted to the National Institute of Justice. Omaha: University of Nebraska at Omaha.

———. 1991. "Measuring Lambda Through Self-reports." *Criminology* 29:471–95.

———. 1992a. "An Experimental Comparison of Two Self-report Methods for Measuring Lambda." *Journal of Research in Crime and Delinquency* 29(1): 102–21.

———. 1992b. "Risk Perception Among Serious Offenders: The Role of Crime and Punishment." *Criminology* 30:575–94.

Hough, Michael, and Pat Mayhew. 1985. *Taking Account of Crime.* Home Office Research Study, 85. London: Her Majesty's Stationery Office.

Huizinga, David, and Delbert S. Elliott. 1986. "Reassessing the Reliability and Validity of Self-report Delinquency Measures." *Journal of Quantitative Criminology* 2(4):293–327.

Humphreys, Laud. 1975. *The Tearoom Trade.* Enlarged edition with perspectives on ethical issues. Chicago: Aldine.

Hunter, Rosemary S., and Nancy Kilstrom. 1979. "Breaking the Cycle in Abusive Families." *American Journal of Psychiatry* 136:1318–22.

Inciardi, James A. 1986. *The War on Drugs: Heroin, Cocaine, Crime, and Public Policy.* Palo Alto: CA: Mayfield.

———. 1993. "Some Considerations on the Methods, Dangers, and Ethics of Crack-house Research." Appendix A in *Women and Crack Cocaine,* ed. James A. Inciardi, Dorothy Lockwood, and Anne E. Pettieger, 147–57. New York: Macmillan.

Inciardi, James A., Anne E. Pottieger, Mary A. Forney, Dale D. Chitwood, and Duane C. McBride. 1991. "Prostitution, IV Drug Use, and Sex-for-crack Among Serious Delinquents: Risks for HIV Infection." *Criminology* 29:221–36.

Intons-Peterson, Margaret, and Beverly Roskos-Ewoldsen. 1989. "Mitigating the Effects of Violent Pornography." In *For Adult Users Only: The Dilemma of Violent Pornography,* ed. Susan Gubar and Joan Hoff. Bloomington, IN: Indiana University Press.

Jacob, Herbert. 1984. *Using Published Data: Errors and Remedies.* Thousand Oaks, CA: Sage.

Jacobs, Bruce A. 1996. "Crack Dealers' Apprehension Avoidance Techniques: A Case of Restrictive Deterrence." *Justice Quarterly* 13:359–81.

Jeffery, C. Ray. 1977. *Crime Prevention Through Environmental Design,* 2d ed. Newbury Park, CA: Sage.

Johnson, Bruce D., Paul Goldstein, Edward Preble, James Schmeidler, Douglas S. Lipton, Barry Spunt, and Thomas Miller. 1985. *Taking Care of Business: The Economics of Crime by Heroin Abusers.* Lexington, MA: Lexington.

Johnston, Lloyd D., Patrick M. O'Malley, and Jerald G. Bachman. 1996. *National Survey Results on Drug Use from the Monitoring the Future Study, 1975–1995. Volume I: Secondary School Students.* NIH Publication No. 97–4139. Rockville, MD: National Institute on Drug Abuse.

Justice Research and Statistics Association. 1996. *Domestic and Sexual Violence Data Collection.* Report to Congress under the Violence Against Women Act. Washington, DC: U.S. Department of Justice, Office of Justice Programs, National Institute of Justice and Bureau of Justice Assistance.

Kaplan, Abraham. 1964. *The Conduct of Inquiry.* San Francisco, CA: Chandler.

Kelling, George L., and Catherine M. Coles. 1996. *Fixing Broken Windows: Restoring Order and Reducing Crime in Our Communities.* New York: Free Press.

Kelling, George L., Tony Pate, Duane Dieckman, and Charles E. Brown. 1974. *The Kansas City Preventive Patrol Experiment: A Technical Report.* Washington, DC: Police Foundation.

Kish, Leslie. 1965. *Survey Sampling.* New York: Wiley.

Kitsuse, John I., and Aaron V. Cicourel. 1963. "A Note on the Uses of Official Statistics." *Social Problems* 11:131–38.

Krohn, Marvin. 1991. "Control and Deterrence Theories." In *Criminology,* ed. Joseph F. Sheley. Belmont, CA: Wadsworth.

Krueger, Richard A. 1994. *Focus Groups: A Practical Guide for Applied Research,* 2d ed. Thousand Oaks, CA: Sage.

Kuhn, Thomas. 1970. *The Structure of Scientific Revolutions,* 2d ed. Chicago: University of Chicago Press.

LaFree, Gary D. 1985. "Adversarial and Nonadversarial Justice: A Comparison of Guilty Pleas and Trials." *Criminology* 23:289–312.

Lane, Roger. 1989. "On the Social Meaning of Homicide Trends in America." In *Violence in America: The History of Crime,* ed. Ted Robert Gurr. Thousand Oaks, CA: Sage.

Larson, Richard C. 1975. "What Happened to Patrol Operations in Kansas City? A Review of the Kansas City Preventive Patrol Experiment." *Journal of Criminal Justice* 3:267–97.

Latané, Bibb, and John M. Darley. 1970. *The Unresponsive Bystander: Why Doesn't He Help?* Englewood Cliffs, NJ: Prentice-Hall.

Lauritsen, Janet L., John H. Laub, and Robert J. Sampson. 1992. "Conventional and Delinquent Activities: Implications for the Prevention of Violent Victimization Among Adolescents." *Violence and Victims* 7(2):91–108.

Lauritsen, Janet L., Robert J. Sampson, and John H. Laub. 1991. "The Link Between Offending and Victimization Among Adolescents." *Criminology* 29:265–92.

Lazarsfeld, Paul. 1959. "Problems in Methodology." In *Sociology Today,* ed. Robert K. Merton. New York: Basic Books.

Lempert, Richard O. 1984. "From the Editor." *Law and Society Review* 18:505–13.

Lempert, Richard O., and Christie A. Visher. 1988. *Randomized Field Experiments in Criminal Justice Agencies.* Washington, DC: U.S. Department of Justice, Office of Justice Programs, National Institute of Justice.

Lineberry, Robert L. 1977. *American Public Policy.* New York: Harper & Row.

Loeber, Rolf, Magda Stouthamer-Loeber, Welmoet van Kammen, and David P. Farrington. 1991. "Initiation, Escalation and Desistance in Juvenile Offending and Their Correlates." *Journal of Criminal Law and Criminology* 82(1):36–82.

Loftin, Colin. 1986. "The Validity of Robbery-murder Classifications in Baltimore." *Violence and Victims* 1:191–204.

Loftin, Colin, David McDowall, Brian Wiersma, and Talbert J. Cottey. 1991. "Effects of Restrictive Licensing of Handguns on Homicide and Suicide in the District of Columbia." *New England Journal of Medicine* 325:1615–20.

Lopez, Patricia. 1992. "'He Said . . . She Said . . .' An Overview of Date Rape from Commission Through Prosecution Through Verdict." *Criminal Justice Journal* 13:275–302.

Luntz, Barbara, and Cathy Spatz Widom. 1994. "Antisocial Personality Disorder in Abused and Neglected Children Grown Up." *American Journal of Psychiatry* 151:670–74.

Lynch, James P. 1990. "The Current and Future National Crime Survey." In *Measuring Crime: Large-scale, Long-range Efforts,* ed. Doris L. MacKenzie, Phyllis J. Baunach, and Roy R. Roberg, 97–118. Albany, NY: State University of New York Press.

McCaig, Linda, and Janet Greenblatt. 1996. *Preliminary Estimates from the Drug Abuse Warning Network.* Advance Report Number 17. Rockville, MD: U.S. Department of Health and Human Services, Substance Abuse and Mental Health Services Administration, Office of Applied Studies. http://www.health.org/pubs/96dawn/ar17.htm   Accessed December 18, 1996.

McCall, George J. 1978. *Observing the Law: Field Methods in the Study of Crime and the Criminal Justice System.* New York: Free Press.

McCleary, Richard. 1977. *Dangerous Men: The Sociology of Parole.* Thousand Oaks, CA: Sage.

McCleary, Richard, Barbara C. Nienstedt, and James M. Erven. 1982. "Uniform Crime Reports As Organizational Outcomes: Three Time Series Experiments." *Social Problems* 29:361–72.

McDonald, Douglas C., and Christine Smith. 1989. *Evaluating Drug Control and System Improvement Projects.* Washington, DC: U.S. Department of Justice, Office of Justice Programs, National Institute of Justice.

MacKenzie, Doris Layton, Phyllis J. Baunach, and Roy R. Roberg, eds. 1990. *Measuring Crime: Large-scale, Long-range Efforts,* 97–118. Albany, NY: State University of New York Press.

MacKenzie, Doris Layton, James W. Shaw, and Voncile B. Gowdy. 1993. *An Evaluation of Shock Incarceration in Louisiana.* Research in Brief. Washington, DC: U.S. Department of Justice, Office of Justice Programs, National Institute of Justice.

Maltz, Michael, Andrew C. Gordon, David McDowall, and Richard McCleary. 1980. "An Artifact in Pretest–posttest Designs: How It Can Mistakenly Make Delinquency Programs Look Effective." *Evaluation Review* 4:225–40.

Mande, M. J., and Kim English. 1987. *Individual Crime Rates of Colorado Prisoners.* Denver: Colorado Department of Public Safety, Division of Criminal Justice.

Marx, Karl. 1880 (July 5). "Workers' Questionnaire." *Revue socialiste.* Reprinted in *Karl Marx: Selected Writings in Sociology and Social Philosophy,* ed. T. B. Bottomore and Maximilien Rubel. New York: McGraw-Hill, 1956.

Mastrofski, Stephen D., and Roger B. Parks. 1990. "Improving Observational Studies of Police." *Criminology* 23:475–96.

Maxfield, Michael G. 1987a. *Explaining Fear of Crime: Evidence from the 1984 British Crime Survey.* Research and Planning Unit Paper 43. London: Home Office.

———. 1987b. "Incivilities and Fear of Crime in England and Wales and the United States: A Comparative Analysis." Unpublished paper prepared for presentation at the Annual Meeting of the American Society of Criminology.

———. 1987c. "Lifestyle and Routine Activity Theories of Crime: Empirical Studies of Victimization, Delinquency, and Offender Decision-making." Introduction to special issue. *Journal of Quantitative Criminology* 3:275–82.

———. 1989. "Circumstances in Supplementary Homicide Reports: Variety and Validity." *Criminology* 26(4):123–55.

Maxfield, Michael G., and Terry L. Baumer. 1991. "Electronic Monitoring in Marion County, Indiana." *Overcrowded Times* 2:5, 17.

———. 1992. "Home Detention with Electronic Monitoring: A Nonexperimental Salvage Evaluation." *Evaluation Review* 16:315–32.

Maxfield, Michael G., and Cathy Spatz Widom. 1996. "The Cycle of Violence: Revisited Six Years Later." *Archives of Pediatrics and Adolescent Medicine* 150:390–95.

Maxwell, Joseph A. 1996. *Qualitative Research Design: An Interactive Approach.* Thousand Oaks, CA: Sage.

Mayhew, Pat, Natalie Aye Maung, and Catriona Mirrlees-Black. 1993. *The 1992 British Crime Survey.*

Home Office Research Study, 132. London: Her Majesty's Stationery Office.

Mayhew, Patricia, Ronald V. Clarke, and David Elliott. 1989. "Motorcycle Theft, Helmet Legislation, and Displacement." *Howard Journal* 28:1–8.

Mednick, Sarnoff, William Gabrielli, and Barry Hutchings. 1984. "Genetic Influences in Criminal Convictions: Evidence from an Adoption Cohort." *Science* 224:891–94.

MEGG Associates. 1996. *A NIBRS Overview.* Richmond, VA: MEGG Associates, Inc. http://www.crisnet.com/m-nibrs3.html#nib_hist Accessed December 23, 1996.

Mercy, James A., Mark L. Rosenberg, Kenneth E. Powell, Claire V. Broome, and William Roper. 1993. "Public Health Policy for Preventing Violence." *Health Affairs* 12:7–29.

Mieczkowski, Thomas M. 1990a. "The Accuracy of Self-reported Drug Use: An Evaluation and Analysis of New Data." In *Drugs, Crime, and the Criminal Justice System,* ed. Ralph Weisheit, 275–302. Cincinnati, OH: Anderson.

———. 1990b. "Crack Distribution in Detroit." *Contemporary Drug Problems* 17:9–30.

———. 1996. "The Prevalence of Drug Use in the United States." In *Crime and Justice: An Annual Review of Research,* ed. Michael Tonry, 349–414. Chicago: University of Chicago Press.

Miethe, Terance D. 1987. "Charging and Plea Bargaining Practices Under Determinant Sentencing: An Investigation of the Hydraulic Displacement of Discretion." *Journal of Criminal Law and Criminology* 78:155–76.

Mikesell, John, and Maureen Pirog-Good. 1990. "State Lotteries and Crime." *Journal of Economics and Sociology* 49:7–20.

Milgram, Lester. 1965. "Some Conditions of Obedience to Authority." *Human Relations* 18:57–76.

Mirrlees-Black, Catriona. 1995. "Estimating the Extent of Domestic Violence: Findings from the 1992 BCS." *Research Bulletin* (37):1–9.

Mirrlees-Black, Catriona, Pat Mayhew, and Andrew Percy. 1996. *The 1996 British Crime Survey: England and Wales.* Home Office Statistical Bulletin. London: Research and Statistics Directorate, Home Office.

Mitford, Jessica. 1973. *Kind and Usual Punishment: The Prison Business.* New York: Random House.

Monahan, John, Paul S. Appelbaum, Edward P. Mulvey, Pamela Clark Robbins, and Charles W. Lidz. 1993. "Ethical and Legal Duties in Conducting Research on Violence: Lessons from the MacArthur Risk Assessment Study." *Violence and Victims* 8(4):387–96.

Mott, Joy, and Catriona Mirrlees-Black. 1995. *Self-reported Drug Misuse in England and Wales: Findings from the 1992 British Crime Survey.* Research and Planning Unit Paper 89. London: Home Office.

Murphy, Linda L., and Richard W. Dodge. 1981. "The Baltimore Recall Study." In *The National Crime Survey Working Papers: Volume 1. Current and Historical Perspectives,* ed. Wesley G. Skogan and Robert G. Lehnen. Washington, DC: U.S. Department of Justice, Bureau of Justice Statistics.

Murray, Charles A., and L. A. Cox. 1979. *Beyond Probation: Juvenile Corrections and the Chronic Delinquent.* Thousand Oaks, CA: Sage.

Myers, Martha A., and Suzette M. Talarico. 1986. "The Social Contexts of Racial Discrimination in Sentencing." *Social Problems* 33:236–51.

National Criminal Justice Reference Service. 1996. "Home Page." Rockville, MD: National Criminal Justice Reference Service. http://www.ncjrs.org/ncjhome.htm

National Institute of Justice. 1988. *Research Program Plan: Fiscal Year 1988.* Washington, DC: U.S. Department of Justice, Office of Justice Programs, National Institute of Justice.

———. 1994. *Program Plan: 1994–95.* Washington, DC: U.S. Department of Justice, Office of Justice Programs, National Institute of Justice.

———. 1995. *Research Plan: 1995–96.* Washington, DC: U.S. Department of Justice, Office of Justice Programs, National Institute of Justice.

———. 1996a. *1995 Drug Use Forecasting: Annual Report on Adult and Juvenile Arrestees.* Washington, DC: U.S. Department of Justice, Office of Justice Programs, National Institute of Justice.

———. 1996b. *NIJ Awards in Fiscal Year 1995.* Washington, DC: U.S. Department of Justice, Office of Justice Programs, National Institute of Justice.

———. 1996c. *Research Plan: 1996–97.* Washington, DC: U.S. Department of Justice, Office of Justice Programs, National Institute of Justice.

———. 1996d. *Solicitation: COMBAT Program Evaluation.* Washington, DC: U.S. Department of Justice, Office of Justice Programs, National Institute of Justice.

———. 1997. *Building Knowledge About Crime and Justice: The 1997 Research Prospectus of the National Institute of Justice.* Washington, DC: U.S. Department of Justice, Office of Justice Programs, National Institute of Justice.

National Institute on Drug Abuse. 1996. *Monitoring the Future Study, 1975–1996.* Rockville, MD: National Institute on Drug Abuse. http://www.nida.nih.gov/NIDACapsules/ncmtfuture.html   Accessed December 26, 1996.

Newman, Oscar. 1972. *Defensible Space.* New York: Macmillan.

———. 1996. *Creating Defensible Space.* Washington, DC: U.S. Department of Housing and Urban Development, Office of Policy Development and Research.

NOP Market Research Limited. 1985. *1984 British Crime Survey Technical Report.* London: NOP Market Research Limited.

O'Brien, Robert M. 1985. *Crime and Victimization Data.* Newbury Park, CA: Sage.

Office of National Drug Control Policy. 1996. *Pulse Check: National Trends in Drug Abuse Spring 1996.* Washington, DC: Executive Office of the President, Office of Drug Control Policy.

Painter, Kate. 1991. *An Evaluation of Public Lighting As a Crime Prevention Strategy with a Special Focus on Women and Elderly People.* Manchester, England: University of Manchester, Faculty of Economic and Social Studies.

Park, Robert E., and Ernest W. Burgess. 1921. *Introduction to the Science of Sociology.* Chicago: University of Chicago Press.

Pate, Anthony M., Mary Ann Wycoff, Wesley G. Skogan, and Lawrence W. Sherman. 1986. *Reducing Fear of Crime in Houston and Newark: A Summary Report.* Washington, DC: Police Foundation.

Patton, Michael Quinn. 1990. *Qualitative Evaluation Research Methods,* 2d ed. Newbury Park, CA: Sage.

Perkins, Craig, and Darrell K. Gilliard. 1992. *National Corrections Reporting Program, 1988.* Washington, DC: U.S. Department of Justice, Office of Justice Programs, Bureau of Justice Statistics.

Petersilia, Joan. 1989. "Implementing Randomized Experiments: Lessons from BJA's Intensive Supervision Project." *Evaluation Review* 13:435–58.

Petersilia, Joan, and Susan Turner. 1991. "An Evaluation of Intensive Supervision in California." *Journal of Criminal Law and Criminology* 82:610–58.

Peterson, M. A., and H. B. Braiker. 1980. *Doing Crime: A Survey of California Inmates.* Santa Monica, CA: RAND.

Podolefsky, Aaron M. 1983. *Case Studies in Community Crime Prevention.* Springfield, IL: Thomas.

Poklemba, John J. 1988. *Measurement Issues in Prison and Jail Overcrowding.* Albany, NY: New York Division of Criminal Justice Services, Criminal Justice Information Systems Improvement Program.

Posavec, Emil J., and Raymond G. Carey. 1992. *Program Evaluation: Methods and Case Studies,* 4th ed. Englewood Cliffs, NJ: Prentice-Hall.

President's Commission on Law Enforcement and Administration of Justice. 1967. *The Challenge of Crime in a Free Society.* Washington, DC: Government Printing Office.

Quade, E. S. 1989. *Policy Analysis for Public Decisions,* rev. Grace M. Carter, 3d ed. New York: North-Holland.

Ramsay, Malcolm, and Andrew Percy. 1996. *Drug Misuse Declared: Results of the 1994 British Crime Survey.*

Home Office Research Study, 151. London: Her Majesty's Stationery Office.

Rasinski, Kenneth A. 1989. "The Effect of Question Wording on Public Support for Government Spending." *Public Opinion Quarterly* 53:388–94.

Reaves, Brian A. 1993. *Using NIBRS Data to Analyze Violent Crime.* Bureau of Justice Statistics Technical Report. Washington, DC: U.S. Department of Justice, Office of Justice Programs, Bureau of Justice Statistics.

Reiss, Albert J., Jr. 1971. *The Police and the Public.* New Haven, CT: Yale University Press.

Reuter, Peter, Robert MacCoun, and Patrick Murphy. 1990. *Money from Crime: A Study of the Economics of Drug Dealing in Washington, D.C.* Santa Monica, CA: RAND.

Reynolds, Paul D. 1979. *Ethical Dilemmas and Social Research.* San Francisco: Jossey-Bass.

Riecken, Henry W., and Robert F. Boruch. 1974. *Social Experimentation: A Method for Planning and Evaluating Social Intervention.* New York: Academic Press.

Robins, Lee N. 1978. "Sturdy Childhood Predictors of Adult Antisocial Behavior: Replications from Longitudinal Studies." *Psychological Medicine* 8:611–22.

Roethlisberger, Fritz J., and William J. Dickson. 1939. *Management and the Worker.* Cambridge, MA: Harvard University Press.

Rosenbaum, Dennis P., Susan F. Bennett, Betsy D. Lindsay, Deanna L. Wilkinson, Brenda Davis, Chet Taranowski, and Paul Lavrakas. 1992. *The Community Responses to Drug Abuse National Demonstration Program: Executive Summary.* Chicago: Center for Research in Law and Justice.

Rosenfeld, Richard, and Scott H. Decker. 1993. "Discrepant Values, Correlated Measures: Cross-sectional and Longitudinal Comparisons of Self-reports and Urine Tests of Cocaine Use Among Arrestees." *Journal of Criminal Justice* 21:223–31.

Rossi, Peter H., and Howard E. Freeman. 1993. *Evaluation: A Systematic Approach,* 5th ed. Newbury Park, CA: Sage.

Sampson, Robert J. 1989. *The Victimization of Juveniles and Young Adults: A Longitudinal and Repeated Cross-section Study.* Proposal submitted to the National Institute of Justice. Urbana, IL: University of Illinois, Department of Sociology.

Sampson, Robert J., and John H. Laub. 1993. *Crime in the Making: Pathways and Turning Points Through Life.* Cambridge, MA: Harvard University Press.

Schmalleger, Frank. 1991. *Criminal Justice Ethics: Annotated Bibliography and Guide to Sources.* New York: Greenwood Press.

Schneider, Anne L. 1990. *Deterrence and Juvenile Crime.* New York: Springer-Verlag.

SEARCH Group. 1995. *NIBRS State Profiles.* Denver: SEARCH Group, Inc. http://www.nibrs.search.org/status.html   Accessed November 13, 1996.

Seidman, David, and Michael Couzens. 1974. "Getting the Crime Rate Down: Political Pressure and Crime Reporting." *Law and Society Review* 8:457–93.

Shaw, Clifford R., and Henry D. McKay. 1969. *Juvenile Delinquency and Urban Areas.* Chicago: University of Chicago Press.

Shearing, Clifford D., and Phillip C. Stenning. 1992. "From the Panopticon to Disney World: The Development of Discipline." In *Situational Crime Prevention: Successful Case Studies,* ed. Ronald V. Clarke, 249–55. New York: Harrow and Heston.

Sherman, Lawrence W. 1992a. "The Influence of Criminology on Criminal Law: Evaluating Arrests for Misdemeanor Domestic Violence." *Journal of Criminal Law and Criminology* 83:1–45.

———. 1992b. *Policing Domestic Violence: Experiments and Dilemmas.* New York: Free Press.

Sherman, Lawrence W., and Richard A. Berk. 1984. *The Minneapolis Domestic Violence Experiment.* Washington, DC: Police Foundation.

Sherman, Lawrence W., and Ellen G. Cohn. 1989. "The Impact of Research on Legal Policy: The Minneapolis Domestic Violence Experiment." *Law and Society Review* 23:117–44.

Sherman, Lawrence W., Patrick R. Gartin, and Michael E. Buerger. 1989. "Hot Spots of Predatory Crime: Routine Activity and the Criminology of Place." *Criminology* 27:27–55.

Sherman, Lawrence W., Jannell D. Schmidt, Dennis P. Rogan, Douglas A. Smith, Patrick R. Gartin, Ellen G. Cohn, Dean J. Colins, and Anthony R. Bacich. 1992. "The Variable Effects of Arrest on Criminal Careers: The Milwaukee Domestic Violence Experiment." *Journal of Criminal Law and Criminology* 83:137–69.

Silberman, Charles. 1978. *Criminal Violence, Criminal Justice.* New York: Random House.

Singleton, Royce A., Jr., Bruce C. Straits, and Margaret Miller Straits. 1993. *Approaches to Social Research,* 2d ed. New York: Oxford University Press.

Skogan, Wesley G. 1974. "The Validity of Official Crime Statistics: An Empirical Investigation." *Social Science Quarterly* 55:25–38.

———. 1985. *Evaluating Neighborhood Crime Prevention Programs.* The Hague, Netherlands: Ministry of Justice, Research and Documentation Centre.

———. 1988. "Community Organizations and Crime." In *Crime and Justice: An Annual Review of Research,* ed. Michael Tonry and Norval Morris, 39–78. Chicago: University of Chicago Press.

———. 1990a. *Disorder and Decline: Crime and the Spiral of Decay in American Neighborhoods.* New York: Free Press.

———. 1990b. *The Police and the Public in England and Wales.* Home Office Research Study, 117. London: Her Majesty's Stationery Office.

Skogan, Wesley G., and Michael G. Maxfield. 1981. *Coping with Crime: Individual and Neighborhood Reactions.* Thousand Oaks, CA: Sage.

Speirs, Verne L. 1988. "Targeting Serious Juvenile Offenders for Prosecution Can Make a Difference." *NIJ Reports,* 211. Washington, DC: U.S. Department of Justice, Office of Justice Programs, National Institute of Justice.

Spergel, Irving A. 1990. "Youth Gangs: Continuity and Change." In *Crime and Justice: An Annual Review of Research,* ed. Norval Morris and Michael Tonry, 171–275. Chicago: University of Chicago Press.

Spohn, Cassia. 1990. "The Sentencing Decisions of Black and White Judges: Expected and Unexpected Similarities." *Law and Society Review* 24:1197–216.

Spohn, Cassia, and Julie Horney. 1991. "The Law's the Law, but Fair Is Fair: Rape Shield Laws and Officials' Assessment of Sexual History Evidence." *Criminology* 29:137–61.

Stewart, D. W., and P. N. Shamdasani. 1990. *Focus Groups: Theory and Practice.* Thousand Oaks, CA: Sage.

Surette, Ray. 1992. *Media, Crime, and Justice: Images and Realities.* Pacific Grove, CA: Brooks/Cole.

Takeuchi, David. 1974. *Grass in Hawaii: A Structural Constraints Approach.* Unpublished Master's Thesis, Department of Sociology, University of Hawaii.

Taylor, Ralph B., Sally A. Shumaker, and Stephen D. Gottfredson. 1985. "Neighborhood-level Links Between Physical Features and Local Sentiments." *Journal of Architectural Planning and Research* 2:261–75.

Turner, Anthony G. 1972. *San Jose Methods Test of Known Crime Victims.* Washington, DC: Law Enforcement Assistance Administration.

Turner, Charles F., Judith T. Lessler, and Joseph C. Gfroerer, eds. 1992. *Survey Measurement of Drug Use: Methodological Studies.* Rockville, MD: U.S. Department of Health and Human Services, Public Health Service, Alcohol, Drug Abuse, and Mental Health Administration.

Turner, Jonathan. 1974. *The Structure of Sociology Theory.* Homewood, IL: Dorsey.

United States Bureau of the Census. 1992. *Statistical Abstract of the United States.* Washington, DC: Government Printing Office.

————. 1994. *Technical Background on the Redesigned National Crime Victimization Survey.* Washington, DC: U.S. Department of Justice, Office of Justice Programs, Bureau of Justice Statistics.

United States Department of Justice. 1986. *Attorney General's Commission on Pornography: Final Report.* Washington, DC: U.S. Department of Justice.

————. 1991. *Crime in the United States 1990.* Washington, DC: U.S. Department of Justice, Federal Bureau of Investigation.

————. 1995. *The Nation's Two Crime Measures.* Washington, DC: U.S. Department of Justice.

Van Kirk, Marvin. 1977. *Response Time Analysis.* Washington, DC: U.S. Department of Justice, National Institute of Law Enforcement and Administration of Justice.

Vera Institute. 1981. *Felony Arrests,* rev. ed. New York: Longman.

Voas, R., J. Rhodenizer, and C. Lynn. 1985. *Evaluation of Charlottesville Checkpoint Operation.* Washington, DC: National Highway Traffic Safety Administration.

Walker, Samuel. 1994. *Sense and Nonsense About Crime and Drugs: A Policy Guide,* 3d ed. Belmont, CA: Wadsworth.

Walker, Wallace Earl. 1985. "The Conduct of Program Evaluation Reviews in the General Accounting Office." *Evaluation and Program Planning* 8:271–80.

Wallace, Walter. 1971. *The Logic of Science in Sociology.* Chicago: Aldine-Atherton.

Ward, V. M., J. T. Bertrand, and L. E. Brown. 1991. "The Comparability of Survey and Focus Group Results." *Evaluation Review* 15:266–83.

Warner, Barbara D., and Glenn L. Pierce. 1993. "Re-examining Social Disorganization Theory Using Calls to Police As a Measure of Crime." *Criminology* 31:493–517.

Weis, Joseph G. 1986. "Issues in the Measurement of Criminal Careers." Chapter 1 in *Criminal Careers and "Career Criminals,"* Vol. 2, ed. Alfred Blumstein, Jacqueline Cohen, Jeffrey A. Roth, and Christy A. Visher, 1–51. Washington, DC: National Academy Press.

Weisburd, David, Anthony Petrosino, and Gail Mason. 1993. "Design Sensitivity in Criminal Justice Experiments." In *Crime and Justice: An Annual Review of Research,* ed. Michael Tonry, 337–79. Chicago: University of Chicago Press.

Weiss, Carol H. 1995. "Nothing As Practical As Good Theory: Exploring Theory-based Evaluation for Comprehensive Community Initiatives for Children and Families." In *New Approaches to Evaluating Community Initiatives: Concepts, Methods, and Contexts,* ed. James P. Connell, Anne C. Kubisch, Lisbeth B. Schorr, and Carol H. Weiss, 65–92. Washington, DC: Aspen Institute.

West, Donald J., and David P. Farrington. 1977. *The Delinquent Way of Life.* London: Heinemann.

Widom, Cathy Spatz. 1989a. "Child Abuse, Neglect, and Adult Behavior: Research Design and Findings on Criminality, Violence, and Child Abuse." *American Journal of Orthopsychiatry* 59:355–67.

————. 1989b. "The Cycle of Violence." *Science* 244 (14 April):160–66.

————. 1989c. "Does Violence Beget Violence? A Critical Examination of the Literature." *Psychological Bulletin* 106:3–28.

———. 1992. *The Cycle of Violence*. Research in Brief. Washington, DC: U.S. Department of Justice, Office of Justice Programs, National Institute of Justice.

Williams, Kent M. 1991. "Using Battered Woman Syndrome Evidence with a Self-defense Strategy in Minnesota." *Law and Inequality* 10:107–36.

Williams, Terry. 1989. *The Cocaine Kids*. Reading, MA: Addison-Wesley.

Wilson, James Q., and Richard J. Herrnstein. 1985. *Crime and Human Nature*. New York: Simon & Schuster.

Wilson, James Q., and George Kelling. 1982. "Broken Windows." *Atlantic Monthly* (March):29–38.

Wilson, O. W., and Roy Clinton McLaren. 1963. *Police Administration*, 3d ed. New York: McGraw-Hill.

Wilson, William Julius. 1987. *The Truly Disadvantaged*. Chicago: University of Chicago Press.

Wolfgang, Marvin E., Robert M. Figlio, and Thorsten Sellin. 1972. *Delinquency in a Birth Cohort*. Chicago: University of Chicago Press.

Wolfgang, Marvin E., Robert M. Figlio, Paul E. Tracy, and Simon I. Singer. 1985. *The National Survey of Crime Severity*. Washington, DC: U.S. Department of Justice, Office of Justice Programs, Bureau of Justice Statistics.

Wright, Richard, and Trevor Bennett. 1990. "Exploring the Offender's Perspective: Observing and Interviewing Criminals." In *Measurement Issues in Criminology*, ed. Kimberly L. Kempf, 138–51. New York: Springer-Verlag.

Wright, Richard T., and Scott H. Decker. 1994. *Burglars on the Job: Streetlife and Residential Break-ins*. Boston: Northeastern University Press.

Wycoff, Mary Ann, Wesley G. Skogan, Anthony M. Pate, and Lawrence W. Sherman. 1985a. *Citizen Contact Patrol: Technical Report*. Washington, DC: Police Foundation.

———. 1985b. *Police Community Stations: Technical Report*. Washington, DC: Police Foundation.

Glossary

aggregate   A grouping of individuals or other units. The word *aggregate* is used in two related ways in social science research. First, units of analysis may be aggregates, or combinations, of individuals. For example, a study of delinquency might examine individual people under age 18 or some aggregate such as a high school class. Second, social scientists usually try to explain or predict aggregates, not individuals. Thus, a delinquency researcher would want to describe the behavior of people under age 18 in general, rather than the behavior of some specific 16-year-old. See Chapters 1 and 4.

attributes   Characteristics of persons or things. See *Variables* and Chapter 1.

average   An ambiguous term that generally suggests typical or normal. The *mean, median,* and *mode* are specific mathematical averages. See Chapter 14.

binomial variable   A *variable* that has only two *attributes* is binomial. Gender is an example; it has the attributes male and female.

bivariate analysis   The analysis of two *variables* simultaneously for the purpose of determining the empirical relationship between them. The construction of a simple percentage table and the computation of a simple correlation coefficient are examples of bivariate analyses. See Chapter 14 for more on this topic.

cluster sample   A multistage sample in which natural groups (clusters) are sampled initially, with the members of each selected group being subsampled afterward. For example, you might select a sample of municipal police departments from a directory, get lists of the police officers at all the selected departments, then draw samples of officers from each. This procedure is discussed in Chapter 9.

cohort study   A study in which some specific group is studied over time, although data may be collected from different members in each set of observations. See Chapter 4 for more on this topic.

conceptual definition   Defining concepts by using other concepts. Recall from Chapter 5 that concepts are abstract, the words and symbols that are used to represent mental images of things and ideas. This means that a conceptual definition uses words and symbols to define concepts. In practice, conceptual definitions represent explicit statements of what a researcher means by a concept. A conceptual definition of "prior record" might be: "recorded evidence of one or more convictions for a criminal offense." See *Operational definition* and Chapter 5.

conceptualization   The mental process whereby fuzzy and imprecise notions (concepts) are made more specific and precise. So you want to study fear of crime? What do you mean by fear of crime? Are there different kinds of fear? What are they? See Chapter 5.

confidence interval   The range of values within which a population parameter is estimated to lie. A survey, for instance, may show that 40 percent of a sample favor a ban on handguns. Although the best estimate of the support that exists among all people is also 40 percent, we do not expect it to be exactly that. We might, therefore, compute a confidence interval (for example, from 35 to 45 percent) within which the actual percentage of the population probably lies. Note that it is necessary to specify a *confidence level* in connection with every confidence interval. See Chapters 9 and 14.

confidence level   The estimated probability that a population parameter lies within a given *confidence interval.* Thus, we might be 95 percent confident that between 35 and 45 percent of all residents of California favor an absolute ban on handguns. See Chapters 9 and 14.

construct validity   (1) The degree to which a measure relates to other *variables* as expected within a system of theoretical relationships (Chapter 5). (2) How well an observed cause-and-effect relationship represents the underlying causal process a researcher is interested in (Chapters 3 and 7). Also see *Validity threats.*

content validity   The degree to which a measure covers the range of meanings included within the concept, See Chapter 5.

contingency table   A format for presenting the relationship among *variables*—in the form of percentage distributions. See Chapter 14 for illustrations of it and for guides to doing it.

control group   In experimentation, a group of subjects to whom no experimental stimulus is administered and who should resemble the *experimental group* in all other respects. The comparison of the control group and the experimental group at the end of the experiment indicates the effect of the experimental stimulus. See Chapter 7.

criterion-related validity The degree to which a measure relates to some external criterion. For example, the validity of self-report surveys of drug use can be shown by comparing survey responses to laboratory tests for drug use. See Chapter 5.

cross-sectional study A study based on observations that represent a single point in time. Contrast with a *longitudinal study.* See Chapter 4.

deduction The logical model in which specific expectations of hypotheses are developed on the basis of general principles. Starting from the general principle that all deans are meanies, you might anticipate that this one won't let you change courses. That anticipation would be the result of deduction. See also *Induction* and Chapters 2 and 3.

dependent variable The variable assumed to depend on or be caused by another variable (called the *independent variable*). If you find that sentence length is partly a function of the number of prior arrests, then sentence length is being treated as a dependent variable.

descriptive statistics Statistical computations that describe either the characteristics of a sample or the relationship among variables in a sample. Descriptive statistics summarize a set of sample observations, whereas *inferential statistics* move beyond the description of specific observations to make inferences about the larger population from which the sample observations were drawn. See Chapter 14.

dimension A specifiable aspect or facet of a concept.

dispersion The distribution of values around some central value, such as an average. The *range* is a simple measure of dispersion. Thus, we may report that the mean age of a group is 37.9 and the range is from 12 to 89. See Chapter 14.

ecological fallacy Erroneously drawing conclusions about individuals based solely on the observation of groups. See Chapter 4.

empirical From experience. Social science is said to be empirical when knowledge is based on what we experience.

environmental survey Structured observations undertaken in the field and recorded on specially designed forms. Note that interview surveys record a respondent's answers to questions, while environmental surveys record what an observer sees in the field. For example, a community organization may conduct periodic environmental surveys to monitor neighborhood parks—whether or not facilities are in good condition, the amount of litter present, and what kinds of people use the park. See Chapter 11.

equal probability of selection method (EPSEM) A sample design in which each member of a population has the same chance of being selected into the sample. See Chapter 9.

experimental group In experimentation, a group of subjects who are exposed to an experimental stimulus. Subjects in the experimental group are normally compared to subjects in a *control group* to test the effects of the experimental stimulus. See Chapter 7.

external validity Whether a relationship observed in a specific population, at a specific time, in a specific place would also be observed in other populations, at other times, in other places. External validity is concerned with generalizability from a relationship observed in one setting to the same relationship in other settings. *Replication* enhances external validity. See Chapters 3 and 7.

face validity The quality of an indicator that makes it seem a reasonable measure of some *variable*. That sentence length prescribed by law is some indication of crime seriousness seems to make sense without a lot of explanation; it has face validity. See Chapter 5.

focus group Small groups (of 12 to 15) engaged in a guided discussion of some topic. Participants selected are from a homogeneous population. Although focus groups cannot be used to make statistical estimates about a population, members are nevertheless selected to represent a target population. Focus groups are most useful in two situations: (1) where precise generalization to a larger population is not necessary, and (2) where focus-group participants and the larger population they are intended to represent are relatively homogeneous. See Chapters 9 and 10.

frequency distribution A description of the number of times the various *attributes* of a *variable* are observed in a sample. The report that 53 percent of a sample were men and 47 percent were women is a simple example of a frequency distribution. Another example is the report that 15 of the cities studied had populations less than 10,000, 23 had populations between 10,000 and 25,000, and so forth.

generalizability That quality of a research finding that justifies the inference that it represents something more than the specific observations on which it was based. Sometimes this involves the generalization of findings from a sample to a population. Other times it is a matter of concepts: If you are able to discover why people commit burglaries, can you generalize that discovery to other crimes as well?

hypothesis An expectation about the nature of things derived from a theory. It is a statement of something that ought to be observed in the real world if the theory is correct. See *Deduction* and also Chapters 2 and 7.

hypothesis testing The determination of whether the expectations that a hypothesis represents are indeed found in the real world. See Chapters 2 and 7.

impact assessment A type of applied research that seeks to answer the question: Did a public program have the intended effect on the problem it was meant to address? If, for example, a new burglary prevention program has the goal of reducing burglary in a particular neighborhood, an impact assessment would try to determine whether burglary was in fact reduced as a result of the new program. Compare to *process evaluation.* See also Chapter 13.

independent variable An independent variable is presumed to cause or determine a *dependent variable*. If we discover that police cynicism is partly a function of years of experience, then experience is the independent variable and cynicism is the dependent variable. Note that any given variable might be treated as independent in one part of an analysis and dependent in another part of the analysis. Cynicism might become an independent variable in the explanation of job satisfaction.

induction   The logical model in which general principles are developed from specific observations. Having noted that teenagers and crime victims are less supportive of police than older people and nonvictims are, you might conclude that people with more direct police contact are less supportive of police and explain why. That would be an example of induction. See also *Deduction* and Chapter 2.

inferential statistics   The body of statistical computations relevant to making inferences from findings based on sample observations to some larger population. See also *Descriptive statistics* and Chapter 14.

interchangeability of indexes (indicators)   A term coined by Paul Lazarsfeld, referring to the logical proposition that if some general variable is related to another variable, then all indicators of the variable should have that relationship. For example, if women are more fearful of crime than men, the women should appear more fearful on every measure of fear. See Chapter 3 for a fuller description of this topic and a graphic illustration.

internal validity   Whether observed associations between two (or more) variables are in fact causal associations or are due to the effects of some other variable. The internal validity of causal statements may be threatened by an inability to control experimental conditions. See also *Validity threats*. Consult Chapters 3 and 7 for details.

intersubjective agreement   That quality of science (and other inquiries) whereby two different researchers studying the same problem arrive at the same conclusion. Ultimately, this is the practical criterion for what is called *objectivity*. We agree that something is "objectively true" if independent observers with different subjective orientations conclude that it is "true." See Chapter 2.

interval measure   A level of measurement that describes a variable whose attributes are rank-ordered and have equal distances between adjacent *attributes*. The Fahrenheit temperature scale is an example of this because the distance between 17 and 18 is the same as that between 89 and 90. See also *Nominal measure, Ordinal measure,* and *Ratio measure.*

latent content   As used in connection with content analysis, this term describes the underlying meaning of communications as distinguished from their *manifest content*. See Chapter 12.

level of significance   In the context of *tests of statistical significance*, the degree of likelihood that an observed, *empirical* relationship could be attributable to sampling error. A relationship is significant at the .05 level if the likelihood of its being only a function of sampling error is no greater than 5 out of 100. See Chapter 14.

longitudinal study   A study design that involves the collection of data at different points in time, as contrasted with a *cross-sectional study*. See also Chapter 4 and *Trend study, Cohort study,* and *Panel study.*

manifest content   In connection with content analysis, the concrete terms contained in a communication, as distinguished from *latent content*. See Chapter 12.

mean   An *average*, computed by summing the values of several observations and dividing by the number of observations. If you now have a grade-point average of 4.0 based on ten courses, and you get an F in this course, then your new grade-point (mean) average will be 3.6.

median   Another *average*, representing the value of the "middle" case in a rank-ordered set of observations. If the ages of five people are 16, 17, 20, 54, and 88, then the median is 20. (The mean is 39.)

mode   Still another *average*, representing the most frequently observed value or *attribute*. If a sample contains 1,000 residents of California, 275 from New Jersey, and 33 from Minnesota, then California is the modal category for residence. See Chapter 14 for more about averages.

multivariate analysis   The analysis of the simultaneous relationships among several *variables*. Examining simultaneously the effects of age, gender, and city of residence on robbery victimization is an example of multivariate analysis. See Chapter 14.

nominal measure   A level of measurement that describes a *variable* whose different *attributes* are only different, as distinguished from *ordinal, interval,* and *ratio measures*. Gender is an example of a nominal measure.

nonprobability sample   A sample selected in some fashion other than those suggested by probability theory. Examples are *purposive, quota,* and *snowball samples*. See Chapter 9.

nonsampling error   Imperfections of data quality that are a result of factors other than sampling error. Examples are misunderstandings of questions by respondents, erroneous recordings by interviewers and coders, and data-entry errors. See Chapter 14.

null hypothesis   In connection with hypothesis testing and *tests of statistical significance*, the hypothesis that suggests there is no relationship between the *variables* under study. You may conclude that the two variables are related after having statistically rejected the null hypothesis.

objectivity   Doesn't exist. See Intersubjective agreement.

operational definition   Specifying what operations should be performed to measure a concept. The operational definition of "prior record" might be: "Consult the county (or state or FBI) criminal history records information system. Count the number of times a person has been convicted of committing a crime." See Chapter 5.

operationalization   One step beyond *conceptualization*. Operationalization is the process of developing opera

operationalization (*continued*)
tional definitions by describing how actual measurements will be made. See Chapters 4 and 5.

ordinal measure A level of measurement that describes a *variable* whose *attributes* may be rank-ordered along some dimension. An example is socioeconomic status as composed of the attributes high, medium, and low. See also *Nominal measure, Interval measure,* and *Ratio measure.*

panel study A type of *longitudinal study,* in which data are collected from the same subjects (the panel) at several points in time. See Chapter 4.

probability sample The general term for a sample selected in accord with probability theory, typically involving some random-selection mechanism. Specific types of probability samples include area probability sample, *equal probability of selection method (EPSEM), simple random sample,* and *systematic sample.* See Chapter 9.

process evaluation A type of applied research that seeks to answer the question: Was a public program implemented as intended? For example, a burglary prevention program might seek to reduce burglaries by having crime prevention officers meet with all residents of some target neighborhood. A process evaluation would determine whether meetings with neighborhood residents were taking place as planned. Compare to *impact assessment.* See Chapter 13 for more detail.

purposive sample A type of *nonprobability sample* in which you select the units to be observed on the basis of your own judgment about which ones will be best suited to your research purpose. For example, if you were interested in studying community crime prevention groups affiliated with public schools and groups affiliated with religious organizations, you would probably want to select a purposive sample of school- and church-affiliated groups. Most television networks use purposive samples of voting precincts to project winning candidates on election night; precincts that always vote for winners are sampled. See Chapter 9 for more details.

questionnaire A document that contains questions and other types of items designed to solicit information appropriate to analysis. Questionnaires are used primarily in survey research, also in field research. See Chapter 10.

quota sample A type of *nonprobability sample* in which units are selected into the sample on the basis of pre-specified characteristics, so that the total sample will have the same distribution of characteristics as are assumed to exist in the population being studied. See Chapter 9.

randomization A technique for randomly assigning experimental subjects to *experimental groups* and *control groups.* See Chapter 7.

range A measure of *dispersion,* the distance that separates the highest and lowest values of a variable in some set of observations. In your class, for example, the range of ages might be from 17 to 37.

ratio measure A level of measurement that describes a variable whose *attributes* have all the qualities of *nominal, ordinal,* and *interval measures* and in addition are based on a "true zero" point. Length of prison sentence is an example of a ratio measure.

reductionism A fault of some researchers: a strict limitation (reduction) of the kinds of concepts to be considered relevant to the phenomenon under study.

regression analysis A method of data analysis in which the relationships among variables are represented in the form of an equation, called a regression equation. See Chapter 14 for a discussion of the different forms of regression analysis.

reification The process of regarding as real things that are not real. This is usually a problem in measurement. See Chapter 5.

reliability That quality-of-measurement standard where the same data would have been collected each time in repeated observations of the same phenomenon. We would expect that the question "Did you see a police officer in your neighborhood today?" would have higher reliability than the question "About how many times in the past six months have you seen a police officer in your neighborhood?" This is not to be confused with *validity.* See Chapter 5.

replication Generally, the duplication of an experiment or other study to confirm its results or to expose or reduce error. The successful replication of a study adds to its external validity. Check Chapter 1; also see *External validity* and *Intersubjective agreement.*

representativeness That quality of a sample of having the same distribution of characteristics as the population from which it was selected. Representativeness is enhanced by *probability sampling* and provides for *generalizability* and the use of *inferential statistics.* See Chapter 9.

sampling frame That list or quasi-list of units composing a population from which a sample is selected. If the sample is to be representative of the population, it is essential that the sampling frame include all (or nearly all) members of the population. See Chapter 9.

secondary analysis A form of research in which the data collected and processed by one researcher are re-analyzed—often for a different purpose—by another. This is especially appropriate in the case of survey data. Data archives are repositories or libraries for the storage and distribution of data for secondary analysis. See Chapter 12.

simple random sample A type of probability sample in which the units composing a population are assigned numbers, a set of random numbers is then generated, and the units that have those numbers are included in the sample. Although probability theory and the calculations it provides assume this basic sampling method, it is seldom used for practical reasons. An alternative is the *systematic sample* (with a random start). See Chapter 9.

snowball sampling A method for drawing a *nonprobability sample.* Snowball samples are often used in field research. Each person interviewed is asked to suggest additional people for interviewing. See Chapters 9 and 11.

stakeholders   Individuals with some interest, or stake, in a specific program. Any particular program may have multiple stakeholders with different interests and goals. See Chapter 13.

standard deviation   A measure of *dispersion* about the *mean.* Conceptually, the standard deviation represents an "average" deviation of all values relative to the mean. See Chapter 14.

statistical conclusion validity   Whether we can find covariation among two variables. This is the first of three requirements for causal inference (see Chapter 3 for the other two). If two variables do not vary together (covariation), there cannot be a causal relationship between them. See Chapters 3 and 7 for more on statistical conclusion validity. Chapter 14 describes the role of sample size in finding *statistical significance,* which is conceptually related to statistical conclusion validity.

statistical significance   A general term for the unlikeliness that relationships observed in a sample could be attributed to sampling error alone. See *Test of statistical significance* and Chapter 14.

stratification   The grouping of the units composing a population into homogeneous groups (or strata) before sampling. This procedure, which may be used in conjunction with *simple random, systematic,* or *cluster sampling,* improves the representativeness of a sample, at least in terms of the stratification variables. See Chapter 9.

systematic sample   A type of *probability sample* in which every kth unit in a list is selected for inclusion in the sample—for example, every 25th student in the college directory of students. We compute k (also called the *sampling interval*) by dividing the size of the population by the desired sample size. Within certain constraints, systematic sampling is a functional equivalent of *simple random sampling* and is usually easier to do. Typically, the first unit is selected at random. See Chapter 9.

test of statistical significance   A class of statistical computations that indicate the likelihood that the relationship observed between variables in a sample can be attributed to sampling error only. See *Inferential statistics* and Chapter 14.

trend study   A type of *longitudinal study* in which a given characteristic of some population is monitored over time. An example is the series of annual uniform crime report totals for some jurisdiction. See Chapter 4.

units of analysis   The what or whom being studied. Units of analysis may be individual people, groupings of people (a juvenile gang), formal organizations (a probation department), or social artifacts (crime reports). See Chapter 4.

univariate analysis   The analysis of a single variable for purposes of description. *Frequency distributions, averages,* and measures of *dispersion* are examples of univariate analysis, as distinguished from *bivariate* and *multivariate analyses.* See Chapter 14.

validity   (1) Whether statements about cause and effect are true (valid) or false (invalid). See Chapters 3 and 7; also see *Validity threats.* (2) A descriptive term used for a measure that accurately reflects what it is intended to measure. For example, police records of auto theft are more valid measures than police records of shoplifting. It is important to realize that the ultimate validity of a measure can never be proven. Yet we must agree to its relative validity on the basis of *face validity, criterion-related validity, content validity,* and *construct validity.* This must not be confused with *reliability.* See Chapter 5.

validity threats   Possible sources of invalidity, or making false statements about cause and effect. Four categories of validity threats are linked to fundamental requirements for demonstrating cause: *statistical conclusion validity, internal validity, construct validity,* and *external validity* (see separate entries in this glossary). In general, statistical conclusion validity and internal validity are concerned with bias; construct validity and external validity are concerned with generalization. See Chapters 3 and 7.

variables   Logical groupings of *attributes.* The variable gender is made up of the attributes male and female. See Chapter 1.

Indexes

■ NAME INDEX

Ageton, Suzanne S., 49, 314
American Psychological Association, 184
Austin, James, 327

Babbie, Earl, 21, 176, A3
Bachman, Jerald G., 135, 397
Bachman, Ronet, 130, 235
Baldus, David C., 97
Ball, John, 233
Banks, Curtis, 189–191
Baranek, Patricia M., 76
Baumer, Terry L., 7, 141, 142, 201–202, 227, 264, 275, 279, 280–282, 288, 293, 300, 305, 316, 328, 329, 335–337, 340, 341, 346
Baunach, Phyllis J., 305
Bennett, Trevor, 266
Berk, Richard A., 9
Bertrand, J. T., 256
Beveridge, W. I. B., 30
Bichler, Gisela, 293
Bichler-Robertson, Gisela, 279
Black, Donald, 123, 305
Blalock, Hubert M., Jr., 410
Block, Carolyn Rebecca, 123, 141, 306
Block, Richard L., 123, 141, 306, 346
Blumstein, Alfred, 39, 76, 133, 293, 295–296, 342, 344–345, 401
Boland, Barbara, 35
Bonney, Charles, 52
Bonta, James, 162, 163–164
Boone, Joe, 108
Boruch, Robert F., 330
Bowie, Norman, 177
Boys, Don, 55
Braiker, H. B., 402
Brantingham, Patricia L., 40, 264
Brantingham, Paul J., 29, 40, 264
Bratton, William J., 346
Brown, Charles E., 4
Brown, L. E., 256
Brownstein, Henry H., 124, 125
Buerger, Michael E., 298, 299, 304
Bureau of Justice Assistance (BJA), 141, 276
Bureau of Justice Statistics (BJS), 123, 129, 130, 132, 304
Burgess, Ernest, 27, 28, 38
Bush, Tracey, 139, 286, 287

Caldwell, Ami, 302
Campbell, Donald T., 51, 54, 55–56, 57, 59, 153, 156, 160, 162, 166, 167, 170, 171, 326
Carey, Raymond G., 347
Caspi, Avshalom, 19
Caudill, Samuel P., 108
Chaiken, Jan M., 57, 59–61, 233, 238, 402
Chaiken, Marcia R., 57, 59–61, 233, 238, 402
Chan, Janet B. L., 76
Chicago Community Policing Evaluation Consortium, 234
Cicourel, Aaron V., 305
Clarke, Ronald V., 43, 162, 164–165,

262, 275, 293, 338, 340, 349, 366–367, 395, 396
Cohen, Jacqueline, 39, 133, 293, 296, 342, 344, 401
Cohen, Lawrence E., 298, 395
Cohn, Ellen G., 8–9, 307
Coles, Catherine M., 275, 306, 346
Cook, Thomas D., 51, 54, 55–56, 57, 59, 153, 156, 160, 162, 166, 167, 170, 171, 326
Cornish, D. B., 43
Cornwell, J. Phillip, 282
Cottey, Talbert J., 337
Couzens, Michael, 305
Cox, L. A., 154
Cuvelier, Steve, 327

Daly, Martin, 39
Darley, John M., 177
Darwin, Charles, 39
Decker, Scott H., 71, 76, 138, 139, 183, 186, 187–188, 228, 270–272, 287–288, 302, 391, A22
Dennis, Michael, 183, 331, 337
Devine, Joel A., 83, 398
Dickson, W. J., 150
Dieckman, Duane, 4
Dillman, Don, 246, 250
Dodge, Richard W., 178
Doherty, Michael J., 282
Donnerstein, Edward, 293
Drayer, Scarlet L., 282

Eck, John E., 141, 324
Eisenstein, James, 30–32, 41, 303
Ekblom, Paul, 366
Elliott, David, 338
Elliott, Delbert S., 49, 60, 137, 233, 314–315
Elliston, Frederick, 177
English, Kim, 402
Erez, Edna, 184
Ericson, Richard V., 76
Erven, James M., 167, 300, 307, 338
Esbensen, Finn, 233

Fabelo, Tony, 99, 100–101, 348–349
Farrell, Ronald A., 99
Farrington, David P., 108, 109, 136, 148, 152, 159, 340–341, 401
Felson, Marcus, 227–228, 274, 298, 395
Figlio, Robert M., 105
Finn, Peter, 327
Fishman, Mark, 293
Frederick, Bruce C., 342, 344
Freeman, Howard E., 323, 326–328, 334, 337, 341, 346, 347
Freeman, Linton C., 370, 372

Gabrielli, William, 39
Gall, John, A16
Gallup, George, 232
Garofalo, James, 304, 365, 395
Gartin, Patrick R., 298, 299, 304
Geerken, Michael R., 109, 306
Gerbner, G., 293
Gfroerer, Joseph, 134, 135, 136

Gilliard, Darrell, 304
Glaser, Barney G., 32, 262
Glueck, Eleanor T., 39, 293
Glueck, Sheldon, 39, 293
Gold, Raymond, 264
Goldkamp, John S., 292
Gordon, Andrew C., 154
Gordon, Margaret T., 312–313
Gottfredson, Don M., 41
Gottfredson, Michael R., 39, 95, 119, 292, 365, 395
Gottfredson, Stephen D., 41, 276
Gowdy, Voncile B., 327, 329
Goyder, John, 252
Grayson, Betty, 313–314
Greenblatt, Janet, 138, 139
Greenstein, Steven C., 342, 344–345
Greenwood, Peter, 4
Gross, L., 293
Gurr, Ted Robert, 40, 296, 304

Haney, Craig, 189–191
Hanmer, Jalna, 254
Hansen, Hugh G., 108
Harries, Keith D., 274
Hart, Barbara, 33
Heeren, T., 110
Hempel, Carl G., 97
Herrnstein, Richard J., 119
Hesseling, Rene, 183
Heumann, Milton, 315
Hindelang, Michael J., 365, 395
Hingson, S., 110
Hirschi, Travis, 39, 95, 119
Holmes, Sherlock, 51
Holsti, Ole, 314
Homan, Roger, 188
Homel, Ross, 142, 262, 284, 285
Hood-Williams, John, 139, 286
Hoover, Kenneth, 37, 38
Horney, Julie, 226, 227, 233, 238, 400–410
Hough, Michael, 234, 366
Huizinga, David, 49, 60, 137, 314
Humphreys, Laud, 181, 188–189, 263, 265
Hunter, Rosemary, 81
Hutchings, Barry, 39

Inciardi, James A., 7, 181, 182, 228
Indiana Department of Correction, 204
Intons-Peterson, Margaret, 293

Jacob, Herbert, 30–32, 41, 295, 299, 303, 304, 305
Jacobs, Bruce A., 177, 192, 228, 271
Jeffery, Ray, 29, 264
Johnson, Bruce D., 70, 177, 182, 238, 270
Johnston, Lloyd D., 135, 397
Justice Research and Statistics Association, 123

Kaplan, Abraham, 36, 95, 147
Kelling, George L., 4, 35, 113, 200, 275, 306, 346
Kilstrom, Nancy, 81

Kish, Leslie, 208
Kitsuse, John L., 305
Krohn, Marvin, 26
Krueger, Richard A., 198, 256
Kuhn, Thomas, 38

LaFree, Gary D., 226
Lane, Roger, 304
Larson, Richard C., 3, 58
Latane, Bibb, 177
Laub, John, 81, 293, 314–315, 398–399
Lauritsen, Janet L., 314–315, 398–400
LaVigne, Nancy, 141
Lazarsfeld, Paul, 62–63, 109
Lempert, Richard O., 9, 184, 337, 347
Likert, Rensis, 236
Lineberry, Robert, 322
Linz, Daniel, 293
Loeber, Rolf, 113
Loftin, Colin, 170–172, 308, 315, 337, 338
Lombroso, Cesare, 39
Lopez, Patricia, 97
Luntz, Barbara, 180, 248
Lynch, James P., 235
Lynn, C., 151

MacCoun, Robert, 40, 75, 177
MacDonald, Douglas C., 347
MacDonald, John, 340
MacKenzie, Doris Layton, 305, 327, 329
Maltz, Michael, 154
Mande, M. J., 402
Marshall, Ineke Haen, 227, 233, 238, 400–410
Marx, Karl, 232
Mastrofski, Steve, 276
Maxfield, Michael G., 7, 76, 102, 109, 110, 114, 125, 204, 226, 234, 247, 275, 278, 293, 298, 300, 305, 307, 314, 316, 328, 329, 335–337, 340, 346, 350
Maxwell, Joseph, 50, 287
Mayhew, Patricia, 43, 234, 254, 338–339, 366
McCaig, Linda, 138, 139
McCall, George J., 228, 263, 265–266, 270, 276, 281
McCleary, Richard, 154, 167, 300, 305, 307, 338
McDonald, Douglas C., 322, 326, 337
McDowall, David, 154, 337
McKay, Henry D., 27–29, 38, 42, 369–370
McLaren, Roy Clinton, 4
Mednick, Sarnoff, 39
MEGG Associates, 128
Mendelsohn, Robert I., 7, 201–202, 275, 279, 293, 300, 305, 335–336, 340, 341
Metro Action Committee on Public Violence Against Women and Children (METRAC), 280
Mieczkowski, Thomas M., 134, 135, 136, 138, 139, 177

Miethe, Terance D., 165–166, 337
Mikesell, John, 77
Milgram, Lester, 191
Miller, Harold D., 293, 342, 344
Mirrlees-Black, Catriona, 239, 254, 286
Mitford, Jessica, 186
Mitter, Eric L., 282
Monahan, John, 177
Morelock, S., 110
Motiuk, Laurence L., 162, 163–164
Mott, Joy, 239
Murphy, Linda L., 178
Murphy, Patrick, 40, 75, 177
Murray, Charles A., 154
Myers, Martha A., 293

National Criminal Justice Reference Service (NCJRS), 3
National Institute of Justice (NIJ), 137, 138, 301, 321, 394
National Institute on Drug Abuse, 135
Newlyn, Andrea K., 327
Newman, Oscar, 42–43, 264
Nienstedt, Barbara C., 167, 300, 307, 338
NOP Market Research, 256

O'Brien, Robert M., 178, 233
Office of National Drug Control Policy (ONDCP), 139, 140
Ohlin, Lloyd E., 148
O'Malley, Patrick M., 135, 397

Painter, Kate, 227, 264, 273
Park, Robert, 27, 28, 38
Parks, Roger, 276
Pate, Anthony M., 4, 58–59, 79, 155, 338
Patton, Michael Quinn, 21, 255, 266, 274
Pennell, Susan, 302
Penrod, Stephen, 293
Percy, Andrew, 239, 254

Perkins, Craig, 304
Petersilia, Joan, 156, 157, 158, 184, 301, 302, 333, 334, 341, 347
Peterson, M. A., 402
Pierce, Glenn L., 369–370, 375
Pirog-Good, Maureen, 77
Podolefsky, Aaron M., 76
Poklemba, John J., 303, 307–308
Posavec, Emil J., 347
Pulaski, Charles, 97

Quigley, Peter, 327

Ramsay, Malcolm, 239
RAND Corporation, 156, 158, 159, 238, 292, 333, 402, 404
Rasinski, Kenneth, 237
Reaves, Brian A., 133
Reis, Janet, 312–313
Reiss, Albert J., Jr., 76, 123
Reuter, Peter, 40, 75, 177
Reynolds, Paul D., 184, 188, 191
Rhodenizer, J., 151
Riecken, Henry W., 330
Robert, Roy R., 305
Robins, Lee N., 81, 82
Roethlisberger, F. J., 150
Rosenbaum, Dennis P., 141, 142, 172, 227, 264, 280–282, 288
Rosenfeld, Richard, 133, 138, 296
Roskos-Ewoldsen, Beverly, 293
Rossi, Peter H., 323, 326–328, 334, 337, 341, 346, 347
Roth, Jeffrey A., 39

Saltzman, Linda E., 130
Sampson, Robert J., 81, 293, 314–315, 395, 396–399
Saunders, S., 254
Schmalleger, Frank, 177
Schneider, Anne, 158
SEARCH Group, 128
Seidman, David, 305
Selvin, Hanan, 210
Shamdasani, P. N., 256

Shaw, Clifford R., 27–29, 38, 42, 369–370
Shaw, James W., 327, 329
Shearing, Clifford D., 263
Sherman, Lawrence W., 8–9, 58–59, 79, 155, 293, 298, 299, 304, 307, 332, 333, 338, 347
Shumaker, Sally A., 276
Silberman, Charles, 96
Simpson, O. J., A6
Singer, Simon I., 105
Singleton, Royce A., Jr., 101
Skogan, Wesley G., 35, 58–59, 79, 76, 110, 113–114, 133, 155, 200, 226, 234, 278, 293, 314, 315, 327–328, 338
Smith, Christine, 322, 326, 337, 347
Smith, R. A., 110
Speirs, Verne L., 327
Spelman, William, 324
Spohn, Cassia, 226, 314–315
Stadler, Stephen J., 274
Stanley, Julian, 153, 156
Stein, Morris, 313–314
Stenning, Phillip C., 263
Stewart, D. W., 256
Straits, Bruce C., 101
Straits, Margaret Miller, 101
Straus, Anselm, 32, 262
Strunk, William, Jr., A13
Surette, Ray, 314
Swigert, Victoria Lynn, 99

Takeuchi, David, 32
Talarico, Suzette M., 293
Taylor, Bruce M., 235
Taylor, Ralph B., 276, 278
Thommeny, Jennifer, 262
Tomsen, Steve, 262
Tracy, Paul E., 105
Turner, Anthony G., 178
Turner, Charles, 239
Turner, Jonathan, 37
Turner, Susan, 301
Tyler, Thomas, 312–313

U.S. Bureau of the Census, 249
U.S. Department of Justice, 122, 123, 124, 293

van Alstyne, David J., 342, 344
Van Kirk, Marvin, 4
Van Winkle, Barrik, 183, 186, 187–188, 228
Vera Institute, 76
Visher, Christie A., 39, 184, 337, 347
Voas, R., 151

Walker, Samuel, 10
Walker, Wallace Earl, 349–350
Wallace, Walter, 34
Ward, V. M., 256
Warner, Barbara D., 369–370, 375
Weis, Joseph, 137
Weisburd, David, 160
Weiss, Carol H., 330
West, Donald J., 108, 109, 136
White, E. B., A13
Widom, Cathy Spatz, 81, 109, 162–163, 180, 248, 297–298, 299, A22
Wiersma, Brian, 337
Williams, Kent M., 97
Williams, Terry, 19, 139, 177
Wilson, James Q., 35, 113, 119, 148, 200
Wilson, Margo, 39
Wilson, O. W., 4
Wilson, William Julius, 29, 75, 369
Wolfgang, Marvin E., 79, 105, 316
Woodworth, George, 97
Wright, James D., 83, 398
Wright, Richard T., 71, 76, 139, 228, 266, 270–272, 287–288, A22
Wycoff, Mary Ann, 58–59, 79, 155, 338

Zdorkowski, R. T., 274
Zhang, Ray, 21
Zimbardo, Philip, 189–191

■ SUBJECT INDEX

Advance Report Number 17, 139
African Americans, drug use and, 77
Agency accountability, measuring crime and, 122
Agency records, 292
  decision making and, 300
  nonpublic, 296–300
  published statistics, 294–296
  reliability and validity and, 304–308
  sampling and, 303
  topics appropriate for, 292–294
  types of, 294–302
  units of analysis and, 302–303
Agency staff, new data collected by, 300–302
Aggregate matching, 163
Aggregates, 13–14
Agreement reality, 3–4
  science and, 5
AIDS, 54–55
Alcohol abuse, 147, 149–150
Alcohol use, 148–149, 153–155, 157–158
  victimization and, 399–400
American Bar Association, 102
  Code of Professional Responsibility, 184
American Correctional Association, 217
American Prosecutors' Research Institute, 292
American Psychological Association, 184
Analysis, 398. *See also* Units of analysis
  bivariate, 362–365
  content. *See* Content analysis

criminal justice research and, 181
  multivariate, 365–370
  policy. *See* Policy analysis
  regression. *See* Regression analysis
  research design and, 88
  research proposal and, 90
  secondary, 314–316
  univariate, 354–362
Anonymity. criminal justice research and, 179–180
Appearance. interviewing and, 247–248
Application, 71–72
  research design and, 88
Applied research, 41
  political context of, 346–350
Approximation, 56
Arrest
  agency records and, 297–298
  domestic violence and, 8–9
Assault, 142, 178, 274
  body language and, 313–314
Association, measurement and, 61–64, 370–376
Attitudes, survey research and, 233–234
Attributes, 15
  exhaustive, 103
  mutually exclusive, 103–104
Authority, human inquiry and, 7–8
Averages, 355–357
Avoidance behavior, 382–384
Axioms, 37

Battered woman defense, 97, 199
Beer World, 198
Bias
  asking questions and, 237
  racial, 10
  sampling, 206–207
  selection, experimental validity and, 154–155
Bibliographic databases, A4–A5
Bigotry, 14
Binomial sampling distribution, 212–217
Binomial variable, 209
Biology, theories of law breaking and, 39
Bivariate analysis, 362–365
Body language, assault and, 313–314
British Crime Survey (BCS), 220, 224–225, 234, 235, 237–238, 239, 254, 286, 366
British Home Office, 234, 254
British Home Office Research Unit, 43
Budget, research proposal and, 90–91
Bureau of Justice Statistics (BJS), 105, 125, 224, 256, 292, 293, 294, 304, 314, A11–A12, A21
Bystander intervention, 177

Caller identification, telephone surveys and, 250
Calls for service (CFS), 298–299
Card catalog, A3
  on-line, A3–A4
Card sort, 252–253

Case studies, 255–256
Causal inference, 397
  experiments and, 152–160
  validity and, 55–61
Causality
  correlation and, 52–53
  criteria for, 50–55
Causal model, probabilistic, 49
Causal reasoning, 5, 18–19
Causal statement, micromediational, 54
Causal time order, experimental validity and, 155
Causation, 17
  in natural sciences, 47
Cause, 47
  necessary and sufficient, 51–54
Census of Children in Custody, 294
Census of State Adult Correctional Facilities, 256
Central tendency, 355–357
  dispersion compared, 359–360
Chicago Police Department, 306
"Chicago School" of criminology, 27
Child abuse, 81, 86, 133, 248
  agency records and, 297–298
  later arrest and, 162–163
Chi square, 382–384
  distribution of, A28–A29
Civil strife, 40
Classical experiment, 148–152
  variations in design, 160–162
Closed-ended questions, 235–236
Cluster sampling, 220
  multistage, 220–221
    with stratification, 221–223
Cocaine, 19, 60, 139, 198
Code of Federal Regulations, 184
Coding, 109
  content analysis and, 311–312
Cohort designs, 165–166
Cohort studies, 79
College Board, 110
COMBAT, 90
Commission on Law Enforcement and Administration of Justice, 4, 128
Community policing, 86
Community prosecution, grounded theory and, 34–35
Compensatory rivalry, experimental validity and, 156
Compensatory treatment, experimental validity and, 155–156
Complete observer, 266
Complete participant, 264
Composite measures, 112–115
Composites, 305
Computer-assisted personal interviewing (CAPI), 239
Computer-assisted telephone interviewing (CATI), 250–251
Computer-based information sources A2–A8
Concept(s), 94–99
  defined, 95
  operationalization of, 61
  theory construction and, 37
Conception(s), 94–99
Conceptual definition, 97–99
Conceptual entrapment, 98
Conceptualization, 67, 95–96, 396
  content analysis and, 311–312
  research design and, 86
Confidence intervals, 209, 216, 376
Confidence levels, 209, 216, 376
Confidentiality, criminal justice research and, 180
Conflict theory, 40
Constructs, 95
Construct validity, 57–58, 110–111
  threats to, experiments and, 158–159
Content, manifest, 312
Content analysis, 87, 292, 308–314
  coding in, 311–312
  illustrations of, 312–314

units of analysis and sampling in, 309–311
Content validity, 110
Contingency questions, 240–241
Contingency tables, 364–365
  bivariate, 370
  multivariate, 369
Continuous variables, 360
Control, interviewing and, 248–249
Control groups, 149–151
Convenience sampling, 227–228
Convergent validity, 110, 136
Conversational interview, informal, 266
Coordination, interviewing and, 248–249
Correctional Populations in the United States, 294–296
Correlation, causality and, 52–53
Court Caseload Statistics, 296
Cover letters, 245
"Crack houses", 181
Creaming, 155, 325
Crime
  conceptions of, 94
  conceptual definition of, 119
  counting, 233
  drug use and, 56, 59–61
  ecological theories of, 42–43
  ideology and politics and, 10
  known to police, 122–128
  lifestyle and, 365–369
  measures of, 143
    issues in, 119–122
    surveys and, 128–133
  mobility and, 29
  newspaper stories about, 312–313
  observing, 141–142
  policy responses to, 41
  social disorganization theory of, 26–28
  social disruption theory of, 26–27
  space-based patterns of, 141
  summary-based measure of, 125
  "victimless", 129
Crime Act, 321, 411
Crime commission rates, 400–410
Crime "hot spots", agency records and, 298–299
Crime prevention, 86
  situational, 43, 339–340
  street lighting and, 264
Crime prevention policy, ecological theories of, 42–43
Crime Prevention Studies, 340
Crime records, incident-based, 141
Crime seriousness, 96–97
  conceptualization of, 99–101
  levels of measurement and, 016
Crime surveys, 140–141
  general-purpose, 235
Criminal justice
  composite measures and, 112
  theory in, 38–43
Criminal Justice Abstracts, A4
Criminal Justice Ethics, 177
Criminal Justice Policy Council (CJPC), 100, 348–349
Criminal justice research
  analysis and reporting and, 181
  anonymity and, 179–180
  confidentiality and, 180
  deceiving subjects and, 180–181
  ethical issues in, 176–184
  ethics and, 22
  legal liability and, 181–182
  no harm to participants in, 177–178
  probability sampling and, 197
  public policy and, 41–42
  special problems in, 182–184
  time and, 69
  voluntary participation in, 178–179
Criminal justice sources, on Internet, A7–A8
Criminal Victimization in the United States, 224, 294
Criminology
  "Chicago School" of, 27

social ecology and, 40
Criterion-related validity, 110
Cross section, 136
Cross-sectional studies, 78

Dade County Police Department, 301
Data
  empirical, collection of, 61
  grouped, 354–355
  qualitative, 20–21
  quantitative, 20–21
  secondary
    advantages and disadvantages of, 316
    sources of, 315–316, A20–A27
  social production of, 305
  sources of, 197–200
Databases, bibliographic, A4–A5
Data collection
  issues in, 200–204
  measurement validity and reliability and, 201–203
  obtrusive and unobtrusive measures and, 203–204
  research proposal and, 90
  through mail, 244–245
Data processing, research design and, 87–88
Death penalty, 97
Deception, criminal justice research and, 180–181
Deduction, illustration of, 30–32
Deductive logic, 29–30
Deductive method, inductive method compared, 33–34, 36
Deductive model, 61–62
Deductive reasoning, 19–20
Defensible Space (Newman), 42
Definitions
  conceptual, 97–99
  operational, 99
  real, 97
Degrees of freedom, 383
Delinquency, 27–28, 37, 38, 48, 60, 61–62, 79, 108, 113, 129, 136, 183, 208, 399–400
  agency records and, 297–298
  ethnicity and, 28
  victimization and, 314–315
Demeanor, interviewing and, 247–248
Demoralization, experimental validity and, 156
Dependent variable, 18, 148, 329
Description, 70–71, 102
Descriptive statistics, 354–376
Desired outcomes, 329
Desistance, 39
Determinism, social science and, 47–49
Deterrence, 41, 86
DIALOG, A9
Dichotomous variable, 148
Diffusion of treatments, experimental validity and, 155
Dimensions, 96–97
Direct observables, 95
Direct observation, 198–199
Discrete variables, 360
Discriminant validity, 110
Disney World, 263
Disorder, index of, 113–115
Dispersion, 357–358
  central tendency compared, 359–360
Dispositional hypothesis, 189
Disproportionate stratified sampling, 220
Distributions, 354–355
  joint, 377
  skewed, 359
Domestic violence, 14, 33, 139, 286, 293, 332–333
  arrest and, 8–9
  underreporting of, 254
Double-blind experiment, 151
Drinking, violence and, 142, 283–285
Drug abuse, 70, 337
  national household survey on, 134–135

Drug Abuse Warning Network (DAWN), 138–139
Drug addiction, 208, 330–331
Drug episodes, 138–139
Drug surveillance systems, 137–140
Drug use, 263, 314
  African Americans and, 77
  crime and, 56, 59–61
  self-reported, 239
Drug Use Forecasting (DUF), 137–138, 301–302
Drunk driving, 72–73, 80, 83, 110, 166–167, 170, 197

Ecological fallacy, 76–77
Ecological theory, 42–43
Economic reductionism, 77
Economics, deterrence and, 41
Educational Resources Information Center (ERIC), A4
Effect, 47
Efficiency, cluster sampling and, 221
Electronic monitoring (ELMO), 275
  home detention and, 6–7, 201–202, 335–337
Element, 208
The Elements of Style, A13
Empirical data, collection of, 61
Empirical research, 4–5
Empirical support, 5
Environmental design, crime and, 264
Environmental surveys, 276–277
Epistemology, 5
EPSEM samples, 207
Equal probability of selection method, 207
Errors
  human inquiry and, 8–11
  of reasoning, 54–55
Escalation, 39
Ethical controversies, 188–191
Ethical principles, promoting compliance with, 184–188
Ethics
  criminal justice research and, 22, 176–184
  juvenile gang members and, 187–188
Ethnicity, delinquency and, 28
Ethnography, 139–140
Evaluability assessment, evaluation research and, 326–327
Evaluation, 71–72
  linking process to, 323–324
  nonexperimental, 340–341
  stakeholders and, 346–348
Evaluation apprehension, 326
Evaluation research, 11, 321
  evaluability assessment and, 326–327
  measurement and, 328–332
  problem formulation and, 327–328
  topics appropriate for, 321–325
Exceptions, social regularities and, 13
Exit polls, 226
Experiential reality, 3–4
  science and, 5
Experiment(s), 147
  causal inference and, 152–160
  classical, 148–152
    variations in design, 160–162
  double-blind, 151
  generalizability and, 158
  randomization and, 152
  selecting subjects for, 151–152
  topics appropriate to, 147
Experimental design, 149
  cohort designs, 165–166
  with nonequivalent dependent variables, 171
  nonequivalent-groups, 162–165, 338
  quasi-experimental, 162–172, 337–340
  time-series designs, 166–170, 338–339
Experimental groups, 149–151
Experimental mortality, 79
  experimental validity and, 155
Explained variation, 375
Explanation, 71, 102

idiographic, 18–19
  models of, 49–50
  nomothetic, 18–19
Exploration, 69–70
Ex post evaluations, 337
External validity, 58–59
  threats to, experiments and, 159–160

Face validity, 110
Fact, theory construction and, 35–36
Fallacy
  ecological, 76–77
  gambler's, 10
  individualistic, 77
Federal Bureau of Investigation (FBI), 70, 108, 120, 123–125, 199–200, 292, 294, 307–308
Federal Bureau of Prisons, 292, 294
Field journal, 275
Field notes, 275–276
Field observations, linking with other data, 278–279
Field research, 32, 87, 262–263
  asking questions in, 266–267
  illustrations of, 280–285
  observer and, 264–266
  preparation for, 267–278
  sampling in, 273–274
  strengths and weaknesses in, 285–288
  topics appropriate to, 263–264
Final sampling unit, 208
Flexibility, field research and, 285
Focus groups, 198, 256–257
Follow-up mailings, 246
Formal organizations, access to, 267–270
Frequency distributions, 354–355

Gallup Poll, 294
Gambler's fallacy, 10
Gamma, 372–373
Gender, marijuana use and, 32–33
General Accounting Office (GAO), 314, 349–350
General interview guide, 255
Generalizability
  experiments and, 158
  field research and, 287–288
Generalized understanding, 73
General Social Survey (GSS), 233, 237, 363
Generic controls, 341
Government documents, A5
Graffiti, 203
Grant proposals, 392–394
Grounded theory, 32, 33, 262
  community prosecution and, 34–35
Group(s)
  control, 149–151
  experimental, 149–151
  focus, 198, 256–257
  as units of analysis, 73–74
Grouped data, 354–355
Gun control, 170–172, 212–214, 256, 302, 315, 337, 338, 377–382
Gun ownership, 362–363

Hawthorne effect, 150
Heroin, 60, 70, 139, 177, 182, 228, 233, 238, 270
Hierarchy rule, 124
History, experimental validity and, 153, 167
Home detention, 70
  electronic monitoring and, 6–7, 201–202, 335–337
  micro model of, 328
Homicide, 129, 170–172, 296, 307
  sexual selection theory and, 39
  workplace and, 366–367
Homosexual behavior, studying, 188–189, 263, 265
Homosexuality, AIDS and, 55
Human inquiry, personal, 5–8
  errors and, 8–11

Hybrid source, 300
Hypotheses
  empirical testing of, 61–62
  theoretical, derivation of, 61
  theory construction and, 37

Ideology, criminal justice and, 10
Idiographic explanation, 18–19, 49–50
If-then statements, 323
Illinois Criminal Justice Information Authority, 141
Illogical reasoning, 10
IMPACT, 329–330
Impact assessment, 324–325
Incident, as unit of analysis, 120, 125
Incident-based crime records, 141
Incident-based police records, 125
Incident-based reporting system, national, 125–128
  information in records, 126
  Uniform Crime Reports compared, 127
"Incivilities", 200, 314
Independent variable, 18, 148
Indexes, interchangeability of, 62–64
Index of disorder, 113–115
Indiana Code (IC), 100, 119
Indicators, 96–97
Indirect observables, 95
Individualistic fallacy, 77
Individual matching, 163
Individuals, as units of analysis, 73
Induction, illustration of, 32–33
Inductive logic, 30
Inductive method, deductive method compared, 33–34, 36
Inductive reasoning, 19–20
Inductive theory, justice policy and, 33
Inference
  causal, 397
    experiments and, 152–160
    validity and, 55–61
  univariate, 376–377
Inferential statistics, 376–385
Informal conversational interview, 266
Informants, 270
Information sources, computer-based A2–A8
Informed consent, 185, 186
Inmate self-report survey, 401–408
Inquiry, personal human, 5–8
  errors and, 8–11
Institutional review boards (IRBs), 184–187, 405
  requirements of, researcher rights and, 187–188
Instrumentation, experimental validity and, 154, 167
Intensive Motivational Program of Alternative Correctional Treatment (IMPACT), 329–330
Intensive supervision probation (ISP), 156–158
Internal validity, 57
  threats to, experiments and, 153–158
International Association of Chiefs of Police (IACP), 245
Internet, 296, 316, A2, A6–A8
Interpretation, 23
Interrater reliability, 109
Interrupted time series, 166
Inter-university Consortium for Political and Social Research (ICPSR), 314, 315, 396, A20–A21
Interval measures, 104–105
Interval variables, 373
Interview(s)
  conversational, informal, 266
  open-ended, standardized, 255
Interviewing
  personal, computer-assisted, 239
  rules for, 247–248
  specialized, 255–256
  telephone, computer-assisted, 250–251
Interview surveys

completion rates and, 252
in-person, 247–249

Jail stay, 102–103
Joint distribution, 377
Judgmental sampling, 225–226
Justice. *See* Criminal justice
Justice Information Center, A9–A10
Juvenile delinquency. *See* Delinquency
Juvenile gangs, 73–74, 274
ethics and, 187–188
Juvenile victimization, offending and, 394–400

Kansas City Preventive Patrol Experiment, 3, 4, 57, 156
Kauffman Foundation, 141
Knowledge, prediction and, 5–6

Labels, 40
Lambda, 371–372
Law, theory construction and, 36–37
Law breaking, theories of, 39–41
Legal liability, criminal justice research and, 181–182
Letters, access to formal organizations and, 268
Level of significance, 382
Level of Supervision Inventory (LSI), 163–164
Libraries, using, A2–A8
Lifestyle, street crime and, 365–369
Likert scale, 236
Literature review, research proposal and, 90
Logic
deductive, 29–30
inductive, 30
Logical support, 5
Longitudinal studies, 78–80, 397
approximating, 80
LSD, 80

Mail, self-administered questionnaires and, 244–245
Mailings
follow-up, 246
warning, 245
Mail surveys, 244–246
acceptable response rates and, 246
Manifest content, 312
Mann-Whitney *U* test, 410
Manslaughter, 129
Marginals, 354
Marijuana, 7, 32–33, 52–53, 80, 236, 241, 245, 363–364
victimization and, 399–400
Market research, 256
Matrix questions, 241–243
Maturation, experimental validity and, 153
Mean, 355
Measure(s)
of association, 370–376
composite, 112–115
interval, 104–105
nominal, 104
obtrusive and unobtrusive
data collection and, 203–204
ordinal, 104
ratio, 105
self-report, validity and reliability of, 136–137, 239
Measurement, 23, 396
association and, 61–64
of crime, issues in, 119–122
criteria for quality of, 106–112
national incident-based reporting system and, 127–128
Uniform Crime Reports and, 124–125
data collection and, 201–203
evaluation research and, 328–332
levels of, 104–105
crime seriousness and, 106
implications of, 105–106

operationalization and, 101–106
reliability of, 107–109
research proposal and, 90
validity of, 109–112
Measuring Crime, 305
Media, Crime, and Justice: Images and Realities, 314
Median, 355–357
Meetings, access to formal organizations and, 269–270
Methadone, 270
Methodology, 5
Miami Police Department, 301
Micromediational causal statement, 54
Micro model, 327–328
Minneapolis Domestic Violence Experiment, 8
Minneapolis Police Department, 298
Mobility, crime and, 29
Mode, 355
Molar statements, 54
Monitoring, measuring crime and, 121–122
Monitoring the Future (MTF), 135–136, 198, 396
Morphine, 139
Multiple regression analysis, 375
Multistage cluster sampling, 220–221
with stratification, 221–223
Multistage sample, 208
Multivariate analysis, 365–370
Murder, 13

National Archive of Criminal Justice Data (NACJD), 315, A21–A22
National Center for Health Statistics (NCHS), 170–172
National Center for State Courts, 292, 296
National Crime Survey, 71, 235
National Crime Victimization Survey (NCVS), 71, 78, 79, 122, 128–132, 178, 195, 198, 223–224, 232, 234, 241, 254, 287–288, 293, 294, 394
redesign of, 130–132
screening questions, 131, 242
National Criminal Justice Reference Service (NCJRS), 3, A5, A9–A12
National Football League, 13
National Hockey League, 95
National Household Survey on Drug Abuse (NHSDA), 134–135, 239
National incident-based reporting system (NIBRS), 125–128
information in records, 126
Uniform Crime Reports compared, 127
National Institute for Mental Health, 233
National Institute of Corrections, 292
National Institute of Drug Abuse, 70
National Institute of Justice (NIJ), 9, 90, 108, 137, 182, 314, 337, 347, 349, 390, A10–A12
data resources program, A22–A23
Research Plan, 391–394
National Institute on Drug Abuse, 135
National Institutes of Health, 348–349
National Jail Census, 232
National Organization for Reform of Marijuana Laws, 245
National Planning Association, 344
National Science Foundation, 47
National Youth Survey (NYS), 233, 314, 396
Natural sciences, causation in, 47
Nebraska Department of Correction, 227
Necessary cause, 51–54
New Jersey Bell, 164
New York Division of Criminal Justice Services, 124
"New York reconciliation", 124
New York State Division of Criminal Justice Services, 342
Nominal measures, 104
Nominal variables, 371–372
Nomothetic explanation, 18–19, 49–50
Nonequivalent-groups designs, 162–165, 338

Nonprobability sampling, 225–228
Nonsampling errors, 377
Normal science, 38
Norms, 13
NOTIS, A3–A4

Objectives, research proposal and, 90
Objectivity
politics and, 348–350
theory construction and, 35
Obscene phone calls, deterring, 164–165
Observables
direct, 95
indirect, 95
Observation, 28–29, 122
direct, 198–199
field, linking with other data, 278–279
field research and, 263
inaccurate, 8–9
making, 198–199
participant, 264
recording, 274–275
research design and, 87
selecting cases for, 271–272
selective, 10
structured, 276–278
theory construction and, 35
units of, 73
Observation unit, 209
Observer, field research and, 264–266
Observer-as-participant, 265
Offender, as unit of analysis, 120
Offending
juvenile victimization and, 394–400
surveys of, 133–137
Offense, as unit of analysis, 120
Office of Juvenile Justice and Delinquency Prevention, 233
Office of National Drug Control Policy (ONDCP), 139
Onset, 39
Open-ended questions, 235–236
Operational definition, 99
Operationalization, 27–28, 67, 99–106
of concepts, 61
content analysis and, 311–312
measurement and, 101–106
research design and, 87
Ordinal measures, 104
Ordinal variables, 372–373
Organizations
formal, access to, 267–270
as units of analysis, 74
Organization theory, 41
Outcomes, specifying, 329–330
Overgeneralization, 9

Panel studies, 79–80, 136
Paradigm(s), theory construction and, 38
Paradigm shifts, 38
Parameter, 209
Parametric tests of significance, 377
Parole risk, predicting, 163–164
Parole violation, 307–308
Participant-as-observer, 265
Participant observation, 264
Pearson's product-moment correlation, 373
Peer group, 37
Pennsylvania Coalition Against Domestic Violence, 33
Pennsylvania Department of Education, 344
Percentage down, 363
Percentaging, 363–364
Perceptions, survey research and, 233–234
Periodicity, systematic sampling and, 218
Persistence, 39
Philadelphia Police Department, 276
Phone calls, access to formal organizations and, 268–269
Photography, 275

Plagiarism, research report and, A16
Plea bargaining, 31–32
Poisson process, 227
Police, preventive patrol, 4
Police Foundation, 4, 8
Police records, incident-based, 125
Policing Domestic Violence: Experiments and Dilemmas, 332
Policy
  crime and, 41
  crime prevention, ecological theories of, 42–43
Policy analysis, 72, 341–346
  topics appropriate for, 321–325
Policy process, 322–323
Policy proposals, survey research and, 234
Political science, theories of law breaking and, 40
Politics
  criminal justice and, 10
  objectivity and, 348–350
Population(s), 73, 208, 217
  modeling, 342–346
  representative of, 207
  research design and, 87
  special, 185–187
  study, 208
  target, 331
Posttesting, 148–149
Poverty, 27
Prediction, knowledge and understanding and, 5–6
Predictive validity, 136
President's Crime Commission, 128–129
Pretesting, 148–149
Preventive police patrol, 4
Primary sampling unit, 208
Principles, 37
Prison, simulating, 189–191
Prison populations, modeling, 342–346
Probabilistic causal model, 49
Probabilistic reasoning, 5
Probability of selection, 207
Probability sampling, 197, 205–207
Probability sampling theory, 210
Probation, 158–159
  intensive supervision, 156–158
Probes, interviewing and, 248
Problem formulation, evaluation research and, 327–328
Process, linking to evaluation, 323–324
Process evaluation, 324–325
Program evaluation, 324–325
  designs for, 332–341
Proportionate reduction of error (PRE), 370–371
Proportionate sampling, 225
Propositions, 37
The Prosecution of Felony Arrests, 294
Prosecution, community, grounded theory and, 34–35
Prospective studies, 81–82
Prostitution, 263
Psychological reductionism, 77
Psychology
  deterrence and, 41
  theories of law breaking and, 39
Public opinion polls, 217
Public order, 40
Public policy
  criminal justice and, 10
  criminal justice research and, 41–42
Published statistics, 294–296
Pulse Check, 139–140
Purposive sampling, 225–226, 274

Qualitative data, 20–21
Quantitative data, 20–21
Quasi-experimental design, 162–172, 337–340
Question(s)
  asking, 198, 255–257, 266–267
    guidelines for, 235–239
  closed-ended, 235–236

contingency, 240–241
  matrix, 241–243
  open-ended, 235–236
Questionnaires, 236
  construction of, 240–243
  interviewing and, 248
  measuring perceived disorder and, 114
  pretesting, 226
  self-administered, 243–246
Quota sampling, 226–227

r, 373
Racial bias, 10
Racism, 348–349
Random assignment, 333, 340
  criminal justice research and, 184
Random-digit dialing (RDD), 249
Randomization, 152
Randomized evaluation designs, 332–335
Random sampling, simple, 218
Random selection, 210, 216
Rape, 97, 226
Rates, computing, 360–361
Ratio measures, 105
Ratio variables, 373
Real definition, 97
Reality
  agreement, 3–4
  approach to, science and, 5
  experiential, 3–4
Reasoning
  causal, 5, 18–19
  deductive, 19–20
  errors of, 54–55
  illogical, 10
  inductive, 19–20
  probabilistic, 5
Recidivism, 57, 86, 94, 99, 293
  defined, 100–101
Reductionism, 77–78
  economic, 77
  psychological, 77
Reference sources, A3
Regression analysis, 373–375
  cautions in, 375–376
  multiple, 375
Regression equation, 373–374
Regression line, 373
Relationships, variables and, 16–18
Reliability
  agency records and, 304–308
  data collection and, 201–203
  field research and, 287
  interrater, 109
  measurement and, 107–109
  self-report measures and, 136–137, 239
  survey research and, 254
  validity and, 111
Reporting, criminal justice research and, 181
Representativeness, 207, 377
Research
  applied, 41
    political context of, 346–350
  criminal justice. *See* Criminal justice research
  empirical, 4–5
  evaluation. *See* Evaluation research
  field. *See* Field research
  market, 256
  measuring crime and, 122
  purposes of, 69–72
  social disorganization theory and, 29
  social science, ethical rule of, 22
  survey. *See* Survey research
  time dimension and, 69, 78–83
Research Bulletin, 286
Research design, 69, 83–89
Research process, 83–85
Research proposal, 69, 89–91
  elements of, 90–91
Research report, A13–A19

Retrospective studies, 80–83
Review, research design and, 88–89

Safety audit, 279–280
Sample
  EPSEM, 207
  multistage, 208
  single-stage, 208
Sampling, 197, 204–205
  agency records and, 303
  cluster, 220
    multistage, 220–221
  concepts and terminology, 207–209
  content analysis and, 309–311
  convenience, 227–228
  field research and, 273–274
  judgmental, 225–226
  nonprobability, 225–228
  probability, 197, 205–207
  proportionate, 225
  purposive, 225–226, 274
  quota, 226–227
  random, simple, 218
  research design and, 87
  snowball, 228
  stratified, 219–220
    disproportionate, 220
  systematic, 218–219
Sampling bias, 206–207
Sampling designs, 218–225
Sampling distribution, 210–212
  binomial, 212–217
Sampling error, 209, 219, 221, 225
Sampling frame, 208–209, 217
Sampling theory, probability, 210
Sampling unit, 208
San Francisco Chronicle, 54
Scattergram, 374
Schedule, research proposal and, 90
School performance, 37
Science. *See also* Social science
  agreement/experiential reality and, 5
  logico-empirical, 11
  as method of inquiry, 1
  natural, causation in, 47
  normal, 38
  traditional model of, 26–29
    deductive logic and, 29–30
  wheel of, 37
Scientific revolution, 38
Seasonality, time series and, 167
Seat belt use, field research and, 282–283
Secondary analysis, 314–316
Secondary data
  advantages and disadvantages of, 316
  sources of, 315–316, A20–A27
Selection bias, experimental validity and, 154–155
Selective observation, 10
Self-administered questionnaires, 243–246
Self-interest, definition of crime and, 119
Self-report measures, validity and reliability of, 136–137, 239
Self-report surveys, 111, 233, 237–239
  inmate, 401–408
Sentinel system, 122
Series victimizations, 130
Sexual assault, 226
Sexual selection theory, homicide and, 39
Shock incarceration, 329
Shoplifting, 122, 141–142, 179, 227, 262, 264
  field research and, 280–282
  situational prevention of, 340
Simple random sampling, 218
Single-stage sample, 208
Situational crime prevention, 43, 339–340
Situational hypothesis, 189
Skewed distributions, 359
Slide show, 398
Snowball sampling, 228
Sobriety checkpoints, 151, 166–167

Social artifacts, 74–75, 292
"Social constraints" theory, 33
Social desirability, self-report items and, 237
Social disorganization, 37
  delinquency and, 28
Social disorganization theory, 27–29, 40
Social disruption theory, 26–27
Social ecology, criminology and, 40
Social regularities, 13
Social science
  determinism and, 47–49
  foundations of, 10–18
Social science research, ethical rule of, 22
Social scientific theory, 11–13
  aggregated behavior and, 13–14
  creation of, 26–38
  social regularities and, 13
Social strain theory, 40
Socioeconomic status (SES), 97–99
Sociology, theories of law breaking and, 39–40
Sourcebook of Criminal Justice Statistics, 294
Specialized interviewing, 255–256
Special populations, 185–187
Split-half method, 109
Sponsors, access to formal organizations and, 268
Staff misbehavior, criminal justice research and, 182
Stakeholders, 328
  evaluation and, 346–348
Standard deviation, 357–358
Standard error, 215
Standardized open-ended interview, 255
Statements, 236
  causal, micromediational, 54
  if-then, 323
  molar, 54
  theory construction and, 37
Statistic, 209
Statistical Abstract of the United States, 367
Statistical conclusion validity, 56–57
  threats to, experiments and, 160
Statistical regression, experimental validity and, 154
Statistical significance
  cautions in interpreting, 384–385
  logic of, 377–382
  tests of, 377
Statistics
  descriptive, 354–376
  inferential, 376–385
  published, 294–296
Still photography, 275
Stratification, 219
  multistage cluster sampling with, 221–223
Stratified sampling, 219–220
  disproportionate, 220
Street lighting, crime prevention and, 264
Structured observation, 276–278
Study population, 208
Subcultures, access to, 270–271
Subgroup comparisons, 362
  multiple, 369–370
Subject(s)
  available, reliance on, 227–228
  deceiving, criminal justice research and, 180–181
  research proposal and, 90
  selecting, 151–152
Subjectivity, theory construction and, 35
Sufficient cause, 51–54
Suicide, 170–172
Supervision, 57
Supplementary Homicide Reports (SHR), 125, 133
Surveillance system, 122
Survey(s)
  asking questions and, 198
  crime, 140–141

  environmental, 276–277
  interview
    completion rates and, 252
    in-person, 247–249
    mail, 244–246
      acceptable response rates and, 246
    measuring crime through, 128–133
    measuring perceived disorder and, 114
    of offending, 133–137
    self-report, 111, 233, 237–239
      inmate, 401–408
    telephone, 249–251
Survey of Inmates in Local Jails, 294
Survey of Justice Expenditure and Employment, 294
Survey research, 232
  quidelines for asking questions in, 235–239
  strengths and weaknesses of, 253–254
  topics appropriate to, 232–235
Survey Sampling, 208
Systematic sampling, 218–219

Tables
  bivariate, 364–365
  constructing and reading, 364
  contingency, 364–365
    bivariate, 370
    multivariate, 369
  multivariate, 365–369
  percentaging, 363–364
Target population, 331
The Tearoom Trade, 188
Telephone surveys, 249–251
Testing, experimental validity and, 153
Test-retest method, 108–109
Theory, 26–27
  conflict, 40
  construction of, 61
    terms used in, 34–38
  criminal justice and, 38–43
  defined, 37
  ecological, 42–43
  grounded, 32, 33, 262
    community prosecution and, 34–35
  inductive, justice policy and, 33
  organization, 41
  sampling, probability, 210
  sexual selection, homicide and, 39
  "social constraints", 33
  social disorganization, 27–29, 40
  social scientific. *See* Social scientific theory
  social strain, 40
Tiananmen Square, 21
Time dimension. research and, 69, 78–83
Time series, 136
  interrupted, 166
Time-series designs, 166–170, 338–339
  interrupted, 170
  with switching replications, 170
  variations in, 168–170
Tradition. human inquiry and, 6–7
Transition zones, 27, 28, 42
Transportation Research Center (TRC), 282
Trend studies, 78–79
Triangulation, 89
Typologies, 112–113

U.S. Bureau of the Census, 71, 78, 110, 128, 130, 132, 232, 249, 254, 294, 295, 297, 367
U.S. Department of Health and Human Services, 184
U.S. Department of Justice, 132
U.S. Postal Service, 244
U.S. Public Health Service, 122
U.S. Supreme Court, 102
Understanding
  generalized, 73
  prediction and, 5–6

Unexplained variation, 375
Uniform Crime Reports (UCRs), 70–71, 78–79, 122, 123–125, 195, 199–200, 295
  national incident-based reporting system compared, 127
United States Code, 119
Units of analysis, 69, 72–78
  agency records and, 302–303
  content analysis and, 309–311
  ecological fallacy and, 76–77
  measuring crime and, 120–121
  reductionism and, 77–78
Units of observation, 73
Univariate analysis, 354–362
Univariate inference, 376–377
Urban zones, 28
USA Today, 55
Using Published Data: Errors and Remedies, 304

Validity, 109–112
  agency records and, 304–308
  causal inference and, 55–61
  construct, 57–58, 110–111, 158–159
  content, 110
  convergent, 110, 136
  criterion-related, 110
  data collection and, 201–203
  discriminant, 110
  external, 58–59, 159–160
  face, 110
  field research and, 286–287
  internal, 57, 153–158
  multiple measures and, 111–112
  predictive, 136
  reliability and, 111
  self-report measures and, 136–137, 239
  statistical conclusion, 56–57
  statistical conclusions, 160
  survey research and, 254
  threats to
    experiments and, 153–158
Vandalism, 9, 203
Variables, 14–16, 209, 362
  binomial, 209
  continuous and discrete, 360
  dependent, 18, 148, 329
  dichotomous, 148
  independent, 18, 148
  interval, 373
  nominal, 371–372
  ordinal, 372–373
  rank-ordered, 104
  ratio, 373
  relationships and, 16–18
  stratification, 219
  theory construction and, 37
Vice, observational studies of, 263
Victim, as unit of analysis, 120
Victimization
  delinquency and, 314–315
  juvenile, offending and, 394–400
"Victimless" crime, 129
Victim surveys, 234
Video cameras, 275
Videotaping, 274
Violence, 262
  domestic. *See* Domestic violence
  drinking and, 142
  field research and, 283–285
  intergenerational transmission of, 80–81
Voluntary participation, criminal justice research and, 178–179

Warning mailings, 245
Western Electric Works, 150
Wheel of science, 37
Workplace, homicide and, 366–367
World Wide Web, A2, A6–A8
Written records, examining, 199–200